The Best of

LONDON

REVISED EDITION

Editor
Colleen Dunn Bates

Contributing Editors
Philip Evans, Diana Stobart

Assistant Editors
Jennifer Rylaarsdam, Margery L. Schwartz

Prentice Hall Travel Editor
Amit Shah

Operations
Alain Gayot

International Coordinator
Sophie Gayot

Supervised by
Christian Millau

Directed by
André Gayot

PRENTICE HALL ▪ NEW YORK

Other Gault Millau Guides Available from
Prentice Hall Trade Division

The Best of Chicago
The Best of France
The Best of Hong Kong
The Best of Italy
The Best of Los Angeles
The Best of New England
The Best of New York
The Best of Paris
The Best of San Francisco
The Best of Washington, D.C.

Published by Prentice Hall Trade Division
A Division of Simon & Schuster Inc.
15 Columbus Circle
New York, New York 10023

Please address all comments regarding *The Best of London* to:
Gault Millau, Inc.
P.O. Box 361144
Los Angeles, CA 90036

Library of Congress Cataloging-in-Publication Data
The Best of London / editor, Philip Evans; assistant editors, Margery L. Schwartz, Diana
Stobart. – Rev. ed. p. cm.
Rev. ed. of: The best of London / Gault Millau ; written by Christian Millau. Rev. 1st ed.
c1986. Includes index.
ISBN 0-13-073180-3
1. London (England)—Description—1981—Guide-books.
I. Evans, Philip, 1943- . II. Schwartz, Margery L. III. Stobart, Diana. IV. Millau, Christian.
Best of London.
DA679.G3313 1989
914.2'04'858–dc20 89-32909

Special thanks to the staff of Prentice Hall Travel
for their invaluable aid in producing these Gault Millau guides.

Printed in Singapore

CONTENTS

A Disclaimer

Readers are advised that prices and conditions change over the course of time. The restaurants, hotels, shops and other establishments reviewed in this book have been reviewed over a period of time, and the reviews reflect the personal experiences and opinions of the reviewers. The reviewers and publishers cannot be held responsible for the experiences of the reader related to the establishments reviewed. Readers are invited to write the publisher with ideas, comments and suggestions for future editions.

LONDON

ALIVE & THRIVING

M any people were as startled as we were after the publication of the first edition of *The Best of London* in 1976 to see the disconcerting pictures of "a new London" starting to appear in the press. There they were, Rolls=Royces crammed with veiled women, crowds of emirs and princes preening in the lobbies of luxury hotels, and groups of the faithful kneeling on the pavement, their faces turned toward Mecca, chanting their prayers. They cleaned out every jeweler's window, ran off with Old Master paintings and bought up noble old estates as casually as if they had been just so many plum puddings. It was as if London had suddenly become a satellite of the Middle East.

At about the same time, like a cloud of vultures, Americans and Continentals swooped down on this promised land of cut-rate cashmere and tweed jackets. London seemed to be on the verge of sinking like a leaky old tub. Thankfully, those fears were unfounded. London is unsinkable: an eternal city that has seen and been through it all, with the uncanny knack of swallowing whatever fate dishes out. London (to continue the metaphor) has a cast-iron stomach that can handle the most brazen eccentricities; people of every nation can pass through or even settle there, and although occasional disturbances may result from the cosmospolitan mix, in the end London always manages to absorb the shock to its system. (We know of some "typically English" restaurants where if you peek into the kitchen you'll see only Chinese cooks.) It has even coped with the declining dollar. At the time of this writing, London's prices seem outrageous to most Americans, but they still adore the place and fill its hotel rooms year-round.

We must agree with Prince Charles that some of London's newest buildings resemble "gigantic gargoyles." But regardless of its appearance, London is still London: Its bowler-hatted businessmen still stalk the City's streets, umbrellas smartly in hand, and the "English eccentric," that doughty breed, is not yet extinct.

On the other hand, 1992—the year of a common European market—is drawing near, to be followed a year later by the scheduled opening of the Euro-tunnel, which will surely make those living in southeastern England feel more like Europeans than English. London, however, is still inhabited by Londoners, with their picturesque traditions, their artlessness, their polished manners, their cordial aloofness, their greatness, their silly phrases, their genius, their courage, their studied idleness and their redder than rose-red roses.

Our guide to London does not claim to tell you all there is to know about the city on the Thames, but if it succeeds in giving you a taste for one of the world's most thrilling and extravagant cities, we shall consider our efforts amply rewarded. For several months, our team of writers visited hundreds of restaurants, hotels, pubs, wine bars, sights and shops of every description (though there are bound to be some gaps in the coverage). A guidebook is never really finished; that is one reason why our writers are never bored, for as soon as they finish one edition, they must get down to work on the next.

Please don't curse our name if your restaurant checks or hotel bills do not correspond to our estimates. Our readers expect a lot of us (as well they should), but we cannot be expected to freeze inflation.

RESTAURANTS

INTRODUCTION

IN PURSUIT OF ENGLISH COOKING

Either the English are less badly off than is genuinely believed, or they are living beyond their means. Whatever the case may be, when a new restaurant opens in London, unless the food is abominable, the place is immediately crammed to capacity. To obtain a table in a top restaurant, would-be patrons must reserve far in advance.

Londoners have always loved to dine out—that's nothing new. What is new is that the English, traditionally known to be formidable trenchermen, have finally discovered the pleasures of eating well; that in itself is a minor revolution. Of course, many of them still gobble down dreadful food, thereby supporting any number of mediocre restaurants that serve peas as large and hard as marbles, chicken that has all the taste and texture of a boiled blotter, and potatoes as fuzzy and fibrous as tennis balls. Many hotels persist in serving the kind of indigestible meals that prevailed during the reign of Victoria. "Luxury" restaurants survive as well, where preening waiters serve flaming food with fancy French names; what passes in such places for grand cuisine is in fact heavy, pretentious, ludicrous food.

While we're on the subject, let's not forget to give a black mark to those so-called French bistros that were decent enough 30 years ago but that have sunk into grimy decrepitude. And there are those "chic" little places where gastronomic dilettantes discover the error inherent in the notion that when you don't know what to do with your life, you can always open a restaurant.

Often misconstrued on British shores, French nouvelle cuisine has suffered in the hands of amateurish chefs, some of whom apparently believe that it's enough to serve raw fish and nearly raw green beans to qualify as the new Michel Guérard. So connoisseurs of bad cooking should take heart: London won't disappoint them; indeed, this very guidebook contains a few addresses that cranks like them will thank us for. But most of you will probably be more interested in the impressive and growing number of establishments daring enough to serve good and even very good food.

For more than a decade now, the restaurants of London have been making tremendous progress. One has only to observe the space devoted to gastronomy in newspapers and magazines to gauge the evolution of British taste. A generation of young gourmets is growing up in Albion, for whom food is more fascinating than cricket, and wine is a consuming passion. London has traveled a long way since the days when a touch of garlic was regarded as daring and one had to travel to Limehouse for decent dim sum. Today London surely boasts the most varied range of ethnic cuisines in Europe. There is now a plethora of food shops, purveying everything from lemon grass and sagara pepper to soft-shell crabs and fresh sea slugs. And there are plenty of restaurants preparing these delicacies. The newest and most popular culinary trend is Thai cuisine; in fact, Thai restaurants have put the rather tired and battle-weary Chinese on their mettle, much like the pike that are put into carp farms to keep them lively and moving. Vietnamese cuisine is new to the city, but we're sad to say that there are as yet few

Vietnamese restaurants of note. Spanish tapas, regional and vegetarian Indian cooking, Cajun/Creole, North African couscous, Caribbean . . . London is undergoing an ethnic-cuisine invasion that even the most bigoted Anglophile cannot defeat—or regret.

We're happy to report that overall, the talent level of London's chefs has risen spectacularly in the past few years. Many new cooks have arrived from the Continent who are considerably more skilled and enthusiastic than their predecessors. With a few brilliant exceptions, notably Escoffier early in this century, the Continent's best chefs would rarely go into voluntary exile across the Channel. Today, since English culinary levels have risen so high, there is really no reason why a good chef should refuse to leave Paris, Brussels, Munich or Geneva for London. The young cooks who take this leap bring with them all sorts of original ideas and modern techniques; it is obvious that the French food (to mention only one example) served in London today is worlds away from the fossilized grand cuisine of not so long ago.

Another point of prime importance is that the British, especially in the prosperous years since 1980, have discovered that it's possible to make a name for oneself, and even reach stardom, as a chef. At last we are beginning to see talented home-grown cooks emerge from Britain's kitchens, chefs who will one day be forces to reckon with. Indeed, we must single out the impressive strides made in the last few years by British chefs working in London, all of whom are reviewed in this book. They include Sonia Blech (Mijanou), Philip Britten (Capital), David Cavalier (Cavaliers'), David Chambers (Oak Room, Le Meridien Piccadilly), Sally Clarke (Clarke's), Paul Gayler (Inigo Jones), Gary Hollihead (Sutherlands), Simon Hopkinson (Bibendum), Nico Landenis (Simply Nico), Rowley Leigh (Kensington Place), Alistair Little (Alistair Little), Brian Turner (Turners), Marco Pierre White (Harvey's), Bryan Webb (Hilaire) and Anthony Worrall-Thompson (Ménage à Trois). And more are found outside of London, including John Burton-Race (L'Ortolan, in Shinfield) and Anthony Blake (Lucknam Park, in Colerne, near Bath).

Curiously, the British are still uncomfortable with the idea that if they would only make a concerted effort, their native cuisine could become a source of national pride. If they do want to forge ahead, English chefs and gastronomes must first go back to their culinary roots. The following pages show that some of them are striving to rethink English cooking and show it to best advantage, lightening and modernizing the dishes along the way.

However small their number, these chefs have one important thing going for them: Britain produces outstanding raw ingredients that lend themselves beautifully to preparations à l'anglaise. Its Colchester oysters, salmon, Scottish beef and lamb are incomparable, as is its delicate Dover sole. English bacon is meaty and savory, English game first-rate, and Aylesbury ducks tender and tasty. And there are at least ten cheeses, not counting Stilton, that deserve the attention of discerning cheese lovers. True, we can't go so far as to say that all British produce is of the same admirable quality. Fruits and vegetables betray a lack of sunshine, and many dairy products are mass-produced. It takes real determination to unearth truly exceptional ingredients—but in that respect, Britain is no different from other industrialized nations.

It's up to the British themselves to develop a national cuisine worthy of note. Are we optimistic about their chances? Quite honestly, yes. In years to come finding good

British food in a city chockablock with French, Italian, Chinese, Thai, Indian and Pakistani restaurants may no longer be a superhuman feat.

ABOUT THE REVIEWS

RATINGS

As in all Gault Millau guides, London's restaurants are rated in the same manner that French students are graded: on a scale of one to twenty, twenty being unattainable perfection. The rankings reflect *only* the quality of the cooking; decor, service, reception and atmosphere are explicitly commented on within the reviews. Restaurants ranked thirteen and above are distinguished with toques (chef's hats), according to the following:

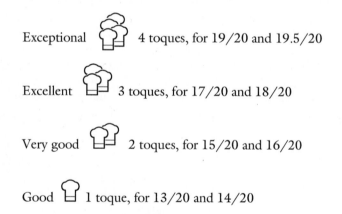

Exceptional   4 toques, for 19/20 and 19.5/20

Excellent   3 toques, for 17/20 and 18/20

Very good   2 toques, for 15/20 and 16/20

Good   1 toque, for 13/20 and 14/20

Keep in mind that we are comparing London's restaurants to the finest in the world—just because the city's best restaurants don't all get four toques doesn't mean they aren't exceptionally good. Also, these rankings are *relative*. One toque for 13/20 is not a very good ranking for a highly reputed (and very expensive) temple of fine dining, but it is quite complimentary for a small, unpretentious place.

PRICES

Unless otherwise noted, the prices given are for a complete à la carte dinner for one, including an appetizer, main course, dessert and service. Whenever possible, we also give prices for fixed-price meals. When noted, a half bottle of wine is also included in the price. It is, naturally, difficult to estimate the cost of wine; for our purposes we've assumed it to be a modest bottle at a modest restaurant and a bit more expensive wine at a more serious place. Lovers of the great Burgundies and Bordeaux will find their bills higher than our estimates.

Most Americans are taken aback by London's prices—prepare yourself for menu shock at many of the city's top-flight restaurants. Gourmands on a budget should keep an eye out for fid-price lunch or dinner menus, which can sometimes be great bargains.

CREDIT CARDS

After the hours for each restaurant, we list the credit cards accepted, if any. "All major cards" includes American Express, Diners Club, MasterCard and Visa.

TIPPING

As in the United States, gratuities are rarely included in the bill. A fifteen-percent tip is generally considered adequate; up to twenty percent may be warranted if the service has been exceptional.

A FEW NOTES

Londoners tend to eat relatively late: 1 p.m. for lunch, 8 to 8:30 p.m. for dinner.

As we noted earlier, many of London's restaurants enjoy tremendous popularity, so reservations are *always* recommended.

Except in the most select restaurants, people wear pretty much whatever they wish when they dine out. A man could, for instance, wear black tie to a simple bistro, and no one would take any notice. As for women, no matter how eccentric their clothing, they never risk being ridiculed, for the simple reason that the English do not stare at their neighbors.

TOQUE TALLY

18/20

Tante Claire

17/20

Chez Nico
The Oak Room

16/20

Bibendum
Capital
Cavaliers'
Le Gavroche
Harvey's
Alastair Little
Le Soufflé

15/20

The Grill and Restaurant
(Connaught)
Inigo Jones
Le Mazarin
Sutherlands
Turner's

14/20

Auberge de Provence
La Bastide
Clarke's
Gay Hussar
Interlude
Kensington Place
Ma Cuisine
Ménage à Trois
Mijanou

13/20

Al Hamra
L'Arlequin
Bahn Thai
Bartons
Blakes
Blue Elephant
Bombay Brasserie
Chez Moi
Crowthers
Thomas de Quincey's
Dragon Gate
Dragon's Nest
The English House
Golden Duck
Grafton
Hilaire
Jamdani

Kundan
The Left Bank
Leith's
Meridiana
Montpeliano
Neal Street Restaurant
Odette's
Pomegranates
Quincy's
Rue St. Jacques
Santini
La Seppia
Suntory
Le Suquet
White Tower
Zen Central

12/20

Boyd's Glass Garden
braganza
Brinkley's
Chaopraya
Chinon
La Croisette
La Dordogne
The English Garden
Friths
Fung Shing
Gavvers
Green's Champagne & Oyster Bar
Hiders
Ikkyu
Au Jardin des Gourmets
Kew Brasserie
Launceston Place Restaurant
The Lindsay House
Magno's
Martins
Maxim
Mélange
Miyama
One Two Three
Orso's
Princess Garden
Rebato's

Red Fort
Red Pepper
The Ritz
River Café
Saga
San Lorenzo
The Savoy River Room
Tiger Lee
Walton's
Valchera's
The Veeraswamy
Zazou

11/20

Joe Allen
Anna's Place
Arirang
Auntie's
Beotys
Le Caprice
The Chanterelle
Chicago Pizza Pie Factory
Chuen Cheng Ku
Corney & Barrow
Cranks
Danieli
Down Mexico Way
Eatons
Eleven Park Walk
La Fantasie Brasserie
Frère Jacques
Garbo's
The Garden
Green Leaves
Ho Ho
Hunan
Hung Toa
Ikeda
L'Incontro
Jensens
Julie's Restaurant
Kaspia
Kensington Tandoori
Lanes
Langan's Brasserie

Ken Lo's Memories of China
Malabar
Mario
Mega-Kalamaras
Michel
Micro-Kalamaras
Mr. Frascati
Mon Plaisir
Piccolo Mondo
Pinocchio
Pitagora
Pollyanna's
Pontevecchio
Le Poulbot
La Rive Gauche
Rules
Salloos
San Carlo
San Frediano
Signor Zilli
Soho Brasserie
Sonny's
Tai Pan
Thierry's
Topkapi
Toto
Tui
Veronica's
Wilson's
Wiltons
Woodlands Restaurant
Ziani Dolce

10/20

Baron of Beef
Bertorelli
Bubb's
Buzkash
Byblos
Cafe Brazil
Café Pelican
Carraro's
Chiang Mai
The Criterion Brasserie
Dal Pescatore

Deals
Ealing Tandoori Restaurant
Giovanni's
The Grill
Jams
Kew Rendezvous
Lemonia
Leonis Quo Vadis
Light of Nepal
Lockets
Low iczanka
Marco's
Masako
Melati
Mr. Chow
Mr. Kong
Monkey Business
Ognisko Polskia
Old Vienna
Poons (Leicester St.)
Poons (Woburn Pl.)

Le Quai Saint Pierre
Rajdoot
Rodos
Tony Roma's—a Place for Ribs
Rowley's
Seven Dials Restaurant
Le Tire Bouchon
Trattoo
The Waterfront

9/20

The Belvedere
Entrecôte Café de Paris
New World
Ovations
The Pavilion Restaurant
Tate Gallery Restaurant
Wheelers

7/20

Cafe Fish

THE WORLD'S CUISINES

AFGHAN

Buzkash

AMERICAN

Joe Allen
Chicago Pizza Pie Factory
The Grill
Jams
Monkey Business
Tony Roma's—a Place for Ribs

AUSTRIAN

Old Vienna

BRAZILIAN

Cafe Brazil

BRITISH

Auntie's

Baron of Beef
Bartons
The Belvedere
Boyd's Glass Garden
braganza
Cavaliers'
Clarke's
Corney & Barrow
The English Garden
The English House
The Grill and Restaurant
(Connaught)
Kensington Place
Kew Brasserie
Launceston Place Restaurant
Leith's
The Lindsay House
Alastair Little
Lockets

Ovations
The Pavilion Restaurant
Pollyanna's
The Ritz
Rowley's
Rules
The Savoy River Room
Seven Dials Restaurant
Soho Brasserie
Sutherlands
Tate Gallery Restaurant
Veronica's
Walton's
Wilson's

BRITISH/FRENCH

The Belvedere
Corney & Barrow
Thomas de Quincey's
The Grill and Restaurant (Connaught)
Kew Brasserie
Launceston Place Restaurant
Ovations
Pollyanna's
The Ritz
Seven Dials Restaurant
Soho Brasserie
Le Tire Bouchon

CHINESE

Chuen Cheng Ku
Dragon Gate
Dragon's Nest
Fung Shing
Golden Duck
Green Leaves
Ho Ho
Hunan
Hung Toa
Kew Rendezvous
Ken Lo's Memories of China
Marco's
Maxim
Mr. Chow

Mr. Kong
New World
Poons (Leicester St.)
Poons (Woburn Pl.)
Princess Garden
Red Pepper
Tai Pan
Tiger Lee
Zen Central

FRENCH

L'Arlequin
Auberge de Provence
La Bastide
The Belvedere
Beotys
Bibendum
Brinkley's
Bubb's
Café Pelican
Capital
The Chanterelle
Chez Moi
Chez Nico
Chinon
Corney & Barrow
The Criterion Brasserie
Crowthers
La Dordogne
Eatons
Entrecôte Café de Paris
La Fantasie Brasserie
Frère Jacques
Friths
Le Gavroche
Gavvers
Grafton
The Grill and Restaurant (Connaught)
Harvey's
Hiders
Hilaire
Interlude
Au Jardin des Gourmets
Jensens

Inigo Jones
Julie's Restaurant
Kaspia
Kew Brasserie
Langan's Brasserie
Launceston Place Restaurant
The Left Bank
Ma Cuisine
Magno's
Martins
Le Mazarin
Mélange
Ménage à Trois
Michel
Mijanou
Mon Plaisir
Ninety Park Lane
The Oak Room
Odette's
Ovations
Pollyanna's
Le Poulbot
The Ritz
La Rive Gauche
Rue St. Jacques
Seven Dials Restaurant
Soho Brasserie
Sonny's
Le Soufflé
Tante Claire
Thierry's
Le Tire Bouchon
Turner's

GREEK

Beotys
Lemonia
Mega-Kalamaras
Micro-Kalamaras
Rodos
White Tower

HEALTH FOOD

Cranks
The Garden

HUNGARIAN

Gay Hussar

INDIAN

Bombay Brasserie
Ealing Tandoori Restaurant
Jamdani
Kensington Tandoori
Kundan
Malabar
Rajdoot
Red Fort
Salloos
The Veeraswamy
Woodlands Restaurant

INTERNATIONAL

Blakes
Le Caprice
Deals
Lanes
Neal Street Restaurant
Pomegranates
Quincy's
Valchera's

ITALIAN

Bertorelli
Carraro's
Dal Pescatore
Danieli
Eleven Park Walk
Giovanni's
L'Incontro
Leonis Quo Vadis
Mario
Meridiana
Mr. Frascati
Montpeliano

Neal Street Restaurant
Orso's
Piccolo Mondo
Pinocchio
Pitagora
Pontevecchio
River Café
San Carlo
San Frediano
San Lorenzo
Santini
La Seppia
Signor Zilli
Toto
Trattoo
The Waterfront
Ziani Dolce

JAPANESE
Ikeda
Ikkyu
Masako
Miyama
One Two Three
Saga
Suntory

KOREAN
Arirang

LEBANESE
Al Hamra
Byblos

MALAYSIAN
Melati

MEXICAN
Down Mexico Way

NEPALESE
Light of Nepal

PIZZA
Chicago Pizza Pie Factory

POLISH
Low iczanka
Ognisko Polskia

RUSSIAN
Kaspia

SCANDINAVIAN
Anna's Place
Garbo's

SEAFOOD
Cafe Fish
La Croisette
Frère Jacques
Green's Champagne & Oyster Bar
Le Quai Saint Pierre
Le Suquet
Tiger Lee
Wheelers
Wiltons
Zazou

SPANISH
Rebato's

THAI
Bahn Thai
Blue Elephant
Chaopraya
Chiang Mai
Tui

TURKISH
Topkapi

VEGETARIAN
The Garden
Woodlands Restaurant

BATTERSEA

⑬ L'Arlequin

123 Queenstown Rd., SW8 - 622 0555

FRENCH

Open Mon.-Fri. 12:30 p.m.-2 p.m. & 7:30 p.m.-11 p.m., Sat. 7:30 p.m.-11 p.m. Closed bank holidays, 1 week in winter & 3 weeks in Aug. All major cards.

L'Arlequin's owner/chef will feel honored, we hope, to see that his is the first establishment listed in our guide to London's restaurants. We compliment his charming wife on her delightful welcome and acknowledge the culinary talents of her spouse. Which is not to say that the food is so brilliant it merits a special trip to Battersea. But if you happen to be in the neighborhood, you could do worse than to wander over to this rather anonymous-looking restaurant, where a clientele heavy on loyal regulars fills two featureless but tidy dining rooms.

Chef Christian Delteil, formerly of the Chewton Glen Hotel, has put together an appetizing menu. Fish soup redolent of saffron, old-fashioned stuffed cabbage, young rabbit with fresh pasta, and cumin-scented sweetbreads with endive keep company with a half dozen dishes based on the market's bounty, which, on a given day, might include salmon baked in parchment with rosemary or, if game is in season, woodcock paired with bitter chocolate. The fixed-price meal is engaging enough, although it doesn't—quite—live up to its promise. We think it is excessive, for example, to apply the adjective *truffé* (truffled) to an otherwise excellent carrot flan topped with the merest sliver of truffle, a flourish that added exactly nothing to the flavor of the dish. On the other hand, truffles (not black, but of the gray summer variety) did contribute their distinctive fragrance to a dish of excellent fresh pasta. Though our pheasant, served in the form of rissoles (like turnovers), was bland (it would have been far tastier roasted or in a casserole), the accompanying cabbage was delicious, as were the frozen nougat dessert and the coffee that followed. A fixed-price menu dubbed "gourmand" commands the stiff tariff of £55 and entitles one to fresh goose-liver terrine, prawns in vinaigrette, young pigeon with cabbage and a chaud-froid (served cold) of raspberries.

A la carte: £30-£45, including wine. Fixed-price menus: £40-£55, including wine.

10/20 Carraro's

32 Queenstown Rd., SW8
720 5986, 720 7079

ITALIAN

Open Mon.-Fri. 12:30 p.m.-2:30 p.m. & 7 p.m.-11:30 p.m., Sat. 7 p.m.-11:30 p.m. Cards: AE, MC, V.

Gianfranco Carraro, who started Rugantino (the popular Soho restaurant) in 1967, moved south of the Thames and opened this restaurant exactly twenty years later. Following the not uncommon teething problems of a new venture, this elegant establishment, which from the outside looks off-puttingly formal, has at last settled down. The £10.95 "executive" fixed-price menu (available at both lunch and dinner) clearly pays homage to the Venetian hinterland, the area of Italy that Carraro hails from. Although the ravioli filled with Mascarpone (cow's milk cheese) and red turnips was not entirely unpleasant, the baccalà (dried cod) with polenta was a complete disappointment: The polenta was unpleasantly soggy, and an overabundance of Provençal sauce smothered the flavors of both the cod and the nuggets of toasted maize (corn). On the other hand, the lamb maremmana (with mustard) formed a pleasing contrast, with just the right amount of mustard, and in the rosette di vitello al funghe prataioli, a wine-and-cream sauce with porcini mushrooms enhanced the noticeably thin sliver of veal. The solid wine list includes a number of half bottles. The background music, even if it is Vivaldi, Mozart and Bach, is inclined to be intrusive.

A la carte: £25, including wine. Fixed-price menu: £10.95.

⑯ Cavaliers'

129 Queenstown Rd., SW8 - 720 6960

BRITISH

Open Tues.-Sat. 12:15 p.m.-2:30 p.m. & 7:15 p.m.-10:30 p.m. All major cards.

After spells at the Grosvenor House and the Dorchester, David Cavaliers opened Pebbles in Aylesbury and then, in 1987, took over the former site of Chez Nico in Battersea's restaurant wilderness. The original space has been extended to create the generous proportions of a grand-hotel dining room, the walls have been covered in trelliswork wallpaper that provides an appealing brightness and, of course, most importantly, the food is delicious. The prices for the fixed menus (£15.50 for lunch and £23.50 for dinner, service included) may look steep on paper, but we've found them to be well worth the sum: The cooking is imaginative—oysters in Oriental spices, little medallions of wood pigeon, steamed veal filet, a pot roast of baby guinea-fowl—and the dishes sumptuous. Even a humble-sounding salad of mixed leaves and grilled scallops arrives in a vast fan of asparagus spears, orange slices and chunks of artichoke. The "south coast bouillabaisse" is a more delicate version of its Mediterranean cousin, fragrant with saffron instead of burning with cayenne; its only flaw is that the luscious heap of fish and shellfish leaves precious little room to float the tiny croutons slathered with rouille (spicy red-pepper-and-garlic mayonnaise). The bread basket houses fine saffron or raisin rolls. Main courses are genuine showstoppers, with intense and variegated flavors and dramatic presentations—for example, the towering rosette of Angus beef and roast shallots caramelized in ruby wine and served with a brilliantly garlicky gratin. All of the meats, in fact, are excellent, and the vegetable sous-chef deserves a medal. After all this come well-chosen and -kept unpasteurized English and Irish cheeses from James of Beckenham, or rococo fruit confections, ice creams (Devonshire or Calvados) and pastries; good coffee and chocolates are £2.50 per person extra. The wine list consists of pages of overpriced French bottles, but we found a reasonably priced Clos du Bois Merlot from California.

A la carte: £25-£30, including wine. Fixed-price menus: £15.50-£23.50.

11/20 Pollyanna's
2 Battersea Rise, SW11 - 228 0316
BRITISH/FRENCH
Open Mon.-Sat. 7 p.m.-midnight, Sun. 1 p.m.-3 p.m. All major cards.

Not many years ago, it would have been a surprise to find any sort of French restaurant in Battersea, let alone a good one. But times change, and today Pollyanna's looks as much at home on Battersea Rise as it would in Shepherd Market. The advantage of Battersea over Mayfair is that people, many of them young and prosperous, actually live there. This provides restaurants like Pollyanna's with a regular clientele, which in turn encourages a consistent standard of cooking and service. We've encountered some inventive dishes here, some of which are listed on a blackboard carried around to the customers—for example, brioche with smoked salmon and scrambled egg, medallions of pork in a sauce of honey and soy sauce with red cabbage and polenta, and partridge in red wine sauce with a purée of celeriac and fresh spinach. We must say, however, that in our experience these dishes haven't always tasted quite as interesting as they sounded on the menu. But the vegetables are crisp, fresh and beautifully presented, and of the desserts, we particularly liked the dark- and white-chocolate mousse. Perhaps we simply have been unlucky in the ordering of our entrées—Pollyanna's clearly enjoys a contented, loyal clientele. Service is excellent—attentive but not pesky, helpful but not overly strident. The house wine is £6.50, but there's also an impressive choice of fine wines that includes, uniquely enough, a proper range of half bottles. On a fine summer evening or a sunny Sunday afternoon, a meal out in Pollyanna's courtyard is hard to beat.

A la carte: £25-£30, including wine.

BAYSWATER

11/20 Hung Toa
54 Queensway, W2 - 727 6017
CHINESE
Open daily noon-11 p.m. Cards: MC.

Hung Toa is still the best Chinese rotisserie in London. At the chopping board in the window stands "Wei-the-Big-Knife" himself, slicing such divine delicacies as burnished duck and crispy pork—all home-roasted—like a card shark cuts a deck. Piled in neat, even portions, and couched on beds of sauced greens or Chinese cabbage, the meat flows endlessly along its path from his knife to the crowded tables. Though roasts are the house specialty, there is also an extensive and varied menu that's strong on seafood and ranges from casseroles to a pork-innards broth. It's authentic stuff, all right. Even the stewed goulash in soy sauce tastes distinctly Chinese. For the budget-conscious, all the roasted specialties are served with rice or noodles for about £3 per platter. Hung Toa, upstairs and downstairs, is packed with diners from every part of the Far East. Those hoping to feast on the famous meats should come early: The full racks of chestnut-colored roasts dwindle in number with alarming rapidity. Consistently good food and an exceptional value. It's fully licensed, but tea seems to be the popular tipple.

A la carte: £9. Fixed-price menu: £18 for two.

11/20 Mega-Kalamaras
76-78 Inverness Mews, W2 - 727 9122
Micro-Kalamaras
66 Inverness Mews, W2 - 727 5082
GREEK
Open Mon.-Sat. 7 p.m.-midnight. All major cards.

It's been a long time since proprietor Stelious Platanos danced on the tables of his neighboring restaurants late at night to wild bouzouki music . . . but both of his authentically Greek restaurants still have a sparkle that's missing from the other pseudo-Greek eating places around town (most of which are actually Cypriot). If the evening is not too busy, which happens rarely, Platanos will take you into his kitchen so you may choose from among the dozens of simmering pots and trays, the way they do in the Greek tavernas back home. And he'll explain why there's so much fish on his menu: Though few fish remain in the Aegean since the islanders used explosives instead of nets to catch them, here in London he can buy all those vanished favorites—red mullet, hake, halibut, cod, sea bream, octopus and, of course, squid, the restaurant's namesake (kalamaras). As a starter, kalamarakia me krassi (in red wine) is delicious, or small barbouni (red mullet), seared and fried in hot olive oil

and served with rosemary-flavored pan juices, is as good as it gets.

Greece is not a rich country, so authentic Greek cuisine includes an enormous number of delicious but inexpensive vegetable dishes, such as imam bayaldi (stuffed eggplant) and another eggplant dish, melitzanes papoutsakia ("eggplant slippers"). And, of course, the kitchen produces such classics as spanakopita (spinach pie with feta cheese, leeks, spring onions and fennel baked in phyllo pastry) and anginares me koukia (small spiny globe artichokes cooked with broad beans, chopped onions, herbs and lemon juice). As for the entrée, relinquish the thought that Greek cuisine consists entirely of char-grilled kebabs, lamb and stuffed vine leaves; instead, we recommend you get the waitress to translate some of the other dishes and try them.

Micro-Kalamaras is more clubbish than its bigger, more expansive Mega brother and is always jammed with Hellenophiles, sitting at the outdoor tables whenever London weather allows, filling the long, empty months until they can return to their own secret corner of the Aegean. The Micro has no liquor license, so bring your own wine; at the Mega, the Greek house wine sells for about £6.25.

A la carte: £20, including wine.

11/20 Mr. Frascati
34 Spring St., W2 - 723 0319
ITALIAN
Open Mon.-Fri. noon-3 p.m. & 5:30 p.m.-11:30 p.m., Sat.-Sun. 5:30 p.m.-11:30 p.m. All major cards.

From the outside, this recently opened restaurant, with its tall windows and white partitions, resembles a conservatory. And this impression is emphasized upon entering when you are confronted with masses of plants and flowers and with tables covered with rose-pink tablecloths. Just south of Paddington Station, Mr. Frascati combines some of the sophistication of a ristorante with the hustle and bustle of a lively trattoria. You can dine al fresco if the weather is warm enough, when the door-length windows at the front are opened. An outstanding specialty of the house is the olive all'ascola, a half dozen green olives filled with meat, egg and herbs and fried lightly in batter. A full range of pasta dishes—including a most satisfying spaghetti alle vongole (with clams) and fettuccine verdi al carciofo, a soothing blend of green pasta and artichoke—is served. If the flavorful chicken breast alla pietro is spoiled by a too-creamy mustard sauce, the calf's liver alla fiorentina (a happy marriage of liver and spinach highlighted with fennel seeds) is extremely succulent, and the veal scaloppine alla milanese (coated in bread crumbs and fried in butter) is wonderfully tender. Avoid the cheesecake. The satisfactory selection of wines, most of which are Italian, includes a bright Frascati 1986. Reservations are advisable.

A la carte: £20-£25, including wine.

11/20 Veronica's

2 Hereford Rd., W2 - 229 5079
BRITISH
Open Mon.-Fri. noon-3 p.m. & 7 p.m.-midnight, Sat. 7 p.m.-midnight. All major cards.

The surroundings and decor are pleasantly floral, and the atmosphere, particularly at lunchtime—when Veronica herself presides with considerable, effortless charm—is friendly and relaxed. On Saturday evenings,

however, it can be a different story, with Veronica out back slaving over a hot stove while her "hench ladies" handle the front of the house. On such occasions, one misses Veronica's gentle touch. The menu, which changes each month, makes for a good read, with each dish described in detail; though brief, it lists enough varied dishes to enable one to put together an interesting meal. Among the intriguing first courses are deep-fried cheese with hot cranberry sauce (a pity the heat did not reach the center of the cheese), delicious roast-cashew pâté, and the mandatory jumbo prawns, which can be had grilled in a garlic sauce or devoured plain. For the main course one can choose between crispy roast duck (which turned out to be too crispy), a perfect filet of sole or an oak-roasted filet of beef. All in all, the cooking is adequate but not brilliant. The wine list is by no means inexpensive, though the choices complement the food nicely. Desserts, sadly, are not successful: runny yogurt brûlée, and brown bread ice cream that is unfortunately just that.

A la carte: £20-£25, including wine.

BELGRAVIA

11/20 Eatons

49 Elizabeth St., SW1 - 730 0074
FRENCH
Open Mon.-Fri. noon-2 p.m. & 7 p.m.-11:15 p.m. All major cards.

Although it's still predominantly a male preserve, we are pleased to report that this worthy, friendly restaurant is increasingly frequented by females. Looking out onto one of the most civilized shopping streets in the neighborhood, the pleasant little dining room's country-house decor of brown Hessian and bird prints is complemented by a conservatory-like extension at the back. The fixed-price menu is moderately priced, and the supplementary à la carte menu changes weekly. The imaginative soups, sound pâtés and terrines and unusual quenelles of fresh and smoked salmon in cream sauce are a treat. We've had good luck ordering the sautéed filet of lamb and kidneys provençale, which were pink and garlicky, and the pork scallop stuffed with red cabbage and raisins. Impeccable poached salmon was part-

nered with a cucumber mayonnaise, and the perfectly roasted rack of lamb with rosemary, a house specialty, was redolent of Provence. The absolute freshness and high quality of ingredients could not be faulted. Over the years, personal, competent management by the owners has enhanced the standing of this popular restaurant. The safe, unsensational wine list is priced with commendable restraint.

A la carte: £25-£30, including wine.

11/20 Hunan

51 Pimlico Rd., SW1 - 730 5712
CHINESE
Open Mon.-Sat. noon-2:30 p.m. & 6 p.m.-11 p.m., Sun. 6 p.m.-11 p.m. Cards: DC, MC.

This small busy restaurant situated among the antiques shops of Pimlico specializes in the incendiary cooking of Hunan, the late Chairman Mao's native province. Owner/chef Peng was one of the co-founders of Taipan, the first restaurant to introduce this fiery cuisine to London. You can make a meal here by choosing first from the list of nineteen appetizers; best bets are the "salt and peppery prawns," the braised lettuce-wrapped parcels of minced pork, and the frogs' legs and dumplings in a hot chili dressing. An array of assorted appetizers also provides a valuable introduction to the menu (just make sure the chef includes the curried won ton puffs in his selection). Adept at seafood, chef Peng makes hot-and-sour prawns, sea bass in the typical chili-and-bean sauce of the region and lobster prepared five different ways. The only disappointment we've experienced has been the camphor-and-tea-smoked duck—a sloppy, inaccurate version of a classic dish. Stuffed phoenix chicken in an earthenware pot is a much better selection. The balanced spiciness says a lot for Peng's skill: The ubiquitous chilis do not swamp the palate, which allows other flavors to reach the taste buds. Drafts of well-chilled white or rosé wine help the food along, and the fainthearted can plead with the staff for blander treatment. The "chef's menu surprise" has a negotiable price.

A la carte: £21, including wine.

11/20 Ken Lo's Memories of China

67 Ebury St., SW1 - 730 7734
CHINESE
Open Mon.-Sat. noon-2:30 p.m. & 7 p.m.-11:30 p.m., Sun. noon-3 p.m. All major cards.

Blond wood, geometric screens, calligraphy on whitewashed brickwork and Bauhaus chairs provide an austere setting for boisterous customers to enjoy their libations. It's been suggested in some quarters that Ken Lo's memories of his native land may be fading (he came to London many years ago via Hong Kong, where he was a tennis champion). The range of fare in this, the parent restaurant, and in the offspring branch in Chelsea Harbour is eclectic to a fault, and the result is that very little gets exactly the right treatment. Cantonese, Szechwan, Pekinese and Mongolian dishes vie for diners' attention; the fixed-price menus lump everything together. Thus, the "Gastronomic Tour" (£20.50 per person) includes Cantonese poached prawns and quick-fried beef, Szechwan bang-bang chicken and aromatic crispy duck and Beijing quick-fried diced chicken. The "Lobster Feast" (£23.50 per person) starts with crackable hunks of the crustacean in a subtle ginger-and-onion sauce and proceeds from there to a Mongolian barbecue of lamb, which when we tried it was over-

cooked, marred by congealing fat and wrapped in iceberg lettuce leaves instead of pancakes. The lettuce isn't a bad idea, but someone in the kitchen should be told about the advantage of draining the lettuce (water dripping all over the plate isn't exactly appetite-provoking). The fruit sorbet was a kind of lemon snowball not recommended for the dentally sensitive. We recommend you drink tea, bottled Budweiser or a wonderfully zingy Sauvignon Blanc from Brownlie Bay View Estate (£13.70). The cover charge of £1 pays for hot towels, chocolates and China tea; the fifteen-percent service charge won't necessarily prevent the waiter from leaving the bottom line of your credit-card slip blank.

A la carte: £30, including wine. Fixed-price menus: £20.50-£23.50.

⑭ Mijanou

143 Ebury St., SW1 - 730 4099
FRENCH
Open Mon.-Fri. 12:30 p.m.-2 p.m. & 7:30 p.m.-11 p.m. No cards.

Don't be put off by the unprepossessing exterior and less-than-glamorous decor of this small, popular restaurant owned by Neville Blech, who's in charge of the service and the wine selection, and his wife, Sonia, who's in charge of the cooking. This is a serious, dedicated place with a kitchen, clearly visible to diners through a plate-glass window, that produces French cooking of some distinction. In addition to the à la carte selection, there are four fixed-price menus: a lunchtime bargain for only £13, a standard menu for £22, a special menu for £26.50 (which includes many of the dishes on the first) and a six-course menu dégustation for £32. A wonderful selection of bread, baked on the premises, precedes the first courses, which include a gâteau of wild duck, a thick chunk of intensely flavored coarse duck pâté with an orange sauce; a julienne of beef en brioche with a sauce of mustard grains and shallots, featuring the lightest possible brioche pastry; and a feuilleté made with a vegetable mousse and fromage blanc in puff pastry, which has a crispness and texture that gives new life to this old nouvelle-cuisine favorite. Among the main courses are pink, succulent grouse (in season) with a whisky-based sauce, and a bold but wholly successful combination of breast of wild chicken with a passion-fruit and Armagnac sauce. An interesting selection of cheeses makes a good alternative to the rich but tempting desserts, which include a chocolate bavaroise (Bavarian cream) with passion fruit, and crêpes with coconut and pineapple. Portions are generous, and the service is knowledgeable and courteous. The exceptional, sensibly priced wine list offers a number of distinguished clarets, carefully chosen wines from Australia and California and a good choice of fine dessert wines, including Château d'Yquem.

A la carte: £30, including wine. Fixed-price menus: £13-£32.

 Pomegranates
94 Grosvenor Rd., SW1 - 828 6560
INTERNATIONAL
Open Mon.-Fri. 12:30 p.m.-2:15 p.m. & 7:30 p.m.-11:15 p.m., Sat. 7:30 p.m.-11:15 p.m. All major cards.

Patrick Gwyn-Jones's cozy, madly eclectic basement restaurant just keeps getting better and better. Currently there are four chefs in the kitchen—Chinese, Portuguese, Spanish and Jamaican—plus a Welshman, if you count Gwyn-Jones, who not only researches his exotic dishes but does much of the preparation (and all of the sauces and pâtés) himself. Yet he still finds time to circulate among his guests to explain the weird and wonderful menu, which ranges from Cantonese roast duck with plum sauce to Jamaican pepperpot and curried goat with plantains. Gwyn-Jones discovered most of the dishes on his travels, and he's particularly proud of the delicious Welsh salt duck—marinated, simmered and served pink with a rich onion sauce—a dish found nowhere else in London. His gravlax (raw salmon filets cured in sugar and salt and seasoned with dill) is famous, and rightly so, but we prefer the thinly sliced raw fresh salmon marinated in lime juice, with a superb parsley and spring-onion dressing. We were less keen on the curried goat, which tasted as you would imagine a wild Highland goat would taste—wild and high—and the snails with cèpes cried out for garlic, though its pastry dome was magnificent looking. Much nicer was the Welsh prawn pâté topped with spiced butter and the giant skewered prawns with a spicy Creole dip of fresh vegetables and herbs. We suggest finishing with a mouth-watering brandy and honey ice cream, or perhaps some ripe Stilton. A superbly

selected wine list contains familiar names from France, Germany and Italy and interesting choices from Australia, California and Chile.
A la carte: £20-£35.

 Santini
29 Ebury St., SW1
730 4094, 730 8275
ITALIAN
Open Mon.-Fri. 12:30 p.m.-2:30 p.m. & 7 p.m.-11:30 p.m., Sat.-Sun. 7 p.m.-11:30 p.m. All major cards.

The pastel shades have long since disappeared. Now this low-ceilinged, white-walled restaurant walking distance from Victoria Station makes use of lengthy mirrors to emphasize its black-and-white elegance, and the walls are decorated with intriguing studies of Italian characters by Venetian photographer Fulvio Roiter. Santini was opened in 1984 by charming Gino Santini, his English wife, Maggie, and Giorgio Rosselli, the talented chef of the group's successful restaurant in Ealing. Since Gino comes from Jesolo, just inland from Venice, and recently published the book, *La Cucina Veneziana*, it comes as little surprise to discover that most of his dishes are Venetian. Mercifully, the menu is not overburdened with an unruly number of selections. Among the successful specialties are wild mushrooms in season and salmon carpaccio with dill, capers, lemon and oil—in this dish, the fresh salmon is sliced finely and cooked in a salamander (broiler) for a couple of seconds. All the pasta is made on the premises; and outstanding examples are the fettuccine in a creamy sauce and the risotto. Among the more successful meat dishes are calf's liver with raw young spinach and roast quails with a wine-and-herb sauce. The house tiramisu (a rich confection of chocolate and liqueur-soaked okra interleaved with creamy Mascarpone) is surely among the best in London. The wine list includes a fine selection of the choicer Barolos and Barberescos and some of the more distinguished French wines (Château Mouton Rothschild '78 for £220), as well as a satisfying number of modest Italian bottles for £11 to £15. Santini offers a special £12.50 business lunch menu that changes weekly. All told, this is a vibrant restaurant in which the staff does its utmost to please.

A la carte: £35, including wine. Fixed-price menu: £12.50 (lunch only).

BLOOMSBURY

11/20 Cranks

9-11 Tottenham St., W1 - 631 3912
HEALTH FOOD
Open Mon.-Sat. 10 a.m.-7 p.m. No cards.

Cranks was the first health-food store in London to open a restaurant. Its original home (8 Marshall Street, W1, 437 9411) is still going strong, and several other branches have since sprung up. The Tottenham Street representative is the newest and the largest, though it remains primarily self-service. On offer is a wide and tempting display of cold salads, quiches, nut rissoles and breads and a daily hot dish, perhaps the tofu-and-vegetable lasagne, which sounds daunting but is in fact aromatic and delicious. The minestrone soup was another, less successful, story: rather tepid with a strange and rather unpleasant mixture of herbs. The bread is delicious if a bit on the heavy, hearty side, and salads are crisp and fresh. Sweets run to such healthful goodies as carrot cake, nut bars, a good fresh-fruit salad and Loseley ice cream. A yogurt, milk and honey drink and, of course, carrot juice are alternatives to the house wines, and there is a nice selection of English country wines. Everything is tastefully served on attractive pottery, and the decor is light and airy. A good place for an unpretentious (though surprisingly filling) lunch or supper.

A la carte: £6-£8.

12/20 Ikkyu

67 Tottenham Court Rd., W1
636 9280
JAPANESE
Open Mon.-Fri. noon-2:30 p.m. & 6 p.m.-11 p.m., Sun. 6 p.m.-10:30 p.m. All major cards.

London's first robato-yaki restaurant (country-style cooking featuring stew-type dishes) is in a cramped basement beneath a stereo shop. Its decor is spartan, with dark wooden screens and token paper lanterns, but its menu is extensive. A page of yakitori (grilled skewered tidbits) lists tongue, heart, liver, gizzard, skin and chicken wings as separate dishes; dishes "in the pot" include chicken and vegetables and boiled tofu with oyster mushrooms. Ikkyu serves the closest thing to rustic Japanese cooking around. For example, we've never seen boiled potatoes like these; they're served as a first course with strips of stewed beef and seaweed. There's also excellent (and quite cheap) crisp asparagus spears in butter, fried eggplant, sumptuous chicken teriyaki and (much more expensive) raw yellowtail. And the fish list is comprehensive: conger, pike, horse mackerel, sardines, tuna and salmon, either grilled, raw (sashimi) or as sushi. The sashimi fixed-price lunch (about £8) is a tremendous bargain and includes: good soup, rice and a bowl heaped with various fish, yellow pickled radish and appropriately incendiary green mustard. The service is brisk and notably congenial. Though there are house wines, sake and Suntory and Kirin beers, the Japanese businessmen who flood the place in the evenings prefer to stick to Kestrel lager.

A la carte: £10-£18. Fixed-price menus: £5-£8 (lunch only).

(13) Jamdani

34 Charlotte St., W1 - 636 1178
INDIAN
Open Mon.-Fri. noon-3 p.m. & 6 p.m.-11:30 p.m., Sat. 6 p.m.-11:30 p.m., Sun. 12:30 p.m.-3 p.m. All major cards.

A new arrival on a prime Charlotte Street site, Jamdani is owned by Amin Ali, the driving force behind many of London's most successful Indian restaurants. He appears to have created yet another winner, since Jamdani is already attracting the young dynamos from nearby BBC Channel 4 and the local film companies and publishers. It is a surprisingly cool oasis nestled among sweatier neighbors—a far cry from the usual brocade-and-flock wallpaper and hot-red velvet banquettes. The decor, by the ubiquitous Fitch and Company, is all cream stone, spare russet stenciling and Arabic-looking chrome. Elegant beige tablecloths and immaculate matching linen napkins adorn the tables, along with spicy papadums and interesting-looking chutneys. The atmosphere is one of extravagant but coolly clinical chic.

Jamdani's cuisine originates from the Dhaka area of Bangladesh, famed for its textiles (some of which are displayed here, albeit discreetly) and eloquently described in the wood-bound menu (which also describes the food so beautifully that one inevitably orders more than one ought to). Of the first courses, the murgh masala chaat—a julienne of chicken strips, cucumber and two sweetish purées—is light, delicious and truly appetizing. The more substantial cashew rolls are heavy with both cashew and cumin and come with the inevitable sweet chutneys. The sweet emphasis is even more noticeable in the sham-e-gujarat, described as a variety of snacks from different Indian regions (it turned out to be a plateful of rather unimaginative cake-like things). Instead, we recommend you try the excellent mini-dosa, or stuffed pancakes. To follow, skip the heavily sauced halibut tikka and try the murgh makhani, tandoori-flavored chicken in a disconcertingly bright orange sauce; despite the frightening color, the flavors combine happily. The lamb pasanda (with almonds and cashews) is rich and tender, and the unusual khargosh achari (hare) in a sinisterly dark chili sauce is tasty but chewy. If you have not overeaten by now, there are Indian puddings and sorbets and fresh fruit for a final taste-buds tickle. For a place serving such interesting and unique food, the wine list is like a Drink-by-Numbers selection, but the house white is excellent and a good value at £6.50. Service is attentive and sharp, as it should be when a fifteen-percent service charge is added to the bill. Jamdani's special £9.95 buffet lunch on Sunday is tempting.

A la carte: £20, including wine. Buffet lunch: £9.95 (Sunday only).

10/20 Poons

50 Woburn Pl., WC1 - 580 1188
CHINESE
Open daily noon-3 p.m. & 6 p.m.-11:30 p.m. All major cards.

The youngest and most glitteringly appointed of the four London restaurants that bear this name is a magnet for tourists from the Russell Square hotels. What they find is a hideously glaring dining room four feet above street level. The tiled floor and ceiling spotlights create an unfortunately harsh setting. On our last visit, the air conditioning failed and something went seriously wrong in the kitchen, triggering a sort of Chinese-style *Fawlty Towers*-like chaos. Admirably encyclopedic though the menu is, with everything from seaweed to whole roast suckling pig, no

restaurant should offer such a range without complete confidence in its ability to pace the dishes throughout a meal. Skewered chicken and wind-dried sausages came in a fairly sorry batter; shrimp dumplings had the telltale glutinous signs of having outstayed their welcome in the steamer; a well-executed Szechwan crispy duck was betrayed by excessively floury pancakes; and brisket of beef with turnips, though nicely sparked with coriander and ginger, had been baked at too high a heat for far too short a time. The whole steamed sea bass, which was intended to be the climax of the feast, arrived looking oddly undercooked, a suspicion confirmed by the waiter who tried to filet it. Ten minutes later it returned overcooked, with much of the skin clinging stubbornly to the flesh. Competent Singapore noodles went some way toward salvaging the evening, as did strawberry ice cream and caramel apples. The wine list includes kindly priced bottles from California and Australia as well as Tsing Tao beer.

A la carte: £25, including wine. Fixed-price menus: £7-£10.

⑬ Rue St. Jacques

5 Charlotte St., W1 - 637 0222
FRENCH
Open Mon.-Fri. 12:30 p.m.-2:30 p.m. & 7:30 p.m.-11:15 p.m., Sat. 7:30 p.m.-11:15 p.m. All major cards.

Rue St. Jacques must have more cordless telephones per square foot (brought in by the customers) than any other restaurant in London. With service that borders on the obsequious, this is a place for some serious ego massaging. From the comfortable reception area, you are ushered to a table in one of several smallish dining areas on two levels; the decor is either pink or green, in either case pleasantly restful. The menu, strong on fish and expensive cuts of meat, with minimal vegetable accompaniment (no hearty stews here), is quite appealing. On our last visit, the homemade rolls were not as fresh as they should have been. Duck and pork rillettes were exquisite, and fish soup was fine and flavorful, with crab and a strong aroma of fennel, but, alas, there was no rouille (that spicy red-pepper-and-garlic mayonnaise de rigueur with Provençal fish soups). Main courses, like the appetizers, arrive hidden under huge silver lids, an affectation we wish were reserved for the tasting menu. Under the lids, one finds prettily arranged food with thoughtful sauces of varying effectiveness. Noisettes of lamb on a bed of spinach and garlic was surprisingly bland, perhaps because the lamb was so undercooked that its juices were unable to run. Desserts are enticing, and the cheese board is outstanding, with most of the selections arriving in superb condition, including a fascinating variety of goat cheeses. Wine is expensive, with much of the list devoted to Champagne, but there are some good half bottles, too. A liter bottle of Perrier is £3.75, which must set some kind of markup record. The fixed-price lunch menu (£17.50), including coffee and petits fours, is a good value, but eating à la carte here is not. Taped music is so quiet as to be irrelevant, but its very existence says something about the ambience, which just fails to live up to that of a top-class restaurant.

A la carte: £35-£45, including wine. Fixed-price menu: £17.50 (lunch only).

⑬ White Tower
1 Percy St., W1 - 636 8141

GREEK

Open Mon.-Fri. 12:30 p.m.-2:30 p.m. & 6:30 p.m.-10:30 p.m. Closed 3 weeks in August. All major cards.

This beloved Greek restaurant opened its doors in 1938. Almost every day the widow of its founder glides among the tables, watching the coolly professional staff do its job. The White Tower occupies a converted Edwardian townhouse that dates from the days when Bloomsbury was well connected to the literary world. The menu ornately describes the daily specials, and mentioned alongside the Greek dishes are several that claim to be international, but the former comprise by far the best bets. The pâtés are most unimpressive, but among the alternatives is a sizable dish of mezes, a Greek mixed hors d'oeuvre that is full of interesting tastes, and an outstanding taramasalata (pink fish roe puréed with bread that has been moistened with milk, olive oil, lemon juice and garlic and served with crusty bread). Then, we can suggest you sample the turbot kebab, robust beef Stroganoff or the dish of the day, perhaps the outstanding roast young chicken

with a delicious, authentic stuffing of cracked wheat, raisins, almonds and orange peel. The menu of predictable desserts is brief, and the wine list is overpriced (the best value is the house wine at £7 a bottle). The White Tower has an atmosphere enchantingly redolent of days past, and if you choose carefully, you can dine here quite well.

A la carte: £25, including wine.

12/20 Zazou
74 Charlotte St., W1 - 436 5133

SEAFOOD

Open Mon.-Sat. 12:40 p.m.-2:40 p.m. & 7 p.m.-11:30 p.m. All major cards.

This extremely popular restaurant, started by the owners of Chez Gérard just down the street, is located in the basement of a house, with its bar and brasserie on the ground floor. It is self-consciously French, with a short handwritten menu specializing in shellfish, particularly oysters, which can be had au naturele (a half dozen for £6) or as part of other dishes. There are a few nods toward nouvelle cuisine in the salad appetizers, one of which consists of celery, spring onions, langoustines and mussels. The obligatory soupe de poissons (fish soup) is mussel-based, with a creamy, saffron-flavored stock, and second and even third helpings are offered. Oysters are featured again in the main courses, though rather less successfully when served with filet of steak in a rich, creamy sauce. The filet of brill, by contrast, is perfectly grilled, flavored only with olive oil (extra-virgin olive oil was also offered from the bottle). The vegetables served in earthenware dishes included deliciously crusty pommes à la dauphinoise and a squash, tomato and fennel gratin. The rich sauces and generous helpings leave little room for dessert, but you'll be tempted by the trolley, which in the past yielded a beautifully crisp tart laden with—in the middle of winter—fresh strawberries. There is also a magnificent cheese trolley with an enormous selection of (primarily) French cheeses in good condition. Good coffee is poured, and the service in general is excellent. The thoughtfully selected wine list includes a house variety for a mere £5.80, but otherwise this is not a cheap place to eat.

A la carte: £30, including wine.

CHELSEA

Bibendum
16

Michelin House, 81 Fulham Rd., SW3
581 5817

FRENCH

Open Mon.-Fri. 12:30 p.m.-2:30 p.m. & 7 p.m.-11:30 p.m., Sat. 12:30 p.m.-3:30 p.m. All major cards.

The sapphire in the crown at the southern side of Brompton Cross, one of London's most fashionable areas, is the Michelin building, which houses this spacious restaurant on its second floor. Bibendum has a wonderfully light and airy atmosphere, with gray carpet complementing the vivid original perfect-blue stained glass that depicts framed caricatures of the bicycling Michelin Man. On our last visit, we were immediately made comfortable; two of us were shown to a flower-bedecked table for four and invited to settle into wonderfully relaxing chairs draped with pale-green cotton covers. Simon Hopkinson, formerly the highly acclaimed chef at Hilaire in South Kensington, moved here to act as both chef and co-proprietor. His repertoire remains enormous—though we noticed minor culinary faults in its early days, Bibendum now ranks decidedly in the highest class.

The generously sized menu lists three soups at its top: a tomato, a deeply rich fish soup and, particularly attractive in warmer weather, a tangy cold curried apple soup with a surprisingly delicate flavor. From the long list of first courses, we sampled an exquisite salad of calf's brains and scallops with marinated sardines and a mild ballotine (rolled mead stuffed with foie gras) served with an onion confit that was far too strong. But an assortment of raw fish, including salmon and halibut, was enhanced with just the right amount of dill. Other exquisite dishes included a chunky halibut with fresh mussels, aromatic saffron, chives and a smooth celeriac purée; chicken with tarragon; and a wonderfully tender veal with anchovy butter. Romantics can order from the entrées for two: roast Bresse chicken, roast guinea-fowl with thyme and lemon, roast lamb with mint

and whole garlic cloves and grilled beef with a béarnaise sauce. The wine list is exceptional, and though many bottles have been marked up severely, bargains, like the house wine, a Côtes de Ventoux '83 for £10.95, do exist.

A la carte: £30-£40, including wine. Fixed-price menu: £17.50.

10/20 Deals

Harbour Yd., Chelsea Harbour, SW10
352 5887

INTERNATIONAL

Open Mon.-Sat. noon-3 p.m. & 6:30 p.m.-10:30 p.m. All major cards.

Owned by Lord David Linley, restaurateur Eddy Lim and Lord Patrick Lichfield, Deals is approached via Kings and Lots roads in the western part of Chelsea, home to many prosperous antiques shops and more than a few prospering, upwardly mobile young Brits. Modern buildings have been rising in Chelsea Harbor lately almost faster than the eye can see, so Deals provides a seemingly constant panorama not of water but of the construction-supply trains that rumble past. The skillful use of blinds would help, though the trains are actually less intrusive than one might think (the place is seemingly always crowded and filled with the excited chattering of its clientele). The Deals design, which has been called "decorator Sing-Sing," favors natural woods. The food is a happy mélange of tastes from Korea, Thailand and Japan. A cutely worded menu (Opening Deals, Mini Deals, Dealer's Choice, Main Deals, Raw Deals, Hot Deals and Side Deals), suggests that you start with spring rolls filled with Pacific prawns, char-broiled Malaysian kebabs served with a spicy peanut dip or a delightful vegetable terrine served with a zesty tomato coulis. Although the spareribs can be distressingly overcooked, the main-course selection also includes a delicious Thai chicken curry flavored with sweet basil and citrus leaves and a chili con carne that invites you to declare your heat threshold. If you have room for more, Deals serves a comely slice of pecan pie.

From a plentiful wine list, we very much enjoyed an '86 Brouilly for £7.95. The staff is bouncy and enthusiastic, and the charming Eddy Lim (he and Lichfield formerly were partners at another Chelsea restaurant, Pier 31) ensures that things always run smoothly.

A la carte: £25-£30, including wine.

11/20 Eleven Park Walk

11 Park Walk, SW10
352 3448, 352 8249
ITALIAN
Open Mon.-Sat. 12:30 p.m.-3 p.m. & 7 p.m.-midnight, Sun. 12:30 p.m.-3 p.m. & 7 p.m.-11 p.m. Cards: AE, MC, V.

Situated in the premises of a former nightclub called Factotum, Eleven Park Walk opened in 1977 and is now a popular spot with wealthy locals as well as with residents from other parts of the city. A light, fresh-looking place, it boasts plate glass that exaggerates the impression of space and Italian food that is some of the best in western London. Among the superior dishes included on the long menu are a bracing penne arrabbiata, a tasty dish of ravioli and tomato enhanced with basil; a superb crespelle ai quattro formaggi, a crêpe-like, four-cheese dish; a wonderfully light chicken breast with lemon; a tender veal chop with butter and sage; and a tender duck filet heightened by black cherries. For Sunday lunch, a special buffet is available.

A la carte: £25-£30, including wine.

12/20 The English Garden

10 Lincoln St., SW3 - 584 7272
BRITISH
Open Mon.-Sat. 12:30 p.m.-2:30 p.m. & 7:30 p.m.-11:30 p.m., Sun. 12:30 p.m.-2 p.m. & 7:30 p.m.-10 p.m. All major cards.

Within pollinating distance of Chelsea's Physic Garden and the site of the annual flower show, The English Garden is inescapably precious. The ground-floor conservatory suffers from lurid dried flowers and too many mirrors. Other rooms are much more successful, notably the private-function rooms upstairs and the garishly floral drawing room. The food, too, is presented in a precious, fussy manner: a proletarian-sounding dish of beef stew and herb dumplings comes in a little bowl with a paper ruff around it, set on a doily-covered plate. In spite of all this nonsense, the food is exceptionally good. The lime vinaigrette on

the smoked-salmon-and-watercress salad is brilliantly balanced; another good first course is the home-smoked saddle of hare. Main courses include roast beef and Yorkshire pudding and such clever combinations as poached chicken roulade with pink peppercorns and cream sauce. The desserts are nice, the selection of English cheeses is not quite substantial enough, the wine list is sensible, with some bargains in the £12-to-£20 range, and the service is obliging. The three-course fixed-price lunch, with coffee, is a great deal.

A la carte: £30. Fixed-price menu: £12.50 (lunch only).

⑬ The English House

3 Milner St., SW3 - 584 3002
BRITISH
Open Mon.-Sat. 12:30 p.m.-2:30 p.m. & 7:30 p.m.-11:30 p.m., Sun. 12:30 p.m.-2 p.m. & 7:30 p.m.-11 p.m. All major cards.

We too are willing to exclaim, along with The English House's owner, Colin Livingstone, "Long live English cooking!"—particularly when it is as lively, inventive and beautifully executed as it is here. Venerable old British recipes have been unearthed, dusted off, pulled apart and intelligently modified for contemporary tastes. Skillfully treated, top-drawer ingredients yield such winning dishes as dressed globe artichokes with a subtle, herb-flecked stuffing, and a Cornish chicken pie that's a stellar rendering of an often hackneyed dish. There are a few uncommon desserts and an attractive little wine list that includes, appropriately enough, an English bottling. All this is offered at exceedingly reasonable prices (there's a fine fixed-price menu for £11). This little haven of happiness is found in Chelsea, behind a vine-covered facade in a comfortable and slightly old-fashioned decor.

A la carte: £35, including wine. Fixed-price menu: £11.

12/20 Gavvers

61-63 Lower Sloane St., SW1
720 5983
FRENCH
Open Mon.-Fri. noon-2:30 p.m. & 7 p.m.-11 p.m., Sat. 7 p.m.-11 p.m. All major cards.

Still enormously popular and having recently been refurbished in muted greens and grays, this cheaper arm of the Roux brothers' empire (which includes Le Gavroche and the

Closerie des Lilas

*T*ime was when life's finer things
such as Hine Cognac were the
preserve of a privileged few.

Today, it is still the true connoisseur who
appreciates the mature, mellow flavour
of Hine.

The dictionary defines a connoisseur as *"one
who is an expert judge in matters of taste".*

And who are we to argue.

HINE

MAISON FONDÉE EN 1763

C O G N A C

BRASH, BOLD GUIDES
TO THE BEST OF THE VERY BEST

Also available:

The Best of Chicago
The Best of New England
The Best of France
The Best of Paris
The Best of London
The Best of Italy

Waterside Inn) now serves lunch and still manages to pack in two seatings an evening, which means that you can either dine at seven and risk being hurried, or at nine and risk having to wait around in a rather drafty doorway for a table to open up. The winning formula is the fixed-price dinner menu that includes a (smallish) kir and a half bottle of red or white wine per person, as well as a plateful of appetizers to get you started and petits fours with your coffee as the finishing touches. Don't expect the food to be of Le Gavroche standards, or anything even approaching it; the sauces can be ordinary and the presentation rather slapdash. Nevertheless, one may eat remarkably well here for the price, and some of the dishes (the black pudding served with apples, for instance, or the rack of lamb with tomato and basil coulis) are excellent. The desserts, on the whole, are rich (cheese is available, for an added cost, as an alternative), and the coffee excellent.

A la carte: £30. Fixed-price menu: £15 (lunch only), £23 (dinner only, including wine).

⑭ Ma Cuisine
113 Walton St., SW3 - 584 7585
FRENCH
Open Mon.-Fri. 12:30 p.m.-2 p.m. & 7 p.m.-11 p.m., Sat. 7 p.m.-11 p.m. All major cards.

After making several halfhearted attempts to leave, Guy Mouilleron eventually sold his interest in this small jewel of a restaurant and departed for France. But he had overseen the business for 25 years, and to ensure that the transition went smoothly, he spent two weeks training new chef Stephane Landwerlin, who he enticed away from Le François. Since the new proprietor, Lucien Celentino, hails from Naples, and his charming wife, Helen Kong, from Shanghai, Ma Cuisine now has a truly international cast. The interior, however, remains the same: paneled walls that display copper pots and faïence plates in a tiny dining room that is a true replica of a southwestern (France) auberge.

Though standards have fallen slightly since the departure of Mouilleron, Ma Cuisine is still a good family restaurant, and it should come as no great surprise that the menu has changed little since his departure. The duck-liver salad with thin slices of breast of duck and mushroom mousse is more than satisfying; pigeon pâté is granted added flavor with an Armagnac sauce; a sea-scallop mousse is enlivened by a white-wine and light-orange sauce; and a boned leg of chicken is given zest with the addition of roasted garlic cloves, fresh tomato and sherry vinegar. Although the tarte tatin has an authentic flavor, the mousse brûlée tasted distressingly bitter when we last tried it. From a dependable wine list, we chose a Pouilly Fumé '86 (£15.40) that proved to be wonderfully fresh.

A la carte: £25, including wine.

12/20 Monkeys
1 Cale St., Chelsea Green, SW3
352 4711
FRENCH
Open Mon.-Fri. 12:30 p.m.-2:30 p.m. & 7:30 p.m.-11 p.m., Sat. 7:30 p.m.-11 p.m., Sun. 12:30 p.m.-3 p.m. No cards.

Situated in one of Chelsea's prettiest backwaters, Monkeys is still presided over by one of its original owners, Tom Benham. His schoolmasterly hauteur is more than offset by his wife's Gallic effervescence. Benham is now squarely installed in the kitchen, which functions smoothly under his spouse's eagle eye. Paneled walls and old prints are reminiscent of a sedate gentlemen's club; fortunately, the food is much better than typical club fare. Benham has always favored small fixed-price menus, with alternative courses marked on the opposite page. Thus, ordering a foie gras salad adds an extra £6 to your bill, and Scottish lobster, cold or grilled, sets you back an additional £8.50. The soups, pâtés and terrines are invariably satisfying. An assortment of fish, fresh and subtly seasoned, confirms Benham's sure touch with seafood, but our favorite nevertheless remains the baked saddle of lamb stuffed with duxelles (finely chopped mushrooms and shallots slowly cooked in butter to form a thick, dark paste) and wrapped in the lightest of pastry. Watch out for game in season, a specialty. Good desserts, a most adventurous cheese board and French drip coffee complete the experience. The three-course Sunday lunch includes traditional roasts of beef, pork and lamb and is an outstanding value. This small restaurant is extremely popular, so reservations are recommended.

A la carte: £30, including wine. Fixed-price menus: £7.50 (lunch only), £25 (dinner only).

12/20 Red Pepper

7 Park Walk, SW10 - 352 3546
CHINESE
Open Mon.-Fri. 12:30 p.m.-2:30 p.m. & 7 p.m.-11:45 p.m., Sat.-Sun. 12:30 p.m.-3 p.m. & 7 p.m.-11:45 p.m. All major cards.

Situated on a narrow street just south of Fulham Road (which in recent years has become home to several good restaurants), Red Pepper is owned by an elegant Indian man who is looking not only to open another branch but has displayed interest in purchasing a Jewish deli. Now that's diversification. Red Pepper has a modern, stylish decor and excellent food. Chef Wong is particularly adept at Szechwan cuisine and patently believes in giving his food a high spice threshold. This was well demonstrated on our last visit by his fine chili prawns, his excellent "salt 'n' pepper" deviled spareribs and his tasty grilled dumplings with a zesty garlic dip. His roster also includes worthy fresh scallops in the shell, steamed with ginger and scallions, crispy beef shreds with carrots and chilis, and good camphor duck, innovatively presented with a sauce and served, like Peking duck, with pancakes and trimmings. All told, Red Pepper serves honest, spicy Szechwan food that is neatly tailored for the European palate without compromising the real flavors.
A la carte: £20-£25, including wine.

⑬ Le Suquet

104 Draycott Ave., SW3 - 581 1785
SEAFOOD
Open daily 12:30 p.m.-2:30 p.m. & 7 p.m.-11 p.m. All major cards.

Ever since Pierre Martin cast anchor on the shores of the Thames, the former Parisian bartender has put together a flotilla of successful seafood restaurants. (The others are La Bouillabaise and La Croisette in Chelsea, Le Quai Saint-Pierre in Kensington and Lou Pescadou on Old Brompton Road.) Le Suquet, however, has the unique advantage of its strategic location: next door to Ma Cuisine and Drayton's wine bar. The atmosphere here, especially after dark, is lively and animated. In the ground-floor room or in the cozy, intimate upstairs dining room staffed by a squad of cheerful waiters, you can peruse the brief menu that stars, naturally, fish, shellfish and crustaceans. You can sample the English and French oysters (Belons, Speciales, Colchesters) or mussels prepared six different ways, excellent

salads of salmon, prawns or scallops, crab feuilletés that are crispy and light, fresh crab and fish soup, or go for one of the fish specials that vary daily according to what looks best at the market. All the seafood is luminously fresh, whether it is simply prepared, like the grilled sea bass and sole, or cooked more elaborately, like the monkfish with Provençal herbs, turbot with a duo of sauces and salmon with stewed leeks. Whatever you choose, you can be sure that the natural taste of the seafood will shine through.
A la carte: £30, including wine.

11/20 Tai Pan

8 Egerton Gdn. Mews, SW3
589 8287
CHINESE
Open daily noon-2:30 p.m. & 7 p.m.-11:30 p.m. All major cards.

This unexpectedly attractive basement on a grim Knightsbridge mews has muted echoes of a pre–World War II ocean liner, with a herringbone-block floor and wooden fans recessed into the ceiling. Four tables, raised on one side of the room, pick up the theme with slatted-wood Lloyd loom ocean-liner chairs from the '20s and '30s. Simon and Garfunkel battle it out, inappropriately, on tape. And the cuisine concentrates on the food of Hunan, the birthplace of Chairman Mao, who "did, after all, live to an advanced age," according to the menu. Diners are invited to indicate their "heat threshold" (spiciness) when ordering, though that's unnecessary if you choose the mild "South West Special Set Feast": spareribs; seaweed; prawns and tofu in sesame; camphor- and tea-smoked duck; prawns in ginger sauce; and seasonal vegetables (Chinese chestnuts, bamboo shoots) in Hunan sauce. General Tseng's chicken and peppers raises the heat with a pungent ginger sauce. .
A la carte: £20.

⑱ Tante Claire

68 Royal Hospital Rd., SW3
352 6045
FRENCH
Open Mon.-Fri. 12:30 p.m.-2 p.m. & 7 p.m.-11 p.m. Closed bank holidays & 10 days at Christmas-New Year's. All major cards.

Tante Claire: The name evokes a cozy, rustic inn deep in the heart of provincial France, with bogus ceiling beams, homey curtains, wrought-iron fixtures and a prize collection of copper saucepans hung amid framed culinary diplomas on a background of flowered wallpaper. Get the picture? Well, it's all wrong. Tante Claire is a supremely elegant restaurant in the middle of London, and its owner/chef, Pierre Koffmann, is a man of urbane tastes. The refinement is immediately apparent from the menus, which are adorned with a Matisse reproduction. And it pervades the unaffected, discreetly polished atmosphere of the small, blond-wood dining room decorated with vividly colored paintings in the spirit of Matisse. A white bouquet perfumes every table.

Another culinary thoroughbred trained in the Roux (of Le Gavroche fame) stables, Koffmann (whose remarkable talents we were among the first to acclaim with a three-toque rating) has obviously surpassed his teachers. With no hesitation whatsoever, we are declaring him the best chef in London, a choice that will not surprise the epicures and socialites who clamor to get their names on the restaurant's endless waiting list.

Listing seven hot and cold hors d'oeuvres, five seafood options and seven meat dishes, the menu is not huge, but it changes often enough so that not even the most assiduous habitués risk boring their palates. You can be sure that no dish will leave you indifferent. The stunning presentations—never fussy or overdone—the impeccable quality of the foodstuffs, the intelligence—indeed the boldness—of the flavor combinations . . . every detail contributes to make a meal at Tante Claire a celebration for the palate, the stomach and the eye.

Koffmann possesses the rare ability to construct his dishes by layering flavors one upon the other, keeping them clear, distinct and unmuddled. Consider, for example, his coquilles St-Jacques à l'encre (in squid ink), a dish so visually striking that one would willingly hang it on one's drawing room wall. Koffmann also brings squid ink, creamed garlic and sweet pepper into perfect harmony with the faintly sweet sea tang of the scallops. It's consummate artistry! And the performance continues at the same rarefied level with superb ravioli, a filling of sweetbreads and foie gras wrapped in the lightest possible pasta; with wild-mushroom consommé, wherein float little cabbage-leaf dumplings stuffed with minced snail; with salmon preserved in goose fat, as tender as a cherub's cheek; with baked red mullet with cumin-spiced cream; and with turbot filets coated in an astonishing lemon-and-cinnamon sauce that nearly overwhelms the taste of the fish. Equally impressive are the pigs' trotters stuffed with sweetbreads and accompanied by a potato gâteau (Koffmann's signature dish), venison with bitter chocolate, young pigeon with a sweet-and-sour elderberry sauce, and a classic roast of Angus beef brilliantly enhanced with a larding of bacon and a fumet of cèpes (essence of mushrooms).

It really is a shame that the desserts aren't quite on a par with the rest (we are thinking in particular of a chaud-froid of crêpes with sour cherries and cocoa ice cream). The coffee, though acceptable, could be better as well. These are mere quibbles, of course. A meal at Tante Claire leaves an enduring and blissful memory, particularly if you splurge on one of the more costly Bordeaux, Burgundies or Côtes-du-Rhônes from the best estates (there's also an ample list of crus bourgeois from the Médoc priced at about £20). Ministering to your happiness is an affable French maître d'hôtel, whose competence is such that we would willingly entrust our stomachs to him for the rest of our days.

A la carte: £50-£60, including wine.

11/20 Thierry's

342 King's Rd., SW3
352 3365, 352 9832
FRENCH
Open Mon.-Sat. 12:30 p.m.-2:30 p.m. & 7:30 p.m.-11:30 p.m. All major cards.

Once upon a time, Thierry Cabane confesses, he used to call his mother in France to check his plats du jour recipes. Today, after more than 25 years of serving good food, Thierry's is one of the most popular and consistent French restaurants on King's Road, complete with that rare status symbol, a massive front door with its own bell. The small split-level restaurant is cozy and unabashedly French, and it positively oozes ambience: red-and-white checkered tablecloths and gilt mirrors, paintings and apocryphal family photographs covering every inch of the terracotta wall. Chef François Rohlion, formerly of Fouquet's, in Paris, appears to have withstood the pace, as have the decorative, bilingual young waitresses, some of whom have been with the suave, saturnine Thierry from the start. "The only one who ever left me was my wife," he sighs.

As ever, the two-course fixed-price lunch is a good value that seldom disappoints, with six starters and six main courses that change weekly. The cleverly composed à la carte menu is riveting in its own right. A perfect cheese soufflé in a busy, crowded restaurant always strikes us as a miracle, and Thierry's always rises to the occasion. Honest fish soup is accompanied by rouille (a spicy Provençal red-pepper-and-garlic mayonnaise) and croutons, and a rich crab terrine is served with herb mayonnaise. The disk of creamy chèvre may be a trifle too goaty for lunch, but the quenelles (mousse-like dumplings) of pike in a light golden sauce are excellent (though we wish they had been a bit smaller). Chef Rohlion is market-wise; at past meals here, both the calf's liver with apples in a dark cider sauce and the medallions of beef with a crock of whipped horseradish cream were a tribute to his expert shopping. Look out for seasonal game, which Thierry's serves with an English flourish and all the trimmings: such tasty things as game chips, spiced sausages and wild mushrooms. To follow, we suggest you sample the heavily brandied petit pot au chocolat, the crème brûlée with a crunchy topping or the soufflé Grand Marnier, which a good many regulars swear is addictive. Eating at Thierry's is a leisurely affair; the handless clocks that abound are meant to induce a sense of gastronomic nirvana. The wine list is short but select. House wines include good Minervois and a Touraine Sauvignon.

A la carte: £25-£35, including wine.

11/20 Toto

Walton House, Walton St., SW3
589 2062
ITALIAN
Open Mon.-Sat. 12:30 p.m.-3 p.m. & 7 p.m.-11:30 p.m., Sun. 12:30 p.m.-3:30 p.m. & 7 p.m.-11:30 p.m. Cards: AE, V.

Toto must be the only Italian restaurant to occupy a former squash court. Down a cobblestone mews, it once formed part of Walton House, a grand residence built in the 1880s. It was from there on September 12, 1908, that one Clementine Hozier set off to marry Winston Churchill. One of Churchill's gifts to her, a carved seventeenth-century fireplace dedicated to Bacchus and big enough to roast an

ox in, forms the centerpiece of the restaurant. Toto is a split-level establishment that resembles a cross between a baronial hall and a conservatory, with an internal balcony and a secluded garden for alfresco eating. The menu is largely Italian, leavened with a few French and English dishes. Service is leisurely, so we prudently called for two glasses of Punt e Mes and emptied a pack of grissino (breadsticks) while waiting.

The wait was worth it: We were rewarded with fine pastas, notably the homemade tagliolini verdi gratinati (thin green noodles with grated cheese) and the risotto with a choice of wild mushrooms or seafood. The chef scores, too, with his fish dishes: generous portions of buttery grilled prawns, impeccable sea bass and turbot with green butter. From the grill emerges poussin (a young chicken), chicken paillard and châteaubriand (for two). Superb carpaccio (thin slices of raw beef filet served with a tasty sauce) and calf's liver veneziana with polenta represent the more traditional Italian offerings. Overall, Toto's is restrained Italian cooking of the Common Market stamp but executed with a sure touch. Scattered among the jungle greenery, the smart clientele glows with affluence, like they're dining on a *Dynasty* set. Dedicated management, with an air of studied gloom, make a welcome change from the customary overdose of Italian brio. A good choice for Sunday lunch. Interesting Italian wines. Reservations are a good idea.

A la carte: £25, including wine.

15 Turner's

87-89 Walton St., SW3 - 584 6711
FRENCH
Open Mon.-Fri. & Sun. 12:30 p.m.-2:45 p.m. & 7:30 p.m.-11 p.m., Sat. 7:30 p.m.-11 p.m. All major cards.

An elegant addition to the gastronomic haven of Walton Street, Turner's is the first solo venture of Brian Turner, formerly of the Capital Hotel. The pearly atmosphere is enhanced by dove-gray-printed upholstery and peach-marbled walls. French touches appear in the Lautrec prints, the engraved-glass screens that separate diners from staff, and the chic black blinds that separate diners from the street. Rippling music and bejeweled customers add to the luxurious ambience in this small (seats 50 or so) place, which can on occasion become oppressively noisy. The most important ingredients at Turner's are the chef/patron himself. He takes true delight in his customers, and without him, the atmosphere could be too slick, too impersonally smart. But his honest camaraderie is happily contagious.

The menu is less startling than we expected, considering the brave gambles Turner made at the Capital, but despite an occasional too-delicate sauce, his cooking remains consistently fine. At our last meal here, the salad of stuffed poached quail was safe but disappointingly bland. The red mullet soup with saffron, on the other hand, was beautifully judged, a richly flavored consommé with a subtly eggy rouille. Other starters included marinated filets of young rabbit, sweetbreads and concoctions of sole and turbot. Among the main courses, the rack of lamb in an herb crust was perfection, the filet of veal on celeriac (celery root) rather undefined. But we scored with the menu du jour, which was roast veal, its portion as generous as its flavor and accompanied by a bouquet of vegetables that was pretty but, apart from the glamorously potted pommes dauphinoise (sliced potatoes baked with milk, egg yolk and nutmeg), rather basic. We were also delighted with Turner's exquisite crab "sausage" and his sea bass on red cabbage. Desserts are stunning, the raspberry charlotte a particularly attractive melting combination of choux (cream puff pastry) and berries.

The selection of Champagnes is respectable, and there are also some excellent Alsatians and well-selected Burgundies on the young wine list, which Turner will undoubtedly continue to develop. Service is exemplary. Real trenchermen could be in danger of going away hungry, but everybody seems to go away happy. Be as daring as you can with your selections and you'll be in for a gastronomic treat; being less courageous, and you risk feeling teased. Don't even think about getting away with paying less than £60 for two.

A la carte: £30, including wine. Fixed-price menus: £13.50-£22.

12/20 Walton's

121 Walton St., SW3 - 584 0204
BRITISH
Open Mon.-Sat. 12:30 p.m.-2:30 p.m. & 7:30 p.m.-11:30 p.m., Sun. 12:30 p.m.-2 p.m. & 7:30 p.m.-10:30 p.m. All major cards.

The decor is self-consciously plush and over-designed, but the food at this expensive restaurant just gets better, thanks to the skill of chef Gary Jones. Of the four courses offered, the first proposes such delicacies as truffled terrine of foie gras and a smoked-salmon mousee. Among the "second dishes," the old-English country soup garnished with boned chicken wings sounds daunting, but the tartelette (they're rather keen on tartelettes here and make them with exquisitely crisp pastry) filled with summer vegetables in a lightly curried sauce was delicious, as was the eggplant dish. Some of the main courses are of ancient origin, such as the eighteenth-century saffron chicken, served with a "ragoo of grapes and cucumbers," but others, like the roulade of veal with wood mushrooms and the soft-boiled eggs in crusty tartelettes with curried crab lean more toward nouvelle cuisine. Although certain meat dishes, such as the scallops of beef, work handsomely, others are less successful (the one constant are the steep prices). Desserts are less original but include homemade fruit ices. There is also a good old-English savory Welsh rarebit, which comes, according to the menu, from an "enigmatic" recipe.

While a Walton's meal from the à la carte menu can hardly be called cheap, the fixed-price three-course lunch menu is quite an extraordinary value. The cooking and presentation are of a high standard, but the ingredients are simple: mussels rather than scallops, pork rather than veal. There's also a special English Sunday lunch and an after-theater fixed-price dinner. Since it opened in 1973, Walton's has consistently provided commendable cuisine. Mint tea as well as coffee is served to cap a meal. And the long wine list presents some fine clarets and an inexpensive house wine.

A la carte: £45, including wine. Fixed-price menus: £15 (lunch only), £19.50 (dinner only, after 10 p.m.).

10/20 The Waterfront

Harbour Yd., Chelsea Harbour, SW10 - 352 4562, 352 4602, 352 4619
ITALIAN
Open daily 12:30 p.m.-3 p.m. & 7 p.m.-11:30 p.m. All major cards.

The aptly named Waterfront is a multilevel, riverfront offspring of the long-established Eleven Park Walk, with a view of Chelsea

Harbour. Comfortable, light, bright and trendy though it may be, The Waterfront misses out on one basic detail: food. Majoring in seafood, supposedly Venetian at that (given that the chef used to work at Cipriani), it features such plain, nondescript dishes as Dover sole and steamed filet of salmon in hollandaise—the hot, garlicky breath of La Serenissima's cooking is conspicuous in its absence. On our last visit, just among the pasta dishes our complaints included: too much tomato sauce overwhelming the taste of the gnocchi verdi, and the sloppy polenta in a tomato sauce embellished with "laminated" shrimp was appalling. There are ten fish dishes on the main-course menu (including John Dory, turbot, lobster and sea bass), but even though the monkfish was served with a tasty lemon-peel sauce, garlic and parsley, the leathery flesh seemed unwilling to depart from its spine, and we were served a saltimbocca that was virtually ruined with too much salt. The ready-made desserts were represented by dry tiramisu that was appreciably lacking in both moisture and liqueur, and semifreddo di vaniglia (vanilla chilled or frozen mousse-like dessert of cream, custard, cake and fruit) that was tepid and boring, something akin to a wartime ice cream. In all, our most recent visit here was such a disappointment that we presumed that Giancarlo Dellaporta, the much-praised chef, must have been on vacation.

A la carte: £25-£30, including wine.

11/20 Ziani Dolce

112 Cheyne Walk, SW3 - 352 7534
ITALIAN
Open Mon.-Sat. 12:30 p.m.-2:45 p.m. & 7 p.m.-11:30 p.m., Sun. 12:30 p.m.-2:45 p.m. All major cards.

Just off Cheyne Walk, down Riley Street, this light and airy restaurant serves authentic Italian food in a pleasant setting dominated by a hand-stenciled ceiling and an abundance of green plants. Marinated salmon is a good starter, as is the delicious strozzapretti fiorentina, dumplings filled with ricotta and spinach and served in a tomato sauce with garlic. The main courses worth trying are the spicy, piquant thin slices of beef with warmed radicchio and rosemary and the tender calf's liver in a white-wine sauce. Since the chef comes from Venice, it is not surprising that many dishes are served with polenta, including stuffed boneless quails and breast of pigeon with a mushroom-and-herb sauce. The piscivorous, however, will prefer the grilled sea bass or the monkfish. Vegetables of the day (broccoli, zucchini and sautéed potatoes are standards) are usually crisp and fresh. For dessert, we prefer the excellent strawberry flan over the cheesecake, which is too creamy and rich for us. Ziani Dolce has moved into the premises that housed its compatriot, Santa Croce, for more than twenty years, and it promises to have an equally successful life.

A la carte: £25, including wine.

CHISWICK

10/20 Cafe Brazil

18 Fauconberg Rd., W4 - 994 9400
BRAZILIAN
Open Tues.-Sun. 11 a.m.-3 p.m. & 7 p.m.-midnight. All major cards.

At this bold new venture in a small row of shops tucked away in the Grove Park area of Chiswick, a short but authentic fixed-price menu offers such mainstream dishes as crab pâté and pork cutlets in addition to the restaurant's specialties: "Grandma's delicacies," a selection of small, crisp stuffed pastries; and "heavenly breasts," chicken breasts served with rice and a pungent, spicy sauce. The desserts are sweet and gooey and not necessar-ily worth the calories, but there is also an exceptional fruit salad. A few wines from Brazil and Portugal are found on the short wine list. The coffee is excellent (as one would certainly hope it would be in a Brazilian restaurant), the service friendly, but the prices are high.

A la carte: £25, including wine.

11/20 Danieli

142 Chiswick High Rd., W4 - 994 2628
ITALIAN
Open Mon.-Fri. noon-2:30 p.m. & 7 p.m.-11 p.m., Sat. 7 p.m.-11 p.m. All major cards.

In 1986 Marcello Danieli, the former head-waiter at Conway's, moved up and across the street to start his own restaurant, which aspires to be more than a humble trattoria. Danieli has the customary plate-glass front and white walls adorned with modern prints—and some tasty food. On top of the standards—pasta, meat, fish—its special weekly menus include a few dishes that must really tax the chef. Poached pike marinated in olive oil, capers and Emmenthal cheese and accompanied by a lightish, tasty polenta proved a subtle primer, and the pancakes filled with dried mushrooms, cooked ham, bread crumbs and béchamel sauce were delicious. Venison marinated in a red-wine sauce with juniper berries, carrots and onions delivered a deep flavor, but the mullet baked in foil with coarsely chopped tomatoes and herbs was less successful, tasting rather metallic. Desserts were ordinary, particularly the amaretti cakes, which were accompanied by a ruinous synthetic cream. The sound wine list accentuated Italian selections.

A la carte: £20-£25, including wine.

12/20 La Dordogne

5 Devonshire Rd., W4 - 747 1836
FRENCH
Open Mon.-Fri. noon-2:30 p.m. & 7 p.m.-11 p.m., Sat. 7 p.m.-11 p.m. Cards: AE, MC, V.

Since it opened in late 1985, La Dordogne has seen three chefs come and go (one of whom, a former cook for President Mitterand, disappeared to Brazil) and suffered through troubled times. By no means discouraged, owner Rachel Bitton expanded the place a couple of years ago to its current seating capacity of 64. And since the arrival of the present chef, Pierre Vincent, from Lyon, the standard of the cuisine has been consistently good. So we can now say that La Dordogne is now truly praiseworthy—much better than just a decent neighborhood restaurant.

Listed on the sensibly midsize menu are such appetizers as a delicious goat-cheese salad on a hot canapé, escalopes of fresh salmon served with herbs and lemon juice, and foie gras marinated in Jurançon, a sweet white wine from the Béarn district in southwest France. Representing the warm hors d'oeuvres are a duck terrine in puff pastry served with a green peppercorn sauce and a tasty fish mousse topped with scallops and served in a butter sauce. Two of the five fish courses are chunks of monkfish in a tomato-butter sauce and escalopes of salmon in a creamy sorrel sauce; among the other main-course entrées are tender lamb cooked in honey and mint, sliced chicken breast served in a creamy bacon-and-mushroom sauce, filet of beef in a Roquefort sauce and duck with a green peppercorn sauce. Cheeses are courtesy of Philippe Olivier. And standouts in the sweets department are the excellent sherbets. The wine list is short but interesting.

A la carte: £20-£25, including wine.

THE CITY

10/20 Baron of Beef

Gutter Ln., EC2 - 606 6961, 606 9415
BRITISH
Open Mon.-Fri. noon-3 p.m. & 5:30 p.m.-9 p.m. All major cards.

Behind the rather spartan exterior of this unremarkably rebuilt City establishment lies a bovine haven for City financiers and their visiting Japanese counterparts, who sink into the red plush banquettes as if to the barony born. The huge, well-stocked bar, the hunting prints, the hanging leaded lanterns and the starched waiters all seem steeped in the club tradition. And women are a rare sight indeed at the Baron of Beef. Lovely white-white table linens, crystal glasses, ornate silver settings and endless waiters are all pleasantly pampering. At our last meal here, a pretty plate of well-tailored amuse-gueules (cocktail appetizers), complete with designer radish and smoked-salmon toasts, heralded the arrival of a new chef. To celebrate this fact, we ordered two dry sherries (which turned out to be Tio Pepe at a hefty £5.70 for two) but passed on the appetizers in anticipation of the weighty entrées to follow. The "specialty" filet steak was a mighty example of the genre, suitable for an NFL tackle, though it could have been more tender. The rich gravy and accompanying artichoke with mushrooms and potato pebbles were fine, and the headwaiter solicitously adapted the bouquet of vegetables to suit our whims.

The beef trolley, however, is obviously an institution not to be tampered with. The gargantuan sirloin was produced, knives flashed and scraped dramatically, and the waiter found it completely incomprehensible that one slice was all a delicate appetite demanded. The disbelief, remonstration, attempts at persuasion and ultimate resignation that followed were on the bullying side of polite. We finally won and were rewarded with a Yorkshire pudding the size of a melon. Our beef was much enlivened by a delicious Saumur Rouge wine (a complete surprise and a bargain at £6.85), and the waiter didn't show his disappointment at our frugal choice, which was something of a relief. When ravishing-looking desserts were paraded in front of us, we fell for an excellent pear charlotte with raspberry coulis and refreshingly crunchy fruit salad (much improvement here). There was also a handsome English cheese board, laid out on yew leaves and served with a flourish. Individual coffee came complete with mints and macaroons, which we thought mighty generous—until the bill came, and we discovered we had been charged for them. A lush, plush place that is much improved, but also much pricier, since our last edition.

A la carte: £30, including wine.

10/20 Bubb's

329 Central Market, EC1 - 236 2435
FRENCH
Open Mon.-Fri. 12:15 p.m.-2:30 p.m. & 7 p.m.-9 p.m. No cards.

Within mooing distance of Smithfield Market, this corner site offers blood-red wood paneling, a somber wood bar, Tiffany lamps and severe white nappery to set off the gray suits of its regular customers. The slight air of dowdiness is as authentically Gallic as the menu. Provençal fish soup and onion gratiné are suitably dense and sustaining, and the main meat courses are vegetarian nightmares: a vast beef filet stranded on a creamy mushroom sauce, a whole pink lamb filet in pastry with a sweetish reduction sauce and haricots verts (green string beans). There are also snails, a goat-cheese salad, sea bream, kebabs and our old friend, grilled breast of duck au poivre. These arrive with generous dishes of undergarlicked potatoes dauphinoise, cheesy cauliflower and watery steamed zucchini. The cheese board arrived to us on our last visit curricular but woefully overfridged, and the

wine list tended toward bottles from Beaujolais, the Loire and the Rhône. The chocolate truffle cake always scores high, but the Kona coffee is vile. Another oddity is that, while taking no credit cards, this place happily accepts personal checks for more than £50.

A la carte: £25, including wine.

11/20 Corney & Barrow

118 Moorgate, EC2 - 628 2898
FRENCH/BRITISH
Open Mon.-Fri. 11:30 a.m.-3 p.m. & 5 p.m.-8:30 p.m. Cards: AE, MC, V.

Down the road from Finsbury Square is the extravagantly designed Corney & Barrow. Below the wine shop, reached by brass-railed stairs reminiscent of all the sybaritic cruises you've never taken, the basement restaurant is a triumph of decor over space, with the eye judiciously confused by a reflective maroon ceiling lit by low-wattage bulbs. Julian Wickham (see also Kensington Place in Notting Hill Gate) has cleverly mitigated the harshness with floral displays, fat columns trailing greenery and well-spaced tables in the dining room. At a central, transverse bar, brisk graysuiters snack with one eye on the constant stream of business news on the video screens. In its own bustling way, this place fulfills the same function as the Dickensian chophouse; and the cooking, as at many other wine-led restaurants, tries its best but never rises above tokenism. A fish-happy lunch menu ranges from a fairly stodgy terrine of smoked salmon and halibut littered with juniper berries to a main course of poached halibut fingers in peppercorn sauce freighted with orange segments. There are also a lobster salad, scallops poached in wine, and a whitefish casserole in lobster sauce that tries to be too many things for too many people. The carnivore is ministered to by veal piccata, grilled lamb kidneys and bacon, and roast lamb. The oenophile will salivate over the weighty, French-dominated wine list rising stratospherically to Château Petrus and tailing off with glasses of Fonseca 1960 port at £10.50 a pop. The homemade bread is good, as are the very English desserts (baked plums in sponge beset by raspberry coulis and cream). Remarkable for such an operation: Five different teas are offered in addition to coffee.

A la carte: £25, including wine.

9/20 The Pavilion Restaurant

Finsbury Circus Gdns., EC2 - 628 8224
BRITISH
Open Mon.-Fri. 12:15 p.m.-3:30 p.m. Cards: AE, MC, V.

Not the easiest of venues to locate, this restaurant (a converted bowling green pavilion in surprisingly leafy surroundings) turns out to be opposite London Wall, a short hop from the Museum of London but so deeply rooted in City atmosphere that it's not likely to be a tourist trap. The incredibly popular wine bar opened in 1984, followed shortly thereafter by the restaurant. Upon entering the building, the unseasoned diner is thrust immediately into the wine bar: a torrent of noise, smoke and Champagne quaffers. Traditional wine-bar food is supposedly available, but animated faces, cigarettes and glasses are all one can see. Its true raison d'être reveals itself upon one's exit: an idyllic view of the bowling green seen through huge picture windows. Those in search of food should leave the stewy bar, via the spiral staircase, to the fairly stewy subterranean restaurant, decorated in two tones of green paint (on brick) with rather baleful lighting. Unfortunately, one can't help but feel the presence of the thundering herd above. Women are in short supply here, and we didn't find a one without a financial background.

The fixed-price three-course menu comprises a choice of five appetizers, five main courses and two desserts or cheese. Rather elderly bread, accompanied by tiny tired crudités with indeterminate dip awaited us on the table at our last visit. It was a hot day, and the dip had acquired a skin that was not endearing. The timbale of Roquefort, rice and bacon was an interesting combination that would have been more interesting sans the rice. A salad of quail eggs was nicely presented if short on greenery and included only two eggs. To follow there was a hearty, unsubtle chicken provençale, generously dished up with umpteen olives, and a filet steak that could have been more tender but was compensated for by a powerful garlic sauce. The vegetables were fine. The summer pudding (fresh raspberries and red currants stewed together, sweetened and pressed in a bread-lined bowl) arrived with cream already poured over it, and sorry, there are no light desserts for weight watchers. The cheese was just okay. The biscuit basket, handed from table to table, contained specimens that would have been happier in a museum. Whatever you might think about the cuisine, the wines are well worth investigating. There are some real gems here. Try the Mâcon Cahrnay from Manciat-Poncet (which outclasses many high-ranking Burgundies and is just £9.35) or the extraordinary Condrieu from Belas Frères (£16.50). It came as no surprise to find that The Pavilion was awarded the 1988 Egon Ronay award for Cellar of the Year.

A la carte: £32, including wine. Fixed-price menu: £23.

11/20 Le Poulbot

45 Cheapside, EC2 - 236 4379, 248 4026
FRENCH
Open Mon.-Fri. noon-3 p.m. All major cards.

Rowley Leigh's departure for Kensington Place in Notting Hill Gate brought to an end an era in which Le Poulbot purveyed the best lunch in the City. On the ground floor, the Brasserie (which doesn't take reservations and is fraught with madding lines) turns out steaks, omelets and daily specials. In the basement (a zone of maroon plush squashed by a white plastic ceiling) is the restaurant proper, which has always been popular among Japanese bankers. Unlike at the Roux brothers' other, more vaunted operations, the menu here is a strict £24.50 fixed-price, including an apéritif and service. Le Poulbot's famous habit of charging woundingly high tariffs for alcohol is evidenced by an increasingly overpriced wine list (on which appears its own label Brouilly 1986 for £13.70, the current best bet) and by the appearance on our bill of an amusing £14 for two humble pear Williams.

Leigh's successor, Philippe Vandewalle, proffers a familiar selection of dishes, which the young French staff sometimes finds difficult to translate for customers. A typical menu presents a choice of two soups—beef consommé and gazpacho—a terrine of foie gras, stewed turbot, pan-fried calf's liver and noisettes d'agneau (lamb) with ratatouille tartelettes. Our last meal here started with fairly limp amuse-gueules, followed by a sloppy mousseline of chicken and Roquefort, whose sauce had far too close and heavy a relationship going with onion, and a decent asparagus salad with battered lamb's sweetbreads and aïoli. Our main courses were a sauté of beef with tarragon, watercress, carrots and squash, and a lattice-grilled filet of sea bream accompanied by a tomato-based sauce. The kitchen's taste exceeds its technique. The food looks so pretty when the silver domes are whipped off the plates—but this isn't the first time good looks have deceived. The cheese board is still a feast.

A la carte: £35-£40, including wine. Fixed-price menu: £24.50 (lunch only).

CLAPHAM

⑬ **Grafton**
45 Old Town, SW4 - 627 1048
FRENCH
Open Tues.-Fri. 12:30 p.m.-3 p.m. & 7 p.m.-11:30 p.m., Sat. 7 p.m.-11:30 p.m., Sun. 12:30 p.m.-3 p.m. All major cards.

Number 45 Clapham Old Town, an English seventeenth-century house with a Turkish carpet lining the winding paneled staircase, has a genuine historical-British atmosphere. Inside, however, is a restaurant that is as French as Bastille Day. None of that rushing the food to the table with desperate enthusiasm. Service is performed like a sacred rite: noiseless, elaborately polite and faintly aloof, with the waiters appearing, when something is needed, as if by magic. Thus expectations of a very good French meal are raised, expectations that are not disappointed. The salmon arrives in a pink sauce tinged with horseradish, a few chives radiating it for decoration, with some tiny peeled tomatoes completing the still life. The cream of mussel soup has the scent and tang of saffron. Tourte de faisan aux champignons sauvages brings pheasant, spinach and oyster mushrooms together, happily enclosed in a pastry case. Roast breast of duck is given life with a sauce of mushrooms, lardons and onions. Don't leave without trying the soufflé au Grand Marnier, which is served with a little bowl of cream and chocolate to add. Also worth tasting is the warm citrus tart with meringue. The fine selection of wines ranges in price from £7 for the house wine to £80.

A la carte: £30, including wine.

COVENT GARDEN

11/20 Beotys
79 St. Martin's Ln., WC2 - 836 8768
GREEK/FRENCH
Open Mon.-Sat. noon-2:30 p.m. & 5:30 p.m.-11:30 p.m. All major cards.

This is old-fashioned Soho at its most relaxed. Originally opened in Kensington in 1945 by Theodore Frangos, Beotys became ideally situated for pre- and post-theater meals, and grew to be extremely popular, when it moved to St. Martin's Lane in 1957. Quite recently the interior was totally redecorated with distressed terra-cotta walls, prints of Grecian deities and new attractive flinty-blue seats, which give the restaurant a grand feeling of vast spaciousness. And the tables are spaced well apart, so there is no need to inhale your neighbors' cigarette smoke or listen to their chatter.

The menu is divided into two sections. One offers such familiar French dishes as duck, entrecôte of beef, mignons de veau (veal) and filet of sole. The other contains some of the more popular Greek-Cypriot specialties, most of which are excellent—notably the kalamarakia (squid cooked in red wine), a fine taramasalata (pink fish roe, puréed with bread that has been moistened with milk, olive oil, lemon juice and garlic and served with crusty bread) and the dolmathes (stuffed grape leaves), which arrives hot and delicious in an unorthodox demi-glace sauce. Among the main courses, our particular favorite is the stifado, a rich casserole of tomatoes, small onions, bay leaves and rosemary, though the arnaki melitzanes, pieces of tender lamb served with eggplant, is outstandingly well cooked, as is the moussaka. In addition to the expected Greek sweets (among them a baklava decidedly not for those with many fillings) is a spectacular crêpes Suzette. Good coffee finalizes the meal, and there are small boxes of Turkish

Delight for customers to take home with them. The Greek food is much more reasonably priced than the French-based section of this hybrid list; the three-course fixed-price lunch is a bargain at £10.50. House wines are £7.50, and there is an expensive but sound wine list. Beotys is Greek for *welcome*—it's a word epitomized here by excellent service that is friendly and solicitous without being in any sense intrusive.

A la carte: £20-£25, including wine. Fixed-price menu: £10.50 (lunch only).

10/20 Bertorelli

44A Floral St., WC2 - 836 3969
ITALIAN
Open Mon.-Sat. noon-3 p.m. & 5:45 p.m.-11:30 p.m. All major cards.

On the street that flanks the world-famous Royal Opera House on its northern side, Bertorelli is a light, airy restaurant that once again has the family in charge and appears to have recaptured the popularity it lost a few years back. On the ground floor the use of mirrors makes the room seem much larger, as does the cunning use of wall lights with royal-blue pedestals; downstairs is an informal bistro with video screens that serves food more speedily. As at many Italian trattorias, the primary concern here is ensuring that the pasta is freshly made and accompanied by interesting sauces. As preludes, there are some interesting dishes, such as outstanding salad with mushrooms, garlic and endive, and crisp Norwegian prawns served with a lemon mayonnaise. Notable pastas include succulent rotelli (twists) in a peppercorn sauce and the delicious house version of spaghetti bolognese. Of the main courses, the veal scaloppine is gratifyingly sharp. The wine list is clearly above average, and the good house wine is priced at just £6.75.

A la carte: £15-£20, including wine.

10/20 Café Pelican

45 St. Martin's Ln., WC2 - 379 0309, 379 0259
FRENCH
Open daily 11 a.m.-2 a.m. All major cards.

Genuine brasseries are still scarce in London, despite the recent relaxation of liquor-licensing laws, but Café Pelican qualifies thanks to its lengthy open hours, extensive menu and physical layout. The narrow front section leads into a snakey wooden bar, which in turn leads beyond glass screens to a cool cream-colored room where the rattling bustle fades to a semblance of tranquility—an aura that is furthered by the presence of a grand piano. The food (such staples as cassoulet, pot-au-feu and blanquette de veau) used to be adequately prepared, if a trifle ambitious, and the service was famously slow. Lately things have changed: The presentation is now attentive, but the cooking can be indifferent. The Provençal fish soup, for example, once boasted a genuine, intense broth; when we last tried it, it was a watery, tomatoey apology with a vaguely fishy aftertaste. Onion soup was similarly anemic and seemingly innocent of beef stock, and it did no justice whatsoever to the accompanying wonderful fresh baguettes. Dry saucisse (sausage) maison and a nicely char-grilled entrecôte with mustard butter came with heaps of fries. All of this suggested a curious reversal of values, because if the food were only a few notches better, the restaurant would have been as packed as the tables in the front bar. More money can be made, of course, from libations, and unless things change, the sumptuously stocked bar will always have more fans than the kitchen.

A la carte: £20, including wine.

9/20 Entrecôte Café de Paris

12 Upper St. Martin's Ln., WC2 - 836 7272
FRENCH
Open Mon.-Sat. 12:30 p.m.-2:30 p.m. & 6 p.m.-11:30 p.m. All major cards.

The Entrecôte presents a simple but effective menu. You select either steak or fish (each prepared differently day to day), which is brought to your table, placed before you on a warming dish and served with delicious french fries. This is followed by a wonderfully garlicky salad. You can then choose from a simple selection of desserts, but the Entrecôte also offers a generous selection of French cheeses. Good wines are available. A relaxed, friendly atmosphere is allied to brisk service.

A la carte: £20, including wine.

11/20 Frère Jacques

38 Long Acre, WC2 - 836 7823
FRENCH/SEAFOOD
Open Mon.-Sat noon-3 p.m. & 6 p.m.-11:30 p.m., Sun. noon-2:30 p.m. & 7 p.m.-10:30 p.m.

Just a few doors from Covent Garden tube station, this French seafood restaurant is perfectly situated to feed those headed to or from the Royal Opera House, or to or from any other theater in the area. We can guarantee that you won't be disappointed by the food—if you don't expect the unreasonable—and the service is excellent. We've enjoyed the appetizers, including a mild terrine of salmon and an excellent carrot soup, which was served properly—hot and not ruined with too much caraway. The filet de lotte Frère Jacques makes for an interesting balance of flavors between the monkfish and the Dijon mustard sauce that brightened both the fish and the accompanying prawns. The assiette de l'amiral au champagne, a selection of brill, salmon and sole filets in which the flavors of the three fish were distinct, makes for a pleasing array, with an accompanying Champagne and lime sauce that was light and fresh (though it could have stood a bit more lime). The accompanying vegetable assortment included nicely al dente broccoli and cauliflower, but we were sad to see the cauliflower covered in the customary dull cheese sauce. The ambience at Frère Jacques is enchanting, an eye-pleasing mixture of posters, prints, tiles and stained-glass windows in the Belle Epoque style. There is a brasserie downstairs and live music from 7:30 p.m. on.

A la carte: £20, including wine.

10/20 Giovanni's

10 Goodwin's Ct., off 55 St. Martin's Ln., WC2 - 240 2877
ITALIAN
Open Mon.-Fri. 12:30 p.m.-2:30 p.m. & 6:30 p.m.-11 p.m., Sat. 6:30 p.m.-11 p.m. All major cards.

Despite its address, the nearest approach to this slip of a path is not via St. Martin's Lane but instead by way of its other adjunct, Bedford Street. Giovanni's is a small but immensely friendly restaurant, with photos of stars on the walls over faded oxblood seats. The standards at Giovanni Colla's restaurant are fairly high, and intended to provide good value for the money, making no pretense to be grander than it is. Bresaola (dried salt beef sliced from the filet, served as an antipasto) is enhanced by delicious green figs; another worthy starter is the spaghetti dish with a wonderfully rich pesto sauce. Veal scaloppine alla pizzaiola is fairly well balanced, and we could really taste the flavor of the chicken in the pollo alla valdostana. It is advisable to reserve a table; Giovanni's is always full, thanks to its pleasant, relaxed atmosphere. The house wine is Piedmontese Baci, but we relished a bottle of Montepulciano d'Abbruzzo 1986, which cost an astonishingly low £5.40.

A la carte: £25, including wine.

⑮ Inigo Jones
14 Garrick St., WC2
836 6456, 836 3223
FRENCH
Open Mon.-Fri. 12:15 p.m.-2:15 p.m. & 6 p.m.-11:30 p.m., Sat. 6 p.m.-11:30 p.m. All major cards.

Paul Gayler is one of London's master chefs. Besides his numerous prestigious gastronomic certificates on the walls, the room is elegant and, with its deep apricot-colored sofas offset by bare brick walls, nylon net curtaining and a plethora of vines, comfortable looking. Unfortunately, our last meal here got off to a disconcerting start when we were brought the wrong wine. Perhaps the waiter was color-blind, or more likely he was too rushed (Inigo Jones is like that at lunchtime), but we didn't allow that small mistake to spoil our meal. The rest of the service proved exemplary. We selected from the three-course fixed-price lunch menu (also offered pretheater, from 5:30 p.m. to 7 p.m.; if you dine after 7 p.m. and choose from the à la carte list, your bill can be easily multiplied two or three times over). From the selection of five starters, we chose the excellent gray mullet salad, potato and French beans and the delicious duck confit with lentils. A special entrée is prepared for each day of the week (calf's liver with sage and Madeira onion sauce, baked salmon, scallop tart with Champagne butter, among them), but we selected instead from the five regular main courses. And we relished the braised wild wood pigeon served with grapes and a sweet-corn pancake, as well as the finely textured pastry case filled with offal in a robust coriander sauce, which combined sharp and bland tastes in a most flavorful contrast. Gayler, an acknowledged master of vegetarian dishes, always offers a couple of meatless dishes. And among the desserts are a subtle pear-and-walnut burnt cream (not too sweet), fresh sorbets (raspberry, lemon) and a weighty chocolate ice cream. There's also a gratifying selection of cheeses. The grand wine list offers few bargains, but there is a most drinkable house Burgundy (£10.95) and a welcome selection of half bottles.

A la carte: £40-£50, including wine. Fixed-price menu: £18.25 (lunch and early dinner only).

Interlude
7-8 Bow St., WC2
379 6473, 836 9864

FRENCH
Open Mon.-Fri. noon-2 p.m. & 7 p.m.-11:30 p.m., Sat. 7 p.m.-11:30 p.m. Closed bank holidays, 10 days at Easter & Christmas & last 3 weeks of Aug. All major cards.

It has been almost ten years now since Jean-Louis Taillebaud, a Roux brothers disciple and trainee, opened this small, chic restaurant on the site of the former Covent Garden ticket office up the street from the Royal Opera House. Interlude de Tabaillau, as it was then known, was an immediate critical success, and when Taillebaud moved on to America, a considerable and devoted clientele feared the worst in terms of gastronomic continuity. In fact, the renamed Interlude has survived two chef changes since Taillebaud, and throughout it has managed to maintain consistently high standards. The setting has scarcely been altered—it's still smart, professional and unfussy, if a touch cramped, particularly for occupants of the tables for two in the front, who, in the best Parisian tradition, rub elbows with diners at tables on either side of them. Rust walls, mirrors, plants and subdued lighting make for a coccoon-like ambience in the evening, and at lunchtime the massive cream-colored pillars of the Royal Opera House loom through the blinds.

The food, from a kitchen now under the direction of Nicolas Bussy, remains sophisticated modern French, notable for sauces that incorporate fruits, wines and cream. An à la carte menu of ten appetizers and ten main courses includes such dishes as terrine of foie gras marinated in port, salmon marinated in dill with a cream sauce, seafood pot-au-feu with a saffron sauce, roast guinea-fowl with a grape-and-Sauternes sauce, and fruit gratin in Pineau des Charentes (a wine that is also served as the house apéritif). The pretheater dinner menu lists fixed-price choices (£9.95 for two courses or £13.50 for three)—a meal might include cauliflower mousse, fried sea bass and

assorted sorbets. There is also fixed-price menus for lunch and dinner; the former is a particularly good value at £19.50—an apéritif, three courses (an excellent rabbit terrine in slightly sickly plum cream sauce, a braised fondant of pork filet in a well-reduced red-wine sauce and a first-class warm apple tart), a half bottle of good Georges Duboeuf Beaujolais or Côtes-du-Rhône from the well-chosen wine list, coffee and petits fours.

A la carte: £40, including wine. Fixed-price menus: £9.95-£24.

12/20 Magno's
65A Long Acre, WC2 - 836 6077
FRENCH
Open Mon.-Fri. noon-2:30 p.m. & 6 p.m.-11:30 p.m., Sat. 6 p.m.-11:30 p.m. All major cards.

This popular restaurant, which started out as a brasserie, has set its sights higher, and in the process becoming more ambitious and expensive. It is always crowded, and the tables could hardly be closer together, but the service is attentive and the food original and prettily served. And as a wonderful bargain, the restaurant offers a pretheater fixed-price menu between 6 p.m. and 7 p.m. that costs a mere £8.95. The regular menu, which is short and changes frequently, includes such tempting starters as vegetable mousse with a basil sauce, and sautéed duck livers with greens and hazelnut oil. Noisettes of lamb are intriguingly partnered with eggplant-stuffed ravioli, and a sensational-looking king ragoût of sole and squid is served in a sauce of the latter's ink. Desserts from the trolley include, in season, fresh figs sauced simply with a raspberry coulis. Excellent cheese board. There are some interesting, reasonably priced French wines on the list, along with a well-priced house wine.

A la carte: £25, including wine. Fixed-price menu: £8.95 (pretheater only).

12/20 Mélange
59 Endell St., WC2 - 240 8077
FRENCH
Open Tues.-Fri. noon-2:30 p.m. & 6 p.m.-11:30 p.m., Sat. 6 p.m.-11:30 p.m. All major cards.

Don't be put off by the unprepossessing exterior or somewhat dingy decor (down to the paper tablecloths). This small, inexpensive restaurant serves unusual, well-prepared food in a style the owners rather charmingly call "cuisine libre." The short handwritten menu lists hors d'oeuvres that include an "envelope aux legumes," vegetables filling a crust of crisp phyllo pastry, and a warm salad with vegetables and strips of beef. Of the main courses, the calf's liver with grapes is tender and precisely cooked, with a good demi-glace but spoiled by unpitted grapes; the lamb noisette with a honey-and-green-pepper sauce is delicious, though a little overspiced. The fact that lamb and duck are offered only "when available" suggests a welcome lack of dependence on the freezer. Desserts include chocolate mousse (very rich, with a white-chocolate topping), profiteroles (small puffs of choux paste filled with whip cream and covered with chocolate sauce) with ice cream, and freshly baked apple pie. The total effect is rather like dining informally at home with food-loving friends. The presentation is not elegant and the service may be a bit erratic, but the food is interesting and cooked with great panache, and the ambience is both relaxing and friendly.

A la carte: £19, including wine.

10/20 Monkey Business

35 The Piazza, Covent Gdn., WC2
379 5803
AMERICAN
Open daily noon-midnight. All major cards.

Described as an American Bistro and Bar, this newly opened downstairs eating place is done up like a safari watering hole. There are murals of rolling African plains, a staff dressed in khaki shorts and bush shirts and life-size models of animals—including a large African elephant welcoming diners by the entrance—dotting the room. It all makes for a jolly, informal atmosphere, and solemn business-lunch types may have the spare chair at their table filled by a large black gorilla, placed there by an exuberant waiter. The menu consists of hamburgers, barbecued spareribs, salads and a few vegetarian dishes, such as enchiladas served with an enticing array of side dishes. The burgers are generous and freshly cooked, the fries large and crisp, and the dressings spicy. Desserts are primarily ice cream–based, and cocktails, liqueurs and specialty coffees are served as well as listings from the short wine list. This is a marvelous place to take children; there's a special children's menu and lots of freebies: balloons, crayons, and a World Wildlife Fund poster. Though clearly more marketing concept than restaurant, Monkey Business

is nevertheless a bright place to eat.
A la carte: £15.

13 Neal Street Restaurant

26 Neal St., WC2 - 836 8368
ITALIAN/INTERNATIONAL
Open Mon.-Fri. 12:30 p.m.-2:30 p.m. & 7:30 p.m.-11 p.m. All major cards.

After seventeen years, this golden example of fine restaurant design looks as good as it did when it opened. Elegant and spacious, with comfortable chairs and David Hockney prints on its walls, Neal Street started a trend that many have since followed. It has had a high profile recently, thanks to its genial co-owner/managing director, Antonio Carlucci, who published a book about Italian cooking and is seen frequently on television. Carlucci, a devout believer in allowing the flavors of a dish to be strong, creates all the recipes. The restaurant's specialties—wild mushrooms and white truffles from Alba in northwest Italy—are at their peaks during October and early November; in fact, both have short, autumnal seasons, leaving many months when the menu concentrates on more standard Italian fare, a far cry from its early, earthy days of game and fish. True, you'll still find a tasty offal soup and a tender venison with a robust flavor enhanced by cèpes, but otherwise the cuisine serves such Italian staples as a vegetable fritto misto (deep-fried in batter), a flavorful crespoline (crêpe-like version) of spinach and ricotta, tender, sliced calf's liver alla veneziana and so on. More satisfying dishes that hail from other parts of the world include a tasty dish of scrambled eggs with smoked salmon, gravlax and crab from Cornwall. Desserts include an outstanding crème brûlée and an authentic tiramisu.

A la carte: £35, including wine.

10/20 Poons

4 Leicester St., WC2 - 437 1528
CHINESE
Open Mon.-Sat. noon-11:30 p.m. No cards.

High-quality plate glass prevents the music from Covent Garden Piazza's mechanized "street performers" from penetrating Bill Poon's flagship restaurant. A small lounge of cane armchairs with the obligatory potted trees and signed movie-star photos introduces a tank of angel fish and a brick-walled dining area with Chinese screens and recessed spot-lights. Busy chefs can be seen behind a curious glass partition at the rear. The chairs are stiffly upright, and there are carnations on the tables, but what you're really paying for is the space. This is a classic example of what happens when a successful Cantonese operation (originating in Soho) gets ideas of gentility: service improves, prices skyrocket, and the cooking becomes lazy and even bland. And there is no soy sauce bottle on the table!

The preciously phrased menu begins with the usual array of duck, chicken, lobster and prawns and climaxes in fixed-price dinners for two to four, ranging in price from £33 to £78. The £39 menu for two kicks off with battered, deep-fried scallops and crab-and-minced-pork rissoles (deemed "Gold Sovereigns" and "White Jade in Onyx," respectively) and progresses to scallop and creamed cucumber soup, which proved to be one of the most unpalatable broths we have ever sampled. Bowls of hot, salty broth (more like wallpaper paste, if truth be told) holding three wan scallops and a few cucumber peelings were briefly tasted and briskly removed. "Bronze Duck" proved to be a tired dish of uncrispy duck wallowing in a puddle of soy. "Prawn Rope" at least had an authentic dash of ginger. Another dish of stewed lychee, red and green pepper, mango, melted bananas and coriander leaf provided a welcome relief from the pervasive tartness and sweetness of the seasoning, and the fried rice with sprinklings of egg and green pepper was exemplary. As a rule, the cooking needs more garlic. The libation to drink here is Tsing Tao beer, even at £2 a bottle. Banana fritters (£4.60 for two) can be a long time in coming, but they're adequately crisped.

A la carte: £20, including wine. Fixed-price menus: £33-£78.

11/20 **Rules**

35 Maiden Ln., WC2 - 836 5314
BRITISH
Open daily noon-midnight. All major cards.
The year Napoléon opened his campaign in Egypt (1798), Thomas Rule opened an oyster bar just south of Covent Garden. It evolved into a restaurant that has been visited regularly by such authors as Charles Dickens, William Makepeace Thackeray, John Galsworthy, H. G. Wells and Graham Greene, and it was the favorite spot of the Prince of Wales in the early years of the twentieth century, when he used to wine and dine Lillie Langtry. Rules is still enormously popular, which may explain why the service is amiable but sometimes forgetful (one bottle of wine took all of twenty minutes to arrive despite three reminders, and a second bottle failed to make an appearance entirely, though the the red-faced waiter was most apologetic). The nicotine-stained walls wear hundreds of cartoons from *Spy* magazine and other publications, along with paintings of sporting events from the eighteenth century. Those decorations, and the plum-colored upholstery, contribute to the almost exclusively male and club-like atmosphere.

The interesting appetizers include mussels in white-wine sauce and smoked eel with creamed horseradish. Entrées have become considerably more gamey in recent years; during the autumn months, Rules serves succulent roast grouse with green peppercorns, tangy wild duck with walnut and ginger, and delicious breast of pheasant with black currants. Also on the menu is delicious smoked eel, and the steak, kidney and mushroom puddings come in portions large enough to send a Grenadier sanguinely into battle. During the months when game fish is in season (March to September), the kitchen prepares wild Scottish salmon and wild sea trout. If you want to stay away from game, we can suggest the skate with black butter, the warm scallop mousse wrapped in lettuce or the steamed sea bass with a fennel butter sauce. The dessert and cheese selection is sparse. The house wines (£6.50 a bottle) are the worthy Pinot Blanc and the Sandeman Bordeaux Superior, but you'll also be tempted by several interesting clarets on the list, such as Château Millet 1982 at £12.50 a bottle. An obligatory port of call for tourists, Rules is indeed a gratifying place to visit.

A la carte: £30, including house wine.

---

*Restaurant prices are for a
complete three-course meal for one
person, including tip. Wine is
included only when noted.*

EALING

⑬ Bartons
7A The Green, High St., W5
840 3297

BRITISH

Open Mon.-Sat. noon-2:30 p.m. & 6:30 p.m.-11 p.m., Sun. 12:30 p.m.-4 p.m. All major cards.

A friend told us about Bartons, a recent creation of Barbara and Tony Yerolemou. We investigated the tip and are happy to report that the Yerolemous have brought to western London a most commendable restaurant. Set back off High Street at the end of a courtyard dragooned with weighty plants, Bartons is built on the two floors of what was obviously a stable in Georgian times. Upstairs is a beautifully fresh room with comfortable taupe chairs, tasteful Victorian prints on the walls and a pleasing array of flowers gracing its center. But what really provides the room with its particular appealing sedateness are the elegant waitresses in white silk blouses and long black Victorian skirts.

Although the official house specialties are game and fish, Bartons cuisine is, in fact, eclectic. Lobster-and-crab bisque tastes fresh and genuine. Assorted mushrooms are served in a cream sauce with a subtle suggestion of mustard. Baked pork filets covered with Stilton and served in an excellent piquante sauce are wonderfully tender. And while the salmon is enlivened by a rich tomato and tarragon sauce, it's easy to understand why the venison marinated in red Burgundy, juniper berries and wild sage, then sautéed and served with an onion marmalade, has become a much-loved Bartons specialty dish. The brandy-flavored crème brûlée is excellent. A compact and decently priced wine list offers some recent vintages—the '87 Mâcon Villages Pinot Chardonnay proved to be a good value at £12.95.

A la carte: £25, including wine. Fixed-price menus: £10.95-£13.95.

10/20 Ealing Tandoori Restaurant
9-10 The Green, High St., W5 - 567 7606, 840 0818

INDIAN

Open daily noon-3 p.m. & 6 p.m.-midnight. All major cards.

At this recently opened brick-exterior tandoori house, the best dishes are the chicken tikka flavored with cardamom, fennel and lemon juice; hasina, tender pieces of lamb marinated in yogurt and cooked in capsicum (chili), tomatoes and onions; and one of the special dishes, mughlai meat served with a saffron cream sauce and nuts. And the restaurant serves more than its fair share of vegetarian dishes. Functional wine list.

A la carte: £10-£15, including wine.

12/20 Maxim
153-155 Northfield Ave., W13 - 567 1791, 840 1086

CHINESE

Open Mon.-Thurs. noon-2:30 p.m. & 6:30 p.m.-midnight, Fri.-Sat. noon-2:30 p.m. & 6:30 p.m.-12:30 a.m., Sun. 6:30 p.m.-midnight. All major cards.

Mrs. Chow (no relation to the trendy Mr. Chow of Knightsbridge, New York and Los Angeles) is probably the only female chef/owner of a Chinese restaurant in London. She also owns Maxie's, a popular wine bar in Knightsbridge that serves good wines along with interesting food. A native of Shantung, Chow specializes in Pekingese cuisine but throws in a few Szechwan dishes to add spice to the menu. Maxim serves some of the best Chinese food outside central London, and to make choosing easier for "foreign devils," there are a staggering eight fixed-price feasts, including an entire vegetarian menu. Highlights from the à la carte menu include traditional Peking duck, steamed scallops in the shell and Szechwan prawns served in a miraculous ginger-flavored glaze. And Chow's hot, crispy, garlickly frogs' legs give their French cousins a run for the money. She's even come up with an enterprising wine list, from which the 1983 Mâcon Clesse drinks beautifully. One linguistic note from the Department of the Mysterious East: Maxim owes nothing to its grand namesake in Paris. It is simply an approximation of "Mei Sin," the restaurant's Chinese name, which translates as "beautiful heart."

Fixed-price menus: £10.50-£19.50.

EARL'S COURT

12/20 Brinkley's

47 Hollywood Rd., SW10 - 351 1683
FRENCH
Open Mon.-Sat. 7:30 p.m.-11:30 p.m. All major cards.

John Brinkley's attractive, mock-Edwardian restaurant, overlooking a trellised garden for alfresco eating, has a long-standing reputation for good, straightforward French food at reasonable prices. (The same kitchen serves the less expensive Wine Gallery next door.) Ex-Odin chef Graham Day is particularly good with mousses and terrines, which are outstanding in texture and flavor: pike with chervil, red mullet with fennel, a hot wild-mushroom mousse and a game terrine with an onion confit. He also makes a great fish soup, saffron-scented and chock-full of squid, scallops and mussels, a light pastry case of creamed sweetbreads on a bed of leeks, and a perfectly cooked dish of calf's liver with sweet braised apples. Among the more adventurous dishes is an intriguing combination of monkfish in a vermouth sauce with a pink-grapefruit garnish. Vegetables are interesting and served in substantial quantities. Top favorites among the desserts are an incredibly rich chocolate-and-brandy loaf and a chestnut mousse striped with crisp caramel. The good wine list features some bargains, as might be expected from an owner who not only drinks in his own restaurant but owns his own wine shop a mere two doors away.

A la carte: £25, including wine. Fixed-price menus: £14-£16.

12/20 La Croisette

168 Ifield Rd., SW10 - 373 3694
SEAFOOD
Open Tues. 7:30 p.m.-10:30 p.m., Wed.-Sun. 12:30 p.m.-2:30 p.m. & 7:30 p.m.-10:30 p.m. Closed 2 weeks at Christmas. All major cards.

La Croisette, the first restaurant launched by Pierre Martin, serves basically the same seafood specialties that are offered at Martin's other places, Le Suquet in Chelsea and Quai Saint-Pierre in Kensington: platters of shellfish and filets of whitefish presented in herb sauces. This basement venue is charming and lively, though it can become cramped; for evenings, reserve a table if you don't want to be sent away disappointed. There is a strong wine list, with an excellent house wine (£7.80).

A la carte: £30-£32, including wine.

⑬ Golden Duck

6 Hollywood Rd., SW10 - 352 3500, 352 4498
CHINESE
Open Mon.-Fri. 7 p.m.-midnight, Sat.-Sun. 12:30 p.m.-3 p.m. & 7 p.m.-midnight. All major cards.

The Golden Duck has been delighting thousands of customers for more than twenty years with its excellent food and reasonable prices. It remains a flourishing concern thanks to the intelligence with which its fixed-price menus continue to feature three leave-it-to-us feasts (bargains at £12.50, £13 and £13.50), in addition to a special six-course vegetarian banquet (£10). At the Golden Duck we are always aware of the hum of anticipation emanating from each of the three sections of the restaurant, which are skillfully partitioned to resemble a Chinese lantern separated by mirrors. The Golden Duck was among the first of the new generation of Chinese restaurants in London to discard the dusty bric-a-brac of dragons and lanterns that clutter so many of these establishments. The redecoration harmonizes nicely with the young, hip clientele that comes here for a good meal that won't annihilate their budget. The Golden Duck has benefited from a sense of continuity under its founder and co-owner, the multilingual Russian Chinese Alexander Shihwarg (a.k.a. Shura), who keeps a caring eye on the cuisine of the current chef, the immensely talented 29-year-old Cheung, who took over in 1986.

Although the restaurant specializes in the cuisine of Beijing, it also creates various hot and spicy dishes from such areas as Hunan to the south and Szechwan to the southwest. Among the delicious appetizers are a light, clear won ton soup served with long-eared ravioli (a house specialty) and a tasty crab-and-sweet-corn chowder; hot canapés of prawn pâté on toast; and fried shredded seaweed with grated scallops. The Golden Duck prides itself on its outstanding dumplings, along with its more-than-satisfying steamed scallops in the shell with ginger or spring onions, mussels in a black-bean sauce, tofu-and-pickle salad (a Buddhist monk's delight), salad of lamb and coriander in a light mustard dressing, lettuce parcels filled with minced beef and braised in a hot "sea spice" sauce, hot and spicy Chengdu prawns and delicious lemon and garlic lamb. There's a sound wine list and an inexpensive house wine.

A la carte: £15-£20, including wine. Fixed-price menus: £10-£13.50.

⑬ The Left Bank
88 Ifield Rd., SW10 - 352 0970

FRENCH

Open nightly 7 p.m.-11:30 p.m. All major cards.

In the house that formerly served as the home of such restaurants as Nick's Diner and Martin's (now moved west of Regent's Park), The Left Bank makes yet another attempt to cultivate the palates of those who live in or choose to visit this area of West Brompton. Bare wooden tables reflect candlelight, and there's a glass conservatory ceiling to complement the eighteenth-century portraits and nineteenth-century animal paintings hanging against pink and beige Osborne & Little wallpaper. The menu changes frequently, but several visits have confirmed that The Left Bank is a restaurant of consistently high standards. Calf's kidneys cooked slowly in a cream-and-chive sauce makes an interesting starter, and the warm salad of sautéed pork served on a bed of green beans and salad leaves is delicious. The filet of salmon, poached and served with a light cream sauce, is excellent; also meriting distinction are the breast of duck roasted and served with a sharp peppercorn sauce, the medallions of pork heightened with an excellent honey and ginger mixture, and the monkfish cooked in a cream-and-lime sauce. A well-chosen wine list is strong on representatives from Bordeaux and Burgundy, and there's an excellent house wine for £6.50.

A la carte: £25, including wine.

11/20 Pontevecchio
256 Old Brompton Rd., SW5 - 373 9082

ITALIAN

Open daily 12:30 p.m.-3 p.m. & 7 p.m.-11:30 p.m. All major cards.

This spacious restaurant seats up to 250 people. Its outside dining area is nearly full during the afternoons, when the main room becomes increasingly noisy. As the evening wears on, the sound of voices starts to rebound off the decorative modern paintings and cut glass. As its name would indicate, Pontevecchio boasts a proprietor who hails from Florence and a menu with Tuscan overtones. The day's specialties, written on the right side of the tall menu, often include the impressively rich house pâté and the gamberetti Pontevecchio, a delightful mélange of prawns, white wine, garlic and chilis. The pesto sauce may be too rich, but the use of spinach in the pancake stuffed with ricotta cheese provides a telling contrast. The petto di pollo lungarno, chicken breast rolled and stuffed with garlic and butter, is light and delicate, and we were also particularly pleased with the grilled lamb with basil and rosemary. The 1984 Brunello di Montalcino from the well-selected wine list was superior, and a bargain at £9.50.

A la carte: £20, including wine.

12/20 Tiger Lee
251 Old Brompton Rd., SW5 - 370 2323, 370 5970

CHINESE/SEAFOOD

Open nightly 6 p.m.-11:15 p.m. All major cards.

The tiny tremors of anticipation experienced by diners may be due in part to the fact that Underground trains run directly beneath this small, elegant Cantonese fish restaurant, whose location is hardly the most salubrious in London. Do not be deterred, however, for Tiger Lee is one of the best Chinese restaurants in the city. Fresh trout glimmer as they fin through the bubbles in the freshwater tank near the entrance, double-doored to shut out the thunder of traffic. Inside, the decor is a cool oasis of calm, as balanced and precise as a Chinese shadowboxer. The short menu is a far cry from the order-by-numbers chop suey and chow mein once associated with Cantonese cooking. Diners may find themselves steered into ordering a well-balanced selection of dishes so that steamed and stir-fried, hot and mild complement one another in proper harmony. If you demonstrate interest in the subject, the precepts of yin and yang (the cool, gentle, female principle and the hot, strong, male one) will be simply explained in culinary terms. Deep-fried prawns, their shells encrusted with salt, crunchy prawn toast, scallops, abalone, delicate deep-fried baskets filled with morsels of chicken, scallops and slivers of smoked raw ham, bean curd cooked in a dozen different ways, perhaps stuffed, deep-fried or steamed with ribbons of fresh vegetables—to many people these dishes will constitute nothing short of revelations. Many combine a delicate blend of fish and white poultry meat; notable among these is the classic Cantonese deep-fried chicken, as crisp and melting as the bed of golden curling shrimp crackers on which it rests. Presentation is superb. Where else in London can you find such a pinnacle of preparation as lightly stir-fried rice wrapped and steamed in a lotus leaf? We must proffer one small criticism: This is an expensive restaurant, and it presumes that the yin half of a couple needs to be shielded from the cruel reality of menu prices. The wine list is high priced and well selected, with the house wine running £9.20. The restaurant holds only about 30, so reservations are essential.

A la carte: £20-£25, including wine.

EUSTON

11/20 Pinocchio

160 Eversholt St., WC1 - 388 7482
ITALIAN
Open Mon.-Fri. noon-2:45 p.m. & 6:30 p.m.-10:45 p.m., Sat. 6:30 p.m.-10:45 p.m. All major cards.

Actually in an area east of Euston known as Somerstown, Pinocchio is the most southerly of two restaurants that have opened recently, both of which are doing a justifiably flourishing trade. Situated near a Nepalese bistro on an unprepossessing road that runs down the side of Euston Station, Pinocchio has a newly opened glass-roofed area at the back, which is a blessing, because the cramped area at the front, with its black blinds, central pillar, wall lights and black ceiling fans, is rather claustrophobic and gloomy. Maurizio Bertasio and his English wife, Linda, opened this friendly little spot in 1986, and it quickly developed into a fine area restaurant. Pinocchio's is a short but authentic Italian menu that includes, for starters, delicious fresh pasta, praiseworthy risotto and tasty carpaccio, in addition to the un-Italian but quite acceptable gravlax. Comprising the small range of main courses are a deliciously tender venison steak and an interesting combination of monkfish, tuna and king prawns in a cream, white wine and garlic sauce. Long may Pinocchio flourish, and let's hope the intrusive music soon ceases to exist altogether.

A la carte: £15-£20, including wine.

FULHAM

 Blue Elephant

4-5 Fulham Broadway, SW6
385 6595, 381 2896
THAI
Open Mon.-Fri. & Sun. noon-2:30 p.m. & 7 p.m.-11:30 p.m., Sat. 7 p.m.-11:30 p.m. All major cards.

A welcome splash of swagger in drab Fulham, the Blue Elephant announces itself to the street with wobbly blue neon and colorful roof tiles. Similarly bold, the bar area is a designer jungle of spot-lit bamboo ceiling, oversize greenery, rattan thrones and background serenadings of Thai ballads (on tape). The dining area, with its two massive skylights riding above the tables and its life-size praying Buddhas reflected in the gold-plated table settings, comes into its own on summer evenings. Widely hailed as the best Thai restaurant in Britain (companion to L'Eléphant Bleu in Brussels), the Blue Elephant serves a cuisine befitting its opulent setting. And it promises that "the magical culinary skills" of chefs Kop and Chang will do wonders with the vast range of seafood—from cod to fish cakes to every form of crustacea under the waves. Fish stew (mussels, prawns, crabs and scallops) is echoed by a piscine soup answering to the name of Floating Market. Menam chicken soup is a brilliantly pungent concoction of chicken, coconut, lemon grass and makrude leaves, spiked with ginger and torpedoed with button mushrooms. The satays are generously chunky, and their accompanying peanut sauce packs a genuine crunch. Scallops farang (stir-fried with an oyster sauce and many vegetables) is fairly muted in this company, as are the stuffed chicken wings. A grandiose brass plateau called the Royal Platter comprises several main courses, such as the cool, acidic salad of chili beef and the succulent, tandoori-like emerald chicken, marinated and wrapped in toey leaves. The wine list is best disregarded in favor of Singha beer. A great restaurant will always attend to details, and that principle is applied here by a sure touch both on and off the table—the prawn crackers, for instance, are the best in captivity. This place is a treat not to be missed.

A la carte: £25, including drinks.

11/20 The Garden

616 Fulham Rd., SW6 - 736 6056
VEGETARIAN/HEALTH FOOD
Open Tues.-Sat. 7:30 p.m.-11 p.m., Sun. 1 p.m.-2:30 p.m. All major cards.

The Garden is based on what promises to be a successful formula: a menu of vegetarian dishes and healthful dishes made with fresh fish, poultry and game. The raw materials are supplied by farmers who rear free-range hens and grow organic produce. The place is more of a cottage garden than a formal one, with some half dozen tables arranged around a small, simple room that is peaceful and intimate without being crowded: nice, thick white tablecloths, extremely comfortable Lloyd loom basket chairs, fresh flowers, greenery and light Mozart or Vivaldi playing gently in the background. The menu changes frequently in harmony with the owners' philosophy of using the fruits of the earth in season. Special recommendations are due, however, to the vegetable moussaka, which is a great deal more flavorful than many of the meat dishes; the airy cheese and spinach puffs, deep-fried croquettes of Brie; and the chicken in lemon sauce. The small wine list is admirably selected: a half dozen lightweight red wines, a couple of good rosés, some delicious, full-bodied white wines and two specialties that merit tasting: Hugh Rock's elderflower and sparkling gooseberry wines. The Garden is a delightful place for a quiet dinner with friends, though it is perhaps a bit

muted for diners in search of distraction. The three-course fixed-price dinner menu varies seasonally along with the regular menu. A pianist performs in the evenings.

A la carte: £20, including wine. Fixed-price menu: £15 (dinner only; supplementary charge for game dishes in season).

12/20 Hiders

755 Fulham Rd., SW6 - 736 2331
FRENCH
Open Mon.-Fri. 12:30 p.m.-2:30 p.m. & 7:30 p.m.-11:30 p.m., Sat. 7:30 p.m.-11:30 p.m. All major cards.

Up in the furthermost reaches of Fulham's gentrified hinterland is Hiders, home of chef Paul Duvall (formerly of Bewicks) and of rich, ultra-nouvelle food. Run by Richard Briggs, the two-floored, attractive Edwardian restaurant is quiet and relaxing at lunchtime, candlelit and bustling at night. It has already become a neighborhood fixture, saving local residents a fortune in gasoline. Why travel west when it's all happening right here? The fixed-price menus (two- and three-course) change every two weeks; voracious eaters can pay a supplementary price for an additional main course. Duvall's food is both fashionable and palatable, but it would benefit from being less baroque. All the old nouvelle-cuisine favorites are served here: seafood feuilleté, chicken mousse with two sauces of red and yellow peppers, duck magret (rare duck breast) and mignons of pork with pink peppercorns and brandy. Only the good cooking and skilled presentation save it from being entirely déjà vu. We particularly liked the delicate cream of parsnip soup with a touch of curry, and the pink lamb cutlets in a garlicky wine sauce. Pan-fried calf's liver with a julienne of ginger and spring onions made a perfect luncheon dish, and the filet of sea bass topped with a mushroom and herb crust was close to thrilling. Game sausage with juniper berries in a sort of Cumberland sauce struck a welcome English chord, but the suprême of chicken suffered from an overdose of anchovies. Luscious desserts include a superb trifle made from amaretto biscuits and fluted with cream, as well as a scrumptious summer pudding. The short wine list features Blanc de Blancs and Rouge de Champclos as house choices.

A la carte: £17-£25, including wine. Fixed-price menus: £12.50-£15.

HAMMERSMITH

10/20 Light of Nepal

268 King St., W6 - 741 3536
NEPALESE
*Open daily noon-2:30 p.m. & 6 p.m.-11:45 p.m.
All major cards.*

Small and rather dingy, with food-spattered menus and crowded tables, this restaurant tends to be overlooked, located as it is alongside its more glamorous Hammersmith neighbors. Nevertheless, it is worth a visit for its special Gurkhali dinner for two, which features a superb spicy soup with small stuffed dumplings and other Nepalese specialties floating in its broth. The rest of the menu is standard tandoori and curry fare, but the spicing is authentic and the portions generous. A dish of assorted seeds and nuts (including betel) is presented at the end of the meal—and it's better than the coffee. Service is lackadaisical.

A la carte: £12-£20.

10/20 Lowiczanka

238-264 King St., W6 - 741 3225
POLISH
Open Mon. & Wed.-Sun. 12:30 p.m.-3 p.m. & 6 p.m.-10 p.m., Tues. 12:30 p.m.-3 p.m. All major cards.

On the first floor of the Polish Social and Cultural Centre, this spacious, unpretentious restaurant caters primarily to expatriate Poles who enjoy the inexpensive and authentic food served in pleasant surroundings. You'll find such international dishes as avocado with prawns and chicken Kiev, but the Polish dishes include a succulent piece of cured herring in a raw-onion and fresh-cream sauce, and a pea-and-smoked-ham soup thick with vegetables. There are also pirogi, little ravioli-like stuffed dumplings, and a hearty bigos, a hunter's stew of Sauerkraut, beef, polish sausage and boiled potatoes. The desserts run to cakes of various sorts, but there are also crisp, light pancakes filled with jam or cream cheese. On our last visit, the service was slow and rather surly, but the food is nonetheless an excellent value and perfect on a cold, hungry day. On Friday and Saturday evenings the place comes alive with music and dancing. Even with wine, it would be hard to spend more than £10 a person.

A la carte: £10, including wine

10/20 Rajdoot

291 King St., W6 - 748 7345
INDIAN
Open Mon.-Thurs. & Sun. noon-2:30 p.m. & 6 p.m.-midnight, Fri.-Sat. noon-2:30 p.m. & 6 p.m.-12:30 a.m. All major cards.

In the section of King Street that runs westward from the Hammersmith Underground station, Rajdoot is the most frequently visited of the area's clutch of immensely popular Indian restaurants. Pink table linens, subdued lighting and spacious surroundings make this a more elegant venue than many of its counterparts, and the food, straightforward northern Indian with some Mughlai specialties, is well above average, with intelligent use made of such spices as saffron in the soup and cinnamon in some curries. A fragrant prawn dish soars above the ordinary, and two of the house specialties—the lamb pasanda, thin slices of lamb filet marinated in spices and yogurt with herbs, and the gosht kata masala, lamb braised with onions, ginger, garlic and garam masala (blend of ground spices)—are exceptional. Tandoori masalas, vegetarian and nonvegetarian thalis and Khurzi chicken or lamb (available with 24-hour notice) are delicious. Strangely, no tea is served, only the customary, rather nasty coffee. Prices are reasonable.

A la carte: £10-£12.

12/20 River Café

Thames Wharf, Rainville Rd., W6 - 381 8824
ITALIAN
Open Mon.-Fri. 12:30 p.m.-2:30 p.m. & 7:30 p.m.-9 p.m. Cards: AE, MC, V.

The River Café, just as its name suggests, overlooks a stretch of the Thames. With plate-

---

Going traveling? Look for Gault Millau's other "Best of" guides to France, Paris, Italy, Hong Kong, New York, New England, Washington, D.C., Los Angeles, San Francisco and Chicago.

---

glass walls and a dark-powder-blue vaulted ceiling, it is a light and sparkling oasis of culture in a section of London that is bereft of such restaurants. More importantly, it serves some delicious food—in fact, it is responsible for some of the most flavorful Italian cuisine in London. Among the appetizers on the short but tidy menu are a delicately balanced saffron soup accompanied by Tuscan bread and sage; three mozzarella crostini (small pieces of toast) served with sun-dried tomatoes, chili and red anchovies; several tasty slices of bresaola (the northern Lombardy specialty of dried salt beef), which are enhanced by rocket (arugula); and a white truffle oil and penne with a bracing sauce. Among the six main courses are grilled

squid with fresh red chili, rocket and french fries; a slice of mouth-wateringly tender grilled calf's liver with polenta and wild mushrooms; pork loin braised in milk and lemon and accompanied by slow-cooked zucchini; a juicy leg of lamb served with rosemary and garlic; and a zesty grilled red mullet with anchovy-flavored tapenade (a purée of capers, anchovies, black olives, garlic and olive oil), grilled fennel and blue lentils. For die-hard carnivores, thick entrecote is presented with french fries and a mixed salad. A short list offers wines that are primarily Italian. Add brisk, friendly service, and you have a restaurant worth seeking out when you're in this part of London.

A la carte: £15-£20, including wine.

HIGHGATE & HAMPSTEAD

(13) Quincy's
675 Finchley Rd., NW2 - 794 8499
INTERNATIONAL
Open Mon.-Sat. 7:30 p.m.-10:30 p.m. Sun. noon-2 p.m. & 7:30 p.m.-9:30 p.m. Cards: MC, V.

A proper restaurant on the borders of Cricklewood and Golders Green, Quincy's combines cooking (which achieves its ambitions with complete success) and service (which is deft, attentive and informed) to make it one of the best neighborhood restaurants in London. It is clear that Sandy Anderson is interested in reviving the English taste for meat with fruit. Take, for example, the pigeon breast with crab-apple jelly or the curried parsnip soup, both of which, thankfully, taste much better than they sound. They are perfectly judged, never cloying, and thoughtfully respectful of their ingredients. Anderson also serves thin raw beef, carpaccio-like, with an anchovy and grain-mustard sauce. His desserts are sumptuous and highly flavored, and his cheese selection is among the healthiest in the city, always at its absolute peak when presented. It should not be astonishing to find, say, a Reblochon or farm Brie in magnificent condition, but it is. This is a restaurant that clearly pays close attention to the details.

A la carte: £20-£25, including wine. Fixed-price menus: £14 (Sunday lunch only), £16.50.

11/20 San Carlo
2 Highgate High St., N6
340 5823, 340 5421
ITALIAN
Open Tues.-Sat. noon-2:30 p.m. & 7 p.m.-11:30 p.m., Sun. noon-2:30 p.m. & 7 p.m.-10:30 p.m. All major cards.

San Carlo, located in Highgate Village, is a reliable, well-run example of London's medium-to-upscale Italian restaurants. Outside are white plaster, full-width windows and a yellow canvas awning. Inside are white walls, modern paintings, handsome unglazed terracotta tile floors and a raised bar area with a little white upright piano. At the back, the pretty walled courtyard houses tables for apéritifs. The clientele is composed primarily of affluent Hampstead/Highgate professionals, who often know one another and the staff. The service is brisk, for the most part efficient and solicitous. Lunchtime business groups and evening family parties testify to San Carlo's ability to draw a steady clientele, but as far as we're concerned, the food is thoroughly competent but in no way outstanding. A good array of antipasti covers the heavy wooden table in the middle of the room, which also bears a ham slicer. Alternative starters include prosciutto, bresaola, carpaccio, mussels, snails and the "chef's specialty," delicious grilled mushrooms sprinkled with parsley, garlic and anchovies. Among the dozen or so pastas and soups is a tasty fettuccine in a salmon sauce. Main courses and desserts are equally middle of the road: a nice fondant of calf's liver in butter and sage, plump veal sautéed with fresh herbs, zabaglione and a trolley full of tarts, cakes, mousses and fruit desserts. Moderately price Sicilian table wines, a reasonable list of classier bottles and large cups of espresso are also offered.

A la carte: £30-£35.

HYDE PARK & KNIGHTSBRIDGE

⑯ Capital
22 Basil St., SW3 - 589 5171

FRENCH

Open daily 12:30 p.m.-2:30 p.m. & 6:30 p.m.-10:30 p.m. All major cards.

What an enchanting room in which to enjoy a meal: Small and intimate, it is decorated in the most soothing colors—peach, apricot, crushed strawberry—and gives off a powerful belle epoque impression, thanks to the tall framed tapestries, vases of flowers, bows, medallions, tapestry-covered chairs and ornate silk curtains. The simplified menu is now all in English, and the service is discreet but effective. The Capital hotel has had some outstanding chefs in recent years, including Richard Shepherd (presently at Langan's) and Brian Turner (who left to start his own restaurant on Walton Street); now comes a third chef of outstanding talent, Philip Britten, who has apprenticed at both the Battersea branch of Chez Nico and the Dorchester. In every dish we've tasted here, the textures were precise and the combination of sauces exact. His cooking is a sort of hybrid of first-rate traditional French (which combines taste and intrinsic exellence) and nouvelle cuisine (that is, with vegetables steamed and meat very lightly grilled or baked). A mousseline of duck and mushrooms is enhanced by a mild cèpes butter sauce. A cream of cauliflower soup, delicate and delicious, is clearly freshly prepared (it includes an egg yolk and is topped with a sprinkling of chives). Such a light, palate-teasing starter sets the appetite humming for the main course, and we have yet to be disappointed in this arena either. Wonderfully tender mignons of beef with a leaf-spinach garnish are served with a delicate béarnaise sauce, and calf's liver is grilled exactly right, topped with wild mushrooms and garnished itself with a pat of au gratin potato. Desserts include a tasty fresh lemon tart and a light mousse of William pears on a whole-meal biscuit base. Our only gripe concerns the wines, which are fearfully expensive.

A la carte: £25-£45, including wine. Fixed-price menus: £17.50 (lunch only), £27.50 (dinner only).

11/20 La Fantasie Brasserie
14 Knightsbridge Green, SW1 - 589 0509

FRENCH

Open Mon.-Sat. 12:30 p.m.-3 p.m. & 7 p.m.-11:15 p.m. All major cards.

Situated in the heart of Knightsbridge, La Fantasie Brasserie is elegantly decorated in an art nouveau style with pastel colors, candles on the tables and house plants. In this pleasant atmosphere a varied and original menu is offered, filled with a number of dishes that are more ambitious than one would expect in a traditional brasserie. However, on our last visit, we had the distinct impression that not all the dishes were prepared to order. But their presentation was excellent, and the French staff is efficient and friendly. On the weekly changing menu you may come across such starters as tasty crab claws with a tartare sauce, and such main courses as rock fish and pineapple fritters, baked breast of chicken with wild mushrooms, and beef filet with a green-pepper sauce. The dessert selection includes a tasty almond meringue cake and a combination of black currant, lime and raspberry sorbets. On the solid wine list are a good many bottles from Beaujolais, Côtes-du-Rhône and Burgundy priced between £10 and £25.

A la carte: £25, including wine.

⑭ Ménage à Trois
15 Beauchamp Pl., SW3 - 589 4252

FRENCH

Open Mon.-Fri. 11:30 a.m.-2:45 p.m. & 7 p.m.-12:15 a.m., Sat. 7 p.m.-12:15 a.m. All major cards.

Since it is situated on a highly fashionable Knightsbridge shopping street, is run by a personality chef and features a "concept menu" of "mainly befores and afters," one might expect Ménage à Trois to be glossy, pretentious and silly, full of posing Eurotrash types who have more money than sense. Fortunately, that's not the case at all. The clientele, while obviously more in the mold of Diana Spencer (a.k.a. Princess Di) than Marks & Spencer, is mixed and jovial and keeps the braying within acceptable limits. The warren-like basement premises are homely and underdesigned, like a sophisticated version of a bustling Left Bank student bistro. The decor—cream-painted brick walls, wicker chairs, banquettes upholstered in a '30s zigzag pattern, a little greenery, framed paintings and photographs that would be considered sexist a couple of miles north in the People's Republic of Islington—is pleasantly ad hoc, and the small piano bar adds a sophisticated note.

Far from being gimmicky, Anthony Worral-Thompson's cooking is full of imagination, skill and, most important of all, that crucial third ingredient: taste. Instead of being listed under the traditional categories—appetizers, fish, entrées and so forth—the dishes are organized by their principal ingredients: cheeses, vegetables, salads, caviars, pasta, shellfish, duck and its foie gras, game, meat and poultry, desserts and chocolate dreams, and a recent addition, "food that chefs enjoy eating" (such substantial country dishes as pot-au-feu, cassoulet and sausages and mash). Within each of the categories is a choice of three dishes of modest size, and one is invited to order as few or as many courses as one wishes. In practice, since all of the dishes are rich, and not that small, three courses make a good, full meal. The dishes, often featuring the "trio" theme—such as the one combining lamb with garlic and rosemary, beef with curried eggplant and veal with a confit of wild mushrooms—are inventive enough to be genuinely interesting but not confusingly fussy. They often take as a starting point a traditional earthy basic, which gives even the most fanciful concoction a certain robust tastiness. Good examples of this are the two dishes named Ménage à Trois, each a trio of hot succulent pastry parcels. The first trio contains Camembert and cranberry, Roquefort and leeks, and Boursin and spinach; the second, lobster and sugar snaps, scallops

and leeks, and crab and cucumber. We also liked the novel and delicious roasted cake of layers of Brie and goat cheese, served with grilled apples and pears and a surprising and successful sesame-flavored oil dressing. Desserts include a first-rate selection of eight chocolate confections and the sweet Mascarpone with hot strawberry fritters, displayed on a white plate painted red and yellow with a vivid strawberry coulis and shining golden corn syrup. The attention to detail extends to the trio of flavored butters—anchovy, blue cheese and red pepper—that are served with bread, and to the massive wine list, tended by a sommelier who is able and willing to dig out odd, interesting half bottles and bin ends on request.

A la carte: £40, including wine.

10/20 Mr. Chow

151 Knightsbridge, SW1 - 589 8656, 589 7347

CHINESE

Open daily 12:30 p.m.-2:45 p.m. & 7 p.m.-11:45 p.m. All major cards.

The sound of the word *ciao* is heard frequently inside Mr. Chow; curiously, the staff at this once-fashionable Chinese restaurant is almost exclusively Italian. This Knightsbridge establishment was originally started in the boisterous '60s, making it one of the oldest Chinese restaurants in London. When it was reopened in the early '80s, however, it was with a European staff, since it was felt that the use of Chinese waiters who could speak only rudimentary English had been the primary cause of the service in the past being brittle and unfriendly. At lunchtime the ground-floor area can accommodate 80, and in the evening the upstairs section (reached by climbing a spiral staircase) is open, doubling that number. The elegance of the place cannot be denied: Full-length mirrors provide an impression of greater depth, and the rooms are broken up into booths that provide a sense of privacy.

As for the cuisine, it is uneven but not without its charms. The starters on the short menu include tangy shrimp in seaweed, with white beans spoiled by an overly harsh, unsubtle sauce. But crispy duck is delicious, and Peking chicken with walnuts interesting. One of the most successful dishes is a wonderfully rich lamb flavored with an onion sauce. Most of the wines are seriously overpriced, but the house wine is a manageable £8 a bottle, and we found a light Bardolino from the Veneto at £10.95. On our last visit, there were lots of vacant tables, suggesting that many of Mr. Chow's old customers had conveyed a final *ciao* and would not be returning.

A la carte: £30-£40, including wine.

⑬ Montpeliano

13 Montpellier St., SW3 - 589 0032

ITALIAN

Open Mon.-Sat. 12:30 p.m.-3 p.m. & 7 p.m.- midnight. No cards.

The food in this small, bright, cheerful and noisy Italian restaurant not far from Harrods is as appealing as the setting. The skillful use of mirrors, white walls, Turkish tiles, colorful flowers, green plants and a large skylight create an impression of space and show off to advantage the attractive people who crowd it day and night. The flamboyant, suspendered owner, Antonio Trapani, directs the kitchen staff and service with the hand of a master (he was trained in both departments). The simple fettuccine is outstanding—perfectly cooked pasta with cream and cheese—as is the rather more complex paglia e fieno, green and white pasta with a tomato and vegetable sauce. Entrées are varied and uniformly excellent: fresh grilled king prawns cooked with precision; a succulent veal chop with butter and sage, which retains the delicate flavor of each ingredient; delicious breast of duck with mango; and wonderfully tender calf's liver alla veneziana that is richly balanced by a white-wine and onion sauce. The cold crêpe dessert is a worthy specialty of the house, but don't neglect the tiramisu—a triumph—or the airy, well-balanced zabaglione. The friendly, efficient waiters are a pleasure to watch as they ensure that the dishes arrive at the table quickly and without fuss. There's a short but well-chosen list of Italian wines.

A la carte: £20-£25, including wine.

Ninety Park Lane

Grosvenor House

90 Park Ln., W1 - 499 6363

FRENCH

Open Mon.-Fri. 12:30 p.m.-2:30 p.m. & 7:30 p.m.-10:45 p.m., Sat. 7:30 p.m.-10:45 p.m. All major cards.

When he suddenly decided to close his Oasis on the Riviera in La Napoule, many of us feared that Louis Outhier (who had earned four toques in our France guide) intended to deprive us of one of the most fabulous dishes created in the last years of this millennium: langouste (lobster) with Thai spices. Thank heaven, we needn't have worried. Outhier's former executive chef, Jean-Marie Meulien, still serves it, at the Hôtel Méridien in Paris. And we sampled it recently in London, at Ninety Park Lane in the Grovesnor House hotel, where the dish tasted even better (if that's possible)—the Asian spices and herbs combined even more subtly with carrot stock to create a divine, foamy sauce that perfectly pointed up the barely cooked crustacean's natural flavor. So sublime was this rendering of the dish that we nearly leapt up from our sofa (the dining room's cushioned banquettes are the last word in voluptuous comfort) to see for ourselves if Outhier, the restaurant's supervisory chef, had by chance taken over the kitchen that evening. No, not a trace of him. The admirable lobster was the handiwork of Outhier's highly talented disciple Hervé Guillaume (who, incidentally, earned four stars from the *Chicago Tribune* while cooking at that city's Le Prince). His wild-mushroom consommé was exquisite; his halibut filet was cooked to perfection and swathed in a delicate basil sauce; and his tender and flavorful filet of beef was enhanced by a remarkable Brouilly wine sauce.

Our meal might have been flawless had the pâté of crab cannelloni not turned out to be quite so heavy, and had the pastries tasted as delightfully delicate as they looked on their elegant showcase. With the exception of an exemplary almond sorbet, most of the desserts were unpleasantly alcoholic. And though the young French sommelier is both charming and competent, the rest of the staff lacks snap and speed. But the long waits between courses allow time to admire the warm, posh dining room, where soft lights, fine china and sumptuous damask napery bear witness to the concern for refined details. (We particularly admired the enchanting nineteenth-century painting of a Chinese port that hangs in the foyer.)

The suave service is capably directed by Signor Rebecchi. The restaurant's kitchen will be completely revamped by the time you read this. Until the revamping we are holding back our rating. We wish chef Guillaume all the luck in the world and hope that Ninety Park Lane will provide meals as memorable as those we so often enjoyed in the past. We must say that the coffee here is some of the best in London, a city where we are often tempted to repeat Abraham Lincoln's legendary retort to a waiter: "If it's tea, bring me coffee; if it's coffee, bring me tea."

Al la carte: £35-£45.

11/20 Salloos

62-64 Kinnerton St., SW1 - 235 4444,
235 6845
INDIAN
Open Mon.-Sat. noon-2:30 p.m. & 7 p.m.-11:15 p.m. All major cards.

This fashionable family run restaurant sits on the first floor of a building on a cobbled mews southeast of the Knightsbridge Underground station. Latticed frames at the windows give a feeling of intimacy, though lately the restaurant has been keeping itself full of patrons, particularly in the evenings (making reservations is almost mandatory). This is understandable, since Salloos, which belongs to Mr. Salhuddin (thus the familiar abbreviation), has friendly, helpful service and prides itself on its cooking. Among the much-praised starters are keema nan (spiced minced meat inside layers of wheat dough baked in a tandoor oven) and tandoori prawns. A number of the main dishes are superb. We can recommend in particular the delectable chicken taimuri, a house specialty; quails marinated in a mild blend of special spices; and the magnificent tandoori lamb chops, which (like many of the tandoor-cooked dishes here) are marinated for 24 hours in spices before being barbecued in the charcoal tandoor. "A dish not to be missed" proclaims the menu, and who can disagree? There's a selection of special wines from Corney & Barrow.

A la carte: £20-£25, including house wine.

12/20 San Lorenzo

22 Beauchamp Pl., SW3 - 584 1074
ITALIAN
Open Mon.-Sat. 12:30 p.m.-3 p.m. & 7:30 p.m.-11:30 p.m. No cards.

This good-looking, spacious restaurant, which has a glass roof that can be opened on hot days to create its own version of al fresco

eating, is still going strong more than 25 years after it opened. It's a nice place for star-spotting, but fortunately the food is good as well. A shortish, genuinely Italian menu features a flavorful minestrone, good carpaccio bianco (marinated raw fish) and Parma ham with melon for starters, along with the seldom encountered but perfectly delicious bagna cauda (a garlic, anchovy, oil and butter sauce) served with generous amounts of crudités, and the equally unusual (in this country) polenta with Gorgonzola. Polenta is also served with grouse as a main course. At our last meal here, the sea bass with basil sauce turned out to be a succulent piece of fish, though disappointingly speckled with an almost indiscernible amount of basil. The desserts are delicious: perfect tiramisu and brandy-laden crêpes San Lorenzo. The wine list, naturally enough, is predominantly Italian. Service is unobtrusive but helpful.

A la carte: £30, including wine.

16 Le Soufflé

Hotel Inter-Continental
1 Hamilton Pl., Hyde Park Corner, W1
409 3131
FRENCH
Open Mon.-Fri. 12:30 p.m.-3 p.m. & 7 p.m.-11:30 p.m., Sat. 7 p.m.-11:30 p.m., Sun. noon-3:30 p.m. All major cards.

When we settled down on the green banquettes in this comfortable dining room decorated in an indefinable style (the curious, pale-yellow wallpaper is so creased that one wonders if it was done on purpose), we found it hard to tell (at least from the surroundings) whether we were in London or Frankfurt or Chicago. We felt no such hesitation, however, about the cuisine's origins. Chef Peter Kromberg presents his menu in French, with English subtitles. The menu is nicely composed, resolutely avoiding all the clichés of "international" cuisine. And none of the options are likely to leave the diner indifferent: What would you say to lobster salad with crab beignets? or a potato souffléed in its skin with smoked salmon and caviar? or a creamy soup of shellfish and crustaceans sparked with lime? or a mixed simmer of fish from the North Sea in a saffron-tinctured broth? or Gressingham duck in a sauce laced with vintage port and Armagnac? or breast of farm-raised chicken with orange butter?

With its four courses, cheeses and assortment of desserts, the daily fixed-price meal (£34.50) is no less tempting than the à la carte selection, and most of the dishes listed live up to their billing—but not all, alas. True, the salmon-and-prawn terrine (partially cooked in the smokehouse) had a subtle yet assertive flavor, the sautéed rabbit with fresh pasta and a garlic-and-basil sauce was savory, and the stuffed veal chop grilled with watercress in a five-spice sauce was an absolute triumph. But the grilled salmon and turbot swam in a bland sorrel sauce, and a delicate filet of sea bass barely held up under its wine-vinegar-based sauce. The dessert cart was respectable but hardly exciting, and the coffee ranked well below average. Chef Kromberg's undeniable—and oft-celebrated—gifts (not to mention the prices) entitle a diner to be demanding; in a lesser restaurant, we might not have even noticed the above-mentioned shortcomings. Rich, and expensive, wine list.

A la carte: £40-£50. Fixed-price menu: £34.50.

ISLINGTON

11/20 Anna's Place

90 Mildmay Park, N1 - 249 9379
SCANDINAVIAN
Open Tues.-Sat. 12:30 p.m.-2:30 p.m. & 7:15 p.m.-10:45 p.m. Closed Aug. No cards.

Anna Hegarty is of Swedish origin, and her Place, located in the area on the northern perimeter of Islington known as Mildmay Park, was once a much-praised high-class restaurant. But this was before it was transformed into a born-again Swedish bistro. It's a pretty, homespun sort of place, the decor marked by flinty blue walls hung with watercolors and decorative plates and, in the back room, a little bar, stools and a plant-filled glassed-in balcony. The small tables are close together, and the blackboard on the wall lists the dishes of the day. Hegarty, blond, friendly and proprietorial, presides over the two dining rooms, chatting up a storm. Downstairs in the kitchen, chef Paul Sykes turns out a reliable selection of solid, well-made dishes, several of which have passed into London gastronomic lore.

Some of the finer items include the famous lax pudding, a rich, delicious baked mixture of layers of salted salmon, onion and potatoes in cream; the tender marinated salmon served with a creamy mustard sauce (mustard features strongly in this cuisine); excellent fresh terrines, such as the one composed of succulent chunks of pike and eel; good fried Camembert served with fried parsley; sweetbreads and kidneys in a creamy mustard sauce; veal roast with dill sauce; and the famous Scandinavian apple crumble, rescued from the flaccidity of its English cousin by a topping of hazelnuts. Some of the main courses are less interesting: a bland, stodgy beef casserole in the ubiquitous mustard sauce, and forgettable turbans of sole stuffed with salmon. The desserts can also disappoint; a massive composition of cheese-filled pastry with jam and ice cream sounded fascinating but defied consumption beyond an exploratory spoon or three. The interesting wine list is complemented by iced aquavit.

A la carte: £20-£25.

KENSINGTON

9/20 The Belvedere

Holland House, off Abbotsbury Rd., W8
602 1238
FRENCH/BRITISH
Open Mon.-Fri. noon-2:30 p.m. & 6:30 p.m.-10:30 p.m., Sat. 6:30 p.m.-10:30 p.m. All major cards.

This should be one of the prettiest restaurants in London, given its location in the former stables of Holland House, which were converted during the nineteenth century into a ballroom and orangery. On summer evenings scents drift over from the lovely geometric flower garden, and families of rabbits putter on the lawns beneath the tall trees. Inside, however, all is far from luxurious, elegant tranquility. The decor of the big, airy ground-floor lounge bar and the upstairs dining area, the latter situated in and around a large square turret that was the Holland House's belvedere, has all the depressing charm of a chain-hotel interior. Lowered ceilings with inset downlighting, cane-style armchairs with predictable pastel upholstery and functional carpeting all contribute to the overall effect: bland, when it could be exquisite.

The food is equally disappointing, especially in view of the not inconsiderable price it commands. The seasonally changing, primarily French menu reads all right, if not inspired: medallions of venison in port and Cognac garnished with beetroot, poached tournedos of beef in a cream-and-spinach sauce, pan-fried veal with fresh lemon and ginger wine, braised suprême of turbot with Noilly Prat and pink peppercorn sauce. But too often the finished product proves to be simply inferior. A starter of chicken quenelles was tasteless, over-gelatined and served sauceless with some salty shredded lettuce; a poached salmon steak was forgettable, and its accompanying garden vegetables (virtually raw string beans, desiccated creamed potato) were redeemed only by a good fresh zucchini fritter. The dessert trolley was similarly reminiscent of a second-rate English market-town hotel dining room. Wines are tolerable, there is no espresso, and the service is perfectly efficient. Rather mystifyingly, 92 malt whiskies are offered on a bagpipe-logoed list.

A la carte: £40-£45, including wine.

10/20 Byblos

262 Kensington High St., W8 - 603 4422
LEBANESE
Open daily 11:45 a.m.-11:45 p.m. All major cards.

You can imagine our concern when we stopped in here on an early Sunday afternoon for lunch to find that we were the only customers in the place. But the meal we had in this small, well-established restaurant, which opened in 1968 and has been much visited by both the British and Middle Easterners, was an authentic Lebanese experience. Exotically decorated with carpet wall hangings and mosaics, the place is particularly popular in the evening, when a limited but interesting menu is pre-

sented. The fixed-price lunch for £7.95 features mezes (small blobs of hummus, taramasalata, tabouli and falafel served with olives and salad), a main course and desserts. The kebabs are juicy and well seasoned, and the lamb dish with okra, called bahmia, is wonderfully spiced. The wines include Château Musar at a bargain price of £10.95.

A la carte: £15, including wine. Fixed-price menu: £7.95 (lunch only).

11/20 Kensington Tandoori

1 Abingdon Rd., W8 - 937 6182
INDIAN
Open daily noon-11:30 p.m. All major cards.

At the northern end of a narrow road that runs south from Kensington High Street stands this intimate restaurant, whose decor is so curious it makes customers feel as though they have stumbled into Alice's Wonderland: drooping vines in greens and russets on the walls, maroon seating that appears to glower, a lowered ceiling and five booths separated from one another by etched-glass dividers. No, the Mad Hatter would not look out of place here. Instead of being served by that extrovert, however, one is tended to by urbane waiters who are aware that they work in a highly respected restaurant that has elicited much praise in recent years for the distinctive quality of its food. Worthy of mention from the intriguing menu are, as a starter, the tandoori plate (chicken and lamb) and, as a main course, the bataire masala (two quails barbecued, then simmered in a cream sauce) and lamb pasanda (sliced lamb cooked in yogurt with peanuts). A well-chosen wine list indicates a sophisticated clientele that cares about such things, and the coffee is excellent. Service is included in the bill.

A la carte: £12-£15, including wine.

12/20 Launceston Place Restaurant

1A Launceston Pl., W8 - 937 6912
FRENCH/BRITISH
Open Mon.-Fri. 12:30 p.m.-2:45 p.m. & 7 p.m.-11:30 p.m., Sat. 7 p.m.-11:30 p.m., Sun. 12:30 p.m.-2:45 p.m. Cards: MC, V.

On our last visit to charming Launceston we were greeted by Nick Smallwood (late of L'Escargot), who is co-owner with Simon Slater (formerly with Zanzibar). The welcome was as warm as the decor: full of flowers and decorated in English country-house colors.

Soon after, we were brought delicious warm rolls to nibble while considering the two fixed-price menus (£9.50 for two courses, £11.50 for three courses) and the à la carte selection, which includes some vegetarian dishes. Among the dishes on the fixed menus are such appetizers as a succulent combination of chicken salad dressed with sesame oil and cured Ashdown ham with melon. These dishes may be followed by sea bream filets on a bed of ratatouille, or wild salmon with apple and shallots in phyllo pastry with sorrel sauce. Among other first courses are a good terrine of sweetbreads with a red-pepper coulis, lettuce-and-clam soup and carrot mousse with lemon sauce. The selection of entrées includes earthy Cumberland sausage with Tewksbury mustard, filet of beef wrapped in bacon with herb butter and roast guinea-fowl with kumquats. An eclectic wine list includes offerings from Australia, California and New Zealand; when we asked for a nice light red, we were presented with a '74 Côtes-du-Rhône (shipper Paul Jaboulet), which proved a perfect accompaniment. Launceston, we can report without hesitation, is a commendable neighborhood restaurant offering good value and excellent service.

A la carte: £25, including wine. Fixed-price menus: £9.50-£11.50.

11/20 Michel

343 Kensington High St., W8
603 3613
FRENCH
Open daily noon-2:30 p.m. & 7 p.m.-11 p.m. All major cards.

Michel has run this small restaurant on the western end of Kensington High Street since 1983. He no longer does the cooking himself, having delegated it to another French chef, Gabi Peuget. The style of the place is that of an upscale bistro offering classic but relatively uncomplicated French bourgeois cooking based on sound ingredients. Examples of starters are fish soup, mussels and escargots, to be followed by rack of lamb glazed with Cointreau, sautéed calf's liver in a lime butter sauce, or filet steak in Roquefort sauce. The à la carte menu changes with the start of each season. There is always a large and tempting selection of cheeses, as well as some interesting desserts, such as peaches cooked in a syrup flavored with pepper and thyme. Come eve-

ning, a good-value fixed-price menu is offered: three courses (and a choice of two dishes for each course) for £14.50. The wine list is short, reasonably priced and concentrates on the Loire and Burgundy; there is also the respectable house wine for £6.60. Friendly and efficient service is provided by predominantly French waiters. The background music, featuring Françoise Hardy and '60s favorites, is sufficiently soft to leave conversation undisturbed. In all, a visit to Michel is a most pleasant way to spend an evening without inflicting too much damage on the wallet.

A la carte: £25, including wine. Fixed-price menu: £14.50 (dinner only).

10/20 Le Quai Saint Pierre

7 Stratford Rd., W8 - 937 6388
SEAFOOD
Open Mon. 7 p.m.-11:30 p.m., Tues.-Sat. 12:30 p.m.-3 p.m. & 7 p.m.-11:30 p.m. All major cards.

Pierre Martin's quintet of restaurants (including La Bouillabaisse and La Croisette in Chelsea, Lou Pescadou on Old Brompton Road and Le Suquet in South Kensington) has become an institution in West London, an area not noted for its attention to seafood. This member of the family, Le Quai Saint Pierre, on the corner of a chocolate-box mews, has the sepulchral gloom of its fellows, with marine prints on the walls and, most bizarrely, an indoor sun awning. The most attractive decorative feature is the obligatory tank of crayfish with safely bandaged claws. The place to sit, lunchtime adulterers excepted, is in the window with its boxed hydrangeas; the wine to drink is an excellently zingy Muscadet; and the thing to eat is the seafood assortment, an operatically minded cornucopia of whole crab, oysters, cockles and mussels riding on a thick cork boat. Nutcrackers are included, as is an unusually stiff, yellowish, mustardy mayonnaise. The turnover of shellfish ensures that it is fresh. However, the cooked fish dishes (turbot, sea bass and so forth) are less successful. We sampled a dish of monkfish au poivre vert, which turned out to be firm to the point of toughness. Seafood crêpes and a scallop feuilleté were unremarkable, save for the dullness of the latter's pastry and the butteriness of its sauce. The house sorbet is a pretty extravaganza of lemon and raspberry ices tricked out with slices of mango, kiwi, strawberries and small black grapes, but the chocolate mousse doesn't work. The espresso is divine.

A la carte: £30, including wine.

10/20 Trattoo

2 Abingdon Rd., W8
937 4448, 937 4602
ITALIAN
Open daily noon-2:30 p.m. & 6 p.m.-11:45 p.m. All major cards.

This fashionable eatery of the '60s that has successfully survived the '80s now serves vaguely nouvelle Italian food in an attractive pink and green interior. The appetizers include such stalwarts as bresaola, carpaccio, snails with garlic butter and a tasty variation of mozzarella. The excellent fresh pasta boasts some original sauces, such as a smoked-salmon and cream concoction; the popular trenette al pesto is also decent. Breast of chicken sorpresa (with a "surprise" filling) and other familiar chicken and veal dishes comprise the main courses, which are served with fresh vegetables. The desserts are not spectacular, and the predominantly Italian wines are reasonably priced.

A la carte: £18-£23. Fixed-price menu: £9.95.

MARYLEBONE

11/20 Garbo's

42 Crawford St., W1 - 262 6582
SCANDINAVIAN
Open Mon.-Fri. noon-3 p.m. & 6 p.m.-midnight, Sat.-Sun. 6 p.m.-midnight. All major cards.

The engaging Ake Lindholm manages this appealing Swedish restaurant, which accommodates 50 and is located on a street just south of Marylebone Road, conveniently close to the Swedish Embassy on Montagu Place. Although its facade is painted a somber maroon, the interior is far more cheering. There are portraits of Carl Gustaf and of Queen Silvia, but most of the artwork runs to etchings of the great Greta Garbo. Opposite these Garbo etchings are black-and-white stills of other Swedish stars: Ingrid Bergman, Oti Anderson, Ingrid Thulin.

The food smells of the sea. For starters, we can recommend the gravlax heightened by a dill-and-mustard sauce, and the spicy herring in a cream sauce enlivened with a frond of dill. Of the main courses, we're fond of the appropriately named planksteak garni (a tender steak cooked on a slab of birchwood, into which juices have oozed) served on a wood slab with duchess potatoes, tomato and parsley. Among the other choice dishes are pan-fried salmon filled with spinach and cooked in a white-wine sauce, delicious Dover sole grilled and served with dill butter, and eel cooked in beer and accompanied with scrambled egg and chives. The wine list is fairly priced, but many (including us) prefer a Swedish lager to complement their meal.

A la carte: £20, including wine.

11/20 Green Leaves

77 York St., W1 - 262 8164
CHINESE
Open Mon.-Fri. noon-2:30 p.m. & 6 p.m.-11 p.m., Sat. 6 p.m.-11 p.m. All major cards.

Inside this friendly little restaurant just west of Baker Street you'll find lace-bordered tablecloths and a Chinese version of flying ducks filling up the wall space. Despite its minuscule dimensions, the place offers an extensive Pekingese and Szechwan menu, and Mr. Tao, the young chef/proprietor, seems unruffled when he emerges from his tiny kitchen for a breather. Appetizers include the ubiquitous fried seaweed and a Chinese version of chicken satay, skewers of moist, tender meat caramelized in a sweet yellow bean sauce. Tao's renowned Ganshow prawns in a balanced tomato-and-ginger glaze improve from being cooked with the lees of rice wine—not easy to come by in London. Dark, pungent strips of sesame beef are sprinkled with toasted seeds, and cold sliced pork boasts a superior sauce of soy and garlic. Specialties include three ways with fresh crab, lobster in a ginger-garlic sauce and sizzling beef on a griddle. Experienced readers of Chinese menus will spot, under the modest title of "steamed small buns," a popular Shanghai delicacy rarely seen in London: round, puckered dumplings bulging with pork, vegetables and juices, served in a bamboo basket. They're definitely worth a tasting; the Chinese like to make a meal of them. There is also a choice of four fixed-price feasts, ranging from £10 to £22 per person. The wine list is adequate, but we prefer sticking to the hot sake. Dinner reservations are recommended.

A la carte: £20, including house wine. Fixed-price menus: £10-£22.

11/20 Topkapi

25 Marylebone High St., W1
486 1872
TURKISH
Open daily noon-midnight. All major cards.

An attractive room decorated with brass plates and hanging lamps, Topkapi is located at the northern end of Marylebone High Street. The menu features a nice selection of meat dishes (chicken and lamb predominate), as well as interesting vegetarian meals that employ eggplant, squash, vine leaves stuffed with rice and some spectacular salads. The mezes (assorted appetizers) are particularly spicy and satisfying. The many good wines featured include a Château Musar '86 and an acceptable house French wine. Because Topkapi is so popular, it is always wise to reserve ahead.

A la carte: £20-£25, including wine. Fixed-price menu: £9.50.

11/20 Woodlands Restaurant

77 Marylebone Ln., W1 - 486 3862
INDIAN/VEGETARIAN
Open daily noon-3 p.m. & 6 p.m.-11 p.m. All major cards.

This South Indian vegetarian restaurant, located on a quiet street across from the Bond Street tube station (there is another branch on Panton Street near The Haymarket, 839 7258), was recently redecorated. A branch of the chain with representatives in Bombay and New Delhi, Woodlands has become extremely popular in recent years. The fried lentil doughnuts in yogurt and the spicy steamed rice cakes are particularly delicious. The fixed-price meals, tasty and filling, consist of a selection of different dishes served on a tray with a chapati and a dessert. There is a short list of reasonably priced wines; the house wine is £6. Friendly and helpful service.

A la carte: £12-£15. Fixed-price menus: £8-£10.

MAYFAIR

⑬ **Al Hamra**

31-33 Shepherd Market, W1
493 1954, 493 6934
LEBANESE
Open daily noon-midnight. All major cards.

In the middle of Shepherd Market, a district notorious for housing members of the world's oldest profession, stands this most dignified and elegant restaurant, the main room of which resembles the saloon of a luxury liner. Tables are set outside when the weather turns merciful; the ambience is always friendly and the service superb: discreet but solicitious. From the excellent 40-item mezes assortment, we can recommend the tabouli and the pita stuffed with mince accompanied by an eggplant dip. Kafta yoghouthieh (minced meat with yogurt, served toasted and accompanied with pine nuts) has an authentic Lebanese flavor, and is served in a round dish fringed with pita pieces. Kafta autabiyeh (minced meat, parsley, garlic and tomato purée grilled on skewers) is simililarly served. The dessert trolley (if you feel tempted) will satisfy any lingering appetite. There is a short wine list, but we prefer the outstanding Château Musar house wine. You'll leave the quiet of the restaurant and emerge into the busy atmosphere of Shepherd Market having paid a small price for a most satisfying big meal.

A la carte: £20-£25, including wine.

12/20 Chaopraya

22 St. Christopher's Pl., W1 - 486 0777
THAI
Open Mon.-Fri. noon-3 p.m. & 6:30 p.m.-11 p.m., Sat. 6:30 p.m.-11 p.m. All major cards.

Located on an attractive passage just north of Oxford Street that has many pubs, restaurants and chic boutiques, Chaopraya serves authentic Thai food, only slightly adapted to Western tastes. Don't be put off by the emptiness upstairs: All the action is in the basement, with its carved wall lights, alcoves and waitresses in traditional dress. The long menu is a bit mystifying; since our last visit, there has been an orgy of deletions (our favorite beef curry with sweet potatoes is no longer offered, but with a choice of 127 dishes, we really had no reason to feel deprived). The menu is also notably short on explanations. What could "kao myo nar goong" possibly mean to the average Westerner? Fortunately, the good-natured staff will eagerly bridge the communication gap.

And we can help as well: Start with the excellent satay, tender meat on bamboo skewers, which taste faintly of charcoal. The egg-flour cake is much nicer than it sounds, a sort of soft, light omelet filled with bean sprouts, pork and prawns in coconut paste—a fantastic combination. Also recommended are dim sum of crab and chicken in a soy-and-vinegar dressing topped with a crisp vegetable relish, and the salad of grilled beef strips in a lime-and-chili dressing. Large parties can have fun with the poh tack, a delicious "boat" of seafood flavored with lemon grass and chilis. For the genuinely mystified, there are some fixed-price feasts. We could identify only lychees among the desserts, but we were lucky with our choices, which were both strange and delicious. The first, a purée of beans and coconut, came garnished with fried onions! The other consisted of little cups sewn from banana leaves filled with smooth coconut cream hiding a core of nutty brown fudge. Exotic cocktails are dispensed from a small bar; and there's a hodgepodge wine list.

A la carte: £20-£25, including wine.

11/20 Chicago Pizza Pie Factory

17 Hanover Sq., W1 - 629 2669
AMERICAN/PIZZA
Open Mon.-Sat. 11:45 a.m.-11:30 p.m., Sun. noon-10:30 p.m. No cards.

Imitation is the sincerest form of flattery, and Bob Payton has many imitators, but his Chicago-style pizza restaurant remains London's best for value, quality and fun. Counteracting the customer's inevitable sense of being just one in a crowd are the cheerful, friendly staff members, who cope with some 350 people every hour. The hostess introduces herself in miraculously audible tones (the teeth-jarring music is punctuated predictably with Ol' Blue Eyes's rendition of "Chicago, Chicago") and weaves you expertly through the crowded tables, explaining the rules of the eating game and leaving you to settle in and order. Choose from a half dozen varieties of the Payton Patent Deep Pan Pizza, with irresistible garlic bread to help you get through the half-hour wait for your pie. A Regular (for two) is about the size of a small car wheel and nearly as thick, and a Large (for three to four) would fit a Cadillac. Customers line up willingly below the raised corral of the bar, where they play vigorous baseball, football and basketball video games. It's all a bit exhausting—all that energy, all those people loosening up with bucket-size Harvey Wallbangers, Chicago Blizzards and various other theme cocktails. Wine is not taken seriously here: Château Chicago Vin looks the same as Coca-Cola without the bubbles or ice. But the Champagne de Lahaye from Epernay "France" can put lots of fizz into parties for £15 a bottle. Otherwise, stay American and drink Budweiser. Reservations aren't taken (how could they be?).

A la carte: £9.

Le Gavroche

43 Upper Brook St., W1 - 408 0881
FRENCH
Open Mon.-Fri. noon-2 p.m. & 7 p.m.-11 p.m. Closed 2 weeks at Christmas. All major cards.

People who tout Le Gavroche as Britain's top restaurant are not only guilty of considerable exaggeration, they are also placing an unfair burden on chef Albert Roux. By according him such a lofty status, Roux's well-wishers virtually invite negative criticism from seasoned epicures who have sampled the creations of Raymond Blanc in Oxford, Nico Ladenis in London, Joël Robuchon in Paris, Michel Guérard in Eugénie-les-Bains, Fredy Girardet in Lausanne and Eckart Witzigmann in Munich. Veteran diners who have been led to believe that Le Gavroche is the summum genus and sanctuary of England's highest culinary art are bound to judge harshly a cuisine that is—admittedly—delicious and well wrought, but that simply does not bear comparison with the sublime achievements of the master chefs mentioned above.

Having said all that, it does indeed seem to us that Le Gavroche has progressed appreciably since Albert's son, Michel Roux, has taken

THE BEST
IN AIR TRAVEL

The best of London and the best of England are connected with the best of France on Air France non-stop flights from Aberdeen, Birmingham, Bristol, Edinburgh, Glasgow, London, Manchester, Newcastle, Southampton.

Air France is the only airline to operate services to the four London airports: Heathrow, Gatwick, Standsted, London City.

Air France offers the best means to reach all of Europe in comfort and style. Travel with Air France to over 100 destinations throughout Europe.

For Reservations
in the U.S.A.:
CALL 1 (800) AF PARIS
1 (800) 237-2747
in New York City:
(212) 247-0100
in London:
(1) 499-8611
(1) 499-9511
or contact your travel agent

AIR FRANCE

on greater responsibilities in the kitchen, bringing a fresh, youthful outlook to this family run restaurant (a below-street-level dining room in an elegant Mayfair townhouse). For the time being, Michel has initiated no revolutionary changes; we still do not know if this young chef possesses a creative talent, and, if he does, whether or not he intends to impose his own stamp on Le Gavroche's cuisine. In any case, he certainly knows how to make the most of the restaurant's superbly fresh and fine raw materials. While the food may not be brilliant or imaginative, it is unarguably appetizing, comforting cuisine bourgeoise, and it is prepared with split-second precision—all the sauces are light, and every flavor is distinct.

Such familiar but eminently toothsome classics as gratinée lyonnaise (onions and potatoes), foie gras à l'ancienne, duck rillettes with a salad of Jerusalem artichokes and smoked salmon roulade stuffed with crab, lead on to more traditional favorites—three fish in a zesty curry sauce, blanquette de veau (veal stew), farm-raised chicken cooked en cocotte (casserole) with thyme-scented lentils, daube of beef, and saddle of young rabbit in its tasty juices, among them. Not terribly original, perhaps (and nothing like the innovative dishes dreamed up by today's world-class chefs), but every entry on the concise menu is a manifestation of expert culinary handiwork.

Our sole reproach is that the prices are awfully steep (£60 to £70, if one steers clear of the pricier bottles on the opulent wine list). The £19.50 fixed-price lunch, however, which includes lobster bisque, game pie with young vegetables, a pear poached in red wine embellished with pistachio ice cream, mediocre coffee and very good petits fours, is a terrifirgain. And those sage diners who order it will enjoy the same attentive service from the exceptionally courteous and efficient staff. We always leave Le Gavroche with that typically British sense of quiet comfort and well-being.

A la carte: £60-£70, including wine. Fixed-price menu: £19.50 (lunch only).

⑮ The Grill and Restaurant
Connaught
Carlos Pl., W1 - 499 7070
BRITISH/FRENCH
Open daily 12:30 p.m.-2 p.m. & 6 p.m.-10:15 p.m. (The Grill is closed weekends & bank holidays.) All major cards.

The Restaurant at the Connaught hotel must be one of the few places left on the planet where waiters change the tablecloths before serving dessert. Our waiter did not go so far as to offer us fresh napkins as well, but that was probably an oversight for which (should the maître d'hôtel learn of it) the unfortunate man will be hanged by his thumbs. So we've decided to let the matter rest. With its oak paneling buffed to a high sheen, its austere elegance, its equally polished patrons (who seem nearly as well bred as the Franco-Italian staff) and its maîtres d'hôtel who smile "Thank you very much" at least 26 times in the course of an evening (we know: we counted) and place before their wards preheated cups into which piping hot coffee is then poured, yes, The Restaurant at the Connaught is surely one of the last true bastions of civilization. As for The Grill, its principal charm is that a grill room is the last place it resembles. It is probably the only place in London where, thanks to a near-total absence of light, lunchtime looks, and feels, like dinner.

To peruse the menu is to take a trip down gastronomy's memory lane: from "Zéphyr de Sole Tout Paris" to "Mousse de Homard Neptune," from "Mignon de Veau Prince Orloff" (with its garnish of "Petits Légumes Frou-Frou") to "Salade Caprice des Années Folles" and "Sauce Pudeur," it's all pure nostalgia. But don't be misled by the Paleolithic terminology. Chef Michel Bourdin, who has manned the Connaught's kitchen for years (after working under Alex Humbert at Maxim's), has dusted off this archaic repertoire so deftly that the results seem startlingly modern. Sauces are light and natural, and presentations are free of needless furbelows. We thoroughly enjoyed the consommé aspic, salmon mousse, turbot en feuilletage, braised oxtail and even the bécasse (woodcock) flambé Empire (perhaps not quite so grand as the one Mario used to prepare in the old days at Lucas-Carton, but memorable nonetheless—particularly for us unfortunate Frenchmen, who now risk prison for hunting this succulent game bird). Emotion also marked the arrival of a majestic trolley bearing an enormous side of beef, alongside steak-and-kidney pie, leg of mutton and other quintessentially English specialties.

Thirty of the 100 offerings that make up the kitchen's repertoire change daily. In all frankness, not every one of them deserves a two-toque rating; some, indeed, are utterly lackluster. For a meal that starts off with game terrine, Scottish salmon or lobster bisque, continues on to rack of Kentish lamb, grouse or roast pheasant, and is brought to a rousing close with bread-and-butter pudding or crème brûlée with wild strawberries (or any of the other "poor" dishes that wealthy folk so adore), you may expect to part with up to £50. To our way of thinking, it's a reasonable sum to pay for an excursion into the deservedly lofty realm of British cooking and polite breeding—more instructive, and certainly more nourishing, than a visit to the House of Lords!

A la carte: £50, including wine.

11/20 Ikeda

30 Brook St., W1 - 629 2730
JAPANESE
Open Mon.-Fri. 12:30 p.m.-2:30 p.m. & 6:30 p.m.-10:30 p.m., Sun. 7 p.m.-10:30 p.m. All major cards.

Near Grosvenor Square stands this friendly and comparatively informal Japanese restaurant, which holds more customers than may initially seem possible, thanks to the sushi bar, where you can watch with delight as the chefs busily slice food into shapes that would send a geometrician into rapture. At lunchtime the best bet is one of the fixed-price meals (but beware of the incendiary green mustard, which the ingenue next to us, to her ensuing horror, mistook for a carving of lettuce and swallowed with a gulp). Menus are in scarce supply—the chefs prefer instead to discuss the food with each diner—but every Japanese specialty is provided to order, and the walls are consequently festooned with messages of thanks and praise from their customers. A very relaxed, and relaxing, restaurant.

A la carte: £25-£30, including sake. Fixed-price menus: £23 and up.

10/20 Jams

42 Albermarle St., W1 - 493 3600
AMERICAN
Open Mon.-Fri. noon-3 p.m. & 7 p.m.-11 p.m., Sat. 7 p.m.-11 p.m. Cards: AE, MC, V.

An affiliate of Jonathan Waxman's acclaimed East 79th Street restaurant in New York, this branch in well-heeled Mayfair opened in 1986 and speedily became a favorite meeting place for those who work nearby and for those who simply want to be noticed.

Although there is another room downstairs, the main room has an engagingly open atmosphere, thanks in part to the visible kitchen at the far end. And that atmosphere is emphasized by dramatic modern paintings, the conservative use of spotlights and a tiled floor that skillfully increases the noise level as the evening progresses. Waxman splits his time between here and New York, so it should come as little surprise that the menus change frequently.

The cuisine and the choice of wines borrow much from California and allow you to eat as much or as little as you please. The starters (£2.95 to £5.95) include a good, fresh soup of the day, gravlax with fresh dill, cured salmon with juniper and a mustard sauce, an intricate dish of red-pepper pancakes with smoked salmon, salmon caviar, crème fraîche and a sweet-corn sauce, and warm goat cheese coated with poppy and sesame seeds on a bed of rice. The least expensive main course (£8.95) is grilled corn-fed chicken with sage butter and wonderful french fries. Some of the more complex dishes that struck our fancy are sautéed medallions of monkfish with deep-fried spinach, red-pepper compote and a shallot and ginger butter sauce. The most expensive items on the menu (£12.50) are the grilled rack of lamb with double-blanched garlic and the goose breast with garlic and mint, mashed potatoes and a plum-bourbon sauce. Some of the wines are good values, but others are heavily marked up. Although the Jams kitchen tends to use excessive amounts of flavors, it does turn out interesting, enjoyable meals.

A la carte: £20-£25, including wine.

11/20 Kaspia

18 Bruton Pl., W1 - 493 2612
RUSSIAN/FRENCH
Open Mon.-Sat. 12:30 p.m.-3 p.m. & 7 p.m.-11:30 p.m. All major cards.

This Franco-Russian restaurant next door to a famous Russian shop is a good place for solo diners, who appreciate bar stools. A branch of the restaurant on rue Madeleine in Paris, this Kaspia is a low-ceilinged, oak-paneled room marked by an ornate fireplace, a stormy seascape by Ignatiavii and glass cabinets containing Russian artifacts and some breathtaking plates. The clientele is what you would expect in an area filled with visitors to Sotheby's and similar auction houses; and like the clientele, the food is rich and pricey. It concentrates on seafood, with caviars taking center stage. In addition to the short menu, which details such dishes as smoked salmon and the different caviars available (pressed, sevruga, osetra and the heavenly beluga), there are also two fixed-price menus. The cheaper one (£20) includes borscht, pirogi (large pastries filled with a savory or sweet stuffing and cut into servings), 30 grams of pressed caviar with blini or toast, cheese or pastries, and coffee; the more expensive one (£30) presents Scotch smoked salmon, 30 grams of sevruga caviar with blini or toast, cheese or pastries, and coffee.

A la carte: £30, including wine. Fixed-price menus: £20-£30.

11/20 Lanes
Inn on the Park
Hamilton Pl., Park Ln., W1 - 499 0888
INTERNATIONAL
Open Mon.-Sat. noon-3 p.m. & 6 p.m.-midnight, Sun. 6:30 p.m.-11:30 p.m. All major cards.

The business people who work in the southern part of Mayfair are well acquainted with the lavish buffets laid out in this warm, spacious dining room in the Inn on the Park hotel. For a sum that varies from £20 to £24, they can select from an impressive array of appetizers, followed by a main course—grilled Scottish salmon, grilled filet of beef, filet mignon—accompanied by french fries and a green vegetable. The higher-priced fixed meal even includes all the Côtes-du-Rhône or Blanc de Blancs one might wish to drink at a single sitting. It makes us wonder whether the business people who work in the southern part of Mayfair have very productive afternoons.

A la carte: £25-£30, including wine. Fixed-price menus: £20-£24.

11/20 Langan's Brasserie
Stratton St., W1 - 493 6437
FRENCH
Open Mon.-Fri. 12:30 p.m.-2:45 p.m. & 7 p.m.-11:45 p.m., Sat. 7 p.m.-12:45 a.m. All major cards.

This large, fashionable brasserie was once upon a time as famous for its food as for its glitzy clientele. But since the departure of Peter Langan (who has since died), standards have slid perceptibly downhill. On our last visit, our table was reserved by one of our party who has the same name as a star in *Dynasty*, and we were given the table next to that of part-owner Michael Caine. We can therefore testify that once the waiter is convinced you are not a celebrity, the service can become irritatingly slow and offhand. The lengthy, difficult-to-read menu, now beginning to look distinctly tatty, the plastic tablecloths and the large numbers of noisy advertising executives who seem to constitute the majority of the diners make visiting the place a less-than-glamorous experience.

Matters weren't helped along when the appetizer of goat cheese, tomato and asparagus arrived—meager in the extreme, with a paper-thin slice of cheese and a single asparagus tip. The pike mousse with prawn sauce was good but lukewarm, and the trout with saffron sauce was so cold that a skin had formed on the sauce. The roast duck with sage and onion stuffing was, in contrast, juicy and plentiful, with well-cooked vegetables, illustrating that the traditional English dishes are probably the best bet here. Lots of nursery desserts—a crisp, lemon-flavored treacle tart (served with real custard), rice pudding—made us feel much better. The wine list is not as long as the menu, though it is strong on Champagnes (for the benefit of the ad execs, no doubt).

A la carte: £30, including wine.

10/20 Masako
6-8 St. Christopher's Pl., W1
935 1579
JAPANESE
Open Mon.-Sat. noon-2 p.m. & 6 p.m.-10 p.m. All major cards.

Masako is a comfortable, rather formal restaurant decorated all in black, white and red. The standards at Masako, however, have been permitted to slide in recent years, and nowadays the restaurant is visited almost exclusively by Europeans and far too few Japanese. Fixed-price meals are the smartest way to go here; they include a smoky-flavored clear soup with bonito shreds, fresh raw fish (including salmon) and crisp tempura. The highlight of the meal is the beef teriyaki, a huge portion served sizzling on a metal platter. If you are eating à la carte, try the sushi, a colorful selection of ten kinds of raw fish, seaweed and sticky sauce; the fried oysters with a spicy dip; and/or the marinated crisply fried chicken nuggets. Fruit and green tea cap the meal. Sake, of course, is the best accompaniment.

A la carte: £40, including sake. Fixed-price menus: £14 and up.

12/20 Miyama

38 Clarges St., W1 - 499 2443
JAPANESE
Open Mon.-Fri. 12:30 p.m.-2:30 p.m. & 6:30 p.m.-10:30 p.m., Sat. 6:30 p.m.-10:30 p.m. All major cards.

A most impressive restaurant on two floors of a Mayfair townhouse, Miyama has a white, windowless dining room with a marble floor and tables divided by a wooden trellis. Located close to many of London's larger hotels, it is popular with Japanese working in the West End (a healthy seal of approval), as well as with Westerners who relish Japanese food. There is a dauntingly large menu and a comparatively cheap fixed-price lunch. A good meal might include clear soup; raw fish beautifully presented in small ceramic bowls; succulent pieces of marinated beef cooked on the plate; a tempura of fresh prawns and vegetables deep-fried in a light batter; and, finally, sukiyaki cooked at the table, containing thin beef and fresh vegetables to dip into the sauces. There's also an extensive takeout menu.

A la carte: £30, including sake.

10/20 Old Vienna

94 New Bond St., W1 - 629 8716
AUSTRIAN
Open Mon.-Fri. noon-3 p.m. & 6 p.m.-11:30 p.m., Sat. 6 p.m.-11:30 p.m. All major cards.

Gird up your lederhosen and stoke your appetite when you make a trip to this dark but jolly Viennese restaurant. The vast menu contains such untypically Austrian food as snails and shrimp cocktail, but a careful search through the pages reveals wurst (which looks and tastes remarkably like Spam) and a few hybrid dishes, such as mushrooms fried in a batter made with Austrian lager (actually quite successful). Dumplings are much in evidence and tend to be of the cannon-ball variety (both in size and weight). The helpings of meat are huge, and the specialties—like the Old Vienna, with steak, veal, pork and sausages, or the mixed grill with Sauerkraut and dumplings—make for hearty, satisfying main courses. The wine list is short and predominantly Austrian,

and the house wine is inexpensive.

A la carte: £20.

12/20 One Two Three

27 Davies St., W1 - 409 0750
JAPANESE
Open Mon.-Fri. noon-2:30 p.m. & 6:30 p.m.-10:30 p.m. All major cards.

At one of our meals here, the manager said to one of our party in Japanese that if Americans came, they were to keep their voices down and not pretend to know too much about Japanese food. So consider yourself warned. One Two Three, which seats 50 people (there are also a few tables outside), is one of the most respected Japanese restaurants in London. The ambience is discreet and sophisticated, washed by unobtrusive piped-in classical music. When we arrived for our last meal here, we found the bar upstairs empty except for about 150 bottles of Chivas Regal on its shelves in various stages of consumption (it's an old Japanese custom for regular patrons to keep their personal bottles, from which they imbibe at each visit). In the restaurant downstairs we were served beef teriyaki of unquestionable high quality, crisp oysters that were soft and juicy inside, a kakuri (simmered pork in soy sauce and sake) that melted in the mouth and an outstanding shrimp and vegetable tempura combination. The dishes are served on attractive china, and the service is well staffed and highly efficient, though decidedly formal rather than friendly.

A la carte: £25-£30. Fixed-price menus: £23-£30 (dinner only).

12/20 Princess Garden

8-10 N. Audley St., W1 - 493 3223
CHINESE
Open daily noon-2:30 p.m. & 6:30 p.m.-11:15 p.m. All major cards.

Chinese restaurants are getting grander by the day. Bigger entrepreneurs with more money to spend are changing the face of Chinese dining around the world, creating restaurants filled with rare woods and fabrics and near-priceless artifacts. The Princess Garden (its parent and namesake opened in Hong Kong in 1952) was conceived in the same grand manner. Geomancers attended its birth to ensure that all elements were in harmony and that the mandatory white lions stood on guard at the entrance. You dine in sybaritic comfort in a spacious room decorated in gentle greens and grays; service is close to impeccable.

The largely northern cuisine features, notably, an entire section devoted to shark's fin, designed to appeal to wealthy feasting Chinese. Below decks are five banqueting suites, each named after an exotic bloom, that seem to be permanently booked. The cooking is competent and polished, if a little short on brio. Appetizers include poached prawns with sesame seed and chili oil, pan-smoked fish and crisp-fried smoked chicken shreds. A number of traditional Chinese soups are offered, and the braised superior whole shark's fin is beloved by money-is-no-object connoisseurs (incidentally, shark's fins in China are graded as meticulously as caviar is elsewhere). The menu reveals such uncommon dishes as beef and mutton casseroles; even that old cliché fried rice is different here, served with a flourish in a pineapple half. We like to end our meals here with the fruit mountain, a mosaic of sliced tropical fruit molded over a cone of crushed ice. On the whole, this is enjoyable food served in a very stylish setting. But you'll pay dearly for both, unless you choose with extreme care. The overpriced wine list drove us happily to sake.

A la carte: £25-£30, including wine.

12/20 Saga
43 S. Molton St., W1 - 629 3931
JAPANESE
Open Mon.-Sat. noon-2:30 p.m. & 6:30 p.m.-10 p.m. All major cards.

You could imagine yourself to be in one of the many small eating houses found on the back streets of Tokyo: This is a simple, bare room dominated by a big teppan-yaki grill and its white-hatted chef. Downstairs is a sushi bar, upstairs a more elegant room for parties. The fixed-price dinners star all the old favorites: sashimi, sukiyaki, tempura, yakitori. A la carte diners can try zensai, a ravishing selection of distinctly colored hors d'oeuvres; darkly braised eggplant rounds, cooked in soy and sake and topped with sesame seeds; glistening pink salmon roe on a bed of finely shredded Japanese radish; and the freshest possible sashimi with shredded daikon, a carrot flower and a dab of hot green wasabi (often referred to as Japanese horseradish). Meanwhile, on the grill, steak, vegetables, salmon and prawns are being expertly sliced and tossed onto its siz-

zling surface for just a few seconds. Try the lethal dish in which the chef wraps thin steak around dozens of braised garlic cloves and chucks it on the grill. Finish with fresh fruit or sorbet, plus cups of green tea.

A la carte: £12-£18. Fixed-price menus: £8-£12 (lunch only), £24-£32 (dinner only).

⑬ La Seppia
8A Mount St., W1 - 499 3385, 629 5446
ITALIAN
Open Mon.-Fri. noon-2:45 p.m. & 6 p.m.-11 p.m., Sat. 6 p.m.-11 p.m. All major cards.

La seppia means cuttlefish in Italian, and from the moment you descend the steep steps to the basement you'll have no doubt that the cuisine accented here is seafood: The sumptuous decor is rife with seafaring statues, a ship's wheel, a rope, anchors and storm lamps. The manager is the knowledgeable Riccardo Fiori; the chef, his older brother Antonio has worked in such acclaimed restaurants as Tante Claire and the Inter-Continental hotel. Appetizers to be on the lookout for are the excellent carpaccio with endive, slivers of Parmesan and a truffle oil dressing, and the fried oysters coated in bread crumbs and served with sour cream and beetroot. Among the main courses are a delicious sea bass with a light marjoram sauce and baked whole Dover sole stuffed with mushrooms. But we prefer to stick to one of the two fixed-price menus, which include many of Fiori's best dishes. The lunch menu starts with a splendid salad of crab and radicchio, moves on to fine tagliatelle with a sauce of clams in their shells, followed by a choice of either baked red mullet in a rosemary sauce or medallions of lamb, and ends with a powerful chocolate terrine. The seven-course "menu d'assagio," with its sensibly reduced portions, includes, among other dishes, layers of wild and smoked salmon with artichokes, rich fish soup, a plate of three pastas (risotto with wild mushrooms, tagliolini and rigatoni), grilled salmon steak with a basil sauce, and buffalo mozzarella and artichoke coated in bread crumbs and deep fried. The short wine list offers almost exclusively Italian wines. It is most unlikely that you will leave disappointed in either the cuisine or the friendly service.

A la carte: £25-£35, including wine. Fixed-price menus: £16.50-£19.50.

(13) Zen Central
20-22 Queen St., W1 - 629 8103
CHINESE
Open daily noon-2:30 p.m. & 6:30 p.m.-11 p.m. All major cards.

If evidence were still needed to prove the recent Chinese urge to gentrify, Zen would secure a conviction on its own. Yet another exercise in upscale minimalism, Zen is an arctic white hall graced on one flank by a curved black bar and on the other by mirrored walls and dribbling water troughs. The dining chairs, black leather hassocks on tubular steel frames, were seemingly designed for people with minimalist legs. In contrast to the setting, the food is opulent and ambitious: double-boiled supreme shark's fin (£30 for two), braised whole abalone in oyster sauce (£22 for two), roasted whole Kwantung suckling pig (with 24 hours' notice). Braised spareribs are paired with plum sauce, roast pigeon with yellow-bean sauce, and fish cakes with coriander. Even baked lobster is prepared six different ways, including tea-smoked; sea bass comes five ways (the latter could taste fresher). Crispy Szechwan duck is irreproachable, and the delicious mound of sea-spiced eggplant and spring onions shows that someone in the kitchen takes vegetables seriously. From the wine list, we can recommend the '85 Rully (£12.50). Watch out for tourists' flashbulbs, even when wielded by the unfailingly obliging black-trousered waitresses.

A la carte: £30, including wine.

NOTTING HILL GATE

12/20 Boyd's Glass Garden
135 Kensington Church St., W8 - 727 5452
BRITISH
Open Tues.-Fri. 12:30 p.m.-2:30 p.m. & 7:30 p.m.-10:30 p.m., Sat. 7:30 p.m.-10:30 p.m. Cards: AE, MC, V.

Boyd's is a small, stylish, rather pricey restaurant with crisp white napery, an attractive glass roof and plenty of flowers and greenery. Owner/chef Boyd Gilmour likes to chat with his customers, a trait not appreciated by everyone, but his original, decorative food is generally appreciated by all. There are two simple fixed-price lunch menus and a longer, more elaborate fixed-price dinner. Some of Gilmour's flavor combinations (grilled salmon infused with dill) are effective, but others, though interesting (parsnip-and-horseradish soup), are not entirely successful. Good bets are the dark, intriguing roulade of pheasant and the haunch of venison marinated in red wine with juniper berries and a gin-and-juniper sauce. The elegant, delicious desserts include a chocolate marquise and an exquisitely light hazelnut parfait served with a tulipe (crisp cookie-like "bowl") of fresh fruits. Malvern water is served throughout the meal and is included in the cover charge, a civilized practice we would like to see more restaurants adopt. The wine list is short but expensive and includes an unusually healthy selection of half bottles.

A la carte: £25, including wine. Fixed-price menus: £14-£16 (lunch only), £27.50 (dinner only).

(13) Chez Moi
1-3 Addison Ave., W11 - 603 8267
FRENCH
Open Mon.-Fri. 12:30 p.m.-2 p.m. & 7 p.m.-11:30 p.m., Sat. 7 p.m.-11:30 p.m. Closed bank holidays, 2 weeks in Aug. & Christmas. All major cards.

It's grown a bit with its success, but 24-year-old Chez Moi is still reliable, with a menu divided into "traditional" and "creative" sections (the latter changes every six weeks, in step with the market). Old favorites sparkle undimmed; the chicken-liver pâté with prunes and the poached egg Christophe (glazed with a cod roe chantilly in a smoked-salmon parcel) continue to delight. So do the boned sole stuffed with a salmon mousseline, and the turbot quenelles in lobster sauce. But the warm scallops with apples and a Calvados sauce doesn't quite make it. Lamb has always been a house specialty: Both the English rack, roasted in a coating of herbs, mustard and bread crumbs, and the noisettes, with mint butter and fresh figs, are impeccable. And we have fond memories of a daily special—rustic homemade duck sausage with beurre rouge and an onion confit—that had us reaching for the Burgundy. You'll surely be as tempted as we were by the rich petit pot au chocolat brimming with orange Curaçao (an old favorite) and the new black-currant mousse in a passionfruit coulis. We prefer to ignore the occasional murmur of nouvelle cuisine emanating from the kitchen—the best of Chez Moi remains the steadfastly traditional, which benefits greatly from the enviable continuity of style and standards. The civil staff and civilized clientele make this one of London's most agreeable restaurants. The sound wine list is almost exclusively French. Reservations are essential.

A la carte: £25, including wine. Fixed-price menu: £12.50.

⒁ Clarke's
124 Kensington Church St., W8
221 9225

BRITISH
Open Mon.-Fri. 12:30 p.m.-2 p.m. & 7:30 p.m.-11 p.m. Cards: MC, V.

This delightful, popular restaurant on the Notting Hill end of Kensington Church Street has its own bakery next door, where its excellent rolls and bread are baked. The decor is cool and elegant, with white linens and fresh flowers, and the cooking is inspired and original. Appetizers—salad of duck livers and lettuce, a sensational crisp tartelette with sage, Parmesan and Mascarpone—are primarily cold. On our last visit we tried two main courses: a thick, juicy grilled salmon steak with a red-pepper sauce and a classic osso buco with the correct seasoning of lemon and parsley. Desserts are primarily fruity in nature, with figs and a redberry compote among them. The interesting, carefully selected wine list is predominantly French (though there are some California representatives) and fairly pricey.

A la carte: £20-£30, including wine. Fixed-price menus: £14 (lunch only), £24 (dinner only).

11/20 Julie's Restaurant
137 Portland Rd., W11 - 229 8331
FRENCH
Open Mon.-Sat. 12:30 p.m.-2:45 p.m. & 7 p.m.-10:30 p.m., Sun. 12:30 p.m.-2:45 p.m. & 7 p.m.-10 p.m. All major cards.

Burrowing relentlessly beneath adjoining properties, this underground restaurant seems intent on undermining the entire neighborhood, which is composed of recently renovated houses whose young inhabitants make up a good proportion of Julie's evening clientele. The increased space translates into a bit more elbow room at the bar and a delightful little drawing room filled with comfy sofas and armchairs. You feel more like a guest at a private dinner party than a restaurant patron. Each vault or alcove is furnished with odd-shaped tables, unmatched chairs, candles, tropical plants and ferns, all set against a background of Gothic panels and mirrors snatched from long-lost washstands. Though diners may sit on rejuvenated church pews, there's nothing dim or religious about the food, the wine or the guests. The cooking is adventurous and, like all good experiments, sometimes fails. But we have been able to find no faults in the appetizers, which include a watercress and cream-cheese mousse and an artichoke croissant. As for the entrées, we have found the chicken suprême with cranberry and lemon sauce preferable to (and prettier than) the filet steak stuffed with duck-liver pâté. Salads are crisp and inventive, and vegetables are fresh and beautifully cooked. Best of all are the desserts: Madeira and orange syllabub (an old-fashioned creamy sweet drink, somewhat like eggnog), lemon roulade with raspberry coulis, parfaits and fresh-fruit sherbets. The choice of cocktails and wines perfectly suits the clientele: Bucks Fizz, Kir Royale, Black Velvet scotch, some good Bordeaux and Burgundies and a representation from California, Germany, Spain, Italy and Australia. You'll also find port, cigars and some excellent white dessert wines, including Château de Rayne-Vigneau '79, sold by the glass and the half bottle.

A la carte: £25-£30, including wine.

⒁ Kensington Place
201-205 Kensington Pl., W8
727 3184
BRITISH
Open daily noon-midnight. All major cards.

Just a stone's throw from the Notting Hill Gate Underground station, Kensington Place is one of the more recent entries in London's restaurant derby, and so far, it deserves to be an immediate front-runner. The restaurant exudes the authentic feel of a European brasserie, with its stool-lined bar at one end and its gigantic mural of a lily pond at the other; in between are tables with chairs that feel far less uncomfortable than they look. One side of the place consists entirely of enormous glass windows that keep the room bright. And there's always an air of lively bustle about the place.

The menu, devised by Rowley Leigh (seduced away from his successful chefdom at Le Poulbot), is packed with winning culinary combinations. Slices of chicken enlivened with a goat-cheese mousse and olives made for an intriguing starter, and the sweetbreads terrine with brioche was a marvel. Hake was enhanced perfectly by mushrooms and a white-wine sauce, and steamed cockerel was cleverly matched with couscous and a hot, flavorful sauce. A light hazelnut-oil dressing gave a green salad a deliciously fresh taste. We can't guarantee that you'll be able to sample the same dishes we did: In this extraordinarily resourceful place, specials change daily and the main menu changes weekly. But we can guarantee that whatever is offered will be fresh, creative and good. Our favorite dessert is the superb lemon tart; in summer, other notable sweets include a raspberry gratin and a delicious wild-strawberry pudding. As one would expect, the service is brisk but never intrusive. The list of carefully chosen wines features a number from the New World. We suggest reserving a table in advance to avoid disappointment.

A la carte: £15-£20, including wine.

(13) **Leith's**
92 Kensington Park Rd., W11
229 4481
BRITISH
Open nightly 7:30 p.m.-11:30 p.m. All major cards.

Prue Leith has forged a considerable career as a cook, restaurateur, food writer and consultant to catering operations (including British Rail and the Orient Express), and her original restaurant, off a Notting Hill mews, reflects her personality: calm, practical, honest, sensible and well endowed with taste, though less so with flair. The restaurant is cool and comfortable, attractive but not beautiful, rather Scandinavian in feel. There are some unfortunate touches, like the oatmeal-textured wall fabric, but most elements are supremely comfortable. The general effect is of a Conran's-designed director's dining room in a Danish bank.

The food suits the ambience, though the strong qualities of its ingredients lifts it to a higher level. Appetizers come either from a trolley carrying such dishes as solid, unflashy salads, terrines and gâteaux of, for example, artichokes in pastry, or from a short menu of soups, melon dishes and such compositions as a "sandwich" that layers oak-leaf salad, smoked tuna, swordfish and a rémoulade sauce between two thin potato galettes, the whole topped with a few juicy gold salmon eggs. The main courses may be delicious, like the tender, crisp-skinned duckling, or faintly disappointing, like the veal scallops in a lime gravy—but they are never less than honest. Ditto desserts (from another trolley), which include blackberry or strawberry tarts on good confectioners' custard, and an excellent lemon mousse. Delicious, imaginative sweet treats are served with your coffee: grapes coated in Cognac-flavored icing, tiny slices of coffee mousse cake and, the best of all these elegant morsels, a single, almost larger-than-life glistening red strawberry—unadorned but perfect. The clientele is discreet, loyal and dotted with captains and lieutenants of industry. The well-selected wine list features some excellent clarets and Burgundies as well as sound, fairly priced house wines.

A la carte: £30-£40, including wine. Fixed-price menus: £22.50-£40.

11/20 Malabar
27 Uxbridge St., W8 - 727 8800
INDIAN
Open daily noon-3 p.m. & 6 p.m.-11:30 p.m. Cards: MC, V.

A few steps west of the Notting Hill Gate tube station, Malabar's is a most un-Indian atmosphere and decor, but its menu is packed with enticing dishes from the Indian subcontinent that decidedly benefit from having been made with fresh ingredients. We can always suggest the murgh chat, pieces of chicken in a lemon-flavored sauce; kahari kebab, rolled lamb cooked with green peppers and onions and served sizzling in an iron kahari (wok); and venison marinated with tamarind. There are also appealing dishes for vegetarians. On Fridays a seasonal fish curry is offered; and on Sundays a buffet lunch is served. Standard wines are offered.

A la carte: £14. Fixed-price menu: £20 (for two).

PICCADILLY

7/20 Cafe Fish

39 Panton St., SW1 - 930 3999
SEAFOOD
Open Mon.-Fri. noon-3 p.m. & 6 p.m.-11:30 p.m., Sat. 6 p.m.-11:30 p.m., Sun. noon-3 p.m. All major cards.

Located on a street to the west of the Haymarket, Cafe Fish was bought by its current owners in 1986. Sadly, however, reality hasn't lived up to the promises made at the time of the takeover. Framed piscine prints swim about a deep dado, but despite the skylight and the hanging ferns, the high-ceilinged room manages to be oppressive. We've never eaten well here, but on our last visit, for Sunday brunch, we felt that perhaps this once well-intentioned operation may have given up trying. The £1 cover charge actually produced something tangible: acidic fish pâté (was it ever smoked mackerel?) and stale French bread. Even more disappointing were the half dozen fines de claires oysters, which tasted decidedly off. Other dishes we sampled that fateful day include immense, adequate bowls of salade niçoise, tasteless cold salmon served with dreadful mayonnaise, and casserole provençale that had been underseasoned and subjected to the culinary equivalent of a flamethrower. The gastronomic bankruptcy of this sorry meal was partially redeemed by the wine list, which groups bottles on the varietal principle, thus enabling sensible suggestions for appropriate accompaniment. Sauvignon Blanc and Chardonnay from California's Clos du Bois, at £9.75 and £10.95 respectively, strike us as evidence of canny buying. Since the basement is already a wine bar and the kitchen plainly can't live up to the detailed menu, the proprietors should consider abandoning all pretensions and sticking to fish and chips.

A la carte: £15.

10/20 The Criterion Brasserie

222 Piccadilly, W1 - 839 7133
FRENCH
Open Mon.-Sat. noon-3 p.m. & 6 p.m.-11 p.m., Sun. 6 p.m.-11 p.m. All major cards.

In the past, this brasserie was covered from floor to ceiling in Formica. Apparently enough was enough, and in 1984 the brasserie re-opened following a face-lift that turned the clock back 111 years to the period when the building was the site of the most popular Turkish baths in London. Now The Criterion Brasserie is indeed a feast for the eyes, an interesting marriage of delights that sees Byzantine art sidling up to art nouveau, complete with potted palms, engraved glass and blackboards revealing the daily specials. Unobtrusive classical music plays in the background, and a pianist performs between 7 p.m. and 11 p.m. You can sit either at the bar or at one of the tables near the entrance and enjoy a smaller menu; or if you have more time, you can dine in relative splendor on the raised platform at the far end of the room. The food is better than average brasserie fare. Somehow we weren't surprised to find the menu generous in its suggestions, offering twenty or so hors d'oeuvres in addition to a similar number of main dishes, among which the brill meunière and the marinated lamb were not one whit less than tasty. House wine is £7.50, and a small wine list includes several Champagnes.

A la carte: £20-£25, including wine.

11/20 Down Mexico Way

25 Swallow St., W1 - 437 9895
MEXICAN
Open Mon.-Fri. noon-3 p.m. & 7 p.m.-11:15 p.m., Sat. 6 p.m.-11 p.m. All major cards.

Ornate blue and gold tiles cling to the walls of this restaurant, which has colorful stained-glass windows and alcoves for its tables. A tiled fireplace stands at one end of the room and a dribbling fountain at the other, and lattice-wood screens divide the room. There are a number of prints of 1930s American cars, and rustic wooden beams are suspended from the ceiling, but one can't help feeling that a latter-day Pancho Villa or Emilio Zapata would find many of these additions most bizarre. The absurdly large menu, approximately three times the size it needs to be, offers a selection of meat, chicken and turkey dishes garnished with the expected tortillas and chiles. Among the few traditional Mexican specialties listed are some interesting vegetarian dishes: mushrooms and onions tossed with hot oil, seasonings and chiles, and a Mexican cheese fondue served with hot flour tortillas. Down Mexico Way makes a special point of drawing attention to the efficacy of using mesquite wood, herbs and spices. To accompany your meal is a small selection of frozen margaritas, with a two-pint pitcher of the strawberry variety running £9.95. The short wine list offers reds and whites from both California and Chile, as well as two Champagnes (one is a Moët Chandon 1982 for £28); the house wines are £7.

A la carte: £20-£25, including wine.

The Oak Room

Le Meridien Piccadilly
Piccadilly, W1 - 734 8000
FRENCH
Open Mon.-Fri. noon-2:30 p.m. & 7 p.m.-10:30 p.m., Sat. 7 p.m.-10:30 p.m. All major cards.

Any doubts engendered by minor hints of vulgarity around the entrance and lobby of this great renovated Edwardian hotel just off Piccadilly Circus should be put aside. The Oak Room is a superb restaurant in every sense of the word. The room, with its vertical acres of pale limed-oak paneling, lovely arabesque wall mirrors, gilded plaster, massive greenery-stuffed flower displays and chandeliers casting nicely calculated glows, is grandiose but in no way forbidding. The furnishings—muted oyster, pink and dusty-blue sofas and carpets, big solid tables with individual golden candle lights, pretty plants and fine silver and crystal—are comfortable and luxurious. And the food of executive chef David Chambers, with the creative consultancy of Burgundian star cuisinier Michel Lorain of La Côte Saint-Jacques in Joigny, is among the best in Britain—and, bearing in mind the sumptuousness of the premises and the value of the hotel's site, it provides a better value for the money than a good many of its high-rated competitors.

The menu divides dishes into Cuisine Traditionelle and Cuisine Créative, though whether this is a particularly useful distinction remains dubious. The former category contains, for example, warm baby pigeon salad flavored with star anise served chaud-froid, and the latter contains roast breast of guinea-fowl in a truffle and wild-mushroom sauce. Both categories, in any case, include dishes of the highest caliber, particularly in the area of sauces. Gazpacho with warm langoustines and zucchini quenelles (dumplings) was rich, tomato-colored and smooth, containing four lightly browned crayfish and four extraordinary pale-green quenelles with a delicate flavor and a texture akin to the lightest, creamiest fudge. A cassolette of baby Scottish lobster—the flesh perfectly cooked and sliced—came in a fabulous sauce made of the entire lobster, shell and all, crushed to a fine, glistening emulsion. Roast suprême of salmon sat in a pungent sauce of its own juices combined with brown veal stock and a touch of Cognac. Meats are paired (filet of lamb and venison in a black-currant sauce; fricassée of sweetbreads and quail flavored with port and wild mushrooms in a pastry crust), worked into elaborate truffle-studded compositions (suprême of grouse served on shredded cabbage and wild mushrooms, with a lettuce-wrapped parcel of grouse stuffing encasing a slice of black truffle, and a potato-encased sandwich filled with a mousse of the legs of the bird) or, if simply roasted, set off with a virtuoso sauce (duckling with lime).

Cheeses and wines are as immaculately selected and presented as the restaurant's high ambitions dictate, as are all the details—from the complimentary appetizer that combines a luscious but homey little morsel of rabbit terrine with a sprig of hazelnut oil–dressed frisée lettuce to the excellent espresso. Chambers's sweet sauces are as good as his savory ones. A gratin of red fruits arrived on a big flat plate, dotted with considerable numbers of prime raspberries, strawberries and blueberries in a magnificently buttery vanilla-scented crème anglaise lightly browned under the grill—simple and perfect. The service, finally, is a model of its kind: sensitive, polished, polite but unobsequious, led by a maître d'hotel who exudes unsnobbish pride in his work and who appears genuinely delighted in the interest, and enjoyment, of his clientele.

A la carte: £60, including wine.

12/20 The Veeraswamy

99-101 Regent St., W1 - 734 1401
INDIAN
Open Mon.-Sat. noon-2:30 p.m. & 6 p.m.-11:30 p.m., Sun. noon-2:30 p.m. & 7 p.m.-10:30 p.m. All major cards.

London's oldest Indian restaurant is redolent of Imperial luxury. The dining room was renovated for its 60th anniversary in 1987, when it was furnished, finally, with comfortable padded chairs and bench-style sofas. A sentry in traditional Indian garb directs diners through the Swallow Street entrance and upstairs to the reception area, where various fruity cocktails await. At lunchtime, you can help yourself from a fine buffet, which always features some sort of fish; its preparation varies daily. The buffet also offers two vegetable dishes, one lentil, one meat and one chicken (nothing is fiery hot). All this—as much as you want—cost £10.50. In the evening, starters include fish, quail and lentil cakes, none of which are priced higher than £3.25. Main courses include scallops, trout or lamb chops cooked in the tandoor oven, brains masala, vegetarian thali and various regional specialties, each of which is accompanied by rice, lentils and a vegetable. The wine list is uninspiring and the service occasionally erratic, but the head waiters will deal smoothly with any problems that should come up. Even more than its high-quality food, it is the atmosphere of The Veeraswamy that lingers. It makes you feel like a star, though the prices are far from astronomical.

A la carte: £15-£20, including wine.

PIMLICO

11/20 L'Incontro

87 Pimlico Rd., SW1 - 730 6327

ITALIAN

Open Mon.-Fri. 12:30 p.m.-2:30 p.m. & 7 p.m.-11:30 p.m., Sat. 12:30 p.m.-3:30 p.m. & 7 p.m.-11:30 p.m., Sun. 12:30 p.m.-3:30 p.m. & 7 p.m.-10:30 p.m. All major cards.

Don't be confused by the address. This plush restaurant lies at the western end of Pimlico Road just before it meets Lower Sloane Street to the north and Chelsea Bridge Road to the south. The younger relative to Gino Santin's other restaurant, the luxurious Santini in Belgravia, L'Incontro is enormously popular, and not merely with such local celebrities as Lord Lichfield and Stefan Edberg (the 1988 Wimbledon men's champion). One wall consists of a long mirror broken up by columns, and the floor resembles high-sheen gray marble that just dares you to slip. Seating is comprised of banquettes in an angry mottled gray and chairs in red, turquoise and gray.

From the long menu, our attention was immediately captured by the dish called "incontro di pasta," an appetizer of four pastas that was for the most part delicious; it included excellent tagiatelle with wild-mushroom sauce and gnocchi flavored a bit too mildly with pumpkin. Veal with a flavorsome mango sauce was quite ordinary, but salmon carpaccio, which had been cooked for just a few seconds, was wonderfully mild and enhanced by dill. Among the small list of desserts, the most noteworthy was a mousse with a black-currant base and a topping of white chocolate. The wine list is nearly an exact division between Italian and others. Downstairs, where the walls display photographs of celebrities, a pianist plays every night from 8:30 p.m., making this decidedly the section of L'Incontro you must visit if you're looking for a lively time.

A la carte: £25, including wine. Fixed-price menu: £12.50.

Le Mazarin

3 Winchester St., SW1 - 828 3366

FRENCH

Open Mon.-Sat. 7 p.m.-11:30 p.m. Closed Aug. 24-Sept. 16. All major cards.

If you can prove to us that you managed to coax a smile or a pleasant word from the formidable woman who runs Le Mazarin, we'll buy you dinner (at another restaurant, of course). For at Le Mazarin, no one seems to care in the least *where* you eat. On our last visit, right next to us, a distinguished-looking couple up and left after waiting nearly half an hour for a look at the menu. The staff—arguably the most disorganized and overworked in all of London—didn't bat an eye. In the normal way of things, success usually encourages restaurateurs to improve service, and to offer their patrons greater comfort. Some even go so far as to reduce the number of tables for the sake of creating more spacious surroundings. But at Le Mazarin, success has had the opposite effect. Its pink dining rooms are packed with tables overflowing into a narrow corridor, where raising one's glass requires the skill of a professional juggler. Yet just as one is beginning to feel a bit exasperated by the whole affair, one spies on the walls Ronald Searle's wickedly funny series of drawings dedicated to wine lovers—and a laugh breaks the tension.

The reasonable prices are another pleasant surprise. Two fixed-price meals—£19.50 and £27.50—feature a vast and delicious selection that ranges from fricassée of lobster with basil and turbot with morels, to free-range chicken perfumed with tarragon and a savory navarin d'agneau (lamb stew) with green lentils.

Before opening his own place in Pimlico, chef René Bayard spent some ten years cooking at Le Gavroche, where he learned how to recognize and employ the very finest ingredients. There too he acquired his taste for familiar French classics ever so slightly adapted to modern tastes. None of the dishes we have tried here ignited our unreserved enthusiasm; indeed, we have noted certain errors of culinary judgment, such as the plate of fresh pasta overwhelmed by a heap of mixed shellfish (lobster, mussels, prawns, clams), a muddle of flavors that canceled out one another, swimming in a Champagne sauce with a barely perceptible tinge of saffron. And some (beautifully cooked) red mullet filets in a tasty, nicely seasoned tomato sauce were absurdly garnished with, of all things, a radish. A sweetish, off taste marred the sauce of our navarin of lamb, which was otherwise tender and delicious, accompanied by lentils simmered to a perfect degree of doneness. Dessert was a complete disappointment: The coffee-and-caramel mousse studded with hazelnuts, which had greatly pleased us on earlier visits, was, on this occasion, oddly insipid, as were the petits fours that arrived with a mediocre cup of coffee.

No doubt Bayard will respond that he turns potential patrons away every day, and that his loyal clientele rave about his cooking. For our part, however, we persist in our belief that success has done little to mellow or improve Le Mazarin.

A la carte: £25-£30, including wine. Fixed-price menus: £19.50-£27.50.

9/20 Tate Gallery Restaurant
Millbank, SW1 - 834 6754
BRITISH
Open Mon.-Sat. noon-3 p.m. No cards.

One of Britain's loveliest restaurants is located in a semibasement. Its walls form a continuous neo-Romantic mural (by Rex Whistler) that projects an impossible panorama of lost cities. At the time of this writing, the Tate Gallery still offered a 1959 St. Emilion for £32 and a 1961 Graves at £19—over the hill, perhaps, but an outstanding value nonetheless. The menu makes a point of warning that all bottles served must be consumed on the premises, and the job of the waitresses is to persuade lunchers to have some food with their wine. This is a problem. The steak, kidney and mushroom pie cannot be faulted, and the roast sirloin of beef is perfectly adequate, but apart from these staples the kitchen can fall on its face. It's not just that some of the fish courses have been overcooked or that the starters tend toward the aberrant (Brie and green-bean terrine, crab tartelettes with vanilla sauce)—this place is obsessed with olde-English recipes that would be better left alone to die a natural death. Umbles Paste, Hindle Wakes and Joan Cromwell's Sallet are calculated to pander to the preconceptions of American tourists who still believe, against most of the evidence, that traditional English cookery is something more than a public relations fantasy. In true catering-school fashion, everything comes with a garnish of parsley, and the selection of vegetables is instantly forgettable. The bread, however, is delicious. .

A la carte: £25, including wine.

PUTNEY

10/20 Buzkash
4 Chelverton Rd., SW15 - 788 0599

AFGHAN
Open Mon.-Thurs. noon-2:45 p.m. & 6 p.m.-11 p.m., Fri.-Sat. 6 p.m.-11:30 p.m., Sat. noon-2:45 p.m. & 6 p.m.-11:30 p.m. All major cards.

Although the service at this dimly lit Afghan outpost can be erratic, the food is authentic, delicious and quite filling. Among the appetizers are two specialties: shoorba, a subtle soup made of fresh cream and yogurt, and ashak, pasta filled with leeks and served with a special cream sauce. The range of main dishes is extensive: For the hungry (portions tend to be generous), we recommend kohi, marinated leg or shoulder of lamb roasted with special spices, or cabrogh, marinated beef barbecued over a clay oven, which equals a T-bone steak in size but is infinitely tastier. Of the vegetables, the dal (numerous types of legumes) and the Afghan-style eggplant are particularly noteworthy. The desserts are pleasantly varied, but you probably won't have room to try them, particularly since you'll be served served a complimentary dessert called naun panja, delicately sugared bread fingers. Also complimentary are the mint dip that arrives once you're seated and the sherbet, brought to the table prior to the main course.

A la carte: £15.

10/20 Marco's

94-98 Upper Richmond Rd., SW15
785 7074, 785 7077
CHINESE
Open Mon.-Thurs. noon-11 p.m., Fri.-Sat. noon-midnight. All major cards.

The first Chinese brasserie in the world, Marco's modern decor is set off by good lighting, and if the dining tables are on the smallish side, at least they are spaced far apart enough so you don't have to listen to the intrusive chitchat of your neighbors. Although the cuisine is mainly Chinese, dishes representing other well-known areas of Southeast Asia are also represented. Appetizers include an extremely tasty vegetable tempura (eggplant, onion rings and green peppers fried in the light Japanese batter), beef satay, chicken satay and Marco's chicken pancake roll. To follow: Mongolian lamb, crispy and served with plum sauce, Singapore curried chicken and an Asian-style omelet with salad. The daily special could be a small portion of ngou pon ha, highly seasoned prawns wrapped in strips of beef, which is oh-so warming. Desserts include chocolate mousse, chocolate gâteau, fruit flan

of the day, ice creams and sorbets. Cocktails are priced from £2.50 to £2.80, and more than 30 wines are listed at moderate prices. Brunch is served every day from noon until 6 p.m.

A la carte: £12-£15, including wine.

11/20 Sonny's

94 Church Rd., SW13 - 748 0393
FRENCH
Open Mon.-Fri. 12:30 p.m.-2:30 p.m. & 7:30 p.m.-11 p.m., Sat. 12:30 p.m.-3 p.m. & 7:30 p.m.-11 p.m., Sun. 12:30 p.m.-3 p.m. Cards: MC, V.

Sonny's, a lively, fresh restaurant found at the northern end of Barnes. The long, thin room is cheered with colorful prints on the inside wall, French windows that let in welcome light and a decorative fireplace at its far end. The menu, short and written in no-nonsense, straightforward handwriting, lists dishes that verify that this is a cuisine offering good value for the money. Among the starters is a delicious fish soup with Gruyère, rouille (a spicy red-pepper and garlic mayonnaise) and croutons; a dish of spicy Merguez sausages; an eggplant and roasted-pepper salad; a flavorful rabbit terrine; and interesting pickled salmon with dill and a creamy sweet-mustard mayonnaise (At £3.95, the most expensive starter). Sonny's serves a fish of the day, along with grilled salmon covered with a layer of prosciutto. Other tasty entrées include whole roast pheasant with a prune-and-chestnut stuffing, an interesting rack of lamb served with beetroot, breast of chicken with tomatoes and olive butter and grilled entrecôte with balsamic vinegar and parsley butter. The dessert menu introduces such delicacies as plum crumble, date-and-lime cheesecake, and good fresh-fruit sorbets. The wine list is moderate but well chosen. This place serves some worthy food, imaginatively cooked and pleasingly served.

A la carte: £15-£20, including wine. Fixed-price menu: £9.50.

REGENT'S PARK

11/20 Auntie's

126 Cleveland St., W1 - 387 3226
BRITISH
Open Mon.-Fri. noon-2:45 p.m. & 6 p.m.-10:45 p.m., Sat. 6 p.m.-10:45 p.m. All major cards.

Formerly a popular tea room, Auntie's metamorphosed into a restaurant during the late 1960s and is now an ideal venue for an interesting meal close to London Zoo and Regent's Park. At the northern end of a busy road near

Great Portland Street, this small, intimate place has an elegant Edwardian facade; inside, the decor is enhanced by prints of all sizes adorning its vivid green walls. Auntie's cuisine—which it calls "traditional British fayre"—is fresh and pleasing without being too complicated. Delicious Arley oak-smoked chicken with a hazelnut-oil-dressed salad and a zesty pâté of Cornish spiced-and-buttered crab are two of the starters. Any self-respecting carnivore will want to order the suitably huge Barnsley lamb chop with mint and an orange sauce. Bangers (sausages filled with ground pork and bread crumbs) and mash are served with cider and applesauce, and poached chicken is paired with a sauce of light white wine, tomato and chives. Of course, there are pies, pies and more pies (beef and mushroom, salmon in a cream sauce and more), and fish lovers are tended to with the catch of the day (trout, mackerel and salmon). Several interesting desserts are featured, including a wonderful summer pudding and a rich, rich chocolate jumble; the Marhayes Manor tipsy fruit trifle was too custardy for us. The carefully chosen wine list has some good English wines—the interesting elderflower wine from Hugh Rock—along with a respectable number of half bottles, including a highly flavored Muscat de Beaumes de Venise. Everything is nicely presented by young women who are charming and attentive without being intrusive.

A la carte: £20, including wine. Fixed-price menu: £15.

Chez Nico

35 Great Portland St., W1 - 436 8846
FRENCH
Open Mon.-Fri. noon-2 p.m. & 7:30 p.m.-11 p.m. No cards.

Nico Landenis is topped only by Raymond Blanc and Anton Mosimann in terms of British culinary stardom and media fame. Since the publication of our last edition, he opened a country-house restaurant near Reading and then sold it, after suffering from a lack of a clientele that appreciated his oeuvre. And his other surviving establishment, on a quiet street in Victoria (48A Rochester Row, SW1, 630 8061), has been simplified to serve tasty food at modest prices. But this place (his fifth restaurant in fifteen years) is a runaway success—reservations must be made a minimum of two weeks in advance, so great are the numbers of people eager to brave Landenis's reputation for inspired gastronomic despotism. (The legends about him include one in which he ejected a party that was noisily insisting on ordering a combination of dishes frowned upon by the maestro). The food, primarily French in inspiration, can be outstandingly good, though it is subject to Landenis's particular idiosyncracies. A dish may therefore not be to your taste, but this will not be due to incompetence on the part of the kitchen—your taste just may not agree with Landenis's. (You may then decide—quite reasonably, of course—that you see no reason to vary your taste to suit the chef.) But all in all, we're quite fond of this accomplished cooking.

A major element of Landenis's style is allowing fine ingredients to speak for themselves, unfettered by too much masking (salt is conspicuous in its absence). This stratagem has its down side, as evidenced by one of the dishes we tried, a remarkably lovely plate of sea bass stuffed with salmon mousse in a langoustine sauce, which was on the tasteless side of subtle—and, to paraphrase Groucho Marx, there wasn't enough of it. When Landenis's perfection pays off, however, it does so handsomely. A dish of roast carré d'agneau consisted of three superb pieces of pink lamb, the circumference of which was coated with a wonderful mixture of mustard, garlic and herbs, served with a succulent cake of grated potato, grilled tomatoes dusted with another fine-herb powder, and plain, delicious deglazed gravy.

Chez Nico's cheeses are among the best in London—you'll be served a plate bearing eight prime specimens, an intelligent combination of classics and novelties: an ice cream–consistency gratte-paille, a musky Reblochon, a perfect salty Roquefort, a sweet farmhouse Brie. . . . Attention to detail is visible everywhere: the small, neatly slashed white rolls served with perfect butter, the crisp potato discs that exactly match the scallops sitting atop them in a first-course galette, the barely singed caramelizing on the orange segments that accompany the sautéed-quail salad. Also visible are hints of arrogance, although one is incited by Nico's reputation to seek them out. The menu described the above-mentioned lamb as served with a garlic purée; when we asked what happened to the missing purée, our waiter first said it was in the sauce (not true) and then said it had been omitted, because Landenis doesn't like to get bogged down in routine.

A la carte: £50, including wine.

10/20 Lemonia

154 Regent's Park Rd., NW1 - 586 7454
GREEK
Open Mon.-Sat. 6 p.m.-11:30 p.m. Closed 2 weeks in Aug. No cards.

Located among a row of shops that links Primrose Hill and Camden Town, Lemonia has been fully occupied almost from the day it opened in the spring of 1979—and it doesn't even take credit cards. What's remarkable about this place is that it's a living testimony to what honest fare and a good neighborhood location can do for business. Not to mention the quality of the cuisine, which is unique among Greek neighborhood restaurants. Interesting dishes include good chicken braised with small onions, tomatoes and wine, and lamb with beans. Moreover, true Hellenophiles love Lemonia's nostalgia-evoking decor: stone walls enhanced by sepia photographs of Greek peasants, wooden benches and much greenery.

A la carte: £25-£30, including wine.

12/20 Martins

239 Baker St., NW1 - 935 3130, 935 0987
FRENCH
Open Mon.-Fri. noon-2:45 p.m. & 6 p.m.-11 p.m., Sat. 6 p.m.-11 p.m. All major cards.

After many years of running his much-liked restaurant on Ifield Road, Martin Coldicott has moved to Regent's Park southwest area. His new restaurant, which has a pale-apricot decor, offers two fixed-price menus with an emphasis on nouvelle cuisine. Warm chicken-liver salad, feuilleté of asparagus and delicious slices of salmon marinated in wine vinaigrette represent the starters; the main courses are strong on fish and game in season, along with an unusual plate of tender, thinly sliced calf's liver, sweetbreads and kidneys. Sauces are particularly fine. The desserts tempt one to splurge on the three-course, rather than the two-course, fixed-price menu: The chocolate and hazelnut parfait is particularly rich and delicious, and there are sorbets and fresh-fruit salads for the virtuous. The reasonably priced wine list includes some good Australian Chardonnay.

A la carte: £25, including wine. Fixed-price menus: £13.50-£16.50.

(13) Odette's

130 Regent's Park Rd., NW1
586 5486
FRENCH
Open Mon.-Fri. 12:30 p.m.-2:30 p.m. & 7:30 p.m.-11 p.m., Sat. 7:30 p.m.-11 p.m. All major cards.

Lively Odette's is decorated in wall-to-wall mirrors, each set into gold frames (some of which are Victorian), ranging in size from from just a few inches square to the eight-foot-long representative along one wall. A delightful conservatory is housed at the rear of the building, a busy wine bar is tucked away in the basement, and a healthy number of thriving shops bustle at its front (the lower end of Primrose Hill).

As for the cuisine, the menu changes regularly, and chef John Armstrong draws happily from foods of many countries. The dishes are delivered to the tables by waiters wearing aprons tied severely at the waist, accentuating the theatricality of the ambience. Crispy duck-leg salad is enlivened by its accompanying slices of ginger, and rich game terrine is enhanced with its accompanying bed of lamb's lettuce; the artichoke heart with tongue and poached quail eggs makes for an interesting flavor combination. On the entrée list, we were happy to discover fricassée of corn-fed chicken with shallots and red wine, which was surprisingly light, and saddle of venison with chestnuts, which possessed an authoritatively powerful taste. The fish courses are represented by baked turbot in an herb crust and suprême of salmon accompanied by cucumber spaghetti and salmon eggs. The short dessert list includes a delicious hot apple and Calvados tart and a trio of exquisite mousses. The wine list, which features many tasty wines from the United States and Australia, is strong.

A la carte: £25, including wine.

RICHMOND

⑬ **Crowthers**

481 Upper Richmond Rd., SW14
876 6372
FRENCH
*Open Mon.-Fri. noon-2 p.m. & 7 p.m.-10:30
p.m., Sat. 7 p.m.-10:30 p.m., Sun. noon-2:30
p.m. & 7 p.m.-10:30 p.m. Cards: MC.*

Husband-and-wife owners Philip and Shirley Crowther serve exceptionally good food with cheerful informality in their pretty and intimate restaurant, which could easily be mistaken for a private dining room. They have been joined in their venture by Andrew and Nicola Eastick, who formerly ran a respected restaurant in Grassmere. You'll first be offered an amusing list of unusual apéritifs, which are served with a plateful of tiny, hot appetizers, before being shown the menu, which includes fixed-price menus at both lunch and dinner. The cuisine tends toward the nouvelle, and the appetizers on the frequently changing menu could include such unique combinations as a Gruyère cheese ramekin served with a tomato-and-basil sauce, or a spinach-and-wild-mushroom roulade with hollandaise. Quality ingredients and skillful sauces are the hallmarks of Crowthers' cuisine. Fattening yummy desserts? Oh, yes: chocolate and Tia Maria ice cream, a hazelnut meringue and a strawberry shortcake served with raspberry sauce. Plenty of good coffee is served with petits fours and the obligatory Muscat de Beaumes-de-Venise. The house French wine sells for £8.50, but the modest wine list is interesting and moderately priced.

A la carte: £25-£35, including wine. Fixed-price menus: £15-£25.

12/20 **Kew Brasserie**

149 Kew Rd. - 940 8298
BRITISH/FRENCH
*Open Mon.-Sat. noon-3 p.m. & 6 p.m.-11 p.m.
All major cards.*

This venture came to life during the summer of 1988 when it took over the space formerly occupied by Oscar's. Though there are still tables that allow diners to eat al fresco in warm weather, the interior, which makes generous use of space-enhancing mirrors, has become rather dim and solemn, with tables too close

together—on our last visit we found ourselves unable to avoid listening in on our neighbors' conversations as we enjoyed dishes from the short, well-planned and skillfully executed menu. If the mushroom feuilleté was a trifle disappointing, the delicious carrot mousse came in an orange-flavored buttery sauce, and the fish soup was no less than excellent. Salmon was served in a creamy white-wine sauce, as well as en croûte, and the bold flavor of the venison was enhanced by a rich, gamey sauce. A flavorful, nicely pink roasted rack of lamb had only thyme as an accompaniment. Several vegetarian main dishes are available, including spinach quiche and an intricate Oriental roll with celeriac and bean sprouts wrapped in a crisp pancake with a honey and soy sauce. Accompanying vegetables are generous, as is the selection of desserts, which may include a tartelette au citron vert (lime), melting and pleasantly sharp, and the intriguingly named gâteau Mogador, rich, delicious and extremely chocolatey. Service is rather slow but most obliging. The thinnish house wine is £7.50 a bottle; we prefer to choose from the well-selected wine list.

A la carte: £20-£25, including wine.

10/20 **Kew Rendezvous**

110 Kew Rd. - 948 4343, 948 1334
CHINESE
*Open Mon.-Thurs. noon-2 p.m. & 6 p.m.-11:30
p.m., Fri.-Sat. noon-2 p.m. & 6 p.m.-midnight,
Sun. noon-2:30 p.m. & 6 p.m.-11:30 p.m. All
major cards.*

Just a brisk walk from Kew Gardens, this rendezvous spot comprises three glass-fronted floors that overlook Kew Road. The private room on the top floor is open only on weekends; in fact, all the floors can be converted to private spaces for banquets and parties. Friendly waiters serve good Chinese food that draws on recipes from both Beijing and the Szechwan province. The crab claws make a tasty starter, and the aromatic crispy duck is served with an interesting sauce, as is the Peking duck. By the end of the meal, the lychees taste as cool as ever, though the yellowish color of the pineapple on our last visit was slightly off-putting. House wine is £7 a bottle, and an endless supply of coffee to drive home on is provided.

A la carte: £12-£15, including wine.

11/20 Pitagora

106 Kew Rd. - 940 0278, 948 2443
ITALIAN
Open Mon.-Sat. noon-3 p.m. & 7 p.m.-11:15 p.m. All major cards.

A light and comfortable place, also within walking distance of Kew Gardens, Pitagora is filled with decorative portraits of yesteryear's film stars—David Niven, Humphrey Bogart, Marlene Dietrich, Frank Sinatra, Yul Brynner, Steve McQueen, Claude Rains. . . . In this brisk trattoria, chef Bruno Piotto aims to provide dishes familiar to loyalists of the Italian mainstays. Snails stuffed with butter and garlic, a particularly memorable plate of saucer-size mushrooms served in a succulent garlic-and-wine sauce, and an abundant, flavorful seafood salad are fine representatives of the house starters. Examples of the many fine pasta dishes on the lengthy menu are spaghetti al pesto with a creamy sauce, risotto dal pescatore with fresh shellfish and (too little) rice, fettuccine in a cream sauce with mushrooms and onions, and cannelloni all'Italia, stuffed with ricotta cheese and spinach. Meat dishes are not ignored; we can recommend the chicken stuffed with butter and garlic, the gloriously tender calf's liver with a butter-and-sage sauce, and the spicy cotechino (pork sausage) with fagiolini beans. Included in the short collection of desserts is an outstanding crème brûlée, which our Italian guest was delighted to be served with an abundant cup of real Italian coffee, a rare encounter in London. The staple wine list accents Italian wines, and the house red and white from Colli del Trasimeno are good values at £6.95. With Giovanni Dechiara as an impressive head waiter, the service is both friendly and attentive.

A la carte: £20, including wine.

12/20 Valchera's

30 The Quadrant, Surrey - 940 0648
INTERNATIONAL
Open Mon.-Sat. noon-2:30 p.m. & 6:45 p.m.-10:45 p.m. All major cards.

This celebrated Swiss-Italian-international restaurant was given a new lease on life a couple of years ago when it was purchased by new owners. After experiencing some early teething troubles, Valchera's has become a worthy place that offers a bargain-basement fixed-price lunch menu. In addition to the sedate main restaurant, two upstairs rooms are ideal for weddings, private functions and business meetings. The cuisine concentrates on traditional English and Continental dishes, prepared from fresh ingredients, and specializes in fish and game. To start we can recommend the tasty mushrooms stuffed with Stilton cheese; an exact example of what smoked salmon should taste like; mussels marinière (cooked in white wine with chopped shallots, parsley and butter); and the rich pâté de la maison. Among the fish courses is an outstanding Dover sole, along with tasty scallops on a bed of spinach. But Valchera's has always prided itself on its ability to cook and serve game. The list of such entrées has a truly international theme, with creations hailing from all parts of Europe—a good chicken Kiev, a worthy osso buco Milanese—but it's the magnificently robust venison, the exquisite roast guinea-fowl and the wild duck (which lacked the stringy texture that so frequently spoils the dish) that stand out in our minds. For dessert try the good crème brûlée or the figs served with cream. The house wines supplied by Georges Duboeuf sell for a bargain £6.75 a bottle, and choices from the carefully assembled wine list include a superb Chassagne Montrachet Les Embrazées 1985 (£26.95) and a Beaune Les Cent Vignes 1979 (£24.50), which is still drinking well.

A la carte: £25, including wine. Fixed-price menu: £11.95 (lunch only).

ST. GILES

11/20 Mon Plaisir

21 Monmouth St., WC2 - 836 7246
FRENCH
Open Mon.-Fri. noon-2 p.m. & 6 p.m.-11 p.m., Sat. 6 p.m.-11 p.m. Cards: AE, MC, V.

Just northwest of Covent Garden, this popular, long-established French bistro gives off a true Gallic flavor. It was recently renovated and refurbished, and though the large log fire in the rear dining room was maintained, the front has been mercifully freed from those drafts that used to cause so much complaining. Thankfully, the courtyard for summertime dining remains. Daily specials are written up on a blackboard, but the à la carte menu is where you'll find the appetizers, including a spicy pâté, a fragrant onion soup and a brandade of mackerel. There is a roughly equivalent number of main courses (entrecôte, leg of lamb, a delicious casserole), which you can wash down with a selection from the rough-and-ready wine list, featuring a remarkably pleasant house wine. The cheese board—the star of the show here—comprises some 30 varieties.

A la carte: £15-£25, including wine. Fixed-price menu: £9.50.

10/20 Rodos

59 St. Giles High St., WC2 - 836 3177
GREEK
Open Mon.-Fri. noon-2:30 p.m. & 5:30 p.m.-11:30 p.m., Sat. 5:30 p.m.-11:30 p.m. All major cards.

Rodos is a cramped, immensely popular Cypriot restaurant that has been run by Loucas Savvides and his family for more than fifteen years. The walls are white and freckled, the seats the color of red wine, and the tablecloths the shade of pink roses. Hot pita bread is delivered throughout the meal. From the substantial menu we can recommend the spanakopita with feta, phyllo pastry wrapped around feta cheese and spinach; loukanika, gloriously spicy sausages; tsadziki, a mixture of cucumber and yogurt; and yahni, breast of chicken cooked with mushrooms, onions and tomatoes in Cypriot sherry. A full range of Greek sweets punctuates a meal that always sets us to dreaming about a trip to Cyprus.

A la carte: £17-£20, including wine.

10/20 Seven Dials Restaurant

5 Neal's Yd., WC2 - 379 4955
BRITISH/FRENCH
Open Mon.-Fri. 12:15 p.m.-2:30 p.m. & 6 p.m.-11:30 p.m., Sat. 6 p.m.-11:30 p.m. All major cards.

The engaging Thierry Niel, formerly the manager at Mon Plaisir, has moved a stone's throw down Monmouth Street and is now manager of this spacious glorified conservatory, which encompasses three floors. The service is simply outstanding—everyone seems singularily interested in the well-being of the customer. And chef Aram Atansyan makes good use of organically grown produce. A delicious avocado dip is served with drinks while you study the menu, and the petits fours that accompany your coffee at the close of the meal are scrumptious, but we're getting ahead of ourselves. The short menu offers some solid choices, such as snails vol-au-vent (in puff pastry) in a red-wine sauce and saddle of hare in a juniper berry sauce. The pretheater fixed-price menu (£10.50) is quite popular, since Seven Dials is within hailing distance of Covent Garden and other famous theaters.

A la carte: £20-£25, including wine. Fixed-price menus: £10.50-£12.95.

ST. JAMES'S

⑭ Auberge de Provence

41 Buckingham Gate, SW1 - 834 6655
FRENCH
Open daily noon-2:30 p.m. & 7:30 p.m.-11 p.m. All major cards.

In 1988 this prestigious restaurant severed its liaison with the St. James's Court Hotel and moved a few doors up Buckingham Gate toward Buckingham Palace. The decor still verges on the vulgar, only a vague approximation of the Provençal style it is trying to achieve, with its white painted arches and various textured paints rudely compromised by an overabundance of wrought-iron railings and dark beams. The welcome is warm, however, and the cooking, now supervised by Yves Gravelier, reaches great heights in some dishes. Though the quail salad with wild mushrooms was a disappointment, a light, creamy lemon-grass sauce enhanced the mussel salad, and the pan-fried filet of John Dory with a sea-urchin sauce was delicious, even if the sauce was a bit sweet. Traditionally, Auberge de Provence has seemed more at ease cooking fish rather than meat, but at our last meal here the baked pigeon with a garlic sauce was entirely successful, and the noisettes of lamb with a "fois gras" (sic) sauce were tender and precisely flavored. The charlotte aux marrons (chestnuts) had a fine texture but not much depth, though it was surrounded by tasty bits of miniature rum-soaked Swiss rolls; better was the fresh, slightly sweet raspberry tart. With coffee came petits fours that tasted as dry and boring as they looked. The exclusively French wine list is selected by Jean André Charial and shipped from Les Baux in Provence; you'll also find a most agreeable house wine, a Côtes-du-Ventoux 1986 for £9.50.

A la carte: £30-£40, including wine. Fixed-price menu: £17.50.

11/20 Le Caprice

Arlington House, Arlington St., SW1
629 2239
INTERNATIONAL
Open Mon.-Fri. & Sun. noon-2:30 p.m. & 7 p.m.-midnight, Sat. 7 p.m.-midnight. All major cards.

Known to its regulars as the Stage Door Canteen, Le Caprice is unquestionably a place for stargazing, home to celebrities, agents and such royal folk as the Dutchess of Kent. The decor is ultra-chic, New York–style, in cream, black, glass and chrome, with white orchids on the tables, the obligatory jazz musician before the piano and even jazzier cocktails emerging from the bar. Brunch on Sunday is great: pitchers of Bloody Marys and Bucks Fizz, eggs Benedict, bagels with cream cheese and lox. Co-owners Chris Corbin and Jeremy King stage-manage the spectacle with style. They know everybody who's anybody—but even if you're nobody, they'll still be nice to you. Evenings are equally glamorous, but don't expect top-flight cuisine. Your best bet is to stick with simple steaks and calf's liver. A short, reasonably priced wine list includes two house wines, a white Trebbiano di Romagna and a red Rhône Principauté d'Orange.

A la carte: £20, including house wine.

11/20 Columbina

4-5 Duke of York St., SW1 - 930 8279
839 3240
ITALIAN
Open Mon.-Sat. noon-3 p.m. & 6 p.m.-11 p.m. All major cards.

Just off Jermyn Street, in a posh shopping area, sits this busy, bustling trattoria owned by the three Ferrari brothers. The dated decor is full of overwrought iron and Chianti bottles, but Columbina continues to serve tasty food, often better than that at some of the trendiest Italian restaurants that everyone's talking about. The choice of antipasti is large and tempting, including a fresh, tangy seafood salad, mozzarella with orange, and garlicky frogs' legs alla francese (which surface, mysteriously enough, only at dinner). Daily pasta highlights are crespoline stuffed with ricotta and spinach and marvelous homemade tortellini in a cream sauce with strips of smoked salmon. We savored a classic osso buco and calf's liver grilled with fresh sage, and habitués tipped us off to the fresh lobster, which is served, when available, at giveaway prices. The dessert trolley often features fresh blackberry and blueberry tarts. The superb Stilton, served in true British style, is no doubt creditable to the restaurant's proximity to the Paxton & Whitfield cheese shop just around the corner. Portions are generous, and prices, mercifully, are as dated as the decor. Lunchtime reservations are a must.

A la carte: £15.

12/20 Green's Champagne & Oyster Bar

36 Duke St., SW1 - 930 4566
SEAFOOD
Open Mon.-Sat. 12:30 p.m.-2:45 p.m. & 6:30 p.m.-10:45 p.m., Sun. 11:30 a.m.-3:30 p.m. All major cards.

If you can't afford to belong to a gentleman's club, this august mahogany-paneled restaurant, smack in the heart of St. James's, is the next best thing. The marble-topped Champagne and oyster bar is lined with suave pinstriped art dealers and dandies swapping racing tips, who down Floquet et Fils (the house bubbly, priced at £12) and excellent West Mersea No. 1 oysters. Next door you can eat divine smoked salmon, lobster and crab, or satisfy your craving for nursery food with shepherd's pie or nice crispy fish cakes in parsley sauce. The roast woodcock is simply delectable. Service, on the whole, is impeccable, and the place is great fun, a delightful addition to a restaurant-saturated region. The well-chosen wine list boasts an assortment of 34 Champagnes.

A la carte: £25, including wine.

12/20 The Ritz

150 Piccadilly, W1 - 493 8181
BRITISH/FRENCH
Open Mon.-Sat. 12:30 p.m.-2:30 p.m. & 6:30 p.m.-11 p.m., Sun. 12:30 p.m.-2 p.m. & 7 p.m.-10:30 p.m. All major cards.

Now you've arrived. The Ritz is simply one of the most beautiful rooms in the world in which to enjoy an enjoyable meal, served by the most charming men. On our last visit, the sun was shining, the ceiling was painted with clouds in the style of Tiepolo, the French windows were wide open—need we go on? Sadly, we must—to say that the quality of the cuisine can be mercurial: sometimes just fine, sometimes frightfully boring. Among the appetizers, we've tried a humdrum duck salad and a rillette of smoked mackerel with avocado sauce that was rich and delicious. Quenelles of salmon and haddock were tasty but too heavy, and a grilled brochette of chicken and shrimp was dry. Featured on the dessert list is a chocolate cake that is truly ambrosial, filled with delicious cherries, cream and rich chocolate. Petits fours consist of two scrumptious coconut-covered chocolate balls and two thin almond-flavored biscuits. From the expensive wine list—£495 for a 1970 Talbot—we very much enjoyed a dry, smooth 1978 Château Cheret-Pitres for less than one-thirtieth of the Talbot's tariff.

A la carte: £40-£50, including wine. Fixed-price menus: £17.50-£26 (lunch only), £39.50 (dinner only).

10/20 Rowley's

113 Jermyn St., SW1 - 930 2707
BRITISH
Open Mon.-Sat. noon-2:30 p.m. & 6 p.m.-11:30 p.m., Sun. noon-2:30 p.m. & 6 p.m.-11 p.m. All major cards.

In this space Thomas Wall, born in 1846, created the famous St. James's Butcher Shop. In fact, the front part of the restaurant is still decorated with ceramic tiles, just as it was during the nineteenth century, when the butcher shop claimed a long succession of royal appointments as pie makers. A Rowley's meal begins with a salad, which is followed by steak (served with rosemary butter) and french fries. Sherbet and cheese is succeeded by coffee, and although the wine list is mundane, we always leave feeling entirely replenished and sated.

Fixed-price menu: £13.70.

⑬ Suntory

72-73 St. James's St., SW1 - 409 0201
JAPANESE
Open Mon.-Sat. 12:30 p.m.-1:30 p.m. & 7 p.m.-9:30 p.m. All major cards.

Reputedly the costliest Japanese restaurant in Europe, Suntory is an expense-account bastion where overheard conversations are as likely to be concerning millions of dollars as millions of yen. Though it is unusual for a gastronomic culture that traditionally segregates its various forms of cuisine, Suntory offers sukiyaki, shabu-shabu (meat and vegetables cooked at the table in stock and served with a seasoned sesame sauce) and sashimi under one roof. Downstairs are private rooms for the elaborate fixed-price kaiseki-ryori meals (no shoes, please). The scrupulously monochrome bar displays its shelves of whiskies (so beloved by the Japanese) like cult objects.

If you visit Suntory, you'll surely spend a few moments wondering, as we did, how anyone can charge £38 for a plate of chateaubriand and prawns. Sitting at the teppan-yaki tables dressed in linen bibs, while a chef sizzles beneath the glaring extractor hood, provides a unique opportunity to see your raw ingredients (steak, zucchini, rice, eggs, prawns, unpeeled mushrooms) magicked into a hot platter in a performance of great deftness and verve; it also provides an opportunity to speculate on the restaurant's food markup. The Royal Teppan-yaki meal (£23) and the Imperial meal (£29.50), which includes mixed seafood, begin with soy-sauced mushrooms and dobin-mushi soup served from individual teapots and climax with fresh fruit and coffee or green tea. It's all quite lovely and tasty, but ultimately it seems like an awful lot of money for such simple cooking. The price of wine is similarly immodest.

A la carte: £40-£50. Fixed-price menus: £20 (lunch only), £27-£42.

11/20 Wiltons

55 Jermyn St., SW1 - 629 9955
SEAFOOD
Open Mon.-Fri. 12:30 p.m.-2:30 p.m. & 6:30 p.m.-10:30 p.m., Sat. 6:30 p.m.-10:30 p.m. All major cards.

Wiltons first opened on King Street across from Christie's auction house in 1742, but it has been in this oak-paneled residence on Jermyn Street for only six years. But you can sense the pinstriped tradition of the place within moments of slipping past the pale-green bar stools at the front and striding through to the main restaurant, with its very Edwardian decor. The menu, like the restaurant, is terribly British and specializes in fish and game. Although the turtle soup, at least on our last visit, was surprisingly tasteless, the oysters were excellent—plain, with mornay sauce or in a cocktail—and the salmon succulent. Among the fish dishes are a delicious Dover sole, haddock with parsley sauce, excellent brill, plaice (a European member of the flounder family), salmon served in several ways and tasty turbot. If you prefer game, Wiltons serves an excellent venison, well aged and tender, and it prides itself on its tasty game birds, such as wild duck and grouse. The wine list is well chosen but pricey, though we uncovered a good bottle of claret for a mere (for this list) £17. Service is orderly and formal.

A la carte: £40-£50, including wine.

SHEPHERD'S BUSH

12/20 Chinon

25 Richmond Way, W14 - 602 5968
FRENCH
Open Tues.-Thurs. noon-2 p.m. & 7 p.m.-10 p.m., Fri. noon-2 p.m. & 7 p.m.-11 p.m., Sat. 7 p.m.-11 p.m. Cards: AE, MC.

Will the third venture of young co-owners/chefs Barbara Deane and Jonathan Hayes prove a success? After serving interesting food first at A Taste of Honey and then at the Perfumed Conservatory, Deane and Hayes have brought their combined talents to a third venue, an elegantly decorated room in the western part of London. Their enthusiasm is infectious; the pair have always found cooking an adventure. The menu here has been sensibly shortened and now lists six appetizers and five main courses, but the chefs still experiment with uncommon mixtures (cardamom sauce combined with a bouquet of Thai asparagus, for one) and garnish their dishes with wild herbs, fresh flowers or seaweeds. Among a number of good dishes we've enjoyed here are sea scallops on a bed of spinach tossed with pine nuts and an endive-butter sauce, deviled kidneys with saffron-scented basmati rice, breast of Norfolk duckling served with a crispy, dumpling-like "purse" filled with smoked chicken, and a beautifully tender lamb filet roasted with lavender and served with young spinach, nettles (a green similar to spinach) and reduced lamb juices. There are also abundant vegetables, such as mange-touts (green beans), tiny corn cobs and new potatoes, all of which are delicious. Desserts are sensational—do not leave without treating yourself to the wonderful bread-and-butter pudding, prepared with fresh seasonal fruits; the delightful parfait of white and dark chocolate; or the crème brûlée encased with spun sugar and a fresh fig tartellette. We could drool on, but you get the picture. Coffee comes with homemade black-and-white-chocolate truffles and candied fresh berries. The wine list is tidily chosen and almost exclusively French, and the house wines from Georges Duboeuf are a good value at £7.

A la carte: £25-£30, including wine.

11/20 Wilson's

236 Blythe Rd., W14 - 603 7267
BRITISH
Open Sun.-Mon. noon-2:30 p.m., Tues.-Fri. noon-2:30 p.m. & 7 p.m.-10 p.m., Sat. 7 p.m.-10 p.m. Cards: AE, DC.

This restaurant reopened a couple of years ago, having closed for six months following a disastrous fire. Just about the identical decor was reinstated—light floorboards and dark wooden panels on the walls—but the color of the painted areas has changed from beige to pale blue, and now the lighting is rather somber. The menus change weekly, and the fixed-price dinners and traditional three-course Sunday lunch remain good values. Appetizers include a small tartelette of Brie and wild mushrooms with a leek and Sauterne sauce that is both tasty and original, and a successful plate of selected smoked fish. Although we found the braised leg and roast saddle of rabbit with a gypsy sauce to be a trifle bland, the breast of pheasant with ham à l'alsacienne, pineapple and Sauerkraut baked in phyllo pastry was excellent. To finish there is an appetizing selection of English and French cheeses, as well as some traditional puddings (desserts) and the unusual but delicious dish of warm figs with an almond mousse. The wine list consists of a good selection of reasonably priced wines from Europe, America and Australia, and a decent house wine.

A la carte: £20-£25, including wine. Fixed-price menus: £15.50-£17.75.

SOHO

11/20 **Arirang**

31-32 Poland St., W1 - 437 6633, 437 9662
KOREAN
Open Mon.-Sat. noon-3 p.m. & 6 p.m.-11 p.m. All major cards.

This long-established restaurant now features an awkward decor that may not be to everyone's liking—a mélange of veneered tables, leather-covered walls and reproduction eighteenth-century chairs. Appetizers consist largely of pickle relishes and salads, to gladden the heart of any vegetarian. Topping the bill, inevitably, is the dreaded kim chee, a peppery, fermented, malodorous mix of vegetables, primarily cabbage (it is such an essential part of their national diet that Korean soldiers carry cans of it into battle). Actually, if you can get past the smell, it is highly addictive, and management touchingly supplies a stick of mint gum to sweeten the breath. Also unusual are koraree, a delicately cooked dish of bracken stalks, and shikumchee, sweetish spinach with garlic and sesame seed. Beef, rather than pork (which the Chinese prefer), is the favorite meat. Bulgogi, the national dish, is thin marinated beef strips cooked at the table on a conical metal plate with a curved rim that catches the sweet and spicy juices. Yuk kwe, Korean steak tartare with a touch of sesame oil, is mixed here with strips of crisp, fresh pear, then shaped into a small volcanic mound with an egg yolk sitting in the crater—bizarre but delicious. Other house favorites include squid in a hot chili and yellow-bean sauce; fried-zucchini sandwiches filled with meat; binotok, a kind of pea-flour pizza; and bul kal beef spare-ribs, promised on the menu to be out of this world. We felt compelled to try the small steamboat of shin sol lo, the "dish of kings" that was once reserved for the Korean royal family but is now available to commoners; we commoners found it nourishing but about as exciting as macaroni and cheese. The finale, fresh fruit and a pot of Korean barley tea, is a nice way to end the meal. Sake is, of course, always a good choice with this kind of food; the management also strongly promotes a number of ginseng-based tipples, claimed to "restore, maintain and build up the whole system of the body."

A la carte: £20, including sake. Fixed-price menus: £6.50 (lunch only), £32 (dinner only, for two).

13 **Bahn Thai**

23A Frith St., W1 - 437 8504
THAI
Open Mon.-Sat. noon-2:45 p.m. & 6 p.m.-11:15 p.m., Sun. 12:30 p.m.-2:30 p.m. & 6:30 p.m.-10:30 p.m. All major cards.

Now that the Kensington branch recently closed its doors, the Bahn Thai chain is reduced to this link. One of the prettiest rooms in Soho, it is surrounded by dark-wood paneling enlivened by multicolored paper parasols hanging beneath ceiling spotlights; this setting is slightly betrayed by some kitsch artwork. The tablecloths are black, and candles constantly threaten to scorch the flowers (the staff will eventually remove them if the table gets too crowded).

Nannyish "guidance notes" on the front of the menu reveal that there are no fixed-price menus, which is a pity. The kitchen leads with seafood—squid, prawns, bass and catfish—and extends itself with dry salt beef, chicken livers and stewed pigs' trotters. Tom kha gai, a spicy chicken soup, incorporates plenty of chicken plus lemon and galanga (a fiery spice), but it overdoses on creamed coconut. As ever with this cuisine, be on the lookout for chilis or pieces of chilis, which may necessitate a call to the fire brigade. The satay, served on triangles of pasty white bread, is curiously stringy though well accompanied by an unusually unsweet peanut sauce. The marinated roast duck dish called bhed yang is tender and excellent. Gai pad khing, Thai fried chicken with ginger and dried fungus, also merits recommendation, as do the richly furnished noodles. Perhaps reflecting the British ownership, the wine list is remarkably extensive, with pages of varietals. But traditionalists need not fear—Singha beer is in plentiful supply.

A la carte: £15, including beer.

(14) La Bastide
50 Greek St., W1 - 734 3300

FRENCH

Open Mon.-Fri. 12:30 p.m.-2:30 p.m. & 6 p.m.-11:30 p.m., Sat. 6 p.m.-11:30 p.m. All major cards.

In Soho the restoration trend in recent years has been toward sharpness and modernism: slick, youthful designs and equally slick cuisines that appeal to the fashion-oriented people who have moved into the district. Nicholas Blacklock, psychologist and former chief executive of a data-processing company, went in a different direction when, about three years ago, he decided to make a career change and opened a restaurant. La Bastide is situated on the ground floor (private dining room above, kitchens below) of a Georgian house that was built and originally occupied 250 years ago by the family of a noted local builder, Frith, who gave his name to the street that runs parallel to Greek Street. The restoration work has since won a Westminster Council award, and indeed the pristine original plasterwork, cornices and shell-molded alcoves are a treat to behold. With the genteel, more-or-less period decor—buffs, creams, tangerines, voluminous curtains—the atmosphere is more representative of Bath than Soho.

Blacklock's French cooking is highly competent and blessed more with the attributes of traditional-family-restaurant or brasserie fare than of haute cuisine. His regular "carte" (menu) features such well-prepared upscale dishes as lobster terrine, crab ravioli, salmon in sorrel sauce, navarin of lamb, duck confit with tomatoes and kumquats, and medallion of veal with lime and shallots. The cheaper, simpler "Soho menu" lists such items as smoked salmon, onion soup, grilled sole, andouillette and entrecôte. Most interesting, however, is the fixed-price "regional menu," which changes monthly but always includes ten or twelve specialties from the featured part of

France at a price of about £15 for three courses or £17 for four. Although there is the inevitable occasional dud, the regional menus are often excellent, and they fill a gap in the coverage of London's many French restaurants, regional though some of them are. A Languedoc menu included a good, salty brandade de morue (salt cod) with a small salad and toast, a pleasant, mild garlic soup and a more-than-acceptable cassoulet. From the Champagne region diners have sampled succulent rabbit terrine in a delicious aspic, fresh, tasty pea soup, an excellent potée with beef, chicken and lamb, floury potatoes and strong, fresh carrots in a rich clear broth, and good rack of lamb in a smooth Champagne sauce. From Provence came a good, oily fondant ragoût of mutton with artichokes, a softly fragrant quail confit with a crisp shredded potato cake, a very creditable (unusual in London) encornete (little squid) stuffed with spinach and pine nuts and baked in a slightly dull cucumber sauce, and, less successfully, a dish of rubbery casseroled fried tripe. Desserts, wines and service are all honest values for the money.

A la carte: £25-£35. Fixed-price menus: £15-£17.

12/20 braganza
56 Frith St., W1 - 437 5412

BRITISH

Open Mon.-Fri. 11:30 a.m.-3:30 p.m. & 5:30 p.m.-11:30 p.m., Sat. 5:30 p.m.-11:30 p.m. Brasserie: open Mon.-Sat. 11 a.m.-11 p.m. All major cards.

A far cry from its previous green-painted Wheeler's incarnation, braganza (with the lower-case *b* on the waiters' uniforms and the crockery), now sports a facade so minimalist that it's difficult to find the place. The old entrance is all window (flung open in summer), leading straight into the Brasserie, above which is the restaurant proper, its stark entrance dominated by vast plaster sculptures in a trendy cold white. The chrome staircase leads optimistically upward, but for the uninitiated, arriving can be intimidating. If she is in place, the immaculately dressed receptionist will look after you. Once in, you can relax a bit.

The downstairs Brasserie is light and friendly, decorated with bright pictures. Though the music can be jarringly loud, the menu sounds mouth-watering: delicate salads of marinated smoked chicken, terrines with exotic vegetables, soups, pasta, special vegetarian platters, cheese and fruity desserts. And all at great prices: Two can eat well here, with a bottle of the house wine, for under £30.

However, what Fitch and Company (the well-known, excellent design consultants) really had designs on was the second- and third-floor dining rooms, past the statues. People journey to the wide, bright second-floor room, with enormous windows, large abstract murals, black tablecloths and nattily shirted waiters, to see and be seen. In spite of the rather clinical lighting, the room manages to feel warm and comfortable (the chairs are inviting), and service is attentive and polite. The menu reads like an expanded, extravagant version of the Brasserie's downstairs, and the food has been designed to perfection, sometimes at the cost of flavor—as with a vegetable terrine we tried, which looked gorgeous but tasted only of peppers. On the other hand, a tender, delicate turbotine terrine with fresh (raw) marinated scallops was a feast for the eye that went down beautifully. The entrées, all immaculately presented by the English chef, Roger Evans, include a lattice of salmon and halibut, as fresh as a daisy, and a well-prepared breast of duck with artichoke. The Sauvignon Trois Mouline '87 is a reasonable £8.20, and desserts include a tangy orange-and-mint "terrine" and superior profiteroles, small puffs of choux paste filled with whipped cream and drizzled with chocolate sauce. All in all, this place turns out a fairly impressive example of designer food.

On the third floor the decor could not be more different—all heavy paneling, oak chairs cushioned with Liberty prints and a stupendously garish painted ceiling that would make Tiepolo do backflips in his grave. Here, the same menu is served to a completely different clientele. Whereas the second floor is all designer clothes, high heels and flashing smiles, the third is home to suits and secrets.

A la carte: £25. Brasserie: £15, including house wine.

10/20 Chiang Mai

48 Frith St., W1 - 437 7444
THAI
Open Mon.-Sat. noon-3 p.m. & 6 p.m.-11 p.m., Sun. noon-3 p.m. & 6 p.m.-10 p.m. All major cards.

Diners unable to get into Alastair Little often find themselves next door at the doyenne of West End Thai restaurants. The double-storefront is deceptive: There is another room in back and yet another in the basement, which can become too close on summer evenings. The necessarily spartan decor is suggestive of a stilt house whose inhabitants have spent their disposable incomes on brass kitsch—and all of this is well complemented by piped-in music. Named after Thailand's northern capital, Chiang Mai boasts a 110-item à la carte menu (including an extensive vegetarian selection) of dishes ranging from the hot and sour to the candidly incendiary. Watching the uninitiated mistaking green chilis for French beans among the fried beef provides a frequent source of merriment for more experienced diners here. Absolute beginners could do worse than to sample one of the four fixed-price menus for two (from £27 to £32), which include excellent sticky rice, a bowl of lychees and acceptable coffee. The most successful items are the wonderful spicy sausages, the generous satay, the meat-and-onion-filled batter cases (ga ton tong) and the fragrant soups with fiery depth charges—among them an exquisite chicken and coconut milk and a hot-and-sour chicken bobbing with Chinese mushrooms. The dry curries tend to be crude and dull, and the kitchen shows signs of overloading at peak hours. This is hardly surprising given the cramped conditions of the site, and it may explain why the attentive, if sometimes overworked, waiters don't always offer the selection of meats, instead just slinging out dish after dish of, say, beef. A decidedly undernourished wine list is best ignored in favor of Singha beer. This is the best introduction to Thai food London has to offer, and is a great café by any standards.

A la carte: £20, including beer or wine. Fixed-price menus: £27-£32 (for two).

11/20 Chuen Cheng Ku

17 Wardour St., W1 - 437 1398, 734 3281
CHINESE
Open Mon.-Fri. 11 a.m.-11 p.m., Sat.-Sun. 11 a.m.-11:45 p.m. All major cards.

The dim sum here is still reputed to be the finest in London, though the illusion of eating in Hong Kong is probably stronger at the New World in Gerrard Place, which positively *teems*, this place is merely packed. Heated trolleys carry a massive array of dumplings (whose stuffings are based primarily on shrimp and pork) and white, sticky rice-flour dumplings; deep-fried pasta and tripe in garlic and black-bean sauce; and such sci-fi creations as lotus leaves stuffed with preserved egg, and duck and water mushrooms in glutinous rice. The prices of these substantial snacks are extraordinarily low, which helps make this food about the most exciting cheap lunch in London. So perhaps it is churlish of us to complain about its flaws. Still, there are fine creations: shredded chicken with al dente asparagus, abalone with fish lips (not on the menu, but ask), hot pots (stews) of eel, salt pork, mushrooms and an entire head of garlic, and ho-fun noodles (broad and soft) with dried beef. The desserts are unusually good for a Cantonese place: a delicious almond bean curd is artlessly topped with tinned "fruit salad," but the sherbets are unadorned and potent.

A la carte: £10-£25, including wine. Fixed-price menus: £10 (lunch only), £14 (dinner only).

10/20 Dal Pescatore

26 Romilly St., W1 - 437 5302
ITALIAN
Open Mon.-Sat. noon-3 p.m. & 6 p.m.-11:30 p.m., Sun. 6 p.m.-11:30 p.m. All major cards.

As its name implies, Dal Pescatore is a seafood restaurant. It came into existence when Franco Carraro sold Rugantino, the restaurant that formerly occupied this site, and went off to open a new place in Battersea. Like its predecessor, it's a small, intimate place, which can accommodate 30 on the street level and an additional 25 in the basement (where there is also a bar). Sitting on a street just north of Shaftesbury Avenue, Dal Pescatore is ideally located to serve pre- and post-theater meals. Lorenzo Bellintani is a commendable head waiter whose meal advice is well taken, and chef Francesco Formica (how's that for a name?), who hails from Sorrento, cooked previously at Mr. Frascati in Paddington.

Dal Pescatore makes a special point of serving fish dishes only when the specified fish is fresh and available. On our last visit, the seafood salad was pleasant, as was the fish soup, and mussels were served in an enhancing tomato and white-wine sauce. Red mullet was done to perfection, though the monkfish in a sauce of white wine, basil and parsley was overcomplicated by the presence of far too many small shellfish. The number of sweet courses is minimal, a testimony to the overriding significance of the main courses. Both red and white house wines come from Montevino and are a mere £5.80.

A la carte: £20-£25, including wine.

⑬ Dragon Gate

7 Gerrard St., W1 - 734 5154
CHINESE
Open daily noon-11:30 p.m. All major cards.

Many Chinese restaurants claim to serve Szechwan food, but Dragon Gate is one of the few to deliver the real thing. It is a small, dowdy place, apparently assembled from a do-it-yourself Chinese-restaurant kit. Outside lies the recently completed Chinatown pedestrian precinct. Inside, the atmosphere is perpetually festive, as might be expected from people who take two weeks to celebrate the New Year. Ceremonial arches, red and gold short posts, a sea of fluttering pennants overhead and tiled telephone booths designed like household shrines recall San Francisco or New York.

As for the cuisine, superb appetizers include chicken in red oil, cold tripe with ginger and Szechwan pepper, and thinly sliced pork loin with a thick soy, garlic and chili dressing. As a side dish, the sweet and relatively mild cucumber in sesame oil cools the palate delightfully. Shrimp in garlic sauce, a test-dish of this fiery regional cuisine, is letter-perfect. Other specialties from the large menu are tea- and camphor-smoked duck, and eggplant in soy and wine sauce. Dumplings are served in a red-pepper sauce or a hot-and-sour broth; don't miss the small steamed, puckered buns stuffed with pork. This is authentic food that would not insult that old Szechwanese survivor, Deng Xiao Ping (in fact, rumor has it that the venerable chef is approaching his 90th birthday; one begins to wonder if there is a connection between an incendiary diet and longevity). You'll need the ice cream and lychees that comprise the dessert offerings to cool your palate, but the underlying finesse of the cooking makes it all worthwhile. For a real taste of Szechwan in London, you can't do better.

A la carte: £12-£25, including wine. Fixed-price menus: £11 (lunch only), £15 (dinner only).

(13) Dragon's Nest

58-60 Shaftesbury Ave., W1
437 3119

CHINESE

*Open Mon.-Fri. noon-3 p.m. & 5 p.m.-11:30
p.m., Sat.-Sun. noon-11:30 p.m. All major
cards.*

Off Chinatown's main drag, this chic new restaurant has a very different feel: heavy doors, beveled mirrors, decorative tiles—stately but not too formal. There is faint neoclassical music in the background, and Shaftesbury Avenue becomes more or less inaudible. The menu is comprehensive but not unwieldy, and the head waiter is welcoming and particularly helpful, guiding you away from certain dishes and toward others with convincing enthusiasm. And the food matches the buildup. Several of the dishes are Szechwan-influenced, labeled with stars to warn of exceptional spiciness. Sizzling dishes have real pungency and freshness: beef, the tenderest filet strips; lobster, served in any of five sauces (we liked the hot garlic and chili best), which costs a mere £12 a pound. And the crispy duck is excellent with buns instead of pancakes enwrapping it. The wine list is long enough; and an Orvieto at £8 has just the right aromatic medium dryness to complement this occasionally fiery food. Service is faultless, with hot towels appearing at suitable intervals. The loos are clean and spacious. The Dragon's Nest feels far more luxurious than most Chinese restaurants, and the food is significantly superior, yet it scarcely costs more. Three of us ate more than we could usually manage, including a lobster dish, and got through two bottles of wine. The bill, service included, was £67.85.

A la carte: £20, including wine. Fixed-price menus: £12, £16 and £18 per person (two-person minimum).

12/20 Frith's

14 Frith St., W1 - 439 3370

FRENCH

*Open Mon.-Fri. 12:30 p.m.-2:30 p.m. & 7:30
p.m.-11:15 p.m., Sat. 7:30 p.m.-11:15 p.m.
Cards: MC, V.*

This light, flesh-colored room has two ceiling fans to keep you cool in warm weather and art nouveau prints to make you feel warmer in cool weather. It also has an interesting menu. Frith's may not have the ambience of an expense-accounters haunt; it's more of a place to entertain friends from work, particularly during fine weather when the garden out back is open. Now that Carla Tomasi has returned as proprietor (she worked here for four years as chef), the food is always full of good flavors, as is immediately demonstrated by the appetizers, which include the lentil, bacon and potato soup (£4) and the tasty smoked filets of eel in aïoli, celeriac and ginger dressing (£5). Partridge with baked garlic and parsnip chips was tenderly cooked and tasted superb. The breast of chicken stuffed with red onions and raisins was heightened by the addition of a tarragon sauce. The vegetables (carrots, leeks and beetroot) were served suitably al dente but had been spoiled by being allowed to become too cool. As for the desserts, although the lemon parfait with caramelized ginger and cranberries was delicious, a dish of glazed nuts and toffee tart was far too sweet, and the tart was almost impossible to cut. Three petits fours for two made for interesting arithmetic and was an unfortunately telling example of the service, which was friendly but also inclined to be forgetful. Shortish wine list, with the house French at £8.50.

A la carte: £30, including wine.

12/20 Fung Shing

15 Lisle St., WC2 - 437 1539

CHINESE

Open daily noon-11:45 p.m. All major cards.

Aspiring to elegance (all cream and green) and a Western ambience (soft disco music), this place is characteristic of the "new style" Cantonese establishments that have opened all over London over the past six years. In recent years, Fung Shing has come up with a creative formula that other Cantonese restaurants have been quick to follow. Don't be misled by its facile smartness; this is a serious restaurant with a chef, Fu Kwun, who is eclectic in his sources and inventive in his methods and who has come up with more than 150 courses (although, given forewarning, he will be delighted to cook any dish you might require). His shredded eel with coriander, his pot stews and his scallops with garlic appear to owe as much to Piedmontese tradition as to that of Canton, and his sizzling beef with garlic and onion reheated at the table on an iron hot plate may have come from Japan. But there is no question about the origin of the deep-fried pigs' tripe with candied pickles or the delicious, liver-filled wind-dried sausages. Reservations are advisable.

A la carte: £15-£20, including wine.

⑭ Gay Hussar
2 Greek St., W1 - 437 0973

HUNGARIAN

Open Mon.-Sat. 12:30 p.m.-2:30 p.m. & 5:30 p.m.-11 p.m. No cards.

The Gay Hussar, one of a dwindling number of gastronomic survivors from a pre–clothes shops-and-ad-men Soho, may have lost its progenitor, the much loved Victor Sassie, but happily, so far little has changed. Chef Laszlo Holecz continues to produce delicious and filling high-quality Hungarian peasant staples, as he has done for the past eleven years. The maroon facade is adorned with shields, and the cozy and crowded interior, with its two floors of paneling, red plush seats, mirrors and china displayed on a rail-high shelf, continues to look charmingly like a cross between an 1890s bistro, a gentlemen's club and a rather disorganized publisher's waiting room, with shelves of volumes written by the restaurant's literary clientele. The older waiters still combine brusqueness, jocularity and a rather distracted desire to please, like stern but well-meaning Transylvanian uncles. John Wrobel, the dapper young Pole who manages the business for its new anonymous owners, has opened up the second-floor private dining room, once the exclusive province of Labour Party and trade union luminaries. They still represent an important element of the Gay Hussar's clientele, but now they share the place with an increasing number of conservatives.

The food is copious, robust and tasty, flavored with paprika, nutmeg, caraway, garlic, dill and cayenne pepper. The soups are either savory, based on meat stocks and vegetables, or more exotic, like the celebrated chilled wild cherry, a pale, semisweet, milky Hungarian specialty. The duck, goose and pork dishes are often accompanied by dumplings, cabbage or potatoes. Classics, such as veal goulash (known here as borju porkolt) are much better than the anemic approximations served in "international" restaurants. Gay Hussar's goulash is rich and creamy-thick, served with lovely little twisted "thimble egg" dumplings. Roast goose and duck are well prepared, rich and delicious, and their roasting juices are used in the preparation of other dishes, such as the

superb scholet (a central European confection of smoked white beans baked overnight in a slow oven into a state of wonderful fatty succulence). Fish dishes range from the fair (poached trout) to the interesting (Hungarian bouillabaisse, roast saddle of carp and fish dumplings in dill sauce). The salads are sometimes sharply dressed (pickled cucumber) to compensate for the richness of the main courses. Desserts are equally substantial and for the most part good. The astonishingly inexpensive wine list features a couple dozen reasonable French bottles, as well as a dozen modestly priced Hungarians and carafes of house red (Cabernet Franc) and white (Chardonnay). You'll also find some vintage Tokays.

A la carte: £25-£30, including wine. Fixed-price menu: £12 (lunch only).

11/20 Ho Ho
29 Maddox St., W1 - 493 1228

CHINESE

Open Mon.-Sat. noon-3 p.m. & 6 p.m.-11 p.m. All major cards.

Ho Ho belongs to the new class of London's Chinese restaurants. Different from the café-like Cantonese emporia of Soho or the frequently despicable chop suey houses of everywhere else, it is elegantly decorated and offers a cuisine that is derived from different parts of China (such as Beijing or Szechwan) but also serves dishes drawn from Malaysia and Singapore. The menu lists classics from Beijing, among them mildly flavored dumplings, crispy lamb with pickled vegetables, and sea bass with ginger and onions. Try the Peking duck or the Szechwan special. A good wine list includes Shoa Sing (sake) drunk hot in the traditional manner. The restaurant can be reserved for private parties. By Soho standards, it's not cheap.

A la carte: £20, including wine.

12/20 Au Jardin des Gourmets
5 Greek St., W1 - 437 1816

FRENCH

Open Mon.-Fri. 12:15 p.m.-2:30 p.m. & 6:30 p.m.-11:15 p.m., Sat. 6:30 p.m.-11:15 p.m. All major cards.

When he sold his mini-empire of restaurants to Kennedy Brookes, Joseph Berkmann held on to his favorite, Au Jardin des Gourmets, which he visits every month. In an elegant art deco setting, you can sink into a comfortable seat, call for a kir and munch a finger of toast smothered in a flavored butter. Since he arrived in 1987, Bocuse-trained Nicolas Picolet (who hails from Romanèche, near Fleurie) has injected a new spark of life into a menu that was growing tired and complacent. Among the appetizers now presented are his delicious cheese soufflé, excellent gravlax and a light pastry with snails and oyster mushrooms cooked in garlic and laced with Pernod. Impeccable Dover sole and an aromatic fish casserole with onions and ginger are two of the laudable efforts we have had the pleasure of sampling; other fashionable main courses include noisettes of lamb on artichoke hearts served with a Madeira, foie gras and truffle sauce, chicken enhanced by a tarragon and lime sauce, and monkfish and lobster with a light butter sauce. Beyond à la carte fare, there are three-course fixed-price lunches and dinners at astonishing prices (the menu changes every three days). The house wine is a bargain at £5.75, and Berkmann has left behind a superb claret-led wine list. Indeed, ever since it came into existence in 1931 as one of Soho's best French restaurants, Au Jardin des Gourmets has consistently offered splendid wines, so it came as no surprise to find it awarded the 1987 Cellar of the Year prize by Egon Ronay. With your dessert, why not try a slightly chilled red Pineau des Charentes, an especially good accompaniment to rich chocolate desserts? By the publication of this edition, the expansion to incorporate the establishment next door should be nearing completion.

A la carte: £25-£30, including wine. Fixed-price menus: £14, £26.75 (five-course "menu des gourmets").

11/20 Jensens

6 Greek St., W1 - 437 2006
FRENCH
Open Mon.-Fri. 12:30 p.m.-2:30 p.m. & 7 p.m.-11:30 p.m., Sat. 7 p.m.-11:30 p.m. Cards: AE, MC, V.

This sedate new restaurant aims at the upper stretches of the market, both in its menu and in its decor (which makes memories of the Old Budapest, its predecessor at this address, difficult to recall). The small dining area seats approximately 30 people and is attractively decorated with ornately framed paintings, elegant chairs, exotic flowers on the tables and

subtle lighting. However, it feels too formal, even uncomfortable, particularly if you are the first to arrive for a meal—you may feel like the walls are hiding two-way mirrors, through which your dining manners are being observed. This feeling of sobriety is further emphasized by the headwaiter, who looks and behaves like an overbearing extra from a production of *The Pirates of Penzance*, with his hands clasped severely behind his back.

The crudités were a delicious preprandial start, but the meal we tried recently had its share of weak points. The warm crouton was delicious, but why was it served on a bed of cooked cabbage? And though the salmon filet was excellent and the guinea-fowl extremely tasty, the kidneys were pink and harsh, and the note of formality was reintroduced when the green beans and carrots were laid on the table in regimented rows. The meal ended on a happier note with excellent sorbets and delightful petits fours. There's a good, if pricey, wine list.

A la carte: £35-£40, including wine. Fixed-price menu: £34 (menu dégustation).

10/20 Leonis Quo Vadis

26-29 Dean St., W1 - 437 4809, 437 9585
ITALIAN
Open Mon.-Fri. 12:30 p.m.-2:30 p.m. & 6 p.m.-11:15 p.m., Sat. 6 p.m.-11:15 p.m., Sun. 7 p.m.-10:30 p.m. All major cards.

Mounted on the tired green facade of Leonis is a royal-blue plaque that announces that Karl Marx once lived here. He surely must be writhing with consternation at the manner in which this long established favorite has become a paradise for the expense-account set, primarily people in the film and record industries. This medium-size restaurant, which has been at its current location since 1926, has its tables well spaced for comfort and privacy, but the food is just average. Don't expect to find any real bargains here.

A la carte: £30-£35, including wine.

12/20 The Lindsay House

21 Romilly St., W1 - 439 0450
BRITISH
Open Mon.-Sat. 12:30 p.m.-2:30 p.m. & 6 p.m.-midnight, Sun. 12:30 p.m.-2 p.m. & 7:30 p.m.-10 p.m. All major cards.

The third in what is becoming a small chain of determinedly British restaurants (others are the English Garden and the English House, both in Chelsea), The Lindsay House is a curious blend of individuality, imagination, camp, culinary talent undermined by an insistence on the theme of English recipes, and a lush unorthodox decor that nonchalantly straddles the boundary into kitsch. The narrow mid-eighteenth-century Shaftesbury Avenue house was languishing (architecturally, that is—no offense to the food) as a Chinese restaurant before its present incarnation, and behind the boxing and paneling were discovered virtually all of its original features, which are now set off by a vivid, indeed voluptuous, decorative scheme: The dark, cozy fire-lit ground-floor sitting room is delightful, all strong reds and greens, and the first-floor dining room is a riot of deep-salmon paint, pale-olive pleated fabric walls, festoons of rich pink and green materials, eighteenth-century mirrors with real candles in their holders and potted azaleas on the tables.

The cuisine derives from the research of writer/broadcaster Michael Smith, who has made a specialty of the modernization of English recipes from previous centuries. In this case, the eighteenth century continuously rears its head (presumably because of the period of the building), giving rise to somewhat arch menu items, such as Brye Favors, parcels of baked Brie with a tomato and basil coulis. The cooking, by Philip Hodgson, is good, but frankly, not all of the recipes are entirely felicitous. Success seems to come in roughly inverse ratio to their degree of Englishness. The cheese "favors" dish, baked in fine pastry, was pleasant, but how English is Brie in phyllo pastry with a tomato-and-basil sauce? Although Hodgson clearly can create a fine sauce—the rich, concentrated mushroom and Madeira cream with a tartelette of wild mushrooms was excellent—he is often saddled with an impossible combination. The roast breast of duckling came covered in a strong, dark, treacly soy-based coating that rapidly became cloying, and the truffled sauce that accompanied a dish of breaded pan-fried lamb cutlets was similarly overpowering. There are subtler flavors: a lemon-butter sauce to accompany the pan-fried salmon and cucumbers, and watercress purée served with veal. A short list of desserts features Stilton, Welsh rarebit, homemade ice creams and sorbets, fruit compotes and a year-round summer pudding.

A la carte: £30.

16 Alastair Little
40 Frith St., W1 - 734 5183

BRITISH

Open Mon.-Fri. 12:30 p.m.-3 p.m. & 7:30 p.m.-11:30 p.m. Closed last 3 weeks of Aug. No cards.

Alastair Little is young, English, university-educated, self-taught as a chef and a familiar face in the glossy magazines. His restaurant opened about three years ago, following his successful stint as chef of a fashionable wine bar/restaurant called 192 Kensington Park Road. This new venture's small stark room—polished wood floor, bare black tables, modern canvases on the white walls, thin-slatted venetian blinds over the plain facade, a high-tech ceiling studded with small, dimmed, bar-shape light bulbs—is normally packed for lunch and dinner throughout the week. Little's hallmarks are eclecticism, simplicity and the perfectionist treatment of first-class ingredients. The daily changing menu generally features twelve appetizers, eight main courses and six desserts. Dishes may be of French, Italian, Eastern Mediterranean, Scandinavian or British origin. At the moment, Little is very much into his "Japanese phase"—as manifested in his sashimi of tuna, John Dory, sea bass and sea bream. He also recently acquired a sushi machine that has made a spot for itself beside the pasta maker.

Concentrating as he does on simple, clear, strong flavors, and endowed as he is with excellent taste in terms of selection and combination of flavors, Little creates some extremely good food. A generous plate of fine carpaccio comes with strong rocket (arugula) leaves, shavings of Parmesan and first-rate olive oil; the much-essayed and not always successful Scandinavian combination of gravlax with a cucumber salad and a creamy mustard sauce is delicious; a tasty caramelized onion sauce may accompany a boudin blanc (sausage) or a solid, strong grouse terrine. Main courses include simple fresh fish (baked sea bream with girolles) and well-made classic meat dishes (a pot-au-feu of tongue, tenderly cooked with fresh vegetables in clear aromatic broth); a grilled filet of lamb with floury mild flageolets (a small, pale-green bean); a steamed breast of chicken with leeks and soy sauce. Desserts feature excellent chocolate mousse cake, lime, lemon, hazelnut and nougatine tarts, good ices and sorbets and well-kept British cheeses. There's more than a representative nod toward the United States among the 40 or so well-selected wines; there are also antipodes (Australian and New Zealand) representatives available and the occasional exotic special, such as a Greek Cabernet Sauvignon called Château Carras. The service is amiable and informal, and the ambience relaxed—if a touch noisy at times.

A la carte: £35.

10/20 Melati

31 Peter St., W1 - 437 2011
MALAYSIAN
Open Mon.-Sat. noon-2:45 p.m. & 6 p.m.-11:30 p.m. All major cards.

Not to be confused with its grander namesake on Great Windmill Street, this café-style restaurant is extremely relaxed and friendly, with authentic Malaysian food that alternately soothes and electrifies the palate. The clientele is, or certainly look, interesting: ballet dancers, fashion designers, artists and habitués of the French pub. One of our main problems here is ordering a meal that doesn't taste entirely of coconut or peanuts, but it can be done. A tried formula begins with grilled satay and peanut sauce, plus a huge bowl of golden Laksa Soup, chock-full of rice noodles, fish cakes, chicken (very hot) and lots of coconut. Beef Siam-style follows, in a gingery dressing, and for contrast, some crunchy chicken with deep-fried garlic and chilis. All the curries are good, but "tiny dry fish" with fried cabbage is to be avoided. There's a nicely soothing pancake filled with creamy coconut. Tiger beer is fine with this sort of food, but there is a nice drinkable house wine as well.

A la carte: £15.

10/20 Mr. Kong

21 Lisle St., W1 - 437 7341
CHINESE
Open daily noon-1:45 a.m. All major cards.

The above telephone number is included only for form. This thriving Cantonese restaurant doesn't accept reservations, but the quality of the food makes the wait worthwhile. In fact, the wait gives the eye the opportunity to grow acclimated to the office-chic of the surroundings. Lack of overdesign is as refreshing as the service, which is conspicuously more helpful than is customary on this street. Nowhere else have we heard a Chinese waiter ask, "Have you had sufficient?" We had more than a sufficient portion of well-judged scallops steamed with their coral on the shell; succulent eel satay (ten sticks served with a more somber peanut sauce than its Thai cousin); an exemplary, crispy aromatic Szechwan duck dish; and a sauté of venison in ginger wine, spiked with fresh ginger and decorated with carrot slices in the shape of various edible animals. The more exotic of these items come from the supplementary chef's menu, which is more adventurous than most in Chinatown. The wine list is as rudimentary as the decor, and the beer is limited to Carlsberg, which is a pity. The meal ends with cubes of watermelon—a eupeptic innovation.

A la carte: £15, including wine. Fixed-price menus: £6.80 to £8.80 per person (two-person minimum), £11 to £13.50 per person (four-person minimum, dinner only).

9/20 New World

1 Gerrard Pl., W1 - 734 0677
CHINESE

On the edge of the new, improved tourist Chinatown, with its New York–inspired pagoda-style phone booths, New World continues the decorative theme with tasseled lanterns beneath a brutalist concrete ceiling. Until 6 p.m. each evening, this vast 500-seat restaurant is thronged with heated dim sum trolleys and a mostly Chinese clientele trying to flag them down. At £1.10 per piece and upward, this dim sum represents as good a value as anywhere in the area. The commensurately vast dinner menu offers fixed-price meals at £5.30 per person, hot pots of belly pork and yam, an extensive vegetarian selection and all the standard (mostly Pekingese) seafood and celebrated exotica (such as braised duck with fish lips or fried shark's fin with scrambled eggs). The kitchen patiently struggles to keep up with demand, but it often seems to be operating with a bucket of glue to which sightly different flavors are added. A handsome plate of lobster in ginger sauce suffered from such a fate, as did fried beef and green pepper in a chili and black-bean sauce. Half of a tired-looking but crunchy Szechwan aromatic duck arrived smothered in grated carrot; Singapore noodles were well stocked with prawns and egg but, bizarrely, tasted exclusively of curry powder.

On the up side, "sea-spiced" eggplant and mushrooms were tasty. If you can stand the briskly assertive and sometimes slapdash service from overworked waitresses, this place is a cheap, quick feed where you can always get a table.

A la carte: £10, including Chinese tea. Fixed-price menu: £5.30.

12/20 Red Fort

77 Dean St., W1 - 437 2115
INDIAN
Open Mon.-Sat. noon-2:45 p.m. & 6 p.m.-11:15 p.m., Sun. noon-2:45 p.m. & 6 p.m.-10:45 p.m. All major cards.

Amin Ali, the owner of the elegant Jamdani and one of the guiding lights of the Last Days of the Raj, opened Red Fort in 1983 and immediately raised Indian cuisine into the ranks of fashionable. Any idea that Indian restaurants are not chic is dispelled by Red Fort. It looks like an upscale Italian restaurant but serves excellent Indian food, described as Moghul cuisine. Upon entering, you are invited—or rather, leaned on—to try one of the inventive cocktails. To start with, we suggest masha (onion stuffed with spicy beans) or momo (minced meat and spices wrapped in pastry). Then move on to the tandoori specialties: chicken tikka, vegetarian thali or rogan josh (spiced lamb braised in yogurt and cream). To accompany your meal, we implore you to try a naan bread, particularly the Peshawari naan, stuffed with almonds. Lassi, a yogurt drink either sweet or salted, is most refreshing. The short wine list includes a house wine priced at £6.95.

A la carte: £15-£20, including wine.

11/20 Signor Zilli

41 Dean St., W1 - 734 3924
ITALIAN
Open daily noon-3 p.m. & 7 p.m.-11 p.m. All major cards.

A compact, busy restaurant with fetching pastel panels on its walls, Signor Zilli opened in the summer of 1988 and serves all the mainstays of Italian cuisine, which are served with a flourish. Among the antipasti are a tasty, wonderfully delicate carpaccio, a stimulating fresh crab and mango cocktail and a lovely selection of fresh fish in white wine with tomato, chili, garlic and saffron to provide some fire. Included in the pasta dishes are an outstanding trenette (flat pasta similar to fettuccine) dish pepped up with steamed clams and calamaretti (squid) in a paper case, and spinach gnocchi served in a fresh lobster and radicchio sauce. The chef will grill, steam or sauté any fish from the large selection listed on the menu; we can recommend the outstanding fresh skate in black butter sauce, a whole red snapper in white fennel seeds and Pernod, and a flavorful fresh turbot enhanced by a pink pepper sauce. On Sundays, a special menu concentrates on traditional lamb and beef dishes; the fair wine list concentrates on favorite Italian representatives.

A la carte: £25-£30, including wine.

11/20 Soho Brasserie

23-25 Old Compton St., W1 - 439 9301
BRITISH/FRENCH
Open Mon.-Sat. 10 a.m.-11:30 p.m. All major cards.

After a disappointing lackluster few months, the Soho Brasserie seems to have returned triumphantly to form. Tourists have taken note of its charms, but faithful regulars will not find themselves overrun. The genial informality of the place is a real tonic, and the service is as friendly as it is unassuming. The decor could do with a bit of freshening, but the menu never looks tired, and the fish, bought daily, is always a good bet. The greatest joy about the Brasserie is that it genuinely seems to cater to every possible appetite—you can nibble on one starter after another (avocado mousse served with crûdités is particularly good), order soup, steak, cheese and chocolate mousse, or nibble on bread and salad. An enterprising vegetarian menu is an added bonus. The seafood salad with tartar sauce was nicely un-Thousand-Is-landed, and the tartar is served in a separate tub, you can opt for vinaigrette instead. The soup of the day was reliably hearty. The vegetarian brochette looked colorful, and there wasn't a limp lettuce leaf to be found. A tender lamb steak arrived with an eggplant compote, celery and onion. and fresh beans were obligingly substituted for the ubiquitous vegetable assortment. Grilled hake with hollandaise did justice to an underappreciated fish, and clams sautéed with thyme sounded a fragrant note at £4.95. The Soho Brasserie is a boon for tourists in an area where most good food costs at least £20 a person—anything less seems to get you only fast food, kebabs or sandwiches. You can zoom in and out of here, before or after matinees, or spend an entire afternoon studying maps and nibbling.

A la carte: £15, including wine.

Sutherlands

45 Lexington St., W1 - 434 3401

BRITISH

Open Mon.-Fri. 12:15 p.m.-2:15 p.m. & 6:15 p.m.-11:15 p.m., Sat. 6:15 p.m.-11:15 p.m. All major cards.

Discreetly situated in the former premises of a functional café in the quieter patch of Soho between Berwick and Regent streets, Sutherlands is a chic young restaurant run by a chic young team (the ages of the chef, the restaurant and the general manager average 26). The menu and wine list are models of eloquent clarity, the buttercup-yellow walls and navy carpet are crisp and elegant, and the modern Italian accoutrements—chunky wedge-shape wall light fittings, abstract stained- and etched-glass ceiling panels and black lyre-backed chairs—are a canny enough mixture of the conservative and the avant-garde to satisfy a broad spectrum of Soho's moneyed media-oriented lunchers. Chef Garry Hollihead has done time at the Savoy, Ninety Park Lane and with Louis Outhier in La Napoule, and his repertoire is suitably rich in nages ("swimming in") of this and that, crustaceans and exotic herbs, but his technique and taste are not outstripped by his aspirations.

A starter of roast langoustines glazed in a lobster mousse on a bed of baby leeks was one of our favorite dishes of the year: five plump Scottish crayfish, cooked just enough, bound into a thin base of delicious pounded lobster, fried crisp on the outside, surrounded by a superb dark game-based sauce and placed on a mound of shredded leek. A main course of tender pink pigeon breasts crowned a bed of shredded cabbage, little browned onions and wild mushrooms and was served with a light but densely flavored sauce of greatly reduced veal stock finished with Californian Muscat. The menu always features a couple of vegetarian dishes. There are interesting English cheeses and well-made desserts (dark- and white-chocolate millefeuille with a pistachio sauce; hot peach soufflé) and a short but eclectic wine list that includes a dozen good, moderately priced half bottles.

A la carte: £40.

10/20 Le Tire Bouchon

6 Upper James St., W1 - 437 5348, 437 2320

FRENCH

Open Mon.-Fri. 7:30 a.m.-9:30 p.m. Cards: MC, V.

As can be deduced from its hours, this informal, bustling, noisy but straightforward restaurant is open for breakfast (endless coffee and good croissants), lunch and early dinner (ideal if you are going to the theater) and certainly has a very engaging Gallic atmosphere. You can enjoy either a one-course snack or a more complete meal, courtesy of a most welcoming staff. You won't find any of that on-a-bed-of and wrapped-in stuff here—this is straightforward bistro fare, complemented by a bistro atmosphere, which is heightened by colorful prints on the walls and tables set chummily close together. The bread is always fresh, the fish soup delicious, the risotto tasty and the cod filet quite succulent. The sherbets are also fine, and the coffee good. The wines, much as you would expect in a place like this, are cheap and cheerful.

A la carte: £20, including wine.

9/20 Wheelers

19-21 Old Compton St., W1 - 437 2706

SEAFOOD

Open Mon.-Fri. noon-11:15 p.m., Sat. 6 p.m.-11:15. All major cards.

Through various changes of ownership, Wheelers has lost the bustle and sharpness it had twenty years ago. The oysters are still as good as you'll find, the grilled fish is reliable, and there is an honorable wine list. But sauces tend to be floury, and the ghastly taped music echoes the middle-of-the-road mediocrity into which this once-famous establishment has fallen.

A la carte: £25-£30, including wine.

SOUTH BANK

9/20 Ovations
National Theatre, South Bank, SE1
928 2033
BRITISH/FRENCH
Open Mon.-Sat. 12:15 p.m.-3 p.m. & 5:30 p.m.-12:30 a.m. All major cards.

Given its superb position, with picture windows overlooking the Thames, and the added advantage of offering dinner before and after the show in an area notoriously thin on eating places, we hoped this restaurant would reflect the excellence of the National Theater. But when we visited recently, a look inside the kitchen made it clear that the staff had departed before the post-theater rush began. This merely confirmed what the lamentable food suggested: Everything tasted like it had been preprepared and then microwaved to serve. The menu is full of trendy, faintly ambitious dishes, such as a salad of warmed (and rubbery) goat cheese or overdone rack of lamb. The expensive, overelaborate, poorly prepared food hardly compensates for the magnificent view across the river or the possibility that some of the actors from the play you've just seen may be dining at the next table.

A la carte: £25, including wine.

11/20 La Rive Gauche
61 The Cut, SE1 - 928 8645
FRENCH
Open Mon.-Fri. noon-2:30 p.m. & 6 p.m.-11 p.m., Sat. 6 p.m.-11 p.m. All major cards.

La Rive Gauche is situated, rather confusingly, near the right bank of the Thames, where the cultural life of the capital is concentrated in the National Theater, the Museum of the Moving Image, the Hayward Gallery and the South Bank concert halls. The restaurant is located a few doors down from the Old Vic Theatre, and its rectangular shape is only slightly softened by potted plants, café scenes by Renoir and the many certificates awarded to the chef. Recordings by Edith Piaf and Georges Brassens serenade faintly in the background. The food is nouvelle and the flavors clean. Though beautifully presented, it is not fussy, and the helpings are adequate for someone who does not regard cookery as a mere art form but comes with a proper appetite.

For starters, there is an excellent selection of smoked fish, including salmon, eel and halibut, a millefeuille of smoked salmon with a dill sauce, and a delicious lobster-and-prawn terrine. The special dishes of the day we have witnessed include slices of roast partridge; ; veal filets with Calvados, apple and cream sauce; and pan-fried tournedos with shallots and a red wine sauce. Each comes with a dish of freshly prepared vegetables. We've found the game dishes to be particularly successful. To follow, try the sorbet of Marc de Bourgogne or, for a real treat, the nougat glacé. You may find the wine list pricey—a half bottle of Chablis at £12 for a half bottle—but a good half bottle of Château Canon Montségur is £6.80, and the house red and white from Georges Duboeuf is £7.

A la carte: £30-£35, including wine. Fixed-price menus: £13.50, £15.50.

SOUTH KENSINGTON

(13) Blakes
33 Roland Gdns., SW7 - 370 6701
INTERNATIONAL
Open daily 12:30 p.m.-2:30 p.m. & 7:30 p.m.-10:30 p.m. Closed Christmas. All major cards.

The food has improved enormously since Richard Sparrow took over the restaurant of this super-chic little hotel. The decor is the height of understated elegance, all black lacquer and glass, black napery and bowls of orchids. Beautiful people abound. The menu still jets dizzily around the globe, ranging from borscht and sashimi to chicken tikka and Szechwan duck. The calf's liver is sizzled intriguingly on a bed of lava rock (whatever that might be), and what used to be gimmicky cuisine is now satisfying and authentic, if rather expensive. Scallops sautéed golden brown with strips of fresh ginger in a cumin-scented sauce were hauntingly spicy, and the sea bass with its julienne of fennel baked in cream and dill had a delicate, soothing flavor. But our favorite remains the crisp Szechwan duck, with its sweet char siu bun, water chestnut garnish and seasoning of roasted salt and pepper. The excellent wine list features few bottles for less than £20, but the house wines are a good value at £11.

A la carte: £45, including wine.

⑬ Bombay Brasserie
Courtfield Close, SW7 - 370 4040
INDIAN
Open Mon.-Sat. 12:30 p.m.-2:30 p.m. & 7:30 p.m.-11:45 p.m., Sun. 12:30 p.m.-2:30 p.m. & 7:30 p.m.-10:30 p.m. All major cards.

A stone's throw south of Gloucester Road Underground station, Bombay Brasserie has established itself as one of London's most well-apppointed and plush restaurants. The decor is unashamedly retro Raj, with elegant chandeliers, lazily revolving ceiling fans and walls lined with large siennaed photographs. A white piano provides live music later in the evening, and a beautiful, huge conservatory is filled with greenery. As the restaurant's name suggests, the menu concentrates on dishes from Bombay and features several Parsi and Goan dishes. Appetizers include such Anglo-Indian staples as mulligatawny soup, a far cry from the thick, brown liquid that often goes under this name, and Bombay Tiffin, a selection of vegetarian pastries and savories. Main courses embrace a number of tandoori specialties and Parsi dishes: a succulent lamb-and-apricot creation with masala spicing, interesting Goan fish recipes and two hot curries ("in deference to the wishes of many of our regular clients, including Faye Dunaway," as the menu self-promotingly informs). The Shikar specialty, boneless quails in a Rajputani

sauce, sadly contained a number of bones but nevertheless was subtly flavored. The somewhat disappointing selection of sweets includes a largely tasteless mango kulfi (the Indian version of ice cream served with crushed nuts). A bottle of Gewürztraminer is a fitting companion to this cooking, and there's always Indian beer. The service is intelligent and helpful, but it can be leisurely.

A la carte: £25, including wine.

11/20 The Chanterelle
119 Old Brompton Rd., SW7 - 373 5522
FRENCH
Open daily noon-2:30 p.m. & 7 p.m.-11:30 p.m. All major cards.

We heave a great sigh of relief each time we dine at The Chanterelle. Relief that no demands are made on the customer, and that the onus is all on the staff to make the event an enjoyable one. Relief that there are plenty of half bottles on the wine list to fit the price of the meal. The setting is darkly Edwardian with art deco overtones; the atmosphere is gentle and relaxing. This oddly amputated piece of the Kensington Public Library holds a special place in the hearts of early English gastronomes. Back in the 1950s, when Elizabeth David was pricking our palates with the idea that food in England could be good, this was the place where many Londoners tasted garlic bread or ratatouille for the first time, and where they could entertain lavishly on a limited budget. Amazingly, you can still do much the same thing here today. Dishes are respectably related to genuine French nouvelle cuisine. At The Chanterelle, necessity is genuinely the mother of invention. Jerusalem artichoke and scallop soup, mussels baked with cream and saffron, sea bream and cassoulets are typical dishes on a menu that changes frequently for the dozens of devoted regulars who eat here more than once a week. On occasion, there is a modest supplement for an exceptional entrecôte steak or sole à la Colbert, in order to maintain standards without skimping. No wonder you must reserve one or two days ahead for a table. The wine list is well selected, balanced and inexpensive.

A la carte: £20, including wine. Fixed-price

menus: £8 (lunch only), £10 (dinner only, after 10 p.m.).

Hilaire
68 Old Brompton Rd., SW7
584 8993

FRENCH

Open Mon.-Fri. 12:30 p.m.-2:30 p.m. & 7:30 p.m.-11 p.m., Sat. 7:30 p.m.-11 p.m. All major cards.

The walls of this extremely elegant dining room display attractively framed prints of scenes from Gallic life. And in attendance in this temple of gastronomy are assiduous, French-speaking acolytes. Those who wonder whether the standards of this well-patronized restaurant may have slipped since its former chef, the renowned Simon Hopkinson, moved on to nearby Bibendum, needn't worry. Bryan Webb, his successor, has maintained the high standards—indeed he has added to them—and the restaurant retains its unique flavor. The three-course fixed-price lunch (for an astonishing reasonable charge) changes daily; the fixed-price dinner changes every two weeks. On our last visit, there was a good, powerfully flavored curried apple soup, extremely filling pancakes stuffed with ricotta cheese and spinach, a flavorful chicken tart served with parsley and lemon, and a tasty game pâté. The perfectly cooked rump of lamb was heightened by garlic and mint, while the hake was enhanced by a grain-mustard sauce that stopped just on the right side of overpowering. Also served that evening was a tasty Gressingham duckling with cider and apples. We weren't offered a choice of salads or vegetables but were authoritatively served new potatoes and a green salad, which admirably complemented the dishes. The raspberry tart was a shock of flavor, and the marquis au chocolat with caramel sauce was rich-rich; the cheese offered as an alternative to dessert was of one type only, rather than a selection. The well-balanced, interesting wine list has some sound, moderately priced wines for the thrifty drinker. We, for instance, enjoyed a bottle of 1986 Côte de Ventoux, the house wine, for £9.50.

A la carte: £25-£35, including wine. Fixed-price menus: £17-£26.

11/20 Mario
260 Brompton Rd., SW3 - 584 1724

ITALIAN

Open daily noon-3 p.m. & 7 p.m.-midnight. All major cards.

Mario, along with the late and lamented Franco, revolutionized Italian restaurants in '60s London. He then went back to Italy, returning to open this cool, stylish and fashionable restaurant, whose whole smoked-glass front slides open for summertime al fresco dining. Customers include plenty of ghosts from the '60s, but the young and beautiful also flock here.

The food had a shaky start, for Mario returned from his homeland with some fancy notions of resurrecting historical recipes from Italy's culinary past. His first chef claimed to be a gastronomic researcher. "I simply couldn't go back to spaghetti alle vongole," he moaned to a disgruntled customer. Today all is back to normal. The winners in the appetizers category: crostini of mozzarella with black olive purée and anchovies; seafood cocktail flavored with coconut; and fried prawns wrapped in lettuce. Of the fifteen pastas, we liked the homemade tortellini ardenese, with ham, endive and cream, and the classical trenette al pesto. For the main course, Mario offers prawns grilled with garlic, calf's liver with orange, and chicken in a pepper sauce. The authentically Italian dessert trolley features luscious tiramisu, a ricotta and candied fruit tart and zabaglione. There is a chauvinistic but upscale Italian wine list picked by Mario himself.

A la carte: £25, including wine. Fixed-price menu: £13.

Meridiana
169 Fulham Rd., SW3 - 589 8815, 589 8825

ITALIAN

Open daily 12:30 p.m.-2:30 p.m. & 7 p.m.-11:30 p.m. All major cards.

Just a brisk stroll south of the South Kensington Underground station, in the direction of Chelsea Town Hall, the ever-fashionable Meridiana has been revitalized during the last few years. A nice fresh room on the ground floor that seats about 40 is the only section open for lunch; in the evenings the basement and second floor are made available, and more than 120 diners can be accommodated. The space is broken up by a central mirrored pillar with baskets of hanging plants, while six large windows with attractive blinds and drapes give the room a spring-like atmosphere. Recently there has been a rapid turnover of chefs; since May of 1988, Alberico Penati was replaced first by Francesco Matzano and then by Angelo Scaglia. But the cuisine remains surprisingly rich with surprises. On our last visit some of the appetizers appearing on the menu were: ravioli filled with fish in a celery sauce, a delicious salad of sweetbreads and prawns on a bed of green beans, and marinated scallops with zucchini. These could be followed by lemon sole with lobster sauce, monkfish cooked with green peppers, tomato and garlic, guinea-fowl served with cabbage and grapes, or lightly fried veal stuffed with spring vegetables. The service is most friendly and efficient. An added inducement is the 10 percent discount the restaurant gives to women lunching alone or in groups on weekdays.

A la carte: £25, including wine.

10/20 Ognisko Polskia

55 Exhibition Rd., SW7 - 589 4670
POLISH
Open daily 12:30 p.m.-3 p.m. & 6:30 p.m.-11 p.m. All major cards.

For those who like their ethnic food laced with nostalgia, we recommend the Ognisko Polskia—which translates as the Polish Hearth Club, or the Hearth, as it is familiarly known. Nerve center, club canteen and watering hole of London's large Polish community, it is located in South Kensington, which preserves a lingering aura of Polish diaspora and stands right in the center of museum land, a comfortable Sunday's stroll from the Brompton Oratory just around the corner. You enter through a hall plastered with a busy but appropriate patchwork of posters. Though strictly a club, the Hearth welcomes nonmembers. The restaurant occupies a noble high-ceilinged room with fine columns and a fireplace, and there's a long bar where you can ice the mood with a

couple of vodkas, plain or flavored. Young and more genial waitresses have succeeded the grand old ladies in black bombazine who once served here (and gave rise to the club game Spot the Countess).

The club fare, however, has not changed much over the years. Homemade pâté, herrings in sour cream, superb stuffed fish in aspic and, of course, the mandatory hot or cold borscht, served in cups, are the highlighted appetizers. Veal with mushrooms and chicken in lemon sauce both had the taste of Polish home cooking, and Scotch filet was offered at the amazing price of £4.75. But the star dish is still flaki, meltingly tender strips of tripe in a full-flavored both, served Warsaw-style, further flavored with paprika, thyme and grated cheese—it's good enough to convert the most devout innards hater. A convenient and inexpensive eatery with lots of charm, Ognisko Polskia is a special place, a place for which we are grateful.

A la carte: £15, including vodka.

11/20 San Frediano

62 Fulham Rd., SW3 - 584 8375
ITALIAN
Open Mon.-Sat. 12:30 p.m.-2:30 p.m. & 7:15 p.m.-11:15 p.m. Cards: DC, MC, V.

This is an Italian trattoria of the sort that was fashionable in the 1960s—marked by hustle and bustle, enthusiastic waiters and almost illegibly handwritten menus publicizing the specials of the day. When we ate here last, the place was cheerful and the food (for the most part) quite nice. The appetizers are pretty much standard trattoria fare, but while the pastas did not taste fresh, they were accompanied by some unique sauces, including one with cream and smoked salmon. The veal scaloppine with a sauce of garlic and tomato had an authentic appeal, as did the liver and wood pigeon, but the steak pizzaiola (fresh tomato sauce with herbs and garlic) was served with an overbearing mountain of tomato sauce. The deserts are a hackneyed lot, including crème brûlée, Black Forest cake and tiramisu. Service can be harried, rushed and not always efficient. Some inexpensive Italian wines are sold here, and the house wine goes for £7.50.

A la carte: £20, including wine.

11/20 Tui

19 Exhibition Rd., SW7 - 584 8359

THAI

Open Mon.-Sat. noon-2:30 p.m. & 6:30 p.m.-11 p.m., Sun. 12:30 p.m.-3 p.m. & 7 p.m.-11 p.m. All major cards.

Tui (the name means kite in Thai) is as cool as its food is hot: ecru walls, comfortable chairs, immaculate napery and only the occasional carved ethnic mask and statue. Modern watercolors on the walls depict Thai vegetables (including the dreaded green chili, prik). The handwritten menu features a number of good appetizers, including traditional satays and steamed dumplings of pork and water chestnuts topped with garlic dressing. The spring rolls are delicious and delicate, but the marmalade-like sauce that accompanies them is far too sweet. A dish of char-grilled, bite-size chicken pieces is served with a sweet chili sauce, and tiny popia spring rolls put the Chinese version to shame. A seafood steamboat of tom yam soup flavored with lemon grass and chilis is not calculated to cool the palate, so we relied heavily on the flint-dry Sancerre Rosé Les Renardins '83 from a small but reasonably priced wine list. The customary array of rice and noodle specials, including mee krob and crisp rice vermicelli with pork and prawns tossed in a tamarind dressing, are served. Dishes appear on stylish, oblong cucumber-green platters, and the service by Thai waitresses in national costume is smooth and leisurely, emphasizing the point that Thai food is not to be bolted down. The selection of vegetables is predominated by broccoli and cabbage, but there is good news for vegetarians: Tui will happily custom-devise entire menus just for you. Tui is a welcome addition to the growing number of Thai restaurants in London, the latest wave of conquest from the East. House wines are a Saumur and a Gamay d'Ardèche.

A la carte: £20, including house wine.

STOCKWELL

12/20 Rebato's

169 S. Lambeth Rd., SW8 - 735 6388, 582 8089

SPANISH

Open Mon.-Fri. noon-2:30 p.m. & 7 p.m.-11:15 p.m., Sat. 7 p.m.-11:15 p.m. All major cards.

Several olés to Tino Rebato and his wife Sheila for having the perspicacity and verve to start this haven in a section of London not celebrated for its interesting restaurants. This most engaging Spanish restaurant/bar is divided in two sections. At the darkened end in the front of the house, you can sit surrounded by sherry casks and enjoy some of the most interesting tapas served in England.

Included in the daily offerings, which are listed on a chalkboard and served on small earthenware dishes, are tripe, songbird livers, eels, sardines, spicy sausages and anchovies (each costs between £1.50 and £3.50). Of course you can also partake of the excellent sherry and Spanish wine inside an area in which customers are not pressed to leave. If, however, you move on through the dim bar, you will enter a restaurant and an altogether new world, one that always appears to be luminous, thanks primarily to spacious glass panels that have been cut into the roof. Among the appetizers we have admired here are prawns in a garlic sauce, three tasty pâtés of game, pork and halibut, and a cold and spicy gazpacho. The main courses which we can recommend: grilled fish, charcoal-grilled lamb cutlets and a tasty paella. For dessert, the caramel oranges are delicious. The Torres house wines are £4.95, but there is a strong list of other wines which are mainly Spanish.

A la carte: £20-£25, including wine.

THE STRAND

11/20 Joe Allen

13 Exeter St., WC2 - 836 0651
AMERICAN
Open Mon.-Sat. noon-12:45 a.m., Sun. noon-11:30 p.m. No cards.

This popular, well-run restaurant is frequented by people of all ages who appreciate the good, quick service from a staff decked out in unisex outfits and black ties. Various shades of brown are brightened up by checked tablecloths and framed theatrical posters. The menu is written up on the wall (you can only hope that you'll secure a good view when you make reservations) and lists such goodies as Maryland crabcakes and avocado with bacon and spinach for starters, followed by prime rib and Southern fried chicken. Several fish courses are also served, and there is a fruity house wine. After all is said and eaten, you should emerge from the depths of the basement feeling that everything is okay with the world.

A la carte: £15-£20, including wine

⑬ Thomas de Quincey's

36 Tavistock St., WC2 - 240 3972, 240 3773
BRITISH/FRENCH
Open Mon.-Fri. 12:30 p.m.-2:30 p.m. & 6 p.m.-11:15 p.m., Sat. 7 p.m.-11:30 p.m. All major cards.

On first, superficial acquaintance, several elements tend to make one suspicious of Thomas de Quincey's. There's the fact that certain members of the Italian staff are not familiar enough with the menu, or with the French it uses (with English subtitles) to describe dishes in detail. But first and foremost, there is the decor. After passing through quite an attractive and elegant little Edwardian-style cocktail bar, you find the dining area to be a large, oblong garage of a room, with bare walls painted a donkey brown and camouflaged with swags of drapery, low lighting and (too many?) prints and paintings, presumably to divert the eye from the air conditioners and exposed wiring lurking above. And yet, for all this (and the ugly carpet), the general ambience is actually rather cozy—and the food is very good.

Chef Philippe Gavelle's menu is interesting, varied and firmly based on high-quality components served in well-conceived combinations—it even reaches that lofty zone in which the extravagant and/or fanciful dish achieves its objectives. A feuilleté of frogs' legs and oysters on spinach in an elderberry wine sauce (ordered with some trepidation) was excellent, the smooth, coffee-colored, curry-tinged sauce complementing the shredded meat, warm oysters and crisp pastry. A compote of rabbit and celery flavored with Alsace plum eau-de-vie was moist and delicious, and the appetite-refreshing sorbet of bitter lemon drenched in whisky, served after the first course, was effective and delectable. Main courses include a half dozen fish dishes and a dozen meat dishes (comprising, sensibly, the option of plain grilled steaks, cutlets, pork and offal). Again, the more elaborate dishes are good: Witness a plate of rabbit, the plump leg roasted in a prune sauce, with four noisettes of the white meat rolled around a prune-studded forcemeat, all served with fragrant green lentils sprinkled with grape oil, a crisp potato croquette, a few sweet, perfectly cooked mange-touts (green beans) and al dente carrot shards. Cheeses are satisfactory but no more, and the waiters are not as knowledgeable about them as they should be. Desserts, however, are quite fine. Wines are predominantly French or Italian and not cheap. The clientele is a mixture of expense-accounters, the celebrating middle classes, some après-theater folk and bon-vivant tourists.

A la carte: £45. Fixed-price menu: £16.95 (lunch only).

10/20 The Grill

30 Wellington St., WC2 - 240 7529
AMERICAN
Open daily noon-3 p.m. & 5:30 p.m.-midnight. All major cards.

This lively restaurant is particularly useful for those going to the theater: The Grill links up Wellington and Catherine streets, so its rear entrance is directly across from the Drury Lane Theatre. It's really more of a passage than a room, with mustard-colored walls hung with mirrors and nineteenth-century paintings, bistro-style checked tablecloths (which confirm the informal, relaxed atmosphere) and helpful, friendly service. Soup is served in gigantic bowls, and the guacomole with corn chips and the goat cheese on toast are just two of the tasty appetizers that work. The menu is aggressively American, so of course large hamburgers are available. Other delicious main course items are chili pie topped with melted cheese and chicken marinated in coconut milk. The small selection of desserts comprises various sorbets and a superb chocolate cheesecake. A pretheater menu is offered between 5:30 p.m. and 8 p.m., details of which are written on a blackboard outside. It's probably wise to reserve ahead if you're going to the theater.

A la carte: £15, including wine. Fixed-price menu: £7.95 (pretheater dinner only).

12/20 Orso's

27 Wellington St., WC2 - 240 5269
ITALIAN
Open daily noon-midnight. No cards.

Alongside Joe Allen's, and part of the same enterprise, Orso's is a friendly basement restaurant that can seat up to 110 people and serves most of the dishes served in any self-respecting trattoria. The manager, Richard Polo, makes a point of visiting each table at some stage of the meal, and his peregrinations are looked down upon by the faces of the theatrical celebrities whose photographs reside on the white-glazed-brick walls. The woodwork has been painted in a grayish Nile green, and the rustic cookery gives a splash of color to each table. The menu delights and dismays. The cuisine changes daily, and many ingredients are flown in from Italy. A dish of noodles with sausage, wild mushrooms and tomatoes made an interesting starter, as did farfalle (bow-tie pasta), which was served with salmon, leeks and cream, and an exceptionally tasty lasagne. The dish of sweetbreads with roasted shallots is exquisitely flavorful, and the grilled chicken with tomatoes, olives and rosemary grew on us with each bite. Certain wines on the 50-strong list are delectable, notably the Chianti Classico Villa Antinori 1981 and the Tenuta di Pomino Frescobaldi 1982; the house wines are a reasonable £7.50 a litre.

A la carte: £25-£30, including wine.

11/20 Piccolo Mondo

31 Catherine St., WC2 - 836 3609
ITALIAN
Open Mon.-Fri. 12:15 p.m.-3 p.m. & 5:45 p.m.-11:30 p.m., Sat. 5:45 p.m.-11:30 p.m. Cards: MC, V.

An offshoot of Luigi Primavera's popular three-story restaurant on nearby Tavistock Street, Piccolo Mondo is an upscale trattoria that opened in mid-1988. The walls of its two floors are covered with a moiré-patterned paper in a delicate shade of watery eggplant. It has a fresh feel to it, that of a restaurant keen to succeed, and it has come up with some interesting dishes that go beyond the standard fresh-pasta staples (which, by the way, are excellent). The wild boar "ham" is extremely rich and tasty, and the breast of chicken stuffed with goose liver and cooked in brandy and lobster sauce is delicious—but its pheasant cousin, cooked in butter and served with a wild-mushroom sauce, was a trifle leathery. We also enjoyed the toothsome small potatoes and the suitably crisp mange-touts (green beans). The service was friendly and attentive, offset a bit by rather inappropriate accordion music. There is a dependable list of Italian wines, with the house wine priced at £6.50.

A la carte: £30, including wine.

12/20 The Savoy River Room

Savoy
The Strand, WC2 - 836 4343
BRITISH
Open daily 12:30 p.m.-2:30 p.m. & 7:30 p.m.-11:30 p.m. All major cards.

Perhaps no one in living memory has gone to The Savoy for the food. Like its more celebrated sister operation, The Savoy Grill, cuisine hardly comes into play in surroundings of such sleek grandiosity. The River Room gets by on decor and cachet, as well as its unbeatable location between The Strand and the Thames. In fact, only a half dozen tables enjoy a view of the river, the rest being disposed in a vast salmon-pink chamber fraught with Corinthian columns and pilasters, curlicued mirrors and a gleaming pagoda-like corner bandstand that Sotheby's would give its eyeteeth to auction. Further echoes of the Edwardian sunset resonate from the heavily worked silver of the hors d'oeuvres trolleys and the similarly resplendent biers trundled about by morose sous chefs. The waiters wear bow ties and tails and are inconsistently attentive.

The à la carte menu is a predictably wallet-thinning affair of lobster, pâté de foie gras, coquilles St-Jacques and all the other plush items that convince the upper-middle classes that they're enjoying life. A typical fixed-price lunch menu (£20) might include chicken velouté and chicken pie Savoy, followed by the dessert trolley. There's also a *menu de régime naturel* trading in grilled chicken and green lentils. On our last visit we tried the pâté de canard au foie gras en croûte (which had a rubbery texture and tasted dauntingly of Spam); the pastry was nearly invisible. The dish was accompanied by a spoonful of stewed cèpes and a pool of red jam that may or not have been the Cumberland sauce advertised. If the person-hours that had gone into sculpting the accompanying tomato rose had been devoted to cooking, maybe the results would have been different. Cold Scottish salmon was adequately poached but ruined by a herb mayonnaise that recalled the guacamole of nightmares. On the other hand, veal mignons were served pinkish, and a panache of vegetables was well balanced. But the almond tart and strawberries and cream were disappointingly unremarkable. The blockbuster wine list, however, is definitely something to write home about: six 1970 clarets for £135 to £160, another six 1975s at a third of that price, and representatives from most of the significant French regions, plus Australia, New Zealand and California. There's also an entire page of whiskies and endless spirits and ports.

A la carte: £40, including wine. Fixed-price menu: £20 (lunch only).

10/20 Tony Roma's—a Place for Ribs
45 St. Martin's Ln., WC2 - 379 3330
AMERICAN
Open daily noon-1 a.m. All major cards.

If you're tired and hungry "doing" the National Gallery, a short walk up St. Martin's Lane and you'll find yourself at Tony Roma's. Part of an established U.S. chain, it opened in the heart of theaterland in 1984. The dark, cavernous New York–style place specializes in barbecued baby-back ribs, arguably the best in London. They're crisp, tender and smoky, and served in the rack, either on their own or with cole slaw, french fries and barbecue sauce. The decor consists of cartoons of royalty and show biz personalities and some rather sad oil paintings. More to the point, there is a long bar that dispenses 78 double-measure cocktails and some American beers. A resident pianist seems to spend most of his time playing "Happy Birthday" for customers.

No one should miss the "king-size" loaf of crisp fried-onion rings as a side order. Specialties of the house, besides the ribs, of course, include barbecued chicken and London broil, and dishes of the day feature such down-home American staples as pot roast and baked meatloaf. Though the place has some of the attributes of a fast-food operation, you are not expected to hurry. In the end, though, it's the spareribs that keep them coming—and they can be so good that Chinese cooks should be forced to come here for a refresher course.

A la carte: £15, including beer.

WANDSWORTH

Harvey's
2 Bellevue Rd., SW17 - 672 0114
FRENCH
Open Mon.-Sat. 12:30 p.m.-2:30 p.m. & 7:30 p.m.-11:30 p.m. Cards: AE, MC, V.

Marco Pierre White—now there's a Pan-European name for you! But this young Anglo-Italian chef, who recently set up shop in a remote neighborhood (a good 30-minute cab ride south of the Thames), wears it with style. A strong personality, with highly individual tastes (witness his tiny all-white dining room embellished with spectacular plasterwork, oval mirrors and portraits reminiscent of Cocteau's), chef White has a real talent, which he has devoted entirely to French cuisine. Like many of his confrères, he learned the basics from (you guessed it) the Roux brothers. But now he's on his own, and his cooking is worlds away from the sort of food served at Le Gavroche. It is much closer in spirit to that of his friend and former co-pupil, Pierre

Koffmamnn (Tante Claire), from whom White borrowed—giving all due credit—a fabulous recipe for stuffed pigs' trotters.

White's à la carte offerings are not numerous, but each dish is calculated to make mouths water. Just consider the salmon millefeuille with a velvety chive sauce, and the fondant of prawns and eel with a sprightly vinaigrette or, in the main-course category, Bresse pigeon with cèpes ravioli and a red wine fumet (essence), and saddle of lamb perfumed with basil and escorted by a sumptuous garnish of veal brains, artichokes and exquisite potatoes. And we are pleased to say that from start to finish, every dish on the fixed-price menu is as good as it sounds. There's a sophisticated salad of warm sweetbreads on a bed of oak-leaf lettuce, and a little timbale of wild mushrooms bathed in a truffled sauce périgueux that is as light as it is flavorful—a welcome consolation for all the nasty, indigestible versions of that sauce you may have previously encountered. Oh,

and we must mention the firm, tender scallop of salmon with sorrel, and the tasty Scottish beef, overcooked by a hair but marvelously savory with its garnish of roasted garlic cloves and bordelaise sauce. A mere glance at the dessert menu is enough to set off anticipatory drooling. What would you say to an ethereal glazed sponge cake with crunchy hazelnuts, or a harlequin de chocolat with cinnamon sauce—a sweet masterpiece that attests to White's taste, technique and sensuous palate.

We can only urge you, therefore, to get on your bicycle or head down to the train station (come evening, cabs in these parts are as rare as hen's teeth), but by any and/or all means, do visit this commendable establishment. The young French maître d' will take excellent care of you. As for the wine list, you are sure to be as pleased as we were to find some eminently worthy wines from the Médoc for under £19.

Fixed-price menus: £20 (lunch only), £29 (dinner only).

WESTMINSTER

⑬ Kundan

3 Horseferry Rd., SW1 - 834 8434

INDIAN

Open Mon.-Sat. noon-2:30 p.m. & 7 p.m.-11:30 p.m. All major cards.

This rather formal and gloomy restaurant is patronized by Scotland Yarders and MPs from nearby Westminster. It must be the only Indian establishment to have a Division Bell (which summons members of Parliament to vote). Nevertheless, the delicious, authentic northern Indian cooking more than compensates for the lack of ambience. Moghul food, with its Persian and Turkish overtones, is the haute cuisine of India, and Kundan, which literally means, "to bring something slowly to a state of perfection," lives up to its name. Everything is succulent, delicately spiced or gently simmered, every lamb is "grass-fed," and dishes tend to be the "choice of aristocrats" or "the Nawab's favorite." Our own favorites are the delicious tandoori dishes with light, crisp naan, the chicken korma (stew) with yogurt and saffron, and a splendid house specialty, lamb jahl-fraizee, started in the tandoor and finished

with a sweet-and-spicy sauce with coriander. Condensed-milk enthusiasts will love the kulfi, an Indian ice cream made from sweetened milk simmered for several hours with a dash of rosewater, and the carrot halvah, candy made of crushed sesame seeds and honey with a distinct fudgy taste.

A la carte: £20-£25.

10/20 Lockets

Marsham Ct., Marsham St., SW1 - 834 9552

BRITISH

Open Mon.-Fri. 12:15 p.m.-2:30 p.m. & 6:30 p.m.-11 p.m., Sat. 6:30 p.m.-11 p.m. All major cards.

With its long, low room bedecked with modern paintings and politicians (since it is one of the few restaurants in London that still sounds the Division Bell, which summons members of Parliament to vote), Lockets has an air of self-conscious dignity about it. Its menu is made up of dishes that will satisfy the most impressive of appetites, dishes that comprised gargantuan meals enjoyed in the seventeenth and eighteenth centuries by the likes of John Verney, Samuel Pepys and the Rev. James

Woodforde. Among the tastier "Fore Dishes and Soups" are delicious lambs' kidneys in a Madeira sauce under a pastry top, and potted prawns with dill. Decent choices from the list of "Fishes, Removes, Made Dishes and Grills" are the pot-roasted squab with cider, tasty smoked bacon and livers. And representing the successful "House Favorites" are boiled silverside (the cut of beef from the crown of the rump) cooked in a tarragon, oil, vinegar and caper sauce, and roast turkey with walnut-and-celery stuffing. The abundant wine list features many half bottles.

A la carte: £30-£40, including wine.

REFRESHMENTS

PUBS

In the introduction to the pubs section of our previous edition, we wrote, "Britain is still in the grip of the absurd, outdated licensing laws that force pubs to close just when you are craving a drink or a bite to eat."

Happily, we can now rewrite the introduction. On August 22, 1988, England followed Scotland's lead and conducted an experiment—and we soon saw licensing laws going European. Pubs now can choose if they wish to stay open in the afternoon. What a revelation! Mind you, it's still a bit of a mess for the potential pint drinker, since "choose" is the operative word, and no one is quite clear which pubs are open and which aren't. This makes it difficult for us guidebook writers, since we're expected to provide precise hours of operation for our readers. At press time, when we'd inquire about hours, pub owners would answer only, "What are they doing next door?" By the time this book is published, however, things will surely have settled down (but because of the confusion and changing schedules, we have *not* included hours in the listings below). And several brewers have taken a positive lead by ensuring that all their brewery-owned pubs remain open in the afternoon. Among the likely effects of this change are: further development of food served all day; an increase in the number of beers containing a smaller percentage of alcohol; and the appearance of more "café" pubs, with their set tables, bistro-style food and sales of wine far outstripping the poor old beer-engines (hand pumps) of the traditional pubs.

Aside from the change in the licensing laws, English pubs are having to respond to other forces of change. In Mrs. Thatcher's market economy, customers are being increasingly tempted to convert to the world of international lagers, including many from overseas—brands like Foster, Castlemaine, Budweiser and Miller, which seem to appear everywhere. The age of the world brand is clearly upon us. Let us only hope that, although a static market, the old faithful English ales will remain as trusted venerable cellarmates to these cool international megastars.

While pubs must, of course, serve the sophisticated retail customers of the 1990s, surely these same customers must retain an appreciation for the core values that have been at the heart of the British pub for centuries. The pub is a center for conversation, friendship, tradition and warmth, and it would be a great loss if the special feel and character of the Great British Pub were to dissolve into a sea of wine bottles and (hitherto unheard of) ice-cold lager.

Authentic British ale—always served draught-style from a hand pump—is called bitter and is served at room temperature; bottled bitter is called pale ale. Americans find this strong, slightly bitter ale an acquired taste, but once acquired, it will become a lifelong favorite. Many neighborhood pubs are loyal to a particular brewery (often a small one), whose ales are aged in casks at the pub itself. The larger ale breweries include Watneys, Whitbread, Courage, Young's and Fuller's. Also popular are the various brands of rich, hearty stouts, the most famous of which is Ireland's Guinness.

Do take the opportunity to search out some of the places that we have listed in the following pages; they're each special in their own ways. And when you visit them, take sufficient time to enjoy the atmosphere and to understand their specific niche in their local communities. Each one is different and reflects the variety of people who choose to be regulars. After all, it's the people who make the pubs. Cheers!

BARNES

The Sun Inn
7 Church Rd., SW13 - 876 5893

The Sun is the "local" of the increasingly fashionable suburb of Barnes. Facing the pond (complete with ducks and bullrushes) and the Common, it has all the ingredients of true village life. The pub recognizes its responsibilities and displays many old prints of local scenes and period furniture. The young, affluent customers come here for the Leeds-brewed Tetley Bitter and superb sandwiches.

BELGRAVIA

The Antelope
22 Eaton Terr., SW1 - 730 7781

When The Antelope was built over 200 years ago, the area was rural and this pub served as the "local." Belgravia has changed substantially since then, but The Antelope continues much the same as ever, providing a quiet haven, good beer and reasonable food for Belgravia residents. Settles and zinc-topped tables make for a warm, welcoming atmosphere.

Grenadier
18 Wilton Row, SW1 - 235 3074

Hidden away in a cobbled mews, just a few yards from Hyde Park Corner, the Grenadier was once the unofficial mess room for the Duke of Wellington's Grenadier Guards. Inside there are prints and paintings of the Duke and his guardsmen throughout. The Bloody Marys are famous, and there's a good selection of traditional beers and bar food.

BERMONDSEY

The Angel
101 Bermondsey Wall East, SE16
237 3608

This famous fifteenth-century riverside tavern is now owned by Trust House Forte, Britain's largest hotel and restaurant company. The downstairs bar has been nicely refurbished, and the restaurant upstairs specializes in fresh fish. On summer evenings at sunset, the view upstream to Tower Bridge is one of the most memorable sights in London; make sure to reserve a table by the window. The neighborhood is fast being developed, but The Angel has managed to keep its character and heritage intact. Courage Best Bitter is the local pint.

BLOOMSBURY

The Lamb
94 Lamb's Conduit St., WC1 - 405 0713

The Lamb is undoubtedly in the big leagues of London pubs. A long-established literary-Bloomsbury spot, it has recently become quite cosmopolitan. However, it continues to share its nineteenth-century theatrical character with its twentieth-century customers, who, judging by The Lamb's popularity, still love it. The opaque-glass "snob screens" still protect those who wish to maintain a little privacy. The beer is Young's—what else, for a pub of such London tradition?

Museum Tavern
49 Great Russell St., WC1 - 242 8987

What better way to relax after a visit to the British Museum than to cross the road, follow the footsteps of Karl Marx, and enjoy the Victorian splendor of the Museum Tavern? There is a wealth of nineteenth-century memorabilia to admire, and if you avoid the expensive ploughman's lunch (bread, cheese, salad, and chutney), the food is a good value. During the summer tables and chairs are set outside.

CHARING CROSS

Sherlock Holmes
10 Northumberland St., WC2 - 930 2644

Savor the "deerstalker, pipe and cloak" memories in this pub, which is filled almost to the point of excess with Sherlock Holmes memorabilia. In addition to being a fascinating shrine for *The Hound of the Baskervilles* fans (the pub is mentioned in the book), it is extremely convenient for Whitehall, The Strand and Trafalgar Square residents and visitors. There is also a popular restaurant upstairs. But however good the Whitbread beer and bar food are, they inevitably play supporting roles to the great detective himself.

CHELSEA

Admiral Codrington
17 Mossop St., SW3 - 589 4603

The Admiral Cod is an institution for thousands of Chelseans, past and present. It is a local landmark not to be missed. The accents and fashions in the Admiral Cod will tell you you're in the heart of "Sloane" country—home of the affluent characters from the Sloane Square vicinity known as the "Sloane Rangers." But the pub does not owe its standing merely to this social status; it also offers excellent beer and imaginative food. The bar is stuffed with memorabilia, the little flower-filled patio is charming, and there's a restaurant as well.

CHISWICK

The City Barge
Strand on the Green, W4 - 994 2148

In the midst of a charming row of cottages and elegant houses bordering the towpath along the Thames, just east of Kew Bridge, stands The City Barge (so named because a fifteenth-century Lord Mayor of London kept his barge moored off this point on the river). Though it suffered extensive bomb damage in World War II, it has gradually been revived with substantial restoration. The food is, for the most part, imaginative and well presented.

THE CITY

The Castle
34 Cowcross St., EC1 - 253 2892

The Castle remains London's only pub with a pawnbroker's licence, although the present landlord prefers to concentrate on good beer and food rather than the niceties of lending cash in exchange for the family jewels. The unpretentious green-tiled exterior doesn't do justice to the unexpectedly pleasant atmosphere found inside. The Castle is quite popular with the butchers from nearby Smithfield market.

Old Dr. Butler's Head
5 Mason's Ave., Coleman St., EC2
606 3504

In the early seventeenth century Dr. Butler, court doctor to King James I, founded this historic inn to serve his "medicinal ale." Today the Old Dr. Butler's Head still stands on a narrow road of half-timbered buildings, and it's a popular hangout with young City workers. With its original paneling, gas lights and fine plate-glass mirrors, even Dr. Butler would be proud of his historic legacy. There's a restaurant upstairs, while downstairs is devoted to the art of drinking good beer.

Old Watling
29 Old Watling St., EC4 - 248 6252

A little "olde worlde" gem in the shadow of St. Paul's Cathedral, the Old Watling has served clerics and City folk since it was rebuilt following the Great Fire of London in the seventeenth century. There are a lot of original features to admire, and the passing of time seems to have had little effect on the Old Watling. A good selection of food is served upstairs, and there's a small, separate game room, if you want to try your skill at darts, cribbage or electronic games. Bass IPA is the featured beer.

Samuel Pepys
Brooks Wharf, 48 Upper Thames St., EC4
248 3048

One of London's favorite riverside pubs, the Samuel Pepys looks across to Southwark. The Charrington brewers created this authentic copy of a seventeenth-century inn from a wharfside warehouse, complete with balconies. The theme throughout is the famous diarist himself; in the Cellar Bar, Pepys's period as Secretary to the Navy is remembered with paintings, knickknacks and other memorabilia. The food showcases imaginative traditional English recipes, but pies and puddings are perennial favorites.

COVENT GARDEN

The Lamb & Flag
33 Rose St., WC2 - 836 4108

You have to search for this delightful little pub on a side street approximately 200 yards from the crowds and entertainment of Covent Garden. Very traditional, it preserves the Regency heritage through its old signs and manuscripts adorning the walls. Courage beers and a superb selection of cheeses are the strong suit here. Arrive early at lunchtime if you want to get a seat.

Punch and Judy
40 The Market, WC2 - 836 1750

Named after the long tradition of public entertainment that has taken place under the arches of St. Paul's, across from the pub, Punch and Judy now offers a marvelous grandstand view of the regular busking shows (performances by street musicians and singers) that take place on the piazza below the second-floor bar balcony. Drinks and food are expensive in this upstairs bar, which attracts a young theatrical crowd. There is also a cellar bar complete with barrels and a stone-flagged floor. The Courage beers are well cared for, as is the large selection of hot and cold bar food—though on busy market days, it sometimes seems to have difficulty maintaining supplies.

FLEET STREET

Black Friar
174 Queen Victoria St., EC4 - 236 5650

A fascinating art deco pub at the junction of Blackfriars Bridge and Queen Victoria Street, Black Friar is immediately recognizable by the unique mosaic tiling on its walls and signs. Inside is a wealth of Victorian marble, brass, stained glass and carving. Among the wide range of traditional ales is the delicious Adnams, from a small regional brewery in Southwold in rural Suffolk. The food takes third place to the atmosphere and excellent beers.

Edgar Wallace
40 Essex St., WC2 - 353 3120

The Whitbread brewery owners decided that this pub should be a living memorial to the great Edgar Wallace, creator of King Kong, so it changed its name from "Essex Head" in the 1970s. The pub is full of the writer's memorabilia: books, letters and pictures. There's a small restaurant upstairs, and bar food is served on the ground floor.

The Olde Cheshire Cheese
Wine Office Ct., 145 Fleet St., EC4
353 6170

Tucked away in an alley on the south side of Fleet Street, The Olde Cheshire Cheese is one of the finest examples of a genuine seventeenth-century London pub. Dr. Samuel Johnson and James Boswell were regulars after it was rebuilt following the Great Fire. The sawdust on the floors, the narrow passages and winding stairs, the atmosphere, the conversation and the traditional Samuel Smith's beers from Yorkshire are far more important than the food. The Olde Cheshire Cheese is closed on weekends.

Punch Tavern
99 Fleet St., EC4 - 353 8338

As Fleet Street has changed from being the center of "Newspaperland" in recent years, so too have the customers of the Punch Tavern, which for so long was a journalists' haunt. The famous cartoon prints from *Punch*, however, still remain in place. The pub, just a few steps off Fleet Street, makes an excellent stop for a quick pub lunch, particularly since the food has improved.

FULHAM

The Duke of Cumberland
235 New King's Rd., SW6 - 736 2777

If you follow King's Road west, past World's End and on toward Putney Bridge, you'll come to Parsons Green on the left. Opposite the Green is one of the bastions of southwest London pubs, the Duke of Cumberland. Owned and lovingly cared for by nearby Young's Brewery at Wandsworth, the Duke is a model of elegant Edwardian drinking. The beer is excellent and the customers young and trendy—both in keeping with local housing developments.

HAMMERSMITH

The Dove

19 Upper Mall, W6 - 748 5405

A rare find if you find yourself in the area of Hammersmith Bridge, The Dove sits on the edge of the Thames and has lovely views up and down stream from the terrace. It offers locally brewed Fuller's beers and has a well-deserved reputation for the choice and quality of the food. This popular 300-year-old riverside pub is well worth a detour.

HAMPSTEAD

Flask Tavern

14 Flask Walk, NW1 - 435 4580

The Flask, located down an alleyway off Heath Street, is a well-known "local" for Hampstead residents, including plenty of actors and writers. In the summer and on weekends it can get crowded, despite the size of the large public bar and saloon. Young's beers are sold, but the Flask no longer sells flasks of Hampstead Heath Spa water, from which the pub name was derived.

Jack Straw's Castle

North End Way, NW3 - 435 8374

This place is one of the famous pubs on the edge of Hampstead Heath. Jack Straw assisted Wat Tyler in organizing the Peasants' Revolt in 1381 and was reputed to have been hanged nearby. In the 1960s the pub was rebuilt, though it retained its distinctive weatherboarding. In addition to a large snack bar area, a carvery sells roast joint meals. Bass and Worthington beers are poured, and in good weather an outside drinking courtyard is used.

HOLBORN

Old Mitre

1 Ely Ct., Ely Pl. (off Hatton Garden), EC1
405 4751

Being hidden away off Hatton Garden is no deterrent to the popularity of this historic old pub, which was once the servants' quarters for the Bishop of Ely. Pinstripe-suited businesspeople and standing room only are the orders of the day at Old Mitre's busy lunchtime sessions, though in summertime the tables on the outside patio add extra space. The bar food is good and simple, and the strong Burton Ale is worth a try. Look out for the preserved trunk of a cherry tree in the bar, which dates back to the sixteenth century. The Old Mitre is closed on weekends.

Princess Louise

208 High Holborn, WC1 - 405 8816

In 1986, when the Princess Louise was voted London's Pub of the Year, it was easy to see why. It has immense character, friendly and efficient service, delicious food including homemade salads, pies and desserts (served upstairs daily) and, in the pub, quality beers brewed by Vaux in northeast England. Despite its greatly increased popularity, it appears to be maintaining its standards. If you're anywhere nearby, it's well worth a detour for a pint of its own Princess Louise Bitter.

ISLEWORTH

London Apprentice

62 Church St., Old Isleworth, Middlesex
560 6136

We're always happy to make a detour to this corner of Old Isleworth to visit the historical fifteenth-century London Apprentice. It takes its name from the dockland apprentices who rowed up to this spot once a year. Inside are elegant Georgian and Elizabethan features as well as a recently added conservatory restaurant that overlooks the river. Traditional English roast beef and other dishes are served. A truly fine pub, of which the Watneys brewers are justly proud.

KENSINGTON

The Greyhound

1 Kensington Sq., W8 - 937 7140

Tucked away in the corner of Kensington Square, just 100 yards or so south of High Street, this pub maintains its deserved reputation for friendly atmosphere and service as well as an extensive food menu. There's a full-size snooker table in the back of the pub. Among the seven real ales offered is one from the Bedford brewery, Charles Wells's magnificently named Bombardier Bitter. You can sit outside in good weather.

KNIGHTSBRIDGE

Grove Tavern
43 Beauchamp Pl., SW3 - 589 5897

This comfortable Victorian pub, originally converted from two townhouses, provides excellent relief from expensive Beauchamp Place shopping. Hot and cold food is served at lunchtime, and both the interesting "Thames Valley Twins"—Brakspear's beer from Henley and Wethered's Bitter from its close neighbor, Marlow—are on sale.

Paxton's Head
153 Knightsbridge, SW1 - 589 2267

This fine Victorian pub was named after the designer of the original Crystal Palace, which was destroyed by fire. The gas lamps, etched mirrors, mahogany and green-velvet chairs are typical of their period. The pub serves lunch daily and is very convenient for Knightsbridge shoppers and visitors to Albert Hall and the various museums on Exhibition Road.

MAYFAIR

The Audley
41 Mount St., W1 - 499 1843

For years The Audley has reflected the style and wealth of its Mayfair surroundings—a pub simply must be confident when it has the Connaught, Dorchester and Grosvenor House hotels for neighbors. A commendable feature of the Audley has always been its food counter, which we are pleased to report is alive and well, laden with thickly filled sandwiches and freshly carved meats. A glass of dry white wine and smoked salmon are more in order here than a pint of beer and a ploughman's lunch.

Guinea
30 Bruton Pl., W1 - 409 1728

A landmark hidden away in the center of Mayfair, the Guinea was named for the old unit of currency worth one pound and one shilling. Today the Guinea is one of the smartest and probably most expensive pub restaurants in the city. Young's beers are justifiably popular, but it's the special Scottish salmon and the beef in the restaurant that really draws the local wealthy residents to the Guinea. The crowds often drink outside in good weather.

The Red Lion
1 Waverton St., W1 - 499 1307

The Red Lion is a favorite haunt for those working in Berkeley Square. Quaint old windows, wooden floors and antique prints give a truly traditional old-pub feel to the Red Lion, which dates from the eighteenth century. As is customary in this area, the food (pies, sandwiches, sausages) tends to be expensive, though most of the lunchtime and early evening customers are there for the company and conversation rather than the food. The clientele includes many wealthy-looking young real estate developers and brokers who love Watneys and Websters beers as well as the Ruddles brew.

Shepherd's Tavern
Shepherd Market, 50 Hertford St., W1
499 3017

Wood paneling, leather seats and ornate glass are the hallmarks of this elegant eighteenth-century pub in Shepherd Market. If you wish to make a telephone call, you sit in a sedan chair said to have belonged to the Duke of Cumberland, younger son of George II. The bar upstairs serves excellent traditional meals, accompanied by Watneys, Websters and Ruddles beers.

PIMLICO

Orange Brewery
37 Pimlico Rd., SW1 - 730 5378

This pub is one of an increasing number of select places in London that brews its beer on the premises. It sells two home brews: SW1 and SW2 (the latter being the stronger of the two). Complementing the interesting beers is a varied menu written out on blackboards. Pies are homemade.

RICHMOND

The White Swan
Old Palace Ln., Surrey - 940 0959

This lovely little pub stands at the end of a terrace of cottages, a few yards from the banks of the Thames. Opposite is the Old Palace and the other magnificent "Grace and Favor" houses (homes given to long-serving members of the Royal household and government staff) that edge Richmond Green. The little walled-garden is a perfect hideaway to enjoy your Courage Best Bitter and generously filled sandwiches in the sun. Note that the swan on the pub sign wears a crown—the pub was originally licensed by Royal Charter in the seventeenth century.

ROTHERHITHE

Mayflower
117 Rotherhithe St., SE16 - 237 4088
This seventeenth-century riverside pub was renamed to commemorate the ship that took the Pilgrims to North America. It was carefully redesigned in the 1960s to repair wartime bomb damage and now proudly perpetuates its authentic nautical character. You can stand on the jetty and gaze across the Thames with a pint of Bass Ale in hand. The Mayflower is unique in that it is the only pub allowed to sell postage stamps—a license that was originally granted for the convenience of sailors.

ST. JAMES'S

Red Lion
23 Crown Passage, SW1 - 930 8067
After you've completed your bidding at Christie's on King Street across the road, make your way down Crown Passage to the charming Red Lion. Being within a stone's throw of Pall Mall and St. James's, you would expect quality, and you won't be disappointed. The choice of salads, quiches, sandwiches and pies at lunchtime is extremely tempting, not to mention the Ruddles County and Websters Yorkshire beers. A popular West End pub—if you can find it.

SMITHFIELD

The Bishop's Finger
8 W. Smithfield, EC1 - 248 2341
Smithfield may well lose its old meat-market character due to real estate development over the next few years, so take the opportunity now to visit the area and enjoy the atmosphere of a butchers' local. The Bishop's Finger is a big

brash pub that becomes quite busy and noisy as the market closes and tradesmen drift across the road. As you would expect in this location, the food is plentiful, very good and very cheap (the jumbo sausages with French bread virtually make a meal). The beers come from a small independent Kentish brewer called Shepherd Neame. If you want a bit more space and comfort, try upstairs.

SOHO

Argyle Arms
18 Argyle St., W1 - 734 6117
Located just a few yards along from the famous Palladium Theatre and quite convenient to Oxford Street, Liberty's store and Regent Street, the Argyle Arms is set apart in summer by its pretty hanging flower baskets. It's a traditional pub with an ornate Victorian bar and etched glass, and it puts a lot of emphasis on selling delicious dishes listed on the huge special-menu boards. Service is fast and friendly.

SOUTHWARK

The Anchor
34 Park St., Bankside, SE1 - 407 1577
The Anchor remains one of the most famous South Bank riverside taverns. The area around the pub is steeped in history—nearby are the sites of the Globe Theatre and the original Clink Prison on Clink Street. It is said that Samuel Pepys watched the destruction of the old wooden city of London during the Great Fire of 1666 from The Anchor. Today it retains much of its heritage and offers a choice of bars and a restaurant as well as a terrace with chairs and tables at water's edge.

Founders Arms
59 Hopton St., Bankside, SE1 - 928 1899
Young's Brewery rebuilt this pub on the site of the foundries that cast the bells for St. Paul's Cathedral and other city churches. Like the Anchor, the Founders has a magnificent view across the river to the City of London. Its large riverside terrace is popular in fine weather, and the selection of bar food is a good value, if unexciting. If you want something more substantial, try its small restaurant. You can reach

the Founders by going south over Blackfriars Bridge and following the riverside walkway east.

The George
77 Borough High St., SE1 - 407 2056
The George is the only galleried coaching inn left in London. Built in 1554 and rebuilt after being destroyed in the Great Fire of 1666, it retains many of its original features: oak paneling, a Parliamentary clock, a 200-year-old beer engine (ale dispenser) shaped like a cash register, and leaded windows. Light bar food is served in the old booths on the ground floor; more substantial fare is upstairs. If you're lucky, you might catch a Shakespeare play being performed in the courtyard.

THE STRAND

Devereux
20 Devereux Ct., WC2 - 583 4562
The Devereux can be reached by turning off Fleet Street opposite the Law Courts, or from Essex Street. Situated in a peaceful pedestrian court by an entrance to the Middle Temple, and surrounded by barristers' chambers, the Devereux was originally the London home of the Earl of Essex. Although it is often crowded, the pub is full of atmosphere and has a pleasant little restaurant on the second floor serving traditional food.

TOWER BRIDGE

Dickens Inn
St. Katherine's Way, E1 - 488 9936
This is a marvelous reconstruction of a warehouse that was moved from its original site nearby to allow for the development of St. Katherine's Dock in the 1970s. All three floors, with flower-covered balconies overlooking the dock, ooze a true seafaring atmosphere: bare boards, scrubbed tables and plenty of bric-a-brac. A wide range of real ales and a selection of food (primarily seafood) are offered.

VICTORIA

Albert
52 Victoria St., SW1 - 222 5577
Walking along Victoria Street from Parliament Square, you'll find the Albert on the right-hand side opposite the Army and Navy store. A large, imposing building, it sits proudly, though it's now dwarfed by the high-rise buildings around it. In days gone by, the Albert was just about the closest pub to Watney's Stag Brewery, but nowadays the beer has to be delivered from farther afield. The London-Victoriana interior provides a no-nonsense ambience for the enjoyment of food and drink.

Slug and Lettuce
11 Warwick Way, SW1 - 834 3313
Slug and Lettuce is a name that has become common on the London pub scene within the last few years; branches have opened in central residential areas like Islington and Westbourne Grove as well as this one in Victoria. The chain's reputation has been built on the quality and imagination of the food: Guinness casserole, salmon fishcakes, spicy sausages and homemade pies and puddings. Look out for the distinctive name—they are all well worth visiting, if you can get a table.

WAPPING

The Prospect of Whitby
57 Wapping Wall, E1 - 481 1095
Those unfortunate victims who were sentenced by the infamous Judge Jeffries to hang in chains at the nearby "hanging dock" would squint in amazement at the recent development of their seventeenth-century smugglers' wharves. Although Wapping and areas east of it are rapidly changing, The Prospect remains intact as a piece of riverside history: Turner painted from here, Dickens was a frequent visitor, and now tourists by the score enjoy the beamed, flagstoned bar. The atmosphere is always lively, and there is a separate restaurant upstairs.

WESTMINSTER

Buckingham Arms
62 Petty France, SW1 - 222 3386
Good pubs take on the character of the people who live and work in the neighborhood; the Buckingham is surrounded by government offices and is much used by civil servants. If you're in the area of Parliament Square, it is a convenient place to enjoy straightforward bar food and a glass of Young's special London-brewed bitter. At busy times the long corridor provides extra places to sit.

Westminster Arms
7 Storeys Gate, SW1 - 222 8520
The Westminster Arms is located just across the road from Big Ben, the Houses of Parliament, the new Queen Elizabeth II Conference Centre and the European Commission offices, so you may well be rubbing shoulders with MPs, Parliament staff and police. The pub even displays a sign, "People wearing boots or dirty clothing not admitted." Downstairs, where the emphasis is on conversation and drinking, there is very little evidence of food. It would be too dark to see what you were eating, anyway. Upstairs more food is available.

WHITEHALL

The Clarence
53 Whitehall, SW1 - 930 4808
If you walk down Whitehall from Trafalgar Square, you'll find this eighteenth-century pub on the left side opposite Horseguards Parade. Surrounded by ministries. The original decor has been embellished with gas lighting, old church pews and sawdust on the floor. Standard bar food is served at lunch and in the early evening.

QUICK BITES

I n recent years, restaurants that serve food quickly and inexpensively have become more prevalent in London (especially in the Covent Garden area). Char-grilled burgers, deep-dish pizzas with flavorful toppings, fresh pasta with interesting sauces, barbecued ribs and other fast, fun foods now tempt Londoners to eat out as never before. Aside from the speed and low cost, both Londoners and visitors love the informality of dress and flexibility of eating times at these places, which have long been common on the other side of the Atlantic. The following comprise a selection of London's best faster-food restaurants, both the oldtimers and the young upstarts, all of which provide simple yet imaginative eating

BELGRAVIA

Upper Crust in Belgravia
9 William St., SW1 - 235 4444
Open daily 11:30 a.m.-11:30 p.m.
An established favorite of Belgravia locals that is badly in need of refurbishment, the Upper Crust nevertheless provides a farmhouse-kitchen atmosphere in the heart of Belgravia. There is always a choice of delicious pies for about £7.50: Turkey with apples and cranberries and steak with pickled walnuts are but two. The £1.25 cover charge includes good vegetables or a salad and the farmhouse bread basket. Try the Yorkshire pudding stuffed with chili-spiced beef as a starter. The house wine is £5.45. About £12; there is a £3.95 minimum per person.

BLOOMSBURY

Heal's
196 Tottenham Court Rd., W1 - 636 1666
Open Mon.-Sat. 12:30 p.m.-2 p.m.
You must make your way upstairs and through the kitchen and bath departments of

this furniture store to find the restaurant, which offers more style than most of its department store competitors. There are always interesting dishes, such as mussels with garlic bread crumbs and tempura with a soy dipping sauce. The house Cabernet Sauvignon is £7.50, and the rest of the wine list is more than adequate. The quality is good, and the young staff serves efficiently. About £15.

Villa Carlotta

39 Charlotte St., W1 - 636 6011
Open Mon.-Sat. noon-3 p.m. & 6 p.m.-11 p.m.

The "Tavola Calda" section of this spaghetti house is a useful spot for a quick meal on this Tottenham Court Road–Oxford Street corner. Huge portions of pasta, made on the premises (in the kitchen on view from the sidewalk), are served by fast-talking Italians. The atmosphere is fiberglass Tuscany, complete with plastic tablecloths. House wine is £5.65 by the liter and £1.20 by the glass. The dance floor in the second-floor restaurant sees a lot of action on Friday and Saturday nights. About £15-£20, including wine.

CAMDEN

Le Bistroquet

273 Camden High St., NW1 - 485 9607
Open Mon.-Fri. noon-11:30 p.m., Sat.-Sun. noon-midnight.

Le Bistroquet serves an excellent Continental breakfast on the weekend. The owner, who comes from Langan's Brasserie, concentrates on such imaginative plats du jour as saffron soup, fresh noodles with basil and cream, navarin of lamb and poached cod provençale. It is quite large, with a noisy French atmosphere. Starters cost about £3, main courses about £10.

Spud U Like

79 Camden High St., NW1 - 589 0744, 387 0960
Open daily noon-midnight.

In this fiber-conscious age, when many of us agonize over calorie and fat intake, we could do little better than to patronize this chain of quick-food restaurants. Compared to a potato filled with a meaty, heavy Bolognese sauce, a Spud U Like spud filled with cheese and chives (£1.40) contains fewer calories and tastes pretty good.

CHELSEA

Henry J. Bean's

195-197 King's Rd., SW3 - 352 9255
54 Abingdon Road, W8 - 937 3339
Open Mon.-Sat. 11:45 a.m.-11 p.m., Sun. 11:45 a.m.-10 p.m.

After going up to the bar to place your order, you wait at your table until your number is called. Satisfying cheeseburgers go for £3.55; make sure to save room for the scrumptious chocolate cheesecake or the good pecan pie.

La Brasserie

272 Brompton Rd., SW3 - 584 1668
Open Mon.-Sat. 8 a.m.-1 a.m., Sun. 10 a.m.-1 a.m.

Probably the first London brasserie, and now firmly settled into its second decade, this place possesses a well-established French atmosphere. The fare changes with the moods and needs of the day. Good coffee and decent croissants (and newspapers on poles) are available in morning; croque monsieurs, pâtés and interesting French specialties arrive for lunch and dinner. House wine is £6.20. About £15.

Chelsea Kitchen

98 King's Rd., SW3 - 589 1330
Open Mon.-Sat. 8 a.m.-11:45 p.m., Sun. noon-11:15 p.m.

A couple of blocks along King's Road from Peter Jones, the Chelsea Kitchen has been a stalwart of good, fresh cooking for many years. Don't expect plush carpets and dim lights—this place has straightforward Formica imitation-wood tables and cheerful waitresses who serve a good selection of casseroles, escalopes, lasagnes and the like. The big boast here is that nothing is frozen. This convenient refuge following an expensive Knightsbridge shopping trip will cost only about £6, including wine.

Dome

354 King's Rd., SW3 - 352 7611
38-39 Hampstead High St., NW3
435 4240
341 Upper St., N1 - 226 3414
Hilgate House, Seacoal Ln., EC4
248 3741
Open Mon.-Sat. 9 a.m.-11 p.m., Sun. 9 a.m.-10:30 p.m.

This cosmopolitan French-style bar is popular with the young, local crowd. Croque monsieurs, baguettes aux saucisses (sausages), omelets with fines herbes and other French classics are served on small marble-topped café tables by waiters in long green aprons. Breakfast is also available all day. The place tends to become full and "pubby" in the evening. About £7-£10.

CHISWICK

Foubert's
162 High Rd., W4 - 747 0210
Open Mon.-Sat. 9 a.m.-11 p.m., Sun. 10 a.m.-7 p.m.
Recently expanded so it now houses a full-size restaurant as well as a wine bar, Foubert's is enormously popular with the denizens of western London. In addition to a variety of main courses, it serves delicious pasta dishes and memorable ice cream sundaes. About £10-£15, including wine.

THE CITY

Birley Sandwiches
14 Moorfields, EC2 - 628 9701
Open 6:30 a.m.-3 p.m.
Birley is the absolute Rolls-Royce of sandwich bars, one whose various combinations of ingredients have been copied by many others. Perhaps its most celebrated experiment came with the mixing of avocado with crispy bacon (how Californian!). Well worth visiting if you feel hungry and are in the area of London Wall or Moorgate. About £1.50 for a hearty sandwich.

Café St. Pierre
29 Clerkenwell Green, EC1 - 251 6606
Open Mon.-Fri. noon-3 p.m. & 5:45 p.m.-10:45 p.m.
Sitting like a pink-and-white wedding cake on the corner of Clerkenwell Green, this hugely popular brasserie (there is a restaurant upstairs) serves such original daily specials as Roquefort cheese mousse on a strawberry coulis and calf's liver with an apple purée, along with such dishes as pasta shells with mushrooms and pan-fried pork with red cabbage. The wine selection is extensive and very well chosen. Lunchtime and weekday early

evenings are particularly busy with local office employees. About £10-£15, including wine.

Food for Health
15 Blackfriars Ln., EC4 - 236 7001
Open Mon.-Fri. 8 a.m.-3 p.m.
Located on the fringe of the City and Fleet Street, this no-nonsense vegetarian restaurant under the arches of Blackfriars Bridge concentrates on feeding loyal office workers nutritious dishes: excellent salads, vegetable curry with brown rice, steamed date-and-walnut pudding and homemade yogurt. It's cheap, simple and well worth a few minutes' walk if you are visiting St. Paul's Cathedral. About £5.

Nosherie
12-13 Greville St., EC1 - 242 1591
Open Mon.-Fri. 8 a.m.-5 p.m.
This popular Jewish restaurant (which opened in 1960) just off Leather Lane is famous for its excellent hot beef sandwiches, Vienna sausages and wursts. It also serves several varieties of soup—the chicken soup is wonderfully spicy. About £10.

Slenders
41 Cathedral Pl., EC4 - 236 5974
Open Mon.-Fri. 7:30 a.m.-6:15 p.m.
A large self-service restaurant just across the road from St. Paul's, Slenders displays an excellent selection of wholesome vegetarian food and juices. It thrives on quick "in and out" midweek office lunches and gets quite busy at peak times. Delicious homemade soups, crisp salads, vegetable casseroles and fruit crumbles are particularly popular. The food is much more inventive than the customary lunchtime snackery. About £6-£8.

HOLBORN

The Café Society
32, Procter St., Red Lion Sq., W31
242 6691
Open Mon.-Fri. 8 a.m.-8 p.m.
This light and lively brasserie, close to the Holborn underground station, serves fresh, thoroughly satisfying breakfast, lunch and dinner dishes. About £10.

KNIGHTSBRIDGE

General Trading Company Café
144 Sloane St., SW1 - 730 6400
Open Mon.-Fri. 9 a.m.-5:15 p.m., Sat. 9 a.m.-1:30 p.m.

This useful café hidden in the basement of the General Trading Company overlooking a little courtyard serves such daily homemade specialties as lettuce soup, turkey and leek pie, and pear and ginger tart. It is just one of proprietor Justin de Blank's excellent operations. About £10.

Harrods Way In Restaurant
85-135 Brompton Rd., SW1 - 730 1234
Open Mon.-Tues. & Thurs.-Fri. 9 a.m.-5 p.m., Wed. 9 a.m.-7 p.m., Sat. 9 a.m.-6 p.m.

Take the elevator or escalator to the fourth floor of the department store and walk through the stylish Way In department to this modern, no-smoking restaurant. Shiny chrome, stools with backs and fresh flowers on the tables set the scene for a choice of interesting dishes that suit all times of the day: charcuterie from the famous Food Hall, hot terrine of lotte, delicious coconut ice cream and freshly squeezed juices. The minimum charge is £3; at about £7, a meal here is a good value.

L.A. Café Restaurant & Cocktail Bar
163 Knightsbridge, SW7 - 589 7077
Open daily noon-midnight.

West Coast–style pizza is served here, in the center of Knightsbridge, in a setting marked by lots of greenery, brass and a big, big cocktail bar. Try a Bullshot Limey cocktail; we can also recommend the good Californian/Mexican rice and refried beans. House wine is £6.50 a bottle. About £8-£10.

Pizza on the Park
11-13 Knightsbridge, SW1 - 235 5273
Open daily 8:30 a.m.-midnight (breakfast until 11:30 a.m.).

Reopened after a several-months' closing, Pizza on the Park is now one of the elegant flagships of the extensive Pizza Express chain, the most reliable source of authentic Italian pizza in London. Mirrors, huge windows overlooking the park (and the traffic) and cool, whitewashed walls make this a pleasant place to escape the hustle and bustle of Knightsbridge, and the setting compensates for the extra 75p or so that has been added to the items on the standard Pizza Express menu: all the usual pizzas, plus a mozzarella-and-tomato salad (with a sprig of fresh basil) served with dough balls and (presumably a concession to the locale) smoked salmon. The house wine is a Frescobaldi for £6.35, but the short wine list also includes an excellent Chablis for £14.50; Nastro Azzuro beer is a good alternative. About £10.

Wolfes
25 Basil St., SW3 - 589 8444
Open daily 11:30 a.m.-midnight.

Exhausted Harrods shoppers can stagger across the road and into this plush restaurant and be served delicious burgers for £4.95. Also great are the potato pancakes with apple sauce. The minimum charge is £6, Saturday £7. A good-value meal is about £6-£10; wine is £7 a bottle or £1.75 a glass.

LEICESTER SQUARE

Chicago Meatpackers
96 Charing Cross Rd., WC2 - 379 3277
Open Mon.-Sat. noon-1:30 a.m., Sun. noon-10:30 p.m.

A theaterland newcomer from the same stable as Chicago Pizza Pie Factory and Chicago Rib Shack, Chicago Meatpackers serves American-style seafood, such as clam chowder, New Orleans blackened whitefish and seafood pasta, along with the inevitable salad bar, barbecued ribs, chicken-and-sausage jambalaya and Key lime pie. Staff dressed in "club" jerseys will take good care of you in the captain's-table atmosphere. About £10.

Stockpot
40 Panton St., WC2 - 839 5142, 839 2010
Open Mon.-Sat. 8 a.m.-11:30 p.m., Sun. noon-10 p.m.

This old favorite is conveniently situated for visits to Trafalgar Square and the Haymarket as well as Leicester Square. Dirt cheap, cheerful and packed with office workers at lunchtime, Stockpot has plain wooden seating and wicker lamp shades. The food is simple and reliable, as customers over the last two decades will testify. Daily dishes usually include moussaka (£1.40), stuffed squash (£1.15) and a baked jam roll (45p). The house wine is an amazing £3.50 a bottle.

MAYFAIR

Chicago Pizza Pie Factory
17 Hanover Sq., W1 - 629 2669
Open Mon.-Sat. 11:45 a.m.-11:30 p.m., Sun. noon-10:30 p.m.

The U.S.A. has come to the West End! Look for the plain red doors on the opposite corner of Hanover Square from the *Vogue* offices. Once inside and downstairs, the American-warehouse theme is fulfilled: brash, noisy, friendly and great fun. The food runs to superb deep-dish pizzas (the two-person size really is enough for two), wickedly antisocial garlic bread and stuffed mushrooms. If you have room, the carrot cake with honeyed whipped cream deserves to fill that last little corner. The place is often very crowded. About £10, and the Château Chicago Vin goes for £5.75 a bottle.

Coconut Grove
3-5 Barrett St., W1 - 486 5269
Open Mon.-Thurs. noon-11:30 p.m., Fri.-Sun. noon-midnight.

A well-established cocktail bar and art deco-style restaurant just to the north of Oxford Street, Coconut Grove serves huge salads, hamburgers and such American-style specialties as deep-fried Camembert and Mississippi mud pie. The Coconut Grove Orgy is a fantasy feast for six people at £54. A normal meal will cost upward of £15, including one of the 40 or so excellent, fun cocktails (about £4.50).

The Crêperie
56A S. Molton St., W1 - 629 4794
Open Mon.-Wed. & Fri.-Sat. 9:30 a.m.-8 p.m., Thurs. 9:30 a.m.-10 p.m., Sun. 11 a.m.-5 p.m.

Just a couple of minutes' walk from Claridge's and Bond Street, this pleasant little courtyard restaurant serves heavenly traditional French buckwheat pancakes, with more than 30 different fillings available. Try the delicious chicken and asparagus or the banana, honey and cream. About £5.

Garfunkels
61 Duke St., W1 - 499 5000
Open daily noon-11 p.m.

A stone's throw from Oxford Street, this place is quick, uneventful but convenient (if you can avoid the line at peak times). The all-you-can-eat salad bar at £3.85 as a main

course is a good value; otherwise, there are quiches, risottos, burgers and a drinkable Valpolicella house wine for £6.30 a bottle.

The Granary
39 Albemarle St., W1 - 493 2978
Open Mon.-Fri. 11 a.m.-8 p.m., Sat. 11 a.m.-2:30 p.m.

It is most unusual in this neighborhood of jewelers, art galleries and the Ritz Hotel to find a good, straightforward, all-day self-service restaurant that serves home-cooked food. The Granary is such a place. It can become terribly crowded, particularly on Saturdays. You help yourself to such bistro dishes as boeuf bourguignon, roast pork in cider sauce, lamb casserole with lemon and mint, and a black-currant charlotte russe. The atmosphere is country kitchen. About £6-£10.

Hard Rock Cafe
150 Old Park Ln., W1 - 629 0382
Open Sun.-Thurs. noon-midnight, Fri.-Sat. noon-1 a.m.

If you prefer to spend your leisure time waiting in lines and eating while being bombarded by eardrum-crushing noise, by all means hurry over to the world-famous Hard Rock. True to its name, the Hard Rock pulsates with loud rock music, much of it oldies, and the walls are covered with rock-music memorabilia. The quality of the food varies greatly, and it is apparent that the Hard Rock's huge international fame has led to a downturn in standards. But we are still fond of the char-grilled burgers (starting at £4) and the "pig sandwich" of hickory-smoked pork (£5.80).

PICCADILLY

Fortnum's Fountain Restaurant
181 Piccadilly, W1 - 734 4938
Open Mon.-Sat. 9:30 a.m.-11:30 p.m.

First and foremost a meeting place and a fashionable place to see and be seen, Fortnum's Fountain always seems to be busy. The staff are friendly but permanently under pressure, so you may get left standing at the door searching for a table or a place at the counter. The menu offers good-quality items, some from Fortnum's own bakery. The fresh sherbets, ice creams and milk shakes are excellent. You can make reservations only after 6 p.m., which explains the occasional long queues. In the evening grilled dishes are served. About £8 for a snack meal and between £12 and £15 for dinner.

RICHMOND

Clouds
6-8 Kingston Hill, Kingston-upon-Thames, Surrey - 546 0559
Open daily 11 a.m.-11:30 p.m.

Just to the south of Richmond Park, this café, with its bentwood chairs and nostalgic atmosphere, serves good char-grilled burgers, along with such classics as barbecued ribs and chicken. The black-currant pavlova (a meringue dessert) with "cascades of cream" is delicious, and the afternoon cream tea is quite popular. About £7.

Pasta Prego
Kew Rd., Surrey - 948 8508
Open daily noon-3 p.m. & 6:30 p.m.-11:30 p.m.

This newly opened fresh-pasta restaurant is just a short walk down Kew Road from the Botanical Gardens. With its light and airy atmosphere and its friendly young staff, Pasta Prego is already gaining a good reputation for its admirable range of pasta dishes. The large plate of tagliatelle al cacciatore (£3.40) is a good value. The amazing tête-à-tête dessert (£2.60), a huge concoction of various ice creams, meringues, fresh fruit and amaretti (macaroons), is covered in chocolate sauce. About £7.

SOHO

Kettners
29 Romilly St., W1 - 437 6437
Open 11 a.m.-midnight.

Fast-food deluxe is found in this century-old building, the flagship of the Pizza Express chain. We can recommend the King Edward topping—four cheeses on a potato base— though we must add that the fare has been inconsistent lately, and the prices can be steep. The house wine is £6.50; for added atmosphere, there is a Champagne bar. From £10-£20.

STOCKWELL

Rebato's
169 S. Lambeth Rd., SW8 - 735 6388
Open Mon.-Fri. noon-2:30 p.m. & 7 p.m.-11 p.m., Sat. 7 p.m.-11 p.m.

Possibly the best tapas bar in the country, Rebato's is a superb place for a snack. If you don't have time to visit the restaurant in the rear of the building, stop here in the tapas bar and sample some of the delicacies on view: trays groaning under the weight of sardines, octopus, spicy sausage, mussels, squid, garlicky prawns and good tripe. Excellent wine and sherry are poured by the glass. About £5-£10.

THE STRAND & COVENT GARDEN

Joe Allen
13 Exeter St., WC2 - 836 0651
Open Mon.-Sat. noon-12:45 a.m., Sun. noon-11:30 p.m.

The menu up on the wall offers such American goodies as Maryland crabcakes or avocado with bacon and spinach, followed by prime rib of beef or Southern fried chicken. Several fish courses are also offered. There is a fruity house wine, and you should emerge from the depths of this basement restaurant feeling that all is well with the world. It's a good idea to book a table before you come. About £10-£15.

Food for Thought
31 Neal St., WC2 - 836 0239
Open Mon.-Fri. noon-8 p.m.

This restaurant embodies the life and character of Covent Garden and is renowned for its genuine, no-frills quality. Although it always seems to be crushingly cramped, its vegetarian cooking continues to be an excellent value. Stir-fried dishes, casseroles and various forms of pasta are typical dishes on the daily changing menu. About £5.

The Grill American
30 Wellington St., WC2 - 240 7529
Open daily noon-3 p.m. & 5:30 p.m.-midnight.

Soup is served in gigantic bowls; other tasty starters include guacamole and corn chips and goat cheese on toast. The decidedly American menu also offers large hamburgers, chili pie topped with melted cheese, and chicken marinated in coconut milk. A short list of desserts includes various sorbets and a superb chocolate cheesecake. About £10.

L. S. Grunts Chicago Pizza Co.
12 Maiden Ln., WC2 - 379 7722
Open Mon.-Sat. noon-11:30 p.m., Sun. noon-10 p.m.

Between the Strand and Covent Garden rests this unmistakable slice of Chicago. Walk in past the mammoth mural of Chicago's Sears Tower and ex-mayor Richard Daley, and experience the friendly and efficient service and the made-to-order deep-dish pizzas. It shouldn't surprise you to learn that there are lengthy waits for tables at peak hours. Amusing cocktails sell for £2.90. About £6—and well worth it.

Maxwells
16-17 Russell St., WC2 - 836 0303
Open Sun.-Thurs. noon-midnight, Fri.-Sat. noon-1 a.m.

Big, brassy and generally full of the trendy young Covent Garden set, Maxwells serves top-quality four- and eight-ounce char-grilled hamburgers (£3.55 for the eight ounce), club sandwiches, smoked ribs and a long list of cocktails. Try the outrageous double-thick chocolate sundae with sprinkles and marshmallows for £1.30. About £8.

Palms
39 King St., WC2 - 240 2939
Open daily noon-midnight.

Italian newspapers cover the walls and baskets of greenery hang from the ceiling in this attractive restaurant located just 100 yards from the Covent Garden Piazza. Linguine, fettuccine, lasagne and other fresh pasta dishes are the house specialties. We've always enjoyed pleasant, informal and speedy service. The Cruise Missile cocktail (vodka, lime and Triple Sec) is a knockout. About £7.

TRAFALGAR SQUARE

National Gallery Restaurant
Trafalgar Sq., WC2 - 930 5210
Open Mon.-Sat. 10 a.m.-5 p.m., Sun. 2 p.m.-5 p.m.

This restaurant has proven to be quite popular with gallery visitors. Situated downstairs in befittingly elegant surroundings, it puts together a help-yourself display of fresh, good-quality hot and cold starters, main courses and desserts (at around £4) as well as vegetarian dishes. Substantial salads are £1, and the house wine costs £4.60 a bottle.

Tony Roma's
46 St. Martin's Ln., WC2 - 379 3330
Open daily noon-12:30 a.m.

Convenient for Trafalgar Square visitors and located next door to the Coliseum (home of the English National Opera Company), Tony Roma's combines a slick, friendly American welcome with fast, professional service. The best dishes are the baby-back ribs (£4.95 at lunch, £6.95 at dinner), onion-ring loaf (£2.95) and filet mignon on a skewer (£5.95). House wine is £6 a bottle, £1.45 a glass.

TEDDINGTON

Spaghetti Junction
20 High St., Middlesex - 977 9199
Open Tues.-Sat. 12:30 p.m.-2:30 p.m. & 6 p.m.-11:15 p.m., Sun. 6 p.m.-11:15 p.m.

Customers come from miles around for the food at this restaurant, which Franco Langella has transformed into a place that positively hums with vitality. Reservations are not accepted, but Spaghetti Junction is well worth a stop for its excellent pasta, pizza and main dishes. Come early on Friday night, when it can get particularly crowded. The house wine is £5.25 a bottle and £1.25 a glass, and a meal will run £7-£10.

WIMBLEDON

MacArthurs
48 High St., Wimbledon Village, SW19
946 4135
147 Church Rd., SW13 - 748 3630
32 The Quadrant, Richmond, Surrey
940 7128
50-54 Turnham Green Terr, W4 - 994 3000
Open daily noon-11:30 p.m.

Located just a few paces off Wimbledon Common in the center of attractive Wimbledon Village, this hamburger joint offers cooked-to-order char-grilled burgers in six-ounce and ten-ounce sizes, priced from £3.50 to £4.85 (for a big bacon cheeseburger). And these burgers are delicious. Starters, specials and salads are also available as well as ice cream and wonderful chewy chocolate brownies. Popular with families. Avoid the wine. About £6-£9. Other branches as noted above.

Pastificio
58A Wimbledon Hill Rd., SW19 - 879 0919
Open daily noon-midnight.

Not too far from the home of tennis, this cheerful Italian restaurant, located on a block full of shops, serves fresh homemade pastas, good pizzas and a nice selection of starters and desserts. We like the popular two-course lunchtime special at £2.99 (for example, creamy chicken soup with mushrooms and herbs followed by linguine ai funghi, pasta with mushrooms and red-wine sauce). The pleasant Italian house wine is £3.05 per half liter. Be prepared to wait at peak times.

TEA ROOMS

A t any time of the day, a cup of tea can fortify, restore and relieve. The traditional afternoon tea as a full meal with sandwiches, toast, jam and cakes is rare these days, though, because of the speed and changing style of modern life. However, when afternoon tea is served with the care, quality, atmosphere and sense of tradition that it merits, it can still be a wonderful treat. To follow are some of the fast-disappearing havens that still offer this particularly satisfying taste of tranquility.

Bendicks
195 Sloane St., SW1 - 235 4749
Open Mon.-Sat. 9 a.m.-6 p.m.

A very flowery, very English country house, this small tea shop, which sells Bendicks's delicious chocolates, serves as a pleasant meeting place for Knightsbridge ladies. Located just along Sloane Street from Harvey Nichols, it isn't far from Harrods. Cream teas are £4.50, and a good espresso is 90p.

Bonne Bouche Pâtisserie
2 Thayer St., W1 - 935 3502
Open Mon.-Fri. 8:30 a.m.-7 p.m., Sat. 8:30 a.m.-6 p.m.

This crowded little café/tea shop is on the corner of Thayer and George streets. You can select from the attractive display of fresh cakes and pastries at the takeout pâtisserie next door, then be served tea by the attentive staff. Afternoon cream tea with scones is £1.65.

Brown's
Albemarle St. & Dover St., W1 - 493 6020
Open daily 3 p.m.-6 p.m.

Surely one of the most English of all London hotels, Brown's has lounges that provide the atmosphere of country house drawing rooms, with paneled walls and luxurious armchairs. Although not cheap, it is an ideal setting in which to enjoy a full range of sandwiches, scones, cakes and pastries with the best-quality tea or coffee. About £6.95.

Connaught
Carlos Pl., W1 - 499 7070
Open daily 3:30 p.m.-5 p.m.

The Connaught, that grand old lady of London's luxury hotels, serves tea in the lounge. Immaculate waiters in tails pour fragrant Chinese Lapsang souchong tea (a most fitting choice) to accompany the trim little sandwiches and perfect pastries from their trolleys. Connaught residents like to take tea, so arrive early to avoid an ever-so-slight crowd. And men should don coats and ties for this hour or so of old-fashioned elegance, which will cost about £6.

Dorchester
Park Ln., W1 - 629 8888

This splendid hotel closed in December 1988 and will not reopen until the spring of 1990. At that time, presumably, afternoon tea will be served in considerable style.

Goring
15 Beeston Pl., SW1 - 834 8211
Open daily 10 a.m.-6 p.m.

Hidden away on a quiet road between Buckingham Palace and Victoria, this privately owned hotel maintains traditional standards of comfort and service. The lounge is an oasis of peace, with heavy curtains and comfortable armchairs and sofas. The set tea (served from 4 p.m.) includes a pot of tea, neatly cut sandwiches, scones and a choice of cake, and is a good value at £4.50,. It's veddy English.

Hyde Park Hotel
66 Knightsbridge, SW1 - 235 2000
Open daily 3:45 p.m.-6 p.m.

In addition to its beautiful view of Hyde Park, with its seasonal moods and constant activity of horses, joggers and the occasional troop of the Household Cavalry, the Hyde Park Room has an Edwardian splendor that complements the fine china, fresh flowers and full-blooded English afternoon tea (£6.25), which is served with efficiency by professional waiters.

Lascelles Old English Tea House
2 Marlborough Ct., Carnaby St., W1
439 2366
Open daily 11 a.m.-7 p.m.

Tea is served all day, along with enormous scones filled with jam and clotted cream. There is also a devilishly tempting selection of homemade cakes, and on warm days tea is served outside. A pot of tea for two is £1.30.

Maids of Honour
288 Kew Rd., Richmond - 940 2752
Open Mon. 9:30 a.m.-1 p.m., Tues.-Fri. 10 a.m.-5:30 p.m., Sat. 9 a.m.-5:30 p.m.

This place is named for a sixteenth-century baker; the story goes that King Henry VIII was so taken with the delicious tarts baked on his behalf by the poor maid of honor that he imprisoned her inside the grounds of Richmond Palace so she would continue to cook them exclusively for him. This wonderfully old-fashioned tea room, with polished oak tables and chairs and elderly waitresses in flowered smocks, is handily situated just opposite Kew Gardens. Coffee and tea are served with freshly baked scones, buns or a scrumptious array of cream cakes, which are brought to the table on an elegant platter to tempt the customer to try more than one. The "maids of honour" themselves, sort of like individual cheesecakes baked in puff pastry, are absolutely delicious. (These can also be purchased in the adjoining shop.) The cream tea (including real clotted cream) is £2.25, and lunches, consisting of such traditional favorites as roast lamb with mint sauce, followed by apple pie and cream, are served for a remarkably modest £4.50.

Maison Bertaux Pâtisserie Française
28 Greek St., W1 - 437 6007
Open Tues.-Sat. 9 a.m.-5:30 p.m., Sun. 9:30 a.m.-1 p.m. (takeout only).

This little shop in the heart of Soho has rightly been considered a gem for many years. Now 117 years old, this delightful place is blessed with many loyal customers, who begin to gather on Greek Street in the early hours. Tea is served with freshly made cakes, biscuits, pastries and scones. On Sundays the café, which seats 36 people, is closed, but the pâtisserie is open if you wish to take their treats home or on a picnic in charming Soho Square. A delight. £3-£5.

Le Meridien Piccadilly
Piccadilly, W1 - 734 8000
Open daily 3 p.m.-5:30 p.m.

A short distance from the Royal Academy, Le Meridien Piccadilly is still gleaming from the £16 million facelift given by the hotel's previous owners, Gleneagles. The old Piccadilly Hotel is now extremely elegant; a harpist plays soothing music while you nibble your tomato sandwiches. What better way to refresh the soul after a busy afternoon of shopping? Afternoon tea costs £6.50 and includes a choice of six different teas.

Muffin Man
12 Wrights Ln., W8 - 937 6652
Open Mon.-Fri. 8:15 a.m.-5:45 p.m., Sat. 8:15 a.m.-4:45 p.m.

Not far from Kensington High Street (near the Church Street end) stands this small but attractive two-story café that is prettily decorated in a style in keeping with the craft shop that occupies the other half of the premises. Breakfast (croissants, or scrambled eggs with ham, toast and marmalade for £4.50) and lunch (salads, double-decker sandwiches) are served as well as tea. There are three set tea menus to choose from, including a Devon cream tea (£3.50) and dainty sandwiches with fresh cream gâteaux (cakes). The service is friendly and informal, and the atmosphere rather hectic, as the staff tries to accommodate the endless stream of customers.

Pâtisserie Valérie
44 Old Compton St., W1 - 437 3466
Open Mon.-Sat. 8:30 a.m.-7 p.m.

This high-quality Belgian pâtisserie always seems to be bustling and full of chatter; it's a favorite with local Belgians and Italians. Choose from the enormous selection of delicious pastries, then squeeze your way to a space at one of the plain red Formica tables. You could be in a little café in the heart of Europe. The coffee is extremely good, and the millefeuilles with various cream fillings are scrumptious.

Pontis
27 James St., WC2 - 240 0588
Open daily 8:30 a.m.-6 p.m.

A quick "in and out" cup-of-coffee-and-cookie shop, Pontis serves delicious cappuccino (60p) and various fresh cookies (about 85p per quarter pound), which once you have tasted will tempt you to order more. A visit here is five minutes well spent.

Swiss Centre
Leicester Sq., Wardour St., W1 - 734 1291
Open daily 8:30 a.m.-11 p.m.

Surprisingly, this area has few pleasant tea and coffee shops. The self-service Imbiss (one of five Swiss Centre restaurants) has its own entrance on Wardour Street. The surroundings are unpretentious, but the cakes, croissants and other pastries, all made on the premises, are excellent. The rich hot chocolate with whipped cream (82p) is particularly welcoming on a cold, gray London afternoon.

WINE BARS

I f you're looking for the largest possible selection of wines from all over the world, you'd be best off if you were British—better still, a Londoner. For in London you'll find the longest, most varied wine lists anywhere. "Oh, but surely, France . . ." people say, forgetting that the French, who live in a major wine-growing country, drink virtually nothing but the national product, just as Italians stick to Italian wine, Germans to German and so on. But in Britain, where the business of wine making is at best a cottage industry and at worst a bad summer's unmitigated disaster, people buy wine from all over the world. It's good for their education and better still for their palates that Brits now have as many as 32 countries (at last count) exporting wine to them.

London is a buyer's market—and, fortunately, there is intense competition among the importing countries trying to sell to British restaurants, wine bars and shops. In addition, foreign-government subsidies on these exported wines often outweigh the duties imposed by British Customs. So sometimes you can buy a top-quality wine in London for less than it sells in France or New Zealand, where it was produced.

Wine has rarely—perhaps never—been cheaper in relation to the price of other goods, particularly beer and spirits. When wine began to cost less than lager, the British reached a watershed; they then joined the wine lovers of the world in accepting wine as both a natural agricultural product and the perfect partner to food. Elitism had nothing to do with it.

Since wine bars serve both food and wine, they're onto a good thing. In fact, since they began to invade the London scene nearly 30 years ago, wine bars have provided good value while offering a much wider choice of wine, sometimes at half the price, than gourmet restaurants.

The most successful and popular are those that know their customers, people who have a healthy appetite for the grape. These are not the sort who want, or need, to be patronized; nor do regulars want to see exactly the same wines on the list month after month, any more than they want the same menu. Consequently, a proprietor's spirit of adventure was a deciding factor in choosing the wine bars listed below.

The long-awaited change in British licensing hours had just gone into effect when this guide went to press. Some London wine bars extended their hours at once to accommodate late lunchers who take their Filofaxes and pocket calculators to the table with them. Others held off in making an immediate change, but they may well have done so by now. Therefore, you may be allowed to linger on longer into the afternoon than indicated here.

Note that most wine bars operate on a first-come, first-serve basis, which can mean a long wait for a table if you arrive for lunch later than 12:30 p.m. Wine bars tend to be much quieter in the evenings, though the choice of dishes is often more limited, the decibel count lower, and the essential bonhomie missing. So come early for lunch, or risk having to perch on the stairs or on an overturned wine cask with someone's elbow in your salad.

Unlike at a pub, few patrons smoke, and you won't find deafening jukeboxes or frenetic video games, which have driven so many from the pubs and into the wine bars. Even in a shoulder-to-shoulder crush like that in the Underground during rush hour, you'll always find the best-tempered customers in London wine bars.

Perhaps the wine has something to do with it.

BATTERSEA

Just Williams
6 Battersea Rise, SW11 - 228 9980
Open Mon.-Sat. noon-3 p.m. & 6 p.m.-11 p.m., Sun. 7 p.m.-10:30 p.m.

Battersea is one of those depressed areas of London that has come up in the world (along with property prices) as young professionals have moved in. This popular wine bar, actually built sixteen years ago, resembles a Spanish wine cellar, with low ceilings and checked tablecloths—and a surprisingly varied range of wines, starting with Just Williams's own Battersea Wine Company representative. There are always a few well-chosen specials listed on the blackboard and a choice of a half dozen reds and whites you can order by the glass. These include a pleasantly fruity house red, the house Champagne (Georges Coulet) and five or six vintage ports. Simple home cooking is the culinary order of the day: pâtés, taramasalata (fish roe purée served as a dip with crusty bread), quiche and a few cold dishes (hot in winter), perhaps a chicken salad. The sauces are well above wine bar standards, and there is a small range of starters and desserts. You can sip a Kir or Bucks Fizz (Champagne and orange juice) in the garden in the back on a fine day. The proprietors also own the excellent Pollyanna's restaurant next door (see Restaurants), should Just Williams get too crowded.

BELGRAVIA

Carriages
43 Buckingham Palace Rd., SW1
834 0119
Open Mon.-Fri. 11:30 a.m.-11 p.m.

It looks a trifle grand once you escape the swirl of traffic outside Buckingham Palace and step inside, but Carriages's prices are reasonable for what you get, and the wine list is a joy. There is heavy emphasis on a dozen top Alsatian wines, a tempting selection of Champagnes if you've had a good day at the races and an enterprising choice of Burgundies and Beaujolais. Decent, less expensive bottlings from Spain, Portugal and Italy are also served, as is a full range of Madeira. Of great help are the capsule descriptions of every wine on the list, making it easy to choose intelligently, even if your vinous knowledge is virtually nil. At least a dozen can be ordered by the glass.

The tables are nestled in small brick alcoves crowned with wrought-iron bars. Special promotions, such as pink wines in the summer or warming reds in winter, are worth looking out for. Tables are often fully booked by noon, so telephone early. You can confine yourself to a snack, such as smoked chicken in phyllo pastry, or splurge on a hearty steak or veal escalopes. Thursday evening attracts the bright and brittle cocktail crowd. Down a Knock Out (gin, dry vermouth and white crème de menthe) or a Suffering Bastard (Cognac, dry sherry and ginger ale), and the world is suddenly a beautiful place.

Ebury Wine Bar
139 Ebury St., SW1 - 730 5447
Open Mon.-Sat. 11 a.m.-3 p.m. & 5:30 p.m.-11 p.m., Sun. noon-2 p.m. & 7 p.m.-10 p.m.

There is always a full house at Ebury, so if you want to eat here—and we think you will—reservations are essential. Because many of the customers are regulars (some have been coming for nearly twenty years, since this was one of the first wine bars in London), there is a distinctly club-like atmosphere. It has one of the most carefully thought-out wine lists in London, with not only an imaginative range

from Bordeaux, Burgundy, the Rhône and the Loire, but also some decent Australians and quite worthwhile Italians. Descriptions of each wine are chatty and informative; look for those available by the glass on the front page of the list. The huge glasses hold a quarter of a bottle each, and the house Champagne is Boizel. English wines include St. George, which the prime minister served to a trade delegation from Japan, bringing in a huge order. The chef is French, and her menu, ranging from duck-leg confit to Norfolk duckling and fisherman's pie, is not only expertly prepared but reasonably priced. If you have room for a sinfully rich dessert, accompany it with an ample glass of the sweet Muscat de Beaumes de Venise, and the rest of the afternoon will seem irrelevant.

Motcomb's
26 Motcomb St., SW1 - 235 6382
Open Mon.-Sat. noon-3 p.m. & 5:30 p.m.-11 p.m.

There are only eleven tables on the ground floor of this small, elegant wine bar just off Sloane Street, and just inside the door is a TV set that's always tuned to the major sporting event of the moment. So if you want to concentrate on your lunch partner, ask for a table as far away from the tube as possible, or reserve a table in the downstairs restaurant. The wines include a half dozen Champagnes and some decent years among the French reds and whites but sadly few half bottles. Italian and Spanish wines are notably cheaper. The regular hot-lunch specials, such as Cumberland sausages and fish pie, are really just deluxe schoolboy noshes for grown-ups. Motcomb's is an almost unofficial club, with oil paintings and cartoons on the walls, cases of wine behind the bar, fans revolving lazily and newspapers to browse through over your port.

Tiles Wine Bar
36 Buckingham Palace Rd., SW1
834 7761
Open Mon.-Fri. noon-4 p.m. & 5:30 p.m.-11 p.m.

If the tourists who watch the Changing of the Guard knew of the existence of Tiles, it would be swamped, situated as it is halfway between Buckingham Palace and Victoria Station. Don't let the chipped paint and carefully cultivated anything-goes atmosphere put you off—it has a far better wine list than do many expensive restaurants. The ground-floor bar is usually taken up by those who order a bottle and never move. Tables are easier to come by downstairs, where the Cabernet Sauvignon–red walls may remind you of Santa Claus's grotto in a department store. Among the wines are a house Champagne from Marniquet and a fine nonvintage Veuve Clicquot Yellow Label. Spanish sparkling wine is half the price of the French Champagnes, and there are some original touches among the white wines, such as a Viura Rioja from Cune, an Italian Chardonnay and Louis Gisselbrecht Pinot Blanc from Alsace. Unusual reds include a Saumur, a Montana Cabernet Sauvignon from New Zealand and the Mirassou Gamay Beaujolais from California. To accompany your wine, we can suggest the chicken-and-nut salad and vegetable roulade in the summer and the vegetable pasta with salad any time. Nicely grilled fish generally figures on the menu, and the kitchen does some terrific American Independence Day dishes in the first week of July: Californian scrambled ham, yummy waffles.

CHELSEA

Bill Bentley's
31 Beauchamp Pl., SW3 - 589 5080
Open Mon.-Sat. 11:30 a.m.-3 p.m. & 5:30 p.m.-11 p.m.

Bill Bentley's is a famous name in fish restaurants, not always associated with wine bars. But you'll find at least 30 wines by the glass if you visit the small, rarefied bar, paneled in dark wood. Much of the food is cold, with oysters de rigueur in season, prompting a glass of the excellent house Champagne. Mussels and potted shrimps are thirst-inducing, so why not refresh the glass? Hot soup is also served, along with cold meats, but upstairs it's seafood all the way, along with a thoughtful wine list that does the fish justice (strong on whites from Burgundy, Alsace and the Loire). You will sometimes find Queen Victoria's favorite tipple from the Rhine: Deinhard's famous Hochheimer Konigin Viktoria Berg Kabinett. Tell your guest that this wine was responsible for naming all Rhine wines "hock," and you'll gain points for your savoir faire.

Charco's
Entrances at 1 Bray Pl. & 27 Coulson St., SW3 - 584 0765
Open Mon.-Sat. 11 a.m.-3 p.m. & 5:30 p.m.-11 p.m.

Great things have happened to Charco's since its recent takeover by the Ebury Wine Bar people. The bilious yellow walls have been replaced by attractive paneling and small mirrors that reflect the new glories. A salad bar has arrived, which includes smoked chicken and smoked trout. A big new picture window provides a good show of King's Road shoppers strolling past, pausing to admire the new decor and deciding whether or not they should stop in for a restorative glass of the house brut Champagne. The wine bar upstairs is dominated by soundly chosen white Burgundies, Loire and Alsatian whites, Bordeaux and Burgundy reds and a sidelong glance at inexpensive Bergerac. A decent Vin de Pays house wine, red and white, comes from the Pyrénées, and there are a few half bottles. Lavish glasses hold a fifth of a bottle. The restaurant downstairs has a daily change of menu devised by chef Joanna Lawrence, a graduate of Leith's cooking school and the former head chef at the Ebury Wine Bar. Her traditional English repertoire includes grilled entrecôte, roast pork with ginger and grilled lamb cutlets. With its outdoor seating banked with flowers, Charco's is the most Mediterranean-looking of London's wine bars, given the right weather.

Draycott's
114 Draycott Ave., SW3 - 584 5359
Open Mon.-Sat. 11:30 a.m.-3 p.m. & 5:30 p.m.-11 p.m., Sun. 11:30 a.m.-2:30 p.m.

Those who accuse Draycott's of being the most yuppified wine bar in London are probably right. With a smart and snappy decor—tiled floors, potted plants and elegant little mirrors set into paneling—it invariably attracts the fashionable set. But that doesn't stop us from enjoying its highly drinkable house red and white from the south of France, which are served, like all Draycott's wines, in monstrous glasses, equivalent to a quarter of a bottle, that you can barely get your hand around. Of the 30 or more wines on the list, 14 are available by the glass. The Fleuron d'Alsace from Gisselbrecht, the Penfolds South Australian Semillon Chardonnay and the Mâcon Clesse Burgundy stand out among the whites; the

Côtes-du-Rhône, the Château Bonnet from Bordeaux and Château La Louvière enhance the reds. A sophisticated lunch menu might offer lotte, pigeon breasts, stuffed quail and stir-fried squid, and reservations are not always necessary. In the evening, the only nonliquid sustenance is filled croissants and baguettes, served hot from the bar. The Sunday brunch (smoked salmon and scrambled eggs or eggs Benedict) is always a sellout, and all the Champagnes are discounted £2 between 5:30 p.m. and 7:30 p.m. daily.

THE CITY

Balls Brothers
2-3 Old Change Ct., St. Paul's Churchyard, EC4 - 248 8697
Open Mon.-Fri. 11:30 a.m.-7:30 p.m.

Even the most traditional wine bar can move with the times, which has been verified by this Balls Brothers establishment, which opened fifteen years ago. (The two brothers own ten such bars throughout London.) The oh-so-1960s decor (Formica tops, pine screens supporting a false ceiling) has given way to a big L-shape bar in warm oak tones, with a display of bottles stacked above and a galaxy of ceiling spotlights. And though the ubiquitous Liebfraumilch was once a best-seller, the bar now sells only eight bottles of it a week. Look for the chalked notice designating the wine of the day, which could be Australia's Penfold Chardonnay, white Galestro from Tuscany or a lovely Chilean Cabernet, Conche y Toro. The best feature is a hugh plate-glass window with views of a roomy square at the southeast corner of St. Paul's Cathedral and an elevated flower bed. A netball (basketball-like game) pitch occupies half the square outside, and when a team is playing, a window seat is hard to find. Balls Brothers ships its own wines, so it cuts out the middleman and is able to pass on lower prices to its customers. The buffet is confined to vast and generously filled sandwiches (the tuna is outstanding). In winter, hot steak sandwiches are served on French bread with garlic butter. Tables cannot be reserved.

Bow Wine Vaults
10 Bow Churchyard, EC4 - 248 1121
Open Mon.-Fri. 11:30 a.m.-3 p.m. & 5 p.m.-8 p.m.

Be thankful that the Bow bells rarely ring—otherwise you'd be deafened while sitting beneath the bell tower in Bow Churchyard, where this famous old wine bar is located. The main attraction is a magnificent wine list that would put to shame many a toqued restaurant. The primary drawback is a heavy, middle-aged, male atmosphere, with the reek of tobacco sometimes smothering that lingering aftertaste of Château Cissac you had begun to savor. The wines run more to Burgundies than clarets (Bordeaux), though the latter include Châteaux Beycheville, Batailley and Lagrange. The United States is well represented by Joseph Phelps and Firestone, and Bow Wine even carries the highly regarded Château Musar from Lebanon. But turn first to the list of remainders (though not all are cheap) and rejoice in the range of a dozen different half bottles, including a few Champagne halves. Occasional Champagne promotions for a particular house can save a pound or two on the bubbly. The lunchtime crowd falls like vultures on the smoked salmon, crab and sweet corn, and the ham-and-Emmenthal sandwiches, so get your order in while stocks last. Hot salt-beef sandwiches will have you feeling like another glass or two for dessert.

Corney & Barrow Champagne Bar
19 Broadgate Circle, EC2 - 628 1251
Open Mon.-Fri. 7 a.m.-10:30 a.m., 11 a.m.-3 p.m. & 5:30 p.m.-11 p.m.

The best view of the new, somewhat harsher face of the City is from Corney & Barrow's most recent Champagne bar, on the site of the old Broad Street station. It is easily approached from the Liverpool Street station, just to its east, by climbing up the concrete, galleried terraces of Broadgate Circle, where the bar crouches behind a semicircle of glass. Only Champagne is served, and most of the grandes marques are on parade. Young, hard-nosed City slickers order by the magnum from the circular beechwood bar and splash bubbly around as if it were soda pop. Food barely exists, apart from thinly cut slices of crab or smoked-salmon sandwiches. There are plans for an ice rink in the arena below, making Broadgate Circle the closest London equivalent to New York's Rockefeller Plaza. In summer, you can move out onto an open-air terrace, taking your Champagne with you. It's worth visiting for a quick sip before taking in a concert or a play among the equally neo-Brutalist architecture of the Barbican.

Great Eastern Hotel
Liverpool St. & Bishopsgate, EC2
626 7919
Open Mon.-Fri. 11:30 a.m.-3 p.m. & 5 p.m.-7:30 p.m.

You'll find this traditional-style wine bar on the busy corner of Liverpool Street and Bishopsgate. An authentic chunk of British Railwayana, it was turned into a rather raunchy beer house before being taken over by Balls Brothers five years ago. A stunning marble staircase and cavernous tile ceiling stopped the developers from knocking it down; otherwise, warm mahogany predominates. A dozen white and red wines are poured by the glass from a large tub in the bar. The wine list is predictably French, boosted by eight German hocks (Rhine wines) and Mosels, and prices are generally reasonable. A highly drinkable house Champagne, Vicomte d'Almon, is a top seller, followed by Louis Roederer, and the choice of five ports and two Madeiras befits a City establishment. About a dozen wines can be ordered by the half bottle, though few bother, since this place is popular with a good many serious drinkers. If you arrive after 12:15 p.m., your sandwich lunch may have to be eaten on the hoof, as seats are quickly occupied. The customary form is to order your sandwich at the door as soon as you arrive, choosing between smoked salmon, gravlax, avocado and bacon and Torbay crab. Fillings are generous. The cheeses tried hard to be British, but there was such an outcry over the much-hated Lymeswold that Brie hastily replaced it.

The Greenhouse
16-17 Royal Exch., EC3 - 929 1799
Open Mon.-Fri. 11:30 a.m.-3 p.m. & 5 p.m.-8 p.m.

Some London mapmakers fail to mark Royal Exchange street, which is a few yards west of Bank, sandwiched between Cornhill and Threadneedle Street among the great City companies, with their well-scrubbed brass plates. The present Royal Exchange building, once the site of the Stock Exchange, houses the London International Futures Exchange, the only trading floor left in Britain where futures are verbally traded. The floor traders and discount brokers are tough, purposeful young people with brass lungs and wildly colored blazers that make them look like refugees from the Henley Regatta. They drink at The Greenhouse, London's smallest Champagne and wine bar, and clutching bottles of grand marque Champagne, they spill out onto the wide sidewalk outside, where there are wooden seats and a forbidding bust of bewhiskered Baron Paul Julius Reuter, the famous journalist. The Floquet house Champagne is light and very good as well as cheap, and there are regular money-saving promotions of particular brands. The menu is strictly limited to king prawns, pies, quails' eggs and (on Wednesdays only) spicy Italian sausage that's a real treat. Table wines, supplied by Green's, the City wine merchant that owns the place, include the Premier Cru Chablis Fourchaume among whites and Louis Latour's Morgon among reds. Service is amazingly deft, changing to near-instantaneous when Wall Street opens and the blazered ones disappear as if by magic in pursuit of making more big money.

The Pavilion
Finsbury Circus Gdns., EC2 - 628 8224
Open Mon.-Fri. 11:30 a.m.-3 p.m. & 5 p.m.-8 p.m. (restaurant closed evenings).

To be able to sip your wine in the heart of financial London, looking out onto a broad green swath, makes the Pavilion unlike any other City wine bar. It was originally a bowling green pavilion before wine-bar wizard David Gilmour converted it, retaining much of the original sporting character. There are splendid framed cartoons of funny looking characters playing French boule ball, and the ceiling's wooden paneling has been extended to the bar. Its light, airy look attracts a good many City yuppies, many of them in corporate finance or insurance, imperiously brandishing their credit cards. A handwritten wine list, enlivened with Gilmour's helpful tasting notes, starts with grandes marques Champagnes, and the excitement mounts with superbly chosen claret, Burgundy and Loire wines. Look for the "second wines" of great Bordeaux houses, some unusual white Rhônes or a Jean Leon Chardonnay from the Spanish Penedes. Every month there's a different theme of wines by the glass, with a choice of two sizes. The daily changing bar menu is prepared fresh in the French-provincial style: flans, terrines and salads. A full, classic French menu is served downstairs, where the old changing rooms once were. And if you order a case of wine from Gilmour's trade list, it will be delivered in London the same afternoon.

Punters

5 Abchurch Yd., Abchurch Ln., EC4
623 2355
Open Mon.-Fri. 11:30 a.m.-3 p.m. & 5 p.m.-10 p.m.

Abchurch Lane, a narrow alley just off the north side of Cannon Street at the London Bridge end, leads to Abchurch Yard, which is home to this wine bar occupying a former bank vault. Note the pressed-steel safe door behind the bar, which leads nowhere but is too heavy to move. Manager Suzie Poyser employs ten women, calls them "my boys" and claims them as one reason why 80 percent of her customers are regulars. The clientele is fascinating, starting with the rich East End salesmen in white socks and trendy ties who lunch at 11:30 a.m. and drink pink Champagne. They give way to the money brokers around noon, followed by the bankers. Tables in small arcades are quickly snapped up by customers sampling the hot or cold buffet. The more leisurely head for the dining room, where they lunch on veal cutlets and smoked chicken with papaw salad. House wines are a red Cabernet Sauvignon de l'Aude and a white Bordeaux, and the wine list is traditionally French, though it also includes eight Australian wines and a few outsiders, such as Portuguese Dao, Chianti riserva, a Marques de Caceres Rioja and a Californian Mountain View. All the big names in Champagne are in evidence, and they're discounted £2 per bottle from 5 p.m. to 6:30 p.m. The choice of decanted ports is substantial. The same faces are seen day after day, and the regulars prefer to keep Punters to themselves—for good reason.

Whittington's

21 College Hill, EC4 - 248 5855
Open Mon.-Fri. 11:30 a.m.-3 p.m. & 5 p.m.-7:30 p.m.

The fame of the à la carte restaurant at Whittington's, where everything is fresh and made on the premises, has almost obscured the fact that it is also one of the City's most atmospheric cellar wine bars, with legends of old London practically seeping from the stones. The building goes back to the days preceding the Great Fire of London of 1666, when Dick Whittington actually lived there. After hiking through the rambling cellars to reach the bar perimeter, but before immersing yourself in the fairly comprehensive wine list, take a look at the short selection of wines by the glass, then note the blackboard specials. If you want a special bottle, take note of the range of petits châteaux from Bordeaux (more imaginative than most) and the Spanish and Italian wines. The kitchen does not stint in its portions of bar food (scampi and steaks), and most customers share tables quite happily, making for a friendly, convivial atmosphere, with perfect strangers sampling and commenting on one anothers' wine choices.

COVENT GARDEN

Bar des Amis
Café des Amis du Vin

11-14 Hanover Pl., WC2 - 379 3444
Open Mon.-Sat. 11:30 a.m.-3 p.m. & 5:30 p.m.-11:30 p.m.; café open Mon.-Sat. noon-11:30 p.m.

Consternation followed when Trust House Forte took over the Bar des Amis in 1988. But the worry proved unnecessary, for it continues on under its own steam just as before. It's still crowded at lunchtime with shoppers, who give way to dinner jackets and sweeping cloaks in the evening, when operagoers arrive in force. Make your way down the steps to the café and you'll find yourself in a diminutive, three-sided bar with a fair range of wines by the glass. The bar is strong on Beaujolais (a characteristic Côte-de-Brouilly and Fleurie from Duboeuf) and French regional wines with lots of character, such as red Chinon. Food might be described as French country style: herby sausages, omelets, pâtés and other charcuterie and a fair range of salads. Don't miss the plat du jour, which is always well chosen, whether it's a mussel salad or a veal sauté. If you don't mind missing the overture at the Royal Opera House, linger on a few extra minutes for the oh-so-French tarte du jour. Reservations are accepted for the brasserie, but not for the bar.

EARL'S COURT

Ashbees
22 Hogarth Pl., SW5 - 373 6180
Open Mon.-Fri. noon-3 p.m. & 5:30 p.m.-11 p.m., Sat. 7 p.m.-11 p.m., Sun. 7 p.m.-10:30 p.m.

Earl's Court is bed-sitter territory, and many of the bed-sits were occupied by Australians until the mid-1970s. When these wine-bar-loving locals departed, a number of wine bars put up their shutters, but Ashbees seems determined to survive. It's easily found opposite Earl's Court tube, between a small walkway and Hogarth Road. A staircase leads to three connecting rooms with a choice of two bars, so it's deceptively spacious compared to the size of its entrance. Wines used to be mainly French, but the list has been enlarged and is now more adventurous. The 70 wines, by the bottle or the glass, now embrace Italy, Spain, Greece and Chile, the food is freshly cooked, and the atmosphere is pleasant and informal. The regularly changing blackboard menu lists crudités, quiches and taramasalata (fish roe purée served as a dip with crusty bread) at fair prices, with French cheeses and pastries to follow. Now and again there's a violinist or guitarist; otherwise music is taped. You can even bring along your own tape, if you've always wanted to be able to say, "Darling, they're playing our song."

FULHAM

Crocodile Tears
660 Fulham Rd., SW6 - 73l 1537
Open Mon.-Sat. noon-11 p.m., Sun. noon-4 p.m. & 7 p.m.-10:30 p.m.

Many of those who began patronizing Crocodile Tears when it opened eight years ago are still regulars. And it's no wonder—it's one of the most popular wine bars in Fulham, full of jolly, extroverted people, who have no doubt booked a day ahead to secure one of the nineteen tables downstairs. There is a substantial wine list if you are buying by the bottle, strong on classic French bottlings but not forgetting Spain, Italy and Portugal. If buying by the glass, you can choose between one that holds two-fifths of a bottle or the smaller size. And ask for the "specials" lists, which usually offer bargains from Australia or California, depending on the most recent fortuitious purchases. The restaurant menu includes a number of dishes of Mediterranean inspiration, such as mezes (Greek mixed hors d'ouevres), feta cheese salad, large garlicky prawns and seafood stew. On a warm day, Pimms served by the glass, jug, large jug or "megajug" fairly hits the spot, and can be enjoyed on the outdoor terrace in back, surrounded by cool greenery.

HOLBORN

Bleeding Heart Wine Bar
Bleeding Heart Yd., Greville St., EC2
242 8238
Open Mon.-Fri. 11 a.m.-3 p.m. & 5:30 p.m.-11 p.m.

Get out your *London A-Z* street directory to locate this wine bar, which is mysteriously tucked away down some stairs in a courtyard between Hatton Garden and Saffron Hill. The hunt will prove worthwhile, because whoever put together this wine list has located good, out-of-the-way bottles from all over the world. You can't go wrong with the Bordeaux, as nearly all the staff is French, though the wines from Italy, Portugal, Spain, California, Australia and New Zealand add tremendous zing and variety to the collection. The house Champagne is Heidsieck Dry Monopole, no less. With so many Fleet Street offices now closed, this is one of the few wine bars where you'll find newspaper reporters from the nearby *Daily Mail* building exchanging the gossip of the day. Photographers and ad agency types add to the buzz and clamor, which reaches a crescendo at Friday lunch, when paychecks come into view. The menu has been given a mighty face-lift in the last few years; especially worthwhile is the fish brochette (all the fish is bought daily from Billingsgate Market). And you can't go wrong with the smoked salmon omelet or the three varieties of French sausage. There's always an inexpensive red and white wine of the day for the budget-minded.

Bung Hole

57 High Holborn, WC1 - 242 4318
Open Mon.-Fri. 11 a.m.-4 p.m. & 5 p.m.-8:30 p.m.

If you make your way east from the top of Chancery Lane along High Holborn, you may be in for a rather nasty architectural shock, as you proceed from the chaste stone gateway of Gray's Inn law courts to the tormented terra cotta of Southampton Buildings and on to a severe red-brick Gothic slab of an insurance office. Opposite the Weather Centre stands the reassuring Bung Hole, with warm wood paneling, sawdust on the floor and flickering candles on the tables. Wines are mostly French, with one or two hocks and Moselles and a fine, soft red Californian Clos du Bois. But look first at the list of special offers, generally five whites and three reds, depending on the owner's lucky purchases. The food is basic (but good) fare: cold meats, smoked salmon, prawns and hot potatoes. For a lunch out, try the newly added, air-conditioned Bung Hole Cellars, which seats 120. Its char-grilled steaks, sandwiches or calf's liver and bacon, along with wine, beer or a restorative drop of Cognac, will help you face the architectural horrors outside.

KENSINGTON

Jimmie's Wine Bar

18 Kensington Church St., W8 - 937 9988
Open Mon.-Sat. noon-3 p.m. & 5:30 p.m.-11 p.m., Sun. noon-2 p.m. & 7 p.m.-10 p.m.

A funny thing happened to Jimmie's. The owners moved it, lock, stock and barrel, from its old site in Kensington Barracks (now torn down) and relocated it a few yards away on the same side of the street. Everything was lovingly and exactingly re-created: the same tables, the same guttering candles, the same slightly tobacco-fumed sporting prints on the walls. They even moved the venerable pews. So the same people go there: local business people for lunch and, in the evenings, an older crowd for whom time, like Jimmie's, has mercifully stood still. The wine list is not quite so short as it was, and there's always a wine of the month, generally a good value, plus a selection of beers. Grills are still done to order over a charcoal fire, and

there are reasonably priced salads, though they're usually a bit wilted by the end of the evening. No one has ever heard of the house Champagne, Roulette, but it's a zingy little number that's extremely popular.

KNIGHTSBRIDGE

Maxie's

143 Knightsbridge, SW1 - 225 2553
Open Mon.-Sat. 11 a.m.-3:30 p.m. & 5:30 p.m.-11:30 p.m.

Since it opened as a Chinese wine bar two or three years back, Maxie's has really caught on—that is, once the news got around that wine really does go with good Peking fare. Don't expect Chinese wine to be offered, though. Most customers opt (and rightly so) for a dryish white wine, such as French Muscadet, Chablis or Mâcon Villages or an Italian Frascati, and you won't go wrong if you follow their example, though a light red Beaujolais sets off a basket of hot spareribs rather well. Whether you sit at the bar or find a table, you have the same choice of food: sole with soy sauce, crab and steamed sea bass with ginger. Sweet-and-sour prawns, spring rolls and sizzling lamb are delicious when devoured with various sauces. There's live music in the evenings (piano or jazz), dancing, too, and the staff is kept running on Thursday and Friday evenings, Maxie's two big nights.

Le Métro

Capital Hotel, 28 Basil St., SW3 - 589 6286
Open Mon.-Fri. 7:30 a.m.-11 p.m., Sat. 7:30 a.m.-3:30 p.m.

Just a few steps behind Harrods, Le Métro is certainly one of London's smartest basement rooms, with a cleverly designed bar surrounded by light paneling that gives a sense of airiness and space. Behind the bar is a machine that preserves wine once bottles are opened, so you can be sure that any of the ten wines you order by the glass will be beautifully fresh. Since the buyer concentrates on top shippers, such as Louis Jadot for Burgundies, top prices must also be expected. With ten first-rate Loire wines to choose from and seven Alsatians, this is not a place for those in a great hurry. So take your time over the lengthy wine list, giving the delicious still Champagne, a wine bar rarity, at least a passing glance. Food from the Capital's kitchens is miles ahead of that of most wine bars, with duck rillettes, filet of lamb and smoked fish pâté recurring on the daily changing menu. You can opt for a full meal or a single course. Le Métro is a haven for shoppers, who sometimes seem a bit subdued, no doubt because their feet are killing them.

LEICESTER SQUARE

Le Beaujolais
25 Litchfield St., WC2 - 836 2277
Open Mon.-Fri. noon-3:30 p.m. & 5:30 p.m.-11 p.m., Sat. 5:30 p.m.-11 p.m.

If you're the kind of Francophile who enjoys picnicking on French rillettes, pâté and spicy Merguez sausage, washed down with an inexpensive bottle of wine, then the fare here is possibly the closest London equivalent you'll find. You can hardly miss the place, given the sign's big, flamboyant lettering, the mullioned window in bottle glass and the enticing garlic smells drifting out of the door. The only un-French thing about the place is serving wine by the glass, so it charges a bit above the going rate for that, given that their glasses are decidedly small. Settle instead for a bottle of Beaujolais—from ten individual vintners—or try a Rhône, Loire or Provençal wine from the handwritten list. The blackboard always pinpoints a wine of the month that is generally worth a try, and both the house red from the Côtes-de-Ventoux and the white from the Loire are eminently drinkable. Fewer than 40 can cram themselves into the available space, and tables cannot be reserved, so sharing with others is commonplace, which makes for a convivial, noisy crowd. Apart from basic picnic food, you might find hot game pie, braised ham and peach or smoked-chicken salad. The Pineau des Charentes from the Cognac area, which is a bit like white port, makes an unusual sweetish apéritif. The 96 club neckties hanging from the ceiling include most of the best regiments, public schools and sporting associations. Give them no more than a passing glance—many a gentleman has seen his cherished tie added to the collection after commenting on the display.

Cork and Bottle
44-46 Cranbourn St., WC2 - 734 7807
Open Mon.-Sat. 11 a.m.-3 p.m. & 5:30 p.m.-11 p.m., Sun. noon-2 p.m. & 7 p.m.-10:30 p.m.

Sometimes described as Leicester Square's most civilized watering hole, the Cork and Bottle is run by New Zealander Don Hewitson—hence the mouth-watering selection of wines from Down Under. The bar is a bit down under the street, in a basement garden center that gets so crowded between 12:30 and 1:30 p.m. that only an early or late lunch can save an onset of claustrophobia. Hewitson is an enthusiast who has 150 wines in stock and changes the list constantly by way of special offers. Sometimes he would have you drink Spanish wines, sometimes Beaujolais, sometimes Californians, sometimes sparklers; you might as well give in quietly and go along with his latest discovery. Every day a different wine of note is poured by the glass, and glasses are the generous quarter-bottle size. The tempting array of dishes on the counter, three of them hot, can include ham and cheese pie, Toulouse casserole, Lincolnshire sausages and Greek salad. Desserts and well-kept French and English cheeses are available for those without waistline problems, and if you order a special bottle for a special occasion, the hosts may insist on serving a couple of complimentary glasses of Champagne to sip while the wine "breathes."

Volker Europa Wine Bar
18 Orange St., WC2 - 930 2905
Open Mon.-Fri. 11 a.m.-3 p.m. & 5:30 p.m.-11 p.m.

With the curtain going up at most theaters at 7:30 or 8 p.m., a quick, filling pretheater meal is not always easy to find. The tiny Volker, just off the Haymarket, is not only perfectly situated in the Shaftesbury Avenue area but also serves such life restorers as delicious pea soup with frankfurters and baked potatoes with such fillings as sour cream, cottage cheese, prawns and herring. The bustling proprietor is a former catering civil servant who ran German Food Centres, so it didn't surprise us to see the distinctly German accent in the food: smoked ham and pepper salami sandwiches, herring rollmop in sour cream sauce. Pâtés, salads and cheeses are also featured. There is no wine list as such, only a blackboard with simple names, such as Soave, Mâcon

Villages and Piesporter (among the whites) and Chianti, Brouilly and Fleurie (among the reds); more guidance really would help. The Champagne list is sizable, including vintage bottles and rosés, and Lanson Black Label is available in any size from a little half bottle to a mighty Nebuchadnezzar (the impossibly unwieldy twenty-bottle size). If the place is packed at lunch, look for a decorative milk churn and perch on that. The more adventurous order rum babas, high-spirited concoctions that are supposed to be swallowed in a single (highly alcoholic) gulp.

LONDON BRIDGE

Hay's Galleria Fish Restaurant and Wine Bar

Hay's Wharf, Tooley St., SE1 - 407 4301
Open Mon.-Fri. 11:30 a.m.-9 p.m. (restaurant also open Sun. lunch).

Once a depressed docklands street on the south side of London Bridge, Tooley Street came up rapidly in the world in 1987, thanks to one of London's most imaginative developments, on the site of the old, waterlogged Hay's Wharf. The galleria, with rows of trendy shops on both sides, has a spectacular glass barrel-vaulted roof. Enter from Tooley Street and you'll find this fish restaurant and wine bar down a few steps on the right. Inside is an agreeable mixture of barristers, City folk from the other side of the river and doctors from two nearby hospitals. Wine is served by the bottle or by the glass, with a fair range of half bottles and a heavy emphasis on French vineyards. Generously cut sandwiches, fairly bulging with crab, chicken or smoked salmon, can be taken to an outside table, where there's a view of London's most eccentric piece of sculpture, *The Navigator*. Made of scrap iron and sitting in sludgy green water, it looks a bit like a foreshortened paddleboat, with mobiles whirling atop the mast and jets of water spewing out from unlikely places. Or you can have a full three-course meal in the fish restaurant downstairs. The menu starts with a choice of a dozen starters, then goes on to well-cooked fresh-fish dishes, which are changed daily and come straight from the market. After dinner, stroll to the river to admire the HMS *Belfast*, moored opposite, and the lights of London reflected romantically on the Thames.

Skinkers

42-46 Tooley St., SE1 - 407 9189
Open Mon.-Fri. 11:30 a.m.-3:30 p.m. & 5:30 p.m.-8:30 p.m.

To find Skinkers, join Tooley Street at the south end of London Bridge, just beside the station, and walk east past the London Dungeon Museum. Next door to the museum, tucked underneath the railway arches, Skinkers is one of 40 wine bars under the flag of the John Davy wine company. The Dickensian formula is the same in each, and it never palls. There are flickering candles, old, brooding casks on sawdusty floors, blackened beams athwart low ceilings and spooky corners ideal for secret business deals. Since it really is a former warehouse, Skinkers is one of the most convincing of the chain. It rambles on past the bar, where you can either fill up on sandwiches or reserve a table for a hearty "olde English" lunch of game pie, smoked chicken or chargrilled steak, preceded by potted shrimp, smoked salmon or pâté. The large selection of wines benefits from John Davy's clever buying. Red and white house wines from Loron are good values, as is the house Rioja. Note the generous glass size—about a quarter of a bottle. There are some 45 clarets on the list, along with 20 or so vintages of Château Latour, spanning the years 1881 to 1971. The house Champagne is Veuve Clicquot Yellow Label, and there is a fine range of vintage ports by the glass or bottle, though you should give 48 hours' notice for proper decanting of the bottles. All in all, Skinkers is a wine lover's fantasy come true.

MAYFAIR

L'Autre

5B Shepherd St., W1 - 499 4680
Open Mon.-Fri. noon-3 p.m. & 5:30 p.m.-11 p.m.

In this eighteenth-century corner of London, among a bustling hive of small houses and shops all painted to the nines, is this tiny bar specializing, most improbably, in Mexican food cooked by a Polish chef. Tostadas, burritos and enchiladas are her forte, along with an imaginative array of seafood and smoked dishes, plus the occasional Polish dish, which is a sure bet. The wines are primarily classic French, but the collection has been enlarged to include Italian Frascati, Chardonnay and Verdicchio among the whites, three worthwhile Italian reds and the outstanding Cune Imperial Riserva Rioja. Or you can order by the generous glassful from a dozen bottles listed on the blackboard over the bar. Another board indicates the bargain red and white bottles of the day; Kir and Bucks Fizz are usually available, too. The atmosphere is nostalgically 1930s, with Noël Coward songs on tape and stills from '30s movies on the walls. Foreign-currency banknotes, no doubt worthless, are pinned to beams. The "specialty" coffee, heavily laced with liqueur or brandy, imparts much inner cheer when the rain's falling heavily outside.

Burlington's

23 Conduit St., W1 - 491 1188
Open Mon.-Fri. 11:30 a.m.-3 p.m. & 5:30 p.m.-11 p.m.

This old salad bar has been turned into a restaurant, where you can settle down to a hot dish or, of course, a salad, for which Burlington's has always been noted. That means the bar, just at the entrance, is where most of the action takes place. Burlington's has a resourceful list of vegetarian dishes, soups, sandwiches and pâtés, accompanied by petits châteaux Bordeaux from rather good vintages, a scattering of hearty reds from the Rhône and lots of lesser-knowns from Italy, Spain, Portugal and South Africa. For an instant uplift, order the dry, sparkling Freixenet Cordon Negro from Spain. Burlington's is an oasis for brave souls meeting the Oxford Street sales head-on, enhanced by elegant surroundings, plenty of greenery and service that is simultaneously brisk and friendly. There's a choice of about a dozen wines by the glass, the price varying according to the size of the glass.

Chopper Lump

10C Hanover Sq., W1 - 499 7569
Open Mon.-Fri. 11:30 a.m.-9 p.m.

The Chopper Lump is light and bright for a Davy house, despite the sawdust on the floors and the doubtful authenticity of the exposed beams. The bar is at the entrance, and the underground restaurant stretches away in the distance (most customers prefer to reserve a restaurant table at least a day in advance, espe-

cially when Oxford Street is en fête with sales or Christmas). Davy's white Burgundy, a Montagny Premier Cru, is an exceptional value among the whites, ditto the house red Graves at the same price. There are more reds than whites on the list, and these are particularly strong on single estate Beaujolais and Burgundies. Clarets are completely reliable. You can drink Champagne and Bucks Fizz by the tankard, and the house Champagne is the elegant Piper Heidsieck. As you've probably guessed by now, French wines rule the roost, though a glass of Sercial Madeira makes an original apéritif, and there are ports from the wood. The cooking is most filling in a thoroughly English sort of way, primarily steaks and cold meats and desserts that are a throwback to an Englishman's old-school dinners of yore. The well-kept Stilton is our preference.

Yates Wine Lodge

11 Avery Row, W1 - 629 1643
Open Mon.-Fri. 11:30 a.m.-3 p.m. & 5:30 p.m.-9 p.m.

You may need one of those large-scale London maps of the heart of the West End, because Yates, tucked in a narrow alley behind Bond Street and off Grosvenor Street, takes a bit of finding. But the safari is always worthwhile, with an escape hatch at the end of the trail from the 1980s into a pre–Great War world of bare boards, mirrors, wood paneling and Pimms No. 1 by the tankard. The menu, produced only at lunch, is simple and a bit stark. But the homemade soup has plenty of flavor, and the home-boiled ham, smoked turkey and meat pies can be greatly enlivened with a bottle of Hill Smith Cabernet Sauvignon from Australia or a Torres Coronas from Spain. The white-wine lover might turn to France for Bourgogne Aligoté or, perhaps, an inexpensive Gewürztraminer. Tried-and-trusted French names dominate the wine list. If you pop in at happy hour (between 5:30 and 7), several pounds will be deducted from the price of a bottle of Champagne. Yates belongs to a Manchester chain of wine bars; it's a no-nonsense sort of place, but there's a crying need for a more detailed wine list.

NOTTING HILL

Meson Dona Ana
37 Kensington Park Rd., W11 - 243 0666
*Open Mon.-Sat. noon-3 p.m. & 5:30 p.m.-11
p.m.*

It's hard to miss this bright, cheerful Spanish wine and tapas bar occupying a key corner site at the north end of otherwise gray and dreary Kensington Park Road. The tables that fill up first on bright, sunny days are those lining the pavement. Spaniards never drink without eating the traditional tapas dishes: grilled sardines, cured ham and garlicky prawns, which you'll find well represented here, along with 25 others, such as kidneys in sherry sauce, wild mushrooms with green peppers and spicy Spanish sausage. They're surprisingly cheap, they're delicious, and the all-Spanish wine list is large and imaginative, from Rioja to Jumilla, Navarra to Ribeiro del Duero. In summer, try a Spanish sparkler from Penedes or a half bottle of San Patricio fino sherry; in winter, a warming red Crianza Rioja. The fuller menu includes such exotica as swordfish steamed with wine and baby squid; the lentil soup is excellent. Meson Dona Ana is crowded to the doors and pretty noisy at peak hours, and tables cannot be reserved. A guitarist puts in an appearance in the evening starting at 8:30.

192
192 Kensington Park Rd., W11 - 229 0482
*Open Mon.-Sat. 12:30 p.m.-3 p.m. & 5:30 p.m.-
11:30 p.m., Sun. 1 p.m.-3 p.m.*

Don't be put off by the unprepossessing entrance, because 192 (just around the corner from the Portobello Road market) boasts an extraordinarily upscale list of wines. Many are from Corney & Barrow, wine merchants to Buckingham Palace, no less. And you have only to go down the futuristic staircase past the horseshoe-shape bar to enter a different world, with a softly lit restaurant serving a full à la carte menu. There is always a featured wine special, which is generally reasonably priced; otherwise, you can choose from pricey Burgundies from well-known shippers, a decent choice of petits châteaux Bordeaux and a much more affordable "House Selection" of German, Portuguese, Italian and Provençal wines.

Stick to these for the best value for the money. The place is crawling with Bright Young Things, many in advertising or the rag trade, so the decibel count rises at peak times. The wild salmon makes a nifty starter, and entrées run to such good things as braised duck, red mullet and grilled veal; everything seems fresh. Those on the wagon will appreciate the real orange juice.

REGENT'S PARK & MARYLEBONE

Boos
1 Glentworth St. & Marylebone Rd., NW1
935 3827
*Open Mon.-Fri. 11:30 a.m.-3 p.m. & 5:30 p.m.-
8 p.m. (closed 3 weeks in Sept. & 2 weeks at
Christmas).*

If you feel like a small pick-me-up after plodding around the Chamber of Horrors at Madame Tussaud's, head for Boos, a chatty, cheerful place where most of the customers are regulars, busy catching up with one another's news since they last met at this Tudor-style wine bar with small tables. There are no extortionate prices on the wine list, and the house wines, such as Willm's Pinot Blanc from Alsace, are helpfully served by the bottle, half liter or glass. There are eight other Alsatian wines, just to show what Francophiles the owners are, and you can go in for some serious drinking among top clarets (these, of course, can never be cheap). Nearly all the food is freshly homemade—from soups and salads to the Alsace onion flan and the mayonnaise on the poached salmon. Order a glass of the sweet, luscious Muscat de Rivesaltes with homemade cheesecake, for which Boos is famous, and you could almost face another round of the Chamber of Horrors.

Odette's
136 Regent's Park Rd., NW1 - 586 5486
*Open Mon.-Sat. 12:30 p.m.-3 p.m. & 5 p.m.-11
p.m.*

Tucked away beneath a busy restaurant and flanked by the abrupt slope of Primrose Hill, Odette's is located in an area near the zoo that's a bit of a gastronomic desert. There are plenty of cozy alcoves in which to sink, and you'll need a minute or two to work through the wine list of 60 names. Your decision is made easier by the useful capsule descriptions of every wine, often indicating the food it partners best. House wines are the red and white Vin de Pays de L'Aude, but the real buff might go for one of the 20 petits châteaux from Bordeaux or browse happily among Australian, Californian, Spanish and Italian bottlings, all shrewdly chosen. The food specials are chalked up on a board behind the bar, though you can hardly go wrong with the regular menu items: pork Cordon Bleu, venison sausage, a steak sandwich or the chef's own Mad Max salad, composed of chicken, tuna, cheese and croutons. The great shuddering roar heard dimly in the distance may denote feeding time for the lions as well. Champagnes run from a sound house nonvintage to the great Bollinger 1976.

Wolsey's Wine Bar

52 Wells St., W1 - 636 5121
Open Mon.-Fri. 11 a.m.-3 p.m. & 5:30 p.m.-11 p.m.

You always get the feeling that customers are firmly ensconced in Wolsey's Wine Bar and that time is of no great object. That could be because the place is well removed from the Oxford Street throngs, just opposite the Independent Television News studios—which explains the occasional television personality in the roomy, semicircular bar. Any wine on the list that sells for less than £8 a bottle is available by the glass, and they believe in big glasses here. A well-balanced selection of half bottles, matching any dish on the menu, is posted on the blackboard; in fact, you soon realize that no wine appears on the list (which is especially strong on the classics) without good reason. The wine bar features a number of vegetarian dishes, supplemented by an imaginative range of French country cheeses, served with salad and bread. Fish, however, is the restaurant's great strength.

Zazou

74 Charlotte St., W1 - 436 5133
Open Mon.-Sat. 11:30 a.m.-3 p.m. & 5:30 p.m.-11 p.m.

You'll find this all-French wine bar and restaurant within a stone's throw of the Post Office (or Telecom) Tower. At its foot, TV folk from Channel 4 and sharp advertising people from Saatchi & Saatchi congregate. You'll find them in their faultlessly cut suits,

talking shop among themselves at the piano/wine bar or heading for the brasserie if entertaining clients. The most popular dishes at the bar are Chinese spring rolls, prawn toast and calamari; other good choices include the salade niçoise and a sampling from the cheese board. Everything else, especially in the restaurant downstairs, speaks with a pronounced French-Mediterranean accent. All wines are French and a bit pricey, with Sancerre and Champagne the common tipple among the jeunesse dorée and the lesser known Mercurey from Burgundy among the pick of the reds. The fish, "fresh from Billingsgate and Boulogne," cannot be faulted; we suggest you order it steamed with fresh ginger, spring onions and soy sauce, or abandon thoughts of further work that afternoon and go for the generously proportioned seafood platter. The young French waiters, all from Marseilles, are still struggling with their English lessons, which, if anything, adds to their charm.

ST. JAMES'S

Biggles

17-22 Masons Yd., Duke St., SW1
930 4859
Open Mon.-Fri. noon-3 p.m. & 5:30 p.m.-11 p.m.

This part of London is full of old yards where the stable blocks used to be when it was the smartest part of town in which to live. Don't be put off by the empty ground-floor entrance hall—everything happens downstairs in a large, spacious area that is nicely divided into two bars, one for eating and one for drinking, with lots of tables. Biggles is quite elegant, comfortable and welcoming, though the wine list is not particularly imaginative; the Bordeaux and Beaujolais are the most interesting offerings. And nothing's particularly cheap, but then this is St. James's. There is the inevitable range of Champagnes but a surprisingly poor choice of ports, and house wines are best avoided. The traditional food isn't cheap either, though it is attractively displayed, and the salad bar looks appealing. Biggles gets quite busy at lunchtime, so if you want to eat, make reservations or be prepared to sit on a stool at the bar.

Crown's

3-4 Crown Passage, SW1 - 839 3960
Open Mon.-Fri. 9:30 a.m.-7:30 p.m.

At least one successful West End restaurateur began his climb to the top on Crown Passage, this charming little alleyway off Pall Mall and within earshot of the sentries stamping away outside St. James's Palace—Bob Peyton opened his Chicago Pizza Pie Factory here in 1977 and cleaned up. Crown's tiny wine bar does a bang-up business at lunchtime, but waitresses seem to be employed only if they smile most of the time, so you won't mind a short wait. Burgundy is the pillar of the wine list—the house wines are a red and a white Burgundy from famed shippers Ropiteau and other choices include Gevrey Chambertin from Mommessin and a Premier Cru Chablis from Fourchaume. The house Champagne is nonvintage Bollinger. For everyday drinking, the Frascati Candida from Italy and the Pinot Blanc from Alsace are nice, tangy whites, and the red Chinon from the Loire is light and fruity. All the food is prepared fresh on the premises, with rather predictable starters followed by racier entrées, such as zucchini and prawns au gratin and beef with orange. A choice of eight salads and hearty English puddings, such as treacle tart and apple pie, complete the menu. Coffee is Italian. The daily menu changes are indicated by beautiful copperplate handwriting on the blackboard.

Green's Champagne Bar

36 Duke St., SW1 - 930 4566
Open Mon.-Sat. 11 a.m.-3 p.m. & 5:30 p.m.-11 p.m., Sun. noon-3:45 p.m.

You don't *have* to order Champagne here, but you may find yourself rather out of place if you settle for ordinary table wine. Green's is companion to the Greenhouse (see The City above), and it's owned by the same wine merchants. But here in St. James's the pace is more sedate and the customers more florid, as befits the West End's most exclusive area, with its clubs, wine shops, art galleries and major auctioneers. So settle into one of the little alcoves and order at least a glass of the house Champagne to wash down some of the best oysters in London. Lobster, crab, salmon and quails' eggs are also impeccable. As you might expect from the seafood cuisine, the emphasis is on white wines, especially the French classics. The restaurant, an extension of the bar, has a broader wine list and is famous for its fish cakes and such traditional British nursery food as shepherd's pie and bangers (sausages) and mash (using, of course, only the most aristocratic sausages). If you come up from the country to sell an heirloom at Christie's or to buy a picture, where else but Green's would do for a discreet celebration? There's often a famous face in the restaurant, where the Royal Family has been known to reserve a table on cook's night off and where Princess Diana once sipped champers (British slang for Champagne) at the bar.

SOHO

Shampers

4 Kingly St., W1 - 437 1692
Open Mon.-Fri. 11 a.m.-3 p.m. & 5:30 p.m.-11 p.m., Sat. 11 a.m.-3 p.m.

If it is possible to be off the beaten path and yet within yards of Regent Street, Shampers has achieved it. You'll find it on a narrow alley patrolled by stray cats between Regent and Carnaby streets, opposite the trash cans at the back doors of the big stores. Once found, it's never forgotten, judging by the number of regulars, many from the glitzy world of advertising and public relations, with a few musicians and important agents thrown in. Shampers is a less crowded version of the Cork and Bottle (see Leicester Square in this section)—it has the same ferociously ambitious wine list, featuring nearly 200 wines from all over the world. If your eyes begin to glaze over at such a choice, concentrate on the value-for-money offers on the blackboard or the bottles displayed in the tub on the bar. In any case, the staff will stop you from making a mistake, so make sure to ask if in doubt. It's advisable to reserve a table (lunchtime reservations are accepted until 12:45 p.m.), especially on Thursday, when the joint really jumps. There's a basement for the overflow, but the emphasis below, as opposed to the quick-bite atmosphere above, is on full table service at greater leisure. The fresh, crisp salads never fail to please, and the hot specials (such as spareribs) are recommended, as is the unusual selection of French cheeses.

SOUTH BANK

The Archduke

Concert Hall Approach, SE1 - 928 9370
Open Mon.-Fri. 11 a.m.-3 p.m. & 5:30 p.m.-11 p.m., Sat. 5:30 p.m.-11 p.m.

Where to eat—before or after—if you're among the concrete buttresses of the South Bank for a play or concert? There are restaurants in the Royal Festival Hall and the National Theatre, but you're best off visiting one of London's most strangely located wine bars, tucked beneath the arches of the Hungerford railway bridge. The menu changes monthly in the restaurant and daily in the wine bar, which is decorated with irreverent Hoffnung cartoons of orchestral musicians. If your seats are in a box or the orchestra section, your budget may well allow for a top Bordeaux or Burgundy; upper-circle types on a smaller budget will find a shrewdly chosen house wine or perhaps a Cooks New Zealand Pinot Gris or California Cabernet Sauvignon. In winter you'll sometimes find hot mulled wine, and in summer you could try on the Archduke's specialty, an infusion of peaches and wine called Rinquinquin. Watch the blackboards by the bar for special promotions, then see what's going on at the buffet. The Archduke is famous for its three kinds of sausages, which are usually accompanied by quiches, pies and freshly made salads. It's a friendly sort of place, with customers chattering away like magpies, pecking one another on the cheek at frequent intervals, then rushing out into the night when they realize how soon curtain call is.

Bar Escoba

102 Old Brompton Rd., SW7 - 373 2403
Open daily 11 a.m.-11 p.m.

If a Spanish tapas bar conjures up a picture of fading Costa Brava posters on the walls and fishnets hanging loopily from the ceiling, the Bar Escoba makes for a delightful surprise. Located between Gloucester Road and Queensgate, this former pub has been converted into London's smartest tapas bar. Someone put a lot of thought into the choice of wines from the Rioja, Penedes and Navarra, but the food may well be your first consideration, especially the star performer, the paella. Designed for the avowed trencherman (or woman), it is a thoroughly nostalgic mix of Mediterranean mussels, shrimp, chicken and rice. For more restrained appetites, there are plenty of tempting tapas dishes, from chorizo sausage to Spanish manchego cheeses, taking in fresh anchovies and monkfish, bacon and mushroom brochettes along the way. Handsome red tablecloths are set off by a mock Surrealist decor of wrought-iron wall sconces by Tom Dixon, seashells and a portrait of Franco hung upside down. Half the clientele are French, German and Spanish, the other half Londoners who miss Spain. For the latter, a lively flamenco band often performs.

THE STRAND & COVENT GARDEN

Blake's

32 Wellington St., WC2 - 836 5298
Open Mon.-Sat. noon-11 p.m., Sun. 11 a.m.-10:30 p.m.

Once the home of the old fruit and vegetable market, Covent Garden has burst forth in the last ten years with boutiques, street markets, restaurants and buskers (street entertainers). Blake's was the first wine bar to arrive in the neighborhood, a bold splash of bright-red frontage opposite the new Theatre Museum. On a busy night, Friday for instance, as many as 700 cram themselves into the basement (live jazz five nights a week) and the top floor at street level, where they proceed to fall on an extraordinary mixture of international dishes—from Mexican guacamole and tacos, to Greek hummus and taramasalata, to English cheeses and meats. There are lots of small, circular tables; on a busy night you're likely to start with friends at one table and end up with another group altogether. It's that sort of place. But it's also one of the few wine bars in town where the lunch hour tends to be quieter than dinner, which makes it the best time to give due attention to the wines, most of which come from the very reputable Les Amis du Vin. There are nearly 50 on the list, with French Bordeaux, Loire and Rhône wines leading the field. The selection of wines of the day is not only listed on the blackboard but described in greater detail on the wine list. If you're celebrating, check out the special vintage-Champagne promotions.

TOWER HILL

Reynier
43 Trinity Sq., EC3 - 481 0415
Open Mon.-Fri. 11:30 a.m.-2:30 p.m. & 5 p.m.-7:30 p.m.

Only a few yards from the Tower Hill tube, the new Reynier wine bar is set on a former bowling alley and reached by navigating a short flight of steps. The wrinkled brows belong to customers trying to decide what to choose from the mind-boggling (700 or more bottles) Eldridge Pope and Reynier lists. After that, it's easy. You pay only the retail price plus £1 corkage and enjoy the wine with cheese, pâté, fruit and coffee. Sixty or so half bottles may spur the indecisive on to making up their minds, but if you're completely stuck, concentrate on the excellent Chairman's range, which includes a light blanc de blanc Champagne, a nice, oaky white Burgundy and a soft, drinkable claret. Some visit Reynier's regularly for a comfortable, armchair sort of tour of the wine areas of the world. Prompt home delivery is offered for those who succumb to temptation on the way out and order a case or two from one of the top wine lists.

WANDSWORTH COMMON

Hoults
20 Bellevue Rd., SW17 - 767 1858
Open daily noon-3 p.m. & 6:30 p.m.-10:45 p.m.

Being once attached to a wine warehouse, Hoults was blessed with an adventurous wine list from the outset. It also boasts a pleasant outlook over Wandsworth Common, which provides a nice splash of green that can be a strong persuader for a few City types to desert their desks and computer screens. Otherwise, locals predominate. Though it is primarily a 90-seat restaurant doing a brisk trade in steak-and-kidney pie, Toulouse sausage and lamb's kidneys in red-wine sauce, you can enjoy a wine bar meal by simply choosing from the main menu and enjoying it at the bar. Chicken ballotine or a plate of cheeses are good choices, but alternatives appear constantly. The French, Italian, Spanish, German and Portuguese wines are thoughtfully chosen, and the Australian Rosemount Chardonnay is worth anyone's while. But don't neglect to glance at the blackboard for the recommended wine of the day. Champagne is Georges Goulet, Brut or rosé, the sparkling wine comes light and frivolous from Bouvet-Ladubay in Saumur, and the ports are Taylors. The restaurant menu is seriously fishy, with salmon, turbot and monkfish often featured. All ingredients are fresh and cooked to order.

WESTMINSTER

Methuselah's
29 Victoria St., SW1 - 222 0424
Open Mon.-Fri. 11:30 a.m.-3 p.m. & 5:30 p.m.-11 p.m.

Look for a bright awning sticking out from the tall, gray, multiwindowed office buildings a few minutes' walk along Victoria Street from Westminster Abbey, and you'll have found the latest acquisition of Don Hewitson of Cork and Bottle fame. The wine list is not quite as breathtaking as Cork and Bottle's, but there is a substantial choice of end-of-stock deals to look out for as well as a superb Australian selection. You step straight off the street into a big, airy brasserie, where customers linger over large glasses of wine and watch the world go by. Do not necessarily stop there, because Methuselah's rambles on into the Burgundy room, where serious eating and drinking is always going on. But the heart of the place is downstairs, where the names of the wines of the day are carefully spelled out in different colored chalks on the blackboard and copies of the boss's book, *Enjoying Wine*, are on sale behind the bar. Lunchtime is always crowded, but evenings are generally more peaceful. Pick up a copy of Hewitson's chatty and amusing newsletter, filled with tidbits about his latest finds, special offers and organized dinners of note. His favorite saying, "Life is too short to drink bad wine," is posted prominently, and it's clear he believes the same thing about food—here, it's light and savory—featuring particularly good terrines, crab salad and Stilton roulade.

The Tapster

4 Brewer's Green, Buckingham Gate, SW1 - 222 0561

Open Mon.-Fri. 11:30 a.m.-3 p.m. & 5:30 p.m.- 8:30 p.m.

Sheer nostalgia for the old coach houses of Victorian London clearly animated the architects when they incongruously tacked The Tapster onto the very modern Rolls-Royce head office in Buckingham Gate. "Waggons and Able Horses Daily for Canterbury and East Kent," says one notice, picked out in spidery gold paint on ye olde artificially blackened beam. And if they couldn't quite reproduce authentic London fog outside, there is a close resemblance of it inside during the crowded lunch hours, when the pipe smokers really get puffing. Bare brick gives way to dark paneling and dim lighting, and faces loom vaguely out of dusky corners. Roast beef and ham off the bone are year-round staples for salads and sandwiches, with game pies, smoked salmon, prawns and carefully chosen English cheeses being other popular selections. Nearly all the wines, poured in generous glasses, are classic French from pretty good houses, and there are several heavy reds to ward off winter's chill. If you have a plot to hatch or someone's character to assassinate, one of the numerous alcoves will do nicely. Americans love it here.

HOTELS

Born-Again Hotels

In recent years, London's hotel market has lurched from great peaks to deep troughs. A strong pound and Americans' fears about European travel have been significant factors. There remain, nevertheless, those regular peaks in demand—whatever the economic or political climate—when it is virtually impossible to get a hotel room on short notice (unless, of course, you are well connected): in May, during the Chelsea Flower Show; in September, during the biennial International Farnborough Air Show (next in 1990); and in November, during the travel industry's trade show.

However, underlying all the external factors working to either encourage or discourage foreigners from visiting London, the city's hotels (of every type and class) have remained stoically in the race, attempting to remain competitive by renovating and redecorating (sometimes massively). Hotel rooms throughout London have been redesigned and upgraded, lobbies have been made more welcoming and less like railway ticket offices, and restaurants have become more informal and competitive in price and quality. There are some stunning new health and fitness clubs, and they're no longer buried in basements but, as at the Hyatt Carlton Tower, are located on upper floors with glorious views that may help alleviate the pain of the workout.

Claridge's and the Connaught still rule supreme over the city's hotels, with their clientele of foreign dignitaries and English aristocracy. The Savoy continues its allegiance to the well-heeled show business guest, while Brown's remains the favorite of America's East Coast elite. But these world-famous places, and a handful of others, are the exceptions. To be successful in the 1990s, top-priced hotels lacking the same reputations are now clearly geared toward particular audiences at particular times of the year (for example, English corporate conferences during the winter and Japanese tourists during the summer). So it's a good idea, when choosing a home base in London, that you uncover these "customer characteristics," for they can be as important as comfortable quarters, a convenient location and fair price.

As London traffic gradually grinds to a standstill, location becomes increasingly important. Being within walking distance of major attractions and flourishing shopping streets can be an important bonus, particularly on a short stay.

We have compiled an assortment of hotels—categorized under the headings Luxury, First Class, Charming, Practical and Airport—with widely differing characteristics but one common value: each fulfills its promises. This, we believe, is the key to having a satisfied clientele. With regard to prices, the combination of recent renovations, a weakened dollar and a strengthened pound means that London is pretty high on the international expense roster. But increased competition means that opportunities for negotiating good deals, particularly in the aspiring upper-level hotels, do exist—so never accept the first price quoted. Ask for special packages, or just flat-out bargain.

As England moves toward the European Economic Community's unification in 1992, it seems that London's planning authorities are finally recognizing the need to allow not only renovation but also the virtual rebuilding of existing hotels. The Dorchester closed in December 1988 and will reopen in April 1990 following a complete internal restoration. And St. George's Hospital, Hyde Park Corner, the old Greater London Council offices opposite Westminster, and St. Pancras Station are all slated to be renovated and converted into new hotels.

But hotels are about more than renovation. They're about warmth, charm and, most of all, service—and in this area, London's hotels are still among the world's finest.

LUXURY

Berkeley Hotel
Wilton Pl., SW1 - 235 6000
Open year-round. 133 rooms, 27 suites, color TV, air cond., pool. All major cards.

The Berkeley is confident, one could even say overconfident, with its heritage and position. It makes few concessions to changes of style; classical traditions and, as the hotel brochure promises, "service of another era" rule. On our recent visit, the food was suitably exclusive, but the service, both in the restaurant and the Perroquet Bar, was over-formalized and cold. But the Berkeley remains a popular hotel for those requiring the highest standards of comfort—particularly in the bedrooms, which are elegantly, and individually, decorated. Among its special features are the rooftop indoor/outdoor swimming pool, sauna, gymnasium and the miniature movie theater called the Minema, which is also open to the general public.

Doubles: from £185, including VAT.

Claridge's
Brook St., W1 - 629 8860
Open year-round. 136 rooms, 53 suites, color TV. All major cards.

Claridge's retains its position as the most distinguished hotel in London. Its quiet quality and superb standards of discreet service find regular favor with the world's royalty and political leaders, who use the hotel as their London townhouse. Everything is subdued but extremely comfortable. Director and general manager Ron Jones, who made such a success at the Athenaeum before his move to Claridge's a few years ago, has continued his winning ways by actually improving on the quality of care demanded by his discriminating guests. London should be proud of Claridge's—it is an ambassador for the best of British traditional service and hospitality. In

addition to the formal restaurant, there's an eatery called the Causerie that offers an excellent smorgasbord buffet.

Doubles: from £200, including VAT.

Connaught
16 Carlos Pl., W1 - 499 7070
Open year-round. 90 rooms, 24 suites, color TV, air cond. All major cards.

The Connaught is one of the Savoy-group hotels that is setting standards for quality British service. Other London hotels have found it difficult (if not impossible) to match its time-tested style. The ratio of staff to guests is very high, and it shows. Quiet, exclusive opulence, combined with a single-minded objective to be totally British, is the predominant style of the Connaught. Both the restaurant and the grill serve superb English and classical French food (at a price). The Connaught is a formal place, and men are expected to wear jackets and ties in the public areas.

Doubles: from £216, including VAT.

Dorchester
Park Ln., W1 - 629 8888

The "fashionable lady of Park Lane" closed in December 1988 and will reopen in the spring of 1990 following a major renovation. The new owners plan to preserve its position as one of the world's ultimate luxury hotels. We await the new Dorchester with interest and excitement.

Grosvenor House
Park Ln., W1 - 499 6363
Open year-round. 425 rooms, 50 suites, color TV, air cond. All major cards.

Built between 1927 and 1929 by famous architect Sir Edwin Lutyens, and overlooking Hyde Park, the Grosvenor House recently underwent major, and necessary, refurbishment. Its owners, Trust House Forte, have restored much of its former elegance and added a new health club. And the Ninety Park Lane restaurant has quickly established itself as one of the finest in London. There is also an informal Italian restaurant and the Pavilion, which overlooks Park Lane and specializes in food served from hot and cold buffets.

Doubles: from £219, including VAT.

Hilton on Park Lane

22 Park Ln., W1 - 493 8000
Open year-round. 446 rooms, 55 suites, color TV, air cond. All major cards.

The 28-story Hilton building commands superb views of London in all directions. The hotel recently was sold to the Ladbroke Company, and it remains to be seen if it can maintain its tremendous consistency that has proved so popular over the years. It is a cosmopolitan hotel with a range of restaurants and bars to satisfy the international visitor. The British Harvest Restaurant serves seasonal English food, and on a clear day, the view from the Roof Restaurant can be breathtaking. The Hilton also boasts a nonsmoking floor and a health club.

Doubles: from £220, including VAT.

Hyatt Carlton Tower

2 Cadogan Pl., SW1 - 235 5411
Open year-round. 224 rooms & suites, color TV, air cond. All major cards.

Currently one of London's top modern international hotels, the Hyatt consistently provides a standard in their facilities and customer care unmatched in the city. Small enough to have character, it's also grand enough to offer guests a substantial range of features. The Peak Health Club is one of the finest in the capital and a marvelous spot for a healthy breakfast. The clubby Rib Room continues to attract customers for its Scotch roast beef, widely considered unparalleled in London. But the real value of the Hyatt Carlton Tower is the pleasing style of service: friendly, courteous and clearly intent on satisfying.

Doubles: from £220, including VAT.

Hyde Park Hotel

Knightsbridge, SW1 - 235 5411
Open year-round. 180 rooms, 19 suites, color TV, parking facilities, air cond. All major cards.

The Edwardian splendor of the Hyde Park Hotel reflects the fashionable society and the military traditions of Knightsbridge. The hotel is still much used by English country families as their London base. The rooms and suites facing Hyde Park have glorious views, and traditional afternoon tea in the Park Room is a most gracious way to spend an hour or so. While the Park Room offers imaginative Italian cuisine (scampi-stuffed artichoke hearts, vegetable-filled ravioli) at lunch and dinner, the Cavalry Grill downstairs maintains its stiff-upper-lip British atmosphere. Trust House Forte, the owners, recently redecorated the bedrooms to complement their varied shapes and Edwardian character.

Doubles: from £220, including VAT.

Inn on the Park

Hamilton Pl., Park Ln., W1 - 499 0888
Open year-round. 202 rooms, 26 suites, color TV, parking facilities, air cond. All major cards.

This Four Seasons hotel has garnered more awards in recent years than any other London hotel. It occupies a magnificent location at the southern end of Park Lane, and its reputation is based on its lofty quality of professional service and excellent standard of international hotel keeping. Seemingly every aspect of the hotel complements its luxurious reputation, including, for example, the Four Seasons restaurant and its alternative-cuisine menus (featuring dishes untainted by flour and butter); Lanes restaurant, with its fixed-price buffets; and the sixteen recently converted rooms with private glass-enclosed balconies. The atmosphere throughout the hotel is undeniably affluent.

Doubles: from £225, including VAT.

Le Meridien Piccadilly

Piccadilly, W1 - 734 8000
Open year-round. 290 rooms & suites, color TV, parking facilities, air cond. All major cards.

In the heart of the West End, 100 yards from Piccadilly Circus to the east and the Royal Academy and Burlington Arcade to the west, sits the youngest of London's luxury hotels. The Gleneagles group spared no expense in its complete restoration of the old Piccadilly Hotel five years ago; it then sold it to France's Le Meridien chain two years later. Enter the hotel now and you are immediately transported to an elegant world with a distinctive, extravagant style of its own. Paul Chambers, executive chef of the Oak Room, is considered one of London's best. The Terrace Garden restaurant is light, sunny and fashionable. And

Champneys health club includes the finest facilities of its kind—large pool, squash courts, even a snooker room—in London.

Doubles: from £220, including VAT.

The Ritz

Piccadilly, W1 - 493 8181

Open year-round. 144 rooms & suites, color TV, parking facilities, air cond. All major cards.

The Ritz is pure fin de siècle glamour, and it pursues this image relentlessly. Fashion shows, tea dances in the flawlessly restored Palm Court and restaurant cabarets are constant reminders of what The Ritz is all about: People come here to see and be seen. The bedrooms are for the most part large, beautiful and full of restored original features (brass beds included); those overlooking Green Park are very special. Be forewarned that it is not cheap here—a glass of nonvintage Champagne recently cost us £6.

Doubles: from £185, including VAT.

Savoy

The Strand, WC2 - 836 4343

Open year-round. 152 rooms, 48 suites, color TV, parking facilities, air cond. All major cards.

The Savoy is a great institution, renowned worldwide for its reputation as the London home of the world's rich and famous. For several years Trust House Forte, Britain's largest hotel company, has been involved in a protracted takeover bid for the Savoy, which is still going on as we go to press. Because the Savoy is the closest deluxe hotel to the City of London, it attracts a substantial business clientele for its restaurant, grill and private dining rooms. The south-facing river-view bedrooms are some of the finest available in the capital. As a mark of recognition for his recent achievements, head chef Anton Edelman recently was made a director of the Savoy Hotel Company. As ever, the Savoy remains a memorable hotel for a very special occasion.

Doubles: from £165; suites: £250-£320; luxury suites: £480-£520, including VAT.

FIRST CLASS

Athenaeum

116 Piccadilly, W1 - 499 3464

Open year-round. 112 rooms, color TV. All major cards.

A polished performer in a prime position on Piccadilly opposite Green Park, the Athenaeum retains its individuality even though it is part of a hotel group (Rank Hotels). Small and luxurious, with excellent bedrooms, it is especially popular with seasoned and demanding international business travelers. Quiet, unobtrusive and professional service has attracted many loyal guests.

Doubles: from £170, including VAT.

Belgravia-Sheraton

20 Chesham Pl., SW1 - 235 6040

Open year-round. 89 rooms & suites, color TV. All major cards.

The personal service we witnessed on our recent visits to this small, club-like Sheraton in the heart of Belgravia was as friendly and professional as that of any of its first-rate competitors. There is a nice, warm feel to this hotel, which has been enhanced by recent redecoration. Since Sheraton acquired the hotel a few years ago, it has begun to acquire a style and identity complementing its surrounding diplomatic and residential area. A stay here is well worth considering, whether for a relaxing cocktail hour in the Library Bar or a comfortable week-long London vacation.

Doubles: from £184, including VAT.

Britannia Inter-Continental Hotel

Grosvenor Sq. at Adam's Row, W1
629 9400

Open year-round. 356 rooms, 16 suites, color TV, air cond. All major cards.

At this good international-standard hotel on the south side of Grosvenor Square in the heart of Mayfair, rooms are comfortable and spacious. There is a popular Japanese restaurant in the hotel called the Shogun.

Doubles: from £167, including VAT.

Cavendish Hotel

Jermyn St., SW1 - 930 2111

Open year-round. 249 rooms, 4 suites, color TV. All major cards.

The original Cavendish Hotel was run for 50 years, until 1952, by the Rosa Lewis, a famous London character and pal of Royalty. The old, established hotel was rebuilt in 1966. Trust House Forte recently renovated much of the place, and it now makes for a most pleasant and comfortable base from which to explore St. James's and the West End. The lunchtime buffet in the Gallery Lounge on the first floor is a particularly fine value, and the restaurant offers seasonal English specialties.

Doubles: from £140, including VAT.

Churchill
30 Portman Sq., W1 - 486 5800
Open year-round. 489 rooms & suites, color TV, parking. All major cards.

This hotel of unequivocal international reputation recently changed ownership. Though consistently teetering on the threshold of the deluxe class, it has never quite fulfilled its promise (perhaps because of its location north of Oxford Street). The ground floor is furnished extravagantly with lots of marble, crystal glass, silk lamp shades and thick pile carpets, and bedrooms are paneled and done up in chintz fabrics. This hotel needs to develop its identity.

Doubles: from £145, including VAT.

Cumberland
Marble Arch, W1 - 262 1234
Open year-round. 905 rooms, color TV, parking facilities, air cond. All major cards.

One of London's largest hotels, the Cumberland is situated at the northern end of Park Lane. The ground floor recently underwent a redesign, and although it remains extremely busy, it is now a much friendlier place. The original "carvery" (fixed-price buffet-style) restaurant is as popular as ever, and there is a newly opened modern restaurant called Austens. Other eateries are Mon, a Japanese restaurant, and the hotel's café, for light meals. The bedrooms are of a good consistent standard.

Doubles: from £108, including VAT.

Hilton International Regent's Park
Lodge Rd., NW8 - 722 7722
Open year-round. 377 rooms & suites, color TV, pool. All major cards.

If, by chance, you are a cricket fan, this is the hotel for you. Ask for a room facing St. John's Wood Road and you will look across to the famous Lord's Cricket Ground. Though a new stand was recently added that obscured the view of the cricket pitch, you can almost hear the leather and willow making contact. The hotel just opened an American-style restaurant called Minsky's, which rather typifies the younger, more informal status that the Hilton is adopting.

Doubles: from £120, including VAT.

Holiday Inn Mayfair
3 Berkeley St., W1 - 493 8282
Open year-round. 190 rooms, color TV, air cond. All major cards.

Recently, this hotel has been acquired as part of the Holiday Inn takeover by Bass, the British brewery. It remains to be seen whether improvements will follow. For the moment, we can only report that there is no change: It is more luxurious than the standard Holiday Inn, but then the prices reflect it. Its attractive location is just off Piccadilly.

Doubles: from £160, including VAT.

Howard
Temple Pl., The Strand, WC2 - 839 7282
Open year-round. 135 rooms, 17 suites, color TV. All major cards.

Pleasantly located at the borders of the City, the West End and the riverside embankment, the Howard, built a decade and a half ago, is often overlooked as a worthy place to stay. Good Thames views from its bedrooms, like its famous neighbor, the Savoy, and a charming little restaurant overlooking a central garden are its highlights. And the standard of service and facilities meet all the criteria of a genuine small-scale first-class hotel.

Doubles: from £198, including VAT.

Hotel Inter-Continental
1 Hamilton Pl., Hyde Park Corner, W1 409 3131
Open year-round. 490 rooms, 15 suites, color TV, air cond. All major cards.

The reputation of this modern hotel is enhanced by its superb location overlooking Hyde Park Corner; its star executive chef, Peter Kromberg, who continues to display his skills in Le Soufflé restaurant; and its popular seventh-floor dinner-dance nightspot, Hamiltons. Otherwise, the Inter-Continental is a typically plush international hotel. The bedrooms are airy and comfortable, as you would expect for the top-of-the-range prices.

Doubles: from £195, including VAT.

London Marriott
Grosvenor Sq., W1 - 493 1232
Open year-round. 229 rooms, 10 suites, color TV, air cond. All major cards.

Marriott's London representative, just across the square from the American Embassy, was designed to suit a visitor's perception of an English country house or a London private club. It is all quite comfortable and relaxing, with deep carpets, brass, chintz covers, paneling and sporting prints. The Diplomat restaurant offers international cuisine and hosts regular food festivals.
Doubles: from £200, including VAT.

Londonderry
Park Ln., W1 - 493 7292
Open year-round. 150 rooms, 13 suites, color TV, air cond. All major cards.

Recently acquired by Trust House Forte, the owners of the nearby Grosvenor House, the Londonderry is Park Lane's "little sister." It enjoys an excellent location but does not offer the facilities (such as a health club) of its prestigious neighbors. The atmosphere on the ground floor is one of enforced grandeur, but the Ile de France restaurant is noted for its truly amazing painted ceiling, good service and interesting international menu.
Doubles: from £145, including VAT.

Lowndes
Lowndes St., SW1 - 235 6020
Open year-round. 80 rooms & suites, color TV. All major cards.

The Scottish brewery owners of this hotel at the corner of Lowndes Square recently spent lavish sums to upgrade the entire place. The convenient location more than compensates for a slight lack of distinction. The bedrooms are compact but modern and most pleasantly furnished. Expect a good upper-middle standard and you will not be disappointed.
Doubles: from £160, including VAT.

May Fair
Stratton St., off Piccadilly, W1 - 629 7777
Open year-round. 309 rooms, suites & studios, color TV, air cond. All major cards.

Opened under grand circumstances by King George V in 1927, the May Fair has in recent years struggled to retain its image and reputation. It has always been popular with a show business clientele. Inter-Continental invested a huge amount of money to give the hotel a total face-lift, particularly the bedrooms and the ultra-luxurious suites. The ground-floor lobby and bar now have a paneled English club feel. As we go to press, Inter-Continental has been sold to a Japanese group, and it remains to be seen what effect this will have on the May Fair's future. It deserves a greater degree of prestige than its current stature among the city's hotels would indicate.
Doubles: from £189, including VAT.

Park Lane
Piccadilly, W1 - 499 6321
Open year-round. 271 rooms, 54 suites, color TV, parking facilities. All major cards.

In 1987 the Park Lane celebrated its 60th anniversary as an independent hotel. Like many of its competitors, it too has recently undergone substantial redecorating—and not a moment too soon. A great many of its features reflect its early twentieth-century pedigree, but the style of architecture, while certainly interesting to some, means that bedrooms vary in size and shape. Most of the rooms have air conditioning.
Doubles: from £160, including VAT.

Portman Inter-Continental
22 Portman Sq., W1 - 486 5844
Open year-round. 278 rooms & suites, color TV, air cond. All major cards.

There is an air of space and confidence about this hotel. It is modern, international and has all the standard features, but it is the design of the ground-floor facilities, particularly the Portman Corner Pub Bakery, that attracts much of the lunchtime and early-evening business clientele. With the headquarters of both the Guinness and the Brewers Society in the square, you would assume the hotel pub to be both imaginative and well run, and it is. The elegant upstairs restaurant, Truffles, offers a good-value lunch buffet.
Doubles: from £166, including VAT.

Royal Garden
Kensington High St., W8 - 937 8000
Open year-round. 411 rooms & suites, color TV, parking facilities, air cond. All major cards.

One of Rank Hotels' flagship properties, the Royal Garden is situated on the edge of Kensington Gardens, close to the royal residences at Kensington Palace. General manager James Brown has been here for years, and his experience is reflected in the confidence with which the hotel presents itself to its guests. The star attractions are the garden-view rooms and the Rooftop Royal restaurant, with its magnificent views over the Palace and gardens.

Doubles: from £148, including VAT.

Royal Lancaster
Lancaster Terr., W2 - 262 6737
Open year-round. 435 rooms & suites, color TV, parking facilities, air cond. All major cards.

This eighteen-story Rank Hotel on the north side of Hyde Park was recently substantially upgraded; it is now extremely plush and offers that international standard of luxury found in many of the world's capitals. The Pavement Cafe, an all-day restaurant, is young and lively. The hotel is sometimes dominated by conferences or crowds attending events in the huge ballroom.

Doubles: from £135, including VAT.

Hotel Russell
Russell Sq., WC1 - 837 6470
Open year-round. 317 rooms & suites, color TV. All major cards.

Located outside the center of the West End in the heart of Bloomsbury, this hotel is becoming increasingly popular because of its splendid Victorian architecture and excellent service. Inside is a wealth of Italian marble, crystal and stained glass, along with plenty of space and elegance. The buffet-style "carvery" restaurant serves traditional English roast beef, and the Brasserie on the Square is French and full of character. Most of the rooms are of fine upper-middle-range quality.

Doubles: from £110, including VAT.

St. George's
Langham Pl., W1 - 580 0111
Open year-round. 85 rooms & suites, color TV. All major cards.

Just 200 yards from Oxford Circus, St. George's is located on the top six floors of a fourteen-story building next to the BBC and All Souls' Church. The Summit restaurant and the hotel's cocktail lounge are on the top floor; the reception desk is on the ground floor. The view west over Mayfair toward Hyde Park from the picture windows of the restaurant on a clear London evening makes it one of the most stunning dining spots in the region.

Doubles: from £120, including VAT.

St. James Court
Buckingham Gate, SW1 - 834 6655
Open year-round. 390 rooms, 70 suites, color TV, pool. All major cards.

The owner, the Indian Taj group, is responsible for the expensive conversion the St. James Court underwent a few years ago. There is now a distinct and elegant style about this hotel. One unusual feature is the Inn of Happiness restaurant, which has quickly earned an excellent reputation for its Szechwan and Cantonese food. Facilities also include a health club with a swimming pool, and Buckingham Palace, the Houses of Parliament and Whitehall are all within easy walking distance.

Doubles: from £159, including VAT.

Selfridge
Orchard St., W1 - 408 2080
Open year-round. 298 rooms & suites, color TV, parking facilities, air cond. All major cards.

If your purpose for visiting London is to shop, you could find no better location to stay than the Selfridge. It is situated immediately behind the famous store of the same name, within 100 yards of the Oxford Street branch of Marks & Spencer and within easy walking distance of Bond Street. We suggest you avoid focusing on the facade upon your arrival, since you might confuse the hotel with the entrance to the adjacent gas station. However, once inside, you'll see that a great deal of care and imagination has been taken to inject the cocktail lounge, Stovers Pub and Fletchers restaurant with themes. Bedrooms have the customary upscale-hotel amenities.

Doubles: from £155, including VAT.

Sheraton Park Tower
101 Knightsbridge, SW1 - 235 8050
Open year-round. 295 rooms, 29 suites, color TV, parking facilities, air cond. All major cards.

Big and brassy in comparison to its Chesham Place sister hotel, this Sheraton nevertheless offers a degree of quality that is much respected by its customers. The design of the hotel, a circular tower, ensures that all bedrooms face outward and have increasingly interesting views on the higher floors. Those staying in the Executive Rooms on floors ten through sixteen have access to a private lounge that offers panoramic views of London.

Doubles: from £172, including VAT.

Tower

St. Katharine's Way, E1 - 481 2575

Open year-round. 834 rooms & suites, color TV, air cond. All major cards.

The Tower was built at the start of the City's building boom of the early 1970s. Its location, with the Tower Bridge immediately in front, St. Katharine's Dock behind and the Tower of London to the side, is unique. And it's a shame that an ugly concrete structure like this could have been erected in such a historic area. However, once inside you will see that the owners have made a genuine attempt to create a more pleasing interior, one sympathetic to the environment. The hotel houses several places to eat, including a fixed-price buffet restaurant and an à la carte spot. Above all, the Tower is the City of London's only truly neighborhood hotel, situated in a fascinating area.

Doubles: from £111, including VAT.

Waldorf Hotel

Aldwych, WC2 - 836 2400

Open year-round. 294 rooms, 16 suites, color TV. All major cards.

The ground floor of the Waldorf fairly oozes a rich Edwardian style and elegance. The Palm Court Lounge, where you can waltz and quickstep at the now-famous Friday and Saturday tea dances, is the focal point of the hotel. Both the Club Bar, where celebrating Law Court victors gather, and the underrated Waldorf Restaurant open onto the Palm Court. Head Chef John Insley, previously at the Hyde Park Hotel, proudly prepares his singular English style of cooking for the restaurant's seasonal menus. In addition, there is the Aldwych Brasserie and the open-all-day Footlights bar. In sum, the Waldorf is a well-equipped place to eat, drink and be sociable—and it's well located near many theaters. The bedrooms, which vary greatly in size and shape, have been much improved.

Doubles: from £139, including VAT.

Westbury

New Bond St. at Conduit St., W1
629 7755

Open year-round. 242 rooms, 15 suites, color TV, air cond. All major cards.

With Sotheby's auction house across the street, Savile Row 100 yards away, and Asprey around the corner on Bond Street, you would expect the local hotel to have real style. The Westbury, behind its 30-year-old exterior, is a true corporate expense-account place. Unlike many of its competitors, it achieves high standards and a certain distinction without having to shout about it. The superb Polo bar and restaurant have achieved enviable reputations. The hotel is particularly popular with Americans.

Doubles: from £155, including VAT.

CHARMING

Basil Street Hotel

8 Basil St., SW3 - 581 3311

Open year-round. 103 rooms, color TV. All major cards.

For nearly 80 years the Basil Street Hotel has been near and dear to the hearts of English country families, a home away from home during their jaunts into the city. It's ideal for those who want to stay near Knightsbridge's best shops but who require the peaceful elegance of a smaller hotel. Furnished with antiques, it prides itself on having the atmosphere of a country house. The same management has been in charge for more than 30 years.

Doubles: from £110, including VAT.

Beaufort

33 Beaufort Gdns., SW3 - 584 5252

Open year-round. 29 rooms & suites, color TV. All major cards.

The Beaufort's proprietor, Diana Wallis, has created a charming English country home, with all the modern comforts, right in the heart of London. There is no formal lobby and no restaurant, but there is an elegant sitting room. The price includes a delicious light breakfast served in your bedroom. This Knightsbridge hotel is an absolute delight, full of warmth and discreet luxury.

Doubles: from £130, including VAT and breakfast.

Blakes

33 Roland Gdns., SW7 - 370 6701
Closed Dec. 24-25. 35 rooms, 15 suites, color TV, sauna. All major cards.

Set in leafy residential South Kensington, Blakes has developed a unique reputation as a small, stylish hotel owned by successful actress/model Anouska Hempel. Its relaxed, trendy atmosphere is popular with international media visitors. Some of the rooms are on the small side, but all are individually and imaginatively furnished. The restaurant serves good-quality designer food in designer surroundings.

Doubles: from £165, including VAT.

Brown's

22 Dover St., W1 - 493 6020
Open year-round. 133 rooms & suites, color TV. All major cards.

James Brown, a butler to Lord Byron, established this hotel more than 150 years ago, and it's still as English as ever, with chintz sofas, grandfather clocks, a wealth of original oak paneling and its celebrated high tea in the hotel lounge (for which there is regularly a line). It spans two well-known Mayfair streets that it shares with art galleries, jewelers and the Royal Institute. In L'Apéritif Restaurant, head chef Martin Davis is responsible for the cuisine, which represents the best of English and French cooking. On occasion, he hosts memorable culinary festivals, to which the likes of Michel Guérard (of *cuisine minceur* fame) are invited to showcase their particular skills. Brown's is always full.

Doubles: from £180, including VAT.

Capital

Basil St., SW3 - 589 5171
Open year-round. 50 rooms, 6 suites, color TV, air cond. All major cards.

A small, modern, privately owned gem in the heart of Knightsbridge, the Capital has a reputation for distinction that is quite out of proportion to its size. And the restaurant, renowned throughout London, recently changed chefs: New head chef Philip Britten is serving superb food.

Doubles: from £184, including VAT.

Dorset Square

39 Dorset Sq., NW1 - 723 7874
Open year-round. 30 rooms, color TV. All major cards.

This new, luxuriously furnished hotel in a Regency building on one of London's most attractive squares is fashionably decorated in contemporary English style, with faux-marbre paint and pretty chintz interiors. It offers both location and comfort at a fair price.

Doubles: from £92, including VAT.

Dukes Hotel

34 St. James's Pl., SW1 - 491 4040
Open year-round. 50 rooms, color TV. All major cards.

A jewel of a hotel, this pretty red-brick building tucked away behind St. James's, a brief walk from Piccadilly, is most welcoming. Management spent a lot of money on the decor, which was done in the lavish style now fashionable in expensive hotels, complete with oil paintings and antiques. But you will pay dearly for the privilege of an excellent stay here.

Doubles: from £152, including VAT.

Durrants Hotel

George St., W1 - 935 8131
Closed Dec. 24-25. 98 rooms, color TV. All major cards.

Durrants is the sort of hotel that people rave about to close friends but don't recommend to others for fear of spoiling it. Its distinguished Georgian facade promises something special, and the promise is delivered by the discreet and friendly service. Recently refurbished, the hotel will be a pleasant surprise; you may well become a regular.

Doubles: from £84, including VAT.

Ebury Court

26 Ebury St., SW1 - 730 8147
Open year-round. 39 rooms. Cards: MC, V.

The rooms here are small, but each is uniquely decorated and furnished, so we always feel as if we're staying in a private home rather than in a hotel. And, in fact, the Ebury Court is made up of several terrace houses. Not every bedroom has a bathroom or shower, but you won't have to walk far to find one. There is a 50-pence-per-tray extra charge for breakfast, but you don't have to leap out of bed to admit the waiter; he has a pass key. If your car is parked at a meter in the vicinity, you simply complete a form to indicate where it is and the porter will feed the meter in the morning on your behalf.

Doubles: £89 (with bath), including VAT and Continental breakfast.

Goring

15 Beeston Pl., Grosvenor Gdns., SW1
834 8211

Open year-round. 90 rooms, color TV. All major cards.

If you're looking for the quintessential English hotel—quiet, comfortable, discreet—the Goring is for you. It was built by the present owner's grandfather in 1910 and has remained under the family's direction ever since. Service is solicitous and considerate. The absence of air conditioning is noticeable only in the summer when, if you open the window, the noise of London's traffic may disturb your sleep. If you are a gent, the erotic drawings in the gents' loo might interest you; women must either forget it or enter under false pretenses. The garden, a rare luxury in the center of London, is to be looked at rather than sat in, which is a pity. The formal restaurant serves the traditional food that the English are so fond of and eat without comment: saddle of hare, Dover sole, steak-and-kidney pie, poached salmon.

Doubles: from £159, including VAT and breakfast.

Halcyon Hotel

81 Holland Park, W11 - 727 7288

Open year-round. 44 rooms, color TV. All major cards.

Question: How many elegant little hotels can one actually describe in detail a full month after returning the room key? Answer: Very few. But the Halcyon, opened recently in Kensington, is one of those rare, truly memorable establishments. The interior is an uncommonly handsome blend of classicism and antiques, of flowery neo-Victorian comfort and intelligently designed, functional bathrooms. The overall scheme is characterized by a light, humorous touch and a taste for trompe l'oeil (ask for a peek of the Egyptian room; it's done up like a luxurious desert camp). Guests are pampered, but never overwhelmed, by a discreet staff. Staying at the Halcyon is like visiting the home of well-off, well-bred, highly civilized English gentry.

The day begins with a delicious breakfast: feather-light waffles with maple syrup and croissants that one would swear were baked in a Parisian boulangerie. Perhaps the biggest surprise awaits in the dining room: If the Brits continue to produce native chefs as talented as 27-year-old James Robins, we shall soon have to abandon all of our pet prejudices about English food!

Our attempts to discover the name of the smart man who purchased this former bed-and-breakfast and transformed it into one of the most fashionable yet discreet hotels in London were in vain. That individual clings even more fiercely to his privacy than do many of the Halcyon's guests. And though it is known that Lauren Bacall, Mick Jagger, Richard Harris, Brian Ferry, Harold Pinter, Tina Turner and the Duchess of Kent stay here when in London, all we could learn of the owner is that he is a businessman for whom the Halcyon is the first stage in a vast scheme to open similar luxury establishments throughout the world.

Doubles: from £132, including VAT.

John Howard Hotel

4 Queen's Gate, SW7 - 581 3011

Open year-round. 54 rooms, 10 suites, air cond. All major cards.

In this quiet, discreet hotel behind a Regency facade near Kensington Gardens, the high-ceilinged guest rooms have been sensitively restored and decorated; double-glazed windows and air conditioning ensure a good night's sleep if you are the sort who is disturbed by traffic noise. The hotel's 50 bedrooms are augmented by 12 apartment-style suites, each with a fully equipped kitchen. In addition to the conventional restaurant, there is a Japanese restaurant.

Doubles: from £107, including VAT.

L'Hôtel

28 Basil St., SW3 - 589 6286

Open year-round. 12 rooms, color TV. Cards: AE.

It was the idea of David Levin, owner of the Capital two doors away, to open a French hotel in London. By that, he meant a small, moderately priced bed-and-breakfast hotel with Continental breakfast thrown in with the price of a room. The result is this charmingly decorated but far from cheap establishment. The lobby is the hotel's sole public area, but the basement has been turned into a wine bar that has proven to be as popular as the hotel.

Doubles: from £115, including VAT and breakfast.

Lowndes Thistle
Lowndes St., SW1 - 235 6020
Open year-round. 80 rooms, color TV. All major cards.

A generously furnished hotel in classical English style. The bedrooms have all the extras that make the difference in price and comfort: shampoo and bubble bath, bathrobes, trouser presses and the like. In the summer the hotel has its own sidewalk café that adds charm to an already attractive establishment.
Doubles: from £184, including VAT.

Montcalm
Great Cumberland Pl., W1 - 402 4288
Open year-round. 121 rooms, color TV. All major cards.

This small hotel in a quiet Georgian crescent near Marble Arch has obvious pretensions of grandeur. The furnishings are distinctly bourgeois in style, but you can be assured of com-

fort and good service. A rarely seen but worthwhile feature, for those who do not like to be parted from the radio, is the radio speaker in each bathroom. Bathrobes are provided.
Doubles: from £168, including VAT.

Stafford
St. James's Pl., SW1 - 493 0111
Open year-round. 62 rooms, color TV. Cards: AE, DC.

Now owned by Trafalgar House, which also owns The Ritz, the Stafford is small and personal. American visitors love to return to the club-like atmosphere and be recognized by the staff. It is extremely comfortable without being lavish. The American bar, where Charles has presided as head barman for decades, is representative of the character of the hotel—caps, ties and pennants adorn the walls. Loyal regulars love it. It's "English to the core" and long may it remain so.
Doubles: from £155, including VAT.

PRACTICAL

Forum
97 Cromwell Rd., SW7 - 370 5757
Open year-round. 908 rooms & suites, color TV. All major cards.

These huge popular hotel towers, which were recently extensively renovated, loom above Cromwell Road west of Central London. At the time of this writing, one slight temporary inconvenience was that the Gloucester Road underground station, which is about 200 yards away, was closed, which meant a long trek to either South Kensington, Earl's Court or High Street Kensington, which are all about equidistant. The alternative is an expensive taxi—but it is hoped that by the time you read these lines the station will be reopened. The recent upgrading of the rooms is reflected in the prices. The hotel houses two restaurants: the Kensington Gardens Café and the more expensive Ashburn Restaurant.
Doubles: from £105, including VAT.

Gloucester
Harrington Gdns., SW7 - 373 6030
Open year-round. 535 rooms, parking facilities, air cond. All major cards.

This large, busy, modern hotel, a few minutes from the South Kensington tube station and the museums on Cromwell Road, hosts a range of restaurants and bars that represents both the foibles and the merits of British catering. At the higher-end restaurant, the cuisine is billed as Continental; the Appleyard Cafe has an American-style coffee shop; the wine bar, Le Château, simulates a French bistro; and the Real Ale Tavern does its best to be all that an English pub should be. Though air conditioned, the rooms are not sumptuously furnished; in a couple of suites, however, nothing has been spared to create an atmosphere of modern luxury.
Doubles: from £138, including VAT.

Great Eastern
Liverpool St., EC2 - 283 4363
Open year-round. 164 rooms, color TV, parking facilities. All major cards.

Probably the only hotel of its kind in London, this former railway hotel was built next to Liverpool Street Station to accommodate rail travelers when trains were the preferred form of long-distance transportation. The rooms are cavernous and the corridors wide, and the hotel is well positioned for East Anglia, the ports of Harwich and Felixstowe and Stanstead Airport, which is currently being reconstructed. The hotel's houses of refreshment include a buffet-style dining room and a lively Ball Bros. wine bar, where a bottle of claret and a sandwich generally are more rewarding than the food at L'Entrecôte, a steakhouse.

Doubles: from £120, including VAT.

Great Northern
King's Cross, N1 - 837 5454
Open year-round. 88 rooms, color TV. All major cards.

Opened in 1854, the Great Northern is considered London's oldest purpose-built hotel—in this case a place built solely to accommodate rail travelers (it's located just behind King's Cross Station, whose trains head for northern England and Scotland). Although the facade still reflects the age in which it was constructed, there is not much inside to impress or charm. The stripped-pine furniture in some of the bedrooms seems scarcely appropriate for a genuine Victorian hotel—which is a shame, when so many modern hotels are trying to look Victorian. But don't be put off. The hotel was built for the convenience of railway passengers. The railways are still with us, and if you have to leave London early from King's Cross or St. Pancras, you will find enough comfort and friendliness at the Great Northern to make it worth your while.

Doubles: £75 without bath, £98 with bath, including VAT.

Great Western Royal
Praed St., Paddington, W2 - 723 8064
Open year-round. 170 rooms, color TV. All major cards.

There are two possible reasons to stay in this former British Rail hotel. One may be a fascination with the architecture of Victorian railway hotels, noted for their magnificent high ceilings, wide staircases and passages and large bedrooms. The other reason could only be the need to make a journey from Paddington Station next door, and a morbid fear of missing trains. The interior has all the typical gloom of railway hotels, and scarcely any of the splendor with which they commenced life.

Doubles: from £90, including VAT.

Grosvenor
101 Buckingham Palace Rd., SW1
834 9494
Open year-round. 360 rooms, color TV. All major cards.

One day, probably when they are all torn down, someone will begin to appreciate Britain's railway hotels. The Grosvenor was built at the zenith of the railway age, as the industrial revolution was settling down to become a way of life and no one was heeding the cost of heating and maintaining vast rooms, wide corridors, sweeping staircases and extravagant casements. Today, largely because there is a shortage of hotel rooms, the Grosvenor is once again in demand. In its public rooms on the ground floor, some thought has been given to matching decor and architecture, but austere contemporary styles reminiscent of the '50s and '60s unfortunately prevail in the empty areas of the floor and the bleak, undecorated walls. Such is the Grosvenor, alongside Victoria Station, a monument to the age of the train in the age of the airplane.

Doubles: from £115, including VAT.

Kensington Close
Wrights Ln., W8 - 937 8170
Open year-round. 537 rooms & suites, color TV. All major cards.

We urge you not to be put off by first appearances here: The rather drab frontage belies the size and character of this large hotel. While on the lower end of the price scale, the Kensington Close is able to offer an excellent health club and a large swimming pool and squash courts. Then there is the small high-quality grill, as well as a café that is open all day. Rooms can be compact, but they're furnished to a consistently good and comfortable standard.

Doubles: from £82, including VAT.

London International
147c Cromwell Rd., SW7 - 370 4200
Open year-round. 415 rooms & suites, color TV. All major cards.

The London flagship of the Swallow hotel group, the London International is part of a northeastern-England brewery company. Like many of its competitors in recent years, the company has invested heavily in improvements, particularly to the ground floor. The hotel's Fountain Brasserie is a popular restaurant by day. Due to its proximity to the exhibition halls at Earls Court and Olympia, the hotel becomes extremely busy when trade shows and exhibitions are taking place at these venues.

Doubles: from £82, including VAT and Continental breakfast.

London Tara
Scarsdale Pl., W8 - 937 7211
Open year-round. 831 rooms & suites, color TV. All major cards.

Next door to the Kensington Close hotel and 400 yards from Kensington High Street, this Aer Lingus–owned hotel offers good value at competitive prices. The ground-floor amenities have had a big boost by the addition of a bar and a café. The hotel also owns La Ruelle, a popular à la carte restaurant on Wrights Lane.

Doubles: from £85, including VAT.

Onslow
109 Queen's Gate, SW7 - 589 6300
Open year-round. 174 rooms, 1 suite, color TV. All major cards.

If you are looking for a smaller hotel at a moderate price, within easy walking distance of Knightsbridge and the Kensington museums, then the Onslow hotel must be on your list. An elegantly converted row of Georgian townhouses, it keeps its promises of comfort and value for the money. The Onslow's furnishings and service are excellent, and located as it is in a residential area, it tends to be quieter than many of the West End hotels.

Doubles: from £91, including VAT.

Royal Court
Sloane Sq., SW1 - 730 9191
Open year-round. 101 rooms. All major cards.

Located next door to the Royal Court Theatre, where back in the '50s John Osborne's

---

Going traveling? Look for Gault Millau's other "Best of" guides to France, Paris, Italy, Hong Kong, New York, New England, Washington, D.C., Chicago, San Francisco and Los Angeles.

---

play *Look Back in Anger* created a revolution on the British stage, is the Royal Court, a hotel of strange contrasts and half-fulfilled promises. The imposing entrance suggests a discreet elegance and luxury, which are not always present in tandem and sometimes missing altogether.

Doubles: from £144, including VAT.

Royal Horseguards Thistle
Whitehall Ct., SW1 - 839 3400
Open year-round. 284 rooms, 6 suites, color TV. All major cards.

This hotel occupies what was once part of the National Liberal Club. The rooms have fine views of the river, St. Paul's, Whitehall and, not far away, Scotland Yard and the Palace of Westminster. A member of the Thistle chain, the rooms are sensible, comfortable and without pretensions of grandeur. The service is friendly and attentive.

Doubles: from £97, including VAT.

Royal Trafalgar Thistle
Whitcomb St., Trafalgar Sq., WC2
930 4477
Open year-round. 930 rooms. All major cards.

Here's a hotel right in the heart of London, within walking distance of Leicester Square and Soho and located just behind the National Gallery. A member of the Thistle chain, the Royal Trafalgar has a practical, businesslike approach, but it manages at the same time to provide friendly and caring service. It's not a serene part of London, so don't expect a quiet night unless you keep the windows firmly closed.

Doubles: from £114, including VAT.

Strand Palace
369 Strand, WC2 - 836 8080
Open year-round. 775 rooms. All major cards.

Located directly opposite the Savoy, on The Strand, and backing onto the renovated Covent Garden Market area, this large and well-known hotel provides a straightforward package with no frills. It's ideal for many of the theaters, Trafalgar Square, Whitehall and, indeed, most of central London's top tourist attractions. The pizzeria and coffee shop are designed to tempt visitors to eat in the hotel.

Doubles: from £82, including VAT.

AIRPORT

L ondon's two major airports (a third, Stanstead, northeast of the city, is currently under reconstruction) have looked after millions of travelers over the past 30 years. Heathrow, reputed to be the busiest airport in the world, is surrounded by gravel pits and a mess of arterial roads and motorways. Gatwick, near the town of Crawley in the middle of the Sussex countryside, is a far more pleasant spot to stay if you wish to avoid traveling between London and the airport. Heathrow, at the end of the underground railway line, is closer to London than Gatwick, but it's actually quicker to take the express train from Gatwick to Victoria Station than to catch the tube (there are no expresses) between Heathrow and central London. If you must stay at Heathrow, there are a number of modern hotels that, with one or two exceptions, are uniformly soulless, a condition forced upon them, it seems, by the essentially transient nature of their guests. The hotels in this category are, on the whole, less expensive than central London hotels and they have similar facilities.

GATWICK

Gatwick Hilton International
Gatwick Airport, Gatwick, West Sussex
(0293) 518080
Open year-round. 333 rooms, 13 suites, color TV, air cond. All major cards.

The Hilton provides the highest standards and the best airport location of any of the Gatwick hotels. Linked to the main terminal by a covered walkway, the hotel is built around an atrium that features a replica of an old airplane. There's also a large pool and health club, as well as two restaurants and two bars. The rooms are of modern top-class Hilton quality.

Doubles: from £97, including VAT.

Post House
Povey Cross Rd., Horley, Surrey - (0293) 771621
Open year-round. 218 rooms, color TV, pool, parking facilities, air cond. All major cards.

Half a mile or so from the airport terminals by free courtesy coach, the Post House stands on a quiet location away from airplane flight paths. There is easy parking and an outdoor pool and terrace for summer relaxation. The restaurant and bar seem to attract about an equal number of local customers and airport travelers. The owners have improved the quality of the bedroom furnishings substantially.

Doubles: from £92, including VAT.

HEATHROW

Ariel
Bath Rd., Hayes, Middlesex - 759 2552
Open year-round. 177 rooms, color TV. All major cards.

One of the smaller airport hotels, the Ariel is constructed in a circular shape, which in part might account for its popularity with travelers and locals alike. It prides itself on providing a more personal service than its larger competitors while fulfilling its promise of comfort and value for the money. The Willow Restaurant serves an extensive buffet, as well as à la carte specialties. At the time of this writing, the building of a seafood restaurant in the hotel's central garden area was beginning.

Doubles: from £90, including VAT.

Excelsior
Bath Rd., West Drayton, Middlesex
759 6611
Open year-round. 609 rooms & suites, color TV, air cond. All major cards.

Trust House Forte recently made drastic improvements here; the Excelsior is to be its flagship airport hotel. There are now a swimming pool and health club as well as a new cocktail lounge in the lobby. Many of the bedrooms have been refurbished and upgraded. The Draitone Manor restaurant is the finest in the airport area, and the large buffet restaurant (featuring roasted meats) is consistently popular.

Doubles: from £100, including VAT.

Holiday Inn
Ditton Rd., Langley, Slough - (0753) 44244
Open year-round. 224 rooms & suites, color TV. All major cards.

Although further away from the airport than its competitors, many people welcome the added travel time to enjoy the standards and facilities of this unusually good Holiday Inn, with its swimming pool, gymnasium and tennis courts. Of course the customary Holiday Inn two-tier restaurant is in place and features a menu based around the display buffet. The quality of the hotel service staff is extremely high—perhaps underwritten by the fact that the company's offices are adjacent to the hotel.

Doubles: from £100, including VAT.

Post House
Sipson Rd., West Drayton, Middlesex 759 2323
Open year-round. 597 rooms & suites, color TV. All major cards.

Located at the junction of the M4 and the Airport Spur highways, this Post House must be one of the best-known hotel landmarks in all of England. It attracts many motorists as well as airport travelers. Always busy, it is a most convenient meeting place. The ground floor provides a good range of facilities, with a fixed-price buffet restaurant, a cocktail bar, a coffee shop (in need of modernization) and a pub bar.

Doubles: from £90, including VAT.

Sheraton Skyline
Bath Rd., Hayes, Middlesex - 759 2353
Open year-round. 355 rooms, 5 suites, color TV, air cond. All major cards.

Clearly the current leader of the Heathrow Airport hotels, this Sheraton provides luxury accommodations in the international large-hotel style. There is an exotic array of ground-floor facilities, centered around the indoor pool: a tropically decorated poolside bar with a swimmers' section, the famous Diamond Lil's saloon, an à la carte restaurant and a coffee shop.

Doubles: from £120, including VAT.

NIGHTLIFE

AFTER DARK

Although London's nightclub scene may appear at first as impenetrable as ever, a resurgence in after-dark entertainment has resulted in a steadily increasing choice of good nightspots for those who make the effort to find them. Londoners' mania for exclusivity is manifested in the strict membership policies of such top-notch clubs as Annabel's and Tramp and the obligatory dress codes at the younger, more ephemeral clubs. At some of these places, temporary memberships for overseas visitors are available in advance, though there's no substitute for cultivating a friendship with an established member who can get you in as a guest. In the latter case, getting in often depends on the clothes you wear—particularly at the trendier clubs, many of which are redecorated nightly to reflect the theme of the evening. Most of the hottest clubs are now almost entirely devoted to one-night stands: A particular group of fashionable acolytes will gather one night of the week, another the next night and so on. Since these groups tend to shift from night to night and sometimes from venue to venue, it is essential to call in advance for information on themes. The casual night owl, member or not, is more likely to gain entry to the middle-range private clubs (which are generally more consistent), as long as it looks like he or she has money to spend and won't be destroying the furniture.

Contrary to popular belief, clubs with restaurants attached frequently serve surprisingly good food for slightly less than you would pay in an ordinary restaurant, since the costs are offset by the club itself. On the other hand, with one or two notable exceptions (e.g., Le Beat Route), drinks are more expensive at clubs than at regular bars, and the cost of Champagne is wicked.

London's nightlife runs the gamut from elegant to wild. The male gay scene comprises a variety of attractive clubs, though similar places for women are rare. The men's clubs, complete with strip acts and hostesses, tend to be sedate, discreet and largely unchanged over the years. Over the last few years, rising young entrepreneurs like Peter Stringfellow have brought fresh blood to the London nightclub scene; the sheer pizzazz and laser-sharp style of The Hippodrome and Stringfellows can now be seen in many other discos that are good values, though far from intimate.

The divisions of fashion and taste have given rise to a plethora of specialty clubs; few worthwhile places these days attempt to cater to all tastes. So your best bet before venturing out into the London night is to decide what sort of entertainment you're in the mood for. Whether it's hobnobbing with celebrities, dancing to the latest beat, listening to jazz, making the scene or meeting the man or woman of your dreams—with luck and a little persistence, you're bound to find it.

The price ranges for entrance to the clubs are as follows: Inexpensive is £5 and under; moderate is £10 and under; and expensive is anywhere from £10 to £100.

DISCOS & NIGHTCLUBS

Le Beat Route
17 Greek St., W1 - 734 6308
Open Mon.-Sat. 9 p.m.-3:30 a.m. Moderate membership & cover charge.

A good, solid club and disco with a proliferation of live acts, Le Beat Route is eternally popular, though the clientele varies from night to night. Drinks are cheap and none too sophisticated, but it's a good place to spot actors who seem to have adopted the place as an end-of-the-week hangout.

Bill Stickers
18 Greek St., W1 - 03437 0582
Open Mon.-Sat. 9 p.m.-3 a.m.

This lively restaurant/bar is decorated in Hollywood kitsch with ersatz chandeliers, zebra-skin chairs and oodles of rococo gilt. Most of the action occurs upstairs, where crowds of Soho night owls cluster around the tables to drink beer or cocktails before going on to other clubs. The small basement dance floor is filled with those who have been refused entry into the trendier nightspots.

Busby's
157 Charing Cross Rd., WC2 - 734 6963
Open Mon.-Sat. 10 p.m.-3 a.m. Moderate membership & cover charge.

The happy-go-lucky atmosphere of this lively, popular venue is in evidence in the music and the patrons. Busby's is lots of fun for the uninhibited, though it tends to get pretty packed and sweaty toward the end of the week.

Café des Artistes
66 Fulham Rd., SW10 - 352 6200
Open Mon.-Sat. 8:30 p.m.-2 a.m. Moderate cover charge.

This smoky den is frequented by a motley crowd drawn from the streets of Earl's Court. A good meeting place for students and night owls, Café des Artistes provides plenty of seats for assignations, varied music and cheap junk food. Sleazy but good.

Café de Paris
3 Coventry St., WC1 - 437 2036
Open Mon., Tues. & Thurs. 9 p.m.-1 a.m., Wed. 10 p.m.-3 a.m., Fri.-Sat. 9 p.m.-3:30 a.m. Moderate membership charge.

Wednesday night is club night, and if you're not here you're nowhere. Formerly held in Maximus, the private party at the Café de Paris is the most exclusive and sought-after invitation in town. Once inside, you'll be able to dance on the same floor as George Michael, Boy George, David Bowie and others of that celebrity caliber.

Crazy Larry's
533 King's Rd., SW10 - 376 5555
Open Mon.-Sat. 9 p.m.-3 a.m. Moderate cover charge.

This trendy, spacious club is located down in the World's End area on the west end of King's Road. The small dance floor gets packed early on with beefy blokes showing off for the girls and one another, but there are plenty of tables at which to sit and ogle while waiting to dance.

The Fridge
Town Hall Promenade, Brixton Hill, SW2 - 326 5100
Open Mon.-Sat. 10 p.m.-3 a.m. Moderate membership & cover charge.

Once the hippest club south of the river, The Fridge was forced to move from its first home to a less salubrious one. Still run well by Andy Czekowski, who began the notorious punk club, The Roxy, in 1976, it is a reliable place to go if you're caught on the wrong side of London. Avant-garde music, poetry and cabaret acts, as well as great cocktails, are still high on the list of priorities.

Gossips
69 Dean St., W1 - 734 4111
Open Mon.-Sat. 10 p.m.-3 a.m. Moderate membership & cover charge.

A mixed bag of a club located in a crypt-like cellar in the heart of Soho. Some nights it's action-packed, others it can be quite dull. Choose carefully and dress any which way—you're bound to fit in. Earplugs are optional.

Gullivers

11 Down St., W1 - 499 0760

Open Mon.-Sat. 9 p.m.-3:30 a.m. Moderate cover charge.

Gullivers has maintained its ambience of American soul over the years. It tends to be popular with music-business types nostalgic for the good old days. It may not be very trendy, but it's a fun place to cry into your Budweiser.

Henry Africa's

9 Young St., W8 - 937 9493

Open Mon.-Sat. 9 p.m.-2:30 a.m. Moderate membership & cover charge.

A real discovery, Henry Africa's is a relaxed, friendly club located just off Kensington High Street. The diverse dance music caters to a broad range of clientele; age makes no difference at Henry Africa's. This is one of those rare clubs where you feel at home as soon as you walk through the door.

Limelight

136 Shaftesbury Ave., W1 - 433 0572

Open Mon.-Sat. 10 p.m.-3 a.m. Moderate cover & membership charge.

This truly unusual nightclub is situated, like its counterpart club in New York, in a converted church. Labyrinthine stairways and corridors lead to the large dance floor, the crypt bar and to one of several intimate reception rooms. It's quite noisy and exceedingly popular on Friday and Saturday nights, when the young bouncers, who resemble muscle-bound models, select the clientele (seemingly at random) from the crowd gathered outside.

Madame Jo Jo's

8-10 Brewer St., W1 - 734 2473

Open Mon.-Sat. 10 p.m.-3 a.m. Moderate cover charge.

Madame Jo Jo's, the first and best transvestite club in town, attracts a varied crowd of free spirits and/or amused observers. It's all very campy and entirely friendly, with beautiful women serving drinks in fishnet tights and leotards—only they're all men. Cabaret and hilarious drag acts complete the evenings' entertainments. Oscar Wilde would have loved it.

Maximus

14 Leicester Sq., WC2 - 743 4111

Open 11 p.m.-3:30 a.m. Moderate cover charge.

This long-established Leicester Square nightclub is no longer as essential as it used to be, but it still lures a large clientele of tourists, who find it entertaining without being demanding.

The Palace

1A Camden Rd., NW1 - 387 0428

Open 9 p.m.-3 a.m. Moderate cover charge.

At this former music-hall cinema turned disco, there's a different theme every night—'60s Night, Disco Night—so we suggest you call in advance. It's a good, fun place with more bars than most discos, though the occasional drunken party can be off-putting.

The Park

38 Kensington High St., W8 - 938 1978

Open Mon.-Sat. 10 p.m.-3 a.m. Moderate cover charge.

At this sophisticated, upscale disco for the post-teenage crowd, the dazzling light system above the dance floor keeps the chic, if anonymous, clientele amused. Four bars and a decent restaurant fuel flagging boppers.

Samantha's

3 New Burlington St., W1 - 734 6249

Open Mon.-Sat. 8:30 p.m.-3 a.m. Moderate cover charge.

Fashions and trends may come and go, but Samantha's remains, like its name, locked in a '60s time warp. This, of course, means that it's about to become highly fashionable yet again, though what the genuine article and the young nostalgia freaks will make of each other is anyone's guess.

Wag Club

35 Wardour St., W1 - 437 5534

Open 10 p.m.-3:30 a.m. Moderate cover charge.

The second-most trendy club in London, the Wag has actually benefited from its dethronement by Maximus. There are fewer poseurs, and while still crowded, the atmosphere is considerably more relaxed and cordial than it was a year ago. One of the few hip clubs that is actually above ground, the Wag retains a certain airiness even when chock-full, which it often is.

Xenon
196 Piccadilly, W1 - 743 9344
Open 10 p.m.-3 a.m. Moderate cover charge.

This good, all-purpose discotheque is well organized if a little soulless. The out-of-date music (disco funk) attracts a large European contingent. For some odd reason the place seems to be particularly appealing to German students.

Zanzibar
30 Great Queen St., WC2 - 405 6133
Open Mon.-Sat. 7 p.m.-2 a.m. Moderate cover & membership charge.

This popular, well-established cocktail bar is decorated in '30s art deco style with lots of pink and gray. Good snacks and full meals are served on request in the evening, and music from the resident pianist or a variety of jazz bands gives it a fresh, Casablanca-style ambience.

GAY CLUBS

Apollo
11 Wardour St., W1 - 437 7301
Open Mon.-Sat. 9 p.m.-3 a.m. Moderate membership & cover charge.

Smart and discreet, this intimate, beautifully run male club has a cool black and chrome decor. It's a perfect place for elegant relaxation.

Bolts Lazers Club
6-9 Salisbury Promenade, N8 - 809 1460
Open Fri. 10 p.m.-3 a.m. Moderate membership charge.

One of the most spectacular gay clubs in London, this Friday-night extravaganza features a migraine-inducing laser show and an enormous light dome. The black, white and chrome decor reflects the atmosphere, which is for serious fun seekers. It's huge, loud, unabashed and a lot of fun. Mixed gay crowd.

Gateways
239 King's Rd., SW3 - 352 0118
Open Wed. & Fri.-Sat. 8 p.m.-midnight, Thurs. 9 p.m.-11 p.m., Sun. 8 p.m.-11 p.m. Moderate membership charge.

The doyenne of lesbian clubs, Gateways is a mural-bedecked basement featuring caricatures of former members. It has the aroma of history and the comfortable shabbiness of an often-frequented retreat. Darts, cards, dominoes, a jukebox, a disco—they're all available, making Gateways the next best thing to an all-female pub. Better, in fact.

Heaven
The Arches, Villiers St., WC2 - 839 3852
Open Tues.-Sat. 10 p.m.-3:30 a.m. Moderate membership & cover charge.

Formerly called The Global Village, Heaven had a recent face-lift that spruced up its rather depraved image. Smarter, more select and less dangerous than a few years ago, the club still boasts one of the best dance floors in town (downstairs), while upstairs the octagonal bar enhances the overall air of cultivated decadence. It's big enough to get lost in yet has a unique and monumental charm of its own.

Napoleon Club
2-6 Lancashire Ct., 123 New Bond St., W1 493 3075
Open Mon.-Wed. 9 p.m.-1 a.m., Fri.-Sat. 9 p.m.-3 a.m. Expensive membership & cover charge.

The upscale gay club for sophisticated swingers and a favorite haunt of well-heeled actors. Aesthetically pleasing in green and brown, the decor includes walls decorated with prints and paintings of the Napoleonic era. There are four bars, a French restaurant (The Bonaparte) and a basement disco.

Stallions

4 Falconberg Ct., off Charing Cross Rd.,
W1 - 437 0047

*Open Mon.-Sat. 6:30 p.m.-3 a.m., Sun. 6:30
p.m.-midnight. Moderate membership charge.*
Difficult to find, but worth the effort, Stallions
is a black-and-red plushy basement club with
mirrored walls that reflect the darkly modern
decor. Soft music plays until 11 p.m., when the
atmosphere changes almost instantaneously,
from the intimate to the charged, and disco
takes over.

JAZZ CLUBS

Mainsqueeze

23 King's Rd., SW3 - 730 0660

*Open daily 8 p.m.-3 a.m. Moderate membership
charge.*

This well-established club is quite popular
with people who like jazz but aren't fanatics.
Situated just off Sloane Square, it provides a
noisy yet friendly alternative to the high-tech
thump of the ubiquitous discotheque.

100 Club

100 Oxford St., W1 - 636 0933

*Open daily 7:30 p.m.-1 a.m. Moderate cover
charge.*

Steeped in tradition, the 100 Club is one of
the most popular and friendly jazz clubs
around. It features a live act nearly every night
that varies from traditional jazz to new-wave
rock. The club serves drinks at pub prices and
Chinese food.

Pizza Express

10 Dean St., W1 - 437 9595

*Open Tues.-Sun. 9 p.m.-1 a.m. Moderate mem-
bership or cover charge.*

At this basement restaurant in Soho, you can
eat pizza and drink wine while listening to an
unusually consistent caliber of modern-jazz
acts. If you don't order pizza you can't have
booze, though you can keep the beat with
coffee or soft drinks. The fresh, clean, friendly
atmosphere attracts some big names from both
sides of the Atlantic.

Ronnie Scott's

47 Frith St., W1 - 439 0747

*Open Mon.-Sat. 8:30 p.m.-3 a.m. Moderate
membership or cover charge.*

Ronnie Scott's is justifiably regarded as the
finest jazz club in London. It houses the worst
jokes (courtesy of Scott himself), the most
lethal Spag Bol (spaghetti Bolognese) and the
warmest ambience. Go with a few friends, snag
a table near the front and forget about getting
to bed early. You may be showered by Champagne from the table behind you, or you may
find yourself the butt of one of Scott's atro-
cious puns, but you're not likely to have a
better time at any other club in town. Top-line
acts from America and Britain play before a
motley crowd composed of seemingly every
type—from stockbroker to salesman, villain to
virgin.

MEN'S CLUBS

Bristol Suite

14 Bruton Pl., W1 - 499 1938 (membership), 499 6522 (reservations)

*Open Mon.-Fri. 9 p.m.-3 a.m. Expensive mem-
bership & cover charge.*

This well-run club for the errant gent has a
mildly sophisticated but comfortable ambience. Its patrons come here to relax in the
music lounge/bar with a friendly hostess or
dine respectably on the international cuisine.

Gaslight of St James's

16 Avery Rd., W1 - 930 1648

*Open Mon.-Sat. 8 p.m.-2 a.m. Moderate mem-
bership or cover charge.*

The topless hostesses who hang out in the
two bars are the principal attractions here,
especially for businessmen from abroad who
don't wish to get too involved. Two resident
bands provide the music, and various cabaret
acts fill up the spaces in between.

Miranda

9 Kingly St., W1 - 437 6695

Open Mon.-Fri. 9 p.m.-3:30 a.m. Moderate membership charge.

Little has changed at Miranda over the years, though it does trade in its hostesses on a regular basis. The latest models make a pleasant accompaniment to the striptease cabaret as well as effective dance partners to the civilized sounds of the four-piece band. In this spacious red-velvet basement, you can dine, dance or simply pour out your sorrows to sympathetic (if expensive) ears.

The Office

16 Avery Rd., W1 - 499 6728

Open Mon.-Fri. 9 p.m.-3:30 a.m. Moderate membership charge.

Discretion is the watchword at this ironically named club. You can dance with one of the many hostesses to subtle music from records or a tinkling piano, having told your wife that you're staying late at The Office. Just hope she never finds that membership card—which, by the way, is less expensive for overseas visitors.

The Pinstripe Club

21 Beak St., W1 - 437 4294

Open Mon.-Fri. 9 p.m.-3 a.m. Moderate membership or cover charge.

The deliberate collison of topless "French" waitresses and an English Victorian decor makes for The Pinstripe's slightly campy air. Topless-club aficionados will enjoy whiling away an hour or two over dinner or a drink, attempting to guess the women's real nationalities. It's surprising how many French waitresses were born in Sweden.

PRIVATE CLUBS

Many private clubs allow American non-members a temporary membership (for a month or two) if they are traveling to London for a short stay. Be warned that you will probably pay more than regular members, though, and you should always inquire first, either by calling or writing to the club. Some places, such as Rags, require a recommendation by two other members.

The Alibi

38 King's Rd., SW3 - 584 7346

Open Mon.-Sat. 6:30 p.m.-2 a.m. Moderate membership & cover charge.

The Alibi is a good place to relax among famous and almost-famous actors and musicians. The eclectic clientele drinks, dances and/or eats at modest prices on wicker chairs bathed in a comfortable decor of pseudo-American pastels.

Annabel's

44 Berkeley Sq., W1 - 629 3558

Open Mon.-Sat. 8:30 p.m.-4 p.m. Expensive membership charge.

The most exclusive club in London and conceivably the most expensive. Distinguished patrons range from members of the aristocracy downward—but not very far—and the staff and members are the stuff of legend (and society columns). Annabel's has the most se-lective menu of any club in town. Like at all the best hotels, the staff is the soul of discretion, making this a good place for wealthy members (male or female) to romance the light of their life—other than their spouses. Membership is currently closed, though overseas visitors can apply for a three-week temporary membership, as long as they do so well in advance. Undoubtedly the Rolls-Royce of nightclubs, Annabel's has a sedate luxury that conceals a great deal of power.

The Bank

108 Queensgate, SW7 - 584 6886

Open Mon.-Sat. 10 p.m.-3 a.m. Expensive membership & cover charge.

This smart and sassy new club in South Kensington has lots of intimate alcoves around its fair-size dance floor in which you can converse or observe. The Bank is popular with the elder statesmen of the show-business and pop-music worlds and the not-so-sweet young things on the make. Arrive on the right night and you might wind up in the tabloids.

The Gardens
99 Kensington High St., W8 - 937 7994
Open Mon.-Sat. 8 p.m.-3 a.m. Expensive membership charge.

The Ferrari of nightclubs: expensive, exclusive and a nice place to be invited. Set in the penthouse of a former Derry and Toms department store, it has a most spectacular view across London. Forget about eating, unless you are on an expense account, and amuse yourself instead by watching the wealthy dancing chic to sheikh. The cocktails are out of this world.

The Hippodrome
Charing Cross Rd. off Leicester Sq., WC2
437 4311
Open Mon.-Sat. 9 p.m.-3 a.m. Moderate membership & cover charge.

Peter Stringfellow's lavish extravanganza is well worth a visit, if only to see the amazing light show over the disco floor and spot celebrities and members of the aristocracy who often pop in for a dance before moving on to someplace more exclusive. A giant video screen, six bars and gorgeous waiters/waitresses are just some of the delights to be sampled in this flamboyant arena, which is better for the occasional visit than the regular gig. Glossy live acts take the stage every night.

Legends
27 Old Burlington St., W1 - 437 9933
Open Mon.-Sat. 10:30 p.m.-3 a.m. Expensive membership & cover charge.

The result of a collison between Hollywood and Mayfair, Legends is peopled by the more anonymous business end of the show-biz spectrum. The cosmetic glamour of its '60s ambience can envelop you after the first cocktail, but it's a different world (and time) outside.

Maunkberrys
57 Jermyn St., W1 - 499 4623
Open Mon.-Sat. 10 p.m.-3 a.m. Expensive membership charge.

This upscale disco club is smart and cool without being too trendy. Though it seems to often take the overflow from Tramp (see below), it remains in a pleasant, if anonymous, class of its own.

151
151 King's Rd., SW3 - 351 6826
Open Mon.-Sat. 9 p.m.-2 a.m. Moderate membership or cover charge.

This slightly less chic version of Stock's (see below) attracts a loud, moneyed set, who tend to dance poorly and wave their City ties around in time to the music. Adequate food is served at the tables clustered around the dance floor. Dancing is only for those of strong dispositions and/or cast-iron feet.

Rags
1 Chesterfield St., W1 - 629 2592
Open Mon.-Sat. 10 p.m.-3 a.m. Expensive membership charge.

Like Maunkberrys, this smartish nightclub tends to take the overflow from Tramp (see below). The listless patrons can dine or dance while wondering if the glitzy blonds at the next table are waiting for an offer they can't refuse.

Roxanne's
11 Harrington Gdns., SW7 - 373 7143
Open Mon.-Sat. 9:30 p.m.-3 a.m. Moderate cover charge.

Despite an attempt to improve its image, Roxanne's still has all the atmosphere of a British Railways waiting room designed by Habitat. A former health club, it has plenty of space and a few intimate corners for catnapping and shop talk. Women tend to dance in threes around a molehill of handbags, ogled by the faded insurance salesmen who prop up the bar. A riot it is not.

Stocks
107 King's Rd., SW3 - 351 3461
Open Mon.-Sat. 9 p.m.-2 a.m. Expensive membership or cover charge.

This handsome, chic nightclub in the middle of King's Road is for the less frivolous night owl. Decorated like a country house, with green wood paneling adorned with huntin' and shootin' prints, it is comfortably formal and has an excellent restaurant that specializes in steak and lobster. Apart from the conservative disco, a pianist plays nightly in an ambience that reeks of Harris Tweed and Chanel No. 5.

Stringfellows

16-18 Upper St. Martin's Ln., WC2
240 5534

Open Mon.-Sat. 8 p.m.-3:30 a.m. Expensive membership or cover charge.

If you feel like a flashy night out, head for Stringfellows, where you can wine and dine upstairs in high-tech splendor, then dance till the wee hours in the downstairs disco, which boasts the most spectacular light show in London. Owner Peter Stringfellow has created an upscale version of his more accessible club, The Hippodrome. Stringfellows is patronized by pop stars, television celebrities and hordes of beautiful blond women. Unreserved in the extreme, the club is an over-the-top experience in tasteless exotica and a mirrored paradise for voyeurs and those who like their entertainment larger than life. Shamelessly sensational.

Studio Valbonne

62 Kingly St., W1 - 439 7242

Open Mon.-Sat. 9 p.m.-3:30 a.m. Moderate membership & cover charge.

Just behind Carnaby Street, La Valbonne (as it was formerly known) is a good, gimmicky disco with a sophisticated light show and very loud music. It's not a good place for an inti-

mate tête à tête, but the regulars seem to have perfected the art of semaphore to get their messages across to the bartender or their loved ones above the heady thump of disco funk.

Tokyo Joe's

85 Piccadilly, W1 - 409 1832

Open Mon.-Sat. 9 p.m.-4 a.m. Expensive membership charge.

A former parking lot, Tokyo Joe's is now a fashionable, intimate nightclub situated along Piccadilly near the Hard Rock Cafe. Lots of alcoves, a small but effective dance floor and a restaurant that serves decent French food add up to an effortlessly enjoyable night out among the anonymously prestigious—wealthy businessmen in particular. Despite the name, Tokyo Joe's tends to be populated by those from the Middle, as opposed to the Far, East.

Tramp

40 Jermyn St., W1 - 734 3174

Open Mon.-Sat. 10:30 p.m.-4 a.m. Expensive membership charge.

Still the discotheque of choice for the young, gifted and wealthy. Tramp's strict membership control has granted it longevity and exclusivity, with no discernible decline in standards.

SHOPS

BUYING LONDON

Although Oxford Street is possibly the largest shopping street in the world, when it's time to shop, the typical visitor to London has traditionally made a beeline for Harrods and Marks & Spencer. And the typical visitor *still* heads straight for these and other large department stores, which have, in fact, changed in recent years—many now house a variety of individual boutiques, such as Jaeger, Dunhill, Burberrys, Hatchards bookstore and George F. Trumper hair salon. But the savvy London shopper shouldn't limit himself or herself to the megastores. The quality and quantity of the city's boutiques have increased enormously. All the top international designers now have their own shops (the only noticeable exception being Christian Dior), and charming shop-lined streets abound.

Covent Garden has become a universal pleasure dome that no visiting shopper should miss. There you can not only shop but eat and drink, go to the theater and the opera, or simply sit in a café and watch the world go by. The core of Covent Garden is the central Market Hall, commonly known as The Market, a sturdy Georgian building with a tall glass roof, where all of London used to obtain its fruit and vegetables; it's now home to a variety of interesting shops selling anything from clothes to food to dollhouses. The always-busy and entertaining Market Hall is surrounded by outdoor stalls selling British crafts. Jubilee Market next door displays crafts, antiques or general goods, depending on the day of the week you visit. Scattered throughout the area are places to get a quick bite, as well as opportunities to listen to good live music.

Near Covent Garden is Neal Street, which has recently emerged as a terribly trendy area. One end has a distinct Eastern touch, and the other offers a sense of nostalgia, particularly at the Comic Showcase, where Batman and Bugs Bunny are beloved and where you'll find an assortment of the most unlikely people digging through the new and old comic books.

Situated throughout London's better and more intriguing neighborhoods are all sorts of marvelous shopping districts, each with its own particular charm and character. These clusters of shops and boutiques represent the best in British and foreign design, workmanship and flair: the West End, including Bond Street, still the home of quality, style and luxury; Piccadilly, presided over by Simpson's, Fortnum & Mason and the Royal Academy; crowded Oxford Street, where scarcely an English voice can be heard in the summer; Regent Street and the little shops on Jermyn Street, where royalty gets its cheeses (and shirts, for that matter); and Savile Row, the bastion of London tailoring. To the north, Chiltern Street, Marylebone High Street and St. Christopher's Place offer modern, idiosyncratic styles of their own. Most shops in these areas stay open until 8 p.m. on Thursdays.

To the southwest lie Knightsbridge, home of Harrods and Harvey Nichols; pretty Beauchamp Place; chic Walton Street; and sedate Sloane Street. Shops here stay open until 8 p.m. on Wednesdays. Sloane Street's old-money, high-society "Sloane Ranger" tradition prevails, despite the new haute-couture shops (Valentino, Saint Laurent, Chanel) at its northern end. The much more traditional General Trading Company and Peter Jones department stores, at which authentic Sloane Rangers register for their weddings, are still holding their own at the other end.

But it is Brompton Cross that has become perhaps the most fashionable shopping area in town. It is home to Joseph's large new store (where London buys the highest of high fashion), Joe's Cafe and Bibendum, all of which are constantly in the news. To the west of Brompton Cross, on Kensington High Street, you'll find a redecorated Barkers department store (now owned by House of Fraser) as well as a series of new shops for the young and the trendy. And along Kensington Church Street you'll find a row of antiques shops that wind their way up to Notting Hill Gate and continue on into Portobello Road.

All in all, London is a shopper's dream come true, an international marketplace with a dazzling variety of goods and an exceptional level of quality. Whether you're seeking the highest fashion or the most rustic antique, you'll be astounded at the breadth of selection.

ANTIQUES

A BEGINNER'S GUIDE TO ENGLISH ANTIQUES

I t is all to the good to have nodding acquaintance with the key words used by antiques dealers to describe various periods and styles. This brief guide will at least enable you to hold your head up high in London's best antiques stores.

TUDOR
1485–1558

Most of the furniture—and there wasn't much of it—was made of oak, elaborately carved and rather bulbous. Linenfold paneling on chests, and virtually anything else accessible on the market today, are about as genuine as a pawnbroker's smile. See "Victorian" for reproductions.

ELIZABETHAN
1558–1603

Not much change: The pieces are still made of oak and still very ponderous, but you will find some early inlaid items, most made of ebony and ivory and most quite small (such things as boxes and caskets). Also in evidence are a few more freestanding smaller pieces, such as side tables and joint stools, but not much of this is genuinely genuine.

JACOBEAN
1603–1660

It's beginning to get very fussy—the legs and uprights of practically everything are decorated with "barley sugar twists." The designs are still fairly heavy, the wood still primarily oak. You'll see gate-legged tables, and chairs with caned backs and seats and lots of carving, copied ad infinitum.

STUART (Carolean)
1660–1689

Most stylistic periods do not match up to the reigning dates of the kings and queens for whom they were named. Much more important than Charles II, for example, was the Great Fire of London (1666), after which everything was rebuilt by Sir Christopher Wren. Many more people became literate during the Stuart period, and desks came into their own. Some furniture was made of solid walnut and beech as well as oak. Delft pottery, pewter and simple silver were popular; today, they're all dreadfully expensive.

QUEEN ANNE
1702–1714

The most important period for practically everything: wonderful silver; furniture with lovely curving lines, made of walnut, lacquer, marquetry and parquetry; tall desks and secretaries; pier glasses; and cabriole legs on chairs, lowboys and tables. The description "Queen Anne" actually describes the furnishings made during the reign of George I.

GEORGIAN
1714–1811

The Georgian period is when everything happened: Not only was mahogany used for almost all furniture, both veneer and solid wood, but all the great names associated with English furniture were designing like mad—Chippendale, Hepplewhite and Sheraton, to name but a few. Robert Adam was around too, building houses to put it all in. In the silver department, David Willaume, Nicholas Sprimont, Robert Hennell, Hester Bateman and Henry Chawner were some of the names to reckon with. Bow, Derby, Chelsea, Bristol, Wedgwood and Spode created wonderful china and ceramics; from this time, also, came air-twist glasses with lovely spiraling stems, along with the famous "Bristol blue." It's not surprising that so much stuff in England's antiques shops is labeled "Georgian." Copies abound.

REGENCY
1811–1830

This ostentatious, gleaming style actually started appearing around 1800, when George III was still on the throne. Masses of gilt mounts on furniture, brass inlay—it's all very stylish stuff, particularly the silver, which is positively massive. Paul Storr is the key name to remember. Mason ironstone china and Minton pottery turn up along with the names that had become prominent in the Georgian period. Blond woods, often inlaid, abounded, with satinwood the best of the lot; designs featured little swags and classical motifs. At the other end of the elegant scale, Windsor chairs, with elm seats and yewwood hoops for backs and arms, became quite fashionable for use in rustic settings (such as the grotto or the folly), which is why such a traditional country-made chair got such a grand name.

VICTORIAN
1830–1900

As if the "proper queen" didn't already have a long enough reign, pieces from the William IV (or "Sailor Billy") era have been absorbed into the Victorian period, which these days is considered fashionable indeed—at least in small doses. But it wasn't so long ago that you couldn't give the stuff away. Some of it is attractive and some of it is horrible, depending on your taste. Balloon-backed chairs were made by the millions, along with bulging sofas and "confidantes," designed so a girl could sit next to a man without touching him. The early years brought quite fine reproductions, particularly of "Chippendale" furniture and "Queen Anne" silver. Later on, there was the birth of art nouveau; pieces from that movement have now become extremely valuable. The same holds true of Doulton and Minton pottery, plant stands and jardinieres in bilious colors, most of them made to decorate conservatories, along with rubber plants and maidenhair ferns. As a sort of flight into the romantic past in the face of the Industrial Revolution, masses of mock medieval furniture and objects were produced, often fondly known as "Jacobean." Also in evidence were quasi-French pieces nicknamed "Louis le Hotel."

EDWARDIAN
1900–1920

This period was virtually barren of new ideas in design, except for a few last flowerings of art nouveau, such as the work of G. R. Mackintosh of the famed Glasgow school. But he had to go abroad in search of recognition, and his stuff is virtually unobtainable in England. Rather ominously like its people and its politics, much of the furniture of the Edwardian period was often thinly veneered on poor-quality woods. Some of it was well made, however, and it has been going up in esteem recently.

ART DECO
1920-1940

This import from France never did as well in England as art nouveau, a native product in spite of its name. Most pieces from the art deco period are still finding their niche as "antiques," with the notable exception of glass. But the glass work was either French (Daum, Galle, Lalique) or American (Tiffany), except for English-made light fixtures, which blossomed at Liberty and have been copied ever since . . . in plastic!

ANTIQUES MARKETS

Antiquarius
135-141 King's Rd., SW3 - 675 6155
Open Mon.-Sat. 10 a.m.-6 p.m.

More than 150 dealers large and small are crammed cheek by jowl in this amazing place. The atmosphere can be guessed by the names—many of the dealers insisting on being called "Mr." or "Mrs.," an attempt, no doubt, to maintain a certain social standing among the Bens and Dans and Ninas. B. Barkoff sells inkwells, knives and forks; Mr. and Mrs. Bach specialize in art deco and art nouveau; Fanfreluchs sells costume jewelry; Mr. Knee and Alexander Tichfield don't have a cohesive selection of "general antiques," but their art deco collection isn't bad; Arita sells Daum, Loetz and Galle glass and those peculiar lamps that look like fly-speckled fungi; Brian Tipping specializes in antique pipes, which he assures us are sanitized before being sold; Salvador Vartuli hunches over crocodile purses and empty dressing cases; and there's even a stall displaying old fountain pens and gasoline-filled cigarette lighters. When trade is slack, you'll find many a game of chess, backgammon and draughts going on as you wander down the narrow aisles.

If reproduction antiques are permitted, then why not reproduction clothes? Two merchants in particular deserve special mention: Eavis & Brown, shimmering in the depths of the market among the clocks and bric-a-brac with a stunning collection of '20s- and '30s-style dresses alight with fiery sequins; and Mr. Gubbins, just inside the King's Road entrance, who makes the most dreamy wedding dresses from oyster satin and wild silk in true period styles, foaming with lace or gleaming with beadwork. Heaps of them are piled like so much crème fraîche in the tiny booth, and you may have one made to order (which takes three months). One more surprise: Nick and Sue Alloway have a neat, well-ordered collection of blue-and-white china to covet and admire.

Bond Street Antique Centre
124 New Bond St., W1
Open Mon.-Fri. 10 a.m.-6 p.m.

The 25 dealers here cover the antiques field from every which way; some are good, some not so good. The Oriental bric-a-brac is pretty costly, but you can find good values in other departments, at such places as Limner Antiques (629 5314), which sells good portrait miniatures, and K. Edwards (629 1670), a small space filled with everything imaginable piled in unlikely heaps: fans, pictures, period costumes, old lanterns, swords, small boxes, statuary draped in beads and textiles. Stanley Beal (499 1041) leans toward the Gothic, with such curiosities as a silver-mounted skull among his silver plate. Schaverein (493 3938) is notable for a crowded display of ephemera and for the owner, who wears a clutter of cigarette cards pinned around his head. Gone are the days when these brightly illustrated and informative little pieces of cardboard served as schoolboys' trading currency—they're much too expensive for that sort of foolishness now.

Chelsea Antique Market
245A & 253 King's Rd., SW3 - 352 5689
Open Mon.-Sat. 10 a.m.-6 p.m.

Down a little alleyway, between a shoe shop and an art gallery, stands the entrance to London's first antiques market, established in the '60s by actors "taking a break" and singers not singing. For the most part, the Chelsea Antique Market today is a shadow of its former self; it's best to turn a blind eye to the various stalls and head straight for the major occupant (and, in fact, the proprietor), Harrington Bros., whose display of beautifully bound volumes arrests the eye at street level and whose print shop is on the second floor. Up a flight of narrow stairs at the top of the building, Harrington's full glory reveals itself: Shelved floor to ceiling are hundreds of rare books. Here a philistine with an empty bookcase can fill it with yards of Dickens, Trollope, Shakespeare and the Georgian poets, for about £2,000, depending on the titles chosen. Bookworms with very clean hands can browse for hours, while collectors can pass an afternoon discussing a single rare book with one or another of the Harrington brothers. They specialize in natural history—there's often a volume or two of J. Gould's *Rare Birds* on the bottom shelf—and also deal extensively in topography. Their maps encompass the entire world ("and the south of England," they add firmly). While the young saleswomen keep business moving smoothly in the three separate Harrington shops, one of the brothers keeps a silent vigil via a closed-circuit television, thus allowing browsers to browse undisturbed but keenly observed.

Gray's Antique Market
58 Davies St., W1 - 629 7034
Open Mon.-Fri. 10 a.m.-6 p.m.

A remarkable place to find in the center of London, Gray's is stacked with stalls ranging from the chic to the shabby (including the shabby-chic, the hippest of all). Pick your way through the crowded alleys and head downstairs, where you'll find The Thimble Society of London and the Button Lady, two homes of tiny, terribly expensive rarities. Arca is filled with ivory fans and a fine collection of walking sticks; David Hogg has locks, padlocks, tools and keys of every size and shape; and Armoury Antiques will let you handle a genuine dueling pistol off the wall, where signs read, "No reproductions—all articles guaranteed genuine." There are cigarette-card specialists, souvenir-mug dealers and shops thick with antiquarian books and prints. Monty Lo, surprisingly, sells not Orientalia but Meissen and Dresden china, and Iona Antiques has lovely

paintings of animals. Like Hansel and Gretel, you may have to come up with some method of marking your trail in this cluttered warren of merchants, so you can return to the object that first caught your eye.

Gray's Mews
1-7 Davies Mews, W1 - 629 7034, 450 7683
Open Mon.-Fri. 10 a.m.-6 p.m.

Just around the corner from Gray's Antique Market, Gray's Mews lacks its neighbor's market atmosphere—it's more like an antiques fair or arcade, with less clutter and perhaps more quality. Here you'll find theatrical memorabilia at Leading Lady, Victorian jet jewelry at Allison's, golf books at Golfiana, mechanical curiosities at Howard Hope and extraordinary novelties of great rarity from the '20s and '30s at Studium (such as the handbag in the shape of a three-funneled transatlantic liner).

AUCTION HOUSES

Bonham's
(W. & F. C. Bonham & Sons Ltd.)
Montpelier Galleries, Montpelier St., Knightsbridge, SW7 - 584 9161

Still a family firm, with young Mr. Nicholas on the board and on the rostrum, Bonham's is a small, intimate auction room frequented primarily by private buyers, many of whom live in the area. Regular auctions are conducted with great conviviality—auctions of paintings, for example, are held to coincide with the Smithfield Fatstock Show, Crufts Dog Show, Chelsea Flower Show and Cowes Week, and all take place in the evening, after a glass or two of chilled white wine is served. Visitors include as many tweed-jacketed owners, breeders and growers as there are buyers from the Bond Street galleries. (Occasionally a venerable, flawlessly trained Labrador snoozes peacefully at the back of the room.) Bonham's has been particularly successful with Lalique; its last sale was held in a luxury-liner atmosphere that beautifully suited the subject. Imaginative and helpful, everyone at Bonham's really seems to care. Worth mentioning as well is its successful little lunchtime café, open to the public and a very good value. The food isn't earth-shattering, but it's all very well prepared, presented and served, and should be remembered by weary Knightsbridge trekkers.

Bonham's New Chelsea Galleries
65-69 Lots Rd., SW10 - 351 1380

This small offshoot of the Montpelier Galleries sells furniture and carpets every Tuesday and paintings every two weeks. It also auctions occasional curious collections of early radios, typewriters and "tomorrow's antiques," which usually offer plenty of opportunity for the brave, the farsighted and the impecunious.

Christie's
(Christie, Manson and Woods Ltd.)
8 King St., SW1 - 839 9060

It was once part of the regular routine of the gentleman about town to pop into Christie's as he might into his own club, with a deceptively innocent air, to check out forthcoming sales in order to stay current on the rise or fall of his family's fortune. Christie's, London's most discreet auction house, still handles the possessions and estates of those listed in *Burke's Peerage*, *Debretts* and the *Almanac da Gotha*. The young ladies and gentlemen manning the front counter in this huge place are charming and well informed, answering endless queries and attending to the occupants of the small private rooms, where items are appraised for possible sale. Even the porters, standing guard over showcases packed with treasures and walls groaning with old masters, are more knowledgeable than many prospective buyers. Well-thumbed catalogs hang from strings for all to peruse, and you can always purchase the glossy new ones produced for major sales; they are packed with illustrations and information, including estimated prices (making them useful rough guides for novices). Call to have a sale calendar sent to you; it will indicate the viewing days, when you may inspect the stuff whether you intend to buy or not.

Christie's South Kensington
85 Old Brompton Rd., SW7 - 581 2231

Christie's little sister has been steadily transforming herself from a glorious hodgepodge of showrooms and salesrooms into a well-organized series of galleries. Once the site of an airplane-engine manufacturer, the main gallery is still called "the Hanger"; pieces of it are cordoned off for small sales. In all this hive of activity there is at least one sale a day in progress, if not two or three, all fairly small

(consisting of a couple of hundred lots or so) and all specialized. This Christie's has bravely pioneered the sale of the many collectibles so highly sought after by fashionable types, from the pottery of jazzy '30s artist/designer Clarice Cliff to papier-mâché. It also sponsors excellent small sales of textiles, costumes, dolls, teddy bears, scientific instruments, early photographs and all manner of unusual items. Regular evening viewings attract crowds of first-time buyers, and both the staff and the clientele are upwardly mobile—many of today's best-known authorities started off somewhere in this great sprawl of buildings.

Lots Road Chelsea Galleries
71 Lots Rd., SW10 - 351 5784

Rather like a repertory theater, this auction house is highly original, enormous fun and a bit of a gamble. Monday evening sales offer a motley collection of weird and wonderful objects, from cast-iron hat stands and old pub tables to majolica, Victorian wash stands, towel rails, dining tables, chairs, Empire-style daybeds and chenille curtains tied up with string. It's possibly the last place in London where bargains can still be found and where decorators with unerring eyes can discover unlikely objects that will transform interiors. Well worth a visit, particularly in summer, when the surrounding area looks a bit less like an industrial wasteland, and the huge chimneys of Lots Road Power Station take on a strange glamour against the hazy summer sky.

Phillips
(Phillips, Son & Neale)
7 Blenheim St. at New Bond St., W1
629 6602

A little hard to find in spite of its tremendous size, Phillips fills and empties no fewer than five sprawling floors of antiques, art and collectibles every two weeks. The atmosphere is a little less upbeat than at Christie's and Sotheby's, and prices seldom hit astronomical records, but in some categories, Phillips is a better bet for both buyer and seller. Its strong suit lies in middle-priced objects with careful attention paid to (and advice given regarding) the sort of pieces that can be swept away unnoticed in a general sale elsewhere. The department comprising books, manuscripts, maps and prints is particularly notable, and the sales of art nouveau and art deco objects are always well cataloged. Costumes, textiles, lace, embroidery and fans are also handled well, as is metalware. Look for the regular sales of good-quality silver, fine jewelry, toy soldiers and mechanical toys; philatelists and scripophiles will appreciate the regular sales of stamps, old bank notes and share certificates, some of which are so decorative that they deserve framing. Don't be alarmed if you find yourself sharing an elevator with a large bronze horse or naked nymph, or if you find the reception area overshadowed by a huge stone statue recently dredged from some moat or lake—it's all part of Phillips's stock-in-trade.

Sotheby's London
34 New Bond St., W1 - 493 8080

The entrance to this venerable institution is hardly wider than the magazine kiosk next door, but inside the vista widens as stairs and hallways lead away in tangled confusion (ask the beaming attendant behind the catalog counter how to find what you're looking for). Behind the street facade of fashionable shops and boutiques, Sotheby's extends throughout the entire block to St. George Street and Conduit Street, where there are entrances to even more galleries and salesrooms. Here you'll find the lesser sales that are held on the first Monday of the month; these accept credit cards and offer a low-cost delivery service. Each sale encompasses furniture, silver, ceramics, glass, clocks, silver, pictures and rugs, all of which can be viewed the previous Thursday, Friday and Sunday, as well as the morning of the sale. As at "the other place" (rivals Sotheby's and Christie's seldom refer to each other by name), a front-counter staff offers advice and valuation, but things are less discreet. Would-be sellers may not care to be embarrassed by a specialist who dismisses grandmother's jet necklace as nothing but vulcanite and barely worth the taxi ride over here; if so, they should insist on being taken up to the particular department itself, where at least a certain amount of privacy prevails. The main galleries often broker large American and Continental collections belonging to jet-set types who still consider London to be the greatest center of fine art and antiques in the world.

STREET MARKETS & FLEA MARKETS

Bermondsey Market
Caledonian Rd., Bermondsey
Open Fri. 5 a.m.-2 p.m.

It is said that if you get to Bermondsey between 6 and 7 a.m. you may find yourself buying something that the seller has no right to. Though it's almost certainly a legend, there was a time when petty thieves unloaded their loot here early in the morning, when the stall holders were set up but the crowds had not arrived. And there's still a feeling of furtiveness, a sense that Fagin's boys are picking a pocket or two in the narrow alleys between the packed stalls on the cobbled square. In fact, this is no place for loitering, but not for crime reasons—there's just no time to dawdle over decision making. The moment you put something down, a hand appears and picks it up, a bargain is struck, and your potential purchase is gone forever. Go in summer, when dawn breaks early, or you'll need a powerful flashlight and a razor-sharp mind under the flapping tarpaulins. Never try to bargain—there's only one price here, and that's the trade price. And never, if you take your purchase into the harsh light of one of the nearby early-morning cafés and find it terribly wrong, attempt to return it. What's done is done. It's pretty tough in Bermondsey.

In the tall old warehouses surrounding the market, you'll discover more stalls—these manned by dealers who have a little more time to talk, though their eyes are always looking over your shoulder, in case a regular should slip past. You can find old kitchen items in larger quantities than at most other places—curious cast-iron bean slicers, herb choppers, wooden bowls, laundry dollies—but don't expect them to be cheap. Old toys and dolls, missing ears and eyes and legs, are heartbreakingly eloquent in their abandonment. As you wander you'll see heaps of pot lids, china galore, beads, fans, walking sticks, art deco objects and tomorrow's new collectibles, if you're smart enough to spot them. Take cash, don't flash it around, keep it in an inside pocket and count your change. Happy hunting!

Camden Lock Antiques Centre
Camden High St., NW1
Open Wed.-Fri. 9:30 a.m.-5:30 p.m., Sat.-Sun. 9:30 a.m.-6 p.m.

Not to be confused with Camden Passage (in Islington), this walled city of glorious junk, under a railway bridge over a canal, is noticeably younger, more left-wing and feminist in orientation than the other street markets. The stock runs to ethnic clothes and oddities, lots of books, toys, festoons of beads and ethnic jewelry, and quantities of art deco, both good and bad. Here are the potential collectors and dealers of tomorrow, with babies on knee and toddlers underfoot, earnest but lighthearted, committed but still unshackled. And here, as at the Portobello Road market (see facing column), is a goodly crowd of out-of-work actors and dancers, turning a penny while they wait for the telephone to ring.

Camden Passage
Camden Passage, N1 - 359 0825
Open Mon.-Fri. 10:30 a.m.-5:30 p.m. Market days: Wed., general antiques, 8 a.m.-3 p.m.; Thurs., books, 9 a.m.-4 p.m.; Sat., general antiques, 9 a.m.-5 p.m.

An aura of gentility and civilized living pervades this extensive warren of arcades, passages, galleries and markets—perhaps because restaurateur Robert Carrier (of Carrier's) brought a certain cachet to the area, perhaps because it is so surrounded with antiques shops that it seems almost like an overflow, perhaps because its wide main street lends it an air of graciousness. Whatever the reason, there are now a dozen different wine bars, bistros and little restaurants tucked in among the dealers; on a fine day it's a delight to spend hours wandering among the wares, pausing for a glass of wine, a slice of quiche or a proper meal. The variety here is tremendous, from such little shops as Pierrepoint Arcade's Sherry Hatcher, which sells tiny silver boxes, scent bottles and the like, to the House of Steel (up near Bermondsey on Caledonian Road), which does a brisk business in architectural salvage: balconies, spiral staircases, garden furniture, fireplaces and metalwork.

Portobello Road
Westbourne Grove, W11
Open Sat. 6 a.m.-3 p.m. Some stalls open Fri. 8 a.m.-4:30 p.m.

Eating cherries from brown paper bags, sampling exotic West Indian takeout food, sipping draft Guinness while sitting on the sidewalk outside one of the many pubs in the district—that's how you may find Portobello Road's dealers, bargain hunters, buyers and sellers of anything and everything. Joss sticks by the bundle, printers' blocks, old lace, silver, gold (and that which passes for gold), antique music boxes, old knives, swords, saucepans, jelly molds, candlesticks—this flea market has it all. The official antiques market starts at the top of the hill, then slides down through the "silver section," where it changes abruptly into a fruit and vegetable market. It then regains its antiques equilibrium, though rather shakily, at its darker, more sinister end, thick with stalls of old clothes, belt buckles, knickknacks and old wind-up Victrolas. On fine days, weaving through it all are all sorts of outlandish young people: skinheads, young bloods with peacock-proud Mohawk haircuts in phosphorescent colors, the leather mob, heavy-metal boys and orange-robed, white-faced Hare Krishna followers. In between are a one-man band, an escape artist who writhes in and out of his well-worn chains, photographers who deposit parrots and monkeys on unsuspecting shoulders and, in winter, hawkers of hot chestnuts and baked potatoes.

Among this dizzying wealth of activity, seemingly unending warrens of antiques arcades wind through blocks of buildings. In the Geoffrey Van Arcade, Pat Nye sells Gaudy Welsh pottery, Quimper and French faïence, needlework samplers and oodles of brass, from snuffboxes and candlesticks to kettle stands, trivets, strongboxes and ember tongs. Peter Delehar, one of the market's oldest inhabitants, sells curious and unusual scientific instruments, the uses for which one can only guess at with alarm. Cohen & Pearce, more of an established shop, deals in Oriental porcelain, Japanese prints and Chinese bronzes. John Page Phillips is a writers' man who sells everything to do with desks and pens: paperweights, pen trays, letter scales, ink blotters and much more. Barham Fine Art is a veritable emporium of mixed dates, styles and continents: Victorian fans, Chinese porcelain, old clocks, writing boxes, watercolors and oils, marbles, bronzes and furniture. John Bull Antiques Ltd. carries silver, Sheffield plate and some of the market's best jewelry (much of the stuff in the stalls is dreadful junk), and is a better bet than the hill's recent crop of Asian silver merchants, who seem to sell copies of copies. In the Dolphin Arcade, Books and Things is exactly that: good-value books, sometimes secondhand and sometimes antiquarian, along with posters and prints. As for the rest of the dealers, of whom there are legion, you pays your money and you takes your chances, as the saying goes. You just might find something that everyone else has missed, but you have to get up mighty early to beat the crowds.

ART NOUVEAU & ART DECO

Chenil Galleries
181-183 King's Rd., SW3 - 351 5353
Open Mon.-Sat. 10 a.m.-6 p.m.

London's first flowering of art deco dealers congregated in this tremendously impressive collection of galleries, whose domed ceiling displays a painting in high art deco style. Many of the less serious dealers have since moved to Antiquarius, leaving this core of specialists. Inside Chenil are the Pruskin Gallery, B. J. Chilton and Judy Daniels, all of whom specialize in art deco objects and jewelry and are well worth a visit. But we've noticed a recent drop in Chenil's standards; some fly-by-night dealers lurk in small booths, buying and selling anything they can lay their hands on, worth it or not. An exception is Nicolaus, son of a well-known country dealer, who's headquartered downstairs, where he displays a fine collection of much-sought-after Minton, Bretby and Moorcroft-Macintyre pieces, as well as some excellent country furniture at quite reasonable prices. His shop is particularly worth watching, since his instinct led him to buy Minton a couple of years before the market for it took off. He's now dabbling in turn-of-the-century Islamic metalware, displaying a sure eye for the appealing and the decorative.

Editions Graphiques Gallery
3 Clifford St., W1 - 734 3944
Open Mon.-Fri. 10 a.m.-6 p.m., Sat. 10 a.m.-2 p.m.

Just off Bond Street's beaten path, Victor Arwas opened the first gallery in London to specialize in graphics and art deco back in 1966. A great authority with many books to his name, Arwas deals in graphics from 1880 to the present day, including many original color lithographs and such prizes as *Affiche* by Toulouse-Lautrec, which today costs about £1,200. He also displays plenty of examples of Preiss, Chiparus and other "modern movement" sculptors, whose work some say is fluid; others call it slimy. Original graphics, woodcuts and etchings can cost as little as £5 or as much as £10,000. The collection is rounded out with examples of fine and applied arts, including art deco glass, ceramics and furniture.

Haslam and Whiteway
105 Kensington Church St., W8 - 229 1145
Open Mon.-Fri. 10 a.m.-6 p.m., Sat. 10 a.m.-1 p.m.

The shop may look small from street level, but down below are showrooms full of excellent examples of British decorative art from 1830 to 1930. Co-owner Michael Whiteway was one of the first dealers to remove the stigma from the label "Victorian," opening people's eyes to the excellent design and workmanship of the nineteenth-century arts and crafts movement. And he is still discovering fine, original pieces by more recent furniture designers and architects, most of whom are still largely unrecognized by the general public. Occasional paintings, pieces of silver, sculpture and stained glass show up.

BOOKS, MAPS & PRINTS

The massive British Museum looms over a warren of small streets lined with bookshops. This area fairly echoes with the ghostly footsteps of the Bloomsbury set, most of whose publishers' offices were located on Russell Square just around the corner.

Mr. Ayres
31 Museum St., WC1 - 636 2844
Open Mon.-Sat. 10 a.m.-6 p.m.

Deep in the recesses of this wonderful emporium, Mr. Ayres can usually be found drinking tea from a thick white china cup, examining his latest acquisitions before relegating them to their appropriate places in the glorious jumble. These may include anything from Indonesian stilt-walking puppets, pottery shards and antiquities to old children's books, prints and piles of ethnographic items. A closer look at the dusty glass-fronted bookcases will reveal a fine selection of private-press volumes from Nonesuch Press, Golden Cockerell, Cresset and the like.

Bell, Book and Radmall
4 Cecil Ct., WC2 - 240 2161
Open Mon.-Sat. 9:30 a.m.-6 p.m.

Located in an alley between St. Martin's Lane and Charing Cross Road, this deliciously time-consuming bookseller specializes in expensive first editions of nineteenth- and twentieth-century English and American literature—for example, a first-edition presentation copy of F. Scott Fitzgerald's *Tender Is the Night*, inscribed by Matthew Josephson, Fitzgerald's first biographer, for £3,250. Considerably less hard on the budget, as well as lots of fun, is the early detective and sci-fi fantasy fiction.

Louis B. Bondy
16 Little Russell St., WC1 - 405 2733
Open Mon.-Fri. 10 a.m.-6 p.m., Sat. 10 a.m.-5 p.m.

This bookish little shop, with steamed-up windows revealing heaps of as-yet-unsorted books, produces in its prospective customers strange demeanors as they try to read the titles sideways in their stacks. The small quarters contain unsteady shelves piled with rare volumes, good secondhand books on foreign art and architecture, some theater, travel, memoirs and classics and a sprinkling of inviting and informative small volumes, such as the invaluable *American Shrines in England*.

For more good reading, see the "Books & Stationery" section later in this chapter.

Pleasures of Past Times
11 Cecil Ct., WC2 - 836 1142
Open Mon.-Fri. 11 a.m.-2:30 p.m. & 3:30 p.m.-6 p.m., Sat. (except 1st Sat. of the month) 11 a.m.-2:15 p.m.

Longing for the shop to reopen after its late-lunch closing, scores of young customers press their noses against the window. Pleasures of Past Times is truly not to be missed. For one thing, it's a very pretty place. For another, its staff is precise and helpful. And its merchandise is irresistible. Models of Mr. Pollet's Theatre, early children's books with illustrations to lose yourself in, fairy tales, adventure stories, books on the theater, playbills, posters, postcards of Edwardian belles and their beaux, Victorian valentines frothy with lace and libidinous sentiment, rag books, pop-ups, cut-outs—every pumpkin is a carriage and every frog a prince in this land of enchantment.

B. Weinreb
34 Museum St., WC1
Open Mon.-Fri. 10 a.m.-6 p.m., Sat. 10 a.m.-5 p.m.

The premises are small but roomy, and the walls display a fine collection of architectural prints and engravings, from detailed elevations and floor plans of eighteenth-century villas to monolithic classical statues. Ben Weinreb was the originator and part author of the comprehensive and highly praised *The London Encyclopaedia*, so it should come as no surprise that his shop stocks a small selection of architectural reference books and often hosts small exhibitions of hand-colored lithographs.

CLOCKS, WATCHES & SCIENTIFIC INSTRUMENTS

G. S. Mathias
R5-R6 Antiquarius Antique Market, 135-141 King's Rd., SW3 - 351 0484
Open Mon.-Sat. 10 a.m.-6 p.m.

Fascinating insight into the care, repair and restoration of antique clocks will reward those who seek out this shop. Behind the display of fine eighteenth-century long-case clocks, and flanked by stacks of lap desks, writing boxes and all kinds of postal antiques, is Gerald Mathias's workshop. Here, between discussions on the relative shapes and sizes of Liverpool long cases (wider and flatter, with moon-phase dials) and the sophistication of Home Counties models (with rocking, cut-steel figures of old Father Time), he tinkers with the movements, dials and spandrels, cleaning and repairing clocks and watches of every shape and size.

Rafferty & Huber
34 Kensington Church St., W8 - 938 1100
Open Mon.-Sat. 10 a.m.-5:30 p.m.

Specializing in clocks with weird movements and striking mechanisms, in addition to art deco "Tudric" pewter-and-copper timepieces (meaning clocks without striking mechanisms), Rafferty & Huber also stocks highly original and complex mechanical instruments. Antique watches and clocks are not only sold here but repaired and restored, too. Though the shop is not large, space is always made for some small pieces of seventeenth-, eighteenth- and nineteenth-century furniture, with particular emphasis on the decorative and unusual.

Strike One Islington Ltd.
51 Camden Passage, N1 - 226 9709
Open Mon.-Sat. 9 a.m.-5 p.m. & by appt.

This Camden Passage clock shop specializes in early English wall clocks, particularly tavern clocks and Act of Parliament clocks. No kitsch, no art deco, just pedigrees made before 1870. English long-case clocks made by the finest makers from 1675 to 1820 sell for nothing less than £3,000, so bring your checkbook. On a smaller scale: little English lantern clocks, skeleton clocks, regulator clocks and barometers. Strike One also boasts a good selection of horological reference books.

Igor Tociapski
39-41 Ledbury Rd., W11 - 229 8317
Open Mon.-Thurs. 10 a.m.-5:30 p.m.

Banks of regulator clocks, dusty skeleton clocks without their protective glass domes, bracket clocks and carriage clocks clutter a small space that's made to seem even smaller by the proprietor, a great bear of a man (which is probably why he is often found sitting on the doorstep with a couple of equally huge and friendly dogs). In the dusty window there are always several extraordinary scientific and astronomical instruments—the odd telescope, small hand compasses and other fascinating gadgets—most of which are protected in worn leather cases.

Harriet Wynter Ltd.
50 Redcliffe Rd., SW10 - 352 6494
Open by appt. only.

A haven for the voyager or would-be time traveler, this shop is filled with globes, astrolabes, orreries, maps of the heavens, the earth and the oceans, and instruments for navigating, shooting the sun and plumbing the depths—each as decorative as a piece of sculpture. They'll have you marveling at the scientific knowledge of our centuries-back ancestors. Books and occasional maps and prints on this specialized subject are also sold, and services include restoration, repair and the proffering of a wealth of knowledge about these quaint and curious objects.

FURNITURE

Heritage Antiques
112 Islington High St., Camden Passage, N1 - 226 7789
Open Wed. 9 a.m.-4:30 p.m., Sat. 9:30 a.m.-5 p.m.

Heritage stocks lots of oak and country furniture and a dazzle of brass, from fire irons and fire tools to jack racks, trivets and footmen from the seventeenth to the nineteenth century. Not all of it is as old as it seems, but if you ask, the staff will tell you straight.

Hotspur Ltd.
14 Lowndes St., SW1 - 235 1918
Open Mon.-Fri. 8:30 a.m.-6 p.m., Sat. 9:30 a.m.-1 p.m.

Obscured today by the vast bulk of the Carlton Tower Hotel, a small street of eighteenth-century townhouses has managed to maintain its integrity, despite the hideous traffic that passes down streets more suited to hansom cabs. Here, Hotspur displays superb eighteenth-century English furniture of modest grandeur, excellent taste and fine quality, all on a scale that suits the elegant proportions of the house itself. Everything is displayed with plenty of space and light, reflected in stunning chinoiserie and rococo pier glasses, whose carved gilt frames are fantasies of birds and waterfalls, festoons of curling leaves and tracery.

Mallett & Son Antiques Ltd.

40 New Bond St., W1 - 499 7411
2 Davies St. (Bourdon House), Berkeley
Sq., W1 - 629 2444
Open Mon.-Fri. 9:30 a.m.-5:30 p.m.

Although Mallett ranks as one of London's oldest antiques dealers, and has some of the finest eighteenth-century furniture in town, the ambience here is generally youthful, upbeat and enthusiastic. Mallett has a flair for unusual and decorative objects; one is likely to find its expansive New Bond Street showroom spanned by an exquisite pair of wrought-iron gates wide enough to admit a carriage and pair, a small grotesque stone carving or a Gothic lantern. It favors not so much ormolu as fine boulle and tortoiseshell inlay—English rather than French taste—and has collections of needlework, tapestries, rare long-case and bracket clocks, some porcelain and pottery, and pictures of sporting or other decorative subjects. At Mallett's other shop in Bourdon House you'll encounter larger pieces of statuary, garden furniture, cast iron, stone and marble, along with Continental furniture that's still much in the English taste.

Partridge Fine Arts Ltd.

144-146 New Bond St., W1 - 629 0834
Open Mon.-Fri. 9:30 a.m.-5:30 p.m.

Entering the doors of Partridge, one steps into a distillation of the classic stately English home. A fire leaps in a grand marble fireplace, and stretching off in the distance is a wide, thickly carpeted passage leading to a broad flight of stairs, which climbs to the drawing room of a state apartment, or so it seems. Below, on either side, doors lead to beautifully furnished and decorated rooms displaying fine English furniture, their walls hung with paintings from the English and Italian schools—the traditional choice of stately English homes. Filling out the rooms are silver on the tables and side tables, ormolu clocks and wall brackets, Waterford glass chandeliers and an occasional tapestry or fine Oriental rug. A rich, thoughtful silence pervades the atmosphere; this is a place where one can ponder, admire and make one's purchases in the calmest, most discreetly luxurious setting in London. Go ahead and exclaim your delight—but quietly, please.

This and That

50-51 Chalk Farm Rd., NW1 - 267 5433
Open Tues.-Sat. 10:30 a.m.-6 p.m., Sun. 11:30 a.m.-5:30 p.m.

A lovely place full of creaking country furniture—stripped pine tables, dressers and chairs, with some oak pieces—This and That offers very low prices on the whole, though these big items can be costly to ship.

GLASS

Brian Beet

3B Burlington Gdns., W1 - 437 4975
Open Mon.-Fri. 10 a.m.-6 p.m., Sat. 10 a.m.-1 p.m.

Wondrous are the ingenious gadgets invented to make drinking simpler: Champagne taps and bottle stoppers, patented corkscrews, cork grips, pocketknives and wire snippers for Champagne, bottle stands, bottle tickets, cellarman's aides . . . and, of course, drinking glasses. Also to be found here are antique books on wine and beer, together with many rare trinkets, most of them valued because of their ephemeral qualities—perhaps celebrating a vintage, a special event or a passing fancy, such as the tobacco box for "discriminating chewers" of Piper Heidsieck's Champagne-flavored chewing tobacco.

Delomosne & Son Ltd.

4 Campden Hill Rd., off Kensington High St., W8 - 937 1804
Open Mon.-Fri. 9 a.m.-5:30 p.m., Sat. 9 a.m.-1 p.m.

Tall, studious-looking Mr. Mortimer considers eighteenth-century glass to still be quite undervalued, and his crystal cave will prove that a fine, representative collection of early drinking glasses will cost one-tenth the price of any comparable span of fine period pieces. He prefers the simplicity of early baluster drinking glasses to the more showy air twists, and always has a wide selection of them, along with fine table glass, richly colored "Bristol" blue and green glass, heavy Irish cut glass, candelabra and chandeliers. Delomosne also has a discriminating selection of English and European porcelain of a delicacy that will please those who delight in the finest glass. Mortimer and staff urge people not to be afraid of collecting glass—if it were really so fragile, how could so much have survived to the present day?

Jeanette Hayhurst

3B Burlington Gdns., W1 - 437 4975
Open Mon.-Fri. 10 a.m.-6 p.m., Sat. 10 a.m.-1 p.m.

When you exit the top end of Burlington Arcade, you'll find yourself facing a small shop in which a triumvirate of dealers conduct their business. Jeanette Hayhurst, one of the three, deals in fine glass and has a "Black Museum" of fakes to demonstrate her extensive, ebullient knowledge of the subject. She recently added iridescent Roman glass to her repertoire of eighteenth-century drinking glasses, decanters, table glass and what are known in the trade as "fancies": a slightly derogatory term for curious, cunning objects fashioned in glass.

Christopher Wray's Lighting Emporium

600 King's Rd., SW6 - 736 8434
Open Mon.-Sat. 10 a.m.-6 p.m.

Of Christopher Wray's three wonderful establishments, the Lighting Emporium is the one that stocks antique light fixtures from the art nouveau and "early Liberty" periods. The place resembles an enormous magic garden with swan-necked flowers drooping bell-like from shelves, tables and walls. This stuff may not be to everybody's taste; some of the ceiling fixtures remind us of old B-movie hotel foyers (round, dim and usually marbled or veined), but others are richly colorful, if not garish.

MILITARIA

Robert Hales Antiques Ltd.

133 Kensington Church St., W8 - 229 3887
Open Mon.-Fri. 10:30 a.m.-5:30 p.m.

Although Robert Hales originally dealt in primitive oceanic and ethnographic art, today he is known for Eastern European, Middle Eastern, Ottoman, Oriental and Indonesian arms and armor. His Ottoman, Mamluk and Qajar swords and knives—jeweled, silver-hilted and jade-handled—are decorative objects in their own right, and his small showroom has as fine a display of kindjals (double-edged Caucasus knives), jambiyas (curved Arabian knives) and kris (short, wavy Malaysian swords) as one is likely to find in

London. Occasionally he finds such rarities as Macedonian warriors' belts, six inches deep and heavily studded with giant carnelians—which, he says, look good on women in black dresses.

Under Two Flags

4 St. Christopher's Pl., W1 - 935 6934
Open Tues.-Sat. 10 a.m.-5 p.m.

Many men in the medical profession play war games and collect militaria. Many are also Scottish. Perhaps that's the reason why the two flags under which Mr. Coutts buys, sells, discusses and discourses are neither English and French nor English and American, but English and Scottish. Rank upon rank of toy and model soldiers of every nationality, regiment and squadron march eternally in step with swinging kilts, tall bearskins, kepis and caps; mounted officers perch atop prancing horses draped in streaming pennants; and entire military bands drum up fighting spirit. Military prints and a small selection of books, commemorative china and small bronzes are other offerings.

MISCELLANY

Commemoratives

3 Pierrepoint Arcade, Camden Passage, N1
Open Wed. & Sat. 10 a.m.-5:30 p.m., Fri. 2:30 p.m.-5:30 p.m.

This place sells glorious, gaudy, flag-waving commemoratives of every kind, from plaques to mugs—and not just those good old Coronation souvenir mugs, either. There are all manner of theatrical and film posters and promotional goodies and, of course, political souvenirs. Some of the rarer pieces may shock you by their prices, which are nonetheless usually justifiable.

Anthea Knowles Rare Toys and Fine Dolls

42 Colebrook Row, N1 - 354 2333
Open by appt. only.

Come here for all those curious wind-up toys, tin plate, clockworks and mechanical inventions that were made for yesterday's children. They're all selling for horribly high prices. (Remember the teddy bear you junked years ago? It's probably worth a fortune now.) This is no place to buy toys for real children;

it's only for those who have remained children at heart while their bank balances have become decidedly mature.

The Patchwork Dog and the Calico Cat Ltd.

21 Chalk Farm Rd., NW1 - 485 1239
Open Tues.-Sat. 10 a.m.-6 p.m.

This shop not only sells authentic antique American and English quilts, it even gives the stories behind the traditional patterns; and it actually runs quilting bees upstairs. The stock runs to large quilts, delicious pillows and cushions, small baby quilts, a whole library of quilting books and beginners' kits if you feel ambitious enough to try it yourself. The Patchwork Dog will also restore and repair beloved old quilts, but be warned that it's a very expensive service—take good care of the one your great aunt left you.

ORIENTALIA

Ciancimino Ltd.

104 Mount St., W1 - 499 2672
Open daily 10 a.m.-6 p.m.

Collectors arriving from distant lands at awkward times of the week can be assured of finding Jean-Claude Ciancimino—a telephone call is all that's needed to summon him downstairs, since he lives above his gallery. Once inside, the unprepared may need resuscitation, for the display of exquisite yet understated good taste is thoroughly breathtaking. Ciancimino clearly understands what Japanese and Chinese works of art are all about, in terms of color, proportion, form and function. He conjures with blocks of rare, important Japanese screens, low tables, sculptures, paintings and carvings, deploying shape and color like an artist. Mixed judiciously with Japanese and Chinese works are fine pieces of ivory-inlaid Indian furniture, drawings and watercolors of flora and fauna from the great subcontinent, and occasionally some textiles or rugs. Behind his heavy horn-rimmed glasses, Ciancimino's face betrays nothing but grand politesse as he modestly smiles the smile of a conjuror whose trick is no trick at all. More showrooms can be found at his original store, Ciancimino Designs Ltd., 307 Kings Road, SW3, 352 2016.

Collet's Chinese Gallery

40 Great Russell St., WC1 - 580 7538
Open Mon.-Fri. 9:45 a.m.-5:45 p.m.

Collet's is a bit of a disappointment for hunters of Oriental antiques and porcelain, since it is bedecked with quantities of Taiwanese trinkets. Nonetheless, it is still a fascinating place to visit. Usually to be found are some reasonably priced netsuke, jade and ivory, probably all made for "round-eye" tourists as early as the eighteenth century but more likely during the nineteenth or even the early twentieth century.

Eskenazi Ltd.

Foxglove House, Piccadilly, W1 - 493 5464
Open Mon.-Fri. 9:30 a.m.-6 p.m., Sat. by appt. only.

There is little to hint at the treasures to be found inside Eskenazi, whose entrance resembles a security-conscious block of luxury apartments. But take the elevator or walk upstairs, and you'll come across one of London's most spectacular showrooms of Chinese antiquities, Japanese netsuke, inro, jades, archair bronzes and early and important ceramics. The display space is huge—some 3,000 square feet on one floor—and the displays themselves are sparse and effective. Bronzes thousands of years old with a jade-like patina, earthenware figures from the Tang dynasty, Ming porcelain and precious pieces of jade from the Warring States Dynasty are just some of the wonders to be seen here. Luigi Bandini runs the Japanese department; Phillip Constantinidi the Chinese department. Together with Giuseppe Eskenazi, they have supplied some 40 major international museums and institutions and have helped to create important individual collections of Japanese and Chinese art. One megarich American collector recently stood at the door at dawn, waiting patiently for the firm's 25th-anniversary exhibition to open so he would be certain of acquiring one more priceless object for his collection—that should give you some idea of Eskenazi's stature in the field of Oriental art and antiquities.

John Sparks Ltd.

128 Mount St., W1 - 499 2265
Open Mon.-Fri. 9 a.m.-5:30 p.m.

During the great and tragic time that culminated in the sacking and looting of Peking in the nineteenth century, John Sparks had agents in China buying rare works of art, porcelain and pottery to ship back to the first great collectors in Europe. In fact, it is quite possible that the pieces of extreme rarity and gigantic value that occasionally turn up at sales in America, Hong Kong and London were originally handled by John Sparks 100 or more years ago. The showrooms, thickly carpeted and hospitable, resemble a series of rooms in a luxurious private house. The staff has a way of picking up priceless objects with such familiarity that one imagines them drinking their morning coffee from the rare, delicate bowls of priceless porcelain. They also tend to remember anyone who has visited, it seems, and next time he or she drops in, the welcome is delightful. But these good people are not name-droppers—they just happen to have dealt with most of the illustrious people in their field.

Spink & Son Ltd.
5-7 King St., SW1 - 930 7888
Open Mon.-Fri. 9:30 a.m.-5:30 p.m.

The first John Spink established his business just after the Restoration, in 1666—presumably after the Great Fire, or his descendants probably wouldn't be around today, administering a business that has grown from a small coin dealership to one of the largest and most all-encompassing antiques establishments in England. Difficult to put in any one category, Spink & Son has been known for centuries as a dealer in Indian, Southeast Asian and Islamic art, artifacts and antiquities. Spink & Son was also buying and selling defunct share certificates from the nineteenth century (and earlier) long before people began to frame them as decorative objects. Here, in a rambling assortment of showrooms, galleries and displays, you're likely to find an outstanding collection of "China Trade" pictures and artifacts, in particular the works of George Chinnery, a self-taught artist who lived in the hongs of eighteenth- and nineteenth-century China. If you get lost navigating the staircases and corridors, the charming salespeople will steer you in the right direction.

Woods Wilson
103 Pimlico Rd., SW1 - 730 2558
Open Mon.-Sat. 10 a.m.-6 p.m.

The tall, audacious figure of Henry Woods Wilson is liable to rise suddenly from behind a Japanese lacquer screen and surprise the casual visitor, albeit with great affability. Woods Wilson recognized the importance of Oriental antiques as decorative objects back in the '60s, and today he is a respected authority on Japanese lacquer in particular, though he still buys with more regard for form and shape than for age and provenance. In his field, just as in most other branches of antiques, the nineteenth century has yielded many objects to delight the collector.

PAINTINGS, DRAWINGS & ENGRAVINGS

Arthur Ackermann & Sons
3 Old Bond St., W1 - 493 3288, 493 7647
Open Mon.-Fri. 9:30 a.m.-5:30 p.m.

In 1813 the founder of this firm commissioned Thomas Rowlandson's series of fiercely anti-Napoleonic cartoons. Today, look for a fine collection of sporting paintings and prints from the seventeenth to the nineteenth century, displayed in showrooms that are as elegant as a well-tailored Bond Street suit. Make sure to take a look at *Ackermann's Repository of Prints*, a skillful, accurate depiction of English nineteenth-century life: a series of beautiful engravings of all the best shops, streets, parks and houses in town, published by Rudolph Ackermann, Jr., back when Regent Street was in the throes of reconstruction and London was packed with visitors to the Great Exhibition of 1851.

Thomas Agnew & Sons
43 Old Bond St., W1 - 629 6176
Open Mon.-Wed. & Fri. 9:30 a.m.-5:30 p.m., Thurs. 9:30 a.m.-6:30 p.m.

One of the most venerable and respected galleries in London, Thomas Agnew & Sons has a long history of buying and selling works by some of the world's greatest artists to important collections and private buyers. The British Museum, the National Gallery, the Metropolitan Museum of Art in New York and the Paul Mellon Foundation have all added to their collections through Agnew: Raphael cartoons, Turner seascapes and landscapes, works by Gainsborough, Reynolds and other such eminences. Once or twice a year, Agnew hosts a loan exhibition from one of England's best private collections; year-round, it shows a range of affordable paintings, watercolors and engravings as well as less affordable sculptures of great beauty and delicacy.

P. & D. Colnaghi & Co. Ltd.
14 Old Bond St., W1 - 491 7408
Open Mon.-Sat. 9:30 a.m.-5:30 p.m.

Imposing though it may look, Colnaghi is remarkably informal. Prospective clients are left to riffle through print folders by themselves, comfortably ensconced on a chair or sofa in one of the anterooms, surrounded by friendliness and fine furniture. Less strictly wedded to the Englishness of so many nearby galleries, Colnaghi has always preferred the Italian and French schools (up to the early 1800s) of painting. But there's more: classic Old Master paintings and drawings; English paintings, drawings, engravings and watercolors; sculptures, bronzes and other works of art. The company goes all the way back to 1760 and the great days of the Grand Tour, when English gentlemen first became aware of "art," and Mr. Colnaghi, an Italian purveyor of fireworks, added prints and engravings to his repertoire, which already included scientific instruments, bronze figures and "modern paintings."

Frost & Reed
41 New Bond St., W1 - 629 2457
Open Mon.-Fri. 9 a.m.-5:30 p.m., Sat. 9 a.m.-1 p.m.

Many eminent collectors owe their tentative beginnings to this extremely friendly, approachable gallery, which nurtures both clients and painters with equal care. Known for its Thoroughbred paintings, Frost & Reed has even suffered breeders and trainers to mentally run their hands down the withers of a Derby winner, only to reject it on some obscure technicality—nothing to do with the painting, but with the horse's tendons or the set of its ears. Tony Neville, the director, can tell a fake Ferneley at ten paces and is full of anecdotes. The downstairs gallery usually has an exhibition of one of Frost & Reed's own artists (in the sense that it has discovered, encouraged

---

Shops can close without warning, so please call before setting out for a particular store.

---

and promoted them). Landscapes, still lifes, animals . . . just don't expect to find modern paintings.

Lane Fine Art Ltd.
86-88 Pimlico Rd., SW1 - 730 7374
Open Mon.-Fri. 10 a.m.-6 p.m., Sat. 10 a.m.-2 p.m.

An interested and perspicacious eye will pick up on the slightly quirky taste running through this collection of primitives, early portraits and oil paintings dating from as early as the fifteenth century through 1830. It could almost be said that Mr. Foley buys "decorators' paintings," and so he does—but there's always an added ingredient that lifts them out of the it-matches-the-sofa-perfectly class and into the serious investment bracket. Not all galleries are fun to visit, but this one is.

Paul Mason Gallery
149 Sloane St., SW1 - 730 3683
Open Mon.-Fri. 9 a.m.-7 p.m., Sat. 9 a.m.-1 p.m.

The bay trees and the awning may mislead the passerby into thinking this is a small restaurant, but Paul Mason, mariner manqué, actually sells marine paintings, from the classy to the delightfully naive. He will discourse at length on his subject, with a fair amount of practical knowledge thrown in, since he is an enthusiastic weekend sailor. By no means in the category of "old salt," Mason flings himself nimbly down the precarious spiral staircase leading to his small display of sailors' work, model ships, prisoner-of-war work and reference books. Upstairs, more sedately, he'll show you decorative prints, his favorite subjects being birds and natural history.

Mathaf Gallery Ltd.
24 Motcomb St., SW1 - 235 0010
Open Mon.-Fri. 9:30 a.m.-5:30 p.m., Sat. by appt. only.

Relatively new on the scene, this small, quiet gallery specializes in paintings with petrodollar appeal, primarily from the nineteenth century. Camels, pyramids, mosques and horizonless deserts fill the walls, punctuated by a rapacious hawk mantling over its prey or sinisterly hooded on a gloved fist. As the taste and perception of its clients have improved, so have the Mathaf Gallery's standards.

Johnny Van Haeften Ltd.
13 Duke St., St. James's, SW1 - 930 3062
Open Mon.-Fri. 9:30 a.m.-7 p.m., Sat.-Sun. by appt. only.

The unusually long hours are due to the international clientele, many of whom arrive at odd hours to buy from this engaging purveyor of fine Dutch and Flemish old master paintings. A tireless searcher for his beloved artworks, Johnny Van Haeften is as likely to be on the Continent or in America as he is in London—yet he always seems to be there when a client calls. Rumor has it that he has a clone, but he categorically denies it. He just works hard and loves Dutch paintings.

POTTERY & PORCELAIN

Richard Dennis
144 Kensington Church St., W8 - 727 2061
Open Mon.-Fri. 9:30 a.m.-5:30 p.m., Sat. 10 a.m.-2 p.m.

This beautifully laid-out showroom displays art nouveau tiles and an excellent range of studio pottery from 1870 to 1950, along with plenty of the work of Hannah Barlow, her sister Florence and most of the named Doulton artists. The place also stocks a good range of reference books on potters and pottery of the period.

Jonathan Horne
66B Kensington Church St., W8 - 221 5658
Open Mon.-Fri. 9:30 a.m.-5:30 p.m.

Tall, gentle, and deceptively mild-mannered, Jonathan Horne has a passion for early English pottery, which he goes to the ends of the earth to obtain. His display is spare, but every piece is important. Included are eighteenth-century Oriental and Continental pottery, early English slipware, tin-glazed Delftware, early Staffordshire and a smattering of early metalwork, needlework and wood carving. Horne's manner is diffident until you show genuine interest—then he becomes generous with both his knowledge and his time.

Rogers De Rin
76 Royal Hospital Rd., SW - 352 9007
Open Mon.-Sat. 10 a.m.-6 p.m.

Collectors of china pigs and cats will find themselves in seventh heaven. Specializing in Wemyss pottery long before the prices began to rise like a soufflé, this small shop is full of beguiling flowered porkers, pigs in clover and a delicately chosen selection of small collectors' items, including little boxes, etuis, vinaigrettes and small enamels, along with pretty Victorian jewelry, cushions, straw work, small pictures, miniatures and silhouettes. It may sound a little too coy, but be assured, it's far from it.

Sampson & Jellinek
156 Brompton Rd., SW3 - 589 5272
Open Mon.-Fri. 9:30 a.m.-5:30 p.m., Sat.-Sun. by appt. only.

This team of specialists travels extensively throughout England and the Continent, buying early pottery, oak, fine brass and needlework as well as early Delft, slipware and Staffordshire. Usually to be found are early ceramic ornamental groups depicting boxing, bullbaiting, menageries and the like—a world away from the commonly seen, poorly made Victorian "flatbacks" depicting Queen and Consort, generals and simpering family groups. Sampson & Jellinek handles only the best and the rarest, including Obadiah Sherratt, Ralph Wood and early Whieldon works, Staffordshire salt-glazed pieces and Prattware.

RUGS

Raymond Bernadout
4 William St., Knightsbridge, SW1
235 3360
Open Mon.-Fri. 9:30 a.m.-6 p.m., Sat. by appt. only.

The Bernadout family is now on its way to its third generation of international rug dealing. One member of the tribe specializes in Caucasians, another in Persians; some deal only in high-priced rarities, others in less expensive rugs, carpets, tapestries and embroideries. In recent years, Raymond Bernadout has branched out, acquiring the premises next door to display English and Continental furniture, paintings, sculptures and works of art (unusual in this country, where the rug-dealing fraternity tends to stick to its area of expertise). Once they're known, Londoners are usually permitted to take the piece they have chosen home to see if it really belongs there. If it persists in looking like an exotic stranger, they may return it and try again—Bernadout is most understanding. He will also arrange to have damaged rugs repaired or a prized Persian cleaned and restored, advise customers on selling, and buy on their behalf at auctions. Rugs like these aren't just life-enhancing, they're a lifetime's preoccupation.

Bernheimer Fine Arts Ltd.
32 St. George St., W1 - 499 0293
Open Mon.-Fri. 9:30 a.m.-5:30 p.m.

One of the recent crop of Continental dealers that arrived in London recently, Bernheimer is located just behind Sotheby's in a tall, elegant eighteenth-century townhouse that has been transformed into one of the most exciting antiques galleries in London. Mr. Bernheimer's knowledge and passionate love of antique textiles, fabrics and Oriental carpets are taken for granted in his native city, Munich, but the impact of his style and taste has yet to be felt in Britain. In true Continental tradition, he does not separate rugs and carpets from furniture and fine art, seeing them instead as part of an overall design. The firm's rug expert, German Bogner, who has been with Bernheimer for 25 years, will soon inaugurate exhibitions of fine, rare Oriental carpets and kilims in the showrooms on the top floor. English tapestries from Soho workshops, tapestries from Beauvais and early Transylvanian prayer rugs are just some of the treasures to be found here, along with large sculptures and carvings from the Renaissance.

David Black Oriental Carpets
96 Portland Rd., Holland Park, W11
727 2566
Open Mon.-Sat. 11 a.m.-6 p.m.

Tucked into the right angle formed by Holland Park Avenue and Ladbroke Grove lies the fascinating little corner of London in which David Black has his shop. Though it isn't large, it manages to contain a wide range of rugs and carpets, primarily of tribal origins. The walls are bright with the primary colors of antique Caucasian rugs and Anatolian kilims, and clients sit drinking coffee on piles of Turkoman, Belouch and Afshar work, to name but a few. The small gallery downstairs usually houses an exhibition on a particular theme: Daghestan prayer rugs, for instance, or Sehna flatweaves, or perhaps needlework and embroidery from the Turkmen Republic. Recently, early Scandinavian and European carpets, cushions and rugs were added to the repertoire. David Black

is a great enthusiast who considers rugs and carpets from nomad tribes to be rare and eloquent works of art, and he's published a number of books on the subject.

Bond Street Carpets
31 New Bond St., W1 - 629 7538
Open Mon.-Fri. 9 a.m.-6 p.m., Sat. 10 a.m.-5 p.m.

Magda Schapira's stock is so large and tightly packed that it usually takes some time for the rugs to be shifted and unrolled for viewing. One is not likely to make any great discoveries in the clutter of carpets, however, for Schapira knows exactly what she has and just how deeply it is buried. Still, her rugs represent a good value on the whole. There's usually a good stock of fairly ordinary kilims of no great age from £60 upward, though there may be a bit of a palaver if a customer wants to see too many of them, particularly the ones at the bottom.

Victor Franses Gallery
57 Jermyn St., SW1 - 493 6284
Open Mon.-Fri. 10 a.m.-5:30 p.m., Sat. 11 a.m.-1 p.m.

With his spiky white beard and piercing black eyes, usually topped with a corduroy Mao-style cap, Vic Franses looks more like a weatherbeaten seafarer than a carpet dealer—until you see his fat cigar. To many Londoners, Franses and his extended, close-knit family are almost synonymous with carpets. He seems to always be in the store, putting his encyclopedic knowledge of the international carpet trade to good use. Carefully lit, well-displayed Persian court carpets glimmer on the walls, and around them is a continual buzz of business activity—telephone calls, family members bringing news of an acquisition, a sale in New York or a shipment from abroad, and customers discussing prices, provenances, color, condition, size and origin, waiting to catch Franses for advice or just a friendly chat. If he doesn't know the answer to your question, one of his family members will.

Joseph Lavian
Block F, 53-79 Highgate Rd., NW5
485 7955
Open Mon.-Fri. 9 a.m.-6 p.m.

Practically everyone in the trade knows Joseph Lavian (pronounces "l'avion"), whose bonded warehouse is bigger than an airplane hangar. But not much of the general public finds its way to his door, at least not without a referral from an interior designer or a specialist dealer who cannot hope to compete in terms of sheer numbers with Lavian's stock. This place is not recommended for absolute beginners, simply because the choice is so daunting that most people freeze at the sight of so many old Caucasian, Turkomen, Persian and Anatolian pile rugs, kilims, runners, needlework and embroidery, shown with the casual speed of those accustomed to handling an extremely valuable rug as if it were a favorite old blanket. Here, hung from rude concrete pillars, one is liable to find a "Bibibat antique Bakhtiyar rug, made by the order of Najaf-Gholi-Khan Samsam-Saltaneh, Prime Minister of Iran during the Quaya Dynasty" not to mention a few French Aubusson Portiers draped over a stack of Perepaedils, Chichis, Gharabaghs and a Kurdi Kazak or two. Lavian is courteous, dignified and immensely patient, leaving you to wander as you will, attended at a distance by a member of his staff, who will silently turn the knotted pile pages for you and, if he sees you falter, will fetch a tray of tea or coffee to resuscitate you for your quest.

SILVER & JEWELRY

Before going off in search of authentic English silver, the novice shopper should know a few things. English "sterling" silver is hallmarked with a "lion passant" (the mark of the assay office), the monarch's head (until 1890) and the maker's mark. Sheffield plate, first made in the 1740s, resembles solid silver but is made of a core of copper onto which a thin layer of silver is heat-fused. It should not be confused with silver plate, which is electroplated (it first appeared about 1840).

Those in search of jewels will want to head for the Hatton Garden vicinity. Most of this area has been torn down and redeveloped, but behind a monolithic office-building complex, the home of London's diamond trade has remained largely undisturbed—a mixture of garish, vulgar shops, splashed with discount offers on engagement rings, and the almost clinical surroundings of the "big boys," whose safes hold jewels and gems of untold value. The pale, gracious building that houses the London

Diamond Club is impenetrable to ordinary mortals, but across the street you'll find the Hatton Garden Auction Room, where the trade puffs cigars and swaps notes in an unintelligible language distilled from Yiddish, English and Middle European. Here the Edney Bullion Company posts a daily chart of wedding-ring sizes and prices, detailing their movement up or down the money market. Val D'Or deals in pearls, D. Pennelier sells Krugerrands, and around the corner on Greville Street, Rubin & Son sells all the tools of the trade, including special pots of cleaning and polishing preparations. In among the cheesy glitter, the antique-jewelry hunter can unearth some worthwhile vendors.

Bond Street Silver Galleries
111-112 New Bond St., W1 - 493 6180
Open Mon.-Fri. 9 a.m.-5:30 p.m.

There is little to encourage the stranger to walk through the small entrance next to Yves Saint Laurent and above Barclays Bank. The stairs are echoing concrete, the elevator is industrial, and the smell redolent of abandoned warehouses and stale cigars. But silver aficionados will be glad they sought this place out. Fifteen silver dealers are spread out on three floors, all of them primarily doing business with the trade, which explains the unglamorous surroundings and their sometimes brusque manner. A & B Bloomstein is a good source for pairs of sauce boats and salvers and canteens of silver of mixed dates and makers, and John Bull Antiques Ltd. carries such things as rare mid-eighteenth-century wax jacks. Much of the stock is tarnished, since the trade doesn't need its sterling and Sheffield plate polished to see its value. Prices are lower than in upscale shops in the district, but this is not a place for neophytes.

Ted Donohue
L25-27 & M10-12 Gray's Mews,
1-7 Davies Mews, W1 - 629 5633
Open Mon.-Fri. 10 a.m.-6 p.m.

Ted Donohue found a way to keep up with the big league in the West End without suffering such high overheads, by occupying this generous space just inside the last door of Gray's Mews antiques market. The display cases carry a delicious variety of objects found by Donohue, who has highly original and perceptive taste. He specializes in politically related objects and pieces of historical interest, silhouette rings and jewelry, seals and miniatures, and he has a special love for moss agate. He also keeps a stock of irresistible "toy" silver that starts at about £100: miniature candlesticks, platters, coffeepots and teapots, primarily from the eighteenth century. And he usually has one or two singular and important pieces on display, such as a "fine necklace of table- and rose-cut diamonds inhabited by birds of paradise, sprays and Sevigne bows," dated 1740 and costing £6,000.

London Silver Vaults
Chancery House, 53-65 Chancery Ln.,
WC2 - 242 3844
Open Mon.-Fri. 9 a.m.-5:30 p.m., Sat. 9 a.m.-12:30 p.m.

More than 150 strong rooms open onto long, cool corridors, making this place look more like a maximum-security prison than a silver market. Don't be put off by the first two or three dealers who inhabit this underground kingdom; they give a first impression of appalling taste and indifferent quality. Keep walking, and seek out William Walter Ltd., which specializes in old Sheffield plate and high-quality sterling silver from the best periods. Here, where you can buy silver less expensively than at most other London dealers, you may encounter Mammon himself, though his goods are cunningly left tarnished to discourage unknowledgeable bargain hunters. A. Bloom will find you matched canteens of table silver at moderate prices. If you visit Silverman's, don't remark on the appropriateness of Mr. Silverman's name, and don't let the words "Aladdin's cave" or "treasure trove" escape your lips—the world-weary dealers sitting among cascades of silver hanging from hooks like strings of onions have heard it all before. If you'd rather see stunning silver in less clinical surroundings, E. & C. T. Koopman & Sons Ltd. (242 8365) has premises above this unique underworld.

S. J. Phillips Ltd.
139 New Bond St., W1 - 629 6261
Open Mon.-Fri. 10 a.m.-5 p.m.

Today the Norton family, five of them, runs Phillips, which opened in 1869. The grand showroom is evocative of Edwardian days and famous society belles, who inspected possible purchases while hidden from view by thick velvet curtains. Fine eighteenth- and early nineteenth-century silver fills the tall showcases, and the antique jewelry is positively mouth-watering: necklaces of pure gold that look like mounds of curled butter; emeralds and rubies, pearls and sapphires; coral, cameos, tourmaline and topaz in rings and clasps, bracelets and brooches—all flashing fire under the high, bright light of the winking chandeliers. Endlessly patient, the people at Phillips realize how difficult these decisions can be, and they're quite prepared to wait.

Sac Frères
45 Old Bond St., W1 - 493 2333
Open Mon.-Fri. 9:30 a.m.-5:30 p.m.

There's plenty of old-world courtesy in this little cave of a shop, still redolent of the last decade of the nineteenth century, when the Sac brothers first opened. Should anyone have had the misfortune to have purchased phony amber (the color of well-sucked barley sugar), the Pickwickian gentleman behind the counter, which glows with authentic, golden-hued amber, will be surprisingly outspoken in condemnation. He will ripple beads and necklaces of this mysterious stone to demonstrate the unequivocal difference between real and fake, and he'll show off a rare collection of amber carvings and antique jewelry of great originality. Here, too, can be found jeweled amber cigarette holders of enormous length, in genuine Jay Gatsby style.

Tessiers Ltd.
26 New Bond St., W1 - 629 0458
Open Mon.-Fri. 9:30 a.m.-5 p.m.

Having one of the few original storefronts remaining on New Bond Street, Tessiers is small and discreet, with a long tradition of restringing milady's pearls and polishing up the family jewels for special occasions, keeping them in their safe between uses. You may be lucky enough to find some fine early porringers (a type of bowl), silver-mounted serpentine tankards, a pair of lovely James Gould candlesticks or a set of four heavy, truly grand candlesticks designed by Ebenezer Coker. The jewelry, which is exceptionally beautiful and unusual, includes stickpins, tie pins, eye-dazzling diamonds of excellent quality and no vulgarity, charming early Victorian rings and brooches and, of course, pearls.

Andrew R. Ullman Ltd.

10 Hatton Gdn., EC1 - 405 1877
Open Mon.-Fri. 9:30 a.m.-6 p.m.

Mr. Ullman's father started this business, which sells a multitude of buyable objects: cuff links by the hundred, lockets, seals, sovereign holders, cameo brooches, gold chains, watch chains, charms for bracelets, small silver pieces, gold thimbles and toothpicks and a few pieces of Middle Eastern and Oriental jewelry. Antique silver brooches and gold chains cost as little as £50, but Ullman expansively adds that he has pieces costing "up to anything you like" in the back. He speaks four languages and is charming in all of them.

BEAUTY & HEALTH

FACE & BODY SALONS

Delia Collins

19 Beauchamp Pl., SW3 - 584 2423
Open Mon.-Fri. 9 a.m.-6 p.m., Sat. 9 a.m.-1 p.m.

This is a serious, expensive salon whose reputation is first class. Delia Collins regards beauty care as a science, and it's a science she's been studying for more than 40 years. Whatever treatment you're interested in, one of the lovely women will take care of you with the utmost deference.

Harrods

Knightsbridge, SW1 - 581 2021, 584 8881
Open Mon.-Tues. & Fri.-Sat. 9 a.m.-6 p.m., Wed. 9:30 a.m.-7 p.m.

Harrods has almost everything imaginable, including an ever-growing department dedicated to beauty: facials, waxing, massage, manicures, pedicures. If your run-down body needs some serious pampering, indulge in the all-day Top-to-Toe treatment, which includes a sauna, half-hour massage, one-hour face treatment, shampoo and set, manicure and pedicure for £65; the Total Look treatment includes the same and more, plus lunch and tea, for £85.

Joan Price's Face Place

33 Cadogan St., SW3 - 589 9062
Open Mon.-Fri. 10 a.m.-6 p.m. (open alternate Wed. 10 a.m.-8 p.m.).

Facials, makeup lessons, Swedish massage and many other body and beauty treatments are offered here. The private makeup lesson (£12.50) will help you make the most of your face, with the help of any of Joan Price's eighteen brands. This well-known beauty parlor is frequented by the smartest ladies in Chelsea.

The Sanctuary

11 Floral St., WC2 - 240 9635
Open Mon.-Fri. 10 a.m.-10 p.m., Sat. 10 a.m.-6 p.m., Sun. noon-8 p.m.

This old banana warehouse has been transformed into a garden of worldly delights (exclusively feminine) with a fabulous Moorish/Spanish decor, including winding paths, many different levels and arcades multiplied by the skillful use of mirrors. The vast white space is decorated with exotic birds, plants and young girls in full bloom. Young, pretty women come here to pass away the hours, read the glossy magazines and get themselves into shape, with snow-white towels (supplied by the management) as their only ornamentation. Use of the swimming pool, whirlpool, steam room and sauna, plus one sun-bed session, is included in the £22.50-a-day price (£15.50 after 6 p.m. and £25.50 on weekends); massages, every imaginable beauty treatment and snacks from the health-food bar are extra.

FITNESS

Dance Attic Studios

214 Putney Bridge Rd., SW15 - 785 2055
Open Mon.-Sat. 9:30 a.m.-8:30 p.m., Sun. 10:15 a.m.-3:30 p.m.

One of London's main dance and rehearsal studios, the Dance Attic offers a wide range of dancing exercises, including aerobics, rebound training, kung fu, self-defense, yoga and performing-arts classes. Compared with the other

London studios, this place is completely chaotic. The floor space has expanded considerably, and now there's a gym. The general facilities, however, are well below average, though the teachers are high class.

Dance Works
16 Balderton St., W1 - 629 6183
Open Mon.-Fri. 8:30 a.m.-10 p.m., Sat.-Sun. 10 a.m.-6 p.m.

Dance Works may not be as famous as Pineapple (see below), but its classes and teachers are just as good. They have an innovative style and are constantly updating and introducing new approaches to physical fitness. The latest novelty here is Natureworks—a highly specialized clinic for complementary medicine, with a special interest in professional dancers as well as those involved in any form of exercise. A one-year adult membership is £50, plus the cost of each lesson (£3), but you can join for just the day or on a temporary basis to check it out. The eleven studios are scattered around a warren of passages and stairs. Also available is the customary selection of stretch-and-sweat classes that have become essential to contemporary life.

The Fitness Centre
11 Floral St., WC2 - 836 6544
Open Mon.-Fri. 7 a.m.-9 p.m., Sat.-Sun. 10 a.m.-6 p.m.

Right next door to The Sanctuary stands this ultimate fitness center, which hosts classes in rock or jazz aerobics or just general workouts. Amenities include the popular Nautilus training equipment and impressively large studios with sprung-pine flooring; exotic plants decorate the white walls. The instructors are enthusiastic and generous. There's a pleasant display of dance and fitness wear, along with plenty of swimsuits during the summer months.

Pineapple
7 Langley St., WC2 - 836 4004
Open Mon.-Fri. 9 a.m.-8:30 p.m., Sat. 9 a.m.-5:30 p.m., Sun. 11 a.m.-4:30 p.m.

Debbie Moore opened this magnificently successful dance studio (which now includes a fashionable clothing store) eight years ago, and it's now the largest dance center in all of Europe. At Pineapple you can choose from 750 different classes each week. Beginners, Royal Ballet dancers and aerobics freaks converge here for workouts. The spacious shop next door sells lycra and cotton fashions for fitness fanatics *and* for the thoroughly modern London gal. There are two other London centers: Pineapple West and Pineapple Kensington.

HAIR SALONS

MEN'S

Daniel Galvin
42-44 George St., W1 - 486 8601
Open Mon.-Sat. 9 a.m.-6 p.m.

A good many young TV and film stars come to Galvin to get their hair tinted and tended. Shampoos and fashionable cuts start at £21.

Harrods
Knightsbridge, SW1 - 581 5236
Open Mon.-Tues. & Thurs.-Fri. 10 a.m.-5:30 p.m., Wed. 9:30 a.m.-7 p.m.

Generations of men have followed one another here, both in and behind the barbers' chairs. Unfortunately, this is all changing, and we fear the Harrods men's salon may be nearing the end of an era. Meanwhile, this is still the traditional English hair salon, where a haircut, shampoo and blow-dry costs £12.

Molton Brown
58 S. Molton St., W1 - 493 5236
Open Mon.-Fri. 10 a.m.-5:30 p.m., Sat. 9 a.m.-4:30 p.m.

Molton Brown remains a popular salon with the young men about town, even though its prices are twice as high as those of the more traditional men's hairdressers: £25 for a cut and shampoo.

Nino-Cuts
23A Frith St., W1 - 734 2171
Open Mon.-Sat. 10 a.m.-7 p.m.

Nino, who owns the popular Bar Italia next door (delicious coffee and Italian panettone), also runs this old-fashioned Italian barbershop, where a shave will cost you £5—unless you are privileged enough to be shaved by Giorgio, in which case the price will be £8. Haircuts are also offered; the stylists offer a modern style of snipping, plus more modern prices than Nino, but they work together in harmony and with great success.

Vidal Sassoon
54 Knightsbridge, SW1 - 235 1957
Open Mon.-Fri. 8:30 a.m.-6:15 p.m., Sat. 8:30 a.m.-5:30 p.m.

A modern hair salon that has managed to remain in fashion for several years now, Vidal Sassoon offers shampoos and haircuts that start at £18. Good products (shampoos, conditioners, hair dryers, brushes, scissors and combs) are sold at moderate prices on the premises.

Truefitt & Hill
23 Old Bond St., W1 - 493 2961
Open Mon.-Fri. 9 a.m.-5:30 p.m., Sat. 9 a.m.-noon.

Surely the most courteous, select and professional barbershop in London, Truefitt & Hill must also be the oldest—it was established in 1805. The Duke of Edinburgh is still a customer (though the barbers go to him). You're likely to meet half the House of Lords at one time or another (the other half goes to Trumper), as well as any number of other well-known heads. You can purchase a full range of toilet preparations—in fact, everything a gentleman may require for his bathroom. A cut and shampoo is £13.85, a manicure £6.30.

George F. Trumper
9 Curzon St., W1 - 499 1850
Open Mon.-Fri. 9 a.m.-5 p.m., Sat. 9 a.m.-1 p.m.

Although things are still the same—that is, famous heads, barbers traveling to the Royal Palace—George F. Trumper has entered modern times at least a bit, as manifested by the hair dying, facial treatments and the like. A pair of ivory-backed natural boar-bristle hairbrushes will now set you back nearly £1,000, and a massive shaving brush—ivory and pure badger—is £500. So a simple shampoo and cut for just over £10 (depending on length) seems like a gift.

WOMEN'S

Burlingtons
Burlington St., W1 - 935 0140
Open Mon.-Wed. 9 a.m.-6 p.m., Thurs.-Fri. 9 a.m.-7 p.m., Sat. 9 a.m.-5 p.m.

With its highly innovative cutting team, Burlingtons leads the market in designer haircuts. Guided by Clive Colman, the newly launched East End salon has met with instant success, proving that today's client wants designer hairstyle at realistic prices, which range from £13 to £25. This includes shampoo, conditioner, cut, blow-dry and refreshments. No frills, just style.

Cadogan Club
282 Sloane St., SW1 - 235 3814
Open Mon.-Fri. 9 a.m.-5 p.m., Sat. 9 a.m.-1 p.m.

Everyone who is anyone comes to the Cadogan Club for a haircut and style. It's not as expensive as you might imagine, and the service is quite friendly, even if you aren't anyone.

Harrods
Knightsbridge, SW1 - 581 2021
Open Mon.-Tues. & Thurs.-Sat. 9 a.m.-6 p.m., Wed. 9:30 a.m.-7 p.m.

This very large salon provides all the traditional hairdressing services, along with a department that specializes in long hair, trichology and wigs. An appointment is not always necessary, but without one you risk being attended to by a newcomer. A cut, shampoo and blow-dry/set by the style director costs about £30.

Molton Brown
58 S. Molton St., W1 - 629 1872
Open Mon.-Fri. 10 a.m.-5:30 p.m., Sat. 9 a.m.-4:30 p.m.

A popular and well-established salon, Molton Brown now offers the Remedy Range—the latest addition to its other famous hair-care products—which comprises a complete treatment for fine, limp and/or damaged hair, using every kind of protein and vitamin imaginable. A one-hour Remedy Range treatment in the hair-care department is £12.50. The usual range of cuts and styles is, of course, also offered.

Vidal Sassoon
54 Knightsbridge, SW1 - 235 7791
Open Mon.-Wed. 9:30 a.m.-5 p.m., Thurs. 9 a.m.-5:30 p.m., Fri. 9:30 a.m.-6:15 p.m., Sat. 8:30 a.m.-5:30 p.m.

Twenty-five years after launching his business, Vidal Sassoon no longer lives in London, but his hairdressing salons and classic Five Point haircut look to go on forever. Several other locations.

Teals

5 Pond Pl., SW3 - 584 0105
*Open Mon.-Wed. & Fri. 9 a.m.-6 p.m., Thurs.
9 a.m.-7 p.m.*

Paolo and Jeffrey still run this cozy salon just off Fulham Road, while Evelyne goes out to tend the hair of Chelsea's debutantes and young wives. These three have been joined by Kathy, who handles the more trendy styles.

Toni & Guy

10-12 Davies St., W1 - 629 8348, 499 2249
Open Mon.-Tues. & Sat. 9 a.m.-6:30 p.m., Thurs.-Fri. 9 a.m.-7:30 p.m.

Toni and Guy Mascolo have built a considerable reputation by producing creative styles and showing a high degree of care for their clients. "Technical treatments" (the Mascolos' name for anything more than a simple cut and blow-dry) cost from £7.50 to £45. Whatever you choose to have done here, be assured it will be undertaken with the utmost proficiency.

SCENTS, SOAPS & TOILETRIES

The Body Shop

54 King's Rd., SW3 - 730 0746
Open Mon.-Sat. 9:30 a.m.-5:30 p.m.

It is The Body Shop's philosophy that products should contain natural materials, of vegetable origin whenever possible, and should not be tested on animals. A range of over 160 products—from peppermint foot lotion to jojoba-oil shampoo—is available in five sizes of refillable bottles. You can sample everything in the shop and buy as little or as much as you need (or can afford). These products make wonderful presents for yourself and just about anyone else—man, woman or child. There are thirteen other Body Shops in London.

Mary Chess

7 Shepherd Market, W1 - 629 5152
Open Mon.-Fri. 9:30 a.m.-5:30 p.m.

Walking into this lovely shop is like walking into the past. It was opened by Mary Chess in the 1930s, and the formulas of the fragrances, all based on natural oils and essences, have remained unchanged. Complementing the six

classic, timeless perfumes—White Lilac, Tuberose, Yram, Chess d'Or, Tapestry and Strategy—are a range of products for the body and boudoir, like the luxurious Roman bath oil. The staff is friendly and knowledgeable, and clients who can't visit the shop in person may order by mail.

Clement's

4-5 & 63 Burlington Arcade, W1
493 3923
Open Mon.-Fri. 9 a.m.-5 p.m., Sat. 9 a.m.-1 p.m.

Clement's sells fine brushes of all sorts, including shaving brushes, penknives in every conceivable variation, and scissors in every possible size, along with flasks, whistles (silent and otherwise) and more. An amazing selection of gifts, particularly for men.

Crabtree & Evelyn

6 Kensington Church St., W8 - 937 9335
134 King's Rd., SW3 - 589 6263
30 James St., WC2 - 379 0962
Open Mon.-Sat. 9:30 a.m.-6 p.m.

This pretty place sells attractively packaged men's shaving cream in wooden bowls, colognes and after-shaves, soaps in beautifully decorated tins, bath gels and salts. It also sells a range of jams and preserves, teas and vinegars, and will make up lovely gift hampers to order.

Culpepper House

21 Bruton St., W1 - 499 2400
8 The Market, Covent Garden, WC2 - 379 6698
Open Mon.-Sat. 10 a.m.-8 p.m.

Smelling of herbs, spices and ginger, this attractive shop carries more than 200 kinds of dried herbs and specializes in plant-based cosmetics and an excellent shampoo made from rosemary and chamomile.

Czech & Speake

39C Jermyn St., SW1 - 439 0216
Open Mon.-Fri. 10 a.m.-6 p.m., Sat. 10 a.m.-5 p.m.

Toilet waters, bath oils, shampoos, scented soaps and talcum powders are the stock-in-trade here. And the packaging is beautiful: frosted-glass bottles with glass stoppers (some in "black opal"), shaving soap in traditional porcelain jars. Czech & Speake also sells an elegant variety of Edwardian bathroom fittings, such as taps, shower heads, hooks and rails and, of course, the rolltop bath with brass claw-and-ball feet.

Floris
89 Jermyn St., SW1 - 930 2885
Open Mon.-Fri. 9:30 a.m.-5:30 p.m., Sat. 9:30 a.m.-4 p.m.

Floris has been "purveyors of the finest English flower perfumes and toiletries to the court of St. James's since the year 1730." Its products are virtually everywhere, recognizable by the distinctive blue and gold packages, on which is displayed the Royal Warrant, of course. The beautiful Spanish mahogany showcases inside this charming, old-fashioned shop were acquired from the Great Exhibition in 1851.

Harris
29 St. James's St., SW1 - 930 8753
Open Mon.-Fri. 8:30 a.m.-6 p.m., Sat. 9:30 a.m.-5:30 p.m.

A famous pharmacy whose preparations include a hand lotion, eye drops, a lemon-scented cream shampoo, a bath oil called His, almond soap, shaving cream and an exceptional bay-rum after-shave.

L'Herbier de Provence
5 Gees Ct., W1 - 629 6726
Open Mon.-Wed. & Fri.-Sat. 9:30 a.m.-6 p.m., Thurs. 9:30 a.m.-7:30 p.m.

Stepping into this shop (which opened in 1988) is like stepping into Provence, surrounded by all the smells of the Midi. Its merchandise—beauty oils, capillary products, aromatic bath oils—is made in France, including a new range of herb-based toiletries designed for men. It also sells vinegars, oils, mustards, spices and herbs imported from France.

Ivan's—George F. Trumper
20 Jermyn St., SW1 - 734 1370
Open Mon.-Fri. 9 a.m.-6 p.m., Sat. 9 a.m.-1 p.m.

Ivan's, under the same management as George F. Trumper of Curzon Street, is an elegant barbershop that offers an interesting collection of wigs for men, shaving brushes and a mustache wax highly regarded by Guards officers and retired colonels. Trumper's men's fragrances are also available.

Neal's Yard Apothecary
2 Neal's Yard, WC2 - 379 7222
Open Mon.-Sat. 10 a.m.-6 p.m., Sun. 11 a.m.-4 p.m.

Neal's "natural" products—for the simply curious or the obsessive professional—include huge jars of herbs, seeds, roots, barks, beans, leaves and powders: Slippery Elm, Pickly Ash Balm, Squaw Vine and Rhubarb Powder. Lovely deep-blue glass bottles containing bath oils, shampoos, herbal teas and remedies jostle for attention in this charming shop.

Penhaligon's
41 Wellington St., WC2 - 836 2150
Open Mon.-Fri. 10 a.m.-6 p.m., Sat. 10 a.m.-5 p.m.
69 Moorgate City, EC2 - 588 3547
Open Mon.-Fri. 9:30 a.m.-5:30 p.m.
20A Brook St., W1 - 493 0002
Open Mon.-Fri. 9:30 a.m.-5:30 p.m., Sat. 9:30 a.m.-4:30 p.m.

Penhaligon's produces some of the best scents found anywhere: for men, the exotic Hamman Bouquet, the discreet citrus Blenheim Bouquet and the Lords line, which was originally created in 1911 for "dashing young blades" and is now available in a medium-size bottle for £24; and for ladies, the lovely Jubilee Bouquet, Victorian Posy and the cool, woodsy Bluebell. The firm is also famous for its toilet waters: gardenia, orange blossom, lily of the valley, violet. Everything is delightfully bottled and packaged. We also like the collection of antique bottles, hand mirrors and silver dressing accessories.

Yves Rocher
7 Gees Ct., W1 - 409 2975
Open Mon.-Wed. & Fri.-Sat. 9:30 a.m.-6 p.m., Thurs. 9:30 a.m.-7:30 p.m.

Yves Rocher stocks a range of cosmetics, perfumes and toilet waters derived from plants. It also has its own beauty center, complete with a friendly staff that is happy to dispense advice. Special promotions are held every month.

The Secret Garden

153 Regent St., W1 - 439 3101
Open Mon.-Wed. & Fri.-Sat. 10 a.m.-6 p.m.,
Thurs. 10 a.m.-7:30 p.m.

Although The Secret Garden was launched in 1987, it exploits the centuries-old (and scientifically proven) benefits of products based on both aromatherapy and herbal disciplines. It sells a comprehensive collection of beauty products, including those for herbal skin care, aromatherapy face and body care and herbal hair care, as well as sun screens, bath preparations, men's grooming aids, women's fragrances, home fragrances and beauty accessories.

Shave Shop

Unit 7 (Floor 1), London Pavilion, 1 Piccadilly Circus, SW1 - 494 1249
Open daily 10 a.m.-10 p.m.
8A Foubert's Pl., W1 - 439 7769
Open Mon.-Fri. 9 a.m.-7 p.m., Sat. 9 a.m.-6 p.m.

An entirely new concept for men, the Shave Shop provides a total body solution "for the man on the move." It stocks its own brand of natural face, body, hair, sun and sport products, all manufactured in England. There is also a fine selection of razors and shaving accessories from around the world. Other branches are opening soon (perhaps by the time you read this) in Covent Garden, Chelsea Harbour and King's Road.

George F. Trumper

9 Curzon St., W1 - 499 1850
Open Mon.-Fri. 9 a.m.-5 p.m., Sat. 9 a.m.-1 p.m.

This fabulous museum of human hair absolutely must be seen. The interior has not changed since 1900, and in the midst of portraits of the Royal Family and a collection of eighteenth-century wigs, you may purchase ivory-handled brushes, lime-tree soap, sponges, shaving brushes and a number of excellent homemade lotions, colognes and after-shaves.

TURKISH BATHS

The Porchester Centre

Queensway, Bayswater, W2 - 798 3688
Open Mon.-Sat. 8 a.m.-10 p.m.

The only remaining Turkish baths in central London, the Porchester baths were built in 1925 and fortunately have been saved from demolition. You can enjoy a wonderful two to three hours of steam in the Russian rooms and Turkish dry-heat rooms before plunging into an icy pool, supposedly the most invigorating aspect of the baths. Body shampoos and massage on a large marble slab are also available. The baths cost £7.50 a session; ladies only on Tuesday, Thursday and Friday, men on Monday, Wednesday and Saturday.

BOOKS & STATIONERY

BOOKS

A bibliophile could wish for no greater pleasure than to burrow into the warren of secondhand bookshops just south of the British Museum, or to wander along Charing Cross Road in search of the latest titles that everyone's talking about. You'll find our favorite booksellers in those neighborhoods reviewed below, along with some other worthy discoveries.

Atlantis Bookshop

49A Museum St., WC1 - 405 2120
Open Mon.-Sat. 11 a.m.-5:30 p.m.

Located on a side street across from the British Museum, this specialist bookshop is devoted to the occult and, in addition, sells the complete works of Jung and books and accessories for clairvoyants (tarot cards, crystal balls), magicians and witches. New and used books share shelf space, and the taciturn owner leaves you to browse at your leisure.

Books for Cooks

4 Blenheim Cres., W11 - 221 1992
Open Mon.-Sat. 9:30 a.m.-6 p.m., Sun. by appt.

Heidi Lascelles owns and manages this attractive haven for cooks, which is home to more than 4,000 cookbooks, ranging from the simplest fare to the most exotic of the world's cuisines. You may get lucky and chance upon an author giving a demonstration in Heidi's small kitchen next door. A must for anyone interested in cooking.

Dance Books

9 Cecil Ct., WC2 - 836 2314
Open Mon.-Sat. 11 a.m.-7 p.m.

The bookstore for dancers and dance aficionados—ballet in particular (in fact, it used to be called the Ballet Bookshop). Owner John O'Brien teaches ballet at Pineapple, and manager David Leonard knows everything there is to know about ballet.

Dillon's Bookstore

82 Gower St., WC1 - 636 1577
Open Mon. & Wed.-Fri. 9 a.m.-5:30 p.m., Tues. & Sat. 9:30 a.m.-5:30 p.m.

Close to London University, this bookshop is a home away from home for university students. It's quite well organized—more than one million books are sorted into eleven departments, each subdivided into five sections—and the knowledgeable staff will help you find whatever you need. Although Dillon's is particularly well known for its academic interests, its general collection also gets exceptionally good marks. It recently took over the Arts Council Shop in Long Acre, devoted to the fine arts, and is in the process of opening several branches throughout London.

Foyles Bookshop

113-119 Charing Cross Rd., WC2
437 5660
Open Mon.-Wed. & Fri.-Sat. 9 a.m.-6 p.m., Thurs. 9 a.m.-7 p.m.

Possibly the largest and most famous bookstore in London, Foyles has 29 departments and a telephone that's permanently busy (even the staff admits it's a mistake to phone). It sponsors monthly literary lunches at the Dorchester Hotel; tickets for these can be obtained here. Credit cards are not accepted.

French's Theatre Bookshop

52 Fitzroy St., W1 - 387 9373
Open Mon.-Fri. 9:30 a.m.-5:30 p.m.

Slightly off the beaten track, French's is nonetheless a mecca for theater lovers. It houses more than 6,000 titles concerning the theater (English and American) and the opera: plays, librettos, histories, biographies and technical works. There are also a great stock of show albums and an amazing selection of sound-effects recordings—from church bells to a wagon carrying a farmer and his barking dog. One can study the books at leisure at a spacious round table. Catalog and mail-order sales.

Hatchards

187 Piccadilly, W1 - 439 9921
Open Mon.-Fri. 9 a.m.-6 p.m., Sat. 9 a.m.-5 p.m.

Quite incomparable for the size and range of its stock and for the competence of its personnel, this elegant Piccadilly shop is London's oldest (1797) and most respected bookseller for the general reader. On the ground floor are hardcovers—fiction, biography, history, religion, humor and travel—and in the basement, paperbacks. Elsewhere in the building you'll find books on art, the performing arts, sports, gardening and cooking, along with classical literature and children's books. Hatchards also provides unrivaled charge-account and mail-order services, shipping books anywhere in the world. Any book published in the U.K. that is not in stock can be ordered; for out-of-print books, Hatchards offers a search service. Several new branches have opened in London during the last few years.

Mandarin Books

22 Notting Hill Gate, W11 - 229 0327
Open Mon.-Fri. 10 a.m.-6:30 p.m., Sat. 10 a.m.-6 p.m.

This excellent general bookstore has served the residents of Notting Hill for more than 25 years. It may appear a little chaotic, but the service is first-class; anything not in stock will be ordered with great efficiency.

Motor Books

33 & 36 St. Martin's Ct., WC2 - 836 5376
Open Mon.-Fri. 9:30 a.m.-5:30 p.m., Sat. 10:30 a.m.-5:15 p.m.

Number 33 stocks everything published on the automobile and motorcycle: rare and modern books, magazines, videos and catalogs. Railway publications are in the basement. Number 36 specializes in military publications. The catalog is free, and mail orders are accepted.

John Sandoe
10 Blacklands Terr., SW3 - 589 9473
Open Mon.-Sat. 9:30 a.m.-5:30 p.m.
Close to Sloane Square and the acclaimed Peter Jones department store, this enchanting little house is crammed with books. But despite their large number everything is well laid out and accessible. John Sandoe, one of London's best-informed booksellers, is usually on hand to advise you in his charming and knowledgeable manner.

Sherratt & Hughes
205 Sloane St., SW1 - 235 2128
Open Mon. & Wed.-Sat. 9 a.m.-8 p.m., Tues. 10 a.m.-8 p.m.
Remodeled and under new management, Sherratt & Hughes, formerly known as Truslove and Hanson, is now part of the W. H. Smith empire. Though the new owners say they intend to maintain previous standards, old T & H customers have found a downward slide in the selection of books on display. But the competitive stationery department still supplies printed notepaper to many diplomatic corps members and famous judges.

Ian Shipley
70 Charing Cross Rd., WC2 - 836 4872
Open Mon.-Sat. 10 a.m.-6 p.m.
Here you can find virtually everything published on the fine arts. Books, art books and exhibition catalogs are squeezed together, just as they might be on your own shelves, with no thought to commercial display. There is also a detailed stock catalog and a search facility that will help track down anything not in stock.

Stanford's
12-14 Long Acre, WC2 - 836 1321
Open Mon.-Fri. 9 a.m.-6 p.m., Sat. 10 a.m.-5 p.m.
A world-famous map shop, which includes a large section for the British Ordinance Survey, Stanford's also possesses a large selection of travel guides and specializes in books on exploring almost every country in the world.

Waterstone's
193 Kensington High St., W8 - 937 8432
Open Mon.-Fri. 9:30 a.m.-10 p.m., Sat. 9:30 a.m.-7 p.m., Sun. & bank holidays noon-7 p.m.
Tim Waterstone opened his first store in 1982, and his success has been staggering; branches continue to spring up all over London. His most recent success is his guide to books, which contains more than 25,000 titles; you simply peruse the guide, place an order, and your books will be shipped anywhere in the world. If you prefer to buy your books in person, free gift wrapping is offered.

Zwemmer
80 Charing Cross Rd. & 24 Litchfield St., WC2 - 836 4710
Open Mon.-Fri. 9:30 a.m.-6 p.m., Sat. 9:30 a.m.-5:30 p.m.
Number 80 Charing Cross Road is filled with books on film, photography and graphic design; across the road, Number 24 Litchfield Street is dedicated to art history, the fine arts and architecture, as well as rare and out-of-print titles. Catalog and mail-order sales.

Zwemmer, Oxford University Press Bookshop
72 Charing Cross Rd., WC2 - 240 1559
Open Mon.-Fri. 9:30 a.m.-6 p.m., Sat. 9:30 a.m.-5:30 p.m.
This shop sells the works of one of the leading publishing houses in the world. In addition to the Bibles, dictionaries, encyclopedias and textbooks for which it has long been famous, the Oxford University Press publishes a wide range of other titles, including classics, poetry collections, plays, literary translations and fine children's books. Catalog and mail-order sales.

STATIONERY

Thanks to the telephone, the art of letter writing in Britain is not what it used to be—but you can still tell a true Englishman (and Englishwoman) by the quality of his or her stationery. The traditional types have their note-paper printed at Smythson. To show that you've really arrived in English society, however, have Harrods print yours. And for original, colorful stationery and wrappings, try the more exotic stock at Paperchase or Scribblers.

Paperchase
167 Fulham Rd., SW3 - 589 7839
Open Mon.-Sat. 9:30 a.m.-6 p.m.

A delightful store with all sorts of attractive stationery in all colors and shapes. Plain colored paper is sold by weight, and there are pretty paper bags and boxes for presents, as well as other party goods—paper tablecloths and napkins in lively designs, for example. Mobiles come in all shapes and sizes, and if you want to frighten your guests away, check out the inflatable skeletons that hang from the ceiling. Prices are quite reasonable.

Penfriend
Bush House Arcade, Bush House, The Strand, WC2 - 836 9809
Open Mon.-Fri. 9:30 a.m.-5:30 p.m.

Pens and anything related to them are sold here—from cheap ballpoints to high-class Mont Blancs and Watermans. The staff will change and adjust any nib to suit your fancy, and if you're so inclined, they'll entice you to purchase one of their silver or tortoiseshell dip pens.

Scribblers
29 James St., WC2 - 240 7640
Open Mon.-Sat. 9:30 a.m.-8 p.m.

One of the most popular stationery shops in London, Scribblers is chock-full of striped, dotted and colored paper, cards, stickers, pencils, exercise books, address books and notebooks—a great selection of bright stationery for those who are more interested in image than on content.

Smythson
54 New Bond St., W1 - 629 8558
Open Mon.-Fri. 9:30 a.m.-5:30 p.m., Sat. 9:15 a.m.-12:30 p.m.

One of the world's most extraordinary stationery shops: The choice, the taste, the quality and the originality of its writing papers and Christmas cards are incomparable. Smythson's products are, understandably, the Queen's choice in stationery.

The Walton Street Stationery Co.
97 Walton St., SW3 - 589 0777
Open Mon.-Fri. 10 a.m.-6 p.m., Sat. 10 a.m.-5 p.m.

Everything in this tiny shop just a stone's throw from Brompton Road is in exquisite taste. Writing paper in every conceivable color, plain or with contrasting borders, can be engraved or printed. Greeting cards and colored ink command high prices. The shop will ship orders, but request that it send your purchase by registered mail.

CHILDREN

CLOTHES

Laura Ashley
7 Harriet St., SW1 - 235 9797
208 Regent St., W1 - 734 5824
Kensington High St., W8 - 938 3751
Open Mon.-Tues. & Thurs.-Fri. 9:30 a.m.-6 p.m., Wed. 9:30 a.m.-7 p.m., Sat. 9 a.m.-6 p.m.

Laura Ashley's romantic, demure, maidens-in-the-country look—which aims to make mothers and daughters look alike—remains as popular as ever. It is now wonder, considering the lovely selection we found. he famous pretty floral cotton fabrics go into the making of delightful dresses for girls up to 12 years old. We were particularly tempted by the lovely velvet dresses with lace collars (£38), the cotton smock party dresses (£32) and the velvet tartan dungarees for babies (£17). Don't miss the charming wool all-in-one outfit with matching gloves (£37).

Bambino

77 New Bond St., W1 - 491 8077
Open Mon.-Wed. & Fri.-Sat. 10 a.m.-5:30 p.m.,
Thurs. 10 a.m.-7 p.m.
1 George St., W1 - 935 9452
Open Mon.-Sat. 10 a.m.-5:30 p.m.

Designer children's wear from all over Europe is Bambino's stock-in-trade, including its own line of unusual, casual all-in-one outfits for newborns up to 14-year-olds. The designs and fabrics are creative, the prices sky-high.

012-Benetton

131 Kensington High St., W8 - 499 8509
Open Mon.-Wed. & Fri. 10 a.m.-6:30 p.m.,
Thurs. 10 a.m.-7:30 p.m., Sat. 10 a.m.-6 p.m.
22 S. Molton St., W1 - 409 1599
Open Mon.-Wed. & Fri.-Sat. 10 a.m.-6 p.m.,
Thurs. 10 a.m.-7 p.m.

Italy's Benetton, one of the world's most popular clothiers of fashionable teens and young adults, now has a line of colorful, sporty clothes for children up to age 12. Benetton is famous for its sweaters and other knitwear, its sweatshirts and leggings, but this store also sells casual trousers, jackets and accessories (hats, gloves and belts). Prices are reasonable for the quality.

Buckle-My-Shoe

19 St. Christopher's Pl., W1 - 935 5589
Open Mon.-Fri. 10 a.m.-6 p.m., Sat. 10 a.m.-7 p.m.

At this children's shoe shop in the heart of the West End, Nick and Lulu Rayne sell fun, fashionable shoes for youngsters under 8 at prices ranging from £5 to £70. Party shoes include pretty satin, patent and moiré selections, and little flower girls will be pleased with the dyeable satin ballet shoes. The Raynes also stock more traditional styles—button, lace-up, T-bar and Velcro-fastening shoes—as well as such accessories as belts, suspenders, hats, bow ties and unique socks.

Cacharel

103 New Bond St., W1 - 629 1964
46 Golders Green Rd., NW11 - 455 7508
Open Mon.-Wed. & Fri. 9:30 a.m.-6:30 p.m.,
Thurs. 9:30 a.m.-7:30 p.m., Sat. 9:30 a.m.-6 p.m.

Although expensive, Cacharel's French children's clothes are good in quality and classic in design.

The Chelsea Design Company

46 Fulham Rd., SW3 - 581 8811
Open Mon.-Sat. 10 a.m.-6 p.m.

The Chelsea Design Company's traditional and smart children's wear includes day dresses in Viyella and Liberty fabrics and taffeta party dresses for girls up to 13. Boys can be outfitted in velvet knickerbockers, Viyella shirts and velvet suits. Prices for a day dress range from £80 to £115. Christening and bridesmaid dresses are also sold.

La Cicogna Roma

6A Sloane St., SW1 - 235 3845
Open Mon.-Tues. & Thurs.-Sat. 9:15 a.m.-6:15 p.m., Wed. 9:15 a.m.-7:15 p.m.

These exclusive Italian fashions for children up to age 16 come from such designers as Valentino, Giorgio Armani, Maria Giovanna, Blue Marine and Antonella Baby. You'll also find beautiful kids' shoes, a small selection of French clothes, maternity clothes and babywear. Prices are as high as one would expect from the designers represented.

Confiture

19 Harrington Rd., SW7 - 581 3432
Open Mon.-Sat. 10 a.m.-6 p.m.

The names sold in this small shop near the Lycée Français include Chippie, Oilily and Kideliz for children up to age 12. The lovely Tartine & Chocolat line is available for children up to 4, and fashionable Pomme d'Api shoes are stocked for kids up to 12. Naturally, merchandise of this sort doesn't come cheap.

Createx

27 Harrington Rd., SW7 - 589 8306
Open Mon.-Sat. 10 a.m.-6 p.m.

Createx's French and Italian good-quality kids' clothes—from Cacharel, Petit Bateau, Osh Kosh and the like—are fairly priced. The selection is broader than the shop's small size would lead one to believe. Createx also stocks DD socks and tights.

Instep

45 St. John's Wood High St., NW8
722 7634
Open Mon.-Sat. 9:30 a.m.-5:30 p.m.

One of the few children's shoe specialists in London. Instep's owner has been in business for seven years and knows everything about children's feet; he and his staff take the time to make sure that you get the right shoes for your child. Though he buys primarily in France and Italy, he also stocks such other well-known makes as Start-Rite and Salamander, along with sneakers (Adidas, Nike), socks and tights from DD and Ergé, leotards and ballet shoes.

Joanna's Tent
289 King's Rd., SW3 - 352 1151
Open Mon.-Sat. 10 a.m.-6 p.m.

The trendiest French names (Oilily, Chippie) are found in abundance at Joanna's Tent: jackets, coats, trousers (£52), fashionable skirts (£45). We also discovered hand-knit sweaters by Alison Robson (£94) and shoes by Pomme d'Api. And the brightly colored ensembles can be paired with matching accessories (belts, gloves, socks).

Kenzo Enfant
130 Draycott Ave., SW3 - 584 1252
Open Mon.-Tues. & Thurs.-Sat. 10 a.m.-6 p.m., Wed. 10 a.m.-7 p.m.

Another high-fashion designer for grownups has jumped into the lucrative children's-clothing market: Kenzo. This exclusive line for girls up to 12 ranges from the casual to the dressy and includes hand-knit sweaters, velvet dresses, suits, cotton jersey play clothes and accessories.

Anthea Moore Ede
16 Victoria Grove, W8 - 584 8836
Open Mon.-Fri. 9 a.m.-5 p.m., Sat. 10 a.m.-1 p.m.

A place for the child whose nanny takes him or her to Kensington Gardens, Anthea Moore Ede stocks gorgeous smocked dresses, adorable sailor suits and every other essential item for upper-class children, including, of course, coats with velvet collars. It sells attractive babywear as well, but be assured that these tiny outfits do not come at tiny prices.

The Nursery
103 Bishop's Rd., SW6 - 731 6637
Open Mon.-Sat. 10 a.m.-6 p.m.

Away from crowded Fulham and King's roads, this most unusual shop sells children's clothes (up to age 6) with a classical country look of its own design and manufacture, made of natural fabrics. There are also a selection of Christmas-stocking fillers or party presents (from 20p to £5), some beautiful traditional

books (like the Babar series), a few pieces of old nursery furniture and antique-silver name brooches (£30). The owner is obviously an antiques lover.

Peek-A-Boo
42 Chiltern St., W1 - 486 2800
Open Mon.-Fri. 10 a.m.-5:30 p.m., Sat. 10 a.m.-1 p.m.

The delightful Peek-A-Boo specializes in clothes for children up to 4 years old. We saw some lovely baby outfits—tiny handmade shirts and matching cardigans, booties and sheets, all of which come in fourteen colors—that would make exquisite presents for a newborn (£20 to £30). For little girls, there are pretty cotton and lace-embroidered party dresses. The handmade hangers also make charming gifts. Everything in this small shop is in excellent taste.

Pinky Blue
102 & 106 Allitsen Rd., NW8
586 0167 (102), 722 6027 (106)
Open Mon.-Sat. 9:30 a.m.-5:30 p.m.

The Pinky Blue shop at number 102, subtitled The Juniors' Boutique, is stocked with French, Italian and Spanish clothing for children 6 to 14 years old. The emphasis is on sportswear (denim jackets for about £40). At number 106, you'll find exclusive, high-quality Continental clothing (both trendy and classic) for babies and toddlers, smocked dresses made in England and hand-knits made to order for the shop. The owner is adamant about using pure cotton and wool fabrics. Beachwear and nightwear are also sold at both shops. At the time of this writing, a new shop was about to open at 6 William Street, SW1.

Pomme d'Api
154B Walton St., SW3 - 584 1596
Open Mon.-Sat. 10 a.m.-6 p.m.

This narrow shop on a pleasant street has consistently retained its high standards since Myriam Bouait opened it in early 1980. She stocks clothes for children up to age 12 from such makers as Switzerland's Molli, France's Daniel Hechter (jeans and parkas), Cacharel and Chippie (well-cut overcoats and more), and Italy's Delfino, Scoubidou and Babymini.

Rowe's
120 New Bond St., W1 - 734 9711
Open Mon.-Fri. 9 a.m.-5:30 p.m., Sat. 9 a.m.-5 p.m.

Rowe's has been dressing the Royal Family on and off since the eighteenth century. Given these credentials, you won't be surprised to find that most of the children's clothing is quite traditional in design, though Rowe's does keep in step with the times with its more modern designs. Even if you can't afford the prices, it's an interesting shop well worth a visit.

Patricia Wigan Designs
72 New King's Rd., SW6 - 736 3336
Open Mon.-Fri. 9:30 a.m.-5:30 p.m.
19 Walton St., SW3 - 823 7080
Open Mon.-Fri. 10 a.m.-5:30 p.m., Sat. 10 a.m.-5 p.m.

A successful young designer of affordable, high-quality clothes for children under 12, Patricia Wigan reveals her half-Austrian, half-Italian heritage in her merchandise, most of which (either the fabric or the finished product) is imported from these two countries. Her beautiful knitwear and matching socks come from Austria; her fabrics come from both Austria and Italy, and from these fabrics she has clothing manufactured to her design in Scotland and Hungary; and a new line of clothes for newborns is manufactured in Brazil. A mail-order catalog is available.

Zero Four
53 S. Molton St., W1 - 493 4920
Open Mon.-Wed. & Fri. 10 a.m.-6 p.m., Thurs. 10 a.m.-7 p.m., Sat. 10 a.m.-5 p.m.

We were happy to find Italian and French children's clothes (up to age 13), along with some lovely English hand-knitted woolens, at this attractive shop close to Oxford Street.

FURNITURE

Dragons
23 Walton St., SW3 - 589 3795, 589 0548
Open Mon.-Fri. 9:30 a.m.-5:30 p.m., Sat. 10:30 a.m.-4:30 p.m.

Dragons' attractive hand-painted children's furniture is now complemented by an equally lovely range of fabrics, wallpapers, bed linens and the like. They're no bargains, but the products are excellent, and the designs are everything a parent thinks his child will love.

Hippohall
47 Palliser Rd., W14 - 602 5436
Open Tues.-Sat. 10 a.m.-6 p.m.

Hippohall will create an entire design package for your child's room—and a most attractive job they will make of it, too. It'll supply everything you need, from the furniture to the wallpaper, the curtains and bed linens to the little accessories. All is done in fresh, naive colors that will brighten any child's environment.

TOYS & GAMES

Children's Book Centre
237 Kensington High St., W8 - 937 7497
Open Mon.-Sat. 9:30 a.m.-6 p.m.

The Children's Book Centre moved from Young World (now closed) to its own premises. It still sells a wide selection of books for all ages (up to 15 or so). Book tokens (from £1 to £20) are also available, as are book-related birthday cards and friezes for children's bedrooms. The staff is helpful and friendly.

Dolls' Hospital
16 Dawes Rd., SW6 - 385 2081
Open Mon.-Sat. 9:30 a.m.-5 p.m.

Although this small shop stocks a range of joke items and toys, its main activity is "curing" ailing dolls (primarily antique) and teddy bears. The "doctors" always provide an estimate before taking on "patients."

The Dolls House
29 The Market, Covent Garden, WC2
379 7243
Open Mon.-Sat. 10 a.m.-8 p.m.

This lovely shop in a lively part of London sells attractive and expensive dollhouses of various styles, either in kits (for about £70) or ready-made (as much as £700 or more), along with an extensive range of furniture and accessories, some of which are handcrafted and by no means intended for children. It's a delightful place certain to enchant the collector.

Early Learning Centre
225 Kensington High St., W8 - 937 0419
36 King's Rd., SW3 - 581 5764
Unit 7, King's Mall, W6 - 741 2469
Open Mon.-Sat. 9:30 a.m.-6 p.m.

If you're looking for excellent value in creative games, puzzles and books, stop into one of the branches of this chain of toy shops. The well-organized stores carry broad selections of several brands (including its own) for children up to 8, with everything clearly displayed on shelves arranged by category. And a good many items are priced under £3. The play area for children helps out mom.

Frog Hollow
15 Victoria Grove, W8 - 581 5493
Open Mon.-Sat. 9 a.m.-5:30 p.m., Sun. 11 a.m.-5:30 p.m.

Frog Hollow is a treasure trove for all ages. The traditional goods include a good selection of little things children can buy with their own pocket money, an extensive display of frogs for the collector, a vast selection of books and tapes and a variety of soft toys. The service is personal and attentive. Prices range from £5 to £500.

Hamleys
200 Regent St., W1 - 734 3161
Open Mon.-Wed. & Fri.-Sat. 9 a.m.-5:30 p.m., Thurs. 9 a.m.-7 p.m.

What can one say about the largest toy shop in the world? On the down side, it can be challenging to find your way around, and the staff is not particularly helpful. Definitely avoid Christmastime if hordes of high-energy children make you nervous.

Just Games
71 Brewer St., W1 - 734 6124
Open Mon.-Wed. & Fri.-Sat. 10 a.m.-6 p.m., Thurs. 10 a.m.-7 p.m.

An excellent place for the game lover: mahjongg, chess, backgammon, Chinese puzzles, Trivial Pursuit—they're all here, along with puzzles and game-related books. The staff is interested and helpful.

The Kensington Carnival
123 Ifield Rd., SW10 - 370 4358
Open Mon.-Fri. 9:30 a.m.-5 p.m.

A one-stop party shop, The Kensington Carnival rents children's party furniture (tables, chairs, benches, catering tables), slides, trampolines and much more. It also sells party accessories of all kinds—favors, prizes and unusual, cheap, amusing gifts. Novelty birthday cakes are baked to order.

The Kite Store
69 Neal St., WC2 - 836 1666
3 Marlborough Ct. (off Carnaby St.), W1
734 4320
Open Mon.-Fri. 10 a.m.-6 p.m.

As its name might imply, this store stocks a most amazing range of kites—myriad shapes, from dragons to flowers—some of which are ready to fly and some of which are kits to be assembled. You can also buy the materials to make your own kite, or have one custom-made for you. Prices range from about 95p for an elementary kite to about £250 for the grandest.

Pollock's Toy Theatres
44 The Market, Covent Garden, WC2
379 7866
Open Mon.-Sat. 10:30 a.m.-6 p.m.

Toy theaters (an excellent way for children to expend their creative energy) are the focus of this shop—specifically, dear little Victorian theaters in cardboard and paper, with all the necessary props and personnel. The theaters are complemented by plays, music boxes, old-fashioned toys, rag dolls, paper cut-out models, teddy bears and more.

The Singing Tree
69 New King's Rd., SW6 - 736 4527
Open Mon.-Sat. 10 a.m.-5:30 p.m.

Absolutely charming (though somewhat cramped), The Singing Tree is full of the most delightful dollhouses and everything needed to furnish them, from basic beds, tables and chairs to wallpaper, curtains, sheets, glasses, decanters, china, pictures and silver objects. (Some of the furniture pieces are exquisite handmade reproduction antiques.) There are even attractive little people who will live in your house. Prices for the most basic dollhouses start at £70 for a do-it-yourselfer and go up to £1,200. Not

---

Shops can close without warning, so please call before setting out for a particular store.

surprisingly, this shop is more for adults than for children.

Steam Age—Basset Lowke
19 Abingdon Rd., W8 - 938 1982
Open Mon.-Fri. 9:30 a.m.-5:30 p.m., Sat. 9:30 a.m.-1 p.m.

Steam engine aficionados will adore this shop, which is stocked with scale models from zero- to seven-inch gauge, along with train-related books, accessories, fittings and kits.

Tiger, Tiger
219 King's Rd., SW3 - 352 8080
Open Mon.-Sat. 9:30 a.m.-6:30 p.m.

This attractive store, with its large display of soft toys in the front, carries items priced for anyone's pocketbook. The less expensive, smaller things are easily accessible for viewing and handling in wire baskets, while the more expensive items are well displayed on the walls and shelves. We're particularly fond of the lovely wooden Noah's Arks and the excellent wooden animal puzzles (from £7.15). Also noteworthy is the good stock of dollhouses, farms and books for the younger child.

Toddler Toys
4 Harriet St., SW1 - 245 6316
Knights Arcade, SW1 - 225 2693
Open Mon.-Tues. & Thurs.-Sat. 9:30 a.m.-6 p.m., Wed. 9:30 a.m.-7 p.m.

The prices of these handcrafted, British-made educational toys start at 10p and go considerably higher. The shop sends goods all over the world; mail-order service is available.

CLOTHES & FASHION

ACCESSORIES

HATS

The bowler, once an indispensable part of the Englishman's wardrobe, is now optional, but it's not considered eccentric. You'll still see it on an impressive number of older heads in the City of London, where it continues to bestow an air if not of intelligence, at least of distinction. But remember that this famous hat is worn only by the traditionally minded London businessman (and by the smartest ladies when fox hunting). Note also that the bowler is worn in London during business hours only—as part of its owner's professional uniform, like his striped trousers and tightly rolled umbrella. A City banker will wear a felt hat in the evenings or a tweed cap during weekends in the country.

Bates
21A Jermyn St., SW1 - 734 2722
Open Mon.-Fri. 9 a.m.-5:30 p.m., Sat. 9:30 a.m.-4 p.m.

The Bates family has run this hat shop since it opened at the turn of the century, and has consistently maintained a high level of quality. The shop successfully combines an authentic old-world setting with up-to-date hats, and it's lined with old newspaper photos of famous people wearing Bates hats. Excellent service at prices that are somewhat lower than those at other famous milliners.

The Hat Shop
58 Neal St., WC2 - 836 6718
Open Mon.-Thurs. 10 a.m.-6 p.m., Fri. 10 a.m.-7 p.m., Sat. 10 a.m.-5:30 p.m.

One of the most successful new hat shops in London, The Hat Shop is a small, cramped place overflowing with hats of all shapes and sizes, mainly for women, but there are a few traditional styles for men. You're sure to find the appropriate decorative headgear for any occasion.

Herbert Johnson
30 New Bond St., W1 - 408 1174
Open Mon.-Fri. 9:15 a.m.-5:30 p.m., Sat. 9:30 a.m.-4 p.m.

Herbert Johnson has moved back to New Bond Street from Old Burlington Street, just a few doors away from its original (1889) location. Founded on the advice of King Edward VII, then Prince of Wales, Johnson has been supplying hats to royalty ever since. Traditional tweed caps are a specialty, but don't overlook the Panamas, homburgs, bowlers and much more. And there's a fine ladies' collection by Sylvia Fletcher.

Stephen Jones
29 Heddon St., W1 - 734 9666
Open by appt. only.

Stephen Jones studied architecture, then became a truck driver and finally wound up in hats. He makes them for today's men and women; indeed, he encourages a woman to take her outfit to his shop so he can create a hat around it. (He has made hats out of such strange things as gelatin and a colander, along with the usual felts and such.)

Lock & Co.
6 St. James's St., SW1 - 930 5849
Open Mon.-Fri. 9 a.m.-5 p.m., Sat. 9:30 a.m.-12:30 p.m.

This shop's appearance hasn't changed since Beau Brummell bought his hats here. Since its founding in 1676, the house of Lock has furnished English high society with top hats, bowlers and fishing hats. It is particularly proud of its fur felt hats (£55 to £70), which have become extremely popular again. It also displays a fascinating collection of antique headwear.

RAINCOATS

Aquascutum
100 Regent St., W1 - 734 6090
Open Mon.-Wed. & Fri.-Sat. 9 a.m.-6 p.m., Thurs. 9 a.m.-7 p.m.

Famous since 1851 for its dashing trench coats and elegant wool coats, Aquascutum makes raincoats that are almost as famous as those from Burberrys. Its collection includes British classics and contemporary clothes for men and women. Among the cashmere, camel and tweed coats you'll find silks, knitwear, shirts, jackets and dresses for ladies and everything for the British gentleman's wardrobe. And the Aquascutum has become the raincoat of choice for Japanese businessmen.

Burberrys
18-22 Haymarket, SW1 - 930 3343
165 Regent St., W1 - 734 4060
Open Mon.-Wed. & Fri.-Sat. 9 a.m.-5:30 p.m., Thurs. 9 a.m.-7 p.m.

Thomas Burberry invented gabardine in the last century, and to this day his name evokes the quintessential raincoat. These classic trenches come in a range of colors, including navy, beige, off-white, lovat and black, all enlivened with Burberrys's signature tan plaid

lining. Countless sensible, conservative types from all around the world wouldn't dream of wearing any raincoat but a Burberry. You'll find Burberrys boutiques in all the major department stores, but for the broadest selection of its merchandise, which now includes luggage and children's clothes, visit these full-fledged stores. Traditional trenches start at £305.

UMBRELLAS & CANES

English umbrellas—especially men's—are the most elegant in the world. They are sold, of course, in all the department stores, but if you take a thoroughly British attitude toward umbrellas and see them not just as useful objects but as a part of a gentleman's essential equipment, then you will show your discrimination by visiting one of these two undisputed leaders in the umbrella field.

James Smith & Sons
53 New Oxford St., WC1 - 836 4731
Open Mon.-Fri. 9 a.m.-5:25 p.m., Sat. 10 a.m.-4 p.m.

Since 1830, the celebrated house of Smith has been supplying umbrellas, parasols, canes and even sword-concealing walking sticks to London's upper crust. It's even been known to produce made-to-order models for its more exacting customers. You'll pay anything from £9.50 to £275.

Swaine, Adeney, Brigg & Sons
185 Piccadilly, W1 - 734 4277
Open Mon.-Wed. & Fri. 9 a.m.-5:30 p.m., Thurs. 9:30 a.m.-7 p.m., Sat. 9:30 a.m.-5 p.m.

At this Royal umbrella supplier, you can choose one to suit your height and bring it back if it needs repairing. It's certainly the last shop in the world that still produces umbrellas of pure silk with gold and silver collars, handmade to ensure that the workmanship is flawless.

JEWELRY

COSTUME JEWELRY

Arabesk Bijoux d'Afrique
156 Walton St., SW3 - 584 3858
Open Mon.-Sat. 10 a.m.-6 p.m.

The only shop of its kind in London, Arabesk is home to some exquisite beaded jewelry handcrafted in Africa according to traditional designs and patterns. The exotic one-of-a-kind pieces of antique Ethiopian silver-and-amber jewelry are an Arabesk specialty. Necklaces, earrings and bracelets range from £5 to £700.

Branche
41 St. John's Wood High St., NW8
586 0613, 586 8638
Open Mon.-Sat. 10 a.m.-6 p.m.
Romayne Narinian, the owner of this elegant art deco–style shop with green lacquered walls and a black marble floor, is half English and half Armenian. She travels to America, Spain, France and Italy to gather her attractive, original collection of jewelry, which includes silver and gold and ranges in price from £14 to £200. Also on sale here are English silver-plated photograph frames (from £23), handmade replicas of antique watches, Michel Jasse's hats from America and hair accessories from France (£5.50 to £50).

Butler & Wilson
189 Fulham Rd., SW3 - 352 3045
20 S. Molton St., W1 - 409 2955
Open Mon.-Sat. 10 a.m.-6 p.m.
Although there's a good selection of antique and art deco jewelry here, the real joys of this place are the bold, crazy, glitzy costume pieces to suit all budgets (from £15 to the neighborhood of £300): snake brooches, chunky necklaces and heart-shape earrings in pearls, jet, brilliant-colored glass and diamanté. You can't help but be captivated by *something* at this innovative jeweler.

The Button Queen
19 Marylebone Ln., W1 - 935 1505
Open Mon.-Fri. 10 a.m.-6 p.m., Sat. 10 a.m.-1:30 p.m.
London's largest and finest collection of antique buttons and buckles lives up to its name—it even sells charming earrings and cuff

Going traveling? Look for Gault Millau's other "Best of" guides to France, Paris, Italy, Hong Kong, New York, New England, Washington, D.C., Los Angeles, San Francisco and Chicago.

links made from old buttons. You'll also find a large stock of modern buttons in this fascinating shop, from which it is impossible to escape without yielding to temptation.

Chantal
2A George St., W1 - 935 0206
Open Mon.-Fri. 10 a.m.-6 p.m., Sat. 10:30 a.m.-5:30 p.m.
Chantal Cornet, the charming French owner, imports all her goods from France and Italy: elegant costume jewelry, mini drawstring leather bags, superb matching gloves, belts and hair accessories. Her costume earrings range from £10 to £35, and necklaces go up to £150. We particularly liked a velvet embroidered evening bag that cost £120. At the time of this writing, another branch was slated to open soon at 262 Beauchamp Place, SW3.

Ciro
178 Regent St., W1 - 437 0993
9 New Bond St., W1 - 491 7219
61A Brompton Rd., SW3 - 489 5584
Open Mon.-Sat. 9:15 a.m.-5:30 p.m.
These shops sell a wide selection of copies and original pieces in cirolite stone (a good faux diamond). Ciro is also famous for its imitation and cultured pearls, and everything in the shop is in eighteen-carat gold or rhodium plate. Prices range from £20 to as much as you wish to spend.

Cobra & Bellamy
149 Sloane St., SW1 - 730 2823
Open Mon.-Sat. 10:30 a.m.-6 p.m.
Decorative art and original costume jewelry dating from the eighteenth century to the 1980s are displayed here, including pieces by Trifani, Boucher and Dior. Two Italian designers work exclusively for the shop, which hosts special exhibitions every two years. Currently it is launching a book on "fabulous fakes," *The History of Fantasy & Fashion Jewellery* by Vivienne Becker (the first English book on the subject). Another location at Liberty's on Regent Street.

Fior
22 New Bond St., W1 - 491 4119
27 Brompton Rd., W1 - 589 0053
Open Mon.-Sat. 9:30 a.m.-5:30 p.m.
Specializing in the art of costume jewelry, Fior offers a broad range of pieces to choose from.

Folli-Follie
45 Beauchamp Pl., SW3 - 589 0552
Open Mon.-Sat. 10 a.m.-6 p.m.

Italian jewelry designer Michel Comte works exclusively for this shop, creating modern and traditional pieces from sterling silver and eighteen-carat gold, with rock crystal and zircon. A new collection is designed twice a year and manufactured in Greece, with sterling-silver watches made to match. Earrings are £25 to £400; bracelets and necklaces are £40 and up.

Kristal
2 S. Molton St., W1 - 408 0179
Open Mon.-Wed. & Fri.-Sat. 10 a.m.-6 p.m., Thurs. 10 a.m.-7 p.m.

A small place on fashionable South Molton Street, Kristal sells jewelry primarily from France and Italy, including some pieces by its own, exclusive designers. There are also sterling-silver pieces from Israel and some gold-plated items containing semiprecious stones. We were tempted by an unusual necklace made of a gold chain with a scent bottle as a pendant, plus matching earrings and bracelet. Prices range from £25 to £250.

Ken Lane
30 Burlington Arcade, W1 - 499 1364
66 S. Molton St., W1 - 584 5299
50 Beauchamp Pl., SW3 - 584 5299
Open Mon.-Sat. 9:30 a.m.-5:30 p.m.

Ken Lane's costume jewelry uncannily resembles the real thing: pearl chokers and earrings set in gold; rhinestones and fake emeralds and rubies. You'll also find clever pieces in bold ethnic styles, like the large gold-plated link necklace with a beaten texture (£45) and its matching bracelet (£25) and earrings (£15). Ken Lane also sells beautiful replicas of the late Duchess of Windsor's personal jewelry collection.

Liberty
210 Regent St., W1 - 743 1234
Open Mon.-Wed. & Fri.-Sat. 9:30 a.m.-6 p.m., Thurs. 9:30 a.m.-7 p.m.

Liberty has two jewelry departments on the ground floor: a small, original selection of "designer" costume jewelry and ceramic pieces, which constantly changes, and, in the Cameo Corner, necklaces of amber and tiger-eye, Chinese jewels of coral and jade, Tibetan necklaces, Indian white metal jewelry, Victorian pieces, contemporary silver and a collection of unusual antique jewelry.

Van Peterson
117 Walton St., SW3 - 589 2155
Open Mon.-Tues. & Thurs.-Sat. 9:30 a.m.-6 p.m., Wed. 9:30 a.m.-7 p.m.

Van Peterson sells fine twentieth-century jewelry, prints (Horst), glass and silver (particularly from the '30s, '40s and '50s), Rolex and Cartier watches (from the '30s) and modern jewelry made to house designs. Take a look at the large selection of old and new silver cuff links in animal designs (£115).

FINE JEWELRY

Adler
13 New Bond St., W1 - 409 2237
Open Mon.-Fri. 9:30 a.m.-5:30 p.m., Sat. by appt. only.

We were dazzled by the modern sophistication of European craftsmanship and the warm blend of Eastern sensuality in Adler designs and creations. There is a spectacular choice of beautiful stones, filled with rich color and set in contemporary and passionate designs. This is jewelry designed for modern life, to be worn day or night.

Philip Antrobus
11 New Bond St., W1 - 493 4557
Open Mon.-Fri. 10 a.m.-4:45 p.m.

Established in 1815, Philip Antrobus made the engagement ring given to the Queen by HRH Prince Philip. It now carries a large stock of antique and Victorian pieces and can design and make special commissions in its workshop on the premises. Expect experienced, friendly service in calm, unfussy surroundings.

Asprey
165-169 New Bond St., W1 - 493 6767
Open Mon.-Fri. 9 a.m.-5:30 p.m., Sat. 9 a.m.-1 p.m.

This dignified establishment is the holder of no fewer than three Royal Warrants. The fine selection of art deco and antique jewelry complements Asprey's own beautifully designed pieces. You don't necessarily have to be as rich as the Royals to shop here, for the price range is wide; and you can be sure they're all quality pieces.

N. Bloom & Son
40 Conduit St., W1 - 629 5060
Open Mon.-Fri. 9:30 a.m.-5 p.m.

Bloom stocks interesting and unusual pieces of old jewelry, especially of the late Victorian, Edwardian and art deco periods, priced from £300 to £30,000. Still family owned, it offers the benefit of 70 years' experience.

André Bogaert
5 S. Molton St., W1 - 493 4869
Open Mon.-Fri. 10 a.m.-6 p.m., Sat. 10 a.m.-5 p.m.

Smart, modern, uncluttered designs (in eighteen-carat gold and silver) are available here at affordable prices ranging from £10 to £5,000. Bogaert also sells well-designed accessories—flashlights, key rings, pens and leather goods.

Boucheron
180 New Bond St., W1 - 493 0983
Open Mon.-Fri. 10 a.m.-5:30 p.m.

This great establishment designs unusual gold jewelry, often set with huge precious stones. But buried in the back of the store is a collection of small pieces (from £300) that are sure to please.

Cartier
175 New Bond St., W1 - 493 6962
Open Mon.-Fri. 9:30 a.m.-5:30 p.m.

Cartier upholds its reputation with a Cartier des Indes ruby-and-emerald, bead-and-tassel belt made between the wars from Indian stones, the clasp made of a great cabochon emerald circled by pavé-set diamonds and four cabochon rubies. It sells for a mere £1 million. For those of more modest means, Cartier offers the very chic "Must" tank watch in eighteen-carat gold over sterling silver, hardly a giveaway at about £450, and, of course, the entire Les Must de Cartier range.

Chatila
22 Old Bond St., W1 - 493 9833
Open Mon.-Fri. 10 a.m.-6 p.m., Sat. 10 a.m.-5 p.m.

Chatila, a branch of the famous Geneva jewelers, opened this magnificent showroom in July 1987. It exhibits a full range of contemporary jewelry and watches, with prices ranging from £500 to more than £1 million.

Chaumet
178 New Bond St., W1 - 629 0136
Open Mon.-Fri. 10 a.m.-5:30 p.m.

Among the classic designs of this great French jeweler you will find some unusual modern pieces, colorful baroque necklaces made of pearls, coral or semiprecious stones and heavy designs chased in gold. Prices begin at about £3,700 for a necklace and £1,000 for a matching bracelet.

Collingwood
171 New Bond St., W1 - 734 2656
Open Mon.-Fri. 9:30 a.m.-5 p.m.

Collingwood, which has been in existence for almost two centuries and has been awarded three Royal Warrants, undertakes commission work and manufactures pieces unusual in shape and cut of diamond. It also stocks famous watch brands and antique/period jewelry from early Victorian/Edwardian to art deco. Prices range from £100 to . . . well, let your imagination soar!

Ebel
179 New Bond St., W1 - 491 1252
Open Mon.-Fri. 10 a.m.-6 p.m., Sat. 10 a.m.-4:30 p.m.

Ebel, known worldwide as "The Architects of Time," has decided to open boutiques in the world's major capitals, starting with London. This is the place to find its two complete watch collections—Sport and Beluga 22—along with classic jewelry by Italian designer Alessandra Gradi, who works exclusively for the Ebel boutiques.

Electrum
21 S. Molton St., W1 - 629 6325
Open Mon.-Fri. 10 a.m.-6 p.m., Sat. 10 a.m.-2 p.m.

A split-level gallery, rather than a simple shop, Electrum sells unique jewelry by 60 or so contemporary designers from all over the world.

Theo Fennell
177 Fulham Rd., SW3 - 352 7313
Open Mon.-Fri. 10 a.m.-7 p.m., Sat. 10 a.m.-5:30 p.m.

Theo Fennell believes jewelry should be a personal statement, so he works closely with his clients to produce original pieces or to rework existing ones into fresh designs. He also specializes in objets d'art, silversmithing and goldsmithing. Any object, from a boat to a house, can be made in any size or metal—we saw miniature jewelry take the form of a Porsche, a French horn, a shotgun, a roller skate, a golf bag with individual clubs, and a solid-silver Colt 45 Peacemaker complete with holster.

Garrard
112 Regent St., W1 - 734 7020
Open Mon.-Fri. 9:30 a.m.-5:30 p.m.
Queen Victoria appointed Garrard crown jeweler in 1843 (the lighter crown seen in her later portraits was designed here in 1870), and for the coronation of George V, Garrard incorporated part of the Cullinan diamond in the Imperial State Crown. Aside from such regal merchandise, the establishment sells an enormous range of pieces in traditional and contemporary settings.

Nicholas Harris
26 Conduit St., W1 - 499 5991
Open Mon.-Fri. 10 a.m.-5:30 p.m.
This fascinating shop houses a large collection of antique jewelry, specializing in "archaeological revival"—nineteenth-century Hellenistic and Etruscan revival pieces—as well as signed twentieth-century pieces by the likes of Cartier and Fouquet. We also saw some of the most amusing and unusual decorative silver in London, including a special collection of nineteenth- and twentieth-century American silver. The collection very much reflects the style of its flamboyant owner.

Hof
23 Old Bond St., W1 - 499 5466
Open Mon.-Sat. 10 a.m.-5:30 p.m.
Hof jewelers specialize in modern eighteen-carat gold and platinum jewelry set with fine stones in unusual designs. And to verify the exact details of a stone's quality, the store supplies certificates for all important diamonds.

Annabel Jones
52 Beauchamp Pl., SW3 - 589 3215
Open Mon.-Fri. 10 a.m.-5:30 p.m.
This shop, well known for delightful modern jewelry that wears well with today's clothes, has recently gone into antique jewelry and silver. Anything you buy here you will surely enjoy for many years, and you can always count on a warm welcome in a comfortable, relaxed ambience. Don't miss the excellent selection of silver and enamel cuff links. Catalog upon request.

Kutchinsky
179 New Bond St., W1 - 629 2876
73 Brompton Rd., SW3 - 584 9311
Open Mon.-Fri. 10 a.m.-5:30 p.m., Sat. 10 a.m.-12:30 p.m.
The classic, restrained designs found here include such stones as sapphires, diamonds and pearls.

Ilias Lalaounis
174 New Bond St., W1 - 491 0673
Open Mon.-Fri. 10 a.m.-5:30 p.m., Sat. 10 a.m.-1 p.m.
This remarkable Athenian jeweler now has a London shop and showroom. Lalaounis's creations, inspired by nature and his ancient Greek forebears, are sometimes deceptively simple, while others are modeled on more complex things, such as ancient Byzantine lace. A necklace and earrings in gold and rubies was inspired by jewels worn by a fourteenth-century king. The beautiful workmanship makes this shop at least worth a look.

Paul Longmire
12 Bury St., SW1 - 930 8720
Open Mon.-Fri. 9 a.m.-5 p.m.
No fewer than three Royal Warrants attest to the Royal Family's fondness for Paul Longmire's superb custom-made presentation gifts made of gold and silver. Cuff-link wearers should consider Longmire an obligatory stop—his collection of antique pieces and his excellent made-to-order models are without peer in London. Also on hand in this handsome, service-oriented shop are charming animal-shape brooches (some studded with diamonds), well-made signet rings and vintage necklaces, earrings and rings made of sapphires, emeralds, gold and the like.

Nigel Milne
16C Grafton St., W1 - 493 9646
Open Mon.-Fri. 9:30 a.m.-5:30 p.m.

Fine jewelry from the Victorian and Edwardian eras shares the spotlight with some beautiful examples from the art deco period, a large variety of small silver items and one of the best selections of antique-silver picture frames in London. The modern-jewelry section features exclusive, delicate and dramatic designs by Kiki McDonough, including Georgian shoe buckles adapted to be worn as bracelets. Prices start at £50 and go up into the thousands.

David Morris
25 Conduit St., W1 - 499 2200
Open Mon.-Fri. 10 a.m.-5:30 p.m., Sat. 10 a.m.-3 p.m.

The distinctively designed jewelry of David Morris elegantly combines classical tradition with modern flair. He executes his exciting, wearable designs to the highest standards, which has helped make him one of Europe's foremost jewelers, with an international clientele that includes royalty. The cool, relaxed elegance of the Conduit Street shop, located in the heart of London's West End, provides a perfect setting for these brilliant jewels.

Richard Ogden
28-29 Burlington Arcade, W1 - 493 9136
Open Mon.-Fri. 9:30 a.m.-5:30 p.m., Sat. 9:30 a.m.-12:45 p.m.

Specializing in lovely antique and investment jewelry, as well as selling clients' jewelry on a commission basis, Richard Ogden is known in particular for its beautiful engagement rings: The famous wedding-ring room houses the largest selection of unique examples in the country. It's a family business with a friendly atmosphere; if you're really lucky, you may meet Mr. Ogden himself—a more charming gentleman would be hard to find.

The Watch Gallery
129 Fulham Rd., SW3 - 581 3239
Open Mon.-Fri. 10 a.m.-6:30 p.m.

Watches and only watches are what you'll find here—from £25 for the fun fashion ones to £30,000 for the heavy hitters. They come primarily from Switzerland (though some of the more fashionable ones are of French design with Swiss movements) and include such names as Jaeger-Lecoultre, Baume-Lemercier, Piguet, Corum and IWC. The inexpensive

digital watches are American. There's a good selection of watch straps, a repair service and even a Champagne bar for the customers.

Watches of Switzerland
Swiss Centre, Leicester Sq., W1 - 734 2878
16 New Bond St., W1 (Piaget watches)
409 2925
5 New Bond St., W1 (Rolex watches)
493 2716
15 New Bond St., W1 (Patek Philippe watches) - 493 8866
Open Mon.-Sat. 9:30 a.m.-5:30 p.m.

The various branches of Watches of Switzerland are "horlogists" specializing in the sale and servicing of the world's finest watches and clocks. The showroom staff consists of trained watch specialists, including technicians who facilitate an efficient after-sales service. The company adheres to traditional values of quality and service. Several other locations.

Young Stephen
1 Burlington Gdns., New Bond St., W1
499 7927
Open Mon.-Fri. 9:30 a.m.-5:30 p.m., Sat. 10:30 a.m.-4:30 p.m.

A specialist in Victorian, Edwardian, art deco and cocktail jewelry, Young Stephen also manufactures commissioned pieces and stocks a small selection of high-quality modern items. Service is friendly and personal.

MENSWEAR

READY-TO-WEAR

Aquascutum
100 Regent St., W1 - 734 6090
Open Mon.-Wed. & Fri.-Sat. 9 a.m.-6 p.m., Thurs. 9 a.m.-7 p.m.

A large, elegant shop, Aquascutum sells good-quality English and imported clothing that is classic yet fashionable. Its traditional trench-style raincoats have become a must for traveling Japanese businessmen, but undoubtedly its most famous client is the former Japanese prime minister.

Austin Reed
103-113 Regent St., W1 - 734 6789
Open Mon.-Wed. & Fri.-Sat. 9 a.m.-5:30 p.m. & Thurs. 9 a.m.-8 p.m.

A man can clothe himself from head to toe in this five-floor store that's stocked with a huge selection of shirts, ties, scarves, socks and other items of good quality and classic style. A more modern line of clothing for younger men sells under the name of Cue. Ready-to-wear and custom-made suits are sold at moderate prices.

Bazaar
4 S. Molton St., W1 - 629 1708
Open Mon.-Wed. & Fri. 10:30 a.m.-6:30 p.m., Thurs. 10:30 a.m.-7 p.m., Sat. 10:30 a.m.-5:30 p.m.

Opening a boutique on S. Molton Street has always been a risky business, but for the last five years Bazaar has survived and even thrived, establishing itself as a primary source of Jean-Paul Gaultier's clothing. Its second shop a few doors away (1 S. Molton Street) sells clothes only by Italian-Japanese designer Giuliano Fujiwara and Marithe François Girbaud. Suits can go as high as £700.

Blades of Savile Row
8 Burlington Gdns., W1 - 734 8911
Open Mon.-Sat. 9:30 a.m.-5:30 p.m.

Elegant ready-to-wear suits, shirts and sweaters, along with made-to-measure suits, sell here at prices that are not as fearsome as those of its neighbors on nearby Savile Row.

Browns
23 S. Molton St., W1 - 491 7833
Open Mon.-Wed. & Fri.-Sat. 10 a.m.-6 p.m., Thurs. 10 a.m.-7 p.m.

Three floors display one of London's most comprehensive collections of top international designers: Romeo Gigli, Go-Silk, Claude Montana and more. The store also stocks Comme des Garçons shirts, which start at £65 but can creep up as high as £400. Look for the fun shoes by a new English designer named Patrick Cox.

Crolla
35 Dover St., W1 - 629 5931
Open Mon.-Sat. 10 a.m.-6 p.m.

The spacious drawing room in this shop makes a perfect setting to display Scott Crolla's successful designs. Crolla sells everything a young man needs to be well dressed, whatever the occasion, and it's all designed by Crolla himself. His original shirts made of several different fabrics (like the one with City stripes on the front and a L. .cy print on the back) sell for £70; velvet trousers are £95 and linen suits £500. Though the styles are extremely modern, customers range from young dandies to gents in their 80s. Crolla also displays an exciting range of womenswear in the back.

Alfred Dunhill
30 Duke St., SW1 - 499 9566
Open Mon.-Fri. 9:30 a.m.-6 p.m., Sat. 9:30 a.m.-5:30 p.m.

A world-famous tobacconist for more than 80 years, Dunhill also clothes a well-heeled international set. Double-breasted blazers, pure cotton shirts, pure linen trousers and such accessories as watches and cuff links sell for well-heeled prices.

Ebony
45 S. Molton St., W1 - 408 1247
Open Mon.-Wed. & Fri.-Sat. 10 a.m.-6 p.m., Thurs. 10:30 a.m.-7 p.m.

A sparkling shop full of elegantly exotic fashions, Ebony sells clothes designed by Piero Panchetti, Calligi Gianelli and Momento Due. Shoes are made especially for Ebony by Casare Paciotti, pure cotton socks by Cavallini. Also worth investigating: its interesting new private-label collection and its always-beautiful leather and silver belts.

Sam Fisher
18 The Market, Covent Garden, WC2
836 2576
Open Mon.-Sat. 11 a.m.-7 p.m., Sun. noon-5 p.m.

After starting in business as a specialist in Scottish knitwear, S. Fisher changed its name to Sam Fisher and now deals only in menswear. Tweeds in winter, linens in summer—Fisher is classical in every sense. It stocks British and Irish designs, boaters and fishing bags, all for the young British traditionalist.

Gieves & Hawkes
1 Savile Row, W1 - 434 2001
Open Mon.-Fri. 9 a.m.-5:30 p.m., Sat. 9 a.m.-1 p.m.

A supplier to the Royal Navy since Nelson's time and to certain regiments in the Army, Gieves & Hawkes is clearly obliged to offer "serious" clothes of impeccable quality. Excellent blue blazers.

Grey Flannel
7 Chiltern St., W1 - 935 4067
Open Mon.-Wed. & Fri.-Sat. 9:30 a.m.-6 p.m., Thurs. 9:30 a.m.-7 p.m.

Complete coordinated elegance can be had for the man who shops here. The owners boast that they can dress a man from head to foot (except for pajamas). A special collection each season combines the traditional with the fashionable without going to extremes. The collections are notable for their knitwear designs—and the most beautiful hand-painted silk ties in London.

Hackett
65 New King's Rd., SW6 - 731 2790
1 Broxham House, New King's Rd., SW6 736 0562
117 Harwood Rd., SW6 - 731 7129
Open Mon.-Fri. 10 a.m.-7 p.m., Sat. 9 a.m.-6 p.m.

Several years ago two Englishmen (Ashley Lloyd-Jennings and Jeremy Hackett) joined forces to create one of the most successful menswear businesses London has seen in quite some time. Their "fogey" style, inspired by designs from the '30s and the '40s, has reintroduced a sense of nostalgia in British men's clothing, which has since been imitated by many a West End designer. From top hat and tails to plus fours, Hackett carries all the clothing accessories a thoroughly English gent could wish for.

Harrods
Knightsbridge, SW1 - 730 1234
Open Mon.-Tues. & Thurs.-Sat. 9 a.m.-6 p.m., Wed. 9:30 a.m.-7 p.m.

The Harrods men's shop carries a vast selection of top-quality ready-to-wear suits, shirts, shoes, coats, knitwear, socks, pajamas and accessories, and it provides a made-to-measure tailoring service.

Jaeger
200-206 Regent St., W1 - 734 8211
Open Mon.-Tues. & Fri.-Sat. 9:30 a.m.-6 p.m., Wed.-Thurs. 9:30 a.m.-8 p.m.

Jaeger's newly designed store maintains its excellent combination of traditional and modern menswear, made of good, beautifully cut cloth. Prices are reasonable, and service is always solicitous in this famous London shop. Several other locations.

Jones
13 Floral St., WC2 - 240 8312
129 King's Rd., SW3 - 352 5323
71 King's Rd., SW3 - 353 6899
Open Mon.-Sat. 10 a.m.-6:30 p.m.

All three locations continue to be successful, and pop stars are loyal to Jones's original designers: Matsuda from Japan, Dirk Bikkemberge from Belgium and Nick Coleman and Joe Casely-Hayford from Britain. The friendly staff and the spaciousness of the Covent Garden store (Floral Street), in particular, make it a pleasure to browse around and even buy—anything from a £700 suit to a £35 pair of Jones-label trousers.

Kent & Curwen
39 St. James's St., SW1 - 409 1955
27 Copthall Ave., EC2 - 374 8333
Open Mon.-Fri. 9:30 a.m.-6 p.m., Sat. 10 a.m.-1 p.m.

Suppliers of clothing to the English cricket team, Kent & Curwen now sells to anyone who wants to wear English colors. Soft white V-necked cricket sweaters go for £50, blue blazers for about £175. It's the English sporty look at its best. Shirts in striped English cotton and suits are available at the City branch, 27 Copthall Avenue.

Piero de Monzi
68-70 Fulham Rd., SW3 - 581 4247
Open Mon.-Sat. 10 a.m.-6 p.m.

This place is definitely reserved for men who have the means to buy themselves the most refined items of Italian fashion. Suits start at £489 and shirts at £75, and house-label shoes go for about £150.

Moss Bros.
21-26 Bedford St., WC2 - 240 4567
Open Mon.-Wed. & Fri.-Sat. 9 a.m.-5:30 p.m., Thurs. 9 a.m.-7 p.m.

Famous as the place to rent formal and evening clothes, but also as a complete men's outfitter known for its hunting and riding clothes, Moss Bros. recently teamed up with Hackett, and they plan to give some "style" to the old Moss Bros. image.

For custom suits, see "Tailors."

Simpson's
203 Piccadilly, W1 - 734 2002
Open Mon.-Wed. & Fri.-Sat. 9 a.m.-5:30 p.m., Thurs. 9 a.m.-7 p.m.

Home of the Daks line, a classic English look, this seven-floor emporium carries all a man needs to clothe himself—not only in traditional style but also from a range of designer labels, such as Armani and Valentino, among others. An excellent selection of accessories as well.

Paul Smith
41-44 Floral St., WC2 - 379 7133
Open Mon.-Wed. & Fri. 10 a.m.-6 p.m., Thurs. 10 a.m.-7 p.m., Sat. 10 a.m.-6:30 p.m.

This tall, elegant, talented English designer has enlarged his premises yet again. Surely the most prosperous among his peers, Smith relaxes at his Tuscany farmhouse when not in his London shop. His are definitely clothes of the '80s: raincoats, suits, trousers, shirts, exotic boxer shorts, bench-made shoes and an entire collection of accessories, including watches, lighters and modern pens. The staff is quite helpful.

Gianni Versace
18 New Bond St., W1 - 493 8787
Open Mon.-Wed. & Fri. 9:30 a.m.-6 p.m., Thurs. 10 a.m.-7 p.m., Sat. 10 a.m.-6 p.m.

Versace's clothes are beautiful, and the way he uses fabrics is extravagant: leather, velvet, soft wools and cashmere. But the prices are beyond belief: suits for £1,000, shirts for £125 and cotton boxer shorts for a mere £50. Only stars can afford to buy here—which they do. The misty, subtle lighting allows you discreet glances at the price tags.

SHIRTS & TIES

Cole's
131 Sloane St., SW1 - 730 7564
Open Mon.-Tues. & Thurs.-Fri. 9:30 a.m.-6 p.m., Wed. 9:30 a.m.-7 p.m., Sat. 9:30 a.m.-5:30 p.m.

Owned by Hilditch & Key of Jermyn Street, Cole's carries the same shirts and blouses. You can get a ready-made cotton shirt for £39.95 (silk, £95) or made-to-measure shirts that start at £75, if you're prepared to wait eight to twelve weeks. Selling one of the most comprehensive selections of Sea Island cottons in town, the place also stocks dressing gowns and nightshirts in cotton and silk. Dozens of terribly English ties are exclusive to Cole's.

Harvie & Hudson
77 & 97 Jermyn St., SW1 - 839 3578
Open Mon.-Sat. 9 a.m.-5:30 p.m.

Very, very English striped shirts in the luxury-class, made-to-measure and ready-to-wear categories. The shop also sells a selection of suits and blazers, and the distinctive broad suspenders as worn by Gordon Gekko in *Wall Street*.

Hilditch & Key
87 Jermyn St., SW1 - 930 4126
Open Mon.-Wed. & Fri. 9:30 a.m.-6 p.m., Thurs. 9:30 a.m.-7 p.m., Sat. 9:30 a.m.-5:30 p.m.

Shirtmakers since 1899, Hilditch normally custom-makes shirts in plain, striped or checkered cotton fabric, but it is continually introducing new designs and recently began to sell shirts made from a cotton-and-wool fabric. Made-to-measure customers can have initials embroidered on their shirts. Though one of the most popular shirtmakers for both men and women, Hilditch has also won renown for its tie collection.

T. M. Lewin & Sons
106 Jermyn St., SW1 - 930 4291
Open Mon.-Fri. 9 a.m.-5:30 p.m., Sat. 9:30 a.m.-5:30 p.m.

The tie specialist, T. M. Lewin offers more than 6,000 club ties (of which more than 2,000 are in stock) and makes virtually all the specialty ties in the country. Don't try to buy ties to which you have no right: The rules here are strict—even the Queen's secretary was refused an elite tie until he had proven his right to wear it. But if you want an "ordinary" tie, or even one made for a special occasion, this is the place to come. You'll be in good company: The Mexican Navy, the Pakistani Army *and* the Sultan of Brunei's polo team, not to mention almost every select club and association in Britain, have their ties made here. Also available: ready-made shirts for gentlemen and ladies' shirts of the same quality.

Lords

66-70 Burlington Arcade, W1 - 493 5808
*Open Mon.-Fri. 9 a.m.-5:30 p.m., Sat. 9 a.m.-
4:30 p.m.*

The oldest shop in the Burlington Arcade specializes in shirts, cashmere knitwear and ties, as well as marvelous paisley dressing gowns. Made-to-measure shirts start at £65, ready-to-wear at £45.

New & Lingwood

53 Jermyn St., SW1 - 493 9621
Open Mon.-Fri. 9 a.m.-5:30 p.m., Sat. 10 a.m.-3 p.m.

Originally estabished in Eton to serve scholars of the most famous English public (meaning private) school, New & Lingwood opened a London branch in 1922 and remains one of the most traditional gentlemen's outfitters supplying custom- and ready-made shirts, hosiery and shoes of the highest quality. According to Tom Wolfe (*The Bonfire of the Vanities*), every Wall Street Master of the Universe must have a pair of New & Lingwood's. First-class service to all.

Sulka

19 Old Bond St., W1 - 493 4468
Open Mon.-Fri. 9:30 a.m.-6 p.m., Sat. 10 a.m.-5 p.m.

London, Paris, New York, San Francisco—the same high standards apply to Sulka's goods wherever you buy them. Shirts: made-to-measure from £100 (silk, £130), ready-to-wear from £55; pajamas: cotton from £80, silk from £125; and the famous Sulka dressing gowns: £450 (satin) down to £350 (lightweight silk foulard). If you really want to spoil someone, consider a deluxe cashmere robe for a mere £1,750, or perhaps you'd be interested in the eighteen-carat-gold-thread gown for £4,400.

Thomas Pink

35 Dover St., W1 - 493 6775
*Open Mon.-Fri. 9:30 a.m.-6 p.m., Sat. 9 a.m.-
4:30 p.m.*

Thomas Pink has expanded considerably since the Irish Mullen brothers began selling their now famous twofold poplin shirts. Three London shops, plus the Bath shop, attract young men who love these delightful soft and luxurious striped shirts, each with a small square of pink cotton sewn at the bottom edge—it's vital to have just that part of the shirt hanging out of one's trousers so it can be seen. At £32 each, they are a real bargain.

Turnbull & Asser

71 Jermyn St., SW1 - 930 0502
*Open Mon.-Fri. 9 a.m.-5:30 p.m., Sat. 9 a.m.-
4:30 p.m.*

This old and traditional establishment is the best of its kind on Jermyn Street, providing fine shirts, dressing gowns and ties. Its many famous clients include the Prince of Wales and Robert Redford, for whom Turnbull & Asser supplied the shirts he wore in *The Great Gatsby*.

TAILORS

W. G. Child & Sons

106 Wandsworth High St., SW18
870 3895
Open Mon.-Fri. 9:15 a.m.-1 p.m. & 2:30 p.m.-6 p.m., Sat. 9:15 a.m.-1 p.m.

Those who make the journey here are rewarded by first-class suits at reasonable prices. The Childs, father and son, were trained on Savile Row. That training and generations of craftsmanship (grandfather, son and grandson still work together) transform the best English cloth into suits that are a match for anything made in the West End. Suits start at £400.

Douglas Hayward

95 Mount St., W1 - 499 5574
Open Mon.-Fri. 9:30 a.m.-6 p.m.

Douglas Hayward is still one of London's most exclusive tailors. At one time rather flamboyant, he has now become more classic, though the style remains recognizably his. Only personally known clients or those personally recommended are accepted. But if you do get through the door, you'll find yourself in one of the most tasteful and friendly shops in London. Suits take four to six weeks and cost from £800.

Huntsman

11 Savile Row, W1 - 734 7441
Open Mon.-Fri. 9 a.m.-1 p.m. & 2 p.m.-5:30 p.m.

The most expensive and the most sporting shop of its kind in London, Huntsman is tailor to kings and princes. A Huntsman suit will last at least twenty years. Some customers still wear

Huntsman suits made in the '30s. But expect to wait four months and pay £1,060 (export price) or more; there is a ready-to-wear line of suits from about £470.

Kilgour, French & Stanbury
8 Savile Row, W1 - 734 6905
Open Mon.-Fri. 9 a.m.-5 p.m.

These are the tailors who make suits for a string of millionaires from all over the world. Fine suits at an export price of £977.

Tommy Nutter
19 Savile Row, W1 - 734 0831
Open Mon.-Sat. 9 a.m.-6 p.m.

The custom tailor to the modern generation: Elton John, Tim Rice (of *Jesus Christ Superstar* and *Ev*ita fame) and Lord Montague are on the list of regular customers. Tommy Nutter's suits can be entirely classic or fairly outrageous; he considers his creations to be traditional with a twist. Among his latest innovations are the double-breasted silk moiré vest and the double-breasted and reversible (from club stripes to paisley) vest worn by several of his nattiest customers. Prices for a made-to-measure suit start at £750 (£652 export price). Nutter also carries a large range of ready-to-wear clothes. One Nutter suit is on permanent exhibition at the Victoria and Albert Museum.

Henry Poole & Co.
15 Savile Row, W1 - 734 5985
Open Mon.-Fri. 9 a.m.-5 p.m.

The oldest of the Savile Row tailors, Henry Poole was established in 1806, became court tailor to Napoléon II and was granted Queen Victoria's Livery Warrant, which it continues to hold under Queen Elizabeth II. The present Victorian building was completed in 1887 and has been occupied by tailors ever since. Poole has always had an international clientele, and its cutters make frequent journeys to the United States and major European cities.

OTHER GREAT TAILORS

Anderson & Sheppard
30 Savile Row, W1 - 734 1420

Mr. Faber at Alan Maitland & Riches
12 Cork St., W1 - 734 3641, 734 5558

Lesley & Roberts
11 Old Burlington St., W1 - 629 6924

Stovel & Mason
32 Old Burlington St., W1 - 734 4855

And, finally, specialists in unusual sizes:

High and Mighty
177 Brompton Rd., SW3 - 589 7454

Outsize Man's Shop
177 Brompton Rd., SW3 - 589 7454

WOMENSWEAR

CLOTHING

A la Mode
36 Hans Cres., SW1 - 584 2133
Open Mon.-Tues. & Thurs.-Sat. 10 a.m.-6 p.m., Wed. 10 a.m.-7 p.m.

Though there are few clothes on display, this large marble-floored shop has plenty of famous designers' dresses: Antony Price, Rifat Ozbek, Lolita Lempicka, Martin Sitbon and Giorgio di Sant'Angelo, to mention a few.

Giorgio Armani
178 Sloane St., SW3 - 235 6232

Emporio Armani
191 Brompton Rd., SW3 - 823 8818
Open Mon.-Tues. & Thurs.-Sat. 10 a.m.-6 p.m., Wed. 10 a.m.-7 p.m.

Armani's two new London stores, which opened in January and February 1989, are quite stunning. His Sloane Street boutique sells his Black Label, Mani and Diffusion lines, which are sleek as ever but much more feminine, with swirls of chiffon marking the eveningwear. Emporio Armani sells all the Armani lines, including the new-to-Britain Emporio label, which purportedly is about 50 percent lower in price and is targeted for young people. Whether he's working with fake tiger fur or denim, Armani always remains discreet.

Laura Ashley
7-9 Harriet St., SW1 - 235 9796
Open Mon.-Tues. & Thurs.-Fri. 9:30 a.m.-6 p.m., Wed. 9:30 a.m.-7 p.m., Sat. 9 a.m.-6 p.m.

Flower-print dresses, Victorian-style blouses (shawl collars made in lace) and the ever-popular pretty white cotton nightgowns are still selling strong here—though since Nick Ashley inherited his mother's business, a new richness of color and pattern has crept into Laura Ashley's well-known country look. Despite the subtle changes, customers remain as faithful as ever.

Basile
21 New Bond St., W1 - 493 3618
Open Mon.-Sat. 10 a.m.-5:45 p.m.

Basile's clothes, initially sold exclusively at Browns, now have their own boutique, which sells womenswear on the ground floor and men's fashions in the basement. The clothes are well made in smooth fabrics and soft colors. Though the prices seem relatively reasonable compared to those of Versace, down the road, it remains difficult to find anything below the £400 mark.

The Beauchamp Place Shop
55 Beauchamp Pl., SW3 - 589 4155
Open Mon.-Tues. & Thurs.-Fri. 10 a.m.-6 p.m., Wed. 10 a.m.-6:30 p.m., Sat. 11 a.m.-6 p.m.

The combination of beautiful clothes and charming saleswomen surely will tempt you to purchase one or several garments from the distinguished selection of designers: Cerruti, Ventilo, Workers for Freedom, Edina Ronay (knitwear), Ralph Lauren and Robert Clergerie (shoes). Although T-shirts are still only £5, nothing else could be called inexpensive.

Bellville-Sassoon
73 Pavilion Rd., SW1 - 235 3087
Open Mon.-Fri. 9:30 a.m.-5:30 p.m.

The most elegant outfits paraded at Ascot, the prettiest ball gowns and wedding dresses—all bear the labels of Bellville-Sassoon or Lorcan Mullany, David Sassoon's new partner, and are the designers preferred by the Princess of Wales and the jet set. The shop and work-shops stand on tranquil Pavilion Road, a charming street not far from Sloane Street. Ready-to-wear dresses sell from £200 to £1,000.

Browns
23-27 S. Molton St., W1 - 491 7833
Open Mon.-Wed. & Fri.-Sat. 10 a.m.-6 p.m., Thurs. 10 a.m.-7 p.m.

You'll find chic, expensive, superb clothes at this famous boutique, including first-class selections from Romeo Gigli, Donna Karan, Genny and the bad boy of Italian fashion, Franco Moschino. Don't miss the delicious swimsuits by Norma Kamali. Recently introduced was the "Labels for Less" salesroom, where elegant fashions from the previous season go for astonishingly low prices: well over 50 percent off the original price, and sometimes as much as 90 percent.

Paddy Campbell
8 Gees Ct., St. Christopher's Pl., W1
493 5646
Open Mon.-Tues. & Thurs.-Fri. 10 a.m.-6 p.m., Wed. 10 a.m.-7 p.m., Sat. 10:30 a.m.-5:30 p.m.

Subdued elegance in dresses, blouses and skirts flow from ex-actress Paddy Campbell's shop in this pedestrian precinct just off Oxford Street. Nothing could be further from theatrical flamboyance than these pleasant, reasonably priced clothes.

Chanel
26 Old Bond St., W1 - 493 5040
Open Mon.-Fri. 9:30 a.m.-5:30 p.m., Sat. 10 a.m.-4 p.m.

Parisian haute couture at its most elegant and sophisticated. Karl Lagerfeld's creations for the house of Chanel include wool crepe suits with gilt chains and leather belts, together with short velvet dresses embroidered with jewels. Chanel's specialties include silk blouses, handbags, black-capped shoes, chains and pearls. The variety of products has increased in recent years.

Don't pass up the chance to invest in some fine British woolens.

The Changing Room
10A Gees Ct., St. Christopher's Pl., W1
408 1596
Open Mon.-Wed. & Fri.-Sat. 10:30 a.m.-6:30 p.m., Thurs. 10:30 a.m.-7:30 p.m.

A gem of a shop that one might easily miss in this small alleyway, The Changing Room is small yet uncluttered, its only decoration being a huge, beautifully framed mirror. The clothing sold here originates with at least fifteen designers, among them such British names as Betty Jackson, Ally Capellino, Sara Sturgeon and Margaret Howell; representing the French are Jean Paul Gaultier and Georges Rech. The stock is primarily daywear. We also saw some very sophisticated belts.

Caroline Charles
11 Beauchamp Pl., SW3 - 589 2521
Open Mon.-Tues. & Thurs.-Fri. 9:30 a.m.-5:30 p.m., Wed. 9:30 a.m.-6:30 p.m., Sat. 10 a.m.-5:30 p.m.

You can find this talented designer's clothing in other London stores, but only here can you see the entire collection, which is a favorite of the Princess of Wales. Though the flattering, elegant designs are never ordinary, prices rarely exceed £1,000. Excellent alterations are performed on the premises.

The Chelsea Design Company
65 Sidney St., SW3 - 352 4626
Open Mon.-Sat. 10 a.m.-6 p.m.

This discreet shop at the north end of Sidney Street, specializing in women's day- and eveningwear, is the outlet of one of the most fashionable designers in town. The tight-fitting suits and dresses are very flattering—and devoid of anything decorative, such as bows or accessories, that might detract from the simplicity of the artful creations. Prices range from £620 up to £2,000 for a long evening gown. Exclusive designs created for the increasing number of royal clients are also shown here. Gorgeous wedding dresses are sold at 46 Fulham Road.

Jasper Conran
37 Beauchamp Pl., SW3 - 589 4243
Open Mon.-Tues. & Thurs.-Fri. 10 a.m.-6 p.m., Wed. 10 a.m.-6:30 p.m., Sat. 11 a.m.-6 p.m.

Jasper Conran, Britain's top designer of 1987, likes to shock his fans with controversial designs. To settle the hemline debate—up and down in the last few years—Conran created the slanted hemline, bias-cut Z-line suits and palazzo pants. Conran's styles cater to all ages, from 16 to 60. Prices range from £20 to £500. Kiehls beauty products from New York are also sold here.

Courtenay House
188 Sloane St., SW1 - 235 5601
Open Mon.-Tues. & Thurs.-Sat. 10 a.m.-6 p.m., Wed. 10 a.m.-7 p.m.

Courtenay's Sloane Street branch concentrates on traditional "Sloane Ranger" fashions (in contrast to the Brook Street shop, which specializes in lingerie): well-cut corduroy trousers, Fair Isles sweaters, warm blouses and, in summer, hand-framed cotton cardigans. A classic country look that suits well-off townies.

James Drew
3 Burlington Arcade, W1 - 493 0714
Open Mon.-Fri. 9:30 a.m.-5:30 p.m., Sat. 9:30 a.m.-4:30 p.m.

In this famous arcade, traditionally devoted to the sale of cashmere and antique jewelry, James Drew stands out for its beautiful silks. The talented Shahla Nawabi-Nouri designs exclusively for James Drew. In addition to blouses (priced from £100 to £195), you'll find silk nightwear and scarves, plus attractive silver and gold cuff links. Numbered among the clients are members of the Royal Family.

The Emanuel Shop
10 Beauchamp Pl., SW3 - 584 4997
Open Mon.-Tues. & Thurs.-Sat. 10 a.m.-6 p.m., Wed. 10 a.m.-7 p.m.

After years of designing only ball gowns and wedding dresses for a select few, David and Elizabeth Emanuel have opened their own boutique to sell elegant suits and dresses. Bows of every color and size dominate their latest evening dresses. Prices for a short cocktail dress start at £700 and go up a long way to £2,500.

English Eccentrics
155 Fulham Rd., SW3 - 589 7154
Open Mon.-Tues. & Thurs.-Sat. 10 a.m.-6 p.m., Wed. 10 a.m.-7 p.m.

No shop could live up to its name as purely as English Eccentrics does. Here you'll find blouses, skirts, shawls, scarves and dresses in the most outrageous designs imaginable, including pigs, unicorns, swirls and swoops of color printed on cotton and woolen fabrics. An imitation hedgehog-skin waistcoat sells for £162.

Nicole Farhi
25-26 St. Christopher's Pl., W1 - 486 3416
Open Mon.-Wed. & Fri.-Sat. 10 a.m.-6 p.m., Thurs. 10 a.m.-7 p.m.

This place offers timeless, elegant clothes from one of London's most respected designers. In summertime, linens dominate the collection; wintertime brings out wool gabardines. Whatever the season, colors are subdued: mushroom, sand, navy, moss green. Diversions is a new, less-expensive line in the same style for younger women.

Feathers
40 Hans Cres., SW1 - 589 0356
Open Mon.-Wed. & Fri.-Sat. 10 a.m.-6 p.m., Thurs. 10 a.m.-6:30 p.m.

It's difficult to compete with Harrods just across the road and the trendy new A la Mode right next door, but Feathers has managed to do quite well by selling all the famous French and Italian designers-of-the-moment: Complice, Byblos, Valentino, Moschino, Claude Montana (leathers and suedes) and more. The staff is as pleasant and helpful as the styles are chic.

Gallery 28
28 Brook St., W1 - 408 0304
Open Mon.-Wed. & Fri.-Sat. 10 a.m.-6 p.m., Thurs. 10 a.m.-7 p.m.

Galleries on three levels display designs from such established names as Alistair Blair, John Galliano, Moschino and Azagury, along with the new Spanish designers, including Purificacion Garcia, Jordi Cuesta, Nacho Ruiz and Pedro del Hierro.

Gorgissima
57 Knightsbridge, SW1 - 235 8414
Open Mon.-Tues. & Thurs.-Fri. 9:30 a.m.-6 p.m., Wed. 9:30 a.m.-7 p.m., Sat. 10 a.m.-5:30 p.m.

Gorgissima is one of the most pleasant shops in London. Attendants welcome you and help you choose from a grand selection of primarily French designers (Nina Ricci, Tiktiner, Dejac, Lanvin and Givenchy), with some Italians thrown in for good measure. With day- and eveningwear a specialty, it also has a strong collection of long dresses and ball gowns to suit all tastes. The semiannual sales (in January and July) are exceptional—the clothes of top-class designers go for astonishingly low prices.

Katharine Hamnett
246 Brompton Rd., SW3 - 584 1136
Open Mon.-Tues. & Thurs.-Sat. 10 a.m.-6 p.m., Wed. 10 a.m.-7 p.m.

One of the many English designers launched to success by Joseph Ettedgui, Katharine Hamnett has hung her merchandise inside a huge white-painted garage. At our last visit, we found that her current collection lacked her former imagination. But a visit here is always worthwhile.

Daniel Hechter
105 New Bond St., W1 - 493 1153
Open Mon.-Wed. & Fri.-Sat. 9:30 a.m.-6:30 p.m., Thurs. 9:30 a.m.-7 p.m.

Daniel Hechter offers a good selection of informal, sporty clothing in dusky hues, and his well-cut designs tend toward the traditional. Prices here are not as high as at shops of other famous Parisian designers. Men's and children's departments are in the basement.

Margaret Howell
29 Beauchamp Pl., SW3 - 584 2462
Open Mon.-Sat. 10 a.m.-6 p.m.

Margaret Howell's beautiful classical clothes—primarily trousers, skirts, hacking jackets and 100-percent cotton shirts and blouses—are exquisitely cut and impeccably finished. It's a pleasure to see this designer back in town after several years' sabbatical.

Hyper Hyper
26-40 Kensington High St., W8 - 937 6964
Open Mon.-Wed. & Fri.-Sat. 10 a.m.-6 p.m.,
Thurs. 10 a.m.-7 p.m.

Hyper Hyper, which has been in business for about six years, just recently gained international recognition as an exciting forum for young British designers. The entire complex houses more than 70 of them, and their energy and vitality have drawn a loyal clientele. The fashions are exotic, the absolute newest looks, for both men and women—from sportswear to eveningwear, and shoes and hats to wild accessories.

Jaeger
200-206 Regent St., W1 - 734 8211
Open Mon.-Wed. & Fri. 9:30 a.m.-6 p.m.,
Thurs. 9:30 a.m.-7 p.m., Sat. 9:30 a.m.-5:30 p.m.

Tweed, flannel, camel hair, cashmere—no matter what the fabric, Jaeger has elegantly simple, well-cut, well-finished clothing. There are several other locations, along with boutiques in such larger stores as Harrods and Harvey Nichols.

Joseph
77 Fulham Rd., SW3 - 823 9500
Open Mon.-Tues. & Thurs.-Sun. 10 a.m.-6 p.m., Wed. 10 a.m.-7 p.m.

Joseph Ettedgui's fashion empire (including such stores as Joseph Bis and Joseph Tricot) not only dominates Sloane Street but has crept down to Brompton Cross via this airy new store, which houses all his products under one roof. Joseph Pour la Maison, Pour la Ville, Tricot and Bis dominate the ground floor, though you'll also find a select collection of clothes by Azzedine Alaia, John Galliano, Katherine Hamnett (a young English designer whose career Joseph helped launch) and Rifat Obzek, a hot new award-winning designer. A spacious glass staircase leads down to the lower level and the Joseph Homme line.

Kanga
8 Beauchamp Pl., SW3 - 581 1185
Open Mon.-Tues. & Thurs.-Sun. 10 a.m.-6 p.m., Wed. 10 a.m.-6:30 p.m.

Lady Dale Tryon (nicknamed Kanga) is her own best advertisement. She combines Chinese fabrics with marvelous designs in one-size-only dresses that fit sizes eight to eighteen. Georgette is one of Kanga's favorite materials

because it doesn't crush and is therefore well suited to her jet-set clientele. Prices range from £180 to £300.

Kenzo
17 Sloane St., SW1 - 235 1991
Open Mon.-Tues. & Thurs.-Sat. 9:30 a.m.-6 p.m., Wed. 10 a.m.-7 p.m.

Kenzo Takada, who hails from Japan but currently makes his home in Paris, is still considered by many to be Europe's most original designer of ready-to-wear fashions for women and men. Although lots of young designers are providing stiff competition, he remains the most Parisian of the Japanese designers. There's a distinct ethnic inspiration in his creations, however, as evidenced by the floral patterns mixed with classic lines. Alas, none of his fashions come cheap; T-shirts hover around the £50 mark.

Karl Lagerfeld
173 New Bond St., W1 - 493 6277
Open Mon.-Fri. 9:30 a.m.-6 p.m., Sat. 9:30 a.m.-7 p.m.

Perhaps the most dominant figure in Paris couture, Karl Lagerfeld is the master of perfectly tailored, elegant clothing at sky-high prices: £800 for a linen suit and £450 for a cotton dress. But the prices seem less excessive when one realizes that this is a distinguished and timeless collection not yet disgraced by obvious trademarks.

Guy Laroche
33 Brook St., W1 - 493 1362
Open Mon.-Fri. 9:30 a.m.-6 p.m., Sat. 10 a.m.-6 p.m.

Guy Laroche continues to conquer the ladies of London with his reasonably priced, classic ready-to-wear line, particularly his daywear. His evening ensembles are more exotic, using reds and bright greens, and most Englishwomen prefer to stick to his more traditional boutique collection.

Long Tall Sally
21 Chiltern St., W1 - 487 3370
Open Mon.-Wed. & Fri. 9:30 a.m.-5:30 p.m., Thurs. 10 a.m.-7 p.m., Sat. 9:30 a.m.-4 p.m.

Long Tall Sally stocks fashionable clothes for tall women, sizes twelve to twenty; everything is designed and cut to fit taller figures. The exceptionally wide range of clothes sweeps from the classic to the contemporary and includes a small limited edition of designer collections. The line comprises daywear, eveningwear, coats, lingerie and sporty casual clothing.

Issey Miyake
21 Sloane St., SW1 - 245 9891
Open Mon.-Tues. & Thurs.-Sat. 10 a.m.-6 p.m., Wed. 10 a.m.-7 p.m.
Issey Miyake is an artist. He earned the ultimate accolade in 1988, when the Musée des Arts Décoratifs in Paris hosted an exhibition of his creations. His stark, stone-floored London shop displays his works of art made from cottons, silks, synthetics, polyurethane and shredded leather, pleated into shapes that many would consider beyond an acceptable limit. Those who actually wear Miyake's designs hail from all corners of the world, from every walk of life—from religious people to movie director David Lean.

Monsoon
194 Sloane St., SW1 - 235 8564
Open Mon.-Tues. & Thurs.-Sat. 10 a.m.-6 p.m., Wed. 10 a.m.-7 p.m.
Indian fabrics in extravagant colors are transformed into exquisite dresses by designers Carol Robb, Julia Riman and Nicole Keir. All are well cut and reasonably priced. Most recently, Monsoon began selling taffeta and velvet evening gowns. Several other locations throughout London.

Piero de Monzi
68-70 Fulham Rd., SW3 - 581 4247
Open Mon.-Sat. 10 a.m.-6 p.m.
For several years, Piero de Monzi was *the* place to go to find chic Italian ready-to-wear in London. He still uses beautiful cloth to make his suits (average cost £700), but now he's competing with such Italian fashion luminaries as Versace, Armani and Ferrè. De Monzi appears to be losing out in the competition, in part because his designs have remained the same.

Next
54-60 Kensington High St., W8 - 938 4211
Open Mon. 10 a.m.-6 p.m., Tues.-Wed. & Sat. 9:30 a.m.-6 p.m., Thurs. 9:30 a.m.-8 p.m., Fri. 9:30 a.m.-6:45 p.m.
After eight years of opening Next shops on London's major streets (Oxford Street, Knightsbridge, Kensington High Street), all of which were successful but lacked a single focused image, George Davies finally got around to opening this large store, in which he brought all of his goods together at last. On the ground floor: Next (for women), Next Men, Next Too (lingerie), Next to Nothing (discounted season-end lines), Next jewelry and Next accessories (briefcases, wallets, personal organizers, lighters, desk accessories, manicure kits and so on, all in black). On the second floor: more fashion for men and women, along with more lingerie, a new children's clothing department and the Next Directory, a mail-order service.

Old England
18 Beauchamp Pl., SW3 - 584 1100
Open Mon.-Sat. 10 a.m.-6 p.m.
This small shop carries an amazing variety of clothes, from trench coats to crepe de chine blouses, which can be made in the color of your choice. In addition, it sells Nicole Farhi suits and an excellent selection of cashmere sweaters; the specialty is cashmere scarves and shawls at remarkably low prices.

Bruce Oldfield
27 Beauchamp Pl., SW3 - 584 1363
Open Mon.-Fri. 10 a.m.-6 p.m., Sat. 11 a.m.-5:30 p.m.
It was the Princess of Wales who finally put Bruce Oldfield in the ranks of Britain's best designers—and he has remained there. His client list now includes such celebrities as Joan Collins and Charlotte Rampling. From the outside, this Beauchamp Place establishment looks rather intimidating, with its darkened glass, but inside the smart attendants greet you with great charm. All Oldfield's designs are a pleasure to look at and try on. Prices are geared toward the celebrities he cares for.

Lucienne Phillips
89 Knightsbridge, SW1 - 235 2134
Open Mon.-Sat. 9:30 a.m.-6 p.m.
Lucienne, as charming as ever, shows the best of the British fashion designers. Her star is Jean Muir, whose ready-to-wear collection favors jersey, wool crepe, leather, suede, cashmere and lambswool. Other names Lucienne is loyal to include Tomasz Starzewski, Alistair Blair and Arabella Pollen. And this is the only shop in London to stock Victor Edelstein's marvelous dresses.

Zandra Rhodes

14A Grafton St., W1 - 499 6695
Open Mon.-Fri. 9:30 a.m.-6 p.m., Sat. 9:30 a.m.-5 p.m.

If you're checking out the fashion scene in Mayfair, don't miss this gorgeous shop. Everything about the exotic designs of Zandra Rhodes is extravagant, including the prices. Flamboyant evening dresses decorated with hand-stitched Indian beads; sophisticated dresses for every kind of party; fantastic colors, from soft pinks and creams to dashing peacock blues and greens—you'll come away with plenty to talk about and dream of owning. And the prices? Daywear starts at about £200, but for one of the classic Zandra Rhodes creations we're talking about spending anything up to £5,000; wedding dresses and ball gowns are even more expensive. On the more affordable end, pretty accessories, including ornate T-shirts and evening bags embroidered with beads, go for about £100.

Ritch Bitch

85 Marylebone High St., W1 - 486 4688
Open Tues.-Fri. 10:30 a.m.-6 p.m., Sat. 10:30 a.m.-5 p.m.

Ritch Bitch specializes in formal dresses for grand occasions, including a great variety of wedding dresses, from the traditional down to the informal, in pure silk, taffeta, satin, lamé, georgette and other luxurious fabrics. Elegant dinner dresses, short cocktail dresses and formal ball gowns complete the collection. You could spend as much as £6,000 on a real stunner.

Saint Laurent Rive Gauche

113 New Bond St., W1 - 493 1800
Open Mon.-Wed. & Fri.-Sat. 9:30 a.m.-6 p.m., Thurs. 9:30 a.m.-7 p.m.
33 Sloane St., SW1 - 235 6707
Open Mon.-Tues. & Thurs.-Sat. 9:30 a.m.-6 p.m., Wed. 9:30 a.m.-7 p.m.

These shops are worth venturing inside for a look at Yves Saint Laurent's unmistakable style, to see why he has dominated the Paris fashion scene for 30 years. His fans keep their YSL ensembles for years, passing them on to their daughters; his clothes are a real investment. His latest designs have introduced a more fluid look, with many materials being cut on the bias.

Scruples

26 Beauchamp Pl., SW3 - 584 8919
Open Mon.-Tues. & Thurs.-Sat. 9:30 a.m.-6 p.m., Wed. 9:30 a.m.-7 p.m.

Hennie Sparkes and Rita Morris opened this lovely boutique several years ago. In addition to their Italian and French designer daywear and a few cocktail dresses, they offer excellent service.

Miss Selfridge

40 Duke St., W1 - 629 1234
Open Mon.-Wed. & Fri.-Sat. 9:30 a.m.-6 p.m., Thurs. 10 a.m.-8 p.m.

Attached to Selfridges (though it has a separate entrance on Duke Street), Miss Selfridge is where young girls and women can go to dress fashionably without spending hundreds of pounds on clothes they'll wear for only one season: coats, shirts, blouses, dresses, skirts, trousers, lingerie, an exclusive makeup line and plenty of sparkling jewelry. Another branch on Brompton Road, and several others in the suburbs.

Swann's Way

8 Hollywood Rd., SW10 - 351 7907
Open Mon.-Fri. 10 a.m -7 p.m.

Lady Holly Rumbold (daughter of Alistair Cooke) and Elspeth Vernon run the only shop in London that sells Anne Dudley-Ward's magnificent Children of the Forest line. The specialty here is luxurious countrywear: full, long classic skirts and pretty, soft high-necked blouses. Loose Empire-style coats with buste backs are a treat to see and try on, but Rumbold's most famous creation remains the theatrical waxed-cotton mac with tartan lining. Swann's Way also carries delicate knitwear in 1920s styles, pinafore dresses by Sarah Keogh and the most original suspenders in London for £15 a pair.

Tall Girls Shop

17 Woodstock St., W1 - 499 8748
Open Mon.-Sat. 9:30 a.m.-5:30 p.m.

Frenchwoman Marie-Hélène Davies took over as managing director four years back and made a success of the Tall Girls Shop, which carries fashionable but classic clothes for tall women and shoes in sizes eight through eleven. The fact that the lovely Princess of Wales is five-foot-ten has helped fashion for tall girls; flat shoes remaining in vogue hasn't hurt either.

Tatters

74 Fulham Rd., SW3 - 584 1532
Open Mon.-Fri. 10 a.m.-6 p.m., Sat. 10 a.m.-5 p.m.

    ːters features stunning evening dresses in turn-of-the-century styles by two very gifted designers, Missie Crockett and Graham Hughes, for a very carefully selected clientele. Each creation is unique: sewn, embroidered, bejeweled by hand, altered or even remade to your measurements. Evening gowns and wedding dresses sell for £300 to £1,500. We also found some gorgeous lace blouses—an unforgettable gold lace sleeveless top—and charming jackets embroidered with sequins and glass beads.

Ungaro

39 Sloane St., SW1 - 235 6951
Open Mon.-Tues. & Thurs.-Fri. 10 a.m.-6 p.m., Wed. 10 a.m.-7 p.m., Sat. 10 a.m.-5:30 p.m.

    This Italian designer operates out of Paris and shows very feminine clothes in unusual fabrics and vibrant colors. The striking place is run by extremely pleasant assistants—and you'll need them to bear prices of £1,000 and up for a day suit. A good selection of accessories includes shoes at £150 a pair.

Valentino

160 New Bond St., W1 - 493 2698
174 Sloane St., SW1 - 235 5855
Open Mon.-Fri. 10 a.m.-6 p.m., Sat. 10:30 a.m.-6 p.m.

    Beautifully made skirts, blouses, suits, jackets and coats in the elegant Valentino style are featured in these spacious and attractive shops. The service has improved considerably; on our last visit the staff was extremely helpful.

Gianni Versace

92 Brompton Rd., SW3 - 225 0515
Open Mon.-Wed. & Fri.-Sat. 10 a.m.-6 p.m., Thurs. 10 a.m.-7 p.m.

    His new shop on Brompton Road, not yet open at the time of this writing, will be Versace's largest store in Europe. It will include men's and children's wear. Many feel that Versace's creations are most distinguished for their stark simplicity. Most recently he's had enormous success with a black, tight-fitting layered skirt; he also sells chic black and white silk lingerie, umbrellas and leather belts and shoes. His products can cost a fortune

(£123 for a personal organizer), but that may help keep him a step ahead of the competition.

Wardrobe

17 Chiltern St., W1 - 935 4086
3 Grosvenor St., W1 - 629 7044
Open Mon.-Wed. & Fri.-Sat. 10 a.m.-6 p.m., Thurs. 10 a.m.-7 p.m.

    Elegant window displays embellish Susie Faux's successful shops. Jil Sander, a top German designer, is the star of the collection; her bags, shoes, suits, dresses and eveningwear all have a classical style. Adrienne Vittadini and Ursula Conzem are also represented, as is Marina Rinaldi (for larger ladies), and there's a small selection of gorgeous Rossetti shoes. A wardrobe-consultancy service costs £100 (discounted when you buy clothes on the same day). Faux will help you create your own wardrobe by coordinating the colors and styles that make you look your best. Not all clothes will come from her shops, naturally, but it is a great service for women moving up into top executive jobs who have not yet found a dashing style for themselves. Wardrobe has its own label, Wardrobe Italia, which includes suits and coats made especially for them in Milan.

Wetherall

1 Burlington Arcade, W1 - 493 5938
Open Mon.-Sat. 9 a.m.-5 p.m.

    Excellent reversible coats in pure new wool and alpaca, some of which are incredibly light. The prices range from £135 to £245 for a purchase you will never regret.

Whistles

12-14 St. Christopher's Pl., W1 - 487 4484
Open Mon.-Wed. & Fri.-Sat. 10 a.m.-6 p.m., Thurs. 10 a.m.-7 p.m.:
20 The Market, Covent Garden, WC2
379 7401
Open Mon.-Wed. & Fri.-Sat. 10 a.m.-6 p.m., Thurs. 10 a.m.-7 p.m., Sun. noon-5 p.m.

    The choice is the same in all six London Whistles. The clothes are imported primarily from France and introduce young Londoners to up-and-coming French designers. Prices are reasonable, though you could pay more than £400 for a Myrene de Premonville suit. Flat shoes are made of leather or suede.

LINGERIE

After Dark
62 Pimlico Rd., SW1 - 730 4483
Open Mon.-Fri. 10 a.m.-6 p.m., Sat. 10 a.m.-2 p.m.

Robina Cayzer, who opened her charming shop ten years ago, tries to provide as an extensive a selection of nightwear as possible—mostly cotton, but a few silk items as well. Nightgowns, slippers and accompanying washbags carry her design. The truly lovely shop also has Victorian lace cushions, covered coat hangers, Floris bath oils, drawer liners, soaps and small Limoges china dishes. Next door is Cayzer's interior design shop, also well worth a visit.

Elizabeth Bolton
20 North End Parade, North End Rd., W14 - 602 1470
Open Mon.-Sat. 9:30 a.m.-6 p.m.

This is far and away the most serious lingerie shop in town. Elizabeth Bolton sold her lingerie to famous stores for three years before she decided to open her own place far from the crowds of central London. Husbands and lovers can come here without fear of being embarrassed. Bolton uses only silk or natural fabrics, and all prints are her own designs. Nightwear and corseterie are her specialty. Briefs from £25; bustiers, £82; nightdresses and pajamas, between £150 and £200; elegant slippers, £50. These days her palazzo-style pajamas are all the rage.

Bradleys
85 Knightsbridge, SW1 - 235 2902
Open Mon.-Tues. & Thurs.-Sat. 9:30 a.m.-6 p.m., Wed. 9:30 a.m.-7 p.m.

Established for over 30 years, Bradleys is probably the oldest and certainly the largest specialty lingerie store in London—carrying your first bra to your last corset and everything else you'll need in between. It has long been known for its fluffy slippers, cotton nightdresses, silk and satin gowns by designers from all over the world and from its own Bradleys label. The enormous variety of lingerie attracts a varied clientele, from members of the Royal Family to Middle Easterners.

Courtenay
22-24 Brook St., W1 - 629 0542
Open Mon.-Wed. & Fri.-Sat. 10 a.m.-6 p.m., Thurs. 10 a.m.-7 p.m.

Beautiful lingerie, silk gowns and pajamas are sold in a soft, misty atmosphere in this Brook Street shop. The La Perla, Malitzia, Simone Perèle, Fantasie and other gorgeous silk and satin lingerie all hail from the Continent.

Fogal
51 Brompton Rd., SW3 - 225 0472
Open Mon.-Tues. & Thurs.-Fri. 9:30 a.m.-5:30 p.m., Wed. 9:30 a.m.-7 p.m., Sat. 9 a.m.-6 p.m.

Hundreds of stockings and tights in all colors and sizes, in nylon, wool, cotton and silk. Some are plain, others decorated. Prices range from £5 to £100 for a pair of cashmere tights.

Night Owls
78 Fulham Rd., SW3 - 584 2451
Open Mon.-Sat. 10 a.m.-6 p.m.

At this delicious and popular little Chelsea boutique, young, pretty women feel tempted to slip immediately into silk pajamas (from £220 to £270). There are lots of different styles, from Chinese to very frilly, as well as a fine variety of dressing gowns, some designed by Jean Muir, astonishing underwear and Elizabeth Bolton Restoration-style slippers.

Janet Reger
2 Beauchamp Pl., SW3 - 584 9360
Open Mon.-Fri. 10 a.m.-6 p.m., Sat. 10 a.m.-5 p.m.

Still selling fluffy and marvelous lingerie at exorbitant prices, Janet Reger may not have quite the glamour appeal it had some years back, but there is still a whiff of Hollywood in the air.

WOOLENS

Berk
46-50 Burlington Arcade, W1 - 493 0028
Open Mon.-Fri. 9 a.m.-5:30 p.m., Sat. 9 a.m.-4:30 p.m.

The huge selection of cashmere pullovers and cardigans in all colors favors Ballantyne's famous products, plain or patterned. Berk also has its own brand of original designs, though it's hard to beat Ballantyne. The service here has been rather off-putting in the past, as attendants tend to hover around in hopes of making a sale, encouraging you to purchase something whether it suits you or not. But if you want cashmere, this is the place to go.

W. Bill

93 New Bond St., W1 - 629 2837
Open Mon.-Fri. 9 a.m.-5:30 p.m., Sat. 9:30 a.m.-4 p.m.

Bill doesn't seem to change much with the passing of time. It remains an old-fashioned, charming shop where you can still find superb hand-knit sweaters and socks and good woolen gloves, as well as tartan and tweed fabrics.

Marion Foale

13-14 Hinde St., W1 - 486 0230
Open Mon.-Fri. 10 a.m.-5:30 p.m., Sat. 11 a.m.-5 p.m.

Hand-knit sweaters and cardigans in subdued colors and elegant designs. Extraordinarily soft lambswool is obviously Marion Foale's priority, so much so that few of her sweaters are made of cashmere. A plain-colored fan-knit cardigan costs £150, but nothing in the shop is priced over £200. Also for sale are a small selection of shirts and blouses from Margaret Howell and belts from J. & M. Davidson.

Noble Jones

12-14 Burlington Arcade, W1 - 493 4830
Open Mon.-Fri. 9 a.m.-5:30 p.m., Sat. 9:30 a.m.-4:30 p.m.

You'll find good woolens (lambswool, camel hair, cashmere) but sadly no more Guernseys, for which Noble Jones was so famous. It has now settled for a more staid style and is dedicated to selling gloves, scarves and capes. The line of children's clothing has also been discontinued.

Moussie

109 Walton St., SW3 - 581 8674
Open Mon.-Sat. 10 a.m.-6 p.m.

A popular shop with North American visitors, Moussie sells exclusive hand-knit sweaters designed by Moussie Sayers. In winter, they are pure wool and cashmere; in summer, cottons and silk combinations. Prices range from £130 to £300. Located just down the road from Harrods, Moussie is well worth the visit.

N. Peal

37 Burlington Arcade, W1 - 493 9220
Open Mon.-Fri. 9 a.m.-5:30 p.m., Sat. 9 a.m.-4:30 p.m.

Although the range of cashmeres is vast, the quality that used to distinguish N. Peal from other cashmere shops has all but disappeared. Prices start at £125 for a plain lady's cardigan and go up to £600 for a special designer cashmere. The service is not as friendly as it once was.

Patricia Roberts

31 St. James St., WC1 - 379 6660
Open Mon.-Sat. 10:30 a.m.-7 p.m.

Patricia Roberts has been selling her outstanding knitwear for nearly twenty years. Her standards have always been high, and fans of her designs can buy the yarns and pattern books at her shop or by mail order.

Edina Ronay

141 King's Rd., SW3 - 352 1085
Open Mon.-Tues. & Thurs.-Fri. 10 a.m.-6 p.m., Wed. 10 a.m.-7 p.m., Sat. 11 a.m.-6 p.m.

If Egon Ronay's name is synonymous with good eating, his daughter's name conjures up high-quality, creative knitwear. All her designs are hand-knit, hence the prices: botany wool creations for £115, pure silk for £350. Edina Ronay has an entire collection of day- and eveningwear, all of which can be seen at her small corner boutique.

Scotch House

2 Brompton Rd., SW1 - 581 2151
Open Mon.-Tues. & Thurs.-Sat. 9 a.m.-5:30 p.m., Wed. 9:30 a.m.-7 p.m.

The shop to visit for a complete selection of everything in Scottish woolens, all of excellent quality at correspondingly high prices. Here you can see a mother transform her children into little Highlanders or watch a young executive turn suddenly into a bagpiper. Other branches.

H. P. Scott Ltd.

56-57 Burlington Arcade, W1 - 493 0578
Open Mon.-Tues. & Thurs.-Sat. 9 a.m.-5:30 p.m., Wed. 9:30 a.m.-5:30 p.m.

Scott sells fine cashmere knits for men from £140 (a little less for women). You'll also find crested buttons for blazers, club ties, college scarves and cuff links. But you need a lot of money to buy your woolens here, though they are of extremely good quality.

Westaway and Westaway

62-65 Great Russell St., WC1 - 405 4479
Open Mon.-Sat. 9 a.m.-5:30 p.m.

The immense selection of knits includes cashmere, lambswool and shetland, kilts and plaids—all at competitive prices. Down the road, at Number 92, is Westaway's Real Shetland Shop, which carries designer knitwear: attractive Fair Isles, 1930s-style vests, handknit or hand-framed, at excellent prices.

DEPARTMENT STORES

London's department stores are absolute musts for the serious shopper. The choice of merchandise is vast, and the prices can be attractive, especially during the sales that draw huge crowds and nightlong vigils by the front doors—no small feat when you consider that the most important sales take place in early January (though there are others in early July, which are well advertised in the newspapers).

Fenwicks

63 Bond St., W1 - 629 9161
Open Mon.-Wed. & Fri.-Sat. 9:30 a.m.-6 p.m., Thurs. 9:30 a.m.-7:30 p.m.

Because this store is smaller than it seems, you can cover the whole place quickly and never get bored. It has women's clothes for all occasions, from track suits to evening dresses, and all the appropriate accessories: shoes, underwear, handbags, hats, costume jewelry and so on. There is nothing extremely luxurious here, and items are rather negligently displayed; but the atmosphere is relaxed. The cheerfulness of the sales staff and the quality of the goods will probably lead you to make a number of purchases that you will not likely regret.

Fortnum & Mason

181 Piccadilly, W1 - 734 8040
Open Mon.-Sat. 9 a.m.-5:30 p.m.

The atmosphere around the food counters of this famous emporium exudes pure luxury: Jams, marmalades, pâtés, cakes, biscuits and teas are all first class. But the emphasis is as much on wrapping and presentation as on the quality of the foods. Our impression is that Fortnum serves the connoisseur who is buying food as a gift, whereas the food halls at Harrods serve the connoisseur who is buying food for himself. There are a wine department of real distinction and a functional, modestly priced restaurant on the ground floor.

There is much more to Fortnum than food, however. On the upper floors you will find a superb selection of elegantly designed gifts, furniture and china; elsewhere, a good selection of womenswear and a small but high-class menswear department. One of the store's greatest attractions is its famous clock on the Piccadilly facade. Get there at noon to watch the display of mechanical pageantry that never fails to charm.

Harrods

Knightsbridge, SW1 - 730 1234
Open Mon.-Tues. & Thurs.-Sat. 9 a.m.-6 p.m., Wed. 9:30 a.m.-7 p.m.

If any store deserves to be described as a world of its own, that store is Harrods. This shoppers' paradise occupies a complete 4.5-acre block in Knightsbridge, where it serves an average of 50,000 customers daily—a high proportion being foreigners who come not only to buy from the remarkable range of high-class goods but also to see the departments, displays and window dressings (the best in London) that have become tourist attractions in their own right. Many of the 230 departments merit separate descriptions of their own.

The magnificent food halls stock every kind of gourmet delicacy imaginable as well as first-class basics. The baker offers 130 types of bread and the fresh pasta, made on the spot, is hard to beat. For the fashion-conscious, Harrods's 34 fashion departments carry everything from classic fabrics and designer labels to more avant-garde styles for the younger set. The latter can be found in Way In, the shop within a store on the fifth floor. The newly designed ground-floor Perfumes Hall, faced in Norwegian charcoal granite and complemented by elements of steel, mirror and back-lit hand-sculptured glass, is also worth a visit.

Many English ladies of the old guard believe the excellence and exclusivity of Harrods have disappeared, and they resist changes that are underway. Undaunted, the store's new Egyptian owners are giving the place a more ornate look, one that will return Harrods to its turn-of-the-century style. They plan to spend £9 million on marble and over £16 million on decorative features. More modern additions will include a basement health club, with every facility imaginable, including squash courts.

Harrods is, above all, the store that provides "all things for all people, everywhere"—from pets to pianos, antique furniture to saunas, fine wines to ice cream machines. And then there is its impressive range of services: a bank, safe-deposit boxes, theater and travel agencies, kennels for your dog while you shop, dry cleaners, an export bureau that dispatches merchandise to every part of the world, and even a funeral service. Harrods' famous January sale causes traffic jams throughout Knightsbridge. Whether you are a serious shopper or a casual sightseer, a visit to London is not complete without a visit to Harrods.

Peter Jones
Sloane Sq., SW1 - 730 3434
Open Mon.-Tues. & Thurs.-Sat. 9 a.m.-5:30 p.m., Wed. 9:30 a.m.-7 p.m.

Ask any English lady to name her favorite department store, and nine out of ten will say Peter Jones. For furnishing fabrics, lighting, glass, china, household goods and kitchen equipment, it offers an excellent selection at reasonable prices. Service is courteous and knowledgeable, and values are excellent. This store is not on the normal tourist beat—and the English would like to keep it that way.

Liberty
Regent St., W1 - 734 1234
Open Mon.-Wed. & Fri.-Sat. 9:30 a.m.-6 p.m., Thurs. 9:30 a.m.-7:30 p.m.

This marvelous place, with its pseudo-Tudor exterior, dark woodwork and thick carpets, is far more than just a department store. In addition to the world-famous Liberty prints and furniture coverings, this leader in contemporary design also offers sumptuous tweeds, mohairs, velvet jackets, kilts, leather goods, an endless selection of scarves, aprons, kitchen utensils, records, Persian rugs and gifts. Particularly interesting is the jewelry department on the ground floor, which sells antique and modern pieces from China and India as well as England.

Marks & Spencer
Oxford St., W1 - 935 7954
Open Mon.-Fri. 9 a.m.-8 p.m., Sat. 9 a.m.-6 p.m.

Represented in every major town in Britain, this remarkable chain of stores has become a national institution. Its St. Michael's label, with its consistent emphasis on quality and value, is enormously popular. At one time Marks (as every Englishman knows it) was known as the place to buy basics—sweaters, shirts, underwear, children's clothes—but now designer fashions have been successfully introduced. Although the decor and displays have become more adventurous, they're still comparatively low-key. You can't try on the clothes, but the salespeople are helpful and well trained and their opinions may be trusted. And if the goods don't fit or otherwise please, you can take them back for exchange or cash refund. There is a first-class food department; many a London dinner party has been prepared entirely from St. Michael's dishes. Marks does not accept any credit cards other than its own M & S card.

Harvey Nichols
75 Knightsbridge, SW1 - 235 5000
Open Mon.-Fri. 10 a.m.-7 p.m., Sat. 10 a.m.-6 p.m.

Only a short walk from Harrods, this smaller store has all the elegance and taste of its more famous neighbor without the crowds. Its reputation stands as high as ever, and it is never uncomfortably crowded, even during peak seasons. The young fashion department in the basement, called "Zone," is a great success. Good hair and beauty salon on the fifth floor.

Selfridges
400 Oxford St., W1 - 629 1234
Open Mon.-Wed. & Fri.-Sat. 9:30 a.m.-6 p.m., Thurs. 10 a.m.-8 p.m.

The biggest store on the biggest shopping street in London, Selfridges is distinguished more for quantity than quality. You will find everything here, from low-priced gifts and souvenirs to furniture and furs. The sheer size of the store consistently pulls in the crowds, but contrary to first impressions, the prices are relatively high when compared to those of other stores.

Simpson's
203 Piccadilly, W1 - 734 2002
Open Mon.-Wed. & Fri.-Sat. 9 a.m.-5:30 p.m., Thurs. 9 a.m.-7 p.m.

Simpson's is still the definitive home of the Daks line of menswear; in fact, there's now a separate Daks Corner Shop on Jermyn Street at the back of the store. Seven floors at Simpson's are dedicated almost entirely to classicly styled menswear, including an impressive collection of sports jackets and trousers. The top two floors are for womenswear: a small but fine selection of international design-

ers, a good lingerie department and, of course, Daks for women, too.

OTHER LARGE STORES

C and A
505 Oxford St., W1 - 629 7272
Open Mon.-Wed. & Sat. 9:30 a.m.-6 p.m., Thurs. 9:30 a.m.-8 p.m., Fri. 9:30 a.m.-7 p.m.

The store is well known for average quality and reasonable prices. Particularly outstanding is the range of inexpensive skiwear.

Dickens & Jones
24 Regent St., W1 - 734 7070
Open Mon.-Wed. & Fri.-Sat. 9:30 a.m.-6 p.m., Thurs. 9:30 a.m.-8 p.m.

This store, part of the Harrods-owned House of Fraser chain, is especially good for women's clothing.

John Lewis
Oxford St., W1 - 629 7711
Open Mon.-Wed. & Fri.-Sat. 9 a.m.-5:30 p.m., Thurs. 9:30 a.m.-8 p.m.

A very large department store famous for the excellent quality and value of its household goods, fabrics and furnishings.

FLOWERS

Felton & Sons
220 Brompton Rd., SW3 - 589 4433
Open Mon.-Fri. 8:30 a.m.-5:30 p.m., Sat. 8:30 a.m.-noon.

This well-known flower shop provides all the customary services and bouquets for every occasion imaginable. Delivery service is, of course, also available.

Flower Power
94 Holland Park Ave., W11 - 229 8788
Open Mon.-Sat. 8 a.m.-8 p.m., Sun. 11 a.m.-2 p.m.

A popular, well-established flower shop that will deliver all over the city. Open for longer hours than most London florists, Flower Power prides itself on having such a large variety of blooms that they overflow onto the Holland Park Avenue pavement.

Edward Goodyear
45 Brook St., W1 - 629 1508
43 Knightsbridge, SW1 - 235 8344
Savoy, The Strand, WC2 - 836 4343
Open Mon.-Fri. 8:30 a.m.-5 p.m.

Goodyear's Brook Street headquarters is next door to Claridge's; it is one of the oldest florists in London, first opening in the 1880s. Today it specializes in English-country flower arrangements, with many flowers coming from country gardens. Court florist Edward Goodyear made the headdresses and bouquets for the Princess of Wales's bridesmaids.

Pulbrook & Gould
181 Sloane St., SW1 - 235 3186
Open Mon.-Fri. 9 a.m.-5:30 p.m.

Lady Pulbrook's small and exclusive shop, which has been in business for more than 30 years, specializes in country flowers, particularly white flowers. And in typically British fashion, the atmosphere is low key, though the service and arrangements are first class.

Molyses Stevens
6 Bruton St., W1 - 493 8171
Open Mon.-Fri. 8:30 a.m.-5:30 p.m., Sat. 8:30 a.m.-1 p.m.
The specialties at this place, one of London's most elite florists, are fresh-cut flowers and made-to-order flower arrangements. In the upstairs studio, you can choose your own dried flowers and watch as they are made up into pretty bouquets. Stevens also has its own famous school of flower arranging.

Sutton Seeds
33 Catherine St., WC2 - 836 0619
Open Mon.-Fri. 9:30 a.m.-5:30 p.m.
Just a step from Covent Garden, this is where serious gardeners come to buy seeds and bulbs for plants of great rarity or rare simplicity.

The choice (self-service) is enormous, ranging from mixed flowers for children's gardens to seeds for vegetables specially developed to withstand freezing temperatures. Detailed catalog and mail-order service.

Kenneth Turner
35 Brook St., W1 - 499 4952
Open Mon.-Fri. 9 a.m.-6 p.m., Sat. 10 a.m.-5 p.m.
Ken Turner has become *the* master flower decorator in London. His specialty—dried floral, fruit and leaf arrangements in perfect taste—has now extended to fresh flowers and just about anything horticultural. His new shop on Brook Street displays not only exotic fresh and dried flowers but marble busts, brass plant holders, glass vases and other flower containers (mostly antiques). There is also a charming array of candles and soaps, all scented with perfumes concocted by the great man himself.

FOOD

BAKERIES

Justin de Blank
46A Walton St., SW3 - 589 4743
Open Mon.-Fri. 7:30 a.m.-6 p.m., Sat. 7:30 a.m.-1 p.m.
The bakery belonging to this well-known caterer and cheese merchant sells excellent whole-grain bread baked in 100-year-old brick ovens, plus several other breads and pastries all baked on the premises. The "millionaire's shortbread" remains a great favorite. Cakes and other treats are made to order.

La Fornaia
66 Notting Hill Gate, W11 - 221 3520
Open Mon.-Sat. 8 a.m.-6 p.m.
The ornately lettered sign is pretty difficult to make out, since the shop used to be a well-known grocer and retains the old front, which still reads: "Tea specialists, wines, spirits, liqueurs." But really this is a genuine Italian bread shop that sells at least fifteen varieties—excellent corn-flour bread, olive-oil bread and

raisin-and-walnut bread, for example—and lots of Italian biscuits (which we found rather dry). La Fornaia also supplies Marks & Spencer's Italian breads.

Gloriette
128 Brompton Rd., SW3 - 589 4750
Open Mon.-Sat. 9 a.m.-7 p.m.
Gloriette's main branch, opposite Harrods, is scarcely larger than its other shops. It has eight small tables in a corner, at which you are served sweet or savory pies (don't forget to ask for them hot) and good Viennese pastries—Linzertorte, Sachertorte, fruit tartelettes, cheesecake. Other locations on Melcombe Street, High Holborn and St. John's Wood High Street.

Louis
32 Heath St., NW3 - 435 9908
Open daily 9:30 a.m.-6 p.m.
The millefeuilles, cream puffs, Viennese pastries and other Austro-Hungarian specialties (such as Sachertorte, Black Forest cake and strudels) are excellent.

Maison Bertaux

28 Greek St., W1 - 935 6240
Open Tues.-Sat. 9 a.m.-6 p.m., Sun. 9:30 a.m.-1 p.m.

Established in 1871 and still going strong, this family-run business, where first-class ingredients go into the making of the best croissants in London, offers delicious pastries: cream puffs, cream cakes, meringues, little tarts. We encourage you to visit the tiny tea room upstairs.

Maison Bouquillon

41 Moscow Rd., W2 - 229 2107
Open daily 8:30 a.m.-9:30 p.m.

Owned jointly by a Spaniard and a Frenchman, Maison Bouquillon abounds with goods from both countries. The pastries—éclairs, croissants, cream cakes and many other delicacies—as well as the sorbets have made Maison Bouquillon famous. You can try your treats at the tea shop next door.

Maison Madeleine

27 North End Parade, North End Rd., W14 - 603 0385
Open Mon.-Sat. 8:30 a.m.-6:30 p.m.

Jean-Claude Magoo from Mauritius and his Trinidadian wife have taken over what used to be Maison Désirée. They plan to open a traditional French café in the back, but in the meantime they are producing a variety of top-quality French pastries, including superb almond crescents that surpass those in the south of France.

Maison Sagne

105 Marylebone High St., W1 - 935 6240
Open Mon.-Fri. 9 a.m.-5 p.m., Sat. 9 a.m.-12:30 p.m.

Established in 1921, this Swiss pastry shop sells delicious walnut cakes, chocolate cakes, meringues, rum babas, strawberry tarts, millefeuilles and macaroons. There is seating for 30 at the back of the shop, where one can indulge in a traditional tea or a quick lunch.

Neal's Yard Bakery Co-operative

6 Neal's Yd., WC2 - 386 5199
Open Mon.-Tues. & Thurs.-Fri. 10:30 a.m.-7:30 p.m., Wed. & Sat. 10:30 a.m.-5 p.m.

All the bread in this bakery is made from 100-percent whole-wheat flour, stone ground from organic wheat bought from the mill next door. There's an excellent selection of breads—naturally leavened, sourdough, sunflower, granary-style, rye—along with healthful, sugar-free cakes (carrot-and-coconut, apricot-and-ginger, tofu), carob brownies and oat-and-raisin biscuits. Simple hot lunch dishes are served daily from noon.

Old Heidelberg

270 Chiswick High Rd., W4 - 994 6621
Open Mon.-Sat. 9:30 a.m.-5:30 p.m.

An attractive German/Swiss-style pâtisserie, Old Heidelberg has a small but excellent selection of cream cakes, all of them made on the premises; wedding cakes are baked to order. The rye bread, baked here as well, is the only bread sold. A pasta and salad bar at the back of the shop stays open every evening from 6 to 11. At Easter, Old Heidelberg makes its own Easter eggs, which look marvelous, though many customers prefer to stick to the first-class cakes.

Pechon Pâtisserie Française

127 Queensway, W2 - 229 0746
Open Mon.-Sat. 8 a.m.-7 p.m., Sun. 8:30 a.m.-6 p.m.

This excellent bakery and pastry shop sells more than fifteen kinds of breads—including superb French baguettes baked in old-fashioned ovens, a mountain of croissants and rolls and a counter full of beautiful tarts, meringues, millefeuilles and palmiers. The tea and coffee room at the back of the shop was recently refurbished. It seems as though everyone in the area flocks here to lunch on quiche, an omelet or the special of the day, which is never more than £3. At the two other branches, on Kensington Church Street and on Chepstow Road, lunch is not served.

CHEESE

Justin de Blank

42 Elizabeth St., SW1 - 736 0605
Open Mon.-Fri. 9 a.m.-7 p.m., Sat. 9 a.m.-2 p.m.

An excellent array of French cheeses and other good-looking, home-cooked foods, salads and roulades. The fresh vegetables sell at very stiff prices.

Harrods

Knightsbridge, SW1 - 730 1234
Open Mon.-Tues. & Thurs.-Sat. 9 a.m.-6 p.m.,
Wed. 9:30 a.m.-7 p.m.

Harrods has the largest cheese department in England—more than 500 varieties, including the best traditional domestic cheeses (Cheddar, Stilton, Wensleydale, Caerphilly)—as well as a wonderful array of French and Italian cheeses.

Jereboams

24 Bute St., SW7 - 225 2232
Open Mon.-Fri. 9 a.m.-7 p.m., Sat. 9 a.m.-6 p.m.

This small shop specializes in wine and cheeses from France and Britain. The French cheeses are chosen by Pierre Androuet, founder of the Guildes des Maîtres Fromager, and Roland Barthelemy and brought to Britain directly from French farmers. The British cheeses, selected for their originality, include Ash Barrow, a goat cheese sprinkled with ash, and Ty'n Grug, a hard Cheddar-type cheese from Wales.

Paxton & Whitfield

92 Jermyn St., SW1 - 930 0259
Open Mon.-Fri. 8:30 a.m.-6 p.m., Sat. 9 a.m.-4 p.m.

Established in 1797, this most famous of English cheese shops stocks more than 300 varieties. Apart from the classics—Cheddar, Stilton, Cheshire, Wensleydale—there are many new soft English cheeses. Valscome from Devon is currently its most popular English cheese. Mail-order service.

CHOCOLATE

Bendicks

195 Sloane St., SW1 - 235 4749
55 Wigmore St., W1 - 935 7272
20 Royal Exchange, EC3 - 283 5843
Open Mon.-Sat. 9 a.m.-9 p.m. (Sloane St. branch also open Sun. 11 a.m.-7 p.m.).

The famous delicious Bendicks bitter mints (bitter chocolate covering a mint fondant) are among the most popular in London, even though they are no longer made by hand. The staff can be rather dry in manner, but in the Sloane Street shop you can escape to the adjacent tea room, where you can sit and relax over a cake or two. We suggest you stick to the mints—the other chocolates are not nearly as good.

Charbonnel et Walker

28 Old Bond St., W1 - 491 0939
Open Mon.-Fri. 9 a.m.-5:30 p.m., Sat. 10 a.m.-4 p.m.

At this elegant shop, whose chocolates bear messages written in gold, you can send a loving gift—and save the price of a greeting card. There's also a wide variety of boxes, some funny, some pretty, some hideous. Charbonnel et Walker is famous for its meltingly soft violet creams wrapped in plain chocolate. One pound of chocolates costs £9.50.

Elena

76 St. John's Wood High St., NW8
586 9525
Open Mon.-Sat. 9:30 a.m.-5:30 p.m.

Belgian chocolates arrive here on a weekly basis. And though no longer the famous Belgian Leonidas, they are still first-class chocolates. Lovely ladies in white gloves fill boxes that are then beautifully wrapped. The price for one pound is £6.80.

Newman's

12 Argyll St., W1 - 439 9297
Open Mon.-Sat 9:30 a.m.-7 p.m.
31 Fleet St., EC4 - 583 4702
Open Mon.-Fri. 9:30 a.m.-5:30 p.m.

Newman's and Bendicks chocolates come from the same factory in Winchester—the two shops are owned by the same company. Unlike Bendicks, however, Newman's does not specialize in mints. It sells its own selection of chocolates in pretty red and gold boxes for £7.40 per pound.

Prestat

14 Princes Arcade, SW1 - 629 4838
Open Mon.-Fri. 10 a.m.-5:30 p.m., Sat. 9:30 a.m.-5 p.m.

The cherries in liqueur and the flavored truffles (coffee, vanilla, rum, orange, whisky) are certainly some of the best in London.

Rococo

321 King's Rd., SW3 - 352 5857
Open Mon.-Sat. 10 a.m.-6 p.m.

This exotic little chocolate shop offers jelly beans and jelly worms as well as traditional English and Swiss chocolates, some of which come in quite extraordinary shapes: alligators, champagne bottles, cars. A mixed selection costs £10.

FISH

Blagdens
65 Paddington St., W1 - 935 8321
Open Mon.-Fri. 8 a.m.-5 p.m., Sat. 8 a.m.-1 p.m.

Wild salmon, farmed salmon, halibut, trout, turbot, live lobsters, cooked crabs, fresh shrimp, any fish in season—these, among others, are enough to make Blagdens the best fish shop in the area. Blagdens also sells poultry: wild duck, English Greyleg partridge, pheasant, Norfolk turkeys and corn-fed free-range chickens. The staff will dress customers' own game, all trussed and larded for cooking.

Chalmers & Gray
67 Notting Hill Gate, W11 - 221 6177
Open Mon.-Sat. 9 a.m.-6 p.m.

Chalmers & Gray is the best fish market in the area (in fact, it's just about the only one); it's first class in every sense. We saw beautifully fresh fish, direct from the coast, laid out on a bed of crushed ice, fresh fish from the Seychelles, smoked Scottish salmon and smoked trout. Poultry and all manner of game are offered in season.

Charles
46 Elizabeth St., SW1 - 730 3321
Open Mon.-Fri. 8:30 a.m.-6 p.m., Sat. 8:30 a.m.-5 p.m.

A good, all-around fish shop with all the standard fish in season as well as live and cooked crabs and lobsters and some game in season.

Samuel Gordon
76 Marchmont St., WC1 - 387 2271
Open Tues.-Wed. 8 a.m.-5:30 p.m., Thurs.-Fri. 8 a.m.-6 p.m., Sat. 8 a.m.-2 p.m.

This local shop sells a fine selection of smoked fish (good Scottish salmon) and the usual fresh fish in season. Mr. Gordon can obtain any fish in season with 24 hours' notice.

Getting hungry? For tasty quick meals, see "Refreshments."

La Marée
76 Sloane Ave., SW3 - 589 8067
Open Tues.-Fri. 9 a.m.-6 p.m., Sat. 8:30 a.m.-3 p.m.

Next door to the Poissonnerie de l'Avenue (which has the same owner) is this good fish shop where a jolly Irishman, Mr. White, will tempt you to buy from his selection of beautiful fresh sea bass, gray mullet, trout, salmon and shellfish. The shop also carries bottled fish soup from France, not to mention poultry and game in season.

D. Morgan
80 Westbourne Grove, W2 - 229 5239
Open Mon. & Sat. 10:30 a.m.-1 p.m., Tues.-Fri. 10:30 a.m.-4.30 p.m.

A curious fish shop this, with little bouquets of flowers all around in summer, green plants in winter and a pretty selection of fresh and saltwater fish, chickens and ducks on a white marble display counter. A board displays the day's specials.

Richards
11 Brewer St., W1 - 437 1358
Open Tues.-Thurs. 8 a.m.-5 p.m., Fri. 8 a.m.-3 p.m., Sat. 8 a.m.-4 p.m.

Far and away the best fishmonger for miles, Mr. Williams is celebrated for the variety and freshness of his fish. Here only the best will do. He provides salmon, skate, turbot, hake, sole, sardines, crayfish, oysters, squid and octopus, which are also sold to London's top hotels and restaurants.

Wheeler's Fishmongers
55 Connaught St., W2 - 723 1612
Open Mon.-Sat. 6 a.m.-3 p.m.

Though the name John Gow remains outside the shop, this is the fishmonger that supplies all the famous Wheeler fish restaurants. With oysters the specialty, you'll also find exceptionally good fish, including smoked salmon, plus the usual poultry.

GOURMET SHOPS

Beetons
3 Abingdon Rd., W8 - 937 3442
Open Mon.-Fri. 9:30 a.m.-6 p.m., Sat. 9:30 a.m.-1 p.m.

Philip Daubeny has taken over from Mrs. Cantlie as the owner of Beetons, and it remains to be seen whether the high standards and marvelously prepared foods that made it such a special gourmet shop will be maintained. Daubeny intends to expand the selection of prepared dishes and pep them up with originality: Coconut-and-spinach soup and seaweed-and-shrimp salad are two of his new dishes.

I. Camisa & Son
61 Old Compton St., W1 - 437 4686
Open Mon.-Sat. 8:30 a.m.-5:55 p.m.
The wonderful smell of an old-fashioned Italian grocery store greets you as you enter this small shop crammed with comestibles from all over Italy: dried mushrooms, olive oil, fresh and dried pastas (plus free advice on how to cook them), cheeses, hams, salamis, grissini, saffron, wines, coffee and anything and everything else Italian.

Finns
4 Elystan St., SW3 - 225 0733
Open Mon.-Fri. 9 a.m.-6:30 p.m., Sat. 9 a.m.-2:30 p.m.
A hospital-like whiteness greets you at Finns, which no longer specializes in fish from Ireland. Instead, it is concentrating on catering for special occasions; its soups, pâtés, roulades and various cold dishes all look astonishingly delicious. The cleanliness and neatness of everything are outstanding, as is the homemade vegetable soup.

Fratelli Camisa
1A Berwick St., W1 - 437 7120
Open Mon.-Wed. & Fri.-Sat. 9 a.m.-6 p.m., Thurs. 9 a.m.-2 p.m.
Though not related to I. Camisa of Old Compton Street, Fratelli Camisa is a quite similar shop. It's less jam-packed with goods, though its selection of cheeses is larger (over 100), and it sells a variety of olive oils, sun-dried tomatoes and fresh pastas. Excellent Felino salami.

Hobbs
29 S. Audley St., W1 - 409 1058
Open Mon.-Fri. 9 a.m.-8 p.m., Sat. 9 a.m.-6 p.m.
Service is impeccable in this shop that temptingly displays all its goods: wines, preserves, spices, Russian caviar, San Daniele ham, scented vinegars, condiments, English farm cheeses and an attractive assortment of French cheeses. Not to mention the large Italian glass jars filled with mushrooms in oil, peppers, green olives and silver onions, and a beautiful selection of pastries from Le Gavroche restaurant. Hobbs picnic hampers grace many top-notch social occasions.

Partridges
132 Sloane St., SW1 - 730 0651
Open daily 8:30 a.m.-9 p.m.
Partridges is a small supermarket of the highest quality. The delicatessen counter includes various types of sun-dried hams, beef, pâté and sausages, plus a special range of salads from the Partridges kitchen; fresh fruit and vegetables are brought in daily from Covent Garden market. There is also a wine department and a pâtisserie counter. The friendly staff apologizes profusely for being closed on Christmas and Boxing Day (December 26). Delivery service is free for purchases of over £30; otherwise there is a £3 charge.

Les Spécialités St. Quentin
256 Brompton Rd., SW3 - 225 1664
Open Tues.-Sat. 9 a.m.-8 p.m., Sun. 9:30 a.m.-5 p.m.
This unique establishment has its own kitchen and five top French pâtissiers who turn out a wide range of tempting pâtisserie, viennoiserie and bread. Terrines and pâtés are made specially in the kitchens of the St. Quentin restaurant. Philippe Oliver, Maître Fromager de France in Boulogne-sur-Mer, offers a large selection of naturally produced cheeses, all of which are laid out on beechwood shelves as ordered by the demanding master. There is also a selection of imported French wines. Congratulations to Hugh O'Neill, who owns both restaurant and shop.

HEALTH FOOD

Alara Wholefoods
58-60 Marchmont St., WC2 - 837 1172
Open Mon.-Thurs. 9 a.m.-6 p.m., Fri. 9 a.m.-6:30 p.m., Sat. 10 a.m.-6 p.m.
Alara looks like a typical health food shop, with its transparent bags of various grains and dried beans, and fruits and spices lying on pine shelves. It also carries cosmetics and medicinal products, water filters and ionizers, books and magazines expounding the benefits of royal jelly, ginseng, essential oils, seaweed and algae.

One of its latest products, from Indonesia, is "tempeh," a high-protein soy-based food that's easy to prepare and, believe it or not, quite tasty.

Ceres
269A Portobello Rd., W11 - 229 5571
Open Mon.-Sat. 10 a.m.-6 p.m.

After several years' break, Ceres is once again baking its own bread on the premises. And it still stocks the usual bags of beans and cereals, sheep's yogurt, tofu and other unadulterated products, as well as a special detergent and fabric conditioner for those who care about the environment. At lunchtime Ceres's several hot vegetarian dishes and special pizzas are sell-outs.

Cranks Health Shop
8 Marshall St., W1 - 437 2915
Open Mon.-Fri. 8 a.m.-6 p.m., Sat. 9:30 a.m.-5:30 p.m.

Cranks has been going strong for almost a quarter of a century now, and it is still maintaining its upscale image among health food shops. Though it carries lots of cookbooks and vitamin tablets, everything appears to be on a smaller scale than during the heyday of the brown-bread brigade. Unfortunately, Cranks's lovely whole-grain shop across the street closed recently.

Earthworks
132 King St., W6 - 846 9357
Open Mon.-Wed. 9:30 a.m.-6 p.m., Thurs.-Sat. 9:30 a.m.-10:30 p.m.

While most of London's health food stores have shrunk and cut down on the variety of goods they sell, Earthworks remains in the old tradition: bulging sacks of grains, cereals, seeds, spices and flours are scattered around the floor. The store extends a long way back to an area displaying pottery and cloth from Third World countries. And there are several tables where you can sit down for a resoundingly healthy vegetarian meal.

Neal's Yard Farm Shop
1 Neal's Yd., WC2 - 836 1066
Open Mon.-Sat. 10:30 a.m.-6 p.m.

Although Neal's doesn't sell anything exotic (except when special fruits are around and it makes organic fruit juices), it has a large selection of vegetables that don't look exciting but are absolutely delicious.

Neal's Yard Wholefood Warehouse
21-23 Shorts Gdns., WC2 - 836 5151
Sydney St., SW3 - 352 6006
Open Mon.-Sat. 10 a.m.-6:30 p.m., Sun. 10 a.m.-5 p.m.

The water clock outside Neal's Yard Wholefood Warehouse on Shorts Gardens has become a well-known London sight, and it has remained the same since the warehouse opened in 1977. Inside, the store has had to change to satisfy the trendy nature of Covent Garden: Products come in smaller sizes, and dried fruits, nuts (shelled or ground), spices, honey, jams and peanut butter are displayed in transparent plastic bags or in glass jars with the origin, contents, weight and price clearly marked on each product. There's also a small selection of cosmetic products, hand and body lotions and moisturizers.

Wholefood
24 Paddington St., W1 - 935 3924
Open Mon. 8:45 a.m.-6 p.m., Tues.-Fri. 8:45 a.m.-6:30 p.m., Sat. 8:45 a.m.-1 p.m.

Originally started by members of the Soil Association, who include the Earl Kitchener and Sir Yehudi Menuhin, this place provides an outlet for organic produce. It offers fresh fruit, vegetables and salads (excellent tomatoes) as well as groceries and dairy produce, bread by Justin de Blank and a large selection of health and nutrition-inspired books and magazines. Down the road stands its companion shop, Wholefood Butchers, one of the few London butchers able to assure its customers that the meat it sells is "untainted." It also sells some unusual products, such as Soay lamb and kid.

ICE CREAM

Bernigra
69 Tottenham Court Rd., W1 - 580 0950
Open Mon.-Sat. 8:30 a.m.-11 p.m.

A giant snack-bar chain has taken over Nicolo Papotto's bar and ice cream shop, but so far all remains the same: He still sells some of the best ice cream in London. There are more than 30 flavors that change continuously. His bar has a cabinet full of trophies, and the wall is covered with framed certificates of all the prizes he has won at the annual Longarone ice cream competition.

Harrods

Knightsbridge, SW1 - 730 1234
*Open Mon.-Tues. & Thurs.-Sat. 9 a.m.-6 p.m.,
Wed. 9:30 a.m.-7 p.m.*

Probably the best selection of top-quality ice creams and sorbets in London. All the famous names are here: Loseley, Country Cooks, Prospero, New England, Dayvilles, Lorier sorbets from France and Dolcevita, plus Harrods's own ice cream for dieters and diabetics. All these produces claim to have no artificial ingredients or color added. Free dry ice with each purchase.

Marine Ices

8 Haverstock Hill, NW3 - 485 8898
Open Mon.-Sat. 10:30 a.m.-11 p.m., Sun. 10:30 a.m.-7 p.m.

This large ice cream parlor sells twenty flavors of ice cream and sherbet, some of which go into the twelve combinations of sundaes. It's a pity the ice cream doesn't taste much better than the mass-produced varieties. The Mansi brothers won gold medals in Milan for their ice creams . . . once upon a time.

MEAT

R. Allen

117 Mount St., W1 - 499 5831
Open Mon.-Thurs. 5:30 a.m.-4 p.m., Fri. 5:30 a.m.-5 p.m., Sat. 6 a.m.-1 p.m.

After 200 years in business, a good number of noble animals have passed through the hands of the white-aproned gentlemen who work in this elegant shop just a few steps from the Connaught. The majordomos from prominent Mayfair homes, whose faces recall high-ranking Cabinet ministers, may be seen placing orders here. If you wish to earn the respect of the personnel, dress as if you're going to the Queen's garden party when you come to purchase a crown of Devon lamb.

Baily Lamartine

116 Mount St., W1 - 499 1833
Open Mon.-Fri. 7 a.m.-4 p.m., Sat. 6 a.m.-10 a.m.

John Baily & Sons has been bought by the French Boucherie Lamartine, and the shop will be refurbished, though the olde-English look will remain. The shop will specialize in French poultry and game but, of course, will continue to sell fine Scottish beef, English lamb and Dutch veal.

Boucherie Lamartine

229 Ebury St., SW1 - 730 4175
Open Tues.-Sat. 7 a.m.-5 p.m.

In 1982, with some help from the Roux brothers, this excellent butcher opened his doors to London's elite. And his remarkable success continues. The beef and lamb are English, but the free-range poultry is imported from France, as are the charcuterie, vegetables (superb fresh haricots verts, mushrooms and tomatoes), cheeses and excellent range of bottled vegetables. Several breads are also imported from France, and a few marvelous pastries come from the Roux brothers' kitchen. Lamartine supplies Le Gavroche, Tante Claire and other restaurants of similar status. Local morning delivery service.

Cobb of Knightsbridge

12 Symons St., SW3 - 730 2198
Open Mon.-Sat. 7:30 a.m.-5 p.m.

Now located just behind Peter Jones (it used to be at the top of Sloane Street), Cobb will cut any meat to your requirements. It sells high-quality fowl and game and a range of delicatessen items, including cheeses, spit-roasted chickens and hams carved from the bone.

Dewhurst

54-56 Elizabeth St., SW1 - 730 1365
Open Mon.-Fri. 7:30 a.m.-5 p.m., Sat. 7:30 a.m.-1 p.m.

This excellent butcher, who has just won an award for "best-kept shop" in the meat trade, is known for the quality of his Scottish beef and his sausages, hand-picked Devon lamb and home-baked ham. The service is exceptionally good and friendly. Yet another first-class food shop for the fortunate residents of Elizabeth Street.

Lidgate

110 Holland Park Ave., W11 - 727 8243
Open Mon.-Fri. 7:30 a.m.-6 p.m., Sat. 7:30 a.m.-5 p.m.

This long-established family butcher shop (since 1850) serves the smart families of Holland Park with impeccable attention. There are always lines outside the shop, which sells range-fed meat and poultry from the shires of England. Lidgate also has a grand selection of homemade pies and outstanding sausage rolls cooked on the premises—so good, in fact, that by 1 p.m. they're all gone. Also offered are several prepared dishes, the most famous of which is the coronation chicken, plus cheeses, salamis and other delicacies.

John Lidstone

12 Lower Belgrave St., SW1 - 730 9373
Open Mon.-Fri. 7:30 a.m.-5 p.m., Sat. 7:30 a.m.-1 p.m.

Butchers by royal appointment to Her Majesty the Queen and the Queen Mother—though you'd never know by the look of the shop, since there is very little to be seen. The quality of the beef is excellent, and the shop sells all the other usual meats: veal, poultry, venison, pheasant, grouse and hare.

Randall & Aubin

16 Brewer St., W1 - 437 3507
Open Mon.-Wed. & Fri. 8 a.m.-5 p.m., Thurs. 8 a.m.-1 p.m., Sat. 8 a.m.-4 p.m.

A store of unmistakably Victorian charm and first-class personnel, Randall & Aubin sells superb meat, cut French style, along with poultry, cold meats and a good selection of groceries.

Slater & Cooke, Bisney & Jones

65-67 Brewer St., W1 - 437 2026
Open Mon.-Thurs. 8 a.m.-5 p.m., Fri. 8 a.m.-5:30 p.m., Sat. 8 a.m.-2:30 p.m.

One of the oldest butchers in London, this establishment opened its doors in 1860 but is now completely modernized. It has blue-tiled walls and huge counters over which English lamb, Scotch beef, Dutch veal, poultry and game in season are sold. Homemade sausages and a particularly inviting display of decorated meat dishes are exhibited in the window.

TEA & COFFEE

Algerian Coffee Stores Ltd.

52 Old Compton St., W1 - 437 2480
Open Mon.-Sat. 9 a.m.-5:30 p.m.

This lovely Soho coffee store, established and run by the same family for more than 100 years, specializes in green and roasted coffee and has a choice of 80 teas. Orders are accepted from all over the world; one Japanese customer has the "Algerian special blend" sent to him

every six weeks. Veluto Nero, the store's current most popular coffee, is roasted for espresso and cappuccino machines, which are sold here along with other coffee-making and grinding apparatus. The staff is wonderfully helpful, and the quality of the coffee is superb.

The Drury Tea & Coffee Co.

3 New Row, WC2 - 836 1960
37 Drury Lane, WC2 - 836 2607
3 Mapham St., SW1 - 928 0144
Open Mon.-Fri. 8:30 a.m.-5:30 p.m., Sat. 8:30 a.m.-1 p.m.

The beans at The Drury Tea & Coffee Co. include 22 blends from Brazil, Kenya, Costa Rica, Colombia, Mexico and Mysore in India, which are ground to customers' requirements. A good choice of teas from Sri Lanka, India, China, Taiwan and Kenya is also available, either original or blended.

L. Fern & Co.

27 Rathbone Pl., W1 - 636 2237
Open Mon.-Fri. 8:30 a.m.-5:30 p.m., Sat. 8:30 a.m.-1 p.m.

Established in 1893, Fern continues to sell coffee of the highest quality. Its main shop is just off Oxford Street, near Tottenham Court Road, but there are several other Fern shops in the suburbs. A range of loose and specialty teas is available.

H. R. Higgins (Coffee-Man) Ltd.

79 Duke St., W1 - 629 3913
Open Mon.-Wed. 8:45 a.m.-5:30 p.m., Thurs. 8:45 a.m.-6:30 p.m., Fri. 8:45 a.m.-6 p.m., Sat. 10 a.m.-5 p.m.

All the scents of the East greet you as you enter this brand-new shop on Duke Street. The Higgins family sells a distinguished collection of pure, unmixed coffees and several blends, all displayed in shining copperware and sold at high prices. Their favorites (and the Queen's, since her coffee is purchased here) are from Tanzania, Costa Rica, Colombia, Mysore, India and Ethiopia. The weighing of the coffee on the three magnificent scales is a spectacle in itself. A select quantity of coffee-making equipment and attractive gift packs, with coffees chosen by Mr. Higgins, are also available. Downstairs you'll find teas from India, China, Sri Lanka and Taiwan.

Monmouth Coffee House

27 Monmouth St., WC2 - 836 5272
*Open Mon.-Fri. 9:30 a.m.-6:30 p.m., Sat. 9:30
a.m.-6 p.m., Sun. 11 a.m.-5 p.m.*

Catherine Mansuy, who runs this shop for
Anita Le Roy, will charm you into buying one
of the several varieties of coffee in stock. The
sources may alternate, but you'll always find
varieties from Costa Rica, Colombia and
Kenya. By offering a small selection (five kinds
last time we were here) in large bags, the shop
can sell enough of each variety to be able to
buy directly from the country of origin and
keep the prices low. At several small tables in
back of the shop you can taste the coffee at a
token price of 20p.

The Tea House

15A Neal St., WC2 - 240 7539
Open Mon.-Sat. 10 a.m.-7 p.m.

This specialty shop sells more than 40 different teas, from traditional Indian and Chinese
varieties to such exotic flavors as apple and
lemon, mango and maracuja, strawberry and
kiwi. There are many accessories for the tea
aficionado, including teapots both attractive
and hideous. Mail order is available for the tea
only.

Twinings

216 The Strand, WC2 - 353 3511
Open Mon.-Fri. 9:30 a.m.-5 p.m.

Thomas Twining became a tea merchant in
the early eighteenth century and his family has
been in the business ever since (nine generations now). The long, narrow shop is lined
with portraits of the Twining family, below
which are shelves filled with more than 100
varieties of the famous teas. In the back of the
shop a small Twining family museum features
photographs, eighteenth-century invoices,
Royal Warrants proclaiming Twinings the supplier to three generations of the Royal Family
and a small selection of teapots and other
tea-drinking apparatus.

Whittard & Co. Ltd.

81 Fulham Rd., SW3 - 589 4261
Open Mon.-Sat. 9:30 a.m.-6 p.m.

Whittard was established in 1886 and is one
of the last surviving great tea merchants. It has
moved from its original shop at 111 Fulham
Road to the depths of Conran's basement. The
staff's service and its knowledge of teas from
Sri Lanka, China, Taiwan, Japan and India are
unparalleled, and the list of unusually exotic
blends is unrivaled. Whittard also offers caf-
feine-free herbal teas and some twenty blends
of coffee. There's also a selection of coffee
makers, tea infusers and canisters.

WINE

London is an exciting place for wine enthusiasts. Big stores and supermarkets (Marks &
Spencer, Sainsbury, Waitrose, Tesco) are now
taking wine seriously as well as providing excellent values at both ends of the price range.
The smaller wine chains (such as André Simon,
Peter Dominic, Oddbine and Cullens) are very
reliable once you're familiar with their stock,
and Majestic Wines Warehouses offer astonishing values. But the most exciting place for
buying top labels in London is at one of the
great auction houses, such as Christie's, 8 King
Street, W1 (839 9060), or Sotheby's, 34 New
Bond Street, W1 (493 8080). Watch out,
though, since it's easy to get carried away when
bidding against the trade buyers for the great
vintages. Our selection of wine merchants
attempts to highlight those with something
special: expertise or an outstanding selection in
a particular region; assistance and advice for
building a cellar; particularly informative lists,
or just the infectious enthusiasm of someone
who knows and enjoys the product that he
sells.

Berry Bros. & Rudd Ltd.

3 St. James's St., SW1 - 839 9033
Open Mon.-Fri. 9:30 a.m.-5 p.m.

The Berry family and its ancestors have occupied 3 St. James's Street since the middle of
the eighteenth century. The shop that stands
there today has changed little in more than 200
years and is well worth a visit, if only to see its
wooden paneling, antique bottles and famous
scales. Don't be intimidated by the surroundings—the staff is courteous and helpful
whether you are ordering twenty cases or
choosing a single bottle. Berry Bros. is particularly strong in its stock of claret and Burgundy, both in the great names, as you would
expect, and the petits châteaux. The German
list concentrates on Moselle and Rhine wines;
Champagne and port are also specialties. There
is a small but sound selection of Berry's own
wines, all of them under £5 a bottle and some

under £3. American visitors will be familiar with Berry's Cutty Sark whisky, exported with notable success to the United States. Berry will also store wine for you and help you build up a cellar for your children or even your grand-children.

Caves de la Madeleine
82 Wandsworth Bridge Rd., SW6
736 6145
Open Mon.-Sat. 9:30 a.m.-8:30 p.m.

Previously part of the Laytons empire, this modest but interesting shop is now independently owned and managed. It caters to the improving tastes and incomes of a newly fashionable part of Fulham, which means the wines are almost exclusively French. Selections from Burgundy, the Rhône and the Loire are better represented than those from Bordeaux. Most are bought directly from the growers, the aim being to provide high quality at less than West End prices (though not much less). Look for Macon Fuissé (£6.80), the Deutz Champagnes and, at the cheaper end of the price scale, the French country wines, where savvy buyers will find excellent values. A range of Armagnacs and Cognacs is also offered. And there's more than just wine—you can also buy cheeses, pâtés and quiches.

Alexander Findlater & Co. Ltd.
77 Abbey Rd., NW8 - 624 7311
Open Mon.-Sat. 10 a.m.-9 p.m.

Alexander Findlater stocks a huge range of Australian wines. You might expect shipping costs to make them relatively expensive, but the majority are priced between £5 and £7 a bottle—and they compare in quality with French wines at twice that price. Drinkers who need advice when faced with this bewildering choice will get it from both the enthusiastic owner and his two highly informative lists (one for Australia and New Zealand and the other for the rest of the world). He particularly promotes wines from such neglected regions as Portugal, Chile, South Africa, Alsace and Gaillac (near the Pyrenees), and he's conducting a crusade among his customers to restore the reputation of German wines, so often blighted by association with the flabby Liebfraumilch. His taste for the unusual even leads him to stock Russian and Chinese beers. The sherries are worth a look as well.

Fortnum & Mason PLC
181 Piccadilly, W1 - 734 8040
Open Mon.-Sat. 9:30 a.m.-5:30 p.m.

Bordeaux (claret), Champagne and vintage port are the highlights of this splendid wine department. The Champagne lover need look no further than this collection, which ranges from a 1961 Krug at £121 a bottle to Fortnum's private label at £11.60. The claret list must be one of the best in London. Though the excellent 1982 and 1983 vintages are particularly well represented, every outstanding vintage since 1961 is available—and for the money-is-no-object claret drinker, Fortnum has top-class wines from the legendary 1929 and 1945 vintages at prices ranging from £235 to £560 a bottle. Almost as distinguished are the red and white Burgundy lists; the Alsatians, often unjustly neglected by wine merchants; and the large selection of wines from California, Australia and New Zealand. Attentive and knowledgeable service makes this department a pleasure to explore, whether you are an expert or an enthusiastic amateur.

Gerry's
74 Old Compton St., W1 - 834 2053
Open Mon.-Fri. 9 a.m.-7 p.m., Sat. 9 a.m.-5 p.m., Sun. noon-2 p.m.

Don't expect frills at this scruffy Soho establishment, but you can count on the friendly air of a family business. The wines are on the lower end of the price scale: a respectable range of the cheaper Italian vintages; Hungarian and Bulgarian wines that are great deals for those who care more about the contents of a bottle than its label; and French country wines. You'll also find a good selection of spirits. The staff knows its stock and will guide you to the bargains.

Harrods
Knightsbridge, SW1 - 730 1234
Open Mon.-Tues. & Thurs.-Sat. 9 a.m.-5:30 p.m., Wed. 9:30 a.m.-7:30 p.m.

The Harrods wine department is not what it used to be. More space has been given to spirits and house wines at the expense of what was once a decent selection of vintage French and German bottles. True, the claret section is still to be commended for its loyalty to the admirable Château Cissac, but the Burgundy selection is thin. Spain, Italy, Australia and even England are represented, but not impressively. At the back of the department you can gaze in wonder at such startling rarities as prewar magnums of Château Latour or Cheval Blanc for upward of £1,000 each. The annual New Year's sale can yield some rewarding bargains, but for the oenophile, Harrods is no longer an essential port of call.

John Harvey & Sons Ltd.

27 Pall Mall, SW1 - 839 4695
Open Mon.-Fri. 9:30 a.m.-5:30 p.m.

John Harvey & Sons, a.k.a. Harvey of Bristol, is best known to the world as a sherry exporter, but it is also an important merchant of wines from Bordeaux, Burgundy, the Rhône and the Loire. Discounts for orders of more than twelve cases indicate that this elegant but somewhat severe Pall Mall establishment caters less to the casual customer than to those ready to establish a serious cellar of claret or Burgundy. It is justly proud of its highly prized Château Latour, whose 1976 vintage is now ready to drink (at £530 a case). Latour's "second wine," Les Forts de Latour, will bring most drinkers almost as much pleasure for a considerably smaller investment (£12 to £34 a bottle). The white Burgundies include a good selection of Macon and Chablis at reasonable prices. Sherry, as you would expect, is a strong feature, and Harvey also carries plenty of noteworthy vintage ports.

Justerini & Brooks

61 St. James's St., SW1 - 493 8721
Open Mon.-Fri. 9 a.m.-5:30 p.m.

The Queen's wine merchant, in the heart of London's clubland, has not always been the most welcoming establishment to the casual passerby, but lately this eminent firm (founded in 1749) has been trying to appeal to a wider range of customers. The shop has been modernized, and the redesigned wine list emphatically states that visitors are most welcome. Take the welcome to heart, for inside you'll find a trememdous selection of the more recent Bordeaux vintages and Burgundies of formidable quality (with prices to match, though a new policy has slightly reduced most prices for single bottles). French wines are still the firm's strength, but it is now venturing into Italy, New Zealand and even England. Although the list is still slanted toward the wealthier drinker (and the investor in wine), the Justerini house wines are cheap and good values. During the twice-annual tastings, many

wines are discounted. Justerini will gladly design a cellar plan for you if you don't mind spending at least £500 on wines for the future.

Laytons Wine Merchants Ltd.

20 Midland Rd., NW1 - 837 8235
Open Mon.-Fri. 9:15 a.m.-4 p.m.

Laytons keeps £2.5 million worth of stock in its ample cellars beneath St. Pancras station and almost as much again in bonded warehouses. Although it primarily supplies restaurants, retailers, wine bars and its own chain of André Simon shops in London, you can now buy directly from the cellars at prices well below what you'd pay for the same wines elsewhere. And though the prices are low, the quality is not. Laytons is deservedly famous in the trade for its Burgundy, particularly its substantial selection of white Burgundies that includes carefully chosen Chablis and Macon wines for less than £7 a bottle, a massive choice of Meursault for about £18 and the finest Montrachet for £17 to £70. The choice of red Burgundies and Rhônes is almost as distinguished. The claret list is rich in the good vintages of the early 1980s, and for the drinker of means, there's a stock of earlier vintages at considerably higher prices. Don't expect to find all these clarets on the printed list, since Laytons is constantly buying small lots from a variety of unexpected sources; let the enthusiastic staff show you its latest finds. U.S. wines are represented by bottles from California's Newton winery, which now appear on The Ritz's wine list.

London Wine Ltd.

Chelsea Wharf, 15 Lots Rd., SW10
351 6856
Open Mon.-Fri. 9:30 a.m.-9 p.m., Sat. 10 a.m.-7 p.m., Sun. 10:30 a.m.-5:30 p.m.

Robert Walker, who recently took over the management of what was previously London Wine Brokers, has brightened up this converted warehouse in the depths of Chelsea and, more important, has improved the range and depth of the stock. His policy is to search for character and value for the money as well as to buy in quite large quantity, which helps keep prices surprisingly low—in fact, the majority of his wines sell for less than £5 a bottle. This policy places some limits on the variety of wines on hand, but nonetheless the selection is full of surprises, particularly in the white Burgundies, the lesser-known French country wines and the Italian wines (Walker's personal specialty). The stock also includes interesting whites from Australia and New Zealand, American bottles from Oregon and California, a small but adventurous choice from Chile, Bulgaria and Portugal, and a remarkabe Château Carras from Greece. The staff will gladly open any bottle for a taste.

La Réserve

56 Walton St., SW3 - 589 2020, 584 9855
Open Mon.-Tues. 10 a.m.-7 p.m., Wed. 9:30 a.m.-8 p.m., Thurs.-Fri. 9:30 a.m.-7 p.m., Sat. 9:30 a.m.-5:30 p.m.

There's an agreeable air of eccentricity about this small, jolly wine shop. You'll find the top names among the wines bought directly from growers in Bordeaux, Burgundy and the Rhône. And Sauternes are given the prominence they so seldom receive; the selection rises up the scale as far as the noble Château d'Yquem 1980, for £87 a bottle. The vintage port collection is strong on Dow and Noval. The house wines, which are often excellent values, include two clarets for £2.95 and £4.20. Popular tastings are organized several times a month at the Ski Club of Great Britain in Eaton Square; each is conducted by an expert and focuses on a single region or variety. The tastings cost £10 to £35 per person, except for the d'Yquem evening, which will set you back a well-spent £85.

The Vintage House

42 Old Compton St., W1
Open Mon.-Sat. 9:15 a.m.-11 p.m., Sun. noon-2 p.m. & 7 p.m.-10 p.m.

Accommodating hours and a wide selection of cheap and cheerful varieties make The Vintage House an excellent place to buy magnums of good, straightforward Italian wines. It also has a good stock of Rioja and lesser-known Spanish wines, and a reasonable showing of Chablis and Alsace. The shop justifies its name with a striking collection of vintage clarets and Burgundies. Château Palmer, Lynch Bages and Montrachet from the 1960s onward lurk in the corner, in contrast to the Chianti and Piesporter elsewhere in the store. The spirits section includes a vast array of miniatures.

GIFTS

Asprey

165-169 New Bond St., W1 - 493 6767
Open Mon.-Fri. 9 a.m.-5:30 p.m., Sat. 9 a.m.-1 p.m.

By far the most luxurious gift shop in London. Not everything is to our taste, but without a doubt it does have many beautiful things. The silver, leather, china and jewelry are sold mostly to the British upper crust, celebrities and wealthy foreigners.

Nina Campbell

9 Walton St., SW3 - 225 1011
Open Mon.-Fri. 9:30 a.m.-5:30 p.m., Sat. 10 a.m.-4 p.m.

This is one of London's prettiest gift shops. Nina's favorite motifs—hearts, sprigs and buds—can be found on slippers, covers and other lined goods. But there are many more beautiful items here, including small tables, gun-metal and brass table lamps with shades made by Nina, Romanian rugs and lovely china. Well worth a visit if you want a particularly delightful gift from London.

The Candle Shop

30 The Market, Covent Garden, WC2
836 9815
Open Mon.-Fri. 10 a.m.-7 p.m., Sat. 10 a.m.-8 p.m., Sun. 10 a.m.-6 p.m.

Opened in 1980, this fascinating place has an incredible array of candles in all sorts of shapes and sizes: Oriental water candles, floating flowers, candles depicting politicians, royalty and hamburgers, smoker's candles—anything you can think of. Prices range from 80p to £35. There's a fair selection of candle holders and other small gifts.

Contemporary Applied Arts

43 Earlham St., WC2 - 836 6993
Open Mon.-Fri. 10 a.m.-5:30 p.m., Sat. 11 a.m.-5 p.m.

Formerly known as the British Crafts Centre, this is not a shop in the true sense of the word. It's an open gallery that hosts a constant turnover of members' work, most of which is for sale and includes glass, rugs, ceramics, fabric, clothing, paper, metalwork, woodwork and jewelry—all selected from the most outstanding craftspeople in England. You're certain to find something original here.

The Covent Garden General Store
111 Long Acre, WC2 - 240 0331
Open Mon.-Sat. 10 a.m.-midnight, Sun. 10 a.m.-7 p.m.

This is a huge bazaar with cheap gifts, both plentiful and varied, such as mugs, teapots, all sorts of tins, posters, stationery, T-shirts and toys. The salad bar in the basement closes one hour before the store shuts down.

The Design Council Shop
28 Haymarket, SW1 - 839 8000
Open Mon.-Tues. 10 a.m.-6 p.m., Wed.-Sat. 10 a.m.-8 p.m., Sun. 1 p.m.-6 p.m.

The Design Council promotes British design, from Jaguars to jewelry, and this multi-level center exhibits and sells all sorts of wonderful goods by top British designers: garden tools, cutlery, glasses, jugs, stationery, leather goods, fabrics, the latest plastic kettles (Russell & Hobbs), napkin rings, ceramics—everything that is British and of top-quality design. Each year Prince Philip awards the Duke of Edinburgh's Designer's Prize to the year's outstanding designer from British Design Award–winning companies. A fantastic place that really shows off the best of the British.

Eaton's Shell Shop
16 Manette St., W1 - 437 9391
Open Mon.-Sat. 9:30 a.m.-5 p.m.

Eaton's is a tiny shop on a tiny street off Charing Cross Road, next to Waterstone's bookshop. It specializes in inexpensive seashells, minerals, stones, fossils, and coral and mother-of-pearl jewelry.

Eximious
10 W. Halkin St., SW1 - 627 2888
Open Mon.-Fri. 9:30 a.m.-5:30 p.m., Sat. 9:30 a.m.-2 p.m.

By appointment to HRH The Prince of Wales, Eximious is an official Manufacturer of Monogrammed Accessories. You can have an initial added to anything you buy in this elegant Belgravia establishment. Address books, guest towels, polished pewter hairbrushes, inkwells, loving cups, photograph frames, mahogany shaving bowls, shoe bags, trays and table mats—everything is in exquisite taste.

Fieldhouse
89 Wandsworth Bridge Rd., SW6
736 7547
Open Mon.-Sat. 10 a.m.-6 p.m.

If you happen to be shopping at Hacketts (which is just around the corner), stop into Rosie Bartlett and Jane Rainey's excellent shop, which boasts a varied collection of gifts for all occasions: Italian pottery at reasonable prices, Indian bedspreads, hand-painted Russian trays, marbled-paper stationery and various toiletries for men and women, including Floris, Crabtree & Evelyn, Royal Yacht and New Age Creations, which makes a wonderful Egyptian bath and massage oil.

The General Trading Co.
144 Sloane St., SW1 - 730 0411
Open Mon.-Tues. & Thurs.-Fri. 9 a.m.-5:30 p.m, Wed. 9 a.m.-7 p.m., Sat. 9 a.m.-2 p.m.

The General Trading Co. is one of the most attractive, elegant and intelligently conceived gift shops in London. Charming young ladies will help you or leave you free to browse throughout the store, which is genuinely well stocked with gifts both large and small, all in the most refined taste: porcelain, etchings, picture frames, bric-a-brac, kitchen utensils. In short, everything that anyone who needs absolutely nothing is sure to treasure.

The Glasshouse
65 Long Acre WC2 - 836 9785
Open Mon.-Fri. 10 a.m.-5:30 p.m., Sat. 11 a.m.-4:30 p.m.

Five young glass artisans—two men and three women, each with a distinct style—display and sell studio pieces here: glasses, decanters, bowls, paperweights, perfume bottles and vases, with prices from £20 to £1,000. You can watch glassblowing in the rear of the shop.

Halcyon Days
14 Brook St., W1 - 629 8811
Open Mon.-Fri. 9:15 a.m.-5:30 p.m., Sat. 9:30 a.m.-4:30 p.m.

The cabinets in this handsome shop display hand-painted enamel boxes by Susan Benjamin, an expert in decorative enamels. There are several collections, each depicting different scenes: summer, flowers of the four seasons, traditional sporting pursuits, specially commissioned boxes, Shakespearean quotations. These objets d'art are perfect to grace any fine lady's dressing table.

J. K. Hill
151 Fulham Rd., SW3 - 584 7529
Open Mon.-Sat. 10:30 a.m.-6:30 p.m.

J. K. Hill sells the works of more than 150 British potters. It guarantees that every piece, from a traditional kitchen pot to a unique figurine or piece of jewelry, is a one-of-a-kind creation. Plates, dishes, mugs, vases and bowls are on sale, along with more intricate jewelry and porcelain figurines.

Naturally British
13 New Row, WC2 - 240 0551
Open Mon.-Sat. 10:30 a.m.-7 p.m.

Artisans from all over the U.K. send their products here: pottery, wickerwork, weaving, knitting, patchwork, traditional pub games, soft toys, beautiful children's puzzles and old-fashioned jams and mustards. All of this is jumbled together on two floors, even spilling out onto the staircase. If you look carefully, you're sure to find some charming presents for just a few pounds.

Neal Street East
5 Neal St., WC2 - 240 0135
Open Mon.-Sat. 10 a.m.-7 p.m.

Neal Street East is an attractive emporium with three floors of reasonably priced Oriental craftwork: kimonos, paper lanterns, calligraphy pens, china ink blocks, black and red notebooks, blue and white china bowls and masses of wicker.

Oggetti
133 Fulham Rd., SW3 - 581 8088
Open Mon.-Sat. 9:30 a.m.-6 p.m.

The ultimate in designer, hi-tech coolness: obligatory black Heuer Formula One watches, Braun travel clocks, Mathiesen wall clocks, Globetrotter suitcases, Zippo lighters, Factory pocketknives (Japan's answer to the Swiss army variety) and Folle 26 staplers (included in the Museum of Modern Art's design collection). Other gifts in stainless steel range from an architect-designed kettle to Aldo Rossi's wrist and fob watches. High prices.

Presents
129 Sloane St., SW1 - 730 5457
Open Mon.-Tues. & Thurs.-Sat. 9:30 a.m.-6 p.m., Wed. 9:30 a.m.-7 p.m.

Presents has a large collection of ceramics, trompe l'oeil pieces and other gifts. We guarantee you'll find something here for that difficult person on your list—perhaps a pretty sewing basket with glazed croissants on its top?

Saville-Edells
25 Walton St., SW3 - 584 4398
Open Mon.-Tues. & Thurs.-Sat. 10 a.m.-6 p.m., Wed. 10 a.m.-7 p.m.

Examine the fine bone-china boxes with amusing inscriptions, Limoges boxes, Lalique glass, leather address books, hand-painted walking sticks. These items are expensive, but the shop is definitely worth visiting.

HOME

CHINA & CRYSTAL

Chinacraft
1 Beauchamp Pl., SW1 - 584 8981
71 Regent St., W1 - 734 4915
7 Burlington Arcade, W1 - 491 7624
Open Mon.-Wed. & Fri.-Sat. 9:30 a.m.-6 p.m., Thurs. 9:30 a.m.-8 p.m.

With more than a dozen stores in London, Chinacraft is one of the largest groups in the china business. The Regent Street store stocks a wide variety of fine English porcelain. The polite staff not only will help you select gift items and/or plan your own dinner service, but, if you ask, will show you the floor devoted to extremely expensive show pieces—bronzes, large (and rather vulgar) pieces of china, beautiful French vases and other Continental pieces. Chinacraft also stocks famous English brands of crystal.

Thomas Goode
19 S. Audley St., W1 - 499 2823
Open Mon. & Wed.-Fri. 9 a.m.-5 p.m., Tues. 9:30 p.m.-5 p.m., Sat. 9:30 a.m.-1 p.m.

Thomas Goode is a beautiful Victorian shop displaying a wonderful selection of china and crystal. Goode has supplied the upper crust of

England and the Continent since 1845. It also has some extremely expensive (and hideous) decorative pieces.

Lalique

24 Mount St., W1 - 499 8228
Open Mon.-Fri. 10 a.m.-6 p.m., Sat. 11 a.m.-4 p.m.

In this grand shop you can see the current products of one of France's great crystal makers—vases, bowls, boxes, glasses, flasks and decanters, all attractively displayed—as well as Haviland and Parlon china from Limoges. The staff is helpful and polite.

Lawleys

154 Regent St., W1 - 734 2621
Open Mon.-Wed. & Fri.-Sat. 9 a.m.-5:30 p.m., Thurs. 9 a.m.-8 p.m.

Lawleys has an amazing selection of fine English china (Royal Worcester, Crown Derby, Minton, Wedgwood, lots of Royal Doulton) and quality crystal (Waterford Edinburgh, Stuart and Webb). It also sells cutlery and gifts in all price ranges, for all tastes. The staff is quite helpful.

Leather & Snook

167 Piccadilly, W1 - 493 9121
Open Mon.-Sat. 9:30 a.m.-6 p.m.

This shop specializes in Royal Doulton and stocks some limited editions. It also carries china and crystal from Waterford and Webb and maintains a large inventory, so most items are available immediately. The shop's basement gallery is dedicated to the International Collectors Club.

Line of Scandinavia

91 Regent St., W1 - 437 6111
Open Mon.-Wed. & Fri. 10 a.m.-6 p.m., Thurs. 10 a.m.-7 p.m., Sat. 11 a.m.-5 p.m.

All the big names from Sweden are represented here, including Bodashop, Kosta Boda and Orrefors. There is a vast selection of attractive modern glasses, jugs, glass bowls and Swedish-designed teapots.

The Perfect Glass

5 Park Walk (off Fulham Rd.), SW10
Open Mon.-Sat. 10 a.m.-6 p.m.

The Perfect Glass is London's only retailer devoted entirely to glassware and crystal. It has an unrivaled selection of glasses, vases, bowls, decanters, candlesticks and more, ranging in price from £1 to £250. Bridal registry, gift wrapping, delivery and many other services are also provided.

Reject China Shop

34 Beauchamp Pl., SW3 - 581 0733
Open Mon.-Sat. 9:30 a.m.-6:30 p.m., Sun. 11 a.m.-5 p.m.

There are three of these shops on Beauchamp Place and another on Regent Street. Although they don't actually sell much reject china anymore, these warehouses do have mountains of china, most of it in perfect condition and offered at lower prices simply because of the gigantic stock. Nineteen brands of bone china and over twenty brands of earthenware from all over the world are piled up in a way that doesn't leave much space for customers. But serious bargain-hunters will surely be pleased. Available, too, are imported crystal and cutlery—and a shipping department.

Rosenthal Studio House

102 Brompton Rd., SW3 - 584 0683
Open Mon.-Tues. & Thurs.-Sat. 9 a.m.-6 p.m., Wed. 9 a.m.-7 p.m.

Rosenthal Studio's motto, "The Original of Our Time," is certainly reflected in its goods. We saw an original tea set by Dorothy Hafner of New York and a unique new series of glasses by Michael Boehm called "Papillon." The glassware and glass bowls are particularly superb. You'll find real works of art here, but be prepared to pay dearly for them.

Villeroy & Boch

155 Regent St., W1 - 434 0249
Open Mon.-Wed. & Fri.-Sat. 9:30 a.m.-6 p.m., Thurs. 9:30 a.m.-7 p.m.

This famous china manufacturer opened a shop on Regent Street in 1986. Along with its own world-famous china, it stocks a selection of crystal and modern cutlery from Sheffield. The shop also offers a range of table-setting accessories, such as napkins and candles from France.

Wedgwood

266 & 270 Regent St., W1 - 734 5656
Open Mon.-Fri. 9 a.m.-5:30 p.m., Sat. 9 a.m.-5 p.m.

Here you'll find the entire Wedgwood line, beautifully displayed, all in one shop.

Wedgwood Gered

158 Regent St., W1 - 734 7262
Open Mon.-Fri. 9 a.m.-6 p.m., Sat. 9 a.m.-4 p.m.

Wedgwood's own products are exhibited on a grand scale, but Coalport, Masons, Doulton, Minton, Derby, Worcester and others are also represented. The price range is surprisingly wide; it's possible to find some pieces at a reasonable cost.

FURNISHINGS & FABRICS

Laura Ashley

198 Regent St., W1 - 235 9278
Open Mon.-Wed. & Fri.-Sat. 9:30 a.m.-6 p.m., Thurs. 9:30 a.m.-7 p.m.

Laura Ashley's famous country-charming floral prints are splashed across yards of fabric and wallpaper and are supplemented with co-ordinating bed linens, lamps, china ornaments and more decorative do-dads. It's a pleasant shop to visit and is a good place to get interior decorating ideas, but take note that prices are not as low as they once were. These fabrics are definitely not for the lover of things contemporary and high-tech.

Colefax & Fowler

39 Brook St., W1 - 493 2231
Open Mon.-Fri. 9:30 a.m.-1 p.m. & 2 p.m.-5:30 p.m.

This little house is full of interesting antique English and Continental furniture displayed in rooms decorated with pretty wallpapers and fabrics. All the fabrics and carpets can be found upstairs. Colefax & Fowler's established and reputable interior designers provide excellent service.

Conran

77-79 Fulham Rd., SW3 - 589 7401
Open Mon. & Wed.-Sat. 9 a.m.-6 p.m., Tues. 10 a.m.-6 p.m.

Terence Conran, famous in Britain for his successful Habitat stores (see facing column) and in America for his equally successful Conran's stores and thriving catalog business, and now moving on to Mothercare and other chain stores, has opened this upscale version of Habitat. Here you can buy furniture, lighting, carpets, fabrics and accessories for your home in Conran's young, fresh, clean-lined style.

Designers Guild

271 & 277 King's Rd., SW3 - 351 5755
Open Mon.-Tues. & Thurs.-Fri. 9:30 a.m.-5:30 p.m., Wed. 10 a.m.-5:30 p.m., Sat. 10 a.m.-4 p.m.

In the attractive showrooms of these two shops on King's Road you'll find everything you need to decorate your home, including Designers Guild's own distinctive fabrics and wallpapers. Although the stores offer complete designer services, the staff is never too busy to make a single pair of curtains out of the pretty fabrics.

Mary Fox Linton

249 Fulham Rd., SW3 - 351 0273
Open Mon.-Fri. 9:15 a.m.-5:30 p.m., Sat. 9:15 a.m.-4 p.m.

Mary Fox Linton has set up her own design studio and shop: two bright showrooms where she displays her collection of fabrics, wallpapers and carpet designs. Some furniture and other interior-design items are also on display.

Habitat

206 King's Rd., SW3 - 351 1211
196 Tottenham Court Rd., W1 - 631 3880
195 Finchley Rd., NW3 - 328 3444
16 King's Mall, King's St., W6 - 741 7111
Open Mon.-Wed. & Fri.-Sat. 9:30 a.m.-6 p.m., Thurs. 9:30 a.m.-7:30 p.m.

In these shops, in Conran (see facing column) and in Terence Conran's excellent catalog you can find everything you need to furnish your home. Furniture styles range from modern Bauhaus to traditional country—all share simple lines and a classic look—and are complemented with a good selection of fabrics and wallpapers. The quality isn't always flawless, but the prices are extremely reasonable.

David Hicks

101 Jermyn St., SW1 - 930 1991
Open Mon.-Fri. 9:30 a.m.-5 p.m.

David Hicks undoubtedly ranks among the most important decorators of his generation. His shop (really more of a showcase) reflects the quality of his designs. You can spend a lot of time here gleaning ideas from the fabrics, rugs, furniture and objets d'art arranged in pleasant, uncluttered surroundings.

Liberty
210 Regent St., W1 - 734 1234
Open Mon.-Wed. & Fri. 9:30 a.m.-6 p.m.,
Thurs. 9:30 a.m.-7 p.m., Sat. 9:30 a.m.-5 p.m.

Long known for its line of printed fabrics, Liberty carries a wide range of furnishing fabrics of every price and quality, as well as selections from other well-known manufacturers and high-quality bed linens.

The London Lighting Co.
135 Fulham Rd., SW3 - 589 3612
Open Mon.-Sat. 9:30 a.m.-6 p.m.

This huge store, redesigned in 1987, offers every type of modern lighting you could dream of. The lamps are made in England and also imported from France, Germany, Italy and Spain.

Osborne & Little Ltd.
304 King's Rd., SW3 - 352 1456
Open Mon.-Tues. & Thurs.-Fri. 9:30 a.m.-5:30 p.m., Wed. 10 a.m.-5:30 p.m., Sat. 10 a.m.-4 p.m.

An excellent variety of fabrics and wallpapers includes florals and geometrics, plus interesting solid colors; everything is of good quality and not too expensive. Some of the materials are designed and printed in England, others imported from France or Scandinavia.

KITCHENWARE

Elizabeth David
46 Bourne St., SW1 - 730 3123
Open Mon.-Sat. 10 a.m.-6 p.m.

Although no longer associated with the famous cook, this little shop carries a fine selection of pots and pans. It also stocks herbs and spices. The staff is helpful.

Divertimenti
45-47 Wigmore St., W1 - 935 0689
139-141 Fulham Rd., SW3 - 581 8065
Open Mon.-Fri. 9:30 a.m.-6 p.m., Sat. 10 a.m.-6 p.m.

Besides its good selection of cookbooks, Divertimenti is well stocked with lovely Italian pottery, French saucepans, casseroles—basically everything one could need in the kitchen. It also sells some electrical goods and all sorts of molds and cutters, and it can supply kitchen furniture. Mail-order and planning services are also available.

Heal's
196 Tottenham Court Rd., W1 - 636 1666
Open Mon.-Wed. & Fri.-Sat. 9 a.m.-5:30 p.m., Thurs. 9:30 a.m.-5:30 p.m.

Together with its large and well-displayed stock of furniture and beds, Heal's boasts an excellent kitchen department stocked with cutlery, china, glass and much more.

The Kitchen Range
299 New Kings Rd., SW6 - 736 3696
Open Mon.-Fri. 9:30 a.m.-7 p.m., Sat. 9:30 a.m.-5:30 p.m.

A pleasant shop that will absolutely delight the enthusiastic cook. The selection of cookbooks, utensils, pans and other equipment is vast. Attractive Bridgewater hand-decorated jugs and plates and a pretty range of white oven-to-table porcelain by Apilgo were among the pieces we particularly liked. The hand-painted Portuguese platters are exclusive to the shop. You'll find service friendly and efficient.

David Mellor
4 Sloane Sq., SW1 - 730 4259
26 James St., WC2 - 379 6947
Open Mon.-Sat. 9:30 a.m.-5:30 p.m.

Fairly rustic in style, David Mellor's pottery, china, glass, wicker, white wood and earthenware are all attractive and reasonably priced. There's a fine selection of good cutlery, as well as a large stock of fun implements one can never be without, such as special forks for piercing sausages. If you're a cookbook fan, you'll find happiness here.

LINENS

And-So-To-Bed
639-640 King's Rd., SW6 - 871 2141
Open Mon.-Sat. 10 a.m.-6 p.m.

Along with the shop's amazing selection of brass and other beds, you'll find good-quality linen in attractive pastel colors by Fremaux, Cerruti, Cacharel, Kenzo, Carrara (a superb cotton set at £200). The wool-alpaca blankets are particularly soft and light. For the bathroom, there's a small selection of towels and bathrobes. All the products live up to the promised high standards.

Descamps
197 Sloane St., SW1 - 235 6597
*Open Mon.-Tues. & Thurs.-Sat. 9:30 a.m.-6
p.m., Wed. 9:30 a.m.-7 p.m.*

A success since its 1980 opening. Primrose
Bordier's pretty linen is always tempting.
Sheets, quilt covers, towels, table linens and
baby goods are all well stocked.

Frette
98 New Bond St., W1 - 629 5517
*Open Mon.-Wed. & Fri.-Sat. 10 a.m.-6 p.m.,
Thurs. 10 a.m.-7 p.m.*
284 Brompton Rd., SW3 - 589 4630
*Open Mon.-Tues. & Thurs.-Sat. 10 a.m.-6 p.m.,
Wed. 10 a.m.-7 p.m.*

A superb collection of sheets, pillowcases,
bedspreads, towels is on sale in these stores.
Each collection comes in different colors, and
everything can be matched, as well as embroidered or monogrammed. The bathrobes are
particularly luxurious.

The Irish Linen Co.
35 Burlington Arcade, W1 - 493 8949
*Open Mon.-Fri. 9:30 a.m.-5:30 p.m., Sat. 9:30
a.m.-1 p.m.*

This small shop has an excellent selection of
the finest linen goods, all of which come from
Ireland and are sent to places like China and
Madeira to be hand-embroidered. All the tableware and bed linens are quite lovely and of
excellent quality—in other words, expensive.

John Lewis
278 Oxford St., W1 - 629 7711
Open Mon.-Sat. 9 a.m.-6 p.m.

We always find good values here. The linen
department, on the second floor, is stocked
with serviceable items in excellent colors at
good prices.

Linen Shop
168 Walton St., SW3 - 589 4033
*Open Mon.-Fri. 10 a.m.-6 p.m., Sat. 10 a.m.-5
p.m.*

This lovely shop sells classic, good-quality
household linens. The designs are attractive
and the prices not excessive. Special requirements in size or color are handled through
special order, and all items can be monogrammed within a few days' time.

The Sleeping Co.
123 Fulham Rd., SW3 - 225 2498
143 Fulham Rd., SW3 - 581 2058
Open Mon.-Sat. 10 a.m.-6 p.m.

The Sleeping Co. now occupies two shops
on Fulham Road. Number 123 sells bath linens, lovely nightdresses and pajamas and Christian Dior towels; number 143 sells all sorts of
bed linens. Fine English cotton sheets,
trimmed and decorated with lace and embroidery, command prices one would expect for
such things. Also in stock are Cacharel and
Desforges sheets. Both shops are attractive and
pleasant and employ the services of helpful
salespeople.

The White House
51 New Bond St., W1 - 629 3521
*Open Mon.-Fri. 9 a.m.-5:30 p.m., Sat. 9 a.m.-1
p.m.*

This establishment certainly doesn't feel like
a shop—it's more like a pleasant room in
someone's house set aside to show quality
goods. The timeless children's clothes, made
popular once again by the Princess of Wales,
are well known. If your budget can handle it,
a visit to the linen department is a must.
Stunning hand-embroidered linen table settings come in prices upward of £1,000 for
twelve place settings. Porthault's cotton voile
sheets with embroidered hems and the pure
Irish linen sheets cost at least £800. Gorgeous
embroidered towels to match.

SILVER

Asprey
165 New Bond St., W1 - 493 6767
*Open Mon.-Fri. 9 a.m.-5:30 p.m., Sat. 9 a.m.-1
p.m.*

The most expensive gift shop in London also
stocks fine silver tableware and cutlery collections. Both real silver and silver plate are
stocked in modern and antique patterns.

Bourdon Smith
24 Masons Yd., SW1 - 839 4714
Open Mon.-Fri. 9:30 a.m.-6 p.m.

Where else can you find items costing thousands of pounds along with silver-plate cutlery
and sugar sifters?

Garrard
112 Regent St., W1 - 734 7020
Open Mon.-Fri. 9 a.m.-5:30 p.m., Sat. 9 a.m.-12:30 p.m.

These crown jewelers have always carried a substantial selection of antique silver tableware. The smaller items and the modern silver and plate will cost a lot less than some of the more distinguished pieces.

Hancocks & Co.
1 Burlington Gdns., W1 - 493 8904
Open Mon.-Fri. 9:30 a.m.-5 p.m.

Specializing in flatware, cutlery and old Sheffield plate, this quiet, civilized shop close to Bond Street also stocks Victorian jewelry.

Harvey & Gore
4 Burlington Gdns., W1 - 493 2714
Open Mon.-Fri. 9:30 a.m.-5 p.m.

This little establishment at the bottom of the Burlington Arcade has exquisite silver as well as some pretty jewelry. The helpful, courteous staff complements the pleasant surroundings.

Kings of Sheffield
319 Regent St., W1 - 637 9888
199 Regent St., W1 - 631 0226
593 Knightsbridge, SW1 - 235 0486
Open Mon.-Fri. 9:30 a.m.-5:30 p.m., Sat. 9:30 a.m.-5 p.m.

Kings is known for its wide selection of fine cutlery, various decorative objects, silverware of all kinds and cutlery cases.

Stanley Leslie
15 Beauchamp Pl., SW3 - 589 2333
Open Mon.-Fri. 9 a.m.-5 p.m., Sat. 9 a.m.-1 p.m.

This small shop is absolutely heaped with silver spoons, forks, knives, boxes, bowls, candlesticks, teapots, coffeepots and every silver item imaginable. From the outside, it looks not unlike a pawnbroker's, but do venture inside, because Leslie is bound to have just what you are looking for somewhere at the bottom of a pile. The extent of his stock is amazing, and he is extremely knowledgeable and helpful about it all.

London Silver Vaults
Chancery House, Chancery Ln., WC2
242 3844
Open Mon.-Fri. 9:30 a.m.-5:30 p.m., Sat. 9:30 a.m.-12:30 p.m.

Vaults is absolutely the right way to describe this location: It is, in fact, a cellar or a depository. There are a number of stalls selling all sorts of goods made of silver or plate, ranging from the unattractive to the exquisite (fine old silver). Well worth a visit, even if only to browse around the stalls. And, who knows, maybe you'll pick up a bargain.

Mappin & Webb
170 Regent St., W1 - 734 5842
65 Brompton Rd., Knightsbridge, SW3
584 9361
2 Queen Victoria St., EC4 - 248 6661
125 Fenchurch St., EC3 - 626 3171
Open Mon.-Fri. 9 a.m.-5:30 p.m., Sat. 9 a.m.-1 p.m.

Well-known for silver-plate cutlery, these Royal Warrant holders also stock 1930s silver. The large range of all-silver items covers a varied price scale. Also sold is the Mappin & Webb collection of lead crystal and fine porcelain, most of it designed exclusively for the shop.

S. J. Phillips
139 New Bond St., W1 - 629 6261
Open Mon.-Fri. 10 a.m.-5 p.m.

One of the few remaining family silver firms in London, S. J. Phillips sells top-quality antique silver and jewelry, not to mention a most interesting collection of snuffboxes. In all, an excellent selection in a pleasant environment, where the assistants take the time and trouble to really assist you in your quest to find that special something. Prices, as always in this trade, reflect the quality of the goods.

Shrubsole
43 Museum St., WC1 - 405 2712
Open Mon.-Fri. 9 a.m.-5 p.m.

Shrubsole is a leading specialist in rare antique-silver pieces and old Sheffield plate. If you are a connoisseur or a collector, you really shouldn't miss this place.

Tessiers Ltd.
26 New Bond St., W1 - 629 0458
Open Mon.-Fri. 10 a.m.-5 p.m.

This old, long-established shop, with its très-élégant facade on New Bond Street, stocks a lovely collection of fine silver tableware and jewelry.

Wartski
14 Grafton St., W1 - 493 1141
Open Mon.-Fri. 9:30 a.m.-5 p.m., Sat. 10 a.m.-noon.

At this shop, where you can see the best collection of Fabergé silverware and jewelry in all of London, the prices are a reflection of the work of the famed Russian jeweler. Wartski also carries other silver items and some good tableware at not-too-outrageous prices.

IMAGE & SOUND

RECORDS

James Asman
28A New Row, WC1 - 240 1380
Open Mon.-Sat. 10 a.m.-6 p.m.

This small shop offers new and secondhand jazz records, including a good selection from the years 1920 to 1940.

Covent Garden Records
84 Charing Cross Rd., W1 - 379 7635
Open Mon.-Sat. 10 a.m.-7:30 p.m.

At this famous address stands one of the largest and most important compact disc stores in London. In fact, no long-playing records are sold, though now the store also deals in first-rate stereo equipment. You can listen to any disc of your choice in one of the booths.

58 Dean Street Records
58 Dean St., W1 - 437 4500
Open Mon.-Thurs. 10 a.m.-6:30 p.m., Fri.-Sat. 10 a.m.-7 p.m.

First-class knowledge and service underline the success of twin brothers Phillip and Martin, who have run Dean Street Records for the last seven years. They have become specialists in original shows, films and nostalgia.

Discurio
9 Gillingham St., SW1 - 828 7963
Open Mon.-Fri. 10 a.m.-6 p.m., Sat. 10 a.m.-5 p.m.

This excellent, long-established shop, specializing in classical records not easily obtain-able elsewhere, is the place for those stricken with nostalgia—for the postwar years, for the 1960s or for the voices of Bing, Frank and Ella. It stocks a good selection of imported records, cassettes and compact discs. The shop dispatches discs worldwide.

Dobell's
21 Tower St., WC2 - 240 1354
Open Mon.-Sat. 10 a.m.-7 p.m.

On a quiet street near Charing Cross Road you'll find one of the leading specialists in jazz and folk music, a good deal of which is imported from the United States. There is also a selection of used records, books and jazz-oriented videos. The folk-music department closes at 6 p.m. Mail-order sales are growing rapidly.

Dress Circle
57-59 Monmouth St., WC2 - 240 2227
Open Mon.-Sat. 10 a.m.-6 p.m.

As well as a selection of records, cassettes, compact discs and videos of stage and film musicals, Dress Circle also offers soundtracks and celebrity nostalgia, posters, programs and cards. A super shop for anyone mad about musicals.

HMV Record Store
150 Oxford St., W1 - 631 3423
Open Mon.-Wed. & Fri.-Sat. 9:30 a.m.-7 p.m., Thurs. 9:30 a.m.-8 p.m.

This new HMV store claims to be one of the largest record stores in Europe, with four floors of records, cassettes, compact discs and video cassettes. Service is often brusque, but the staff is knowledgeable.

Harold Moore's

2 Great Marlborough St., W1 - 437 1576
Open Mon.-Sat. 10 a.m.-6:30 p.m.

This charming old shop specializes in classical music. On the ground floor are all the most recent recordings; in the basement you can find old, rare and/or secondhand ones. If the record you're looking for isn't available, the highly competent staff will suggest other stores you can try or will even do the searching for you.

Our Price Records

102 Notting Hill Gate, W11 - 229 6796
Open Mon.-Sat. 9:30 a.m.-10 p.m., Sun. 11 a.m.-9 p.m.

Though there are more than 30 branches throughout London, nowadays this is the company's principal location (it was formerly on Oxford Street). A popular place, it sells all the music in vogue, often at lower prices than its competitors. The staff will order anything not already in stock.

Ray's Jazz Shop

180 Shaftesbury Ave., WC2 - 240 3969
Open Mon.-Sat. 10 a.m.-6:30 p.m.

Ray Smith used to work in the record department at Colletts Bookstore just around the corner. When it closed in the 1950s, he bought out the jazz section and has kept it going ever since. He has an excellent selection of new and used records, cassettes and compact discs, and his surely must be one of the few record stores in all of London which are still selling genuine 78s.

Virgin Megastore

14-30 Oxford St., W1 - 631 1234
Open Mon. & Wed.-Sat. 9:30 a.m.-8 p.m., Tues. 10 a.m.-8 p.m.

This huge store stocks an excellent selection of new releases in rock, reggae and the popular chart sounds. There are extensive mail-order

and export services, as well as a novelcafé where you can relax—if you can cope with the noise level.

VIDEOS

Knights Video

118 Knightsbridge, SW1 - 581 0568
Open Mon.-Sat. 10 a.m.-9 p.m., Sun. noon-9 p.m.

Here you pay a subscription of £40 a year plus £3 a day for the rental of any film. If you are not a member, the price is £5.95 per day plus a £50 deposit. All films are in VHS format. The Knights list is extensive, and all tapes are for sale.

Selecta-Video

23 Beauchamp Pl., SW3 - 581 4422
176 Queensway, W2 - 727 9070
Open Mon.-Sat. 10 a.m.-2 p.m. & 3 p.m.-10 p.m., Sun. 11 a.m.-2 p.m. & 3 p.m.-9 p.m.

The membership system here is complicated. Gold membership: You hand over £195 annually but pay nothing more unless you are late returning your film. Silver membership: You pay a £25 joining fee plus a £5 annual membership, and then rental charges of £2 to £2.50 per night. Nonmembers must leave a £50 deposit on any video they rent plus £3 per day. But there is a great selection, and if you wish to purchase any movie, the staff will obtain an unused copy for you.

Video Shuttle

309 Fulham Rd., SW10 - 352 7986
Open Mon.-Thurs. & Sun. 10 a.m.-10 p.m., Fri.-Sat. 10 a.m.-midnight.

A lovely shop with the best selection of video cassettes in London. For a subscription of £30 a year, you can rent a movie for £2.50 a day or £4.50 for three days. If you are not a subscriber, you must pay a £50 deposit. You can also get a life subscripton for £50. All tapes are available in both VHS and Betamax formats.

LEATHER

Etienne Aigner
6-7 New Bond St., W1 - 491 7764
Open Mon.-Fri. 9:30 a.m.-5:30 p.m., Sat. 9:30 a.m.-5 p.m.

Chic and practical items are available here: silk-lined, hand-stitched calf gloves in classic colors, £40, and in pigskin for men, £60; handbags, portfolios, shoes, brass and leather initial key rings. A collection of smart luggage in leather and lightweight plasticized linen, with leather and brass trim, costs from £583 to £648, and a smaller leather tote bag sells for £325. Just about everything here displays the trademark, a sort of upside-down metal horseshoe, and, in some cases, the company signature as well.

Céline
28 New Bond St., W1 - 493 9000
Open Mon.-Tues. & Thurs.-Fri. 9:15 a.m.-5:30 p.m., Wed. 9:15 a.m.-6 p.m., Sat. 9:15 a.m.-4:45 p.m.

Heavy gilded clasps decorate Céline's handbags, which you either like or you don't. In either case you cannot but accept the fact that the leatherwork and its standard of finish are substantially above average. Also above the norm: smart shoes for men and women in two-tone or crocodile, ladies' suits and dresses in soft leather and many fine-crafted accessories. One thing it's not is cheap.

Alfred Dunhill
30 Duke St., SW1 - 499 9566
Open Mon.-Fri. 9:30 a.m.-5:30 p.m., Sat. 9:30 a.m.-4:30 p.m.

Dunhill has broadened its use of leather since its tobacco-pouch days (circa 1912). Today's leather collections include men's coats, luggage, small leather goods and belts. The three collections are the Oxford, in black and tan calfskin; the Cambridge, hand-tooled in soft black calfskin with tan stitching and pigskin linings; and the Warwick, in black and brown box calf. The professional and courteous staff will explain each line.

Salvatore Ferragamo
24 Old Bond St., W1 - 629 5007
Open Mon.-Sat. 9:30 a.m.-5:30 p.m.

Salvatore Ferragamo's world-famous shoes, leather bags (and clothes) are expensive, but the quality is superb and the pieces literally never fall out of fashion. The vast selection of shoes ranges from patent leather to satin and suede for the evening to python-skin shoes in vivid colors (the 1989 line). Bags are designed to match the shoes.

Foster
83 Jermyn St., SW1 - 930 5385
Open Mon.-Fri. 9 a.m.-5 p.m., Sat. 9 a.m.-noon.

This excellent Mayfair bootmaker, for men only, also sells smart briefcases (£185 to £550) and suitcases. Special-order suitcases can be made in two to three months.

The General Leather Company
58 Chiltern St., W1 - 935 1041
Open Mon.-Sat. 10 a.m.-6 p.m.

Superb leather and sheepskin garments for men and women are manufactured in London by this company, according to its styles and patterns. Individual garments can be made to measure or re-created from older models (£350 for a sheepskin jacket, £900 for a full-length sheepskin coat). A small selection of leather travel bags is also sold, and repair work is available.

Gucci
27 Old Bond St., W1 - 629 2716
Open Mon.-Fri. 9 a.m.-5:30 p.m., Sat. 9 a.m.-5 p.m.

There is nothing new to say about the baggage in plasticized canvas, or about the bags, wallets and briefcases made by this competent manufacturer—who is clever enough to let his customers do his advertising for him, carrying his initials boldly about the world for free. A two-suiter with compartments for shoes, shirts and toiletry kit costs £265. The all-leather luggage includes an elegant pigskin collection. And the waterproofed canvas styles with leather trimming include a matching baby carry-cot for £415—trust the indulgent Italians to cater to the bambino in such style.

Henry's
201 Regent St., W1 - 437 6579
Open Mon.-Sat. 9 a.m.-6:30 p.m.
185 Brompton Rd., SW3 - 589 7119
Open Mon.-Tues. & Thurs.-Sat. 9 a.m.-6:30 p.m., Wed. 9:30 a.m.-7 p.m.

In addition to its own luggage collection, Henry's carries most of the big international names: Delsey, Longchamps, Lancel. Henry's also stocks smart handbags and most leather accessories, such as wallets, address books and change purses.

Hermès
155 New Bond St., W1 - 499 8856
Open Mon.-Fri. 9:30 a.m.-6 p.m., Sat. 10 a.m.-5 p.m.

The excellent selection of handmade pieces includes the most popular models from the Paris shop; for example, we were particularly taken with the timeless Kelly handbag that dates from 1949. Of course, Hermès also specializes in printed silk scarves and ties. Prices are inevitably on the high side, but service is in keeping with this great establishment. Try the small branch (closed on Saturday) in the City for last-minute gifts (3 Royal Exchange, EC3).

Loewe
25 Old Bond St., W1 - 493 3914
Open Mon.-Fri. 9:30 a.m.-5:30 p.m., Sat. 9:30 a.m.-5 p.m.

"LO-AH-VEE"—there, that solves the mystery of how to pronounce the name of this famous Spanish leather dealer, whose elegant products include boots, shoes, coats and briefcases. The rustic "1846" collection in bottle-green suede and natural hide ranges from a £120 shoulder bag to a £410 large suitcase. Suede and leather trousers come in many colors, and there are also blouson jackets and all sorts of accessories. As usual, all things bright and beautiful are bruised with the Loewe logo.

Mulberry
11-12 Gees Ct., St. Christopher's Pl., W1
493 2547
Open Mon.-Sat. 10 a.m.-6 p.m.

The accessories here suggest a traditional English look: hunting and shooting satchels, printed leather belts and a new collection of luggage in rubberized cotton with leather trim. To give you an idea about the prices . . . £120 for a 28-inch suitcase; the bags and belts are affordably priced, beginning at £35 and £10, respectively.

Pickett Fine Leather
41 Burlington Arcade, W1 - 493 8939
Open Mon.-Fri. 9 a.m.-5:30 p.m., Sat. 9 a.m.-4:30 p.m.

Pickett will make wallets, briefcases and luggage to order in just about any color and design you could dream up. There are literally hundreds of wallets, card holders and notebooks in seemingly every possible size, not to mention smart leather handbags, briefcases and overnight cases. Pickett also has a repair service, and the basement holds the silk collection of Georgina Von Etzdorf.

Revelation
170 Piccadilly, W1 - 493 4138
Open Mon.-Sat. 9 a.m.-6 p.m.

In this very attractive shop, the selection of luggage and leather accessories is arranged on two floors. On the ground floor: leather wallets and purses of all kinds, ties, belts, umbrellas and a variety of leather gifts and key rings. In the basement: a fantastic and well-displayed selection of suitcases and attaché and document cases. Famous names here include Delsey, Antler and Samsonite.

Louis Vuitton
149 New Bond St., W1 - 493 3688
198 Sloane St., SW1 - 235 3356
Open Mon.-Sat. 9:30 a.m.-6 p.m.

Louis Vuitton. The name is associated with travel in the grandest manner. Beautifully made trunks sell from £1,850 to £4,555. Soft and hard suitcases go for £300, carryalls start at £135, and those indispensable pet traveling cases are a mere £230. Scattered like snowflakes over almost *everyzing* is the LV logo. Look for the stunning new line of leather purses, wallets, handbags (blessedly sans logo) that comes in a rainbow of colors from beige to deep blue and green (£140 to £425).

SPORTING GOODS

ALL SPORTS

Lillywhites
Piccadilly Circus, SW1 - 930 3181
Open Mon., Wed. & Fri.-Sat. 9:30 a.m.-6 p.m., Tues. 9:45 a.m.-6 p.m., Thurs. 9:30 a.m.-7 p.m.

Europe's largest single sports retailer has six floors devoted to all kinds of sports equipment, clothing and footwear. Some departments are clearly better than others, but then that is inevitable with a store of this size. The emphasis on gear shifts with the seasons; what isn't in stock can be ordered for you. Service can be erratic.

FISHING

Farlow
5 Pall Mall, Royal Opera Arcade, SW1
839 2423
Open Mon.-Wed. & Fri. 9 a.m.-5 p.m., Thurs. 9 a.m.-6 p.m., Sat. 9 a.m.-4 p.m.

An unlikely style of shop on this smart street, Farlow exudes all the warmth, friendliness and unhurried, knowledgeable assistance that one would expect of a small family business in a small market town. It isn't hard to understand why it has been chosen as supplier to the Royal Family. Its two top carbon-fiber salmon rods will cost you about £300, with a cane trout rod going for about £135. It also sells carbon boron rods and a full range of tackle for all types of fishing and all types of conditions. Down the arcade is its other shop, stocked with an excellent selection of outdoor clothing—for fishing in the summer and shooting in the winter. Farlow claims to have the largest selection in London, and we don't doubt it. Above all, the staff will offer excellent advice and mail anything you order anywhere in the world. In between the two shops, the owners have opened a small art gallery specializing in sporting pictures and run by a great country enthusiast, Peter Keyser.

House of Hardy
61 Pall Mall, SW1 - 839 5515
Open Mon.-Wed. & Fri. 9 a.m.-5 p.m., Thurs. 9 a.m.-6 p.m., Sat. 9 a.m.-4 p.m.

One of the most prestigious houses in the angling-supplies field, House of Hardy recently reintroduced cane rods, some of which can cost up to £600; a carbon trout rod will cost between £100 and £150. The fly reels are the finest (and probably the most expensive) in the world. House of Hardy can outfit the angler with clothing and equipment for any waters, any fish. Service is quite agreeable.

HUNTING

Boss & Co.
13 Dover St., W1 - 493 1127
Open Mon.-Fri. 9:30 a.m.-5 p.m.

Boss & Co. makes some of the best side-lock shotguns in the world (all bores start at £16,000 a pair and have a two-and-a-half-year wait) and remains a specialist in single-trigger guns. It does carry some secondhand guns, all of which are reconditioned in Boss workshops before being put up for sale.

William Evans
67A St. James's St., SW1 - 493 0415
Open Mon.-Fri. 9 a.m.-5 p.m.

In 1980 William Evans left Purdey to set up his own shop. It was a good move. The staff is friendly and helpful in this old paneled gun-lined shop not far from St. James's Palace. (Plans are afoot to update the shop while maintaining the old-world atmosphere.) The customer ledger reads like *Burke's Peerage*, but the staff will see to anybody—provided you have £27,000 and the patience to wait three years for a pair of shotguns. (A new model is being designed that will take just eighteen months.) Accessories include marvelous hand-knit pure-wool socks.

Holland & Holland
33 Bruton St., W1 - 499 4411
Open Mon.-Fri. 9 a.m.-5:30 p.m.

This highly civilized shop, where the Duke of Edinburgh has his rifles made, produces magnificent side-lock shotguns (a pair will cost you about £30,000 and take up to two and a half years to receive), magazine rifles and even double-barreled rifles in impressive calibers (one only wonders what giants could handle them). Also sold are antique, secondhand and imported rifles and guns, plus a complete range of hunting clothes and accessories.

James Purdey & Sons
57 S. Audley St., W1 - 499 1801
Open Mon.-Fri. 9 a.m.-5 p.m.

If they disagree about their rifle makers, at least the Queen and the Duke of Edinburgh have the same gunsmith: Purdey. The dream of every sporting shot is to own a pair of Purdeys. And it's a dream anyone who is prepared to wait two and a half years and pay £39,000 or so can realize. The Mayfair premises are quiet, unfussy and dignified, not at all intimidating, and the staff is most courteous and helpful. In addition to the side-lock ejectors of all calibers, Purdey makes highly prized double-barreled rifles. Each Purdey gun is a collector's item, and there are even stories of people buying them, greasing them up and putting them in the bank in place of gold. But the real pleasure of Purdey lies in the handling of its magnificent French walnut stock, the feel of its silky, beautifully worked metal and the testing of its perfect mechanism. Purdey cartridges are loaded in Birmingham to exacting specifications. The shop also carries outdoor footwear and clothing, including cotton boxer shorts with an ingenuous cartridge design.

J. Roberts & Son
66 Great Suffolk St., SE1
734 7611, 836 1108
Open Mon.-Fri. 9:30 a.m.-6 p.m.

Roberts has amalgamated two famous gunsmiths: Cogswell & Harrison (established in 1770) and John Rigby & Co. (established in 1735). Unlike other gunsmiths' premises, you cannot simply walk into this shop to browse: Only genuine inquiries are accepted. Roberts is a supplier of Spanish guns; a pair will cost you approximately £5,000. It also manufactures its own guns at a slightly lower price, plus double-barreled rifles and magazine rifles. The Rigby side of Roberts supplies rifles and cartridges to the Queen.

RIDING

Gidden's
15D Clifford St., W1 - 734 2788
Open Mon.-Fri. 9 a.m.-5:15 p.m., Sat. 10 a.m.-1 p.m.

This family has been making saddles, harnesses and boots for the Royal Family, Her Majesty's cavalry officers and the most distinguished riders in the kingdom since the nineteenth century. You can also find ready-made items at quite reasonable prices.

Swaine, Adeney, Brigg & Sons
185 Piccadilly, W1 - 734 4277
Open Mon.-Wed. & Fri. 9 a.m.-5:30 p.m., Thurs. 9:30 a.m.-7 p.m., Sat. 9:30 a.m.-5 p.m.

Here you'll find everything for the horse and the rider (except the horse), as well as shooting equipment, fine leather goods, picnic baskets and Brigg's flawless umbrellas. On the first floor we were guided knowledgeably and with humor through the saddle, riding-boots and racing-colors departments. The staff will even help you design your own colors. The gun-and-shooting department is in the basement. Superb range of gentlemen's whips.

SAILING

Captain O. M. Watts
45 Albemarle St., W1 - 493 4633
Open Mon.-Fri. 9:30 a.m.-6 p.m., Sat. 10 a.m.-5 p.m.

This famous store continues to maintain the high quality of its products and the intelligent advice offered to its customers by the friendly staff. Here you will find absolutely everything a sailor needs—aside from a mermaid.

SKIING & CLIMBING

Alpine Sports
215 Kensington High St., W8 - 938 1911
Open Mon.-Sat. 10 a.m.-6 p.m.

One of the main specialists in skiwear and equipment in London, Alpine has everything you'll need for a ski holiday, and in summer it specializes in climbing equipment. The staff is extremely knowledgeable, with many having considerable climbing experience. In fact, two employees went on an Everest expedition in 1985.

Snow & Rock
188 Kensington High St., W8 - 937 0872
Open Mon.-Sat. 10 a.m.-6 p.m.

Ski and trekking gear at reasonable prices. We advise any skier wishing to look sophisticated on the ski slopes to choose from Snow & Rock's exciting range of ski and après-ski clothes from Sweden, Finland, Austria, France, the United States and Germany. The selection of camping equipment, however, is not as extensive as it should be.

YHA Adventure Shop
14 Southampton St., Covent Garden, WC2
836 8541
Open Mon.-Wed. & Sat. 9:30 a.m.-6 p.m., Thurs. 9:30 a.m.-7 p.m.

Undoubtedly the most comprehensive range of mountaineering equipment in London: parkas, sleeping bags, tents, ropes, waterproof trousers, backpacks, boots, cooking utensils and dried food, plus an excellent selection of books and maps and even a photograph booth, so you can apply for immediate membership in the association. In September the stock changes—skiing equipment takes over.

TOBACCONISTS

Astleys
109 Jermyn St., SW1 - 930 1687
Open Mon.-Fri. 10 a.m.-6 p.m., Sat. 11 a.m.-2:30 p.m.

A mecca for the world's pipe smokers, this small shop has been making pipes for over a century, and it has on display an extraordinary collection of antique hand-carved pipes, some with famous heads—Queen Victoria, Napoléon and Gladstone among them. If they were only for sale, they'd have little trouble finding buyers. A good selection of ordinary briars is available for £18 to £50, and straight-grain briars are £75 to £750. For those who love the cool smoke of a meerschaum pipe, there are beautifully carved antique bowls in human-head, animal and bowl-in-claw shapes. In addition, Astleys sells a good selection of its own pipe tobacco, cigars, tobacco pouches and humidors. It also reconditions and repairs pipes, because, as it claims, "A foul pipe is injurious to health."

Benson & Hedges
13 Old Bond St., W1 - 493 1825
Open Mon.-Fri. 9:30 a.m.-5 p.m., Sat. 10:30 a.m.-5 p.m.

One of the oldest stores on Bond Street, Benson & Hedges redecorated a few years ago and now has a new wood interior. Messrs. Benson and Hedges began the business on this site in 1870, rolling cigarettes by hand in the basement. Gentlemen's gifts, leather goods and an exclusive collection of menswear may distract you from the serious issue of selecting from a fine gathering of Havana cigars, pipes and other smokers' paraphernalia.

Bonds
330 Oxford St., W1 - 493 1025
Open Mon.-Wed. & Fri.-Sat. 9 a.m.-7 p.m., Thurs. 9 a.m.-8 p.m.

This big shop on busy Oxford Street markets world-famous cigars from Cuba and other countries. There is also a good selection of pipes: Dunhill, Peterson, James Upshall, Falcon. A fine choice of smokers' gifts includes humidors, cigar cutters, cigarette and cigar cases (silver ones, too) and leather goods.

John Bumfit
337 High Holborn, WC1 - 405 2929
Open Mon.-Fri. 8:30 a.m.-6 p.m.

John Bumfit is located in the thirteenth-century timbered Staple Inn building. An excellent variety of fine pipes, both British and imported, keeps its customers returning. The humidified cigar room holds an extensive choice from all parts of the globe. Expert help and friendly guidance are provided.

Davidoff of London
35 St. James's St., SW1 - 930 3079
Open Mon.-Sat. 9:30 a.m.-6 p.m.

You will find the entire range of Davidoff cigars in this luxurious shop, as well as one of the largest selections of the best Havana cigars (stored in perfect condition) in all Europe. To complete your ruin, there are 30 types of humidors and Davidoff's selected Cognac, considered a perfect accompaniment to cigars.

Alfred Dunhill

30 Duke St., SW1 - 499 9566
Open Mon.-Fri. 9:30 a.m.-5:30 p.m., Sat. 9:30 a.m.-4:30 p.m.

Alfred Dunhill opened his first tobacconist shop at 30 Duke Street, St. James's, in 1907. Eighty-some years later, on the same site, stands this super-smart store. Following redecoration in 1987, most of the ground-floor space is now devoted to menswear, leather goods, watches and other accessories. But pipe smokers can still blend tobacco from the impressive Dunhill stock. In the Humidor Room, on the first floor, cigars (including Dunhill's Havana line) are kept in Cuban cedar cabinets at the precise temperature and humidity to ensure prime condition; the Humidor Room also contains some 300 private lockers used by Dunhill's most devoted customers. We're also fond of the huge selection of pipes and, of course, the famous Dunhill lighters—the newest line has a stainless-steel-and-gold finish and is priced from £120. The staff seems most welcoming, not at all pushy or resentful toward the "just looking" brigade.

James Fox

2 Burlington Arcade, W1 - 493 9009
Open Mon.-Fri. 9 a.m.-5:30 p.m., Sat. 9 a.m.-1 p.m.

This venerable shop, founded in Dublin and now located a few steps from Bond Street, specializes in Havana cigars—Punch, Monte Cristo, Rey del Mundo and so forth, along with a number of sizes and brands exclusive to James Fox. It also carries its own selection of perfectly preserved cigars from the rest of the world. The staff will gladly store your own private stock of cigars until you are ready for them. Under the same management as the cigar department at Harrods.

Robin Gage

Unit 7, Talina Centre, 23 Bagley's Ln., King's Rd., SW6 - 731 1370
Open Mon.-Sat. by appt.

Rosewood or cormandel, 100 years old or brand-spanking new—this superb selection of humidors starts at £650 and goes up to £1,000. Another specialty is the Club Fender Seats, custom-designed for clients around the world to fit their fireplaces.

Inderwick

45 Carnaby St., W1 - 734 6574
Open Mon.-Sat. 9 a.m.-7 p.m.

Whatever your pipe requirements, Inderwick can probably satisfy them. It was responsible for making George V a four-smoke pipe, but you may just want a larger bowl or a longer stem. Pipes made to measure, available from £60, have become a specialty, and it's a specialty we like to encourage, since handcrafted quality is becoming increasingly rare. Inderwick also stocks plenty of ready-made pipes and most brands of tobacco.

Robert Lewis

19 St. James's St., W1 - 930 3787
Open Mon.-Sat. 9 a.m.-5:30 p.m., Sat. 9 a.m.-noon.

This elegant, traditional shop is packed with fine cigars from all over the world, stored in the same scented boxes in which they were shipped before the war. Lewis ranks, with Davidoff, as Europe's principal importer of Havana cigars. Churchill bought his Romeo and Juliettes here. And it is here that the world's most demanding tobacco lovers come to order their blends. Needless to say, the customer is treated with all due consideration in a place where the buying of a box of cigars or a tobacco pouch assumes the same importance as the purchase of a Bentley.

Sullivan Powell

34 Burlington Arcade, W1 - 629 0433
Open Mon.-Fri. 9 a.m.-5:30 p.m., Sat. 9 a.m.-4:30 p.m.

This is London's only surviving Turkish-cigarette specialist. Sullivan Powell makes seven varieties, but it no longer manufactures them to individual special order (the block for the gold engraving on the cigarette band costs too much). Two pipe tobaccos, one of them a rare blend of Oriental and Virginia tobacco, are also sold here, together with one of the largest varieties of pipes, including some rare meerschaums, in London.

Desmond Sauter

106 Mount St., W1 - 499 4319
Open Mon.-Fri. 9 a.m.-6 p.m., Sat. 9:30 a.m.-3:30 p.m.

The walk-in humidified cigar room houses a full range of the finest Havana cigars, including the rare and expensive Cohiba. There's also a good selection of cigar cutters, which includes an ingenious bull's-eye cutter that makes a circular incision without unwrapping the outer leaf (£19.50). Pipes include the new Ashton range, exclusive to Desmond Sauter. Crocodile cigar cases and lighters make lovely gifts for the connoisseur.

G. Smith & Sons

The Snuff Centre, 74 Charing Cross Rd., WC2 - 836 7422
Open Mon.-Fri. 8:30 a.m.-6 p.m., Sat. 9 a.m.-6 p.m.

Snuff is ground tobacco with pure, essential oils added, such as bergamot, carnation, jasmine, sandalwood or, in the case of medicated snuffs, menthol and eucalyptus. There are three main groups—dark, moist, coarse snuffs; medium snuffs (recommended for the beginner); and light, dry, finely ground snuffs. According to A. Steinmetz, writing in 1857, there are twelve operations in the taking-a-pinch-of-snuff process, including: rapping the snuff box, presenting it to the company (passing it around), sniffing it with precision and without a grimace, and closing the box "with a flourish." To those who can master the art of the sniff without sneezing and/or falling prey to watery eyes, snuff is said to be refreshing and invigorating, to provide relief from colds and catarrh and to stimulate the mind. Smith blends by hand some 50 varieties of snuff, and it sells its own vintage tobaccos and the essential accessories, such as gold snuff spoons and antique boxes.

SIGHTS

I nstead of attempting to do in a few pages what could fill (indeed, has filled) guidebooks of encyclopedic proportions, our look at London's sights focuses on the lesser-known places and on landmarks that lie well off the beaten path but are nevertheless well worth exploration. As for such acclaimed sights as St. Paul's Cathedral and Westminster Abbey—which under no circumstances should you miss—we'll leave those to the historians and architectural critics. Please don't limit your sight-seeing to only the classics—visiting the quixotic catalog of places we've described below will give you a rewarding insight into the social history of London.

CHURCHES

London's first great church-building period after medieval times (there were some 100 churches in the square mile of the City before the 1666 fire) was during the seventeenth and eighteenth centuries; sadly, only a few of these great buildings have survived the ravages of time, fires and wars. Many of the City churches designed by Sir Christopher Wren, Nicholas Hawksmoor and the two George Dances, senior and junior, were gutted during World War II. In fact, 19 of the 50 churches built by Wren were destroyed by bombs or fire. Listed below is a collection of our favorite survivors, excluding St. Paul's Cathedral and Westminster Abbey, which, as we noted above, are must-sees that deserve more space than our format allows.

All Hallows, London Wall
83 London Wall, EC2 - 638 0971

Known to exist in some form as least as far back as the twelfth century, the church escaped destruction in the Great Fire, was rebuilt from 1765 to 1767, was damaged during World War II and was rebuilt again in 1962. Although its exterior is simple, its interior is very ornate, with fluted Ionic columns rising up to an elegant ceiling.

Brompton Oratory
Brompton Rd., SW1 - 589 4811

A magnificent Italian altarpiece and the high altar from St. Servatious Maastricht are just two of the splendors of this church, which was built from 1878 to 1884.

Christ Church
Commercial St., Spitalfields, E1

Built in 1720 and one of the finest of Hawksmoor's churches, Christ Church was a place of worship for Huguenot refugees, thus the many French names on the gravestones. Though there were some frightful nineteenth-century alterations, Hawksmoor's masterpiece has survived, but it's not currently in regular use.

Queen's Chapel
Marlborough Gate, off Pall Mall, SW1

The first classical church in England, Queen's Chapel was designed by Inigo Jones. Building began in 1623 when the Infanta of Spain was announced as the intended wife for Charles I, but it was stopped when it was learned that the wedding negotiations had collapsed. The chapel was completed in 1627 for Henrietta Maria, whom he did marry, and refurbished for Charles II's Catholic wife, Catherine of Braganza.

St. Bartholomew the Great
West Smithfield, EC1 - 606 5171

The oldest church in London, dating from Norman times, St. Bartholomew has a seventeenth-century brick tower that contains the oldest set of bells in all of London. The church is as beautiful as Westminster Abbey but visited only a fraction as often. On a small street called Cloth Fair to the north, a picturesque wooden house dating from the seventeenth century (no. 41) is still standing.

St. Clement Danes
The Strand, WC2 - 242 8282

There was a church on this site as early as the tenth century (thus the reference to Danes). Although it escaped damage in the Great Fire, in 1679 it was declared unsafe. Enter Christopher Wren: St. Clement Danes is the only one of his buildings—apart from St. Paul's Cathedral—to have an apse. It was bombed in 1941, and the reconstruction was finally finished in 1958.

St. Ethelburga-the-Virgin
68-70 Bishopsgate, EC2 - 588 3596

The smallest of the City's churches, it was rebuilt in 1775 and houses some interesting paintings.

St. George's
Bloomsbury Way, WC1 - 636 5572

A Hawksmoor church completed in 1731, St. George's has a most extraordinary steeple on its west tower that is stepped like a pyramid.

St. Helen's
Bishopsgate & St. Helen's Pl., EC3
283 2231

Said to have been built originally by the Roman Emperor Constantine on the site of a pagan temple when he was converted to Christianity in the fourth century, St. Helen's is packed with fascinating curiosities, among which is a memorial window to Shakespeare, who is known to have lived in the parish. Most of the church building you see today was built in the thirteenth century. It's one of London's grandest old churches.

St. Katherine Kree
Leadenhall St., EC3 - 283 5733

Built originally in 1280 and rebuilt in 1630, this church escaped the Great Fire and suffered only minimal damage in World War II. Spectacular plaster ceiling.

St. Martin-in-the-Fields
Trafalgar Sq., WC2 - 930 1862

A church site since at least 1222, St. Martin-in-the-Fields was first rebuilt in 1544 and then again by James Gibbs, from 1722 to 1726. A good many people of note were baptized (Francis Bacon), married (Thomas Moore) and buried (Nell Gwyn, Charles II's mistress) here.

St. Paul's
Covent Garden, WC2 - 836 5221

Designed by Inigo Jones, St. Paul's (not to be confused with the famous cathedral) was the first new Anglican church built in London after the Reformation and was consecrated in 1638. It was damaged by fire in 1795 and restored soon after by Thomas Hardwick. Known as the "actors' church," it houses memorials to many theater greats.

Temple Church
Inner Temple Ln., EC4

Like Westminster Abbey, Temple Church is exempt from episcopal jurisdiction and is under direct ownership of the monarchy. Most of the building was built before 1300. Although damaged badly during World War II, it has now been fully restored.

Wesley's Chapel
49 City Rd., EC1 - 253 2262

Methodists from all over the world make pilgrimages to this chapel, built in 1788 by John Wesley, the founder of the Methodist church. Next door is John Wesley's House (see "Curiosities" below), which contains a well-stocked library of Methodist-related volumes.

Westminster Cathedral
Victoria St., SW1 - 834 7452

London's principal Catholic church was built between 1895 and 1903 by John Francis Bentley, who derived many of his ideas for the cathedral from a trip he took to Italy in 1894.

CURIOSITIES

Some of these sights are out of the way and may require an advance phone call to obtain precise directions and admission fee information, but all will prove to be well worth the effort.

Apothecaries' Hall
12 Blackfriars Ln., EC4 - 236 1189
Open Mon.-Fri. 10 a.m.-6 p.m.

Aside from a few modifications, this building remains almost entirely unchanged after

300 years. Inside are a well-preserved paneled room where the Society held its meetings, 1671 banisters and an ormolu candelabrum from 1736.

Banqueting House

Whitehall, SW1 - 930 4179
Open Mon.-Sat. 10 a.m.-5 p.m., Sun. 2 p.m.-5 p.m.

The first purely Renaissance building in London, the Banqueting House was designed by Inigo Jones and completed in 1622. The ceiling, painted by Rubens, was commissioned by Charles I. The building was used for various court and state ceremonies; on January 30, 1649, Charles I walked through the Banqueting House and out of a window to be beheaded. After a fire in 1698, it was converted by Christopher Wren into a Royal Chapel.

Bethnal Green
Museum of Childhood

Cambridge Heath Rd., E2 - 980 2415
Open Mon.-Thurs. & Sat. 10 a.m.-6 p.m., Sun. 2:30 p.m.-6 p.m.

The museum is being developed as a museum to commemorate childhood and is notable for its collections of toys, games, dolls, dollhouses and children's costumes. We also enjoyed seeing the wedding dresses and Spitalfields silks (once a local industry).

Carlyle's House

24 Cheyne Row, SW3 - 352 7087
Open Mon. & Wed.-Sat. 10 a.m.-1 p.m. & 2 p.m.-6 p.m., Sun. 2 p.m.-6 p.m.

Thomas Carlyle moved into this house in 1834 and died in the drawing room in 1881. Visitors entertained by Carlyle and his wife included Ruskin, Dickens and Tennyson, and it was up in the attic that he wrote *The French Revolution, Latter Day Pamphlets* and *Frederick the Great*. The house is almost as Carlyle left it, with his hat still hanging on a peg in the hallway. Its neighboring row of captivating Queen Anne houses, built in 1703, has been home to celebrated occupants: George Eliot (number 4), Dante Gabriel Rossetti (number 16), Isambard Kingdom Brunel (number 98), Hilaire Belloc (number 104) and J.M.W. Turner (number 119).

Cleopatra's Needle

Victoria Embankment, WC2

This granite obelisk was presented to the British in 1819. Originally cut from the Aswan quarries in 1473 B.C., it held sway over Heliopolis until 14 B.C.. At that time it was moved to Alexandria. There it stood, in varying degrees of deterioration, for more than nineteen centuries until, as a gift from Egypt, it was towed at great expense by sea to London, finally sailing up the Thames in 1878. Most remarkable, perhaps, is what was preserved for posterity in the time capsule that was buried beneath it prior to its installation on the Embankment: that morning's newspapers, a set of coins, a box of pins, a razor, several Bibles in different languages, a railway guide and, strangest of all, photographs of twelve of the prettiest Englishwomen of the day.

The Cricket Memorial Gallery

Marylebone Cricket Club, Lord's Ground, NW8 - 289 1611
Open Mon.-Sat. 10:30 a.m.-5 p.m.; guided tours & admission at other times by appt.

For cricket aficionados, these new displays at Lord's Ground illustrate the history of the game (including the Ashes—the World Series of cricket).

Cumberland Terrace

Cumberland Terr., NW1

Built between 1826 and 1828, these are the finest of Nash's terraces. Apartments and houses have now been built behind the original facade, but this remains a highlight for architecture fans.

Cutty Sark Clipper Ship

King William Walk, Greenwich, SE10
858 3445
Summer: open Mon.-Sat. 10:30 a.m.-5:30 p.m., Sun. noon-5:30 p.m.; winter: open Mon.-Fri. by appt., Sat. 10:30 a.m.-4:30 p.m., Sun. noon-4:30 p.m.

The last of the China Tea Clippers, the Cutty Sark was built in 1869. Don't miss the Long John Silver figurehead collection.

Dickens' House

48 Doughty St., WC1 - 405 2127
Open Mon.-Sat. 10 a.m.-5 p.m. Closed bank holidays.

This house was occupied by Dickens and his family from 1837 to 1839. Memorabilia displayed includes manuscripts, furniture, autographs, portraits, letters and first editions.

Docklands
Isle of Dogs - 515 3000

This virtual city within a city has been nurtured in the East End of London over the past few years. Docklands is a development encompassing the Isle of Dogs, the Royal Docks and Surrey Docks, an area that fell into great decay in the last couple of decades; it represents the most massive construction project London has known since the Great Fire of 1666. The master plan comprises 22 buildings over 71 acres and will cost approximately £4 billion. To tour this fascinating area, call the number above or Docklands Light Railway, 538 0311.

Michael Faraday's Laboratory and Museum
21 Albemarle St., W1 - 409 2992
Open Tues. & Thurs. 1 p.m.-4 p.m.

This laboratory, where some of the world's most important scientific discoveries were made, has been restored to its 1845 appearance. An adjacent museum houses a unique collection of original equipment arranged to illustrate the most significant aspects of Faraday's contributions to the advancement of science.

Fenton House
Hampstead Grove, Hampstead, NW3
435 3471
Easter Mon.-end Oct.: open Sat.-Wed. 2 p.m.-6 p.m.

The Benton-Fletcher collection of early musical instruments and the Binning collection of porcelain and furniture are on display in this William and Mary house.

Foundling Hospital
40 Brunswick Sq., WC1
278 2424
Open Mon.-Fri. 10 a.m.-4 p.m. Closed public holidays & when rooms are in use for conferences.

The building of the Thomas Coram Foundation for Children houses more than 150 paintings, prints and the like, including works by Hogarth, Gainsborough and Reynolds; historical records; musical scores by Handel; furniture and clocks; and mementos from the

Foundling Hospital, which was established in 1739.

Grange Museum
Neasden Ln., NW10
452 8311
Open Mon.-Tues. & Thurs.-Fri. noon-5 p.m., Wed. noon-8 p.m., Sat. 10 a.m.-5 p.m. Closed bank holidays.

This local-history museum is housed in the stable block of a large farm that was built in the early 1700s and converted into a Gothic cottage around 1810. The permanent display covers various aspects of life in the area, including a Victorian parlor, a 1930s lounge and an Edwardian draper's shop, along with a display of souvenirs of the British Empire Exhibition, which was held at Wembley from 1924 to 1925. The garden is open for picnics.

Guinness World of Records
The Trocadero Centre, Piccadilly Circus, W1 - 439 7331
Open daily 10 a.m.-10 p.m.

This exhibition brings to life the amazing, outstanding facts and feats from the world-famous book, using the latest in video screens, multiscan computers and other breathtaking displays.

Ham House
Petersham, Richmond, Surrey - 940 1950
March-Oct.: open Tues.-Sun. 2 p.m.-6 p.m.; Nov.-Feb.: open Tues.-Sun. noon-4 p.m.

Built in 1610 and altered at various times during the seventeenth century, the Ham House shelters a fine collection of late Stuart furniture.

The Heralds' Museum at the Tower of London
Tower of London, EC4 - 709 0765
April-Sept.: open Mon.-Sat. 9:30 a.m.-5:30 p.m., Sun. 2 p.m.-5:15 p.m.

This museum traces the development of heraldry through the ages. On display are manuscripts, a herald in full figure, jewelry, arms, china and paintings, all of which show the application of heraldry from medieval times through the present day. Entrance is included in the admission fee to the Tower of London.

Heritage Motor Museum
Syon Park, Brentford, Middlesex - 560 1378
April-Oct.: open daily 10 a.m.-5 p.m.; Nov.-March: open daily 10 a.m.-4 p.m. Closed Dec. 25-26.

Comprising the finest collection of uniquely British cars on display, these 100 vehicles represent the history of the British automobile industry.

Highgate Cemetery
Swain's Ln., N6

Consecrated in May 1839, and a great tourist attraction thanks to its grand views of London, Highgate was once the fashionable place to be—six feet under—which is hardly surprising, since it was magnificently laid out and included Gothic buildings, Eygptian columns, landscaped gardens and catacombs containing cast-iron doors and stone shelves for the coffins. Having fallen into desperate decay, it is currently being restored by the Friends of Highgate Cemetery.

Historic Ship Collection
East Basin, St. Katherine's Dock, E1
481 0043
Open daily 10 a.m.-5 p.m. Closed Dec. 25 & Jan. 1.

This collection includes six unique, historic ships berthed afloat, among which is Arctic explorer Captain Scott's *Discovery.*

Hogarth's House
Hogarth Ln., Great West Rd., W4
994 6757
Open Mon. & Wed.-Sat. 11 a.m.-6 p.m., Sun. 2 p.m.-6 p.m. (until 4 p.m. in winter). Closed first 2 weeks of Sept. & last 3 weeks of Dec.

Artist William Hogarth's country house for fifteen years now displays copies of his paintings, engravings and other memorabilia.

IBA's Broadcasting Gallery
70 Brompton Rd., Knightsbridge, SW3
584 7011
Tours Mon.-Fri. 10 a.m., 11 a.m., 2 p.m. & 3 p.m.

This gallery re-creates nearly a century of radio and television history. Children under 16

are not allowed; advance reservations are essential.

Imperial Collection
Central Hall of Westminster Abbey, SW1
222 0770
May-Nov.: open Mon.-Sat. 10 a.m.-6 p.m.; Dec.-Feb.: open Mon.-Sat. 11 a.m.-5 p.m.

This collection of more than 100 pieces of royal regalia and crowns—all in perfect facsimile—is worth more than £2 million. There's also a wall gallery of prints of former kings and queens.

Dr. Johnson's House
17 Gough Sq., EC4 - 353 3745
May-Sept.: open Mon.-Sat. 11 a.m.-5:30 p.m.; Oct.-April: open Mon.-Sat. 11 a.m.-5 p.m.

The great man lived here, near Fleet Street, from 1749 to 1759, and it was here that he compiled his dictionary. Memorabilia including a first edition of the famous dictionary, prints, several paintings and busts of Dr. Johnson, as well as many well-known books of the era are on display.

Living Steam Museum
Green Dragon Ln., Brentford, Middlesex
568 4757
Open Sat.-Sun. & Mon. bank holidays 11 a.m.-5 p.m.

This museum is home to giant beam engines, a type of pumping engine widely used in Victorian times (the earliest built in 1820). Operating under steam, these are the largest of their kind in the world. Working forge, traction engines, scale models.

London Dungeon Museum
28-34 Tooley St., SE1 - 403 0606
April-Sept.: open daily 10 a.m.-5:45 p.m.; Oct.-March: open daily 10 a.m.-4:30 p.m.

Gruesome exhibits of torture instruments from medieval England—along with such new special-effects attractions as The Fire of London—provide a gory look at the past. *Some* kids love it, set as it is in a series of dark, slimy vaults beneath London Bridge and an Underground station, with recorded sounds of screams and moans. But for young and squeamish kids, and for the faint-hearted, it is not a pleasant outing.

The London Toy and Model Museum
23 Craven Hill, W2 - 262 9450, 262 7905
Open Mon. bank holidays & Tues.-Sat. 10 a.m.-5:30 p.m., Sun. 11 a.m.-5 p.m.

The extensive permanent display of commercially made model trains, mechanical toys and nursery items based on two world-famous collections is housed in a fine Victorian building. The working trains, including a garden railway, are delightful.

London Transport Museum
Covent Gdn., WC2 - 379 6344
Open daily 10 a.m.-6 p.m. Closed Dec. 24-26.

Horse-buses, motor buses, trams, trolleybuses and Underground rolling stock, plus unique working exhibits.

Madame Tussaud's
Marylebone Rd., NW1 - 935 6861
Summer: open daily 9:30 a.m.-5:30 p.m.; winter: open daily 10 a.m.-5:30 p.m.

Madame Tussaud was born in 1761 in Strasbourg and emigrated from France to England in 1802. During the French Revolution she was ordered to make death masks of guillotine victims, and when her employer died she inherited his wax exhibition. Nowadays Madame Tussaud's is full of masks of famous characters from history as well as of celebrated contemporary entertainers.

Marble Arch
Marble Arch, W1

Designed by John Nash in 1827, the famous arch used to stand in front of Buckingham Palace and came to its present site in 1851. Don't be foolhardy and attempt to pass through it—this unusual privilege is retained only for the Royal Family.

The Monument
Monument St. & Fish St. Hill, EC3
626 2717

Built in 1667 to commemorate the Great Fire of London of the previous year, this generically named monument was designed by Sir Christopher Wren and rises to 202 feet; it's thought to be the highest single stone column in the world. In 1842, following a rash of suicides, the gallery at the top was enclosed by an iron cage. You'll have to climb 311 steps to reach the gallery, but the view is worth it.

William Morris Gallery
Water House, Lloyd Park, Forest Rd., Walthamstow, E17 - 527 5544
Open Tues.-Sat. 10 a.m.-1 p.m. & 2 p.m.-5 p.m.

This eighteenth-century house was the boyhood home of William Morris. Collections include textiles, wallpapers, designs and the like by Morris, the pre-Raphaelites and other contemporaries. The Frank Brangwyn collection of pictures and sculpture by nineteenth-century (and other) artists, including the donor himself, are also on display.

Orleans House
Riverside, Twickenham - 892 0221
Open Tues.-Sat. 1 p.m.-5:30 p.m., Sun. 2 p.m.-5 p.m. (Oct.-March: open until 4:30 p.m.), bank holidays 2 p.m.-5:30 p.m.; Jan.: open noon-4:30 p.m. Closed Dec. 25-26 & Good Friday.

All that remains of the Orleans House is James Gibbs's baroque Octagon Room, circa 1720, located in a beautiful riverside setting. The former carriage store, now converted into an art gallery, hosts temporary exhibitions.

Pudding Lane
Pudding Ln., EC3

The Great Fire of London started in a bakery on this very spot September 2, 1666.

Statue of Achilles
Park Ln., W1

When this statue was unveiled in 1822, it caused quite a stir, particularly among the terribly upright Women of England, who discovered that they had unwittingly sponsored the first public male nude statue in England.

Telecom Technology Showcase
135 Queen Victoria St., EC4 - 248 7444
Open Mon.-Fri. 10 a.m.-5 p.m.

Just to the south of St. Paul's Cathedral, this unique, permanent exhibition traces more than 200 years of telecommunications history. Major exhibits include Victorian exchanges, wartime reconstructions and displays showing the digital revolution, fiber optics and satellite technology.

Thames Flood Barrier Visitor's Centre
Unity Way, Woolwich, SE18 - 854 1373

An exhibition of photographs, models, videos and informative displays about the history and construction of the Thames Flood Barrier, which was built to protect the city from potentially damaging river floods.

John Wesley's House
49 City Rd., EC1 - 253 2262
Open Mon.-Sat. 10 a.m.-4 p.m.

The founder of Methodism moved into this house in 1778 and died there in March 1791. Next door are Wesley's Chapel (see "Churches") and its museum of Methodism, a shrine visited by people from many countries. Across the road is Bunhill Fields graveyard, where William Blake is buried.

The Wimbledon Lawn Tennis Museum
All England Club, Church Rd., Wimbledon, SW19 - 946 6131
Open Tues.-Sat. 11 a.m.-5 p.m., Sun. 2 p.m.-5 p.m. Closed public & bank holidays & Fri.-Sun. prior to annual championships.

Fashion, trophies, replicas and memorabilia are on display, representing the history of lawn tennis. An audiovisual theater shows films of the all-time great matches. During championships, admission is restricted to those attending the tournament.

Wimbledon Windmill Museum
Windmill Rd., Wimbledon, Common, SW10 - 788 7655
Easter-Oct.: open daily 2 p.m.-5 p.m.

The history of windmills and windmilling is told here in pictures, models and the machinery and tools of the trade.

MUSEUMS & GALLERIES

British Library
Great Russell St., WC1 - 636 1555
Open Mon.-Sat. 10 a.m.-5 p.m., Sun. 2 p.m.-6 p.m. Closed Dec. 24-26, Jan. 1 & bank holidays.

The Reference Division of the national library, itself a part of the British Museum has its own exhibition galleries, in which you can see the Magna Carta, the first folio edition of Shakespeare's plays, Samuel Pepys's shorthand notes of conversations, Jonathan Swift's tiny writing, Jane Austen's original manuscript of the last two chapters of *Persuasion*, fourth- and fifth-century Greek manuscripts, the Gutenberg Bible, a manuscript of *Beowulf* from about A.D. 1000, and countless other fascinating books, manuscripts, maps and musical manuscripts, including pieces by Handel, Mozart and Beethoven. Temporary exhibitions on specific topics are mounted regularly.

British Museum
Great Russell St., WC1 - 636 1555
Open Mon.-Sat. 10 a.m.-5 p.m., Sun. 2 p.m.-6 p.m. Closed Dec. 24-26, Jan. 1 & bank holidays.

The British Museum, which houses the British Library and the national museum of archaeology and ethnography, was founded in 1753 after Sir Hans Sloane requested in his will that Parliament purchase his collection of antiquities and natural history for £20,000—less than half the amount he had spent acquiring it. The collection was originally located in Montague House in Bloomsbury, but a century later, after the collection had grown vastly, a new and larger building was urgently required. In 1852 the present version of the British Museum came into existence, when Robert Smirke added on behind its original building. Since then, various additions to the museum have had to be located elsewhere in London. (And additions have been necessary, especially since the 1911 passing of a Copyright Act decreeing that a copy of every book, periodical and newspaper published in Great Britain be deposited in the museum.)

The museum's departments (Greek and Roman, Egyptian, Ethnography, Prehistory and Roman Britain, Western Asiatic, Asia, Coins and Medals, Medieval, Prints and Drawings) hold treasures far too numerous to do justice to in this limited space. We can mention only a few personal favorites—the legion of mummies and busts of ancient Egyptians and

Romans, the Sutton Hoo Burial (objects that belonged to a king who lived circa A.D. 600), a Viking hoard of jewelry, 67 chessmen made in Scandinavia from pieces of walrus tusk during the twelfth century, gold cups made in Paris in 1380 that belonged to the kings of England and France, a sixteenth-century violin, a log book of the *Victory* and Captain Scott's diary—but you'll surely have your own favorites after spending several enthralling hours here.

Cabinet War Rooms

Clive Steps, King Charles St., SW1
930 6961
Open Mon.-Sat. 10 a.m.-5 p.m., Sun. 2:30 p.m.-6 p.m.

The Cabinet War Rooms are the most important surviving part of the emergency underground shelter built to protect Winston Churchill, his war cabinet and the chiefs of staff of Britain's armed forces against air attacks during World War II. Situated in the basement of the Government Offices, beneath a slab of protective concrete, the rooms were in use from August 27, 1939, until the Japanese surrendered in 1945. The suite of nineteen historic rooms includes the Cabinet Room; the Transatlantic Telephone Room, from where Churchill could speak directly to President Roosevelt in the White House; the Map Room, in which information about operations on all fronts was collected; and the Prime Minister's Room, which served as Churchill's emergency office and bedroom until the end of the war.

Chiswick House

Burlington Ln., W4 - 994 0508
March 15-Oct. 15: open daily 9:30 a.m.-6:30 p.m.; Oct. 16-March 14: open daily 9:30 a.m.-4 p.m. Closed Dec. 24-26 & Jan. 1.

This handsome villa, designed by the Earl of Burlington and built from 1725 to 1729, is a

Going traveling? Look for Gault Millau's other "Best of" guides to France, Paris, Italy, Hong Kong, New York, New England, Washington, D.C., Los Angeles, San Francisco and Chicago.

miniature version of Palladio's Villa Rotonda outside Vicenza. It was used initially to display works of art and to entertain such celebrities as George Frideric Handel, Jonathan Swift and Alexander Pope. William Kent designed the rooms, which are adorned with beautiful plaster ceilings and fireplaces; outside are some fine statues by J. M. Rysbrack. In its gardens remain a waterfall, a large conservatory, an Ionic temple, a Doric column and statues of Caesar, Pompey and Cicero brought from Hadrian's villa at Tivoli—the only reminders of what was once a magnificent and ornate landscape.

The Commonwealth Institute

Kensington High St., W8 - 603 4535, 602 3257
Open Mon.-Sat. 10 a.m.-5:30 p.m., Sun. 2:30 p.m.-6 p.m.

Founded during the heyday of the British Commonwealth in 1887, this museum offers details concerning the geography, history and political development of the many Commonwealth countries. There are regular exhibitions of work by contemporary artists as well as a useful information center.

Courtauld Institute Galleries

Somerset House, WC1 - 580 1015, 636 2095
Open Mon.-Sat. 10 a.m.-5 p.m., Sun. 2 p.m.-5 p.m. Closed bank holidays.

Among these galleries of the University of London are the Lee Collection, which is composed of works by Botticelli, Goya, Rubens and other masters; the important Princes Gate Collection of Old Master paintings and drawings, which includes some remarkable pre-Renaissance works; Courtauld's famous collection of French Impressionist and post-Impressionist paintings, including major works by Cézanne, Van Gogh (*Self-Portrait*), Gauguin, Monet and Manet (*Bar at the Folies-Bergère*); and the Fry Collection, which boasts nineteenth- and twentieth-century British and French paintings.

Dulwich College Gallery

College Rd., SE21 - 693 5254
Open Tues.-Sat. 10 a.m.-1 p.m. & 2 p.m.-5 p.m., Sun. 2 p.m.-5 p.m.

Blitzed during the war, this gallery (designed by Sir John Soane and built in 1814) was carefully restored. It contains a fine collection of old masters, which was bequeathed by Edward Alleyn in 1626 and greatly expanded in 1811, when Sir Francis Bourgeois left 371 paintings to Dulwich College. The collection includes paintings by Rembrandt, Rubens, Poussin, Gainsborough, Reynolds, Van Dyck and Cuyp, along with many Italian representatives.

Geffrye Museum

Kingsland Rd., Shoreditch, E2 - 739 8368
Open Tues.-Sat. 10 a.m.-5 p.m., Sun., Mon. & bank holidays 2 p.m.-5 p.m. Closed Dec. 25-26 & Good Friday.

Originally fourteen almshouses built in 1715 to house widows of former members of the Ironmonger's Company, these buildings were bought at the beginning of the twentieth century and turned into this now-famous museum. The permanent display of period rooms shows the development of the middle-class English home from about 1600. There is also a reference library of books and periodicals on the decorative arts.

Geological Museum

Exhibition Rd., SW7 - 589 3444
Open Mon.-Sat. 10 a.m.-6 p.m., Sun. 2:30 p.m.-6 p.m.; library open Mon.-Fri. 10 a.m.-4 p.m.

As you'd guess from the name, this museum illustrates the earth's history and the general principles of geological science, along with the regional geology of Great Britain and the geology and mineralogy of the world. The collection of gemstones and jewels is enough to break any woman's heart. Special exhibits are arranged from time to time.

Guildhall Art Gallery

Guildhall, King St., EC2 - 606 3030
Open Mon.-Sat. 10 a.m.-5 p.m. Closed Dec. 24-26 & Jan. 1.

A gallery that shows frequent exhibitions of works by young British artists, Guildhall Art Gallery is located on the site of the old Guildhall Chapel (built in 1444 and torn down in the nineteenth century), next door to Guildhall, seat of the City of London's municipal government since the fifteenth century. The present Guildhall building was started in 1411 and finished in 1439; in 1501 kitchens were added in back, to better prepare the lord mayors' public feasts.

Gunnersbury Park Museum

Gunnersbury Park, W3 - 992 1612
March-Sept.: open Mon.-Fri. 2 p.m.-5 p.m., Sat., Sun. & bank holidays 2 p.m.-6 p.m.; Oct.-Feb.: open daily 2 p.m.-4 p.m. Closed Dec. 24-26.

Set in a large park, this local-history museum for the London boroughs of Ealing and Hounslow was built in the beginning of the nineteenth century as a spacious country house for the Rothschilds. Its various departments cover such subjects as archaeology, social history, domestic life, toys and dolls, costumes, transportation (including Rothschild carriages), crafts, and industries, particularly laundry. Eighteenth-century landscaper, architect and painter William Kent is reputed to have worked in the gardens.

Imperial War Museum

Lambeth Rd., SE1 - 735 8922
Open Mon.-Sat. 10 a.m.-6 p.m., Sun. 2 p.m.-6 p.m.; reference departments open by appt. Mon.-Fri. 10 a.m.-5 p.m.

Founded in 1920 as a memorial to the sacrifices of World War I, the Imperial now illustrates and records details of the two world wars, along with all other military operations involving Britain and the Commonwealth since 1914. A wide array of weapons and equipment is on display—aircraft, armored fighting vehicles, field guns and small arms—complemented by displays of models, decorations, uniforms, posters, photographs and paintings.

Jewish Museum

Woburn House, Upper Woburn Pl., WC1 388 4525
Open Tues.-Thurs. (& Fri. in summer) 10 a.m.-4 p.m., Sun. (& Fri. in winter) 10 a.m.-12:45 p.m.

Opened in 1932, the Jewish Museum contains a collection of more than 1,000 objects relating to Judaism and Jewish history.

Keats House

Wentworth Pl., Keats Grove, NW3
Open Mon.-Sat. 10 a.m.-5 p.m.

Poet John Keats lived and wrote in this Hampstead house from 1818 to 1820; it was under a mulberry tree in this garden that some say he composed his celebrated "Ode to a Nightingale." The house today holds Keats' books, letters and various memorabilia relating to his life.

Kenwood (The Iveagh Bequest)

Hampstead Ln., NW3 - 348 1286
April-Sept.: open daily 10 a.m.-7 p.m.; Feb.-March & Oct.: open daily 10 a.m.-5 p.m.; Nov.-Jan.; open daily 10 a.m.-4 p.m.

The paintings housed at Kenwood include a magnificent Rembrandt self-portrait painted late in his life, Vermeer's *Lady Playing a Guitar* and works by Van Dyck, Hals and Cuyp as well as eighteenth-century English paintings by Reynolds, Romney and Gainsborough. There are some glorious views of London from the gardens to the south.

Leighton House Art Gallery and Museum

12 Holland Park Rd., W14 - 602 3316
Open Mon.-Sat. 11 a.m.-5 p.m. (open until 6 p.m. during exhibitions); garden open April-Sept. Closed bank holidays.

This was the home of Frederick Lord Leighton, a former president of the Royal Academy and a famous Victorian artist. He lived here until his death in 1896. Leighton House was designed by Royal Academy member George Aitchison. His unique collection of Islamic tiles by William de Morgan is displayed on the walls of the Arab Hall, and the walls of the Victorian interiors, recently restored to their original appearance, are hung with paintings by Leighton himself, along with those done by Millais, Watts and Burne-Jones. Fine sculpture by Leighton, Brock and Thorneycroft can be seen in the house and garden.

Linley Sambourne House

18 Stafford Terr., W8 - 994 1019
Open Mon.-Sat. 10 a.m.-5 p.m., Sun. 2:30 p.m.-6 p.m.

A fascinating survivor of a late-nineteenth-century "artistic" interior, this house is filled with its original decorations, furniture and pictures, preserved almost unchanged from the time of their first owner, Linley Sambourne (1845–1910), chief political cartoonist at *Punch*.

Marble Hill House

Twickenham, Surrey - 892 5115
Feb.-Oct.: open Sat.-Thurs. 10 a.m.-5 p.m.; Nov.-Jan.: open Sat.-Thurs. 10 a.m.-4 p.m. Closed Dec. 24-25.

A complete example of an English Palladian villa, Marble Hill House displays early Georgian paintings and furniture.

Museum of London

London Wall, EC2 - 600 3699
Open Tues.-Sat. 10 a.m.-6 p.m., Sun. 2 p.m.-6 p.m. Closed Dec. 23-26, Jan. 1 & bank holidays.

The Museum of London, opened in 1976, presents a 250,000-year visual history of the London area. The chronologically arranged exhibits include the lord mayors' coach, models and room reconstructions, everyday tools, various upper-class extravagances, treasures excavated from the Temple of Mithras, paintings and relics of the Great Fire experience, eighteenth-century prison cells and nineteenth-century shops.

Musical Museum

368 High St., Brentford, Middlesex 560 8108
April-Oct.: open Sat.-Sun. 2 p.m.-5 p.m.

A unique collection of player pianos, organs, orchestrations and music boxes, all of which are in working order. A galaxy of famous musicians comes to life from music rolls, which are ably and wittily introduced by Frank Holland.

National Army Museum

Royal Hospital Rd., SW3 - 730 0717
Open Mon.-Sat. 10 a.m.-5:30 p.m., Sun. 2 p.m.-5:30 p.m.; reference collections open Tues.-Sat. (except Sat. bank holidays) 10 a.m.-4.30 p.m. Closed Jan. 1, Good Friday, May 5 & Dec. 25.

The only museum dealing with the British Army in general during the five centuries of its existence, the National Army Museum also features the story of the Indian Army till 1947, along with paintings, uniforms, weapons, equipment, mementos and regimental colors.

The National Gallery

Trafalgar Sq., WC2 - 839 3321
Open Mon.-Sat. 10 a.m.-6 p.m., Sun. 2 p.m.-6 p.m. Closed Dec. 24-26, Jan. 1, Good Friday & May 1.

The National Gallery was founded in 1824, when George IV and a wealthy connoisseur persuaded the government to purchase 38 major paintings by Raphael, Rembrandt and Van Dyck from philanthropist John Julius Angerstein. The collection grew over the next few years and had to be moved from Angerstein's house in Pall Mall to its present site. The museum was built in 1838 and now houses the nation's collection of European paintings from 1200 to 1900. The gallery's first director, Sir Charles Eastlake, was a confirmed Italophile and regular visitor to Italy who purchased no fewer than 139 paintings, including works by Paolo Uccello, Leonardo da Vinci, Giovanni Bellini, Titian, Tintoretto and Salvator Rosa. Eastlake died in Pisa in 1865, but the collection continued to expand, with the addition of works by Dutch and Flemish masters as well as major works from France and Spain. It lost, however, many works by British painters (including masterpieces by Gainsborough, Constable, Stubbs and J.M.W. Turner) to the newly opened Tate Gallery in 1897. The National Gallery hosts many exhibitions centered on specific aspects of its huge collection, and it offers an excellent educational service, including quizzes, audiovisual shows and lectures for adults and children.

National Maritime Museum

Romney Rd., Greenwich, SE10 - 858 4422
Mon.-Sat. 10 a.m.-6 p.m., Sun. 2 p.m.-5:30 p.m. (until 5 p.m. in winter). Closed Dec. 24-26, Jan. 1, Good Friday & May 1.

This national museum, which recently took over some additional display space at the Old Royal Observatory in Greenwich Park, explores British maritime history via paintings and prints (by Hogarth, Reynolds, Gainsborough and others), ship models, portraits and mementos of such distinguished navigational figures as Captain Cook and Lord Nelson, navigational instruments and charts, history of astronomy, medals, a large library with a reference section and information service and a fine collection of manuscripts. Don't miss Neptune Hall, which houses the paddle tug *Reliant*, a boat-building shed, the Barge House and a fine collection of boats.

National Portrait Gallery

St. Martin's Pl., Trafalgar Sq., WC2
930 1552
Open Mon.-Fri. 10 a.m.-5 p.m., Sat. 10 a.m.-6 p.m., Sun. 2 p.m.-6 p.m. Closed Dec. 24-26, Jan. 1, Good Friday & May 5.

Just around the corner from the National Gallery, this national collection includes portraits of the famous and infamous of British history—paintings, sculpture, miniatures, engravings and photographs.

Royal Academy of Arts

Burlington House, Piccadilly, W1
734 9052
Open daily 10 a.m.-6 p.m.

Major on-loan exhibitions from around the world are mounted here throughout the year. Of particular note is the annual June–August Summer Exhibition, when works primarily by British artists are displayed and can be purchased.

Royal Air Force Museum

Aerodrome Rd., Hendon, NW9 - 205 2266
Open Mon.-Sat. 10 a.m.-6 p.m., Sun. 2 p.m.-6 p.m. Closed Dec. 24-26, Jan. 1, Good Friday & May 5.

The only national museum that tells the complete story of this particular branch of the military, the Royal Air Force Museum houses some 40 aircraft as well as galleries depicting aviation history from the Royal Engineers of the 1870s through the RAF of the 1980s. The uniforms of the service are displayed, along with a unique range of memorabilia, medals, orders, navigational and other equipment, bombs, missiles and weapons, paintings and drawings, model aircraft, service cars and other transport, escape aids, early workshop scenes and more.

Royal College of Music, Department of Portraits

Prince Consort Rd., SW7 - 589 3643
Open Mon.-Fri. by appt.

This small museum contains an extensive collection of portraits of musicians, including some 200 original portraits and many thousands of prints and photographs. It also houses the college's important collection of concert programs.

Science Museum

Exhibition Rd., SW7 - 589 3456
Open Mon.-Sat. 10 a.m.-6 p.m., Sun. 2:30 p.m.-6 p.m. Closed Dec. 24-26, Jan. 1, Good Friday & May Day Mon.

Millions of visitors have seen these historical collections portraying the sciences of mathematics, physics and chemistry and their applications, along with the developments of engineering, transportation, communications and industries. Many exhibits are accompanied by a taped commentary.

The Shakespeare Globe Museum
1 Bear Gdns., SE1 - 928 6342
Open Tues.-Sat. 10 a.m.-5:30 p.m., Sun. 2 p.m.-6 p.m.

This permanent exhibition covers London theater from 1576 to 1642, including a full-size replica of the 1616 stage and plans for the International Shakespeare Globe Centre's reconstruction of the Globe Theatre.

Sir John Soane's Museum
13 Lincoln's Inn Field, WC2 - 405 2107
Open Tues.-Sat. 10 a.m.-5 p.m.; lecture tours Sat. 2:30 p.m. (no groups); group tours by appt. Closed bank holidays.

Built by Royal Academy member Sir John Soane in 1813 as his private residence, this museum contains his collection of antiquities and works of art. In addition to being a prominent architect, Soane was a passionate collector of drawings by such celebrities as Wren and Adam, and the Picture Room contains fascinating works by Piranesi, Hogarth, Canaletto and Watteau. A small gem of a place that is well worth visiting.

Tate Gallery
Millbank, SW1 - 821 1313, 821 7128
Open Mon.-Sat. 10 a.m.-5:50 p.m., Sun. 2 p.m.-5:50 p.m. Closed Dec. 24-26, Jan. 1, Good Friday & May 1.

Built in 1897, the Tate is home to the national collections of British painting (from the sixteenth century to about 1900) and modern art (paintings and sculpture, both British and foreign, from Impressionism to the present day). Major works from the "golden age" of British painting (Gainsborough, Reynolds, Romney); an illuminating display of paintings by George Stubbs; special collections of Blake, Turner and the pre-Raphaelites; and a large collection of contemporary prints are featured. Free lectures, films and guided tours are offered, as are special activities for children during school vacations.

Tower of London
Tower Hill, EC3 - 709 0765
March-Oct.: open Mon.-Sat. 9:30 a.m.-6 p.m., Sun. 2 p.m.-6 p.m.; Nov.-Feb.: open Mon.-Sat. 9:30 a.m.-4 p.m. Closed Dec. 24-26, Jan. 1 & Good Friday; Jewel House closed Feb.; closing dates may vary.

Dating from Norman times (and added to and altered for centuries thereafter), the Tower of London has performed many services—from protecting the city from invaders to holding prisoners within its walls. Today its primary job is that of tourist attraction. And a worthy attraction it is. The Tower was the temporary home of many famous prisoners (including Sir Walter Raleigh, the poet Charles of Orleans) and the last place on earth seen by the Duke of Clarence, the little princes (murdered in 1483) and a legion of visitors to the scaffold (Anne Boleyn, Lady Jane Grey, Catherine Howard, Thomas More, the Duke of Monmouth). It's no wonder Macaulay said of the Tower's burial site that there "was no sadder spot on earth." On display today are the Crown Jewels (including the 108-carat Koh-i-noor diamond and the 530-carat Star of India, the largest cut diamond ever), historic relics, uniforms, armories and dungeons. The Crown Jewels can be found in the Jewel House, inside the Waterloo Barracks at the northern part of the Tower.

Victoria and Albert Museum
Cromwell Rd., SW7 - 589 6371, 581 4894
Open Mon.-Sat. 10 a.m.-5:50 p.m., Sun. 2:30 p.m.-5:50 p.m. Closed Dec. 24-26, Jan. 1 & May 5.

One of the world's great museums, the Victoria and Albert holds 145 rooms filled with collections of fine and applied arts from an incredible number of countries, encompassing most significant periods and styles. Don't think you can absorb it all in a quick afternoon—like Paris's Louvre, it is a place to return to again and again. The policy of Sir Henry Cole, the first director, was "to assemble a splendid collection of objects," a task that was duly—and superbly—performed. The European collections are made up primarily of art from early Christian times to the twentieth century and include major works by Turner and Constable and the celebrated *Tapestry Cartoons* by Raphael, which were purchased in 1623 by Charles I when he was still Prince of Wales and which have been here on loan from the Royal Family since the time of Queen Victoria. As for the rest—that's for you to discover.

Wallace Collection
Hertford House, Manchester Sq., W1
935 0687
Open Mon.-Sat. 10 a.m.-5 p.m., Sun. 2 p.m.-5 p.m. Closed Dec. 24-26, Jan. 1, Good Friday & May 1.

This outstanding museum shows works of art that were given to the nation by three generations of the Seymour-Conways (the three Marquesses of Hertford). The collection and its home, Hertford House (in which all three generations resided), was bequeathed in 1897 by Lady Wallace after the death of her husband, Sir Richard Wallace, the illegitimate son of the third Marquess of Hertford. It is a "frozen" collection (it can neither be added to nor lent out) consisting of paintings of the French, Spanish, Italian, Flemish, Dutch and British schools. Amazing miniatures, sculpture, superb French furniture, ceramics and other works of art are also on display.

Wellington Museum
Apsley House, 149 Piccadilly, W1
499 5676
Open daily 10 a.m.-6 p.m., Sun. 2:30 p.m.-6 p.m. Closed Dec. 24-26 & Jan. 1.

Built between 1771 and 1778, Apsley House, the London home of the Duke of Wellington until his death in 1852, is well worth visiting. The house contains many of his trophies, uniforms, decorations, batons and other gifts presented to him by grateful royalty, along with more than 90 paintings from the Duke's collection, including works by Ribera, Velásquez, Murillo, Goya and Correggio.

Whitechapel Art Gallery
80-82 Whitechapel High St., E1 - 377 0107
Open Tues. & Thurs.-Sun. 11 a.m.-5 p.m., Wed. 11 a.m.-8 p.m. Closed bank holidays.

The art nouveau–style Whitechapel Art Gallery, built in 1899 by Charles Harrison Townsend, reopened after modernization and extension in 1985. It has no permanent collection but is noteworthy for the major exhibitions it hosts, generally of modern and contemporary art. An extensive community-education program for adults and children includes public tours, lectures, workshops, audiovisual programs and studio visits.

PARKS & GARDENS

Several counties in southeastern England took a phenomenal pounding when an unexpected hurricane screamed through the area on the night of October 16, 1987. In some areas, particularly around Sevenoaks in Kent (the epicenter of the storm), factories and offices were closed down for several days. The damage was so severe that for months afterward trees lay across fields like gigantic fallen matchsticks, for all the world resembling the photographs of those traumatic scenes on the Somme during World War I. The storm wreaked the most havoc on the gardens and parks just south of London, where an estimated 15 million trees were lost. Many parks and gardens within London also felt the brunt of the storm,

though no opportunity has been missed to replace the fallen trees. Nonetheless, the storm's mark can still be detected.

Battersea Park
Battersea, SW11 - 228 2798
Open daily 6 a.m.-dusk.

In 1829 the Duke of Wellington and Lord Winchelsea fought a duel on this very spot. Before the park's official opening in 1853, the grounds had already provided centuries of amusement: A rough ale house used to attract the more rowdy Elizabethan citizens, who could also enjoy pigeon and sparrow shooting nearby; in later years, gypsies camped in the fields, and droves of revelers visited for Sunday

789011

fairs. After it was designated as a city park, a lake and subtropical garden were laid out, and by 1896 it saw hordes of bicyclists indulging in their latest craze. In 1951 the Festival of Britain Gardens were planted. Today, the park also holds a children's zoo, playing fields, a running track, tennis courts, a boating lake and botanical garden. A fairground opens every Easter Sunday and runs until September.

Bushey Park
Kingston-upon-Thames, Surrey - 977 1328
Open daily 6:30 a.m.-midnight.
Bushey encompasses a magnificent avenue of horse chestnut trees that were laid out by Sir Christopher Wren on the orders of William III. Londoners used to picnic here under the chestnut blossoms on Chestnut Sunday (the Sunday nearest May 11). At the northern end stands Bushey Park House, which was built during the reign of George III. Deer and sheep graze unruffled (well, almost) among the visitors.

Chelsea Physic Garden
Royal Hospital Rd., SW3 - 352 5646
April-Oct.: open Wed. & Sun. 2 p.m.-5 p.m.
Established by the Society of Apothecaries in 1676, Chelsea is the second-oldest physic garden in the country (the first is in Oxford). It boasted the first warmed greenhouse in England, built in 1681. The famous cedars of Lebanon were planted here in 1683, though one died in 1903, and since 1683 there has been a mutual exchange of plants and seeds with botanic gardens all over the world. Botanical research is still carried on, and among its features is the earliest rock garden in the country made from stone from the Tower of London and lava from Iceland bought by Sir Joseph Banks. The herb garden contains ancient and modern medicinal and culinary plants; a 30-foot-high olive tree, the biggest in Britain, produces plenty of edible olives; and, of course, innumerable exotic shrubs and trees from all over the world.

Chiswick House
See Chiswick House in "Museums & Galleries" earlier in this chapter.

Crystal Palace Park
Sydenham, SE19 - 778 7148
Open daily 8 a.m.-half hour before dusk.
The famous prehistoric monsters, made of brick and iron and covered with stucco, were created by Waterhouse Hawkins (1854); *Guy the Gorilla*, created in black marble by David Wynne (1961), can be found by the lake. The park now has some of the best sports facilities in the country, including a huge stadium, a sports hall, an Olympic swimming pool and a dry ski slope to complement the 200 acres of gardens, with boating lakes and a zoo.

Dulwich Park
Dulwich, SE21 - 693 5737
Summer: open daily 7 a.m.-11 p.m.; winter: open daily 7:30 a.m.-dusk.
Once a favorite haunt of duelists, Dulwich is now more famous for its rhododendrons, azaleas and heather-filled rock garden.

Finsbury Circus Gardens
Finsbury Circus, EC2 - 236 6920
Open 7 a.m.-sunset.
A smart bowling green and occasional summertime band concerts attract the City's office workers with their sack lunches. Finsbury is the largest open space in the City and is home to many fine shrubs and trees.

Green Park
The Mall, SW1 - 930 1793
Open daily 5 a.m.-midnight.
Charles II made this into a Royal Park, laying out the walks and building a snow house in which to cool drinks in the summer. The site can still be seen as a mound with a plane tree on top opposite 119 Piccadilly. By the eighteenth century, the inevitable duelists had arrived, and highwaymen held up Horace Walpole (and many others). Balloonists favored the park to make their ascents, and among many spectacular fireworks displays was the 1784 show, accompanied by music composed by Handel, that celebrated the Peace of Aix-la-Chapelle.

Greenwich Park
SE10 - 858 2608
Summer: open daily 7 a.m.-11 p.m.; winter: open daily 7 a.m.-dusk.
Henry VIII had a particular fondness for this park, which from 1515 was used to provide game for the royal hunts; and Elizabeth I was presented with magnificent entertainment here that included a dramatically realistic mock battle. Later, Charles II commissioned Louis XIV's landscape gardener, Le Nôtre, to redesign the new Royal Park. The Queen's House

became the new focal point of the tree-lined avenues; behind the Queen's House runs a border of greenery nearly 1,000 feet long, matched only by the one at Buckingham Palace. The panoramic view from Greenwich Hill is famous, as is the park's Meridien Building, which is set smack in the middle of the zero-degree longitude line. An absolute must on a pleasant day.

Hampstead Heath
NW3
Open daily 24 hours.

These 800 acres have always been a popular spot for local residents and visitors alike. As well as having good facilities for riding, it is one of the best places for kite flying, and on any breezy weekend you can see just about every style of kite. One of the finest groves in London is the park's Judge's Walk, and there are spectacular views to be seen from the high ground by Jack Straw's Castle.

Holland Park
Kensington High St., W8 - 602 2226
Open daily 8 a.m.-sunset; flower gardens open daily 8 a.m.-midnight.

Originally the private park of Holland House and bombed during World War II, Holland Park now displays in its 55 acres more than 3,000 species of rare British plants and trees. The flower gardens are lit in the evening until midnight.

Hyde Park
W1, W2 & SW7 - 262 5484
Open daily 5 a.m.-midnight; no cars allowed after dusk.

Opened to the public at the beginning of the seventeenth century (deer were hunted here until 1768), Hyde Park became the rendezvous for fashionable society during the reign of Charles II. Work on the Serpentine Lake started in 1730, and in 1814, as part of the peace celebrations after the Napoleonic wars, the battle of Trafalgar was realistically re-enacted on the lake. The Great Exhibition of 1851 was held in the park's Crystal Palace, and since 1872, in a section known as the Speakers' Corner (by Marble Arch), anyone and everyone has been granted the right to pontificate on any subject—provided they are not obscene, blasphemous or likely to incite a riot.

Inns of Court Gardens
WC1, WC2, EC4
Open daily 24 hours.

Lincoln's Inn, originally a Dominican monastery, was given to the Earl of Lincoln when the monks moved to Blackfriars; Gray's Inn Gardens were laid out in 1586 by Francis Bacon and were used for hunting and archery; and Temple Gardens were written about by Shakespeare (*Henry VI, Part I*) and Dickens (*Martin Chuzzlewit*). These three combine to make the Inn of Court Gardens.

Regent's Park
NW1 - 486 7905
Open daily 5 a.m.-dusk.

Regent's Park originally formed part of Henry VIII's hunting area, although it wasn't until John Nash designed the park and laid out nearby Regent's Street in 1812 that the terraced houses sprang up in the area. The park opened to the public in 1838. Queen Mary's Rose Garden was originally the garden of the Royal Botanic Society, whose annual flower shows were held here until 1932. Currently there are more than 40,000 bushes and climbers, with each bed containing one variety. There is also a small lake, paths lined with flowering shrubs and a rock garden. The famous Regent's Park Zoo, with its spectacular aviary, draws thousands of people every year, and the Open Air Theatre provides a delightful setting for Shakespearean comedies on summer evenings.

Richmond Park
Richmond, Surrey - 940 0654
Open daily 5 a.m.-dusk.

Two ponds in this large park keep anglers amused with stocks of pike, bream, carp, roach and eels; another pond is popular with those who favor model boats. There is plenty of wildlife: red and fallow deer, rabbits, squirrels, hares. Cricket pitches and soccer fields, two golf courses and tennis courts are on hand for those with sporting inclinations. The truly splendid oaks in the park are survivors of the medievel forests.

Royal Botanic Garden
Kew Rd., Richmond, Surrey - 940 1171
Open daily 10 a.m.-dusk; summer: open daily 10 a.m.-8 p.m.

Principally a scientific institution, the Royal Botanic Garden is concerned with the accurate identification of living and dried plants from all over the world. The Herbarium, sadly not open to the public, contains more than 5 million dried and pressed plants. Temples and alcoves built in the eighteenth century survive, as does the stunning Orangery, which was designed by Sir William Chambers in 1761, and the Great Pagoda, which stands ten stories high. The museum, designed by Decimus Burton and opened in 1857, contains a collection of exhibits on botanical subjects. The huge Glasshouse pavilions house exotic palms and orchids, and outside in the gardens is a constantly revolving show of flowers and shrubs. Although during the 1987 hurricane the 200-year-old Chinese Tree of Heaven smashed onto the roof of King William's Temple, and many other trees were lost or damaged, the garden remains an absolute must for anyone who is even remotely interested in anything to do with flowers, plants and trees.

St. James's Park
SW1 - 930 1793
Open daily 5 a.m.-midnight.
The oldest of London's parks, St. James's was a marshy field attached to a leprosy hospital until Henry VIII drained it and started to graze deer among the trees. Later James I laid out formal gardens that included a menagerie and an aviary (hence Birdcage Walk is the southern boundary). Charles II, some 50 years later, built an avenue of trees among which he could play a type of croquet called pall-mall (hence the name of London's famous street, Pall Mall). By Queen Anne's reign, matters had begun to deteriorate, and the park became notorious for prostitutes; it was only in the nineteenth century that the park began to get cleaned up and the canal was remodeled to its present graceful curve.

Syon House
Brentford, Middlesex - 560 0881
Open Mon.-Fri. 10 a.m.-6 p.m., Sat.-Sun. 10 a.m.-6:30 p.m.

Redesigned by Lancelot "Capability" Brown in the eighteenth century to include lawns, a lake and woods, these gardens, just across the Thames from Kew Gardens, still have some mulberry bushes that came from Persia and, although planted as long ago as 1548, still bear fruit. The great conservatory, which contains an aviary and aquarium, was built by Dr. Charles Fowler in the 1820s. Also within the estate is the London Butterfly House (560 0378), which has an extensive exhibition of butterflies from all parts of the world. Entrance to the exhibit is #1.90 for adults.

THEATER

London is celebrated for presenting as comprehensive an output of plays and musical dramas as is performed in any other world capital city. For decades, plays that began life on the British stage have earned plaudits for their brilliance and have gone on to make decisive contributions to the worlds of film and television.

Given the apparently limitless interest on the part of the public that the British theater has fostered, it should come as no surprise to learn that not a year goes by without some new theater opening or some other undergoing a massive refurbishment.

The Royal Opera House in Covent Garden (240 1066) is one of the foremost venues for opera in the world; the Coliseum on St. Martin's Lane (836 3161) presents a substantial list of operas sung in English; and Sadler's Wells on Roseberry Avenue (837 1672), is always worth a visit for its resident ballet company and Gilbert and Sullivan light operas.

When you think of the theater of the spoken word, think of the National Theatre on the South Bank (928 2252), which stages diverse plays in its three theater houses (Olivier, Lyttleton and Cottesloe). The Barbican Theatre (see below) also mounts fine productions, some of them coming straight from debuts (with the casts intact) at Stratford-upon-Avon. In addition to these famous bulwarks of British theater, theater upon theater in the West End stages outstanding plays. The Aldwych (836 6404), the Haymarket, the Royal Court in Sloane Square and the Shaftesbury (836 6596) consistently present worthwhile performances. If you return home without taking in a play or three, you'll regret it.

As for concerts, music lovers have a grand selection, including the Royal Festival Hall, the Queen Elizabeth Hall and the Purcell Room, all on the south bank of the Thames (928 3191). And, of course, there's the famous Albert Hall (589 8212) just the south of Hyde Park, between Kensington High Street and Knightsbridge.

If you don't wish to deal with ticket agencies or go through your hotel concierge, your best bet is the Leicester Square Ticket Booth in the heart of the theater district, which sells tickets for half price on the day of the performance (from noon to 2 p.m. for matinees and 2:30 p.m. to 6:30 p.m. for evening shows). Many theaters have adopted the excellent idea of performing late-afternoon matinees once or twice a week, usually at 5 p.m.

Below are listings of some of London's more notable theaters.

Barbican
Barbican, EC2 - 638 8891

Since the Barbican Centre for Arts and Conferences opened in March 1982, its theater, which boasts wonderful acoustics, has staged many productions that were shown during the previous season at Stratford-upon-Avon. The roster also includes interesting and topical modern plays.

Drury Lane Theatre Royal
Drury Lane, WC2 - 836 8108

Yet another beautiful old London theater, Drury Lane was built more than 200 years ago, yet it is nonetheless big enough to stage some of London's best ballets, operas and musicals. Its most recent success was a glittering production of *42nd Street*.

Globe Theatre
Shaftesbury Ave., W1 - 437 3667

Designed in 1906 as the Hicks Theatre, this respected theater became the Globe in 1909. Since then it has specialized in comedies and farces. Among celebrated past presentations have been *The Lady's Not for Burning* by Christopher Fry and *A Man for All Seasons* by Robert Bolt.

Haymarket Theatre
Haymarket, SW1 - 930 9832

This very grand, world-renowned, centrally located theater came into existence in 1720, and from 1735 to 1737 it was administered by novelist Henry Fielding, after which it fell into a state of disrepair. The succeeding century saw it experience both good times and bad, but since 1837 the Haymarket has remained in the forefront of London theater. Today it regularly stages glossy productions of beloved classics, featuring performances by some of the major names in the acting profession.

Old Vic Theatre
Waterloo Rd., SE1 - 928 7616

In the early nineteenth century, the Old Vic, officially named the Royal Victoria Theatre, was a haunt for ruffians and prostitutes. In 1914 it was acquired by the legendary Lilian Bayliss, an outstanding missionary of the arts who gave the theater new life. Then, in 1963, under the guidance of Sir Laurence Olivier, it became the founding home of The National Theatre, until its new theater (see below) was built. The Old Vic is now used to stage some glorious productions of new plays, and it still boasts a rich atmosphere.

The Olivier
National Theatre, South Bank, SE1 928 2252

The Olivier is the largest theater of the National Theatre Company complex (the other two being the Cottesloe and the Lyttleton). Just up the road from the Old Vic, it showcases a consistently good standard of acting and works by the world's greatest playwrights. It is also able to stage an impressive range of special effects.

The Orange Tree
45 Kew Rd., Richmond, Surrey - 940 3633

This "fringe theater" in back of a pub puts on first-rate productions of European plays that are rarely seen in Britain. Be warned that its seats are very hard.

Royal Court
Sloane Square, SW1 - 730 1745

Ever since its inception as a small local theater occupying a former chapel, the theater on this site has been in the news. In Victorian times it achieved fame as the home of the comedies written by Pinero, and in the first years of this century it staged the plays of Bernard Shaw. Bombed in 1940 and reopened in 1952, the Royal Court next became known as an avant-garde theater under the director-ship of George Devine, who staged the first production of John Osborne's *Look Back in Anger* (1956). The theater hosts productions of new works from both Britain and abroad.

OUT OF LONDON

BATH

SIGHTS

Bath, a mere hour and fifteen minutes from London by train, or two hours by car, is most definitely worth a visit—not only for the beauty of its architecture but for the excellence of its restaurants and shops. A day spent strolling around the city should include an inspection of the magnificent Roman baths, a look at the fine medieval abbey nearby and a visit to the incomparable eighteenth-century streets designed by John Wood and his son, John Wood the Younger: the Circus, Brock Street and the Royal Crescent. You can also visit The Pump Room, where coffee and tea are served to the accompaniment of a string trio, and you can sample the spa water that made Bath such a fashionable center for cures in Roman times as well as during the eighteenth century, when the city became a favorite haunt of the haut monde, who held magnificent balls and gatherings in the town's assembly rooms.

RESTAURANTS & WINE BARS

There are a number of first-class restaurants in Bath as well as lots of wine bars, cafés and pubs. Many of the wine bars set tables outside during the summer, allowing for relaxed alfresco dining.

Clos du Roy
Box House, Box, Wiltshire
(0225) 744447
FRENCH
Open daily noon-2:30 p.m. & 7 p.m.-10 p.m. Closed 2 weeks in Aug. & 2 weeks in Jan.-Feb. All major cards.

The talented Philippe Roy has moved his much-praised restaurant out of Bath a few miles east to Box House, a picturesque three-story Georgian building in the pleasant little village of Box. The meal we enjoyed in one of the three new dining rooms proved that Roy remains an adventurous soul. Besides his à la carte menu, he offers an irresistible fixed-price "menu surprise," which is the main outlet for his showmanship: lobster stuffed with Gruyère and morels, grilled venison on croutons with framboise, pears poached in Champagne and served in a puff pastry case, dates stuffed with pistachios. The accompaniments are simple and superb: exquisite fresh breads and rolls, the most wonderful unsalted French butter you can imagine and an astounding variety of greens—not just lettuce and radicchio but fuschia and pansy leaves, sorrel and salad burnet. Touches like these (and the trou normand—a sorbet interlude swimming in Calvados) are master strokes. The wine list is primarily French, with some fine young Bordeaux and a small selection of Spanish, Californian and Australian wines.

A la carte: £45-£50, including wine. Fixed-price menus: £24.50-£27.50.

Homewood Park Restaurant
Hinton Charterhouse
(0221) 223731
BRITISH
Open daily noon-1:30 p.m. (Sun. to 2 p.m.) & 7 p.m.-9:30 p.m. Closed Dec. 23-Jan. 6. All major cards.

If you can't stay at this elegant, peaceful country house (see "Hotels") set on well-groomed grounds five miles south of Bath, be sure to visit for a meal. You'll be warmly welcomed, installed in a comfortable dining room, and served commendable food. Lunch is a pleasant, fairly simple affair, offering a set three-course meal (£16) that includes a ragoût of scallops and oyster mushrooms and a spiced tomato soup. The dinner menu is longer and more elaborate, but both meals rely heavily on the restaurant's excellent fish. Monkfish is served with an unusual ragoût of leeks, for instance. Game, too, is strongly represented; venison in a rich, gamey sauce with figs, duck breast served with lentils and a cream sauce, and pheasant in a surprisingly subtle horseradish and walnut sauce. The usual selection of tiny new potatoes, crunchy mange-touts (green beans) and zucchini is offered. Desserts are strong on chocolate with such delights as a three-chocolate mousse with crème de menthe, for instance. Good sorbets, an extensive, attractive cheese board, including a number of West Country varieties, and excellent coffee, with homemade petits fours, make for an elegant finish. Badoit mineral water is served throughout the meal to complement the long and interesting wine list, which includes a number of Australian and Californian wines as well as a strong French selection.

A la carte: £40, including wine.

⑭ Lucknam Park Restaurant

Colerne - (0225) 742777

FRENCH

Open daily noon-2:30 p.m. & 7 p.m.-10:30 p.m. All major cards.

Everything about this opulent country hotel radiates elegance, from the 200 handsome acres outside to the impeccably furnished bedrooms inside. Yet the greatest treasure of Lucknam Park might very well be its brilliant young chef, Anthony Blake, whose cooking is both flamboyant and confident. His six-course gourmet fixed-price menu includes an exquisite carpaccio, duck breast with bacon, veal on a bed of creamed leeks, and an almost perfect melon sorbet. The à la carte menu is equally inventive, offering parfait of goose liver with poached apples and asparagus, lobster mousse wrapped in spinach, and brill and salmon braids with a Champagne sauce. The wine list is eclectic, to say the least, but the cheese board is almost exclusively British. The hotel has two dining rooms, which are open to non-residents for lunch and dinner. The larger of the two dining rooms is spacious, perhaps too spacious for comfort, and decorated in rather dull and muted colors, more suited to a conference than an intimate gathering. We prefer the smaller dining room (which seats 40), a plush, ornately decorative setting.

A la carte: £40-£50, including wine.

10/20 Moon and Sixpence

6A Broad St. - (0225) 60962

BRITISH/WINE BAR

Open daily noon-2:30 p.m. & 5:30 p.m.-10:30 p.m. Cards: AE, MC, V.

Centrally situated, this wine bar is particularly attractive during the summer months, when meals are served in the flower-filled courtyard, with its fountain murmuring in the background. The main selection is from an assortment of cold salads, smoked-fish pâtés, quiches and pies. Upstairs, a restaurant offers a more formal menu, with such main courses as filet of lamb with a red-currant and garlic sauce and stir-fried pork with peppers, water chestnuts and zucchini. A glass of Pimms costs £1.45.

A la carte: £18, including wine. Fixed-price menus: £9.75-£10.75.

12/20 Popjoy's

Sawclose - (0225) 60494

BRITISH

Open Tues.-Fri. noon-2 p.m. & 6 p.m.-10:30 p.m., Sat. 6 p.m.-10:30 p.m. Cards: AE, MC, V.

Slightly overshadowed in recent years by more fashionable newcomers, this pleasant, genteel restaurant beside the theater nevertheless has a lot to offer, including good value. Upon ringing the brass doorbell of the elegant Georgian townhouse, you are admitted cordially. Apéritifs and coffee may be taken in the attractive upstairs drawing room, which has a fire in winter, a sweep of floor-length floral curtains hiding a series of elegant windows along the street wall, comfortable, nonshowy period furniture (the only jarring elements are the small, modern pine-block tables) and a discreet little bar at one end.

The manager, Mark Heather, dispenses cocktails and brings plates of workmanlike appetizers—little pâté à choux made with cream cheese and chives, tartlettes of smoked fish and so on. Most likely, an adjacent party will include locals entertaining foreign visitors, which means you'll probably overhear stories of Georgian-era Bath (Julian Popjoy, a courtesan, was the mistress of Beau Nash, Bath's famous society master of ceremonies). Downstairs is the dining room, which, in terms of dimensions and decor (deep-red walls, white woodwork, chandeliers, oil paintings), is slightly heavier and less relaxing than the upper room.

The food is pretty good, though certain items promise more than they deliver. Two of the sauces we tried were rather humdrum: lemon, thyme and leek cream with ravioli of rabbit (delicious filling, rather flaccid pasta) and a coarse brown shellfish sauce served with an excellent crisp feuilleté of lobster and finely diced greens. Main courses typically consist of well-chosen, well-prepared meat or fish with competent and imaginative accompaniments: perfectly cooked, tasty grouse with a disappointingly weak pistachio mousse in a pastry shell, six plump ribs of fine lamb with a herb-mustard crust and an anemic pearl barley and vegetable "broth" sauce. Desserts are similarly hit-and-miss: a chocolate combination of an excellent rich, mousse-like "truffle cake" and a dull sponge cake in a pleasant nutmeg-flavored crème anglaise, along with a nice warm tartlette of autumn fruits in a sabayon glaze. The generally adequate wine list contains the odd find, such as an unusual and enjoyable bottle of moderately priced Beaujolais rosé. All in all, the imperfections are counterbalanced by the ambience and overall quality.

A la carte: £25-£30.

11/20 **Woods**

9-13 Alfred St. - (0225) 314812
FRENCH
Open Mon.-Sat. noon-2:15 p.m. & 6:45 p.m.-10:15 p.m. Cards: MC, V.

A light and airy room with racing prints on the walls, a blackboard on the far wall (nestled between some old *Spy* magazine cartoons) that lists the specialties of the day and large round pine tables characterize this pleasant restaurant, which offers a more reasonably priced meal than many other Bath restaurants. There are several fixed-price menus; the two-course lunch is a particularly good value. The generous dishes include a saffron-flavored fish soup, a nutty, rough-textured hot mushroom pâté, a spicy lamb-and-almond casserole and prawns served with a fresh orange butter sauce. In the evening the ambience is a little more formal, with pink linen tableclothes and more elaborate fixed-price dinner menus, which begin with a plate of crudités.

A la carte: £15, including wine. Fixed-price menus: £7.50 (lunch), £10.50 and £12.50 (dinner).

HOTELS

Homewood Park

Hinton Charterhouse - (0221) 223731
Closed Dec. 23-Jan. 6. 15 rooms, TV. All major cards.

Only five miles south of Bath, Homewood Park is an ideal place to stay if you're looking for tranquility and some good food (see "Restaurants"). Built mainly in the eighteenth and nineteenth centuries and set in ten acres of gardens and woods, Homewood offers a charming welcome from its young, enthusiastic owners. All fifteen rooms have private bath-rooms, and the elegant lounge/sitting room, complete with log fire, is guaranteed to provide the atmosphere of a private country house.

Singles: £55-£100; doubles: £85-£100.

Lucknam Park

Colerne - (0225) 742777
Open year-round. 30 rooms, 9 suites, tennis, croquet, spa. All major cards.

Lucknam Park is the province of lavish cars and the result of great expense—more than £4 million reputedly went into its recent refurbishment, which transformed a run-down country house into heavenly hotel, located on the edge of the Cotswolds six miles northeast of Bath. Even in an area remarkably well served with grand country hotels, Lucknam Park stands out, set as it is in 200 acres of parkland. From the moment you roll down the avenue of ghostly beech trees and glimpse the wisteria-clad frontage, you know you are in safe hands. Inside, the grand dimensions of the rooms, the subtly varied furnishings and the acres of marble all speak of calm, old-fashioned luxury. And to make the experience thoroughly blissful, the restaurant is outstanding (see "Restaurants").

Doubles: from £100.

Priory Hotel

Weston Rd. - (0225) 331922
Open year-round. 21 rooms, color TV, pool. All major cards.

A little out of the way but worth seeking out, the Priory is the most attractive hotel in Bath. There are only 21 guest rooms, and each has a private bathroom and color TV. Extras include a restaurant and a lovely garden with terraces and a pool.

Singles: from £60.50; doubles: up to £99, including Continental breakfast.

Royal Crescent Hotel

Royal Crescent - (0225) 319090
Open year-round. 45 rooms, color TV. All major cards.

Magnificently located in the center of Bath's most famous crescent, this ultra-luxurious hotel was recently refurbished. It boasts four-poster beds, antique furnishings and an eye-catching sixteenth-century tapestry from Brussels. The amenities include a whirlpool, a croquet field and an elegant garden.

Doubles: £110-£155; suites: £205-£230.

BRIGHTON

SIGHTS

Only an hour by train from London, Brighton was a town that witnessed immense prosperity in Regency times (1820–1837) and is now a center for the most civilized of entertainments, including the Brighton Festival (in May), at which many celebrated stars of classical music perform, including such talents as Yehudi Menuhin, André Previn and James Galway. Brighton's rise to fame was as a sort of late-eighteenth-century Saint-Tropez, where the beautiful people and their hangers-on came to have fun. Royal patronage by the Prince of Wales (who later became Regent and then King George IV) boosted it into the stratosphere of chic. In the 1820s it was the most fashionable town in Europe. Its social cachet faded gradually after 1840, when the railway drew in the masses, but it has never been entirely abandoned by the style makers and VIPs, and Brighton still holds an astonishingly broad appeal. Its raffish character makes it a popular home for actors, media people and antiques dealers.

Brighton's Regency buildings—painted stucco with lots of classical ornaments, canopied bow windows and pretty ironwork—set the tone, but the ocean wind makes maintenance a nightmare. The town's two grand set pieces are found on the two streets located at either end of the seafront: Lewes Crescent in Kemptown and Brunswick Square to the west (actually in the neighboring town of Hove). From the comfortable cafés and bars of the recently revived Palace Pier, the view of the West Pier against the atmospheric Channel skies can be magical. In the fascinating and well-kept Clifton Hill area, a short way up from the middle of Brighton, lies the picturesque core of the old fishing town, known now as the Lanes, full of every kind of antiques shop and boutique. And below the fine Victorian train station is an area bubbling with specialty shops and youthful enterprises.

Above all, what makes Brighton worth a visit is the Royal Pavilion, the Prince Regent's seaside palace in the middle of the town, which between 1787 and 1823 grew from a farmhouse into one of the world's great fantasy buildings, with its Indian domes and minarets on the outside and colorful, spectacular chinoiserie inside. The banqueting room alone is a brilliant coup de theâtre.

RESTAURANTS

Neither Brighton's inhabitants nor its visitors have been effective in calling forth more than a few restaurants of interest. Middle- to lower-rank establishments proliferate like weeds after rain, but good ones tend to come and go like rare mushrooms. Below are the town's best representatives.

9/20 D'Arcy's
29 Market St. - (0273) 25560
SEAFOOD
Open Mon.-Sat. noon-3 p.m. & 7:30 p.m.-10:30 p.m., Sun. 7:30 p.m.-10:30 p.m. All major cards.

Tucked into an old fisherman's cottage on Market Street, D'Arcy's epitomizes much of Brighton's more pretentious eating establishments—coy and cottagey rather than stylish. The starters include a good bisque, and though the ballotine of halibut with shrimp sauce was insipid, the scallops with mange-touts (green beans) had a proper balance of flavor, texture and color. Halibut reared its head again among the main dishes, as did sole and monkfish, which were fresh and adequately if somewhat unimaginatively cooked, served with a good selection of fresh vegetables. From the limited dessert offerings, the chocolate mousse was about as light and fluffy as a piece of Brighton Rock, and the crème caramel aroused no comment. From a serviceable wine list we chose a white Pinot Grigio.

A la carte: £25, including wine.

10/20 Food for Friends
17A-18 Prince Albert St., The Lanes
(0273) 202310
VEGETARIAN
Open Sun.-Thurs. 9 a.m.-10 p.m., Fri.-Sat. 9 a.m.-11 p.m. Cards: V.

Right in the center of town is this paradise for vegetarians. Restaurateur Simon Hope's seemingly inexhaustible inventiveness and eclecticism make his vegetarian restaurant one of the most popular eateries in Brighton—even for carnivores. And its prices are excellent. Visiting vegetarians shouldn't miss it.

A la carte: £5-£8.

12/20 **Old Ship Hotel**

Kings Rd. - (0273) 29001
FRENCH/BRITISH
Open Sun.-Thurs. 12:30 p.m.-2:30 p.m. & 7 p.m.-9:30 p.m., Fri.-Sat. 12:30 p.m.-2:30 p.m. & 7 p.m.-10 p.m. All major cards.

Given the Old Ship's oceanfront setting, it's no surprise that much of its cuisine is drawn from the deep. Bendt Schroeder is a capable chef who makes good use of the local seafood, and he prepares a four-course fixed-price dinner menu for £16.50 that includes some imaginative dishes, including a starter of smoked-halibut-and-pink-peppercorn terrine with an avocado purée. The second course usually brings you a cream of celery soup or a generous dish of moules (mussels) marinière, which contains perhaps a little too much cream but is nonetheless delicious. Main courses include such local specialties as roast Sussex turkey with mushrooms in a red wine and shallot sauce and grilled fresh salmon with a saffron, chive and cucumber sauce; all entrées are served with plenty of vegetables. The good selection of desserts includes a faultless crème caramel, never an easy dish to perfect in a large hotel kitchen, and the well-chosen wine list holds many good bottles of Burgundy. Service is friendly but a little uncertain; the Saturday night live music from the bar next door is somewhat intrusive; but the old-world charm and elegance of the place make up for little imperfections. (Also see "Hotels.")

A la carte: £25, including wine.

12/20 **Swan's**

21 Norfolk Sq. - (0273) 721211
FRENCH/BRITISH
Open Tues.-Sun. 7:30 p.m.-10 p.m. All major cards.

Swan's comes to the rescue of Brighton visitors whose stomachs don't want to risk disappointment. About three or so years ago, Graham Swan and Ron Ulyatt settled down to providing well-composed fixed-price menus that, while neither recherché nor particularly thrilling, offer fully mastered dishes—this is accomplished cooking that seems virtually effortless. A starter of mussels and prawns on a bed of pasta with an onion-herb-garlic sauce was perfectly prepared. So was the chicken livers on a bed of mange-touts (green beans). Neither could we fault the roast poussin (baby chicken) with honey and almonds and the lamb's kidneys in a sauce of wine, mushrooms and cream. Desserts range from a superior bread-and-butter pudding to an unexceptional chocolate mousse. The wine list is, like everything else, thoughtful and an impressively good value, though some of the vintages are still rather young. And the prices of the three-course dinners are hard to beat. When we add that the presentation is impeccable and the service is provided by the proprietors, who communicate the pleasure they take in their pastel place (which is cool, neat and handsome, like its customers), you'll understand why reservations are well advised.

Fixed-price menus: £11.95 and £13.95.

HOTELS

Old Ship Hotel

Kings Rd. - (0273) 29001
Open year-round. 24 suites, 130 rooms, color TV. All major cards.

Among the many hotels along the oceanfront, the Old Ship is almost certainly the oldest. Dating back, in parts, to the sixteenth century, it was a popular rendezvous during the Regency period, when assemblies held in the ballroom several times a week were attended by the beau monde of the Brighton season. The hotel, of course, has since been enlarged and modernized, but the magnificent ballroom is still used for functions and conferences. The suites and bedrooms, many with wonderful views of the ocean and Brighton's two piers, are quite comfortably furnished. See "Restaurants" for details on the restaurant.

Singles: £55; doubles: £75; suites: £115.

Restaurant prices are for a complete three-course meal for one person, including tip. Wine is included only when noted.

CAMBRIDGE

SIGHTS

Described by noted travel writer Arthur Eperon as "a city for strolling and browsing," Cambridge has its own distinct atmosphere, created by the university and college buildings set in some of Britain's most beautiful countryside. And Cambridge is a mere 54 miles from London, less than two hours by train or car.

Most tourists descend on the city in summer, when most of the university's students are temporarily out of residence (off campus), earning extra money in their local supermarkets, acting as couriers or trekking through the world's least accessible regions. Visitors in the summer, therefore, will have to concentrate on the physical environment. Cambridge is a city of open spaces, mercifully spared from heavy industry, where the colleges stagger under the weight of flowers and greenery, where head porters are greeted with as much respect as if they were professors of mathematics, and where the buildings sit sweetly in ancient settings—even those that date from this century.

The beginnings of Cambridge University are uncertain, but teachers and students may have been present as early as 1200. Some certainly arrived in 1209 from Oxford, after riots there that followed the hanging of three students; they found a town that had been colonized first by the Romans, then by the Anglo-Saxons, then by the Danes. (Indeed, the church of St. Bene't, which was started in 1025 and is the oldest building in the city, still has its Anglo-Saxon tower.)

You can wander around the colleges free of charge, but there may be some exhibits or buildings that will charge a small entrance fee. The hours that the colleges are open to the public are usually prominently displayed by the porters' lodges. These do vary, however, so make sure to check first. For general information about the university, including opening hours, call (0223) 874000.

THE COLLEGES

Following the Norman Conquest of 1066, several small monastic houses were established in and around Cambridge, some of which were to evolve into colleges in the next century. The students were only 14 or 15 years old, and brawls with local townspeople were an everyday occurrence. So in 1231 Henry III issued a decree that all students should be under the control of a master. During the following two centuries, however, relations between the Crown, the university and the city continued to deteriorate, and particular difficulties arose when Henry VIII demanded that his marriage to Catherine of Aragon be declared invalid, which the Catholic Church, of course, opposed. Eventually, the university gave way to Henry's demand and broke with the Church. All things considered, Henry was responsible for more good than harm, founding Trinity College in 1546 and creating chairs for civil law, physics, Hebrew and Greek. Erasmus, the great humanist and teacher, also came to Cambridge at that time.

The best time to visit the colleges is at the end of the academic year, during May Week, which actually takes place in June. Festivities, concerts and May Balls are held, and you shouldn't miss the intercollegiate rowing races, known as the Bumps. Degree ceremonies take place later in June for graduating students.

You should allow at least a full day to visit the colleges. If you don't have time for everything, the most outstanding ones are **St. John's, Trinity, Clare, King's, Queens', Corpus Christi, Peterhouse** and **Jesus**, but all are charming and interesting in their own way.

To the north of the city is **Magdalene College** (pronounced *Maudlin*), which was founded in 1542 by Lord Audley, the Lord Chancellor of England. Some of its early buildings have been altered; for example, the sixteenth-century Dining Hall was rebuilt in the eighteenth century. If you have time, step into First Court's picturesque library, which contains a magnificent collection of books and manuscripts bequeathed to the college in 1703 by diarist Samuel Pepys, a former Magdalene student.

Crossing the Cam by Magdalene Bridge and traveling south down Bridge Street, you come to the Church of the Holy Sepulchre. Dating from the beginning of the twelfth century, it is one of only four round churches still existing in England. Opposite the church is **St. John's College**, founded in 1511 by Lady Margaret Beaufort, mother of Henry VII, on the site of a hospital that dates from the thirteenth century. Enter its First Court through a richly decorated gateway that bears the ornate, gilded coat of arms of the foundress and is surmounted by a statue of St. John the Evangelist. The chapel is nineteenth century, but the hall dates from the sixteenth century and contains its original hammerbeam roof. The Second Court has well-preserved buildings of Elizabethan brick; on entering the Third Court you can glimpse on the second floor the Old Library, built during the seventeenth century. You'll next encounter The Bridge of Sighs, built in 1831, which links the older and newer parts of the college. New Court provides a look at the Cambridge Backs (the grounds between the colleges and the Cambridge River). Some of St. John's famous former students include Charles Darwin, William Wordsworth and Samuel Butler.

Next to St. John's is **Trinity College**—with more than 700 students, it's the largest in Cambridge—a result of the amalgamation by Henry VIII in 1546 of King's Hall and Michaelhouse, both founded in the fourteenth century. It is the only college whose master is appointed by the Crown. Its principal gateway, which houses statues of Henry VIII, James I and Anne of Denmark (and their son), leads to the Great Court, which was constructed between 1597 and 1605 under the supervision of the master at that time, Thomas Neville. Then the largest court in either Oxford or Cambridge, it boasts a most beautiful octagonal fountain fed by pipes originally installed by the monks. To the south is a statue of Queen Elizabeth I, and on the north side lies the Tudor chapel, home of a fine statue of Sir Isaac Newton by Roubiliac. The hall, the largest in Cambridge, has a hammerbeam roof, contemporary paneling and, in back, a vast kitchen that dates from 1605. Next you'll pass into Neville's Court (completed in 1614), where you'll find the library, built by Sir Christopher Wren between 1676 and 1685 and one of the most famous in England. It contains decorative carvings in limewood as well as some interesting statuary, notably one of Lord

Byron. Famous former Trinity college students have included Alfred Lord Tennyson, Lord Byron, Thomas Babington Macaulay, Isaac Newton and Jawaharlal Nehru.

After Trinity, you'll come to **Gon**ville and Caius College (pronounced *Keys*), founded by Edmund Gonville in 1348, then refounded and enlarged by Dr. Caius in 1557 (which explains the college's medical tradition). Its main features of architectural interest are the three gates that symbolize the three stages in a student's life: the Gate of Humility, the Gate of Virtue and the Gate of Honour; this last one leads to Senate House Passage, where the worthy student finally receives his degree. This passage continues on to Old Schools, which began life as university lecture rooms in the Middle Ages, were altered and enlarged in the eighteenth century and now house the university's administration. The Senate House, built between 1722 and 1730, is the seat of Cambridge's university government. Just beyond that is Trinity Hall, founded in 1350 by the Bishop of Ely to help fill the vacancies in clergy trained in civil and canon law that had occurred because of the Black Death two years earlier. It has been restored and enlarged, but its original medieval character can still be found in the little court that abuts Garret Hostel Lane.

South of Trinity Hall stands **Clare College**, first founded in 1326 and much altered in 1346 by Lady Elizabeth of Clare, a granddaughter of Edward I. The present seventeenth-century buildings replaced the original ones, which were destroyed by fire. You'll get a fine view of the college and gardens as you cross Clare Bridge, which dates from 1640 and is the oldest bridge in Cambridge. The wrought-iron gates are also particularly good examples of the craftsman's skill; they were constructed in 1715.

King's College was founded by Henry VI in 1440. In 1443, the college received a charter that provided for a provost, 10 priests, 6 clerks, 16 choristers and 70 scholars, at that time the largest college by far in the university. Its chapel, built in the years from 1446 to 1515, has an unforgettable interior, with fan vaulting and stained-glass windows (the most complete set to survive from Henry VIII's time). The quality of the carving in the wooden screen and choir stalls is also superb—some say unsurpassed anywhere in Europe north of the Alps.

Rubens's masterpiece, *The Adoration of the Magi*, now adorns the chapel as an altarpiece; it was given to the college in 1961.

St. Catharine's College, next to King's, was founded in 1473 by the then-provost of King's, but its present buildings date from the seventeenth century and later. Across from St. Catharine's is **Corpus Christi College**, which was founded in 1352 by two of the town guilds—which is particularly interesting because it shows that the benefits of education were beginning to be perceived not only by kings, bishops and nobles but by ordinary townsfolk as well. Corpus Christi's Old Court gives a good idea of what the medieval colleges looked like, and the library in New Court contains a famous collection of Anglo-Saxon and later illuminated manuscripts. Christopher Marlowe was one of the many famous Corpus Christi alumni.

Returning to St. Catharine's, farther down Trumpington Street, if you turn onto Silver Street and then right onto Queens' Lane, you will discover **Queens' College**. Queens' was founded three times, first in 1446 by the rector of St. Botolph's Church, then again in 1448 by Margaret of Anjou, wife of Henry VI, who was no doubt trying to emulate her husband's founding of King's. Finally, in 1465, it came under the patronage of Elizabeth Woodville, wife of Edward IV. The college is therefore called Queens', not Queen's. It is the most complete and intimate example of a Cambridge college. The First Court of red brick was completed in 1449. The Great Gatehouse fronting Queens' Lane contains the rooms used by Erasmus. Cloister Court, as its name suggests, has cloister arcades in brick; it also contains the President's Lodging, with its splendid half-timbered Gallery. To the west lies the Mathematical Bridge, built in 1749 and so called because its structure is held together without nails.

Farther down Trumpington Street toward the Fitzwilliam Museum is **Peterhouse**, the oldest of the Cambridge colleges, founded in 1281 by Hugh of Balsham, Bishop of Ely, to house a master and fourteen students. Most of the buildings forming the college today date from the Restoration, and alteration work carried out in the eighteenth and nineteenth centuries.

Crossing Trumpington Street and returning back to the town, you'll arrive at **Pembroke College** (on the corner of Pembroke Street), which was founded in 1347 by Mary de Valence, Countess of Pembroke. Its original chapel was converted into a library when Sir Christopher Wren designed the present chapel, which was erected in 1663, thus giving Cambridge its first purely classical building.

As Pembroke Street continues its name changes to Downing Street. At the far end of Downing Street is **Emmanuel College**, founded in 1584 by Sir Walter Mildmay, then Chancellor of the Exchequer, on the site of a Dominican priory. Construction was completed on the chapel, also designed by Sir Christopher Wren, in 1674. The college has some fine gardens you can walk through.

Continuing toward the center of the town, you'll come to **Christ's College**, founded in 1505 by Lady Margaret Beaufort, who also founded St. John's six years later. Her coat of arms is splendidly carved on the gatehouse. John Milton was a student here.

Beyond Christ's and onto Sidney Street is **Sidney Sussex College**, founded in 1594 by Lady Frances Sidney, Countess of Sussex, on the site of a friary. To this day the college retains its connections with the Sidney family—the present head of the family, Sir William Philip Sidney, Viscount de L'Isle, holds the position of Hereditary Visitor of the college. Most of the college's buildings were altered in the nineteenth century. The gardens were first landscaped in the eighteenth century and are among the finest in Cambridge. The chapel also dates from the eighteenth century, with some later additions. Oliver Cromwell, who arrived here in 1616, was one of Sidney's better-known students.

Turning onto Jesus Lane, we arrive at **Jesus College**, founded in 1496 by John Alcock, Bishop of Ely; the college symbol of a cockerel is derived from his name. Jesus College was built on the site of a suppressed Benedictine nunnery, St. Radegond. The chapel has a mid-thirteenth-century chancel, a fine painted ceiling and stained-glass windows designed by the pre-Raphaelite artists Sir Edward Burne-Jones. Other parts of the old nunnery, notably the cloisters and chapter house, have also been incorporated into the college's buildings. Famous students have included Samuel Taylor Coleridge and Thomas Malthus.

MUSUEMS

Cambridge and County Folk Museum

2 Castle St. - (0223) 355159

Open Tues.-Fri. 10:30 a.m.-5 p.m., Sat. 10:30 a.m.-1 p.m. & 2 p.m.-5 p.m., Sun. 2:30 p.m.-4:30 p.m.

Housed in the old White Horse Inn, which dates from the sixteenth century, this museum presents exhibits that show the life, work and history of the area's people from medieval times to the early twentieth century.

Fitzwilliam Museum

Trumpington St. - (0223) 69501

Lower Galleries: open Tues.-Sat. 10 a.m.-2 p.m.; Upper Galleries: open daily 2 p.m.-5 p.m.

The Lower Galleries contain classical antiquities, manuscripts, textiles, ceramics, glass, armor, coins and applied arts, while the the Upper Galleries house paintings, sculpture, furniture and a fine collection of fans. Elsewhere in the building are a good shop and an attractive tearoom where tea, coffee, cakes and light lunches are served.

Scott Polar Research Institute

Lensfield Rd. - (0223) 66499

Open Mon.-Sat. 2:30 p.m.-4 p.m.

Interesting exhibits on polar exploration and life in polar regions can be found at this institute's museum.

RESTAURANTS

At last there are signs that Cambridge's years in the gastronomic wilderness may be coming to an end. Several restaurants have recently opened with menus of interest to the discerning, though they tend to be located outside of the parts of the city usually frequented by the casual visitor. A couple of exceptions are included below, along with the more notable of the town's many pubs and wine bars, which serve a wide range of pub grub, such as sandwiches, meat pies, pasties, rolls and Scotch eggs.

12/20 Midsummer House

Midsummer Common - (0223) 69299

BRITISH

Open Tues.-Fri. noon-2 p.m. & 6:30 p.m.-9:30 p.m., Sat. 6:30 p.m.-9:30 p.m., Sun. noon-2 p.m. Cards: DC, MC, V.

This new restaurant is removed from the city center, beside the river, close to the college boathouses and next door to the Fort St. George pub (see below). Perseverence in tracking it down will be well rewarded. A stylishly converted and enlarged river-keeper's cottage (where the man hired to maintain river property lived), Midsummer House serves cuisine of a kind new to Cambridge, and therefore greatly welcomed. The three- and five-course fixed-price menus change every three weeks, depending on the season. Typical starters are fresh noodles in a light cream sauce with sweetbreads and shrimp, or forest mushrooms in parsley sauce en croûte. You may choose from five or six main courses, perhaps including pigeon breasts with a mousse of foie gras braised in cabbage and mushrooms, or salmon in a tangy Champagne sauce with glazed leeks. Nouvelle cuisine–style vegetables are served with entrées. Desserts are works of art: a mousse of white and dark chocolate, a terrine of autumn fruits with Bordeaux in a vanilla sauce and a dark chocolate cake with a Champagne sabayon. Coffee and petits fours are £1.50 extra. The substantial wine list includes a fair selection of half bottles but tends to be on the expensive side. Ask for a table upstairs, where the character of the nineteenth-century rooms is charmingly preserved. Reservations are essential.

A la carte: £20-£30, including wine. Fixed-price menus: £17.50 and £25.

10/20 Restaurant Angeline

8 Market Passage - (0223) 60305

FRENCH

Open Mon.-Sat. noon-2:30 p.m. & 6 p.m.-11 p.m., Sun. noon-2:30 p.m. All major cards.

Tucked away next to the Arts Cinema, this pleasant, comfortable upstairs restaurant is a great place for the connoisseur of rooftop views. It has a separate bar/lounge and a comprehensive wine list. At lunchtime the daily specials are displayed on a chalkboard; typical examples are monkfish stew, lamb cutlets with a fresh, spicy pepper sauce and quiche with leeks and ham, all of which run

£3.40, including a glass of wine. A more extensive range of dishes is available in the evenings, both from the à la carte menu and from the list of nightly specialties, and a selection of homemade sweets or cheeses of a more conventional nature rounds off the meal.

A la carte: £10.

PUBS & WINE BARS

Brown's Restaurant
23 Trumpington St. - (0223) 461655
Open Mon.-Sat. 11 a.m.-11:30 p.m., Sun. noon-11:30 p.m.

This is Brown's third branch, the other two being in Oxford and Brighton. Located conveniently close to the Fitzwilliam Museum, it is light, airy, noisy and crowded, with hardly any diners under the age of 30. A wide range of dishes is available from both the standard menu and daily blackboard specials: pastas, numerous salads and a memorable chicken pie. Sandwiches are substantial. A meal, including wine, will run £10 or more.

Fort St. George Public House
Midsummer Common - (0223) 354327
Open daily noon-2 p.m. & 6 p.m.-9:30 p.m.

Good soups and hot and cold daily specialties like salads, sandwiches, quiche, savory pies and sausage rolls are served in this picturesque sixteenth-century pub catering mostly to vegetarians. The outdoor bar is popular in summer, as is the attractive garden.

Shades Wine Bar
1 King's Parade - (0223) 354907
Open Tues.-Sat. 11:30 a.m.-2:30 p.m. & 6 p.m.-11 p.m.

Shades has an engagingly informal atmosphere, a good selection of wines by the glass and an appealing assortment of salads, cold meats, pies, fish and meat pâtés and the like. More substantial dishes, including steaks and casseroles, are served upstairs in the small, charming restaurant.

HOTELS

Garden House
Granta Pl., off Mill Ln. - (0223) 63421
Open year-round. 117 rooms. All major cards.

Most pleasantly located in gardens beside the river, this modern hotel has by no means broken new ground in the decoration of its rooms. Nonetheless, it is quite comfortable and has attractive reception rooms. Some of the guest rooms have river views.

Singles: £63-£68; doubles: £75-£80, including Continental breakfast.

University Arms
Regent St. - (0223) 351241
Open year-round. 115 rooms. All major cards.

This old, Edwardian-style hotel is located right next to Fenners' cricket pitch, a ten-minute walk from the colleges. It has been entirely renovated, but though the rooms are large, comfortable and equipped with bathrooms, the decor is uninspired.

Singles: £42; doubles: £57, including English breakfast.

HAMPTON COURT

SIGHTS

Hampton Court Palace
(01) 977 8441

A little more than eight miles southeast of London, Hampton Court Palace is rich with great historical and architectural interest, not to mention the numerous artistic masterpieces it houses; it's well worth the short out-of-town trip.

Ministers and nobles should never build palaces for themselves that are larger and more handsome than those of the monarch. This precept was foolishly ignored by Cardinal

Thomas Wolsey during the sixteenth century, to his great regret. In 1514 Wolsey, a minister to Henry VIII, purchased a former priory that belonged to the order of St. John of Jerusalem, admirably located on the banks of the Thames. He decided to turn it into a sumptuous palace unlike any other, a foolish idea given the hot-blooded nature of his ruler. When the construction was well under way, some fifteen years later, the intemperate monarch issued a stern request that the esteemed minister kindly make him a gift of the splendid building—or else. And by that time the king had already taken up the hobby of removing the heads of those who displeased him.

Once the "gift" was made, Henry VIII tore down part of what had been constructed, and added several wings to the building. He installed a tennis court, the oldest surviving court in the world. With its 1,000 rooms, Hampton Court Palace became the most sovereign of residences, which it remained until the death of George II in 1760.

Signs marked with arrows placed around the buildings will help you find your way without too much difficulty. We can't possibly describe everything of interest about the palace so we'll limit ourselves to some notes about our favorite features.

From the Great Gatehouse at the entrance, a passage leads to the Base Court, decorated with terra cotta medallions that date from the sixteenth century. At the back, the Anne Boleyn Gateway leads to the Clock Court, where you'll find an astronomical clock built in 1540 for Henry VIII. On the right is the colonnade constructed a century later by Sir Christopher Wren, from which you can enter the state apartments to view their magnificent collection of furniture, paintings and tapestries.

Worthy of particular note are Cardinal Wolsey's apartments; the painting, *Holy Family*, by Correggio in the Audience Chambers; works by Holbein in the King's Dressing Room; and in the nearby Queen's Closet Room, *The Massacre of the Innocents* by Brueghel the Elder and *Adam and Eve* by Cranach. The Brussels tapestries, modeled after cartoons by Charles Lebrun depicting the story of Alexander the Great, decorate the Queen's Gallery; in the Queen's Private Chamber hang several fine Flemish paintings, including *The Garden of Eden* by Brueghel. The King's Gallery houses several paintings by

Holbein and more Brussels tapestries, these based on cartoons by Raphael. In the Communication Gallery you can view *The Windsor Beauties* by Sir Peter Lely, and in the Haunted Gallery, the ghost of Catherine Howard (Henry VIII's sixth) is said to dwell. Close beside it stands the handsome chapel where Henry VIII secretly (and successively) married Catherine Howard and Catherine Parr. Finally, a staircase leads you to the Great Hall, built by Henry VIII himself and the site of his famous banquets. It later became a theater where, among others, Shakespeare's troupe performed. From here you can go onto the cellar of Henry VIII, and then to the immense Tudor kitchen.

These are just some of the sights to look out for. There is still the Banqueting House and, even more interesting, the Lower Orangery, where Andrea Mantegna's series of nine tempera paintings, *The Triumph of Julius Caesar*, is exhibited. Executed between 1485 and 1492 for Francesco Gonzaga, the Duke of Mantua, this series was purchased in 1628 by Charles I. And try to make time to visit the Chapel Royal, a building that dates to 1135 (though it was not until 1529 that Henry VIII took over the lease that had been granted to Cardinal Wolsey by the Knights Hospitallers of St. John of Jerusalem). Henry added many of its elegant features, including a new vaulted roof. Though many monarchs since the sixteenth century have deserted Hampton Court Palace for other venues, the Chapel Royal remains a most rewarding building to visit.

The palace's gardens were originally created by Cardinal Wolsey in a blend of Dutch, French and Italian styles. The rose garden is located in the Tilt Yard, where the knights jousted, and on the south side of the palace are the formal Tudor gardens. The Great Vine, planted in 1769, still produces some 600 bunches of grapes each season. Other features include Wren's Chestnut Avenue and Broad Walk, the Wilderness, the Great Fountain, the Pond and the Privy Gardens. And don't forget the celebrated Maze, which was planted for William and Mary with hornbeam, cypress and flowering shrubs; holly and privet were added later. It is said that when you are fed up with being "lost" in the Maze, if you turn twice to the right, then keep going left, you just might make it home in time for tea (sorry if we ruined it for you).

OXFORD

"Oxford is on the whole more attractive than Cambridge to the ordinary visitor; and the traveler is therefore recommended to visit Cambridge first, or to omit it altogether if he cannot visit both," wrote Karl Baedeker (founder of the first series of modern guidebooks) in 1887. Much has changed in the century since the publication of his famous travel guide, but one thing that even the most fervent advocate of Cambridge must admit is that during the last 30 years, Oxford has been much better favored with good restaurants and hotels.

SIGHTS

Close to London (58 miles) and well served by fast trains and buses, Oxford is an architectural feast boasting almost every architectural style, from Saxon church towers to modern student accommodations. What's more, Oxford is of manageable (even walkable) size. It hums with intellectual effort, strains with sporting competition, bustles with cultural activity (music, drama, opera, ballet, film) and is teeming with industrial activity, from the ancient craft of printing to the making of automobiles. It is a city in which young minds are enriched by ancient buildings—their architecture and history—which are in turn given life by the enthusiastic students.

Oxford is lucky to enjoy swaths of undeveloped land that run right through the city, primarily following the Cherwell and Isis rivers. These make for most attractive walks through Christ Church Meadow (south), the University Parks (north), Addison's Walk and Angel Meadow (east) and Port Meadow (west), which leads over the Thames to the Perch, a pub that serves lunch.

It wasn't until the tenth century that Oxford became important, first as a road junction and river crossing (a map of England verifies its central location) and later as a meeting place for national councils. William the Conqueror fortified the town and added the castle from which Queen Maud escaped across the snow in 1139. Henry I stayed in Oxford frequently, and his sons Richard Lionheart and John were probably born in Beaumont Palace (at the west end of what is now Beaumont Street).

It is difficult to establish the exact date of the birth of Oxford University. It is known, however, that there was much communication between Oxford and the older University of Paris, which began sending scholars to lecture to Oxford students late in the eleventh century. The cessation of communications with Paris in 1167 (for political reasons) helped to stimulate the university's growth. At present the university is made up of 35 colleges, 8 of which are for graduates only and all but 3 of which are now coed. The largest has about 400 students and the smallest 200, with some 9,000 undergraduates and 3,000 postgraduates altogether. Another 2,500 people—all those in official research, teaching and administrative posts—are members of the university's Congregation (a sort of parliament). Each college is run by a governing body that includes all its fellows (senior lecturers and professors, known as "dons") and its head, who might be called Warden, Principal, Master or President. The fellows elect their head, and the head and fellows elect new fellows. Students are selected by examination (Oxford and Cambridge are alone among English universities in giving their own private entrance examinations). Those who perform best are awarded scholarships, and wear longer gowns.

The university does have its own administration, headed by the vice-chancellor, though the fact that he also remains head of a college reflects the perpetual balance that is maintained between the individual colleges and the university. The university awards degrees and arranges lectures, but it is the colleges that work out the individual study programs over the three or four years of a student's undergraduate life.

The academic year is divided into three terms of eight weeks each: Michaelmas (October to December), Hilary (January to March) and Trinity (April to June). This is short by other university's standards, so a great deal of activity must be packed into these terms, especially in the summer, when examinations as well as numerous social festivities and dramatic activities create an even more frenetic atmosphere. May and June are particularly lovely, lively times to visit Oxford, though an increasing amount of cultural activity is taking place during summer vacation.

As at Cambridge, there is no fee to wander the grounds, but there may be a small fee to enter certain buildings.

THE COLLEGES

A good place to start a tour of Oxford's historic colleges is at Carfax, which means the crossing of the four ways, derived from either the Latin *quadrifurcus* or the French *quatre voies*. Located at the intersection of Queen Street, High Street and St. Aldate's, the tower at Carfax is all that remains of the fourteenth-century Church of St. Martin's, the rest having been demolished in 1896 to relieve traffic congestion. If you're lucky enough to time it right, you'll see the clock's moving figures when it strikes the hour. Walk south for about 50 yards to find the information center across from the Town Hall, which can provide you with maps and details of current goings-on in Oxford.

Continuing down St. Aldate's, you will be met by Tom Tower and **Christ Church**, Oxford's grandest college. The tower, erected by Sir Christopher Wren in 1682, houses a six-ton bell called Great Tom that rings 101 times (one for each foundation member of the college) every night at 9:05 p.m. (five minutes west of Greenwich time). This used to be the signal for all college gates in Oxford to be closed. The grandiose plans of Christ Church's founder, Cardinal Thomas Wolsey, were never entirely realized after his fall from political power. The most striking example of this is the Great Quadrangle (Tom Quad), which, as the remaining plinths and arcades show, was originally intended to be a cloister. Henry VIII dismissed Wolsey but supported his foundation, and in 1546 established the college chapel as Oxford's cathedral, making it one of England's smallest cathedrals and the only one that also administers a college. The cathedral itself (the entry is at the southeast corner of Tom Quad) dates from the twelfth century; notice in particular the solid Norman pillars, though numerous additions have been made over the centuries.

Returning along St. Aldate's, if you turn right on Blue Boar Street and cross Canterbury

Square, you'll arrive at **Corpus Christi College**. Founded in 1517 by the Bishop of Winchester, this small college was one of the first at which Greek was taught. The quad has a pretty sundial (1581) to which a perpetual calendar was added in 1606. Its library is one of the most picturesque in Oxford.

A little farther along Merton Street is **Merton College**. Founded in 1264 by Walter de Merton, a powerful baron, it is one of Oxford's oldest colleges. The hall has a fine thirteenth-century door, and a 1416 porchway decorated with statues of Merton and Henry III leads to Mob Quad, Oxford's oldest quadrangle, with its magnificent, late-thirteenth-century Gothic chapel and the oldest library in England. Don't miss the garden, bounded by the City Wall, which offers a view of Christ Church Meadow. Opposite the entrance to Merton is the tennis court, one of the few courts in England where tennis is played as it was in the age of Henry VIII. The Great Hall, next to the cathedral, is accessible by a fine staircase with a remarkable fan-vaulted ceiling. The huge hall houses a large collection of portraits, including those done of William Penn and C. L. Dodgson, who was a fellow of the college as well as the author of *Alice in Wonderland*, under the pen name of Lewis Carroll. If you have time, walk out through the Memorial Gardens to the Christ Church Meadow and the river, the site of the intercollegiate boat races.

Returning past Corpus Christi up King Edward's Street, you'll emerge opposite **Brasenose College** (see the Brazen Nose knocker behind the High Table in the hall and the nose on the front gate) and the church of St. Mary the Virgin. This has been the university's church since the fourteenth century; its circa-1280 tower affords an excellent view of Oxford. The bishops Latimer, Ridley and Cranmer, all Protestant reformers, were tried there under Catholic Queen Mary in 1555–1566 and subsequently burned at the stake on Broad Street.

Next to the Church is **All Souls College**, founded in 1438 by King Henry VI and dedicated to the victims of the Hundred Years' War. It is the foremost of the graduates-only colleges. A large proportion of the university's full professors in nonscientific subjects are attached to this college, which selects by a tough procedure just a few extremely able fellows each year. The Front Quad hasn't changed since 1443, and on the first floor of its east side is the Old Library, now a lecture room with a light, intricately plastered ceiling on which the bright colors of heraldic shields stand out in the fine plaster molding. At the northern end of the North Quad stands the magnificent Codrington Library.

Opposite All Souls is **University College**, which claims to be the oldest college in Oxford. It was first endowed in 1249, and indeed its claim to have been first founded by King Alfred was upheld in court in the eighteenth century. The memorial to the poet Shelley, who was expelled from the college in 1811 after circulating a pamphlet called *The Necessity of Atheism*, is on the right of the first quad.

Opposite, and a little way down High Street, is the domed gate of **The Queen's College**, so called because of the patronage of the English queens. Like its founder, Robert of Eglefield, many of its students used to come from northern England, and they found it difficult to travel home during short vacations, so a tradition of dinners at Christmas and New Year's evolved. On Christmas Day a boar's head is brought into the dining hall in procession, while on New Year's Day the bursar gives each diner a needle and thread *aiguille et* fil, a pun on the name of the founder.

If you continue west down High Street, you'll pass on the right the **Examination Schools**, focus of considerable attention, anxiety and eventual celebration in early June, during and after the students take their final examinations here. Beyond is an outpost of Stanford University (on the right by the traffic lights).

Across the street is **Magdalen College**, one of the richest and biggest of the Oxford colleges, spreading over 200 acres. Founded in 1458 by William Waynflete, a Bishop of Winchester and Lord Chancellor of England, and with alumni as varied as Cardinal Wolsey and Oscar Wilde, it has enjoyed a mixed history: Though staunchly royalist during the Civil War, it did battle with James II, who wanted to appoint a Roman Catholic as president; in the eighteenth century it sank into a torpor. The eighteenth century did, however, contribute the stately New Building, in 1733, as fine a neoclassical building as any in Oxford. It stands behind the deer park and to the west of the Cherwell River, the water meadows and Addison's Walk, which is at its best when covered in the first flowers of spring. The original college buildings are close to the road and main entrance. The chapel, the cloister with its vaulting and the hall with its early-sixteenth-century linenfold paneling and Jacobean screen merit a visit. But Magdalen's crowning glory is its bell tower that, in its newly cleaned state, shines and gleams as an Oxford landmark. On the morning of May 1 at 6 a.m. the college's choristers sing a Latin hymn, the sound wafting down to the crowds of students who gather below. The choir, one of Oxford's finest, also sings regularly during term. Under Magdalen Bridge punts can be hired, and opposite Magdalen are the Botanic Gardens, with a handsome building and a lovely garden with exotic plants in greenhouses by the river.

Walking back eastward up High Street, turn right onto Queen's Lane just before Queen's College and you'll pass **St. Edmund Hall**, which now holds full college status but until 1957 was the oldest surviving of the residence halls in which Oxford students lived before any colleges were founded (at one time there were 27 such halls on High Street alone). The unassuming entrance leads to a charming quadrangle. On the corner of Queen's Lane is the Church of St. Peter-in-the-East, a Norman building from the first half of the eleventh century, with its fourteenth-century tower. Like a number of churches in Oxford, it is deconsecrated and used as a college library.

As you continue up the lane you will pass the solid Long Room of **New College**, the original house of easement (latrines and cesspool) of that college. Look at the gargoyles on the next building on the right to observe the caricatured physiognomies of New College's recent and current fellows.

Around the corner you can enter New College itself, the first Oxford college to accept undergraduates. It was the newest in Oxford when it was founded in 1379 by William of Wykeham, Bishop of Winchester, who had already founded an affiliated preparatory school in Winchester, from which for 600 years many students have come to New College to continue their education. The chapel is imposing, with fourteenth-century glass, a *Lazarus* by Epstein (best seen from the altar) and an El Greco on the north wall by the altar rail. From two slits in the south wall of the ante-chapel, the warden could observe the proceedings. The quadrangle was the first in Oxford, setting the style for the future with the chapel and hall on one side, living quarters on another, and the library and wardens' lodgings on the two remaining sides. The top story was added in 1675 and fits more easily with the Garden Quad, completed in 1711 and opening out to the garden that is bounded by a section of the original city wall. Beyond this at one time was the city's burial pits for those who died during the plague. Just outside the wall as it turns from west to south, students are now housed in what was the first workshop of William Morris, the English equivalent of Henry Ford. If you exit New College through its northern late-nineteenth-century building you can turn left onto Holywell, an eighteenth-century street where you'll see the oldest music room in Europe (1742), on the right.

The King's Arms Pub, haunt of many students escaping from the nearby libraries, is located at the crossroads. The New Bodleian Library is opposite, with holdings of some five million books. It is linked to the famous Bodleian Library itself by a tunnel under the street. The imposing building on the other corner is the Clarendon Building, erected in 1713 for the University Press from the profits earned from Clarendon's *History of the Great Rebellion*. Although the press is now housed elsewhere, meetings to decide whether or not to publish a book are still held in this building every two weeks during the term.

Next to the Clarendon Building is the Sheldonian Theatre, built as a venue for such secular university functions as degree-bestowing ceremonies, especially the ceremony for honorary degrees at the end of the summer term. The Sheldonian also housed the printing presses of the University Press until they were moved to the Clarendon in 1713. It was paid for by Gilbert Sheldon, then Warden of All Souls, and the plans were drawn up by Sir Christopher Wren; the huge ceiling represents a major engineering feat. The figures surrounding the Sheldonian are emperors and philosophers, and it was last restored in the early 1970s by Michael Black, a local sculptor of international repute.

Next to the Sheldonian is the Old Ashmolean, a marvelous example of late-seventeenth-century architecture. Built in 1683 to house the book collection of famed bibliophile Elias Ashmole, which was subsequently moved to the New Ashmolean, it is now once again

the Museum of the History of Science, home to a splendid collection of astrolabes and other instruments. For information about the museum, call (0865) 278000.

Behind the Clarendon Building is the north wing of the Bodleian Library, one of the oldest, largest and finest in the world. In 1598 a bibliophile named Sir Thomas Bodley decided to establish this library, which was opened in 1602 and later expanded into the present quadrangle. It contains almost two million volumes and thousands of rare manuscripts. A copy of every book published in the U.K. must be deposited there. For information about the library, call (0865) 277000. The door in the Bodleian's west wing leads into the Divinity School, built between 1427 and 1490 in fine perpendicular Gothic style. Here the most famous scholars of the day, including Erasmus, lectured on theology.

South of the Bodleian quadrangle is Radcliffe Square, dominated by the Radcliffe Camera, an imposing building started in 1737 and funded to the tune of £40,000 by Dr. John Radcliffe. It is the oldest round library in England and is used as the history reading room.

On the west side of the square is a lane leading to Turl Street, a covered market full of butchers serving the daily eating requirements of all the colleges. On Turl itself are three colleges: **Lincoln**, founded in 1427 and the college of John Wesley (the founder of Methodism), **Jesus**, founded in 1571 with a strong Welsh connection and the college of Lawrence of Arabia, and **Exeter**, founded in 1314.

Turl emerges onto Broad more or less where Cranmer, Latimer and Ridley were burned at the stake. Opposite is the fine wrought-iron gate of **Trinity College**, founded in 1555 and renowned for its expansive lawns and the handsome Grinling Gibbons carving in its chapel.

Next to Trinity is **Balliol**, one of the leading producers of politicians and colonial administrators. It was founded in 1263 by John of Balliol. Illustrious members of the college have included Adam Smith, Matthew Arnold, Arnold Toynbee, Harold Macmillan, Graham Greene and Edward Heath. Balliol is more distinguished by its alumni than by its uninteresting architecture.

Turning right around Balliol and past St. Mary Magdalen on the left we emerge onto St. Giles, a most handsome boulevard. **St. John's College**, the first on the right, is one of the richest of Oxford's colleges. With its location at the northernmost end of the university at the end of the sixteenth century, it seemed natural for St. John's to purchase the Manor of Walton immediately north of the city. The dons moved to this area when they were first allowed to marry in the mid-nineteenth century and needed houses for their families and servants; most of the streets of North Oxford are owned by St. John's. The early-seventeenth-century Canterbury Quadrangle, with its colonnades, and the garden, with its lawns and rock gardens, are the college's prize exhibits. Opposite St. John's is the Taylorian Institute, built in 1845 with money left by architect Sir Robert Taylor to further the study of modern languages. The institute shares its large site with the Ashmolean Museum, which also houses the Ruskin School of drawing and the Tradescant family collection, which Elias Ashmole inherited and then donated to the university in 1677. The museum also houses an important collection of Greek vases; the unique collection of Minoan art donated by Sir Arthur Evans, who unearthed this civilization at Knossos on Crete; the admirable Asian Arts Room; an Egyptian sculpture gallery that includes antiquities from Tutankhamen's tomb; a wonderful collection of antique jewelry, including the magnificent Alfred (The Great's) Jewel; a fine collection of Michelangelo and Raphael drawings, in addition to fourteen Rembrandt drawings; a selective collection of the works of Pissarro; and notable paintings by Uccello, Renoir, Picasso and Matisse.

At the far end of handsome eighteenth-century Beaumont Street is **Worcester College** and its pretty, three-sided "quadrangle," with fifteenth-century architecture on the south and eighteenth-century on the north and east. If you turn right up Walton Street you'll pass **Ruskin College**, founded originally as a college for older students and now the home (since 1832) of the University Press.

Those interested in neo-Gothic architecture, the pre-Raphaelites, Rhodes Scholarships and/or science should turn north at the King's Arms crossroad. Take a look through the wrought-iron gate at Trinity's magnificent lawns on the left and pass the walled garden of Rhodes House on the right. This is the home of the trust that administers the international Rhodes Scholarships program.

Just ahead to the north are the University Museum on the right and **Keble College**. The museum was built in 1855 from designs by John Ruskin and is strongly influenced by his love for Venice. The exhibits are used primarily for teaching students in zoology, geology and mineralogy, but they also include some vast prehistoric skeletons and the head and foot of a dodo (an extinct, heavy, flightless bird). Attached is the Pitt Rivers Museum, full of anthropological material, a collection based on what was left by General Pitt Rivers in 1885. It also contains some items collected by Captain Cook. Keble College was founded in 1870 as a memorial to John Keble, a cleric who devoted much of his life to the new High Church Anglican theological movement. It is built of red brick, with patterns made of stone and blue and yellow bricks. The chapel contains colored mosaics and a Holman Hunt painting, *The Light of the World.*

To see modern academic architecture look for: **St. Catherine's College**, built in the meadows near where Cherwell River meets Isis River, and **Wolfson College**, a graduate college built on the banks of the River Cherwell in North Oxford. The colleges founded for women students are: **Lady Margaret Hall** (1878), **Sommer**ville (1879), **St. Anne's** (1886) and **St. Hugh's** (1886), all located north of the city center, and **St. Hilda's** (1893), to the east.

RESTAURANTS

12/20 Al-Shami

25 Walton Cres. - (0865) 3110066
LEBANESE
Open daily noon-midnight. No cards.

Making a welcome change from European, Indian or Chinese cuisine, this restaurant offers a tempting range of hors d'oeuvres from the Middle East, either hot or cold, including a variety of spicy sausages and minced meat, tabouli, baba ghanouj and hummus. These dishes come with a huge plate of crudités. Main courses can be bland, except for the marinated ones or those seasoned with lemon juice, but the desserts are delicious. From the adequate wine list, the Lebanese wine is probably the best value, especially the Château Musars.

A la carte: £17, including wine.

10/20 Browns

5-9 Woodstock Rd. - (0865) 51195
BRITISH
Open Mon.-Sat. 11 a.m.-11:30 p.m., Sun. noon-11:30 p.m. No cards.

Airy and light, though often quite full and noisy, Browns is a trendy eating hall for all ages. The food runs to salads, sandwiches (including clubs, BLTs and Reubens), pastas and a fixed-price menu of the day. It's also open for morning coffee and afternoon tea.

A la carte: £10.

12/20 The Cherwell Boathouse

Bardwell Rd. - (0865) 52746
FRENCH
Open Mon. 7:30 p.m.-11:30 p.m., Tues.-Sat. noon-2:30 p.m. & 7:30 p.m.-11:30 p.m., Sun. 1 p.m.-2:30 p.m. & 7:30 p.m.-11:30 p.m. All major cards.

Another Oxford landmark, The Cherwell Boathouse is worth a visit on summer evenings, when Oxford takes its picnics and Champagne onto the river in flat-bottomed punts. If you haven't the courage to try punting, you can watch from the comfort of your dinner table in this unpretentious but attractive room (the other side of the boathouse rents the punts). Its reputation these days rests mainly on its extensive wine list, the result of owner Tony Verdin's passion for wine. Unfortunately, the food is not quite up to the same standard, but it is not without its high points. A fixed-price menu might consist of a choice between a substantial cauliflower soup or profiteroles stuffed with crab mousse to start, followed by roast lamb with a Soubise sauce or escalopes of veal with a ginger wine sauce, lemon soufflé or a butterscotch-cream flan, cheese, fruit and coffee. Some fine wines are on sale at nonexorbitant prices, and the fair house wines cost £4. Reservations are a must.

A la carte: £15-£20, including wine. Fixed-price menu: £12.50.

11/20 Gees

61 Banbury Rd. - (0865) 53540
INTERNATIONAL
Open Mon.-Sat. noon-2:30 p.m. & 6 p.m.-11 p.m., Sun 11 a.m.-4 p.m. Cards: MC, V.

Opened in late 1988, Gees is housed in the spacious greenhouse that formerly belonged to Raymond Blanc's Le Petit Blanc. Among the starters are a flavorsome carpaccio, grilled goat cheese salad and sautéed king prawns; main courses include various types of chicken, salmon, steak and duck. The service is professional and pleasant. Gees is the perfect choice when you want something in between a neighborhood joint and an expensive, fancy place.

A la carte: £15.

Le Manoir aux Quat' Saisons

⑰ Oxfordshire, Great Milton
(0844) 68881
FRENCH
Open Tues. 7:15 p.m.-10:30 p.m., Wed.-Sat. 12:15 p.m.-2:30 p.m. & 7:15 p.m.-10:30 p.m., Sun. 12:15 p.m.-2:30 p.m. Closed Dec. 24-Jan. 21. Cards: MC, V.

Le Manoir is one top-class restaurant that can still boast *le patron mange ici*—though at the prices he charges, owner/chef Raymond Blanc may soon be the only person who can afford to eat here. Blanc's lovely, rambling Cotswold stone manor house has a firmly established international reputation, and the clientele regularly includes American, Japanese and European gourmets who have come to sample what is reputedly England's finest (French) cooking. At the end of the evening, the slim figure of the chef/TV celebrity appears, clad in gleaming white, to make his rounds, chatting with regulars, saying hello to first-time visitors and finally sitting at a corner table for a light supper washed down with his excellent house Sancerre. The house and grounds are beautiful, of course, and the traditional warm, peach-and-cream dining rooms (two connected areas, the larger much more pleasant and with more character than the smaller) are comfortable and elegant enough. The lounge, where one may take apéritifs and coffee, is plush and cozy, with pastel sofas, good paintings and flowers, but its smallness creates a slightly awkward atmosphere; parties sit too close together to be able to ignore one another. The service is expert and unfussy, handled by professional young men in blazers and ties, though it is not perfect: A dry martini was served on the rocks without being so requested. (The little snacks that accompanied it, mainly assorted pastries, and the amuse-gueules of grapefruit, white crab with ginger and avocado that preceded dinner were both relatively mundane.)

Although we have encountered disappointments, the products are of the highest standard, and dishes can be memorable. A starter of tagliatelle with wild freshwater crayfish in a tarragon-scented juice contained some of the best pasta we've ever tasted, in a mild, understated sauce. A dish of plump black morels, the ends "stuffed" with a tangy chicken mousse, came with perfectly cooked young asparagus spears in a rather faint sauce of wine and marc of Gewürztraminer. Beautifully roasted breast of Barbary duckling, its sauce of cooking juices enriched with maize syrup, ginger and lemon, was quite good, but what really stood out was its accompanying "croque" of onions and coriander—a crisp, thin pastry bundle, burnt on top and filled with rich, sticky candied onion. A plate of pan-fried veal kidneys and snails in a sauce of Hermitage red wine was pleasant but nothing more, though the accompanying pungently herbed wild rice was memorable. Cheeses, as well they should be at a place like this, are excellent: a beautifully strong Maroilles, exquisite Brie, good chèvres (the French from Oliver, the English from Rance) and a tasty "twice-baked" soufflé of Cabecou goat cheese served with a hazelnut oil–dressed salad. Desserts include a substantial and exotic Grand Marnier soufflé served hot on a pancake with a fine concentrated sauce of orange butter. The wine list is serious and pricey, but not always cripplingly expensive—choosing a delicious white Côtes-du-Rhône from Jaboulet and a fine Crozes Hermitage kept our bill down to a mere £78 a head.

A la carte: £70-£100.

11/20 Munchy Munchy

6 Park End St. - (0865) 245710
ASIAN
Open Tues.-Sat. noon-2:10 p.m. & 5:30 p.m.-9:40 p.m. No cards.

Tony and Ethel Ow's popular restaurant offers a different choice of spicy or mild Southeast Asian dishes daily. Two or three dishes with rice serves two generously. We suggest you arrive early, for the restaurant is smallish (only 42 seats) and tends to fill up quickly. The Ow's don't have a liquor license, so bring your own wine or beer; corkage is 40p per person. As its fame has increased, so have its prices, but Munchy Munchy still serves some of the most interesting food in Oxford.

A la carte: £10-£12, excluding wine.

10/20 The Nosebag

6 St. Michael St. - (0865) 721033
VEGETARIAN
Open Mon. 9 a.m.-6 p.m., Tues.-Thurs. 9:30 a.m.-10 p.m., Fri.-Sat. 9:30 a.m.-10:30 p.m., Sun. 9 a.m.-6 p.m. No cards.

Our favorites here are the delicious vegetarian lasagne and baked potatoes with a variety of fillings. Good soups, salads, hot dishes, fresh bread and oh-so-tempting desserts are also served in a cafeteria-style upstairs restaurant. The place tends to be a bit noisy at lunchtime, but it is a pleasant spot for a simple meal and a drink.

A la carte: £6-£8.

11/20 Restaurant Elizabeth

84 St. Aldates - (0865) 242230
FRENCH
Open Tues.-Sat. 12:30 p.m.-2 p.m. & 6:30 p.m.-11 p.m., Sun. 12:30 p.m.-2 p.m. & 7 p.m.-10:30 p.m. All major cards.

Twenty-five years ago Oxford's best (and only) French restaurant was the place to be taken for an end-of-term extravagance when wealthy parents came to town. Now owned and run by a charming Spaniard and efficiently staffed by his countrymen, it exudes an air of genteel decline, enlivened with a view of Christ Church. Overshadowed in recent years by its outstanding nouvelle cuisine rival, Le Manoir aux Quat' Saisons, it has nevertheless begun to reestablish itself as a good classic French restaurant. Specialties include delicious light salmon quenelles (a starter) and a good choice of game accompanied by rich but not oversweet sauces. Duck with apricots is served in two stages: The tender breast followed by the crisp leg. Desserts are rich and filling; among the best are a crème brûlée with a pleasingly fluffy custard base, topped by crisp caramel, and a chocolate mousse that is a meal in itself. The cheese selection can be disappointing, but the wine list is excellent (the best value is undoubtedly the old reserve Rioja).

A la carte: £30-£35, including wine.

PUBS

There is an enormous number of pubs in Oxford. According to your mood, try the very busy King's Arms across from the entrance to the New Bodleian, where the undergraduate and graduate worlds meet; the ancient Turf Tavern, tucked away down a passage close to New College; The Bear (dating from 1242) behind Christ Church, with its collection of 3,000 ties, each with the name of a school, college, club or regiment; The Eagle and Child (Bird and Baby) on the west side of St. Giles, where Tolkein and company used to meet; or The Welsh Pony by the bus station, where Dylan Thomas was often drunk. These pubs serve simple, satisfying, very inexpensive food: sandwiches, meat pies, salads, Scotch eggs.

HOTELS

Randolph Hotel
Beaumont St. - (0865) 247481
Open year-round. 109 rooms, color TV. All major cards.
This neo-Gothic Trust House Forte hotel is *the* place to stay in Oxford, though in recent

years it has not been particularly distinguished except for its excellent location at the center of town. We're happy to report that a thorough renovation was begun just as we went to press, so perhaps by the time you read this the formerly bland rooms will have been given new life and charm. Its dining room (built in 1864) is spacious, with huge windows overlooking Beaumont Street, The Ashmolean, Martyr's Memorial and St. Giles. It's a good place for a tasty breakfast or a business meeting; it offers a three-course lunch for £8, afternoon tea and drinks in the warmly paneled bar.
Doubles: from £65, including VAT.

Other hotels in descending order of price are:

Linton Lodge, 13 Linton Rd.
(0865) 53461
Cotswold Lodge, 66A Banbury Rd.
(0865) 512121
The Old Parsonage, 3 Banbury Rd.
(0865) 54843

STRATFORD-UPON-AVON

More than a half million people visit this charming market town every year. They come to see Shakespeare's birthplace, the Memorial Theatre, Ann Hathaway's Cottage and other sites of pilgrimage. They do not, however, come for the food. With a couple of honorable exceptions, dining in Stratford is not a rewarding experience.

SIGHTS

On Henley Street you will find William Shakespeare's birthplace, a double-fronted house bought in 1556 by John Shakespeare. It now houses a museum that includes a Shakespeare first folio from 1623, furniture and paintings from the seventeenth century and other books, manuscripts and prints of the period. Open summers, Monday to Saturday 9 a.m. to 6 p.m., Sunday 10 a.m. to 6 p.m.; winters, Monday to Saturday 9 a.m. to 4:30 p.m., Sunday 1:30 p.m. to 4:30 p.m. Entrance

fee for adults is £1.70, 70p for children. Phone (0789) 204016 for more information.
On High Street is Harvard House, built in 1696, which belonged to the mother of John Harvard, founder of Harvard University. Open June to August, Monday to Saturday 11 a.m. to 4 p.m. Entrance fee for adults and children is £1.
Close to the Town Hall is New Place, a fine Tudor building where Shakespeare lived from 1610 until his death in 1616. Shakespeare is buried in Holy Trinity church, located on the bank of the Avon. Also along the river is the Royal Shakespeare Theatre, which was built between 1920 and 1932. For theater information, call (0789) 295623.
Ann Hathaway's cottage is found in Shottery, a village about one mile west of Stratford. The house is preserved almost exactly as it was in the seventeenth century. Open summers, Monday to Saturday 9 a.m. to 6 p.m., Sunday 10 a.m. to 6 p.m.; winters, Monday to Saturday 9 a.m. to 4:30 p.m., Sunday 1:30 p.m. to

4:30 p.m. Admission for adults is £1.60 and for children 60p. For more information, call (0789) 292100.

Other useful Stratford phone numbers are the Shakespeare Birthplace Trust (0789) 298365 and the Tourist Information Centre on High Street (0789) 293127.

RESTAURANTS

10/20 Shepherd's
Stratford House, Sheep St.
(0789) 68288
BRITISH
Open Tues.-Sat. noon-2 p.m. & 6 p.m.-11 p.m. All major cards.

Shepherd's, the restaurant attached to the friendly, Georgian-style Stratford House hotel, is a small, lively place that serves attractive English food for lunch and dinner. Along with the à la carte menu, there are such daily specials as artichoke mousse with an asparagus sauce, roast guinea-fowl with a red-currant and lime sauce, rack of lamb and filet mignon with a green peppercorn sauce.

A la carte: £20-£25, including wine.

PUBS

Dirty Duck
Waterside - (0789) 297312
Open Mon.-Sat. 11 a.m.-3 p.m. & 6 p.m.-10:30 p.m., Sun. noon-2 p.m. & 7 p.m.-10:30 p.m.

The only reason to come to this famous pub is to play the game of actor-spotting, since the pub is quite close to the Royal Shakespeare Theatre. You will rarely be disappointed, particularly just after a performance.

Slug and Lettuce
29 Guild St. - (0789) 299700
Open Mon.-Sat. 11 a.m.-3 p.m. & 6 p.m.-10:30 p.m., Sun. noon-2 p.m. & 7 p.m.-10:30 p.m.

An imaginative menu, fresh food, cheery service, an entertaining decor and a splendid choice of English beers. All this and a silly name too!

HOTELS

The Alveston Manor
Clopton Bridge - (0789) 204581
Open year-round. 108 rooms, color TV. All major cards.

This hotel is big, reliable and easy to find. It is also next to a busy road junction, which is not the most tranquil of settings. But the atmosphere inside is surprisingly cozy, with small oak-paneled rooms, creaky stairs and deep carpets. The rooms all have private baths or showers.

Singles: from £62; doubles: from £76.

The Arden
44 Waterside - (0789) 294949
Open year-round. 65 rooms, color TV. All major cards.

A peaceful spot located within a few yards of the theater and the Avon river. The accommodations are comfortable, and the private garden is a delight.

Doubles: from £62.50; family rooms: from £83.

Billesley Manor
Billesley - (0789) 400888
Open year-round. 41 rooms, color TV. All major cards.

For those prepared to hang the cost and enjoy themselves, this stately hotel four miles west of town provides both luxury and fine cooking. The Tudor house's discreet extension contains, among much else, a swimming pool and two tennis courts. Around it are spread eleven acres of parkland.

Singles: from £65; doubles: from £80.

Ettington Park Hotel
Alderminster, near Stratford-upon-Avon
(0789) 740740
Open year-round. 42 rooms, 7 suites, color TV. All major cards.

Five miles south of Stratford lies this monstrous building, with its gables, arches and carved stonework looking like the fantasy of some mad millionaire. Sadly, Ettington Park falls considerably short of expectation. Lavish restoration work has left it looking vulgar and pretentious, with artificial log fires, fine bindings bought by the yard and so on.

Singles: from £70; doubles: from £105; suites: from £140.

Stratford House
Sheep St. - (0789) 68288
Open year-round. 10 rooms, color TV. All major cards.
This genuinely friendly little hotel, located smack in the middle of town, was recently refurbished. The converted Georgian house is now quite comfortable, with rooms done in floral fabrics. To find the entrance, you must duck down an inconspicuous alleyway. Attached to the hotel is an appealing restaurant, Shepherd's (see "Restaurants").
Singles: from £45; doubles: from £50.

WINDSOR

SIGHTS

The romantic outline of Windsor Castle, which can be seen from the M4 highway just past Heathrow Airport, owes more to its nineteenth-century reconstruction than to the original medieval stronghold. But both the castle and its surrounding town are essential sights for the visitor to London, and can be easily reached in half an hour by car. The town itself, a charming mixture of narrow cobbled streets and handsome Georgian terraces, is attractively located on the banks of the Thames and dominated by the vast bulk of the castle, which covers an area of more than thirteen acres. While in town, visitors should not miss the Madame Tussaud display at the railway station, which includes a reconstruction of a royal train and commemorates Queen Victoria's arrival by rail during the Queen's Diamond Jubilee in 1897. It's open daily from 9:30 a.m. to 5:.30 p.m.; admission is £2.85 for adults and £2 for children. For more information, call (0753) 857837.

Eton
(0753) 863593
The town of Eton, just over the bridge that spans the Thames river, is home to England's most famous public (i.e., private) school, Eton College. Founded by Henry VI in 1440, it has some 1,100 pupils, of whom 70 are King's Scholars (recipients of scholarships awarded by competitive examinations); the remainder, fee-paying students, are known as Oppidans. Students still wear the famous Eton wing collars and tail coats, and attend the school secure in the knowledge that nineteen prime ministers were former Etonians.
The school buildings, some of which are ancient, can be visited during the school holidays (primarily summertime, Christmas and Easter). The Lower School dates from 1500; the Eton Tower that leads into the school yard and the fine perpendicular chapel both date from the early 1500s.

Windsor Castle
The State Apartments are open to the public when the Royal Family is not in residence. Also open to visitors are St. George's Chapel, with its display of state coaches and harnesses, part of the Queen's considerable collection of Old Master drawings, and Queen Mary's Dolls' House. Hours vary, but in general the State Apartments and St. George's Chapel are open from mid-October to mid-March, 10:30 a.m. to 3 p.m., mid-March to mid-October, Monday to Saturday 10:30 a.m. to 5 p.m., Sunday 1:30 p.m. to 5 p.m.
The castle, built by William the Conqueror after the invasion of 1066, is a fine and unusual example of motte and bailey design, divided by ramparts into three sections known as the Upper, Middle and Lower Wards. From the terraces there are dramatic views down to the river and access to the State Apartments. Queen Mary's Dolls' House, made in 1922 for the princesses and containing miniature furniture, china, cutlery, glass and even a library of real miniature books, is entered on the left. To the right, a staircase leads to the richly decorated rooms that were re-created during the extensive restorations carried out from 1820 to 1830 by George IV. The Grand Staircase

houses a huge display of armor and weapons, and from here the visitor proceeds to the King's Drawing Room (several paintings by Rubens), the Queen's Ballroom (paintings by Van Dyck of King Charles I and family), the Waterloo Chamber, the King's State Bedchamber (several canvases by Canaletto) and the dazzling St. George's Hall, its ceiling covered with the arms of the Knights of the Garter, the monarchy's oldest order of chivalry. The banners, helmets and crests of the Knights of the Garter, who still meet here once a year for a service of dedication, can be seen in St. George's Chapel. This magnificent chapel, one of the finest examples of the perpendicular style in Britain, was begun in 1477 and completed in 1528 by King Henry VIII. It contains the tombs of several kings.

Windsor Great Park

Covering an area of more than 4,800 acres, the park can be reached by turning left at the Henry VIII gateway onto High Street and continuing along Park Street to the northern end. The park's roads are accessible only by foot, but the A328 Ascot road borders the park and leads on to Virginia Water and Ascot. The Great Park contains two royal residences, Royal Lodge (home of the Queen Mother) and Cumberland Lodge, as well as the beautiful Valley Gardens, the Savill Gardens and Smith Lawn, site of summer polo matches.

RESTAURANTS

While gourmets are encouraged to visit the Waterside Inn at Bray-on-Thames and L'Ortolan at Shinfield (both close by), Windsor itself offers no restaurants of note; instead, the visitor would do well to patronize one of the several pubs and wine bars in town. We'd suggest that you avoid the tourist-trap eateries on the cobbled streets opposite the castle and venture instead into town, where you'll find a number of passable cafés as well as several fast-food chain restaurants.

BRAY-ON-THAMES

Four miles north of Windsor and twenty-three miles west of London, Bray-on-Thames has received considerable culinary fame as the home of the Roux brothers' acclaimed Waterside Inn.

Waterside Inn

Ferry Rd., Maidenhead
(0628) 20691, 22491
FRENCH
Open Tues.-Sun. noon-2 p.m. & 7 p.m.-10 p.m. Closed Sun. dinner mid-Sept.-Easter & Dec. 25-Feb. 15. All major cards.

This is without a doubt one of the prettiest settings for a restaurant, right by the water's edge, with a permanent cabaret of ducks and swans, flickering lights on the water, boats, and plumed willows trailing in the water. In such a setting of English simplicity, the Roux brothers' famous soufflé d'oeufs poches aux fines herbes (poached-egg soufflé with fine herbs) strikes just the right note, and indeed most of the hors d'oeuvres are delightful and elegantly and decoratively presented, from the warm terrine of salmon and hake in a saffron sauce to the delicious ballotine of duck in a pistachio sauce, accompanied by a lovely mixed green salad. Past meals have resulted in disappointing main courses—suffering from affectation and lapses in technique—but our last trip here proved entirely successful. Everything, from the starters mentioned above to the flavorful Gascony chicken with tangy wild mushrooms, the excellent lamb and the succulent duck from France's Vendée region, was thoroughly enjoyable. We then relished selections from the well-chosen cheese tray, and indulged in the admirable peach tart and warm strawberry soufflé.

There are a few caveats. The £40 (minimum) fixed-price menu *exceptionnel* at dinner "can only be prepared for a minimum of two persons. No change is possible without extra charge." And "if a starter or a crustace is required as a main course, there will be a charge of 50 percent extra." But since it isn't explained what the 50 percent is based on, it's hard to know what one is letting oneself in for.

And to ask, one feels, would be in the tackiest of taste. At the Waterside Inn the customer must toe the line. But we can't be too critical. After all, the connoisseur's wine list is wide ranging in both content and price, with a particularly fine collection of investment-quality French wines. And the Roux brothers deserve the highest praise for their generous policy of encouraging their talented sous-chefs to strike out on their own, with the blessing and encouragement of their masters. England has been greatly enriched by the gastronomic endeavors of the Roux brothers.

A la carte: £60, including wine. Fixed-price menus: £21.50-£26 (lunch), £40 and up (dinner).

SHINFIELD

Half an hour from London's Heathrow Airport, an hour from the city itself, and twenty miles west of Windsor, Shinfield should be added as an obligatory visit for any gastronomic tour of the Thames Valley.

L'Ortolan

17 The Old Vicarage, Church Ln., near Reading, Berkshire - (0734) 883783

FRENCH

Open Tues.-Sat. 12:30 p.m.-2 p.m. & 7:15 p.m.-10:30 p.m., Sun. 12:30 p.m.-2 p.m. Cards: AE, MC, V.

This is the place that celebrated chef Nico Ladema opened and abandoned after a year to return to London, complaining that the local populace was insufficiently appreciative of his talents, preferring prawn cocktails and steak (and doubtless cheese before dessert), washed down with lukewarm Lambrusco. More likely he simply wasn't flashy enough, because under its present chef/proprietor, self-proclaimed "star" John Burton-Race, it appears to be doing a roaring trade with healthy quantities of big-spending locals as well as Japanese and American gastro-tourists. (Incidentally, the roaring comes as much from the kitchen as the front of house—the team has a reputation for high-strung volatility.)

Shinfield is well-positioned for London and Heathrow (ten minutes from the M4 highway at Junction 11) as well as the Western Home Counties and Oxford. The 1848 house is pleasant, solid and mellow, in red brick with stone casement windows, a sweep of gravel drive, flower-edged lawns and, inside, a deep-peach decor that is perfectly appropriate without being strikingly original. There are tables outside the drawing rooms for summer drinks and a new conservatory dining-area extension at the rear. The staff, led by Marie-Christine, Burton-Race's French wife, is young and sharp, although unexplained waits and minor slipups can occur.

The cuisine is highly ambitious, complex and quite good, but not world-class. "I am bent on creating a new strain in cooking and flavors," declares Burton-Race in the restaurant's brochure. No matter how determined he may be, certain dishes are longer on showy creativity than on substance. Sauces are subtle and interesting but sometimes a little diffuse in taste. Nonetheless, all of the following were laudable: a crêpe of young sweet corn filled with slices of pan-fried foie gras and confit of shallots, with a sherry vinegar sauce; a piccata of prawn tails on a bed of undercooked ratatouille bound in a sweet-pepper and tomato coulis, served with a beurre blanc sauce; a delicious steamed squash blossom stuffed with a delicate sea bass mousse; a simple but exquisite little granité of Sancerre served as a palate freshener before the main course; a tasty plump squab roasted and placed on a truffle-and-bacon-spiked choucroute, served—in the manner of a current favorite of British haute cuisine—with a potato-disc galette sandwich (in this case made of the bird's liver combined with foie gras); and an austere but fresh filet of John Dory poached in basil and served with a Burton-Race specialty, a tomato and sweet-pepper coulis. Among the desserts were an excellent lime sorbet, a good trio of white, coffee and dark chocolates and a well-textured white-chocolate mousse.

A la carte: £55-£60, including wine.

HOTELS

Castle Hotel

High St. - (0735) 51011

Open year-round. 85 rooms, color TV. All major cards.

This pleasant, old-fashioned Trust House Forte–owned hotel is situated just opposite the castle. The rooms are comfortable and the service efficient.

Doubles: from £95.

Oakley Court
Windsor Road, Water Oakley, Maidenhead
(0628) 74141
Open year-round. 91 rooms. All major cards.
  Oakley Court is a grand hotel in a huge
Gothic folly. The hotel is set on 30 acres of
grounds bordering the Thames river some
three miles west of Windsor on the A308
highway. The restaurant serves sumptuous and
original food; dinner runs about £30, including wine.
  Doubles: from £113, including breakfast.

YORK

SIGHTS

  A little more than two hours away by high-
speed train from London and only a bit more
by road, York is well worth visiting, set as it is
in glorious countryside. York's first walls were
Roman, but though substantial fragments of
these remain, it is the medieval wall, nearly
three miles long, that now circles the old city.
A number of York's streets have names ending
in "gate," the Viking name for "street," and
Stonegate, which existed long before the Vik-
ings appeared, is kept free of traffic so its rich
medley of medieval and Georgian architecture
may be enjoyed in peace; this ancient thor-
oughfare has become a most delightful shopping street. The Archbishop of York is the
second most senior post in the Church of
England, and York Minster (open during the
summer from 7 a.m. to 8:30 p.m.) is one of
the finest cathedrals in Europe. Its nave was
begun in 1291 but was not finished until the
middle of the fourteenth century. Work on the
north transept was begun in 1220, while the
entire South Transept, with its magisterial
Rose Window, was eventually reopened in November 1988 after being struck by lightning in
July 1984.

Other attractions worth viewing are:

The Jorvik Viking Centre
Coppergate - (0904) 6432111
*April 1-Oct. 31: open daily 9 a.m.-7 p.m.; Nov.
1-March 31: open daily 9 a.m.-5:30 p.m.*
  Visitors are whisked back 1,000 years in time
via an exact reconstruction of a street from
medieval Jorvik (the Viking name for York).

National Railway Museum
Leeman Rd. - (0904) 621121
*Open Mon.-Sat. 10 a.m.-6 p.m., Sun. 11 a.m.-6
p.m.*
  Displays of Britain's railway heritage, from
the smallest railway-motif waistcoat button to
the 190-ton British-built steam locomotive,
recently returned home after 45 years' service
in the mountains of China. The full-size rolling
stock of diesel, electric and steam locomotives,
arranged on two original turntables, allows the
visitor to view an ever-changing display covering more than 150 years of British railway
history.

*Going traveling? Look for Gault
Millau's other "Best of" guides to
France, Paris, Italy, Hong Kong,
New York, New England,
Washington, D.C., Los Angeles,
San Francisco and Chicago.*

HOTELS

Middlethorpe Hall
Bishopthorpe Rd. - (0904) 641241
*Open year-round. 31 rooms, color TV. All major
cards.*
  Located in the southern end of the city, this
fashionable eighteenth-century country house
is set on 30 acres overlooking the racecourse.

It offers an elegant atmosphere and has an excellent restaurant. The rooms, all with private baths, have been completely redecorated and are spacious comfortable. The hotel will suggest interesting tours of the local countryside, including Castle Howard, seen on TV's *Brideshead Revisited*, and the glorious Yorkshire Dales.

Doubles: £78-£110, including breakfast.

The Royal York Hotel
Station Rd. - (0904) 653681
Open year-round. 110 rooms, color TV. All major cards.

The Victorian-style Royal York is conveniently located near the main railway station. Many of the rooms have splendid views of the city, and room service is excellent.

Doubles: £75-£83, including breakfast.

BASICS

AT YOUR SERVICE

TRAVELERS' INFORMATION

British Tourist Authority, Thames Tower, Blacks Rd., W6, 846 9000.

City of London Information Centre, St. Paul's Churchyard, EC4, 606 3030.

London Visitor & Convention Bureau, 26 Grosvenor Gardens, SW1, 730 3488. Information desks are also located at Harrods, Selfridges, Heathrow Airport and Victoria Station.

Tourist Information Centre: Platform 15, Victoria Station, 246 8041. Open daily 9 a.m. to 8:30 p.m.

FOREIGN EXCHANGE

One pound (£1) is divided into 100 pence (p), with coins of 1p, 2p, 5p, 10p, 20p and 50p. There are bills for £5, £10, £20 and £50.

The best exchange rates are offered at London's banks. This means that you'll have to do your exchanging during bankers' hours, which are Monday through Friday from 9:30 a.m. to 3:30 p.m. A few branches, however, stay open on Saturday. The Barclays at 74 Kensington High Street, W8, is open Saturday morning, and the Lloyd's at 399 Oxford Street, W1, is open from 10 a.m. to 3 p.m.

HOLIDAYS

Like all good Europeans, the British love their holidays. Most businesses and institutions (even some restaurants and hotels) close on Christmas, Boxing Day (December 26), New Year's Day, Good Friday, Easter Monday, May Day (first Monday in May) and the bank holidays: the last Monday in May and the last Monday in August.

TELEPHONE NUMBERS

Ambulance, 999
American Embassy, 499 9000
Automobile Association, 954 7373
British Rail, 928 5100
Canadian Embassy, 629 9492
Fire, 999
French Embassy, 581 5292
Kidsline, 222 8070

London Regional Transport, 222 1234
Police, 999
Post office, 601 9064
River Bus (ferry), 474 5555
Sportsline, 222 8000
Telephone Directory, 921 8888
Ticketmaster, 379 6433
Time, 123
Weather, 246 8091

VALUE ADDED TAX

Britian slaps a Value Added Tax (VAT) of fifteen percent on almost every item you might purchase (books, food and children's clothes excluded). This tax does not apply, however, to goods taken out of the country, so if you make a substantial purchase with VAT added, bring your passport with you and ask the shopkeeper for the appropriate VAT form to show Customs. For the refund, be prepared to show the customs officer at the airport both your purchase and the VAT form, which he will stamp and instruct you to mail at the nearby receptacle. It's a rather bothersome procedure, but it will save you a considerable amount of money.

GETTING AROUND

AIRPORT

London is served by two major international airports, Heathrow and Gatwick. The easiest way to reach central London from Heathrow is, of course, by cab (about a 40-minute drive, which will cost you about £17), but the Underground, or tube, is much more economical and almost as convenient, unless you are laden with luggage. The Piccadilly line will carry you from Heathrow right into the heart of town (with stops at Knightsbridge, Hyde Park, Piccadilly and Covent Garden, among others), where you can catch a cab to your hotel. Gatwick is farther from the city than Heathrow, making cabs prohibitively expensive for most travelers. The easiest, most direct transportation to and from Gatwick is offered by British Rail via the Gatwick Express, which takes just 30 minutes to reach Victoria Station in town. Call 928 5100 for information.

BOATS

Charming boat rides leave Westminster Pier, Charing Cross Pier and Festival Pier daily for trips both up and down the Thames. The itinerary includes the Tower of London, Greenwich, Kew and Richmond (the last two in the summer months only). For more information call 730 4812. There is also a boat trip to Hampton Court that leaves from Westminster and lasts half a day. Departure times are at 10:30 a.m., 11:15 a.m. and noon, returning at 3 p.m., 4 p.m. and 5 p.m., respectively.

BUSES

London buses—red for those serving the Greater London area, green for districts twenty miles outside London—are practical, inexpensive, comfortable and frequently scheduled. Though touristy, the world-famous double-decker Imperial bus offers an ideal way of seeing London that shouldn't be missed (take note that smoking is permitted only on the upper deck). Ask the driver when you board what the closest stop is to your destination. When waiting for a bus, check the sign to see if the stop is a "request" one—if it is, the driver will expect a signal from you if you want to be picked up.

Twenty night bus lines are in operation in the center of London. If you plan on being in London for more than a few days, pick up one of the travel cards issued by London Regional Transport. These may be purchased at the following Underground stations—Euston, Heathrow Central, King's Cross, Oxford Circus, Piccadilly Circus, St. James's Park and Victoria—British Rail stations and some newsstands; prices vary depending on the number of days the card will serve you. They permit unlimited travel on the Underground and the buses in certain areas of the city, night or day.

For more information about London's bus system, call 222 1234.

CABS

London's beloved cabs are nearly all Austins, black and shiny with an unmistakably haughty air. They are available for hire if the yellow light above the windshield is lit. All black taxis have meters that the driver must use on all trips within the Metropolitan Police District (including most of Greater London and Heathrow Airport), but for longer trips—to Gatwick Airport, for instance—the price should be negotiated with the driver beforehand. (A reasonable rate from Mayfair to Gatwick is £35-£40; to Heathrow it's about £22-£25.) Expect to pay extra for large pieces of luggage, trips between 8 p.m. and 6 a.m., on weekends and during national holidays.

Taxis are roomy and comfortable, with near-opaque dividers between the front and back seats, which, along with most drivers' discretion, assures complete privacy. London's drivers are as courteous as cabbies are in any other major city, sometimes more so, and they possess an almost encyclopedic knowledge of the city's bewildering tangle of streets—which explains why they so seldom need to look up your destination in the indispensable *A to Z London* map book (which, by the way, you should pick up for yourself). Nonetheless, you are well-advised to provide them with as much detail as you can regarding your destination, since the same name might belong to streets in districts as far away from each other as Chiswick in the west and Hornsey in the east.

For longer taxi rides, this advice becomes doubly important. An Italian lady, eager to do some shopping at Selfridges, asked the driver to take her to Oxford, but omitted to add the word "Street." It was only when the driver started to drive west on the M40 highway that she realized that she was headed for the university town.

CARS

If you're limiting your travels to within London, a car will be more bother than it's worth; cabs, buses and the tube will get you around more easily and less expensively. But a car is a good idea if you plan on exploring outlying areas and/or continuing on through England.

Rental-car prices differ greatly according to the company, the make of car and the season. All the companies have some sort of basic daily, weekly or monthly charge, sometimes inclusive of mileage, and they all require a deposit. Most also require that you be over 21 and have held a driver's license, valid for use in the United Kingdom (American licenses will suffice), for at least a year.

The major rental firms are:

Avis Rent-a-Car, 35 Headford Pl., SW1, 245 9862. Open daily 7 a.m. to 8 p.m. For worldwide reservations contact Trident House, Station Rd., Hayes, Middlesex, 848 8765.

Budget, many branches, 441 5882. Open Mon.-Fri. 8:30 a.m. to 6 p.m., Sat. 9 a.m. to 12:30 p.m.

Hertz, Radnor House, 1272 London Rd., SW16, 679 1799. Daimlers are a specialty, either self- or chauffeur-driven.

The major limousine firms are:

A1 Cars, Kings Cross, WC1, 278 5225. Supplies black and white Rolls-Royces, Daimlers and Mercedeses, along with personal bodyguards and multilingual drivers. Open daily 24 hours.

Patrick Barthropp, 1 Dorset Mews, Wilton St., SW1, 245 9171. Rents Bentleys, Silver Spirits and Silver Spurs complete with liveried chauffeurs. Open daily 7:30 a.m. to 10:30 p.m.

UNDERGROUND

London Regional Transport takes in more than £75 million a year from foreign tourists—more than a quarter of this from Americans—which goes to prove that taxis aren't the only way to effectively get around London. Besides, in taxis you often spend good money going nowhere, since they operate on time traveled as opposed to distance traveled, and cars traveling through the center of London too often get stuck in traffic jams. Subway trains, however, race along under the streets regardless of how much traffic is tied up in gridlock above.

Knowing precisely where you are going is important when traveling by Underground, since one platform is often used for trains serving different routes. It's a system that can cause unpleasant surprises for careless travelers.

A few notes about traveling on London's marvelous "tube": —Luminated signs indicate the destination of each train as it enters the station.

—Tickets may be purchased from automatic vending machines as well as from ticket booths; the price of a ticket depends on the length of the ride.

—There is only one class of subway car.

—Smoking is forbidden.

—Children under 16 pay half price.

—Dogs may travel on the Underground if a half-price ticket is purchased for them.

—Rush hour is from 7:30 to 9:30 a.m. and 4:30 to 6:30 p.m.

—Trains stop running about midnight, but each line is different. Make sure the line you need runs late before you find yourself stranded at 1 a.m.

—More information can be obtained by calling London Regional Transport at 222 1234.

GOINGS-ON

"When a man is tired of London, he is tired of life; for there is in London all that life can afford," proclaimed Samuel Johnson in 1777. We're inclined to agree—there never seems to be enough time to take advantage of all that London offers. Below is a collection of its more intriguing annual events.

JANUARY

First-second week: Epiphany—gold, incense and myrrh are offered in the name of the Queen (Chapel of St. James's Palace).

Second week: London International Boat Show.

Late Jan.: Jorvik Viking Festival starts in York.

30th: Wreath placed at the foot of the statue of Charles I, who was beheaded 340 years ago (Charing Cross).

FEBRUARY

Second week: English Folk Dance and Song Society Festival (Royal Albert Hall).

Second week: Crufts Dog Show (Earl's Court).

MARCH

Early March-early April: *Daily Mail* Ideal Home Exhibition (Earls Court).

13th: Commonwealth Day.

Late March: Oxford-Cambridge Boat Race (sculls), on the Thames (Putney to Mortlake).

Late March: Easter Sunday Parade (Battersea Park).

APRIL

First week: Seagram Grand National Steeplechase (Liverpool).

Third week: Burlington House Antiques Fair (Royal Academy).

23rd: St. George's Day. London Marathon.

30th: Shakespeare Memorial Service (Southwark Cathedral).

MAY

First three weeks: Brighton Festival (Brighton).

Mid-May: Glyndebourne Arts Festival.

Mid-May: Football Association Cup Final (Wembley).

Late May-26th: Chelsea Flower Show (Hospital Road).

Late May–early June: Bath International Festival of Music (Bath).

JUNE

First week: Ever Ready Derby (Epsom).

Early June: Opening of the Royal Academy Summer Exhibition.

Mid-June: Fine Arts and Antiques Fair (Olympia).

17th: Official Birthday of the Queen; Trooping the Color (Whitehall).

21st: Midsummer's Day, Summer Solstice.

Late June–early July: The All England Lawn Tennis Championship (Wimbledon).

Late June–early July: Henley Royal Regatta.

JULY

Early July: Royal International Horse Show (Wembley).

Early July: British Grand Prix Auto Race (Silverstone).
Mid-July: City of London Festival.

Third week: British Golf Open Championship (Royal Troon, Ayrshire).

Last two weeks: Stratford Festival (Stratford-upon-Avon).

Late July: Start of the Henry Wood Promenade Concerts (Albert Hall).

Late July: Glorious Goodwood Horse Races.

Late July: Birmingham Festival (Birmingham).

Late July-early Aug.: Cowes Week (sailing).

Late July-mid-Aug.: Buxton Festival.

AUGUST

First week: Hickstead Derby Show Jumping.

Mid-Aug.-Sept.: Edinburgh International Festival.

Mid-Aug.-Dec.: Grouse Hunting Season.

SEPTEMBER

First week: Burghley Horse Trials.

Mid-Sept.-late Oct: Annual Show of East London Artists (Whitechapel Gallery, E1).

Mid-Sept.: Last Night of the Proms (Royal Albert Hall).

Mid-Sept.: Opening of The Great Autumn Show (RHS Hall, Westminster).

OCTOBER

1st-Feb. 1: Pheasant Hunting Season.

First week: Horse-of-the-Year Show (Wembley).

Mid-Oct.: London Motor Show (Earl's Court).

Late Oct.: British Philatelic Exhibition (Olympia).

NOVEMBER

First week: London–Brighton Veteran Car Rally.

Second week: Lord Mayor's Procession and Show (City).

Second week: Remembrance Sunday Ceremony at the Cenotaph.

DECEMBER

First week: Royal Smithfield Show (Earls Court).

6th: Lighting of Christmas Tree (Trafalgar Square).

Mid-Dec.: International Show Jumping Championships (Olympia).

26th-28th: Christmas Carols in Westminster Abbey.

31st: New Year's celebrations (Trafalgar Square, Piccadilly Circus).

MAPS

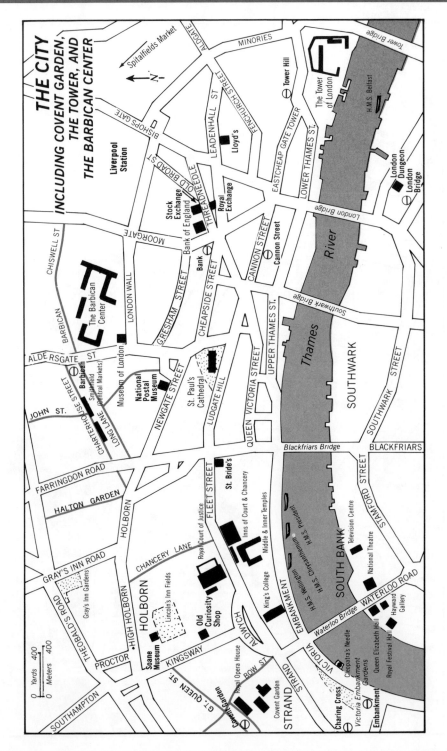

THE CITY
INCLUDING COVENT GARDEN,
THE TOWER, AND
THE BARBICAN CENTER

Spitalfields Market

—N—

MINORIES

ALDGATE

LEADENHALL ST

FENCHURCH STREET

Tower Hill

The Tower of London

The Tower of London

Tower Bridge

H.M.S. Belfast

BISHOPS GATE

Liverpool Station

OLD BROAD ST

Lloyd's

EASTCHEAP GATE TOWER

LOWER THAMES ST.

London Dungeon

London Bridge

Stock Exchange

Bank of England

Royal Exchange

THREADNEEDLE

London Bridge

MOORGATE

Bank

CANNON STREET

Cannon Street

River

CHISWELL ST

GRESHAM STREET

CHEAPSIDE STREET

UPPER THAMES ST.

Southwark Bridge

BARBICAN

The Barbican Center

LONDON WALL

Thames

SOUTHWARK

ALDERSGATE ST

Barbican

Smithfield (Central Markets)

Museum of London

QUEEN VICTORIA STREET

SOUTHWARK STREET

JOHN ST.

CHARTERHOUSE STREET

LONG LANE

National Postal Museum

NEWGATE STREET

St. Paul's Cathedral

LUDGATE HILL

SOUTHWARK

FARRINGDON ROAD

Blackfriars Bridge

BLACKFRIARS

HALTON GARDEN

FLEET STREET

St. Bride's

STAMFORD STREET

HOLBORN

Royal Court of Justice

Inns of Court & Chancery

Middle & Inner Temples

H.M.S. Chrysanthemum H.M.S. President

Television Centre

GRAY'S INN ROAD

CHANCERY LANE

Lincoln's Inn Fields

King's College

EMBANKMENT

H.M.S. Wellington

SOUTH BANK

National Theatre

THEOBALD'S ROAD

HIGH HOLBORN

HOLBORN

Gray's Inn Gardens

Old Curiosity Shop

ALDWYCH

WATERLOO ROAD

Hayward Gallery

Waterloo Bridge

0 Yards 400
0 Meters 400

PROCTOR

KINGSWAY

Soane Museum

Royal Opera House

BOW ST.

STRAND

VICTORIA

Cleopatra's Needle

Queen Elizabeth Hall

Royal Festival Hall

SOUTHAMPTON

GT. QUEEN ST.

Covent Garden

Covent Garden

STRAND

Charing Cross

Victoria Embankment Gardens

Embankment

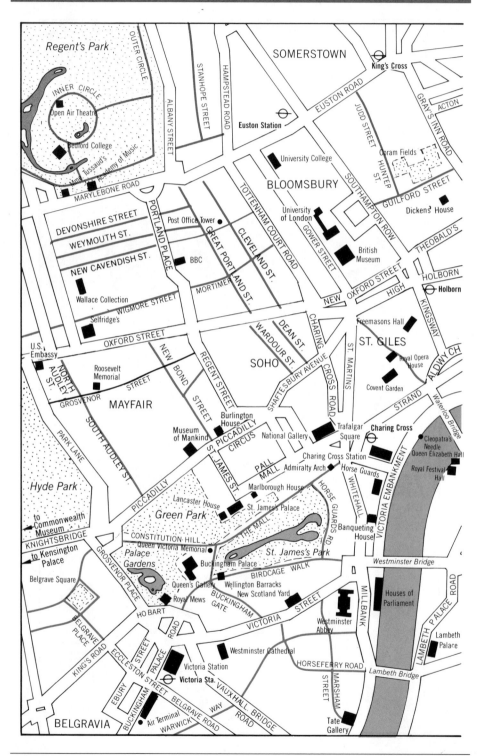

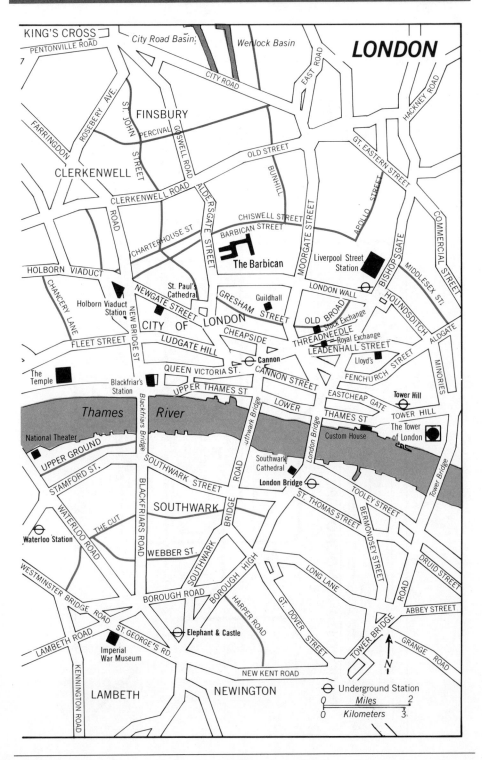

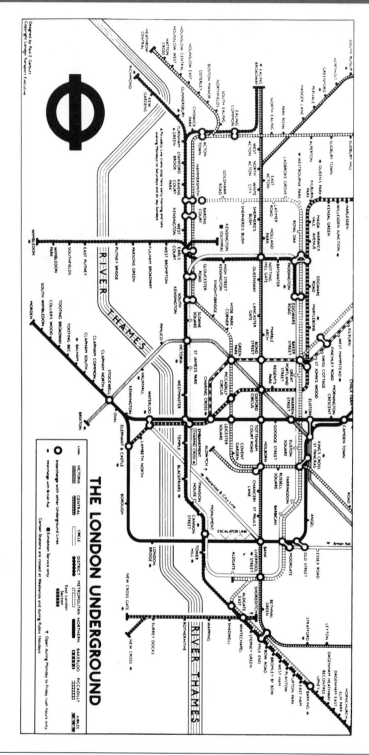

THE LONDON UNDERGROUND

INDEX

C

I

J

K

L

The Gault Millau series of guidebooks reflects your demand for insightful, incisive reporting on the best (and worst) the world's most exciting destinations have to offer. To help us make our books even better, please take a moment to fill out this anonymous (if you wish) questionnaire, and return it to:

Gault Millau, Inc., P.O. Box 361144, Los Angeles, CA 90036

1. How did you hear about the Gault Millau guides: bookstore, newspaper, magazine, radio, friends or other (please specify)?

2. Please list in order of preference the cities (or countries) about which you would like to have a Gault Millau guide, aside from the already existing destinations.

3. Do you refer to the Gault Millau guides in your travels or for your own city?

A. (Travels) ....   B. (Own city) ....   C. (Both) ....

4. Please list, starting with the most preferred, the three features you most like about the Gault Millau guides.

A. ....   B. ....

C. ....

5. What are the features, if any, you dislike about the Gault Millau guides?

6. Please list any features you would like to see added to the Gault Millau guides.

7. If you use any other guides than Gault Millau, please list below.

8. Please list the features you most like about your favorite guidebook series if it is not Gault Millau.

A. ....   B. ....

C. ....   *Please turn over*

9. How many trips do you make per year for business and for pleasure?

Business: International: .... Domestic: ....

Pleasure: International: .... Domestic: ....

10. Please check the category that reflects your annual household income.

$ 20,000-$39,000 .... $ 40,000-$59,000 ....
$ 60,000-$79,000 .... $ 80,000-$99,000 ....
$ 100,000-$120,000 .... Other (please specify) ....

11. If you have any comments on the Gault Millau guides in general, please list them in the space below.

We thank you for your interest in the Gault Millau guides, and we welcome your remarks and recommendations about restaurants, hotels, nightlife, shops, services and so on.

MORE GAULT MILLAU "BEST" GUIDES

Now the series known throughout Europe for its wit and savvy reveals the best of major U.S., European and Southeast Asian destinations: New York, Washington, D.C., Los Angeles, San Francisco, Chicago, New England, Hong Kong, London, Paris, France and Italy. Following the guidelines established by the world-class French food critics Henri Gault and Christian Millau, local teams of writers have gathered inside information about where to stay, what to do, where to shop and where to dine or catch a quick bite in these key locales. Each volume sparkles with the wit, wisdom and panache that readers have come to expect from Gault Millau, whose distinctive style makes them favorites among travelers bored with the neutral, impersonal style of other guides. There are full details on the best of everything in these destinations, including restaurants, quick bites, nightlife, hotels, shops, the arts—all the unique sights and sounds of each area. Filled with provocative, entertaining and frank reviews, they are helpful as well as fun to read. Perfect for visitors and residents alike.

Please send me the books checked below:

☐   The Best of Chicago $15.95
☐   The Best of France $16.95
☐   The Best of Hong Kong $16.95
☐   The Best of Italy $16.95
☐   The Best of London $16.95
☐   The Best of Los Angeles $14.95
☐   The Best of New England $15.95
☐   The Best of New York $14.95
☐   The Best of Paris $16.95
☐   The Best of San Francisco $14.95
☐   The Best of Washington D.C. $14.95

PRENTICE HALL TRADE DIVISION
Order Department—Travel Books
200 Old Tappan Road
Old Tappan, New Jersey 07675

In U.S. include $2 shipping UPS for first book, $1 for each additional book. Outside U.S., $3 and $1 respectively.

Enclosed is my check or money order for $ _____

NAME _____

ADDRESS _____

CITY _____ STATE_____ ZIP _____